LATIN AMERICA
A HISTORY

THE MACMILLAN COMPANY
NEW YORK · CHICAGO
DALLAS · ATLANTA · SAN FRANCISCO
LONDON · MANILA

BRETT-MACMILLAN LTD.
TORONTO

LATIN AMERICA
A HISTORY

by

Alfred Barnaby Thomas

PROFESSOR OF HISTORY
UNIVERSITY OF ALABAMA

THE MACMILLAN COMPANY
NEW YORK

To My Students

PREFACE

This survey of the history of Latin America is aimed to bring out the human forces operating in its culture and the continuity of its development. The character and contribution of Indian civilizations, often thought of as frozen in monuments, are in fact continuing influences in many countries still strongly Indian. The arrival of the Spaniards and Portuguese was not a devastating conquest; it was part of the European process of transferring the culture of the Old World to the New. Blending with the Indian and importing the Negro, Spain and Portugal created a distinctive American civilization.

Many have wondered why Latin America, with a tradition of centralized government among Incas, Aztecs, Spaniards, and Portuguese, nevertheless so universally formed republics after Independence. The answer is simply that by that time, Latin America had absorbed the then new intellectual, economic, and political ideas propagated by the French, given form by the British, and made effective by the Americans in the northern republic.

After Independence, Latin America, in spite of frequent civil wars in the nineteenth century, reflected at base a growth of a middle class inspired by ideas of nationalism, liberalism, and orderly republican government. Late in the century immigration of European laborers strengthened the democratic tradition, for, while they arrived empty-handed, they were not empty-headed. The victims of autocratic government in Europe, many were veterans of a struggle for liberty. They came in the tradition of all Europeans—seeking freedom in the New World.

The twentieth century has seen the struggle against the remnants of a colonial autocracy and illiteracy, carried on by an ever-growing number of Latin Americans intent upon establishing democratic institutions and modern economic organization. Constantly inspired by the example of the United States, Latin America, though distinct in language and institutions, has shared with her great neighbor a common history and, today, common economic and international interests.

The organization of the material in this book rests upon four simple divisions: "Colonial Latin America," the "Wars for Independence," "Modern Latin America," and "Inter-American Affairs." In the modern period, for the sake of clarity, the areas of Latin America are classified on the basis of relationships existing between the various countries. Argentina, Uruguay, Paraguay, and Brazil, designated as the Atlantic Republics, have had their history linked from colonial times. Chile, Bolivia, Peru, and Ecuador—the Pacific Republics—have each had a history more common to themselves than that which occasionally touched their neighbors beyond the Andes. Colombia, Venezuela, Cuba, the Dominican Republic, and Haiti—the Caribbean Republics—have from the beginning shared the Caribbean Sea. Central America, Panama, and Mexico are physically together on a separate continent; all have felt strongly the influence of the United States. Over the two continents, for more than a century, has been woven a web of inter-American relations. Today these twenty Latin American nations and the United States, inspired by common ideals and facing common problems, have created a great inter-American organization aimed at fashioning a better life for all the people of the New World.

It is hard to separate the contributions of many people who in one way or another have helped in the preparation of this book. I am glad to acknowledge my debt to the late Professor Herbert Eugene Bolton. I had the valued experience, as a student, of listening to him expound in detail his now commonly accepted thesis, the unity of New World history. Dr. Leslie Spier, distinguished anthropologist, first made me aware of the vital importance of Indian culture as a force in American history. The reading of his valuable book, *Timeless Mexico,* and frequent conversations with Hudson Strode, my colleague in the Department of English, have given me new insights into the history of Mexico. I am indebted to the University of California, the John Simon Guggenheim Memorial Foundation, and the American Council of Learned Societies for grants which made possible study of Latin American source materials in the archives of Spain, France, Great Britain, and Mexico. Dr. Charles E. Nowell of the University of Illinois has kindly answered questions on sixteenth century exploration problems. Dr. W. Stanley Hoole, University Librarian, and the staff of the Library of the University of Alabama, have been unfailingly helpful. John C. Galloway, Jr., of the University of Alabama Art Department, has shown me many kindnesses. I wish to thank Miss Herta Breiter of the Delphian Society, Chicago, for permission to use materials I have published in the *Delphian Quarterly* on Latin America. I greatly appreciate the assistance of my daughter, Ann Thomas Mock, in preparing the Index.

To my wife, Muriel Goodburn Thomas, I am deeply indebted for her valuable suggestions and her critical reading of the manuscript. My children, Ann, Peter and Sarah, have from the beginning been an inspiration to me in the writing of this book.

ALFRED B. THOMAS

University of Alabama

TABLE OF CONTENTS

COLONIAL LATIN AMERICA

THE WARS FOR INDEPENDENCE

MODERN LATIN AMERICA

Section I. The Atlantic Republics:
Argentina, Uruguay, Paraguay, and Brazil

Section II. The Pacific Republics:
Chile, Bolivia, Peru, and Ecuador

Section III. The Caribbean Republics:
Colombia, Venezuela, Cuba, Haiti, and
the Dominican Republic

Section IV. Central America, Panama, and Mexico

INTER-AMERICAN AFFAIRS

MAPS

MAPS

COLONIAL
LATIN AMERICA

Chapter I

THE INDIAN CULTURES
OF LATIN AMERICA

Part I. EARLY MAN IN THE NEW WORLD

The discovery of the New World by Columbus had its chief significance in putting an end to American isolation. Since 1492 every passing decade has tightened the bonds between Europe and the New World. Before 1492, as one author described it, America was a "secret laboratory of culture" (Macgowan). Here for centuries unnumbered civilizations had evolved totally unrelated to that of Europe. A few "flying saucers" in the form of Indian canoes had reached the Old World, washed up on European coasts, but no one suspected their meaning.

Origin. When did this New World civilization have its origin? From the day of Columbus' return, men have speculated upon this question. At that time it did present an embarrassing question. Scripture had already accounted for all races, a fact which led sixteenth century philosophers to question whether or not the Indian were a human being and, if so, whether he had a soul. History established that the Indian was human. In our more advanced times we have, to answer the question of origin, relied upon various branches of science, anthropology, archaeology, geology, and such things as tree rings and carbon 14. In doing so, the scientists have allowed themselves considerable elbow room. They place the date of the arrival of man in the New World anywhere from 4,000 to 100,000 years ago. The most generally accepted period is that from 10,000 to 25,000 years.

Those who advocate a comparatively recent arrival, under 10,000 years ago, point to the lack of satisfactory "finds" to establish the age of American man. Those who believe that aboriginal Americans had a much longer history, possibly 25,000 years, offer strong presumptive evidence. One is the great variety of Indian languages which have evolved on the two continents, namely, 160 linguistic stocks and 1,200 dialects. None of these thus far has been conclusively shown to have had any connection with European or Oriental languages. Moreover, these languages represent a greater number than those existing in all other parts of the world. Obviously the length of time required for the evolution of so many tongues must have been very great.

Again, the American Indian exhibited a greater variety of characteristics than the entire Caucasian race. Some authorities claim that even 25,000 years would hardly suffice to bring about such a wide differentiation. Surprisingly, American man cultivated a greater variety of food plants than all the rest of the world combined. Obviously, allowing considerable time for man during the Upper Paleolithic Age before he developed agriculture and a much longer period for the Neolithic when he began to domesticate plants, an extremely long span must be assumed for the highly developed state of agriculture among the principal culture areas of the American Indian. Some believe, too, that given the necessarily small groups who migrated into the New World from the Orient, their increase in numbers, estimated at between 8,000,000 and 30,000,000 in 1492, and their slow spread over the two continents from the Bering Strait to the Strait of Magellan, some 11,000 miles, required a vast span of centuries.

Arrival. The difficulty in establishing a fairly specific date of the earliest arrivals arises from the remarkable absence of human remains, given the large population of the two continents, in association with extinct animals of identifiable age. Before 1927 half a dozen fairly reliable instances established the existence of ancient man in the New World. The first of these a German scientist discovered in the Lagôa Santa cave, Minas Gerais, Brazil, in 1838. The remains were those of a long-headed, heavy-browed man buried among the bones of extinct animals. Other discoveries followed, possibly older in time, in a near-by cave; still others came to light in Ecuador and in caves along the Strait of Magellan. In North America finds uncovered near Trenton, New Jersey, had a likeness to those of Lagôa Santa, and in Minnesota the remains of a girl found in deposits having an age of some 20,000 years led to the belief that Minnesota man had an antiquity of some 8,000 to 12,000 years.

Folsom Man. The decisive discovery, however, that provided positive proof that man had existed in association with extinct animals occurred in Folsom, New Mexico, in 1927. There an archaeologist found a point of a spear embedded in the ribs of an extinct bison. The excellence of the workmanship of the point testified to a long previous history and enabled scientists with other data to estimate the age of Folsom man from 13,000 to 25,000 years, that is, the Upper Paleolithic. This belief found further support a few years later (1936) with the discovery of spear points and other artifacts definitely older than those of Folsom in the Sandía Cave, New Mexico. Since 1927 human bones, spear points, milling stones, charcoal, horn, shell, and flaked tools, found either alone or in association with the mammoth and mastodon, bison, sloth, camel, horse, and other extinct animals, have also testified to the existence of early man at various places on both continents.

Pre-Indian Groups. The remains of these ancient men also established that the Indian, if we accept that term to define the migrants characterized by the Mongoloid roundhead, were preceded by a race or races of men definitely longheaded. These have been called by one authority (Macgowan) Australoid-Melanesian. The latter were the earlier arrivals, while the Indian came later. Some estimate the time of the arrival of the American Indian in the first millennium preceding the Christian era. Thus there is in the prehistoric record of early man in America a gap of several thousand years. The prehistory of the people we call Indian can be traced fairly well back from 1492 to around 1000 B.C. Between the latter date and Folsom man, say 13,000 years, the record is shadowy.

Migration Routes to the New World. An interesting dispute flourishes among the anthropologists as to how man reached the New World. Some believe a migration took place across the islands of the South Pacific to South or Central America. However, while not ruling out occasional Polynesian voyages over such a route, the bulk of opinion still holds that the chief highway of migration was by way of Bering Strait. It has been pointed out that 40,000 years ago and again 18,000 years ago, retreating Wisconsin glaciations opened corridors which made possible several avenues from Alaska into the continent.

As the migrants moved southward, they fanned out across the North American continent, although the main stream seems to have continued southward through the Rocky Mountains and along the west coast. In time the invaders pushed through Mexico and Central America, across Panama and into South America, where they repeated the process of occupation that characterized the northern continent. In this long period of movement these early men relied upon hunting and fishing until circumstances of which we know nothing led them to domesticate plants and a few animals—the dog in North America and the llama in South America. The length of time all this development consumed is unknown.

But it would seem clear that when the Indian arrived, there had been a long evolution in the cultivation of land and the creation of social institutions.

In any event if we now refer to these occupants of the New World as Indian, they had by 1492 cultivated more than twenty different food plants, of which there were more than 700 varieties of maize, besides utilizing more than a dozen others that grew in a wild state and exploiting a variety of fibers, dyes, gums, and drugs. With these crops testifying to the long evolution of agricultural skills, the American Indian had erected upon that basis in Latin America four significant civilizations, the Maya, the Toltec-Aztec, the Chibcha, and the Inca. Taken together they are considered by one authority (Kroeber) so distinct from the remaining primitive groups as to merit the name, "Nuclear Culture."

Part II. THE NAHUA AND MAYA CIVILIZATIONS

Nahuan: Toltec-Aztec Culture. In northern Mexico some of the southward-moving prehistoric invaders halted and remained in that arid region. Their primitive nomadic society, for the lack of a better name, is known as the Chichimec, an adaptation of an Aztec word for the barbarians of the north. In time other invaders pushed through the Chichimec lands to enter the valley of Mexico, where they gave up their nomadic existence and devoted themselves to the art of agriculture. There they created a culture underlying all others throughout central and southern Mexico, known as the Archaic. Beyond the central valley still others pushed southward and westward toward the Pacific coast. These, known as the Totonac and Zapotec, were probably the first in Mexico to begin a civilized existence. But within the valley the earliest group of whom we have a fairly reliable account is the Nahua.

Nahua Culture: Toltec. The Toltecs had reached the Chichimec region at an early but unknown time, whence they emerged in the eighth century to enter the valley of Mexico. Their first home, it is believed by some authorities, was at Tula about fifty miles north of Mexico City, where they constructed their pyramids and temples decorated with advanced forms of art. Moving farther south, they apparently conquered the inhabitants of the valley and founded their principal center at Tectihuacan. Here they established a high rank as builders among the American Indians. Their city, some twenty-five miles from present Mexico City, had within it the great Pyramid of the Sun, that of the Moon, and a galaxy of palaces and public buildings besides dwelling places for the population.

The Pyramid of the Sun, one of their greatest achievements, has a base of some 37,000 square feet and rises to a height of 137 feet. Its outside is covered with large slabs of stone, either plain, painted, or sculptured. Mounting from the plaza to a temple atop the Pyramid is a magnificent stone stairway. Notable, too, was the temple of their principal god, Quetzalcoatl. This deity represented by a carved image of a feathered serpent ranks Toltec sculpture high in this aboriginal art.

Corresponding to the Temple of the Sun was the even larger pyramid erected by the Toltecs at Cholula. There the Temple of the Sun covered a surface, some 42,000 square feet, about equal to that of the great pyramid of Cheops at Gizeh. Located in the valley of Cholula, it presided over a large number of lesser ones that dotted the valley. In other parts of the valley of Mexico, the Toltecs left their record in temples and pyramids, a building achievement that compares with the best that Indian America produced.

Little is known of Toltec life. They began writing in symbols and possibly invented the great stone calendar, a national treasure of present Mexico. They were musicians, astrologers, and early Nahuan scientists. They carried agriculture to a high degree, displaying great skill in constructing drainage systems. Their god, Quetzalcoatl, was a beneficent one, not a god of war. He was remembered in their traditions as a wise ruler under whom the Toltecs prospered. He is pictured as a White God, who, driven out by his enemies, promised some day to return from an eastern land. This legend handed on to the Aztecs proved later a valuable weapon in the hands of Cortés.

Nahua Culture: Aztec. Like the Toltecs, the Aztecs moved in tribal groups from the northern Chichimec country into the valley of Mexico, Anáhuac. Legend dates them as emerging late in the twelfth century from Aztlán, their traditional home in the north. After two centuries of migration they arrived in the valley and settled along the great lake of Tezcoco. Here they founded Tenochtitlán, later called Mexico City.

A gifted group, the Aztecs slowly gained ascendancy over the neighboring tribes and intermarried with the conquered Toltecs, whom they held in high esteem. By the end of the fourteenth century, when the Portuguese were just beginning to push toward Africa, the Aztecs had selected a supreme ruler, advised by a council, as chief, whom the Spaniards later called emperor. Outstanding was Montezuma I, who

ruled from 1440 to 1469. Not only did he broaden the conquests of the
Aztecs, but built the great causeway which extended for ten miles across
the lake. Fitted with complicated floodgates, the dike both controlled
the level of the lake and made water available for neighboring towns
in the dry season. His successors Tizoc and Ahuitzotl completed the
great *teocalli* or temple which filled the center of Tenochtitlán. Thus
when in 1502 Montezuma II ascended to the chieftainship, the Aztecs
had brought their civilization to its highest peak. The evolution of this
culture, whose future achievements could only be guessed at, ended a
few short years later when Cortés arrived in 1519.

Government. Building upon Toltec foundations and influenced by
the Maya adjoining them on the south, the Aztecs left behind them material and cultural monuments that testify to the vigor and diversity of
their civilization. In government they created a confederacy among the
tribes surrounding Lake Tezcoco. They soon dominated it, extending
their conquests from coast to coast, to the Chichimec frontier in the
north, and southward into the Maya regions of Central America.

Their highly organized system of government rested upon a theocracy over which a supreme ruler (frequently but not necessarily of the
priestly clan) governed with the aid of a council drawn from the Aztec
and confederated tribes. The Aztecs maintained, however, their historic
social organization based upon clans, *capullis*, which in turn were rooted
in a communal system of land ownership and use. Each clan, of which
there were twenty in Tenochtitlán, owned its own land and administered
its own affairs through a council of old men. While communal ownership dominated, the conception of private ownership was emerging at
the time of the conquest. The clan closely associated with the Aztec war
organization had its own war chief along with its civil head. Under each
of these two leaders, members of the clan received careful training in
military science and agriculture. Clans sent representatives to the tribal
government to sit in the larger council. Each clan had its agricultural,
war, and other gods for whom the members erected temples and carried
on elaborate ceremonies of worship.

The central government levied taxes upon the conquered tribes in
the form of young men and women used as sacrifices for their terrible
war god, Huitzilopochtli. Other tributes were paid in feathers and food.
To collect these they sent at regular intervals tax collectors, whose
authority did much to keep the subjected tribes under control. However,
the Aztecs allowed a wide range of economic activity within their dominions. Their traders, penetrating all corners of their empire, became an

important agency in bringing about the conquest of tribes who refused to admit them.

Construction. As builders the Aztecs resembled the Romans in the massiveness of their structures and in conveying to the beholders a sense of power. The most famous example of their temples was the great *teocalli* raised in the heart of Tenochtitlán to their war god, Huitzilo-pochtli. Begun almost immediately at the time of their occupation of the island, they added to it in the succeeding centuries until it was completed in 1487. A vast, stone-faced pyramid, it covered over 90,000 square feet and rose to a height of 150 feet. Among the rubble beneath the stone slabs which covered its sides, the Aztecs buried treasures as offerings to their god. Unfortunately, the Spaniards searching for these leveled the vast mound. Today in Mexico City the cathedral and other public buildings in the adjoining blocks cover the foundations of the *teocalli*. To carry on the work connected with this temple, the Aztecs constructed seventy-eight lesser buildings. Around this vast center of religious worship, the city of Mexico grew up, estimated at the time of the conquest to have between 200,000 and 300,000 inhabitants.

Agriculture and Industry. In agriculture the Aztecs carried on the work of the Toltecs, who had long before cultivated the principal crops of maize, beans, maguey, and chile, as well as various fruits. Irrigation ditches, dams, and other works were carried on with the simplest of tools. Their industry was extremely varied. Featherwork, gold, silver, and coppersmithing, textiles, ropes, clothing which they dyed in brilliant colors, pottery, many items made from bone, and the manufacture of paint were among the most common products of their labor. Fairs were frequent. The greatest was in Tenochtitlán itself, described by the most fascinating of the Spanish chroniclers, Bernal Diaz:

Every kind of merchandise had its separate spot for sale—gold and silver ware, cotton and henequén cloths, twisted thread, tanned and untanned skins of tigers, lions, red deer, wild cats, and other beasts of prey, beans, sage, cacao and other vegetables, fowls, rabbits, deer, dogs, and other meats, fruit of all kinds, cooked foods, honey and honey pastes, every sort of earthen ware, and copper, brass and tin, furniture such as tables, benches, cradles—but why do I waste words when I cannot note down the details of this great market! [1]

The Arts. In the higher levels of culture the Aztecs evolved a form of writing by using pictures and hieroglyphics. They preserved their work in books, which they manufactured and collected into large libraries. Unfortunately, most of these the Spaniards destroyed in their

[1] Kate Stephens, *The Mastering of Mexico,* New York, 1916, pp. 166–167.

religious zeal, but some have survived. In science they worked out the
principles of astronomy and had reduced their calendar, which is believed
to have been derived chiefly from the Toltecs or possibly the Mayas, to
a great stone carved with all the symbols reflecting their cosmogony.
This famous calendar reveals a carefully worked out system for recording
time in which the year is composed of eighteen months, each with
twenty days, with provision for five additional days. Four weeks of five
days each made up a month.

In the construction of their temples they showed themselves familiar
with engineering principles. The sculptures with which they adorned
their temples and the decoration of pottery with formalized designs but
painted in brilliant hues reveal a high development of both arts. In music
they evolved many types of wind instruments. This vast amount of learning the priests transferred to selected youths instructed in schools in the
various fields of science, writing, religion, philosophy, military instruction, poetry, music, and painting.

Other Mexican Groups. In near-by Tezcoco, founded probably before Mexico City, a variegated culture equaled if it did not exceed that
of the Aztecs. Personified in its greatest figure, Nezahualcoyotl, it reached
its height about the time of Montezuma I. A great builder, the Tezcoco
ruler devoted himself to the arts of peace and frowned upon human
sacrifice.

To the south of the Aztec center as far as Tehuantepec another significant Indian group, the Zapotec, left remains of their culture, which
takes high rank in Indian civilization in the New World. Its most outstanding ruins are at Monte Alban and Mitla. Monte Alban, a few miles
from Oaxaca, is a remarkable site of mounds and pyramids built by
leveling a near-by mountain. In 1932 in one of the tombs there the Mexican archaeologist, Alfonso Caso, uncovered the richest archaeological
treasures ever found in the New World. Some 500 items in number included jade, gold, turquoise, and pearl necklaces, a golden breastplate,
earrings, armlets, a golden crown, and other precious jewels.

Some thirty miles to the east of Oaxaca was the other great Zapotec
religious center, Mitla. While Mitla is rich in the variety of the decorations of its buildings, it is best known for the mosaic in relief which
adorns the façade of its temples.

The Mayas. In southern Mexico, Tabasco, Chiapas, Campeche, Yucatan, and Guatemala, with outlying centers in Honduras and British Honduras, is the region of the greatest Indian civilization in North America—
the Maya. Lost in the antiquity of Indian movements are the Mayan

predecessors who laid down in this area of Mexico and Central America
the basic Archaic culture. Possibly as early as 500 B.C. the Mayas as a
people began to create their distinctive culture. In common with all primitive people their beginnings were in agriculture. They developed maize
long before they learned to cultivate maguey, henequén, cotton, and
other food and fiber plants.

We have no record, as in the case of the Aztecs, of a Maya invasion
into their homeland. Some indications suggest an earlier location in northern Vera Cruz, where lived Huaxtecs who spoke Maya. But these were
separated by a wedge of other intruding groups from their Maya kinsmen
of Central America. Although there is no agreement among experts, a
conjectural date of 162 A.D. has been given for Maya occupation of
southern Vera Cruz. Their oldest known city was at Uaxactún in Petén,
Guatemala.

The Maya in the South. The evolution of Maya history produced two
periods defined on the basis of their characteristics. The first group of
cities to appear in the fifth century A.D. with distinctive culture were in
the southern part of the Maya area. These ranged from Copán in western
Honduras northwestward to Palenque in present Chiapas. Tikal and
Uaxactún in Guatemala were the most northern of the early cities.
Palenque, covering a large area, typified early western Maya culture. In
sculpture the famous panels of the Temple of the Sun reveal a simplicity
of technique that ranks them with the best of the Greeks. In the exquisite
stucco ornamentation of its temples, Palenque brought that art of decoration, bas-relief, to its highest development among the Mayas.

Far to the southeast, Copán exceeded Palenque in the number and
variety of its pyramids, temples, and elaborate inscriptions. Because it
was a great religious city, it was also a center of art represented in its
famous stelae (carved stones). But above all, Copán was the city in
which Maya science and mathematics flourished. The most remarkable
achievement in their science was their calendar. The Mayas had, in fact,
four systems for measuring time. One recognized a year of 365 days,
another of 360 days, and a third of 260 days, while the fourth was a
lunar year. The systems used for different purposes were a check upon
one another. In their calculations of time they devised a mathematical
system which resulted in the discovery of the zero, a concept unknown
to Europeans until centuries later.

One of the most striking advances was in the field of astronomy,
where they measured time by a lunar count and reckoned the year of
the planet Venus with astonishing accuracy. The Mayas, writes Thomp-

son, "were well aware that the Venus year was actually less than 584 days. They knew the length to the second decimal point. . . ." Their system of recording time "was so accurate that had the Maya Venus calendar continued to function uninterruptedly up to the present day, the error over this period of over a thousand years would not have amounted to more than a day. . . . When one recollects that the Mayas were dependent solely on the naked eye for their observations, one is astounded at the grasp they had on the movements of the heavenly bodies." [2]

In near-by Quirigua, a few miles north of Copán, were a people unwarlike and devoted to peace. Their sculptured remains reveal no trace of human sacrifice or other savage customs. Found here, where energies were devoted to peace rather than war, was the Great Dragon or Great Turtle, the masterpiece of both Mayan civilization and American Indian art. Sculptured on a stone weighing some twenty tons, the entire surface of this huge rock is covered with a mass of intricate detail. The main theme, centrally located on the widest side of the stone, is an elegantly clothed figure sitting in the wide-open jaws of a reptilian monster. The opposite side reveals the carved face of a god, possibly that of the netherworld, while on the remaining two sides are the richly carved arms or flippers of a great turtle which gave this monumental piece of art its name. Across the top is the deeply incised face of another Mayan god surrounded with artistically carved figures intricately linked with the designs on each of the four sides.

The Mayas in the North. By 870 A.D. this older culture in the south ended suddenly after some 400 years of brilliant civilization when the Mayas evacuated their lands to move northward into Yucatan. Scholars have advanced a variety of theories to explain the event, the most widely accepted of which is soil exhaustion. A growing population, testified to by the large number of cities, and extensive irrigation systems combined with soil erosion eventually, it is thought, brought the Mayas to the verge of starvation with evacuation the only alternative. Other theories suggest changes in climate (but this is largely discounted), waves of pestilence, and revolt against the priest class, who, it is assumed, ruthlessly drove the population into the vast Maya building program.

Primitive Maya settlements in Yucatan are as old as those in the southern area, but emergence of the north as a great cultural region did not begin until about the middle of the sixth century A.D. The Mayas

---

[2] J. Eric Thompson, *The Civilization of the Mayas*, Field Museum of Natural History, Leaflet No. 25, Chicago, 1932, pp. 56–57.

migrated along the west and east coasts and established a compact group of settlements in upper Yucatan, of which Tulum in 560 was one if not the earliest. About 711 A.D. the Itzas in northwestern Yucatan ended their migration near two large wells, a fact which gave their settlement the name of Chichén Itzá. There for about 150 years they cultivated the land, built their homes, and constructed magnificent public buildings featured by corbeled arches and a wealth of geometric designs. Just before 900 A.D. the Itzas moved to the west coast of Yucatan, where they remained in obscurity until after the middle of the thirteenth century, when they again returned to Chichén Itzá. By this time, deeply influenced by Aztec and Toltec culture, the Itzas and the dwellers of the Mayan cities of Uxmal and Mayapán formed an alliance which ended wars between them and brought on a period of prosperity lasting approximately 200 years.

Maya Achievements in the North. The achievements of the Mayas in the north found their greatest expression in their building and architectural designs. Outstanding examples at Chichén Itzá were the Temple of the Tigers, the Temple of the Warriors, the Caracol, and the Castle *(El Castillo).* Strong evidence of Nahua influence is seen in the universal use of the plumed, feathered serpent, the Quetzalcoatl of the Toltecs, but known among the Mayas as Kuculcan. The Pyramid at Chichén Itzá provides excellent examples of their sculpturing art in the two carved heads of the feathered serpent at the base of the northern stairway, one of the four which led to the well-preserved temple surmounting the structure. The use of this design was not confined to temples; practically all Maya buildings show the feathered serpent in relief for decorative effect on exterior surfaces, in doorways, and on stone lintels. At Uxmal, considered one of the most perfect of Mayan ruins, is the magnificent Palace of the Governor, characterized by a wealth of geometric designs that rival if they do not excel Mitla in beauty. So, too, Mexican influences are believed reflected in the metal working art among the Mayas as well as in new methods of warfare, particularly the use of the bow and arrow, and in the construction of ball courts. The latter, however, may have a South American origin.

In this later period the Mayas also developed writing to a point in which their hieroglyphic symbols represented ideas, a stage recognized as that preceding the use of characters to denote sound. Their priesthood had recorded their traditions in thousands of manuscripts, but unfortunately the Spanish fathers in their excess of religious zeal destroyed all of them except three, which, known as Codices, survive as treasures of

great historical value. At the same time, however, the Spaniards preserved the Mayan language, but in Spanish symbols, and much material
concerning Mayan lore in what are known as the *Books of Chilam Balam.*
Of equal if not greater significance is the *Popol Vul* or *Sacred Book* of
the Quiché-Maya. It contains a voluminous record of the myths, traditions, and history of the Quiché-Maya and is regarded as one of the
remarkable intellectual productions of the Indian race.

Decline of the Mayas. The great period of prosperity ended about
the middle of the fifteenth century when civil war among the allied cities
first destroyed Chichén Itzá. Mayapán thereupon assumed the leadership, but her harsh rule in turn led to her overthrow. Mayan cities after
that time descended into feudal warfare into which the Aztecs projected
their power and began the conquest of the western region. Natural disasters that swept the peninsula added to the decline of the culture, so
that when the Spaniards first reached Yucatan in 1511 the second great
cultural era of the Mayas had already ended.

Part III.   PRE-INCA AND INCA CULTURES

The Indians of South America. Long before the Maya, Toltec, and Aztec
cultures took form, the steady migration of Indians had filled the valleys
of the Andean mountains. Thence they had feathered outward into the
jungles of the Orinoco and the Amazon, and settled in the Brazilian Highlands and in the La Plata-Patagonian area southward to Tierra del
Fuego. In Peru the predecessors of those Indians who laid down the
Archaic culture have been found in the southern coastal regions of Arica.
There a primitive people depended upon fishing and gathering of shells.
Archaic culture appeared in the north in the Chicama and Virú valleys,
where agriculture was practiced but the making of pottery had not yet
begun. This culture, still unnamed, has been estimated to have existed
as early as 1000 B.C.

Pre-Inca Cultures: Chavín. Ranked by some as the mother center and
as the first important culture to influence Peru is that of Chavín. Located
in the valley from which it derives its name in north central Peru, it
lay athwart roads going north and south and those running to the coast.
The pre-Incas at Chavín cultivated the land and built their temples in
an area of some 30,000 square meters. Their pottery shows a distinctive
art, but their carving of stones ranks them as unique in South America.
Represented in a stone head and a famous stela or obelisk, their art,
which sought to inspire fear and a sense of power, reveals a strong feeling

for composition. From this center it is believed Chavín influenced the art and life of both the coastal towns and far-off Quito.

Apparently following Chavín in point of time, two remarkable cultures geographically close, but distinct in their arts, evolved along the southern coast of Peru. One of these, Paracas, a cemetery near present-day Pisco, is famous for its mummy mantles, considered "one of the textile wonders of the world for magnificence and technical skill" (Kroeber). Too, Paracas mummies, hundreds of which have been recovered intact, provide evidence of a knowledge of trepanning the skull, a practice long thought to have been of Inca origin. About 100 miles beyond Paracas is the Nazca cultural area, notable for its pottery of brilliant hues and simplicity of shape.

Possibly contemporary or somewhat later than the Nazca-Paracas cultures and restricted to several small valleys along the northern coast of Peru was the Mochica civilization. Remarkable for the large number of pyramids made of adobe bricks, it produced in the Temple of the Sun the largest structure built by pre-Incas in Peru. While little is known of these people, they effectively revealed their spirit in their pottery decoration and painted fragments of their frescoes adorning their temples. One of the latter depicts an idea frequently voiced in modern times, the revolt of tools and implements against their masters, men! But their pottery cast in the shape of human heads has depicted in the sculptured faces a startlingly lifelike quality. Pathos, humor, suffering, satire are shown so vividly that their art hardly finds an equal among all the primitive master artists of the New World.

Tiahuanaco. Possibly a thousand years after Chavín culture had touched so much of Peru to be succeeded by more localized centers, Paracas, Nazca, Mochica, the next dominating cultural force in pre-Incan times was that of Tiahuanaco. Located in the closed basin of Lake Titicaca, its high altitude and treeless plains offered little base for agriculture. Nevertheless, Tiahuanaco ruins are considered the most remarkable in South America and the most mysterious. Probably built by the Colla, a hardy mountain tribe, Tiahuanaco occupied in this area one of the important crossroads leading from the coast and into the interior of the continent. Denied the benefits of agriculture, the Tiahuanacans exchanged with their neighbors their mountain products, the wool of the llama, alpaca, and vicuña, and pottery for food and wares needed for their daily life. Near-by the Lake of Titicaca became a place of worship known as far as the articles of Tiahuanacan commerce traveled.

Tiahuanaco seems to have been a great commercial center. There is a striking absence of religious and military monuments as well as homes. No great fortresses dominated its plains. The ruins of the principal site are in a rectangular shape, bordered by columns now broken, huge stone statues or idols, with stairways leading into what was evidently the central market. Distinguished from Chavín art, which put so much emphasis upon fear-inspiring stone figures and monuments, Tiahuanaco art shows evidence of a more sophisticated people who encased their ideas in rigid and formalized shapes. These found expression in sculpture, architecture, metallurgy, and ceramics. The most perfect example of this style is the famous stone gateway at Tiahuanaco. Formalistic in the extreme, its monolithic proportions are balanced and symmetrical while the sculpturing, a frieze in low relief, is done with a skill reminiscent of that of Middle America. The principal carved figure is Viracocha, the deity bringing rain, portrayed by tears from heaven to the earth. Lesser figures carved in rows on either side seem to be moving toward him acknowledging his power. While this center was probably the heart of Colla culture, the whole of the Titicaca basin abounds in ruins whose stories are unknown; but excavations indicate this region as one of the richest archaeological sites in the New World.

When Tiahuanaco declined, more localized cultures sprang up. In southern Peru were the Ica and Chinca. But more striking was the Chimú civilization on the northern coast. This culture, succeeding the long disappeared Mochica, eventually fell under the Incas, who overthrew Tiahuanaco in southern Peru. With its center near present-day Trujillo, Chimú culture is believed to have extended some 450 miles along the coast. Like the earlier Mochica, the Chimú built hundreds if not thousands of mounds and adobe brick pyramids. They decorated their temples with elaborate geometrical designs and showed in their pottery-making both the influence of the free-flowing earlier Mochica designs and forms adopted from Tiahuanaco, besides experiments distinctly their own.

Their great city, Chan-Chan, located a few miles outside of present-day Trujillo, was probably the largest one built by aboriginal Americans. Inside its high walls of earth were corridors, plazas, and halls. Thousands of Indians from remote areas came there to trade and worship. By this date, 1200–1400, metal, copper, and bronze were used in the making of agricultural tools, while silver and gold were molded into decorative pieces. At the time when the art and architecture of Chimú were declining, they fell under the rising power of the Incas.

Hundreds of miles to the south of Chan-Chan was another significant pre-Inca culture, probably the most important of the early religious centers—Pachacamac. Located near the ocean in the Lurín River Valley a few miles south of Lima, the huge ruins of this city include a great pyramid of the Sun Temple. Of lesser size was a temple devoted to the god himself, Pachacamac. By some he is believed to have been the coastal counterpart of Viracocha and therefore linked to Tiahuanaco. The ruins also reveal a large market place where Indians gathered from remote districts to exchange food, textiles, and pottery. Near-by and possibly indicating further its religious character are huge cemeteries, part of a remarkable series of burial grounds along this part of the coast of Peru, to which apparently Indians brought from afar their dead to be buried.

Cuzco: Pre-Inca. Dominating Cuzco and the valley of the Urubamba, where the Incas were to establish their cultural home, were an unknown people who, apparently succeeding Tiahuanaco, were builders of monolithic structures. To defend their strategically located city of Cuzco, they built at an unknown time four great fortresses. Protecting Cuzco itself was mighty Sacsahuaman, regarded as one of the greatest engineering and military achievements of the American Indian. A few miles to the east and a thousand feet above the Urubamba River they constructed Pisac, the first in a series of three to defend the valley and approaches to Cuzco. The excellence of its perfectly cut stone construction as well as the beauty of the stones themselves find no equal in Inca architecture. Twenty-five miles northward from Pisac is Ollantaytambo, a massive fort hewn into the living rock of the mountain. Here, too, clings the story of Ollantay, a drama of love and battle, dating from the time of the Incas and believed by some to be the most authentic piece of existing Indian folklore. Still farther north and constructed high above the gorge of the Urubamba are the now famous remains of the great fort of Machu Picchu.

The monumental remains of all these four forts are characterized by monolithic slabs of stone laid in place in a series of terraces. The lower terrace of Sacsahuaman, for example, presents a face of these monoliths half a mile in length. Everywhere they show evidence of later Inca construction where the earlier walls were overlaid with Inca masonry or repairs have been made. Little is known, in fact, of the actual origin of these edifices. Some attribute them to Tiahuanaco builders; others believe they are products of the immediate predecessors of the Incas themselves who carried on the tradition of stone-cutting.

Inca Culture. Upon this broad base of pre-Inca civilization from Ecuador to Chile, the Incas, of whose history we have some record, imposed their own distinctive culture. The Incas belonged to the great

Quechua tribe which reached from northern Chile to southern Colombia, enclosing within it as a major exception the Aymaras, located in southern Peru and Bolivia. Their origins are veiled in tradition. These stories, however, as well as the sixteenth century Spanish accounts of Inca history leave much to be desired. It is believed with reason that the Incas made their entry into the Cuzco region about 1200 A.D. from the south, when two tribes combined to overthrow the pre-Inca control at Tiahuanaco and Cuzco. The Incas then refounded Cuzco under their leader, Manco Capac, in the middle of the thirteenth century.

In the next three centuries they conquered the isolated pre-Inca cultural areas and for the first time established a unified government over this Andean region. At the same time they invaded the territory of many primitive neighboring groups and enslaved them in the *mitaya* system of forced labor, later continued by the Spaniards. By the middle of the fifteenth century Inca control extended from Quito in Ecuador to central Chile, a distance of some 1,500 miles, and eastward into the Brazilian wilderness and northern Argentina of today. It is believed that within this vast region lived possibly 4,000,000 to 6,000,000 Indians.

While the following description of the Inca administrative system is the accepted one, serious doubts have arisen concerning the efficiency of this society. Broadly speaking, the Incas divided their area into four vaguely defined administrative districts. The political, military, and religious capital was at Cuzco. Northward through central Peru and Ecuador was a second area, the coastal region composed a third, and that beyond the Andes a fourth. The people as a whole were divided into ten classes and assigned duties corresponding to their physical capacities and ages. The lowest unit was the *Chunca,* made up of ten families presided over by an official whose duties were to care for and control them. The next highest unit, the *Picha,* was composed of fifty families in turn subordinate to the *Pachaca,* a unit of one hundred families. Thus the system, a decimal one, continued up to the *Hunu,* comprising 10,000 households, and the *Tucuiricuc,* 40,000 households. The heads of the two latter groups apparently were the governors of provinces into which the four departments were divided. Over the latter the *Apu-cuna* were the highest officials next to the Inca himself.

Probably the best explanation of this highly rigid system of control over the population rested upon the simple necessity of guaranteeing an adequate food supply. The vast area of the Incas was in the main a desert. Only in the river valleys, the Urubamba, Apurimac, Lurín, Marañón, the Rimac, and a few others, were conditions of soil and water sufficient to provide food. Thus terracing, which had been practiced extensively by all the pre-Inca people, continued to be a major feature of the Inca culture. Moreover, by thus exercising a strict control over the population, the Incas were able to provide food for those who did not cultivate the soil. These were legion: the vast military organization, the far-flung priesthood, and the equally large number of adminstrative officers, who, moreover, were all tax-exempt.

The system thus established facilitated the collection of tribute and the distribution of supplies, tools, and seed to the working population. Broadly speaking, all men, except those in the exempted categories, between the ages of twenty-five and fifty years, called *Purics,* were liable for work. Youths and children were given lighter duties, and those above fifty relieved of heavy tasks. Taxes were as varied as the needs of the Inca government. These were paid in products characteristic of the various regions. Some sent corn and cocoa, others sea food and manufactured goods, while all districts were called upon for personal and public service by individuals. Tribute came also in the form of livestock, the alpaca and the llama, textiles, metals, pottery, weapons, and gold and silver ornaments. It is impossible to judge the tax burden, but in view of the large numbers that were exempt the working population obviously carried a heavy load. It is believed, however, that poverty was nonexistent and that the aged and ill were cared for under the system.

Upon this economic base rested the structure of Inca society. At the pinnacle was the Inca, called the *Sapa Inca.* He was at once the military, religious, and civil chief, the head of the Inca tribe, and the earthly representative of their principal deity called Pachacamac or a more ancient figure, Viracocha. About him were a higher and a lesser nobility. The higher stemmed from the Inca tribe itself; the lesser, called *Curacas,* were drawn from the chiefs of the conquered tribes. Upon this nobility the Inca drew for the priesthood, the judges, military governors, and all the higher administrative officers. Thus a gulf, impossible to cross, existed between the masses and the Inca nobility.

The cement which held together these classes and the vast area of Inca control was the carefully cultivated religious practices based upon age-old superstitions and long-established beliefs. While little is known of the pre-Inca religions, everywhere evidence testified to the worship of the sun. The Incas called themselves the Children of the Sun, a fact not surprising among people living eternally on the high cloudless plateaus of the Andes. But their religious thinking had carried them beyond the status of mere sun-worshipers. They envisaged the sky's golden orb of light as the outward manifestation of a still greater intelligence which had created the sun and all other things. This being they called Pacha-camac or Viracocha. To him they erected their great Temple of the Sun in Cuzco and richly decorated it with golden images of the god. The Inca himself they considered the earthly representative of Viracocha, so that in their conquests all were taught to look toward Cuzco, where the Inca wielded the power of the sun. Throughout the empire they erected temples to the sun and staffed them with a priesthood and virgins who kept the sacred fires burning. They maintained elaborate ceremonies of fasting, prayer, and animal sacrifice. Their prayers were in harmony with the great concept of a single being and yet reflected the melancholy environment of their desert dominions. Their supplications to Viracocha, beautiful and thoughtful, have the moving power of the greatest passages of the Old Testament.

The material culture of the Incas, like that of the Aztecs in Mexico, owed much to their predecessors. In the cultivation of the land the Incas followed existing methods of terracing, practiced from Mexico to Chile, fertilized the soil, and utilized elaborate irrigation systems of canals and aqueducts. They continued the earlier tradition of stone construction in their houses and temples, bringing this art to a high perfection. The later Incas gave up the use of monolithic stones, but showed great skill in cutting and fitting stones of quadrangular shape and laying them in courses. The curving wall of the Temple of the Sun, upon which the Spaniards constructed the Monastery of St. Dominic in Cuczo, is one of the finest examples of their skill. A network of roads held together their vast region. Two main highways provided the base: one, beginning in Colombia, ran through the central areas of Ecuador, Peru, and Bolivia, where it branched with one artery going toward present-day Argentina and the other to Chile; the second began near Tumbez, near the present Ecuadorian border, and ran along the coast southward to end in central Chile. The principal connection between the two apparently was a high-way which ran westward from Cuzco through present Vilcas-Huamán and joined the north-south coastal road. Lateral connections provided access to all parts of the empire. Along these highways the Incas erected hostels at fixed intervals for the comfort of travelers, soldiers, runners of the Inca, and officials.

In art the Incas excelled in gold, silver, bronze, and coppersmithing. So skillful were they that the golden and silver flowers in the Inca's garden at Cuzco deceived the invading Spaniards until a soldier chanced to pluck one. The gold images and decorations in the Temple of the Sun were executed with finesse that approached that of the Renaissance. They showed equal abilities in the manufacture, decoration, and sculpturing of pottery, typified in the aryballus, graceful in shape and beautifully painted in colors that followed precise geometric designs. In textiles, with only cotton and wool available to them, they wove garments and tapestries with designs often original in conception and beautifully executed. However, in this art they never equaled the handiwork of the weavers of Nazca.

It is a startling fact that the administration of the great Inca empire was carried on with no other device for recording data than the *quipu*. This invention was a simple collection of threads of different colors and lengths upon which knots were tied to keep population, tax, and military records and all accounts of civil administration. The use of the *quipu* implied a knowledge of arithmetic, while their use of stone in house and temple construction indicated an understanding of geometrical and mechanical principles. In other fields of science they had inherited the art of trepanning and understood the use of a number of drugs including quinine and cocoa. In astronomy they were familiar with a number of the planets and had developed a calendar system, unrecorded, with their new year starting June 21. They recognized twelve months of thirty days each to which they added five days annually and a sixth every four years. In spite of these advances, the Incas developed no form of writing, neither picture-writing nor hieroglyphic.

While now it is not customary to accept as historical fact the line of "100 Inca kings," we are fairly certain of the history of the Incas who immediately preceded Atahualpa, whom the Spaniards overthrew in 1533. After Manco and Viracocha had conquered and refounded Cuzco, Cusi, the son of Viracocha, carried Inca conquests northward to the valley of Cajamarca and southward to Tiahuanaco. Shortly after 1400 he was succeeded by his son, Tupac Yupanqui, who continued the Inca conquests into central Chile and pushed the advance northward into Ecuador to occupy Quito. A great administrator, he strengthened his empire by building roads, bridges, and military posts and making alliances with tribes too powerful to subdue. In 1475, after governing sixty years and giving the Inca empire the form it was to retain until the arrival of the Spaniards, he was succeeded by Huayna Capac.

Huayna completed the subjugation of Quito, but blackened his record with the ruthless extermination of the Cara tribe, which had heroically resisted conquest. Living much of his life in the region of the

Caras, he finally established his military headquarters at Quito, where he died in 1527. Out of his fondness for Quito, the old Inca laid the basis for a civil war. His Cara wife bore him a son, Atahualpa, while his legal wife at Cuzco gave him several, of whom Huascar was entitled to succeed. Before his death Huayna named Huascar as his successor over the undoubtedly more able and ambitious Atahualpa. Civil war ensued. By 1530 Atahualpa had defeated Huascar, seized the royal mantle of Inca power at Cuzco, and established his military headquarters at Cajamarca, the better to control an empire torn by civil war. There in 1532 he received Pizarro about whose activities he had long been intensely curious.

Other South American Indians. North of the Inca area in present-day Colombia emerged the Chibcha culture. Its center was in the valley of the Magdalena River, but related tribes extended to the edge of the Amazonian jungle, westward to the Pacific coast, through Panama, and along the Atlantic coast of Nicaragua and Costa Rica. The Chibchas, also known as the *Muisca*, had developed agriculture, raised a variety of crops, and had made marked progress in the use of stone in the construction of temples and well-carved idols. In science they understood arithmetic, evident in the use of the vigesimal system, knew how to build suspension bridges, and paved highways.

In their material life the Chibchas wove fabrics of excellent quality, made pottery, and understood the use of dyes. The abundance of precious and semiprecious stones was the basis of their lapidary art, in which they exhibited great technical skill. Their key location at the top of the continent gave them a foundation for an extensive trade which reached from Ecuador to Central America. They used weights and measures and evolved a thin gold disc for use as money, the only known instance of this practice in the New World.

The principal gods were the sun, the moon, and the earth, together with a variety of lesser deities. Their heaven they placed in the center of the earth, believing that the gossamer webs of spiders carried the soul downward to their paradise. This assumption gave rise to the interesting ceremony associated later in history with the story of the "Gilded Man" or *El Dorado.* For ages unknown the Chibchas had gathered along the shores of Lake Guatavita on the occasion of inducting their chief into office to show respect to their earth god. The chief, powdered with gold dust, leaped at the height of the ceremony from a flower-decked raft into the lake, while the worshipers cast into the water their offerings of gold and silver ornaments and precious stones. The Chibchas buried their chiefs in sepulchral mounds which, where not already looted, have given up precious stores of gold and silver. These as well as jewels and gold and silver ornaments recovered from the lake have furnished many fine examples of Chibchan art.

In government the chiefs of the Chibchan territory in the Magdalenan region had evolved into two separate communities. At the head of each was a ruler, *Zipa* in the south and *Zaque* in the north. Their constant conflict, like that in Peru, facilitated later the Spanish conquest, although some integration was taking place between the two groups, who recognized at the time of the conquest a high priest as peacemaker.

The rest of South America boasted no great civilizations such as those of the Andean region. Certain primitive Indian groups, however, did exercise an influence in the areas later occupied by Spain and Portugal. The Arawaks, whose home was in the Orinoco basin, spread widely and are thought by some to have carried over vast regions important cultural traits. Northward the Arawaks reached across the Caribbean Islands to the tip of Florida; southward the Arawak language spread through central Brazil and into limited areas of Peru and Bolivia of today. Some authorities believe that the Arawaks transferred to other tribes the use of manioc, cocoa, and the rubber ball game. Others suggest that the Arawaks possibly contributed to the rise of the higher Andean cultures by a migration from the Amazonian valley.

The Caribs, deadly enemies of the Arawaks, lived in the eastern Orinoco basin on the Caribbean Islands and extended southward into northern Brazil. A warlike tribe which practiced cannibalism, the Caribs offered a serious obstacle to European occupation of their regions. Of more significance for the history of Brazil were the Tupí Indians. These dwelt along the southern bank of the Amazon and in a huge arc on the Atlantic coast to southern Brazil, where they extended inland, closely associated with the Guaraní along the Paraná River Valley. The Tupí raised manioc, yams, peppers, maize, squash, tobacco, and peanuts, under somewhat wasteful methods. Their houses were simple, palm-thatched huts, though some were large enough to accommodate a number of families. They wove baskets and made cloth. Dwelling along rivers, they made canoes and supplemented their religious ceremonies. Because of their location along the coast and in the south, where the Portuguese later colonized, the Tupí had a greater influence upon Brazil than other tribes of that colony. The Tupí-Guaraní language became, in fact, the *lingua franca* of colonial Brazil.

In Paraguay the Guaraní had their principal centers east of the

Paraguay River, practiced agriculture, hunted, and fished. Unlike the Tupí, they were a gentle people. It was apparently their easily learned language that the Tupí adopted and which came into common use in Brazil. To the south were the warlike and cannibalistic Charrúas of Uruguay and the pampas Indians of Argentina.

Southern South America had as its most distinctive group affecting later history the Araucanians. These lived west of the Andes in southern Chile below the Río Maule, in a territory of some 60,000 square miles thickly populated. They used wood for house construction and cultivated maize, potatoes, ground nuts, and pepper beans. They manufactured a coarse clothing from the wool of the llama and knew how to make clay and wooden pottery. They were a people of fine physique, brave in war and of great endurance. Their military abilities had stopped Inca expansion south of the river Maule. Significantly, their later wars and occasional periods of peace, when trade flourished, welded the Spanish settlers and the Araucanians into the vigorous Chilean people of today.

Indian Contributions. While the New World Indian civilizations, existing at the time Columbus arrived, still remain largely a mystery, there is no doubt of the reality of their contributions. They had in their great centers of culture domesticated a variety of foods which have come into world-wide use. Their knowledge of herbs and medicinal plants they gave to the Spaniards, who made them known in Europe. The mining activities of the Aztecs, Chibchas, and Incas had stored up a great treasure. More important, they had disclosed, in the discovery of gold and particularly silver in quantity, the precise minerals which became the basis for the rapid expansion of the capitalistic system in the Old World. While the Spaniards transported these metals to Europe, it was Indian muscle that dug them from the ground.

Indian culture, apparent in existing architectural ruins, in fine textiles, ceramics, and pottery, testified to a capacity for artistic creation which is only today in Mexico coming into full flower. Their folk tales, dances, and songs, too, have become part of the cultural tradition of the New World. In scientific endeavor they exhibited a capacity comparable to that of the Europeans. The Maya calendar has never been equaled in accuracy. The technique of brain surgery was practiced by the Incas and their forerunners centuries before it was known in Europe. Their use of anesthetics likewise was totally unknown in early modern Europe. Their technical skill in the use of dyes has remained unsurpassed.

It is an unhappy fact that while Europeans quickly learned to exploit the labor of these gifted aborigines, their descendants in many countries of Latin America have not yet found the key to unlock the obvious capacities of the Indian. Toward this treasure of human achievement the process of European expansion had been moving for more than three centuries before Columbus. Its arrival in the New World left the question: What would have been the future evolution of Indian society if it had been left untouched?

Gulf of
Venezuela
CURACAO
I. OF MARGARITA
TRINIDAD I.

Gulf of
Darien

Lake
Maracaibo
Apure
Orinoco
Caroni

ATLANTIC

OCEAN

Magdalena
Meta

R.

R.

Caqueta
R.

Rio
Negro

GUIANA HIGHLANDS

Orinoco
R.

MARJÓ ISLAND

Gulf of
Guayaquil
Marañon
R.

Amazon
R.

Amazon
R.

R.

R.

R.

Tocantins
R.

The
Sertão

Ucayali
R.

Madeira

Tapajós

Xingú

São Francisco R.

BRAZILIAN

Lake
Titicaca

MATTO
GROSSO
PLATEAU

HIGHLANDS

Pilcomayo

Chaco

R.

R.

R.

ATACAMA
DESERT

Paraguay
R.

Paraná

PACIFIC

Pampa

Parana R.

Uruguay
R.

R.

L. dos
Patos

ATLANTIC

Aconcagua
23,080

Rio Negro

L. Mirim

OCEAN

Biobio R.

Rio de la Plata

OCEAN

Colorado
R.

Gulf of
Bahía Blanca

ARCHIPELAGO
OF CHONOS

PATAGONIA HIGHLANDS

Gulf of
St. George

FALKLAND IS.

Straits of Magellan

Cape Horn

ANDES   MOUNTAINS

PHYSICAL MAP
OF
SOUTH AMERICA

Scale of Miles
0   200   400   600   800

26

Chapter II

THE EUROPEAN BACKGROUND
AND THE DISCOVERY
OF AMERICA

Part I. EUROPEAN BACKGROUND: MEDITERRANEAN
EXPANSION

Spain merits the honor of the effective discovery of America. The movement which culminated in the Spanish achievement, however, had a long history of Mediterranean expansion. It began with the Phoenicians in the ancient world, continued under the Moslems and the Crusaders, burst the bonds of the Mediterranean under the Portuguese, and finally came to a head in the voyage of Columbus. Describing the unity of this process of expansion which inevitably led to the discovery of the New World is the purpose of this chapter.

The Ancient World. The growth of civilization in the ancient centers of Mesopotamia and Egypt spread trade along the littoral of Syria and Palestine. As carriers the Phoenicians were the first to make commerce sea-borne. The coming of the Greeks into the ancient world about 2000 B.C., upsetting Phoenicia's profitable barter with the Minoan Cyclades and the Black Sea, turned Phoenicians westward. Their arrival along the coast of Spain from Tyre about 1200 B.C., to trade with the Tartesos on the Strait of Gibraltar marked the first step in the westward expansion of the Mediterranean.

The Tartesos whom the Phoenicians found settled at the mouth of the Guadalquivir River had already explored the Atlantic as far as Britain. They and not the Phoenicians were the first to go to the western ocean from the Mediterranean. After founding Gades (Cádiz) about 1100 B.C. as a market for silver and tin the Phoenicians turned southward along the African coast and discovered the islands of Madeira, from which they brought back purple dye. The Canary Islands, too, fell within the scope of their explorations; the finding of Carthaginian coins on the

Azores has suggested the possibility of the discovery of that group by the ancients. Meanwhile, other Phoenicians from Tyre founded Carthage about 800 B.C. Thenceforth they absorbed the trade of southern Spain, destroying the Tartesos in the process by 500 B.C.

In the following centuries, the Carthaginians not only made few Atlantic explorations, but effectively discouraged oceanic navigation. Some time after 500 B.C. to insure their control in the west, they closed the Strait of Gibraltar and spread throughout the Mediterranean horror stories of the Atlantic which persisted down to the time of Columbus. More effectively, the Carthaginian-Roman treaty of 348 B.C. prohibited the Romans and the Greek Massilians from navigating beyond the Pillars of Hercules.

The overthrow of Carthage and the Roman conquest of the Iberian Peninsula were disastrous to the extension of geographical knowledge of the Atlantic. However, the tradition lingered. Seneca's famous prophecy that by leaving Spain one could voyage to Asia foreshadowed the Colombian achievement of fifteen hundred years later. But Roman interests in the Atlantic were largely intellectual; the Greek spirit of actual exploration languished.

To the east, however, both Greeks and Romans continued their voyages and travels. The Greeks explored the coast of India and established connections in historic times with the Orient and the western Mediterranean. The Romans, while eschewing Atlantic expeditions, sent their explorers deep into Africa. Egyptian traders under the Romans discovered Madagascar, coasted past India and Ceylon, and reached the Strait of Malacca. During the first three centuries of the Christian era, the Romans had direct relations with the Orient via the interior of Asia. After that time, while there are no known records of individual Romans visiting China and India, the trade between the Orient and the Mediterranean persisted in the hands of intermediaries. That Rome could satisfy Alaric's famous levy in 404 for 4,000 pieces of silk raiment and 3,000 pounds of pepper illustrates the vigor of the commerce.

Moslem Expansion Westward. The decline and fall of the Roman Empire brought a slow extinction to this trade. But in the seventh century the rise of Islam renewed Mediterranean expansion. By 900 A.D. the Moslems had reached India and soon after entered the East Indies, China, and Japan. To the west they voyaged the Atlantic to rediscover the Canary Islands and explore the coast of Africa. At the beginning of the next century, 711 A.D., they began the conquest of Spain and the invasion of southern Italy. A civilized people, they brought the scientific achievements of the Greeks to the West as well as the commercial products of the Orient.

Norse Expansion. Contemporaneously with the expansion of the Moslems in the Mediterranean area, the Scandinavians embarked upon travels that carried them east into Russia to the Black Sea and to the west into the Atlantic Ocean. After 850 A.D. their trips to Iceland were frequent. Eric the Red just before 900 A.D. reached a land he named Greenland in the hope of attracting settlers there. In the next century other vikings touched Labrador. By 1000 under Leif Ericson these hardy northerners had found a coast covered with trees, inhabited by a bronze-skinned people who navigated the seas in small, hide-covered boats. This land, called Vinland, was possibly the New England coast. But certain it is that the Norsemen founded settlements farther north in Labrador, whence their articles of trade and use spread far and wide into the interior of the North American continent.

These Norse voyages did not lead to the effective colonization of the New World. They do have significance for the exploration of the Atlantic Ocean and as a link in Mediterranean expansion. Colonization of Greenland carried on continuously into the fifteenth century brought Norse voyages to the attention of the Portuguese. In that century the Portuguese made North Atlantic expeditions of which we know little, beyond the fact that they reached Greenland which the Portuguese called Labrador. Not without their interest, too, were the voyages of French fishermen, long before Columbus, across the North Atlantic to the cod banks of Labrador.

Economic Expansion of the Mediterranean. While Norse expansion is indeed part of the general picture of European expansion, the renewal of economic contacts by the Moslems between the Orient and the Mediterranean more directly led to the discovery of America. The Arabs brought to the West new agricultural products, peaches, lemons, rice, sugar cane, oranges, the silkworm and the mulberry tree, cotton, hemp, flax. Pre-eminently a trading people, they introduced the West to Oriental spices, rugs, robes stitched in gold and silver thread, damask, muslin, satins, perfumes, glassware, clocks, musical instruments: necessities and luxuries.

By the year 1000 A.D. this Moslem trade with the Orient took on an added significance. By that date the disturbed conditions following the fall of the Roman Empire and the barbarian invasions had disappeared. Feudal states emerged. With them came the rise of medieval towns, which, based upon a growing trade and new industries, prepared the

way for the dynamics of capitalism and middle class. These cities imported Moslem goods and sent them by traders into western Europe.
Feudal nobility, made wealthy by the labor of peasants, provided a huge
market for these goods. They welcomed bright-colored tapestries to cover
the bleak interior of the castles; Oriental rugs to replace evil-smelling
straw; fine linens, damask, and silk for clothing and furnishings; precious
jewels and richly woven robes for adornment. At the same time the growing middle class in the towns was an expanding market for the identical
goods. The wife of the merchant prince modeled her dress and house
furnishings upon those of the lady of the castle. She could not be less
well turned out.

In this booming Mediterranean commerce, Italy occupied a strategic
position. Genoa, Florence, Venice, and other cities sent their medieval
galleys to the eastern Mediterranean. There they established colonies,
built navies to protect their sea-borne traffic and delivered the precious
eastern wares over Alpine routes into southern Germany, up the Rhone
River into France, through the Strait of Gibraltar to Lisbon on the
Tagus, to London on the Thames, and into the mouths of the Rhine,
Elbe, and other German rivers. This commerce met that of the Norsemen.
From Russia they brought ermine for royalty, fish for the vast market
encouraged by Catholic fasting, tall pines for shipbuilding, resin, tar,
pelts, and other northern products. Thus by the twelfth century a vast
network of land and sea routes indissolubly connected the European
market with the trade routes of the Orient.

It was inevitable that this commercial contact with the Orient should
attract European travelers, missionaries, and explorers. Thus in 1246 Juan
Pian de Carpini, sent by Pope Innocent IV, visited the Great Khan of
the Mongols, who had recently invaded Russia. Shortly after (1253–
1254), William de Rubruquis, the emissary of St. Louis of France, reached
the court of the Great Khan. But more famous and significant for his
later influence on European expansion was Marco Polo. Taken to the
Orient by his father and uncle between 1271 and 1295, Marco Polo
followed the well-known route through the Black Sea and across the
steppes of Asia to Pekin. He remained in China in the Great Khan's
service for over ten years, occupying high posts and observing Chinese
life in the late thirteenth century. On his return he voyaged down the
coast of China and passed through the Malay Straits and on to India,
whence he found his way back to the Mediterranean through the Per-
sian Gulf. Later Columbus, influenced by Marco Polo's book, sought in
vain for a strait that would lead to India. Besides Marco Polo, mission-

aries reached China, notably Fray Odoico de Pordenone; by the middle of the fourteenth century, a Catholic bishop was residing in Pekin.

The Crusades. Keeping pace with the expanding commercial development of Europe was the growth of the Christian church. By 1100 most of western Europe had been converted to Christianity, and the church was looking for new fields to conquer. Its vast, fervent missionary organization saw in Islam not only a threat to its own expansion but an opportunity to win new converts. A precedent for attack on Islam existed in Spain, where for two centuries the church had carried on a crusade against the Moslems. Thus in the late eleventh century, when the Seljuk Turks molested Christian pilgrims journeying to the holy places in Palestine and threatened the overthrow of the Eastern Empire, the church led the way in launching the Crusades.

Scientific Advances. The Crusades gave renewed impetus to the economic expansion of the Mediterranean. Fleets that carried Crusaders to the eastern shores came back loaded with Oriental goods. Italian cities established colonies in Egypt, Palestine, and Constantinople, as they had previously in Marseilles and Barcelona and Lisbon. Out of the urge for profits, ship construction improved. The primitive craft of the early Middle Ages gave way to larger ships; sails, greater deck space, and larger holds were added. The old double rudder was replaced by a single one, a viking contribution. Inevitably, nautical science advanced rapidly. Italian mariners noted the outlines of the Mediterranean coasts on charts called *portolani,* the earliest step in the science of cartography. By the middle of the fourteenth century, 1339, Dulcert had constructed his map. Not only did it include western Europe and the Mediterranean Sea, but showed quite accurately the leading cities of Mesopotamia, as well as the main outlines of the Near East. Even more striking for its remarkable accuracy was the Catalan map of the Mediterranean made in 1375 for Charles V of France. So, too, mariners gradually abandoned the practice of holding close to the coast and stood out to sea, relying on new inventions, the compass and the astrolabe.

Portuguese Expansion. By the end of the fourteenth century the growing demand for Oriental goods, improved ship construction, and new scientific tools made possible the next major step in Mediterranean expansion: the advance into the Atlantic. Here Portugal took the lead. Many factors motivated her expansion. The Italian monopoly of the Mediterranean blocked her way through that sea. When John I in 1385 expelled the Moslems who had long dominated Portugal, the vigorous Portuguese middle class in Lisbon kept up their trading contacts across the Strait of Gibraltar. This commerce awakened the Portuguese to the possibilities of extending their power along the Atlantic coast of Africa. The church, too, supported the monarchy and the middle class in this new venture, for it had long nursed a hope of rescuing a Christian legendary figure, Prester John, lost somewhere in the depths of Africa. Early in the fifteenth century, Prince Henry, called the Great Navigator, harnessed these forces to further his scientific interests in the unknown world to the south. He believed that a route could be found around Africa to the Orient.

Prince Henry: Africa. Assigned the governorship of Algarve in the south of Portugal, Prince Henry began his program with the founding of a school for pilots at Sagres. Here he gathered Italian and Portuguese scientists, cosmographers, geographers, mathematicians, and others to train pilots for their voyages southward. The first leg of Portuguese expansion put them, in 1420–1430, into possession of the African coast as far as Cape Bojador and the island of Madeira. In 1434 Gil Eannes doubled the troublesome cape to open a route toward the Gulf of Guinea. In 1427 they discovered and occupied the Cape Verde Islands and by 1455 had established posts on the Senegalese coast. By this date, too, they explored the Guinea coast itself, uncovering a treasure of gold and ivory. The Negroes that they enslaved there began the history of that unfortunate practice in western Europe. Because of the strategic importance of the Cape Verde Islands the Portuguese colonized them to raise crops supplying the growing number of ships going to and from the Guinea coast.

The death of Prince Henry in 1460 delayed Portuguese exploration beyond the Gulf of Guinea for twenty years. The rich haul of gold, ivory, and slaves made Portuguese captains loath to push beyond for purely academic reasons. However, with the coming of John II to the throne in 1481, exploration began anew. Between 1482 and 1483 Diego Cão discovered the Congo River, explored the coast of Angola, and entered Walfish Bay.

Bartolomeu Dias. King John, with a scientific outlook, also mindful of Portugal's economic interest in getting to India, noted the relationship of the Cão voyage to what was known from Italian and Moslem maps of the location of India. He accordingly planned with care for the next expedition. As a preliminary, he sent Pedro de Covilhã in 1485 to establish relations with Ethiopia and follow the coast of East Africa southward to Safala Bay opposite Madagascar. Covilhã, too, was to report back regarding the most suitable route to India and the ocean pathways to reach the spice lands of the Orient. At the same time he prepared the expedition headed by Bartolomeu Dias to continue the exploration of the west coast of Africa. The Dias expedition, 1487–1488, after reaching Walfish Bay, continued southward over the protests of the frightened crew and in the face of adverse weather. Dias, in fact, sailed unknowingly beyond the cape and discovered it as he turned north. King John, delighted with the news, named it the Cape of Good Hope for the promise it held of reaching India.

Portuguese Atlantic Expeditions. In these years, 1420–1488, the Portuguese had an incidental interest in western and northern Atlantic exploration. Between 1439 and 1443 they discovered and colonized the Azores. Soon the inhabitants there focused royal interest on the possibility of exploring westward in search of lands which rumor and fable had constantly reported. The Portuguese monarchs gave encouragement, but little else. Nevertheless, these reports of mythical islands were so insistent that they were frequently recorded on fifteenth century and later maps. The most famous of these was the Pareto Map of 1455, which among other islands located one called Brazil. Legend gave this bit of land the rather unusual distinction of being migratory. Accounts sited it in many places, frequently off the coast of Ireland. Apparently, too, the Portuguese in the fifteenth century made voyages from the Azores into the north Atlantic and reached Greenland, which it is believed they called Labrador. So firmly are Portuguese and some Brazilian historians convinced that one of these voyages reached Labrador in the New World that they credit the explorer, João Vaz Corte-Real, with the discovery of America in 1472, twenty years before Columbus!

This Atlantic activity of the Portuguese, however, does have a twofold significance. One result was that out of this environment of Portuguese training and association with the prevailing beliefs of land to the west came Columbus to make his famous proposal. Of lesser importance, this Portuguese interest in the north Atlantic provided a background which satisfactorily explains the known expedition which the Portuguese, Gaspar Corte-Real, made in 1500 to Labrador.

But this western exploration was in fact a side issue to the Portuguese monarchs. Their great dream was an African-controlled route to the eastern Spice Islands. Thus upon the return of Dias in 1488, King John II laid plans for the expedition he was now convinced would reach India. In the midst of these preparations the king received the shocking news of Columbus' discovery of lands to the west. This event and other reasons delayed the departure of the expedition until 1497, when Vasca da Gama finally set sail on the epoch-making voyage which carried Portuguese power to India.

Part II. COLUMBUS AND THE DISCOVERY OF AMERICA

With the Italians in control of the Mediterranean routes to the Orient and Portuguese power extended along the coast of Africa, but one avenue remained to reach the Orient westward across the Atlantic. Looming large in men's thinking of the times were the voyages of the Portuguese northward into the Atlantic and southward around Africa's huge shoulder. Columbus was but one of many who believed that by sailing west one could reach the Spice Islands.

The Life of Columbus. Columbus, the man, is a mystery. Associated with the world's best-known event, he is least known himself. Except for the few years before and after 1492, when he rose to heights of fame, little can be said of him with certainty. Even the date of his birth is placed variously from 1434 to 1454, though 1451 seems to be most widely accepted. Most authorities agree, too, that he was born in Genoa, a wool carder's son. However, since the principal authority used to establish his birthplace is his own simple statement, "I am a Genoese," it may be possible to infer that Columbus was born in one of the Spanish Genoese colonies and not in Genoa proper.

Little if anything trustworthy is known of his early education. When Columbus entered the services of Portugal is likewise unknown. But his seeking the advice of Paolo Toscanelli, who wrote a famous letter in 1474 advising a voyage to the west, though the authenticity of that letter has been questioned, may indicate he was in Portugal before 1474. That he was there by that date is accepted. It is believed also that Columbus made a voyage to the north, possibly, but not known for certain, in 1477. Better authority indicates that he did sail to Guinea in 1482. Certain it is he married in Madeira in 1480 Felippa Moñiz, the daughter of Bartolomeu Perestrello, the governor of Porto Santo, where his first son, Diego, was born.

How and when Columbus developed his first ideas of sailing westward is not known. That he had studied the question is apparent from his marginal notes on his copy of Marco Polo's travels and his perusal of the *Imago Mundi* of Pierre d'Ally and other volumes dealing with the Orient. Undoubtedly, too, he was deeply influenced by the stories he heard from Portuguese navigators who had voyaged the Atlantic. Gómara, the historian, reports that a pilot who had discovered land to the west of Madeira died in Columbus' house and left with him an account of the voyage.

After his return from Guinea, Columbus appealed to John II in 1483 or 1484 for permission to explore to the west. The king, at the moment sending out his own expedition in that direction, refused. Two years later in 1486, seeking the aid of the Spanish monarchs, Columbus met rebuff again. He did, however, make the valuable acquaintance of the Pinzón brothers and other wealthy merchants of Cádiz and Sevilla. Finally, in 1492, through the intercession of the queen's former confessor, Columbus was given an audience. The queen, much impressed with his religious fervor and personal qualities, agreed to finance the expedition in part.

The First Voyage. The famous capitulations drawn up on April 17, 1492, in Granada made Columbus the admiral of the ocean-sea and viceroy and governor-general of the lands he discovered. They gave him the rights to contribute an eighth part to any other expedition sent to the New World, to appoint governors and lesser officials, and to receive a tenth of the gold, silver, and other wealth from the new lands. Columbus himself put up an eighth part from loans negotiated with Martín Alonzo Pinzón and other Genoese and Florentine merchants of Cádiz and Sevilla.

When ready to sail from Palos the expedition carried 120 aboard the *Santa María* or *Gallega,* the *Pinta,* and *Niñá.* Following Portuguese precedent, Columbus took with him as cartographer the great Juan de la Cosa. Leaving Palos on August 3, he followed the well-known route to the Canaries, whence, after a halt, he sailed on September 6 to the west. The route of his voyage shows that he probably sailed southwestward and along the southern edge of the Sargasso Sea, rather than farther north as usually believed. Somewhat to the southeast of the island chain, the Lesser Antilles, he turned northwestward to make his landfall, now agreed upon, on Watlings Island in the Bahama group on October 12, 1492.[1]

In a spirit of thankfulness he called the island San Salvador. Voyaging southward he discovered Cuba, where he gave the name of Indians to the natives flocking to the shore. Sailing eastward along Cuba's northern coast, the expedition discovered mountainous Haiti and named it Española. On its northern coast after the *Santa María* was wrecked, he

[1] Columbus' route suggested here is based upon William Herbert Hobbs, "The Track of the Columbus Caravels in 1492," *The Hispanic American Historical Review,* Vol. XXX, No. 1, Part I (February) 1950, pp. 63–73.

took possession and left a few men as a colony, La Navidad. Turning homeward, Columbus sailed to the Azores, thence to Lisbon, and arrived at Palos, March 15, 1493. Columbus' return was greeted with the wildest enthusiasm. The Sevilla and Cádiz merchants, excluded from the Mediterranean and from the African coast, now believed that a way to the Indies was open to untold wealth. The monarchs, too, thinking that the East Indies and not a New World was within their grasp, accorded Columbus highest honors.

The Line of Demarcation. The success of Columbus and Ferdinand's vigorous plans for a second voyage filled John II of Portugal with misgivings. He had questioned Columbus closely at Lisbon and feared that the discovery in the west might block Portugal's route to the Orient from the Cape of Good Hope. He accordingly proposed to the Spanish monarchs a division of their spheres by a line drawn *east* and *west* along the parallel passing through the Canary Islands. South was to be Portuguese territory; north, Spanish. Columbus had already warned his monarchs of John's antagonism, but they needed little urging to assert their claims. Upon news of Columbus' return they had immediately appealed to Pope Alexander VI, a Spaniard, for recognition of their ownership of the new lands, a practice Portugal had long followed to fortify her title to the African coast.

Taking the Portuguese proposal of a line, the Spanish monarchs suggested to the Pope that it should run rather *north* and *south*. The Pope accordingly issued the famous bull, *Inter Caetera,* which drew a line of demarcation north and south 100 leagues west of the Cape Verde Islands. Not satisfied with this bull, the Catholic kings secured three others in quick succession, which wiped out all papal approval of Portugal's African discoveries and gave Spain the exclusive right to navigate the eastern seas. This invasion of Portuguese territory was too much for John II, who promptly notified the Spanish court that his control of the approaches to Cádiz would make impossible any further Spanish voyages to the west. The Catholic kings could not take this threat lightly, for looming in the background was the possibility of a Portuguese alliance with the recently expelled Moslems. Accordingly, Ferdinand and Isabella agreed to the negotiations out of which came the Treaty of Tordesillas in 1494. It moved the line of demarcation 370 leagues west of the Cape Verde Islands and recognized Portuguese claims to the east of the line and Spain's to the west. Thus Portugal secured the fruits of her long labor and, unknown to her, the eastern part of the still undiscovered Brazil.

Columbus' Fixed Idea: the Three Voyages. When Columbus set out on his second voyage in 1493, he had two objectives. One was to begin the occupation of Española; the other, more important in his mind, was to continue his search for a strait that would lead to India. With his colony safely deposited on the island, Columbus renewed his explorations. In May he discovered the island of Jamaica, turned north to encounter the Isle of Pines, and coasted westward along the shore of Cuba. Evidently discouraged by the long voyage westward, he gave up the search a short distance from the southwestern tip. Returning to Española, he shortly set sail for Spain, where he arrived in March, 1494. Although Columbus' influence was waning, the Catholic monarchs outfitted him with six ships for a third voyage.

His route this time, beginning May 30, 1498, took him to the Cape Verde Islands and then southwestward, a decision possibly influenced by his conversations earlier with John II of Portugal who believed land lay to the south. His voyage carried him to between five and ten degrees south latitude, whence he turned northwest to discover the continent of South America in the region of the Orinoco River. He named it the Land of Grace and the large island, near the mouth of the river, Trinidad after a fancied resemblance of its mountains to the three holy persons. He explored the mouth of the river, the Gulf of Paria, and the neighboring islands of Margarita and Cubagua. Enchanted by the beautiful aspect of the land, Columbus convinced himself that the Orinoco flowed from Paradise. However, since Marco Polo had said nothing of a great continent, Columbus apparently believed he was too far south. Sailing for Española on his way to Spain, he found his colony seething with discontent under the royal governor, Bobadilla, who sent the great admiral home in chains.

Discouraged, lacking funds, and surrounded by enemies, Columbus held on to his great idea. By 1502 he set out again with four ships, accompanied by his two sons. Apparently believing that his second voyage was in the right direction but too far north, he sailed westward from Española south of Jamaica and discovered the coast of present-day Honduras. Following its shores he reached Costa Rica of today, which he named Veragua. There he abandoned the search, November 26, 1502. But striking evidence of the influence of Marco Polo is apparent in Columbus' statement that he believed that the mouths of the Ganges were but nineteen days' sail away. Back in Spain in 1504, dispirited as he saw others favored by the king, he died in Valladolid in 1506.

Columbus' great work, the discovery of America, brought the long process of European expansion to the New World. It is a striking fact that in the very year of the discovery, the Spanish monarchs had themselves brought another process to its end—the unification of Spain. Thus Spain stood ready at the moment to take full advantage of the New World that Columbus had laid at the feet of its rulers. Her preparation for the task came from the long wars against the Moslems, the creation of institutions in Spain to govern and colonize, and a royal leadership that finds few equals in the history of western Europe.

Part III. THE IBERIAN BACKGROUND

Roman and Moslem Contributions. Behind the successful effort to unite Spain lay a long history of peoples who had contributed to the complex civilization of the Iberian peninsula. Especially upon the Spanish and Portuguese people, Roman and Moslem culture left deep imprints, carried later in many forms to the New World.

Roman Contributions. In the 600 years of Roman colonization, from 200 B.C. to 400 A.D., the conquerors spread over the peninsula, intermarrying with the original inhabitants, the Iberians, the Celts in the north, and the remnants of Greek and Phoenician settlers. The Romans with their strong sense of government set up Spain's administrative divisions. Through the Visigothic codes, the basis of Spanish law, they bequeathed the vast body of Roman law to the peninsula. Throughout Spain they built roads, aqueducts, monuments, great public and private buildings, and magnificent cities. This tradition of constructive colonization, Spain revealed later in her own vast work in the New World. So, too, Christianity, imbedded in a powerful church, became more Catholic than Rome.

Moslem Contributions. Excepting the time of barbarian occupation, between the Romans and the unified Spanish and Portuguese nations lay the almost 800-year history of the Moslems. Invading in 711 under Gebel Tarik, they finally were expelled in 1492. Because many facets of this culture were slowly absorbed by the conquerors during the reconquest, it has a special significance in relation to both Spain and Latin America. Moslem government was a theocracy with religious and political power combined in the head of the state. This tradition undoubtedly facilitated the establishment of the later politico-religious autocracy of the Catholic monarchs. While there never developed in Spain a hierarchical feudal organization, Moslem society was fundamentally feudal. The priesthood and warriors made up the aristocracy.

The land was cultivated by peasants bound to the soil. Slavery existed. Nevertheless, the society had a flexibility unknown among the feudal Christian kingdoms of western Europe. Nonnoble merchants had considerable power. Scientists, poets, and writers were honored. It was precisely in these fields of economic and social patterns that the Moslems contributed greatly to Spain and, through her, many influences in Latin American culture.

Agriculture and Industry. Moslem merchants brought to Spain the whole range of Oriental and African products. From India came rice, tumeric, sugar cane, and oranges; Syria provided peaches, lemons, and apricots; Persia sent the mulberry tree and the silkworm. From northern Africa entered cotton; from Arabia, melons, the date palm, and the grapevine. These crops the Moslem farmer tended with a scientific care unknown until centuries later in western Europe. The Moslems introduced horses from Arabia and sheep from Armenia. The cattle range industry first appeared on the plains of Andalucía, whence it spread to the whole peninsula and later, under Spain, to America.

The Moslems created a vast range of industries. Products of their handicrafts, such as decorative tile work, pottery, enamelware, textiles of cotton, wool, and muslin, tapestries, carpets, rugs, silks, and velvets were widely marketed. Toledo was famous for its swords and steel; Córdoba for its shields and leather; Murcia for its iron and brass foundries. Spain, too, inherited from Bagdad its paper-making industry, later a royal Spanish monopoly.

Science and the Arts. In science the Moslems, along with their own, brought both Greek and Oriental achievements to Spain. Greek conceptions of geography, to which the Moslems added those of the Chinese and Hindus, were expanded upon by their own explorations. Their travelers penetrated south through Africa to the Equator and east to the Pacific Ocean as far as Japan. Abn Zaid in 920 condensed the accounts of Moslem travelers to China and India three and one-half centuries before Marco Polo made his journey. In astronomy the Moslems, a seafaring people, had already constructed the best instruments for navigation, including the astrolabe and sextant. It is believed by some, also, that they brought the compass from China, after which it was long known in the Mediterranean.

Moslem medical lore and descriptive accounts of the medicinal properties of plants laid the foundation for later scientific development of many fields of medicine. This tradition carried over among the Spaniards, who later added much to medical knowledge by their accounts of the drugs and herbs of the New World. In other fields of science, notably mathematics and chemistry, the Moslems were pre-eminent. Much of their knowledge they gave to the Spaniards through the Moslem university at Córdoba. Moslem tolerance, too, permitted Spanish Jews, many of whom were scientists, to live within their culture and to extend it to those parts of the Christian world ready to receive it.

The Arts. To the Roman architectural tradition the Moslems added the colorful and substantial house, castle, and mosque construction. In the field of historical writing they established a strong tradition, producing biographies, histories of individual states, and universal histories. This pattern a galaxy of Spanish historians continued with accounts of the conquest of the New World, reflecting strongly Moslem influence in this art. Among the Moslems, too, poetry was highly developed. Ibn Hazam in the eleventh century wrote one of the world's masterpieces in his long poem dedicated to love. This taste for poetical expression flowered among the Spanish people, who carried it to Latin America, where spontaneous poetical compositions testify to the fertile influence of their Moslem background. So too, in folklore, in the dance and music, Moslem culture left deep traces in southern Spain, whence these arts were translated to the New World to become part of the Latin-American cultural tradition.

The Unification of Spain and Portugal. After the Moslem occupation in 711 A.D., Spain dissolved into a pattern of feudal states. In the south were Andalucía and Granada; on the Mediterranean Sea, Valencia and Catalonia; in the center, Castile; to the west, Estremadura and Portugal; and across the north from west to east, León, Galicia, Asturia, and Aragón.

When the reunification movement began about 900 A.D., the Emirate of Córdoba covered most of Portugal and Spain. Its northern boundary corresponded roughly to a line drawn due east across the peninsula from Oporto on the Atlantic Ocean. In the far northeast was the County of Barcelona, while between it and the Emirate were a group of independent Moslem states. In the far north was the tiny kingdom of Navarre; to the northwest was the kingdom of León. With Crusaders from France to aid their forces, the kings of these small Christian states began the long struggle to drive the Moslems back to Africa. Between 910 and 970 the kingdom of León expanded eastward, building castles to hold the country which became known as Castile. Before the end of the tenth century, however, the Counts of Burgos had separated Castile from León. In the next century, 970–1065, came the union of Navarre and Castile and the conquest of León, so that by the latter date Ferdinand I of Castile had united the two countries to become king of Castile and León. In the east by 1037 the kingdom of Aragón had expanded along the Pyrenees and wedged itself between Barcelona and Navarre.

The Unification of Portugal. Beginning in 1055 Ferdinand I of Castile began the conquest of the territory of present-day Portugal from the Moors, organized the north into a county, and made Coimbra the capital. After 1093 Henry of Burgundy with French knights arrived to aid Ferdinand I, in return for which the king rewarded Henry with the County of Portugal and a daughter in marriage. His successor, Affonso Henriques, founder of the Burgundian line in Portugal, tried to win control of Castile, failed, and in turn found his territory reduced to Castilian subjection. By 1143, however, he had been proclaimed king in Portugal and succeeded in eliminating Spanish control in the Treaty of Zamora which recognized Portugal's independence of Spain, that is, Castile. An extremely able man, Affonso continued the wars against the Moslems, captured and annexed Lisbon in 1147 and drove the Moslems south of the Tagus.

In the next two centuries the successors of Affonso continued the drive against the Moors and had largely expelled them by 1340. At the same time they encouraged the agricultural development of the country, overseas trade, and naval development, greatly stimulated by the Portuguese contact with Italian traders at Lisbon. In 1385 John I, who established the new line of kings, the Avis, resisted Castilian efforts to conquer Portugal and finally defeated his enemies at the battle of Aljubarrota in 1385. In the following year, to strengthen both overseas trade and Portugal against Spain, John negotiated the Treaty of Windsor, which began the world's oldest alliance. To seal the bargain, John I married Philippa, the daughter of John the Gaunt of England. During this reign, too, the Portuguese, under the brilliant son of John I, Henry the Navigator, began their career of expansion around Africa.

The Unification of Spain. Meanwhile in Spain itself the process of unification was going forward. In the century and a half after the union of Castile and León, the Christian kingdoms had advanced across the plains of Castile to defeat the Moslems in the decisive battle of Navas de Tolosa in 1212. With the Moslems pushed beyond Toledo, Madrid became the capital of the two united kingdoms. In the northeast the kingdom of Aragón had expelled the Moslems from that area and by 1212 had extended its boundaries as far south as Valencia. After 1212, with the Moslem states themselves disintegrating, the advance of Castile to the south was rapid. By 1266 the Moslems had taken refuge in their last bastion, Granada. Strongly intrenched in its mountainous fastness, they resisted for more than two centuries all efforts to dislodge them. The decisive event that opened the way for their overthrow occurred in 1469 with the marriage of Isabella of Castile and León to Ferdinand of Aragón. The two most powerful Christian kingdoms thus united, the sovereigns launched an offensive in 1482. Ten years later the fall of Granada ended Moslem power in Spain.

The Growth of Royal Institutions. For some six centuries, from 900 to 1492, Spain presented a picture of a feudal nobility, privileged towns, the church, and the monarchy struggling for power within a framework of religious wars: Christian against Moslem. During the Middle Ages, Castilian towns enjoyed a broad local autonomy. It derived from the practice of kings granting privileges *(fueros)* to individuals, usually in groups, who, conquering land from the Moslems, founded towns and governed the neighboring regions. These priviliges included exemption from royal laws in conflict with local ones and the right to elect officials, usually property owners, called *regidores.* These exercised wide powers over collection of taxes, raising armed forces called *hermandades,* regulating use of lands and trade, and otherwise doing whatever was necessary to govern. The towns also had the right to elect representatives to the *Cortes.*

After the marriage of Ferdinand and Isabella, however, the rulers of Castile and Aragón succeeded in undermining many of these municipal privileges. The most effective royal agent was the *corregidor,* an official appointed by the king to cooperate with town governments. In time this officer superseded the local officials in power, particularly through seizing control of the *hermandades.* Under Isabella these militia organizations were converted into a royal army; the *hermandades* themselves became known as *La Santa Hermandad.* The rulers, too, discouraged the exercise of the right to elect representatives to the *Cortes,* a right entirely lost after the revolt of the Spanish *Comuneros* in 1521. Also adding to the control of the king over towns was the use of *pesquisidores* or investigators sent on tours of inspection of municipalities and provinces.

The feudal nobility had an origin in the breakup of the Roman Empire under the Visigothic conquests. Like the towns, they, too, had established deeply intrenched privileges. The rulers of the small Spanish feudal states were forced to recognize these, especially among the richer barons, known later as grandees. The lesser ranks of the nobility, the *hidalgo* and *caballero*, had rights, too, recognized by kings. The grandees could set aside royal laws on their domains, collect their own taxes, and grant privileges to towns. Against these and other feudal powers, the kings struggled. In Castile the conflict became especially bitter after the Battle of Navas de Tolosa, and culminated in a settlement reminiscent of that between King John and the nobles of England in 1215. The Castile charter, known as *Las Siete Partidas,* 1256–1265, recognized the hereditary character of the king of Castile, the divine source of his authority, and the obligations of his subjects to him. At the same time it put limitations upon his authority of such broad character that the nobility was enabled to form entailed estates as a means of preventing royal seizure of lands upon the death of the feudal owner.

However, by 1492 the Spanish kings had gone far in making their political power supreme. The royal army gradually formed out of the *hermandades* weakened the feudal lords who with their retainers were incorporated into the royal forces. After the marriage of Ferdinand and Isabella, feudal decline went forward so rapidly that Ferdinand was able to take over the grand masterships of the military orders of Calantrava, Santiago, Alcántara, Knights Templar, and the Knights of St. John of Jerusalem. The nobility had not lost all of its privileges by 1492, but Spanish rulers were sufficiently strong to hold a firm rein on the conquerors in far-off America.

The church presented a similar problem to the medieval kings of Spain. The clergy which took part in the wars against the Moors shared in the rewards. Kings granted land to the church, as did the nobility. In time the church gained important privileges, such as exemption from some royal tax measures directed at the nobility, the exercise of judicial, legislative, and executive authority on the church's domains, and even the maintenance of armies. The richness of the church's lands led to constant struggle for appointment to ecclesiastical offices. With this framework of land and religion, the great military orders of the church had their origin. Thus the attack of the monarchy upon the nobility was directed equally against the power of the church when these orders were absorbed by Ferdinand. Further, the Catholic monarchs by diplomacy established control over appointment to church offices, collection of tithes, and papal communications. These powers, confirmed by the papacy, became known as the *real patronato,* or royal patronage. In the final phase of the Moslem war, the Inquisition, re-established from 1477 to 1483 in Castile, effectively drove out of Spain all Moslems and Jews who refused to become

Christians. Transferred to the New World, the royal patronage gave the monarchy control over the colonial church.

The judicial system probably contributed as much to the forces centralizing the power of the monarchy as did the army. Its chief officer, the *adelantado mayor* during the unification period, moved about the king's provinces to hold court, hear grievances, and extend royal justice into local regions, provincial and municipal. After 1469 Isabella herself played a leading part in strengthening the royal courts. The *audiencia*, frequently presided over by the monarchs themselves, became the supreme judicial body. *Audiencias* of lesser importance, established in each of the administrative districts, both undermined the local feudal courts and made the nobility more pliable to royal authority. In the sixteenth century the laws of the monarchy were finally codified into the *Recopilación* (Digest) of Castile, 1567. These recognized the existing basis in legal form of the rights of the crown obtained in the preceding centuries against towns, nobility, and church. By that date the Castilian Digest had also become the foundation of colonial law and remained so until the latter was codified in the *Recopilación de las Leyes de Indias* (Digest of the Laws of the Indies), issued in 1680.

Royal Officials. The long process of unification gradually produced officials who carried out the king's will in the areas over which he had established royal authority. On the frontier against the Moslems, an individual volunteering to conquer lands became known as an *adelantado* and was granted wide powers for the purpose. Successful, the *adelantado* exercised his authority in the newly won territory. As the frontier moved forward, the conquered lands in the rear were reduced to provinces over which the king appointed governors. A number of provinces grouped together were commanded by a captain-general. Eventually larger regions, usually fitting a well-defined geographical area, became viceroyalties. Throughout the newly conquered territories, the king took care to secure royal lands for himself, distributed in such fashion as to guard against revolt. Strengthening royal power at every point were the visitor-generals, who made frequent and often unannounced visits to all parts of the realm. Their authority, superseding that of the highest officials, including the viceroys, enabled them to investigate and if necessary make reforms on the spot in taxation and in administrative, judicial, and even military affairs. Their reports and recommendations presented on their return to the monarch kept Spain's rulers in close touch with the administration of their kingdom. This institution played a significant role in colonial government.

The long wars against the Moslems had created powerful centralized institutions under a strong monarchy. These, in essence frontier wars, were followed by colonization of conquered lands. The extraordinary coincidence of the discovery of America by Columbus with the surrender of the Moors at Granada in 1492 opened the way for the continuation of frontier conquests and colonization in the New World. Spain thus was uniquely prepared to carry out an historic task which effectively transferred all aspects of her civilization to colonies destined to become eighteen of the twenty states of Latin America.

Chapter III

COLONIZATION: THE CARIBBEAN AND NORTH AMERICA, 1493-1610

Part I. EXPLORATION OF THE COASTLINE

Introduction. In the fifty years between 1493 and 1543 Spain explored the coastline of most of the New World. The dominating idea behind this extraordinary movement was the search for a strait which would lead to the East Indies. America was an obstacle. Only the Orient was important. The first in the service of Spain to reach the mainland was Amerigo Vespucci, who discovered the North American continent along the Central American coast in 1497. His claim, however, that he reached as far north as Cape Hatteras is not accepted. John Cabot, his contemporary, landed at Cape Breton in the same year, but England did not press the search.

Exploration of the South American Coastline. In the next year, 1498, Columbus opened the exploration of South America with his discovery of Trinidad and the probing of the mouth of the Orinoco River. In 1499 Alonzo de Ojeda and Vespucci explored the coast from the eastern tip of Brazil to the Gulf of Maracaibo. On the northern coast, noting Indians living in huts above the water, Ojeda named the region Little Venice or Venezuela. The next significant advance came from the interest of King John II of Portugal. After sending out Pedro Alvares Cabral in 1500 to claim Brazil, King John dispatched Vespucci, who in 1501–1502 made his third and greatest voyage to examine in detail the coastline of eastern South America. Moving southward from Cape San Roque he discovered the Río de la Plata. Beyond, he continued his voyage, following the indentations of the continent as far as the present-day Gulf of St. George, forty-seven degrees south latitude. By this time he was convinced that the continent he coasted was not that of Asia but a New World. The account of this voyage published in Europe so impressed a contemporary geographer, Martin Waldseemüller, that he gave just recognition in 1507

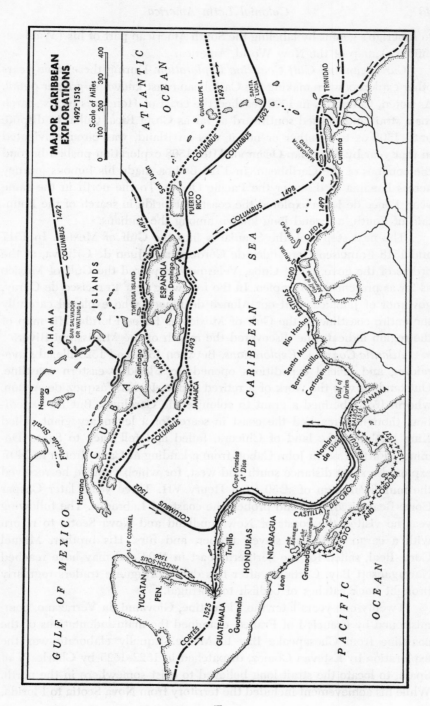

MAJOR CARIBBEAN
EXPLORATIONS
1492-1513

Scale of Miles

0 100 200 300 400

ATLANTIC OCEAN

GUADELUPE I.

SANTA
LUCIA

TRINIDAD

COLUMBUS 1493

COLUMBUS 1493

COLUMBUS 1502

MARGARITA
ISLAND

Cumaná

San Juan

COLUMBUS 1492

PUERTO
RICO

OJEDA 1499

COLUMBUS 1498

ESPAÑOLA

Sto. Domingo

TORTUGA ISLAND

Curaçao

Aruba

OJEDA 1500

Isla de Aves

Rio Hacha
BASTIDAS 1500

Santa Marta

Barranquilla

Cartagena

Gulf of
Darien

CARIBBEAN SEA

BAHAMA ISLANDS

SAN SALVADOR
OR WATLING I.

Nassau

Santiago

COLUMBUS 1493

COLUMBUS 1492

CUBA

JAMAICA

Havana

Florida Strait

COLUMBUS 1502

COLUMBUS 1502

Cape Gracias
A' Dios

Nombre
de Dios

PANAMA

BALBOA 1513

VERAGUA

CASTILLA DEL ORO

San Juan R.

1521

1521

1521

CORDOBA 1517

AND

DESOTO

GULF OF MEXICO

YUCATAN
PEN.

I. OF COZUMEL

CORTÉS 1525

PINZON-SOLIS 1506

GUATEMALA

Guatemala

HONDURAS

Trujillo

NICARAGUA

Lake
Managua

Lake
Nicaragua

Leon

Granada

San Juan R.

PACIFIC OCEAN

ATLANTIC OCEAN

to Amerigo's genius by labeling the South American part of his (Waldsee-müller's) map of the New World, America.

Caribbean and Gulf Coastline Exploration. During these same years other explorers were making the Caribbean coast known in greater detail. As noted, Columbus in 1502 reached the coast of Honduras in his search for a strait and pushed southward as far as Costa Rica. Cuba, in dispute until 1508 as to whether or not it was an island, was circumnavigated in that year by Sebastián Ocampo. After 1508 exploration pushed beyond the confines of the Caribbean. In 1513 Balboa made his famous journey across Panama to discover the Pacific Ocean. To the north in the same year, Ponce de León explored the coast of Florida in search of the Fountain of Youth, a legend long known among the Indians.

The next step took the Spaniards into the Gulf of Mexico. In 1517 and 1518 Francisco Hernández de Córdoba and Juan de Grijalva, at the orders of the governor of Cuba, Velásquez, explored the Gulf of Mexico as far as present-day Tampico. In the following year Francisco de Garay, governor of Jamaica, sent out Alonzo de Pineda who explored carefully the entire coastline of the Gulf of Mexico as far as Florida. His map of the region indicates he discovered the mouth of the Mississippi River.

Atlantic Coastline Explorations. Between 1521 and 1525 illegal slave-raiding and official expeditions opened up Florida's eastern coastline. Outstanding was the work of a retired Judge, Lucas Vásquez de Ayllón, who in 1523 obtained a grant to colonize the Carolinas. But his expedition, though it reached the coast in search of a legendary giant called King Dotha in the land of Chicora, failed and fell back to Santo Domingo. Farther north John Cabot, from a landing at Cape Breton in 1497, explored a short distance south and west, for which venture he received the munificent sum of £50 from Henry VII. Three years later Gaspar Corte-Real discovered and probed the coasts of Labrador. The following year he visited the coasts of Newfoundland and Nova Scotia to return with a cargo of Indian slaves, timber, and furs. His brother, Miguel Corte-Real, sailed for the northern coast in 1502 and may have reached Narragansett Bay. Certainly after this date Portuguese traders regularly brought back catches of codfish to Portugal.

Twenty-one years later the Florentine, Giovanni da Verrazano, commissioned by Francis I of France, examined the main indentations of the coastline from Chesapeake Bay to Maine. Equally elaborate was the exploration by Estevan Gómez, dispatched in 1522–1525 by Charles V of Spain, to locate the strait long believed to exist somewhere in the north. While his achievement included the territory from Nova Scotia to Florida, it did not kill the legend but it did tie up northern and Caribbean exploration to complete the coastline survey of North America.

The Voyage of Magellan. Meanwhile, in South America a similar search for an opening through the great land mass had gone steadily forward. Vespucci believed such a strait would be found. His successor, Juan Díaz de Solís, continued the search in 1515 and explored the opening of the Río de la Plata. Unfortunately, Solís himself fell a victim to cannibals, but his survivors influenced Magellan, already profoundly interested in the idea of a water route to the east. Disappointed in Portugal, Magellan turned to Charles V, who supported the great undertaking. Leaving Sevilla in August, 1519, and accompanied by Antonio Pigafetta, the chronicler of the expedition, Magellan followed the South American coast already made familiar by Vespucci and Solís. The discovery came on October 20 when the expedition, taking refuge in what appeared to be a bay, proved in fact to be in the long-sought strait. Pushing through its narrow walls, Magellan emerged after a rough battle with the elements into the western sea, which, in contrast with the stormy Atlantic, he named the Pacific Ocean.

The explorers, now reduced to three ships, sailed confidently on, convinced that India was not far away. After months of suffering they landed on the Philippine Islands, April, 1520. Here disasters piled upon them. Magellan himself died in battle with the natives; sickness carried off many of the crew. Undaunted, the expedition, now reduced to one ship, the *Victoria*, under Juan Sebastián El Cano, began the long voyage westward to Spain. Hunger, sickness, and storms accompanied their endless journey across the Indian Ocean and along the African coast. At the Cape Verde Islands, desperate for food, El Cano sent a party ashore only to have them seized by the Portuguese. Finally, on September 7, 1522, with but eighteen men left of the original two hundred and fifty, El Cano brought his ship into the Spanish port of San Lúcar. Besides achieving the first circumnavigation of the world, this remarkable voyage finds few examples equaling the courage of its leaders and men.

Magellan's voyage not only proved the world round; it established that America is a continent apart from Asia. Before 1521 only Vespucci had grasped that fact. But Magellan's achievement is best seen as the culminating event in the panorama of coastline exploration. By that date, with Cortés' discovery of Mexico's vast riches, America was becoming valued for itself. The Orient receded into the background of Spanish thinking. The way was now opened for the primary colonization of the two great continents of the New World.

Part II.   COLONIZATION OF THE CARIBBEAN, PANAMA, AND CENTRAL AMERICA, 1493–1525

The West Indies. When Columbus returned from his first voyage, Ferdinand and Isabella lost no time in taking possession of the new lands. They appointed Juan Rodrigo de Fonseca, Bishop of Sevilla, later a bitter enemy of Columbus, to make the preparations for colonization. For this undertaking Columbus himself raised the funds. They embarked on September 25, 1493, with a fleet of seventeen vessels, filled with 1,200 settlers and 300 crew members and outfitted with all the necessities for establishing their homes in the New World: cattle, horses, sheep, pigs, chickens, a large array of building tools, seeds for cereals and fruit trees. The colonists themselves came from all classes, artisans, soldiers, lawyers, merchants, missionaries, and aristocratic adventurers. Upon arrival they found La Navidad deserted. But Columbus again established the new colony, Isabella, himself carefully laying out the town and superintending the building of houses on the northern coast.

From Isabella some eagerly explored for wealth in the interior where gold was reported. Sickness, discontent, and Indian revolt in 1495 decided Bartolomé Columbus, in charge after Columbus set sail for the west, to move to the southern coast. There in 1496 he founded the first permanent European settlement in the New World—Santo Domingo. Conflicts among the colonists and the abuse of Indians led Isabella in 1499 to replace Columbus as governor with Francisco de Bobadilla, who sent the admiral back home in chains. However, Bobadilla himself proving unsatisfactory, Isabella next sent out in 1502 Nicolas Ovando with 2,500 colonists. Given wide power for reform, Ovando introduced the *encomienda* system, which so stimulated the flow of immigrants to the island that by 1509, when Diego Columbus became the next governor, Española had between 10,000 and 12,000 Spaniards living in seventeen towns and on many plantations. By this date, too, tobacco, cotton, and stock raising had become the basic sources of wealth of the colony.

From Española colonization spread to the neighboring islands. In 1508 Ponce de León occupied Puerto Rico with its principal settlement at San Juan. Diego Columbus in 1509 dispatched Juan de Esquivel to colonize Jamaica. Three years later in 1511 Diego de Velásquez began the colonization of Cuba. With him went figures later to gain great fame: Bartolomé de las Casas, the Apostle of the Indians, Pánfilo de Narváez, the explorer of northern Florida, and Cortés, the conqueror of Mexico.

Cuba's conquest was a bloody one accompanied by torture of the natives, the burning of Indian towns, and the massacre of defenseless women and children. Las Casas, who saw these things, was outraged. He began his famous crusade to save the Indians by condemning Narváez to Hades. Thereafter he returned to Spain to seek the monarch's aid. Meanwhile, the pacification went on to become virtually complete by 1514 when Velásquez founded Santiago; two years later, Havana rose at the other end of the island.

Beginning of Colonial Institutions: the Encomienda. The discovery of the New World with its inhabitants, the Indians, forced the crown to fashion a policy in regard to the natives. In the early years of the settlement of Española, Columbus had begun the practice of enslaving Indians and sending them to Spain. Isabella, after a delay of some years, abolished Indian slavery, but the traffic was not effectively ended until 1542. At the same time the colonists who arrived after 1493 virtually enslaved the Indians on the islands to provide food and workers in the mines. With such slavery abolished, however, Ovando in 1502, faced with the stark necessity of feeding the colonists, sought and received from the queen authority to establish in 1503 what became known as the *encomienda* system. The royal order laid down in effect that the natives could be gathered into villages under supervision of a trustee, given lands, and could also be forced to work in the construction of buildings, in mines, and in the cultivation of the soil. For this labor they were to be paid as free men and not as serfs. The trustee on his part was to civilize, Christianize, and protect the Indians. He was entitled in return to collect a tax or tribute. Thus the individual who received a grant of Indians became known as an *encomendero,* and the institution itself the *encomienda.* Such a grant of Indians in *encomienda* did not carry with it ownership of the lands. Reduced to its essentials, an *encomienda* was a right to demand services and collect tribute from the conquered people. In the sixteenth century the word *repartimiento* was frequently used as a synonym for *encomienda,* but the former, in fact, had a more general meaning and was not always equivalent to *encomienda.*

In spite of royal wishes, virtual enslavement of the Indians continued, which, together with ravages of European diseases and punishment for trifling offenses, led to their extermination in the islands. By 1514 only 14,000 remained in Española. The story was repeated on the other islands, so that by the end of the sixteenth century the Indians had disappeared. The *encomienda* was replaced by the institution of Negro slavery. On the continent, where Indians in agricultural areas were long accustomed to similar work systems under Indian empires, they survived.

Political Institutions. Columbus exercised a monopoly of political power until 1499, when the Spanish monarchs sent out the first royal officials. Bobadilla arrived as commissioner or investigating judge, that is, *pesquisidor,* in that year. Ovando had the title of governor, with powers over all dominions in the islands and on the mainland. Diego Columbus, with more elevated authority, was both an admiral and governor-general of the Indies. These experiments, however, eventually gave way to a permanent governing authority, the *audiencia* of Santo Domingo, established September 14, 1524, with four judges, one of whom was president, a financial officer, and a fiscal and several lesser officials.

Local Institutions. Local government in the islands began with the establishment of *cabildos* in 1507, when fourteen towns of Española petitioned and received from the king the same privileges as those of Spain. Broadly speaking, the principal cities had twelve *regidores,* the small towns, villas, and pueblos had six, while villages, *lugares,* had three or four and an *alcalde ordinario.* At first elective, all offices came to be bought and sold. The duties of the officials involved policing the towns, building public works, inspecting jails, meat markets, and hospitals, proclaiming laws and decrees, settling municipal rights in land, communicating by petition with the royal government, and maintaining militia for the protection of the towns.

Significance of the Caribbean. The West Indies became the first base in the New World for the colonization of the mainland. The islands produced the first slave-holding society resting upon a plantation economy. The social structure spread to the periphery of the Caribbean along with the institution of slavery. The islands became and remained the first economic center of the New World for almost 300 years. Through them moved the trade between the mother country and her empire on the mainland. There pirates of other nations "on the make" flocked to prey on this commerce. Later, New England rested the principal base of its triangular trade upon the West Indies. The West Indies, too, became the strategic center of the New World. Spain's hold on these islands against all attacks guaranteed her continued possession of the colonies on the mainland. No nation, though many tried, was able to break down this portal to the empire. Succeeding Spain as the chief New World power, the United States likewise made the Caribbean the center of her strategic defenses.

The Colonization of Panama. The early voyages of Ojeda and others, rich hauls of pearls and gold, and slave raids drew Spanish attention to the possibilities of colonizing Panama and Central America. The earliest attempt at Panama was that of Columbus in 1503 at Veragua. Alonzo de Ojeda and Diego de Nicuesa next launched a project in 1509, but their settlements on the northern coast suffered from sickness, internal conflicts, and Indian attack. By 1511 the remnants of these efforts settled at Darién on the isthmus, with Vasco Nuñez de Balboa as governor.

Soon intrigued by Indian stories of a great sea beyond the mountains, Balboa in 1513 led his famous expedition through the jungles to the heights of Darién. Back in Spain the king rewarded Balboa with the title of *adelantado,* but made Pedrárias de Avila governor and captain-general of the territory then called Castillo del Oro. Pedrárias, fearful of Balboa, had him arrested and executed on thinly veiled charges of treason in 1517. Two years later, following Balboa's plans, the governor transferred the colony at Darién to found Panama on the southern side of the isthmus. At the same time he established Nombre de Dios on the Atlantic side and built a road across the region.

The Colonization of Central America: Nicaragua. Between 1519 and 1523 Pedrárias sent expeditions which explored the coast running to the northwest as far as the Gulf of Fonseca. These brought back pearls, gold, and stories of a powerful king ruling a land called Nicaragua. Pedrárias next sent out Francisco Hernández de Córdoba in 1524, who with Hernando de Soto founded in 1527 Granada on Lake Nicaragua and León on the coast. Missionaries baptizing Indians in the interior came upon the San Juan River, an outlet to the Caribbean.

By this date Pedrárias lost his governorship of Panama but secured that of Nicaragua. At his direction Martín Estete re-explored the San Juan River and founded a settlement at Cape Gracías de Dios on the Caribbean coast. Disappointed in the wealth he hoped to find in gold, Pedrárias developed a lucrative slave trade between Nicaragua and Panama. Before he died in 1530, the vigorous old conqueror tried to elbow his way into Pizarro's undertaking in Peru when the latter sent for de Soto to aid in his conquest. In Honduras he met rebuff at the hands of Cortés.

Honduras. Cortés in Mexico, hearing of Pedrárias' designs on Honduras, sent Cristóbal de Olid with a fleet from Cuba to take possession of the territory. Landing on the coast, Olid founded a villa, Triunfo de la Cruz, but turned traitor to Cortés. Infuriated, the latter sent Francisco de las Casas, who treacherously killed Olid and afterward established Trujillo in Cortés' name. Not satisfied with these events, Cortés himself marched in 1525 to Honduras, a feat regarded as one of the outstanding explorations in North America. With little difficulty he won the submission of the Indians, but found no great civilization he had hoped for.

Guatemala and El Salvador. In December, 1523, Cortés sent his able lieutenant, Alvarado, to conquer Guatemala, of whose riches he had rumor. On his march south, Alvarado won the support of the principal Tehuantepec tribe and quickly reduced the coastal region to subjection. Turning next to the old Maya area, he met stubborn resistance from the powerful Quiché tribe. Resorting to ruthless war, he defeated the Cakchiquels and destroyed their principal strongholds. Moving to the coast, he continued his harsh conquest of the natives to initiate the history of El Salvador under Spain. Back in the interior, his campaigns crushed remaining Maya resistance. Thereafter Guatemalan colonization is first marked by the founding of the city of Santiago, July 28, 1524, later renamed Guatemala City. The conqueror now gave out lands and Indians in *encomienda* to his followers and encouraged the immigration of other Spaniards.

Costa Rica. Unlike other colonies of Spain in the New World, Costa Rica saw no spectacular conquest. No European heroes marched across its lands. The comparatively small numbers of Indians discouraged large land ownership. Its population, as a consequence, grew slowly as Spaniards of little means steadily filtered into the area from Panama. There they cultivated small plots in its rich western valleys and built towns and villages. While not of outstanding importance in the colonial period, this body of small landowners were destined to create after independence a vigorous democratic society.

Part III. CONQUEST AND COLONIZATION OF MEXICO, 1519–1535

Cortés. If a novelist had imagined the conquest of Mexico by Cortés, his story would have been dismissed out of hand as too fantastic. The achievement of a handful of men overthrowing an empire of an estimated 2,000,000 to 4,000,000 people does seem incredible. Knowing the causes does not deny the wonder of Cortés' leadership. Cortés inspired both profound devotion and intense hatred. His zeal in religion was tempered by statesmanship. He combined his unquestioned courage with military abilities of a high order. More, his unusual literary gifts preserved for history in his *Letters to the Emperor Charles V* an understanding and penetrating account of the civilization he was overthrowing.

Origin of the Expedition. Arriving in Española in 1504, Cortés joined Velásquez in the conquest of Cuba. Restless, he begged for permission to head the next undertaking to the west. Reluctantly the governor agreed. Cortés' unexpected energy in preparing the expedition and the whisperings of his enemies aroused Velásquez' misgivings, and he revoked Cortés' authority at the last moment. Not a man to lose all without a struggle, the future conqueror defiantly set sail from Santiago in November, 1518.

With him in a fleet of twelve ships were some 600 Spaniards, 200 Indians, some Negroes and Indian women as slaves. Invaluable in the later conquest were sixteen horses and several artillery pieces. At Cozumel Island off the Yucatan peninsula, Cortés rescued Gerónimo de Aguilar, a Spaniard who knew the Mayan language. Farther along inside the Gulf at Tabasco he landed, defeated the natives, and forced them to recognize the king of Spain as their lord. Here, too, he took with him Doña Marina, an Aztec slave whose knowledge of the Aztec language aided his later plans. From Tabasco, Cortés cast anchor next in a bay which he called Vera Cruz, today San Juan de Ulúa.

Here at Vera Cruz, Cortés was first challenged by Montezuma. The latter sent him presents and a request to leave the land. Unfortunately, Montezuma sweetened his invitation to depart with gifts that made the Spaniards gasp: two large circular plates the size of cart wheels, one of gold, the other of silver, engraved to represent the sun and the moon. Besides, a caravan brought enough grains of gold to fill a helmet, twenty gold ducks, pearls and other jewels, as well as huge bundles of finely woven cloth and feather work. To the demand that he leave, Cortés answered with a forthright request for an audience. Brushing aside the objections of some faint-hearted followers, he burned his ships to ward off mutiny and ordered the founding of a post, confidently named Villa Rica de Vera Cruz, May, 1519. To the municipal government organized with Francisco de Montejo at its head, he tendered his resignation as captain-general and accepted the title anew from his creation. A ship arrived at this moment and he seized it to send to Charles V the cart wheels of gold and silver, dispatching at the same time the first of his famous *Letters* describing the great empire he had discovered, recounting Velásquez' unreasonableness, and praying for the office of captain-general of New Spain.

The Invasion. The Totonacs, among whom he had landed, he overawed with cavalry charges and deafening explosions of artillery. With their alliance assured, Cortés began on August 15, 1519, his famous march to Mexico City. On this invasion the Spaniards profited both from the discontent among the tribes subjected to Aztec rule and from the growing fatalistic conviction of Montezuma that Cortés might be Quetzalcoatl, the White God, whose reappearance in the east during his reign was prophesied. Of no little importance, too, was the aid of Doña Marina, whose role as a spy among the Aztecs furthered the belief that Cortés had the insight of a god.

Montezuma unavailingly alternated trickery with presents to persuade Cortés to leave the country. Among the Tlascalans, not far from Mexico City, who had never bowed to Aztec power, Cortés had to prove himself by battle, god or not, that he was worthy of a Tlascalan alliance His hard-won victory convinced these proud people, so that they willingly joined the invaders against their enemy. Soon after when Cortés crossed the high Sierra Oriental, Montezuma, resigned to defeat, opened the gates of Mexico City to him. After receiving royal honors, Cortés treacherously seized the Indian ruler, having learned in the islands that the capture of a chief paralyzed the tribe itself.

In the midst of these successful maneuvers, Cortés learned that Pánfilo de Narváez, the agent of Velásquez, had arrived with a fleet at Vera Cruz and had sent messengers to Montezuma warning him that Cortés was a mere usurper. The latter acted with his characteristic speed. Leaving Pedro de Alvarado in command in Mexico City, he marched to rout Narváez. At Cempoalla under cover of a torrential downpour, Cortés' hardened veterans attacked with such force that they quickly overcame the camp's carelessly defended positions. The next day the majority of Narváez' 900 followers, persuaded by Cortés' "tongue of honey," deserted to return with him to Mexico City.

Meanwhile, in Mexico City the Aztec Indians, led by a new chief, Cautémoc, attacked Alvarado. Cortés, returning, directed the retreat along the causeways leading out of the city, but suffered such heavy losses that the incident became known thereafter as *La Noche Triste* (The Sad Night). Back at Tlascala, Cortés constructed a fleet of vessels which, transported and assembled on the lake, drove off the Aztec canoes and deprived the Aztecs of their food supply. By August, 1521, when Cortés could no longer restrain his men, the Spaniards attacked. Although the Indians were weak from hunger, they fought bravely from street to street and house to house and did not surrender until their capital was in ruins, their gods knocked from their pedestals, and Cautémoc himself was a prisoner.

Expansion of the Conquest. Even before he had captured their capital, Cortés had already sent expeditions into other parts of the Aztec empire. In 1520 Diego de Ordáz, seeking a strait and a better harbor than Vera Cruz, explored the Coatzacoalcos River and the interior of the Isthmus of Tehuantepec. In 1521 Sandoval founded Medellín below Vera Cruz and Espíritu Santo on the Coatzacoalcos. Meanwhile, Alvarado invaded Tehuantepec and took possession of the Zapotec region, where Cortés had hoped to find an interoceanic highway. Beyond Tehuantepec, Alvarado conquered, as we have seen, the regions later known as El Salvador and Guatemala. In 1525 Cortés himself went to Honduras, where he established his authority in opposition to that of Pedrárias. Chiapas meanwhile fell before Captain Diego de Mazariegos, who founded Villareal, later known as San Cristóbal. Independently of Cortés, Francisco de Montejo, with a royal commission as *adelantado,* invaded Yucatan in 1527. For more than fifteen years the Mayas fought against their subjection to the Spaniards. In 1535, successful temporarily, they drove Montejo out of the peninsula. But returning with reinforcements, he founded Campeche in 1540 and Mérida, later the capital, in 1542. After that date the Mayan tribes succumbed one after another to Spanish control.

For the regions farther west and south, Cortés, using Aztec tax rolls as a guide, dispatched a series of expeditions which conquered the Aztec territories from Tehuantepec to Colima. Orozco in 1521 captured control of Oaxaca, while Cristóbal de Olid in 1522–1524 led a conquering expedition through Michoacán to Zacatula and beyond to Colima, already founded by Sandoval in 1523. To the northeast Cortés himself led an expedition to block the pretensions of Garay, governor of Jamaica, in that region. There he defeated the Huastecas, founded Pánuco, and drove Garay from the coast.

Cortés turned next to the northwest, for he believed, like Columbus, that India was not far away. In 1532 he sent out Hurtado de Mendoza, who explored the Gulf of California and the coastline as far as the Río Fuerte. In the next year Jiménez' discovery of pearl fisheries at the tip of Lower California inspired Cortés himself to found there La Paz in 1535. The colony did not last, but it did initiate the history of Lower California. Aroused by the reports of Alvar Núñez Cabeza de Vaca, who had explored in the north, Cortés dispatched Juan de Ulloa, who rounded the Gulf of California, discovered the mouth of the Colorado River, and made his way along the Pacific coast of the peninsula to explore half of its length.

During these years while Cortés was directing the conquest and occupation of Mexico, he also displayed his statesmanship by organizing its first government. Recognition of his merits came to him in 1522 when Charles V appointed him captain-general of New Spain. In the same year he established the first municipal government of Mexico with Pedro de Alvarado as its first *alcalde mayor*. In the conquered provinces his lieutenants set up the first provincial governments. The most constructive aspect of Cortés rule was his modification of the *encomienda* system by prohibiting the judiciary from holding Indians in *encomienda*. His measure banning Spaniards, except priests, from entering Indian towns was later adopted for the empire by the Spanish king. Too, he brought the first missionaries, the Franciscans, to New Spain to begin conversion.

The Founding of the Viceroyalty of New Spain. In spite of Cortés' great contributions to the empire, Charles V, whose policy was to replace conquerors with royal officials, began reducing his powers. Seizing upon Cortés' violation of royal orders in granting *encomiendas,* the emperor sent a royal commission in 1526 to hold a *residencia,* an investigation, into Cortés' conduct. In the following year the arrival of a royal *audiencia* drastically curtailed Cortés' powers. When, however, he went to Spain to protest, the king received him with honors, making him Marqués of the Valley (Valley of Mexico). Meanwhile, the *audiencia* ruled so harshly that Charles V appointed a new one, which arrived with Cortés in 1530. While he explored in the northwest, the new *audiencia,* under Fuenleal, restored peaceful conditions and founded the Puebla de los Angeles. In Spain the monarchs planned the final removal of Cortés from the scene with the establishment of a new authority, a viceroyalty. In 1535 they sent out Don Antonio de Mendoza as viceroy and personal representative of the emperor. Again Cortés returned to Spain to protest that he had conquered for his monarch "more provinces than he had cities," but to no avail. Cortés remained in Spain, while Mendoza went ahead with his great work of establishing the viceroyalty.

Part IV. THE ADVANCE INTO THE INTERIOR AND INTO
THE PACIFIC OCEAN, 1521–1610

Exploration of Florida. The success of Cortés set other strong-willed men to find another Mexico in the interior of North America. Ponce de León, after his initial exploration, undertook colonization in Florida in 1521, but his settlement of 200 men failed before Indian attack. Five years later in 1526 Ayllón made his ill-fated attempt on the Carolina coast. Pánfilo de Narváez, who had inherited the grants of León and Garay, launched in 1528 a major effort with 600 men. Entering Florida near present-day Tampa Bay in April, he explored north to Apalache while his fleet moved along the coast. No gold rewarded them while Indians, antagonized by slave raiders, drove them back to the coast near St. Mark's Bay. His ships dispersed, more than half of his men dead, Narváez set sail for Pánuco on the Mexican coast in five horsehide boats. Only one boat survived the storms of the Gulf. In it were Alvar Núñez Cabeza de Vaca, a Moorish servant, Esteban, and two others.

Cast ashore on the coast of Texas near Galveston, the four began a famous odyssey from the Texas coast to Culiacán on the other side of the continent. For six years Cabeza de Vaca pushed his way westward, a slave in one tribe, a medicine man in another, and an ambassador for a third, arriving at his destination in April, 1534. His account of his travels opened the history of Texas and revealed one of the major explorations of North America.

De Soto. Meanwhile, in Spain, Hernando de Soto, with the rank of governor of Cuba and captain-general and *adeltando* of Florida, fitted out a fleet of ten ships to carry his colony of 600 to Florida. Landing at Tampa on May 30, 1539, de Soto set out to find the golden-hatted Indians of Cale. But these along the Suwannee River disappointed him. Pushing westward, he rediscovered Pensacola Bay and turned northeastward, where, near Augusta, Georgia, of today, he looted the graves of the Cufitachiqui Indians of 350 pounds of pearls. Continuing northward, he marched over the Smoky Mountains into Tennessee. Returning southward again through present-day Alabama, he halted somewhat north of present-day Mobile Bay, where he met strong resistance from the Mavila Indians. Turning again, he explored northwestward to reach in the spring of 1541, near present-day Memphis, the Mississippi River, his greatest discovery, although the mouth of that stream had been known since Pineda's voyage. Believing his fortune lay beyond the great river, he crossed it to explore large parts of Arkansas. With no reward for his tremendous effort, he determined to return to Cuba for reinforcements but died in the spring of 1542, to be buried in the Mississippi River. Moscoso, his successor, attempted a return journey through Texas, but gave it up to float down the Mississippi River to the Gulf of Mexico and ultimately reach Mexico.

The Coronado Expedition. Meanwhile, in Mexico, Viceroy Mendoza sent out Fray Marcos de Niza to test out Cabeza de Vaca's reports of

rich Indians in the north. Fray Marcos reached southern Arizona, where
Esteban, his guide, went to investigate the pueblo of the Zuñis. When
his messenger did not return, the cleric hastened back to Mexico City
to report that great cities did in fact exist in the north.

Brushing aside Cortés' claims, Viceroy Mendoza sent Francisco
Vásquez de Coronado, the governor of New Galicia, to make the discovery. From Compostela in February, 1540, Coronado led northward
a brilliantly outfitted expedition of almost 300 men and 1,000 Indian
allies. Paralleling his route by sea, Hernando de Alarcón sailed with
three ships along the coast of the Gulf of California and entered the
Colorado River. When Coronado reached the Zuñi pueblo, its poverty
was seen to fall far below the great hopes raised by Fray Marcos.
Disappointed, Coronado next moved eastward to the Rio Grande River
to winter at Tiguex, near present-day Isleta. Again the simple dwellings
of the Pueblos and their parched fields dashed the Spaniards' dreams.

In the spring of 1542 a strange character, whom the Spaniards
dubbed the "Turk" because his Apache headdress reminded them of the
Turks in Europe, told Coronado of Gran Quivira, a rich land to the
east. Hopefully the adventurers followed the "Turk" onto the plains as
far as the headwaters of the upper Red and Brazos rivers. Here, surrounded by "nothing but cattle and sky," the leaders, convinced of the
"Turk's" duplicity, asked other friendly Indians the location of Quivira.
These pointed northward. Still hoping to find great cities, Coronado with
thirty horsemen crossed the plains of Oklahoma to reach the mud huts
of the Wichita Indians along the great bend of the Arkansas River.
From here, finally discouraged, he returned to Mexico. But this great
exploration opened the history of the Southwest and left a precious
historical record of the Pueblo and other Indian cultures from Sonora
to the Arkansas River.

Exploration of the Pacific. Not only did reports of riches in the north
lure Spaniards into great exploits, but belief in a strait led them to
explore the western ocean. In 1527 Cortés sent Alvaro de Saavedra
across the Pacific Ocean to the Moluccas. Twelve years later Alvarado,
Cortés' lieutenant, prepared a new expedition. On his death Viceroy
Mendoza dispatched in 1542 Ruy López de Villalobos to find a route to
the East Indies to compete with the Portuguese in the spice trade. Like
the earlier undertakings, this venture failed but became another step in
the exploration of the Pacific.

To the north, where belief in a strait existed, Mendoza sent in 1542
Juan Rodríguez Cabrillo with two ships. He discovered San Diego Bay

and the Santa Bárbara channel, but missed the long curving shore of Monterrey and the fog-drenched mouth of San Francisco Bay. Beyond, he reached the thirty-eighth parallel, where adverse winds turned him back. On his death his pilot, Bartolomé Ferrelo, renewed the voyage northward along the coast of present-day Oregon. Here his ships, no longer seaworthy, forced his return.

The Colonization of Northern Mexico: New Galicia. In the half century after the Coronado expedition, the Spaniards found in the soil beneath their feet untold wealth. While discoveries of silver deposits became the main factor in the colonization of northern Mexico, its beginnings were in the work of Núño de Guzmán, who, conquering the tribes on the west coast in 1529–1535, established Culiacán and became governor of the province of New Galicia. Guzmán's harsh treatment of the Indians brought on their revolt in 1541 in the Mixton area, a struggle which took the lives of missionaries and destroyed crops. When the rebellion was finally put down and the way cleared for prospecting, Spaniards learned from friendly Indians the secret of the Aztec gold and silver deposits. In 1543 significant discoveries near Compostela launched the first mining rush to the northwest. Three years later in 1546 Indians told Juan de Tolosa the location of the great vein of silver at Zacatecas. In January, 1548, an accident revealed the rich deposits at Guanajuato, and brought the discovery of the "mother lode" of Mexico in 1558.

Viceroy Mendoza, encouraged by this news, called for prospecting nearer Mexico City. At Pachuca, north of the city, discoverers came upon the deposits destined to become one of Mexico's greatest silver mines, Real del Monte. The lively interest generated by these discoveries brought improvement in mining methods in 1557, when Bartolomé de Medina, using mercury to extract silver from ore, originated the "patio process," a method making possible the exploitation of lower grades of ores.

New Vizcaya. In these years Francisco de Ibarra was conducting explorations in northern New Galicia, where his prospectors, whom he outfitted with horses, slaves, food, and equipment, discovered a group of rich deposits. In 1562 Ibarra became governor and captain-general of a new province, New Vizcaya, carved out of the vast region north of New Galicia. In 1563 he founded Durango, which long remained the military capital in the northwest. At near-by Nombre de Dios he encouraged the development of a rich food-producing area. Throughout the province he sought to bring in cattle to provide food in the arid regions of the north. In the far north his men founded Santa Bárbara, later significant in the colonization of New Mexico on the Conchos River in 1564. Not satisfied with these achievements, Ibarra, one of the great colonizers of Mexico, made a series of explorations which opened up anew Sonora and Sinaloa along the coast. At the time of his death in 1570 he had established many new towns, brought a large number of mines into production, and begun a thriving cattle industry.

Las Charcas and New León. Meanwhile, a third line of expansion was moving northeastward from Mexico City. From Guanajuato colonization advanced northward, but halted before the powerful resistance of the Guachichiles Indians. However, continuous discoveries of small silver deposits and military campaigns eventually overcame their opposition. The district called Las Charcas had its principal center by 1576 at San Luís de Potosí. About 1575 Francisco de Urdiñola is reported to have made settlements near present Saltillo. At the same time he sent expeditions which colonized at Parras, a rich grape-growing region.

New León. Farther east along the coast of the Gulf, Cortés himself had begun expansion there with the founding of a settlement in 1527 in the Pánuco district. When rich silver deposits were reported, Luis de Carabajal in 1579 sought a grant to this territory now called the kingdom of New León. Energetic and able, Carabajal established a colony in that year of some 200 men at Pánuco and explored northward. South of the Rio Grande he settled León, later Cerralvo, and San Luis, near modern Monterrey. Besides mining, slave-trading became a profitable business in the area. With new settlers attracted to the region, Carabajal founded New Almadén and planned other settlements. But his royal contract was prejudicial to many, and his enemies hailed him as a Jewish heretic before the Inquisition, which condemned him to exile and ordered some of his relatives executed.

By 1580 the area of northern Mexico, except Sonora, had been colonized at key points. The search for silver had been the primary motive of the occupation. But need for food had brought into the north cattle which ranged in its many valleys. The new towns and herds, soon subjected to Indian attack, required forts or presidios at strategic points. In this work the church founded missions to win souls. Thus northern Mexico became a frontier of mines, cattle, military posts, and missions, characteristics which Spanish expansion in the next two centuries carried deeply into the American Southwest.

The Founding of Florida. The occupation of Florida resulted from the colonization of northern Mexico. The growing volume of silver carried back to Spain by way of the Strait of Florida required by 1565 the occupation of the Florida peninsula to provide haven against pirates and hurricanes. After de Soto, Fray Luis Cáncer in 1549 became a martyr to his belief that kindness could convert the natives. Ten years later, increasing piratical raids in the Gulf demanded the colonization of Florida. Planning took two years, but on June 11, 1559, Tristán de Luna left Vera Cruz in command of an expedition of thirteen vessels carrying 1,500 colonizers, 500 soldiers, and Negro and Aztec servants. After landing at Pensacola the Spaniards saw a hurricane destroy their ships and food supply. Moving to Mobile Bay, Luna sent out parties which brought food from the Coosa region in the interior. However, bickering and lack of reinforcements from Mexico forced the abandonment of the attempt to colonize the Gulf coast in 1561.

After a long history of failures, Spain finally colonized Florida in 1565. The immediate cause was the effort of the French to establish a colony, Fort Caroline, on the St. John's River after René Laudonnière and Jean Ribaut had failed at Port Royal in 1562. This invasion Spain viewed in the light of half a century of French piratical attacks upon Cuba and her treasure fleet. To end the threat, Pedro Menéndez de Avilés, long experienced in fighting pirates along the Cuban coast, was made *adelantado* of Florida and captain-general of Cuba. Sailing in 1565 with 500 fully equipped colonists, he founded St. Augustine in September of that year. He promptly destroyed Fort Caroline, an action, however, avenged by de Gourges at San Mateo, a post left on the site of the French fort.

Menéndez' other constructive work included a careful survey of sites on the peninsula and the founding of a settlement in the south at Tegesta. In the north he called upon the Jesuits who, under Father Alonzo Reynoso, extended their missions along the Georgia and Carolina coasts, then called Guale. Father Juan Bautista de Segura ventured to plant a mission as far north as the Chesapeake Bay on the site of later Jamestown, but the Indians martyred the pioneers. In the west Menéndez dispatched Juan Pardo to explore a route to Mexico, but the effort failed. Florida, thus colonized, became the first step in a defensive barrier in the north to protect the empire along its "borderlands."

The Colonization of the Philippine Islands. Also in the nature of a defensive outpost at the other extreme of the empire, as well as to share in the wealth of the East Indies, Spain colonized the Philippine Islands. To carry out the project, Miguel López de Legazpi and Fray Andrés de Urdaneta, pilot, left Mexico in November, 1564. Arrived in the islands, they struggled for seven years with the natives and the Portuguese, establishing Manila finally in 1571. The seat of government was created in 1583 in the *audiencia* of Manila, but made dependent upon the viceroyalty of Mexico.

Spain developed a rich commerce with the Orient, somewhat restricted in 1580 when Portugal established the sole right to trade with Japan. Missionaries from Spain, however, worked in the Island Empire during 1592–1593. With China, Manila trade produced silks, porcelains, teakwood, spices, and other valuable Oriental goods. The Philippine Islands, too, contributed their quota, all of which found its way to Mexico after 1580 when Urdaneta discovered the northward flowing Japanese current. Thereafter for 200 years the Manila galleon followed the great circle route to the coast of California and thence to Mexico. On this long journey visits ashore to secure water, fresh vegetables, and trade with the Indians at Cape Mendocino, Monterrey, and San Diego made this coast known before Jamestown was founded on the other side of the continent.

Spanish activities in the Pacific late in the sixteenth and early seventeenth centuries attracted the attention of her competitors, the English, Dutch, and French. Leading these late-comers was Francis Drake who, sailing into the Pacific in 1577–1580, attacked the undefended coast of Chile, seized a rich treasure from the Peruvian fleet on its way to Panama and raided the coast of Mexico. Along the coast of California he anchored in what is now known as Drake's Bay, where he named the land New Albion and took possession, before sailing for home, in the name of his queen. Sir Thomas Cavendish, following Drake's route in 1586, had the luck to capture a Manila galleon along the coast of California.

This invasion drew Spain's attention to the necessity of exploring California's coast anew to find a haven for the galleons. Thus in 1595 Sebastián Rodríguez Cermeño attempted the work, but his ships were unequal to the task. In 1598 Sebastián Vizcaíno, who had founded a colony at La Paz, the scene of Cortés' attempt, explored the inside coast of the Gulf of California, but came to grief. Philip II, annoyed, peremptorily ordered a new effort. Vizcaíno, profiting from his first failure, set out again on May 5, 1602, with Fray Antonio de la Ascensión as diarist. Discounting the latter's belief that Lower California was an island and that Quivira, the region Coronado explored, could be reached as well as the Strait of Anian, Vizcaíno proceeded up the west coast. He explored Magdalena Bay, rediscovered that of San Diego—made known sixty years before by Cabrillo—and probed the shore line carefully until he sailed into the wide curving bay of Monterrey. Designating that as the most suitable for the Manila galleon, which it thereafter used, he sent two of his vessels northward, which reached as far as the forty-second or forty-third parallel. His excellent reports on his return, somewhat exaggerating the agricultural wealth and the size of the Indian settlements at Monterrey, set plans afoot to occupy the region. These, however, did not materialize and were not revived until a century and a half later when a Russian threat to the coast brought occupation.

The Colonization of New Mexico. New Mexico owed its origin to a variety of causes. Primarily it represented the next step northward in Spanish expansion from the mining area of northern Mexico. Too, Drake's prevarication that he had found the western mouth of the Strait of Anian worried Spanish officials, who favored another advance northward. Missionaries longed to bring the Indians ranging the plains into the fold of the church. Slave raiders north of Santa Bárbara brought back exaggerated reports of the wealth of Indians living in houses and gave the region the name of "New Mexico." Coronado's explosion of this myth had been forgotten.

The expeditions of Fray Agustín Rodríguez in 1581 and Antonio de Espejo in 1582 re-explored the Pueblo region made known by Coronado, and brought back evidence of silver deposits and missionary opportunity. With enthusiasm kindled for colonization, Juan de Oñate was finally selected to lead the undertaking. Setting out in February, 1598, with a colony of 130 soldiers and their families, servants, Franciscan missionaries, and several thousand head of cattle, horses, and other animals, Oñate followed the Rio Grande to make his first settlement at the pueblo of San Juan far up the river. While his colonists built homes, Oñate conquered the stiff-necked Pueblos, a feat celebrated in the only epic poem of European conquest in North America, written by a gifted member of Oñate's company, Gaspar de Villagrá.

Disappointed in the poverty of his territory, Oñate ranged far and wide from the Colorado River to the plains of Kansas seeking riches that would justify the high hopes men had had in naming the region New Mexico. By 1606 Oñate, discouraged, gave up the governorship, but his work was well done. The colony remained a new outpost on the "borderland" of Spain's empire in the north. Pedro de Peralta, the new governor, founded Santa Fé in 1610. Thereafter Spanish colonial culture intertwined with the picturesque customs of the Pueblo Indians to write a colorful page in the history of the Southwest.

In the century during which Spain had advanced deep into North America, her pioneers were also exploring new lands and carving out domains in the southern continent.

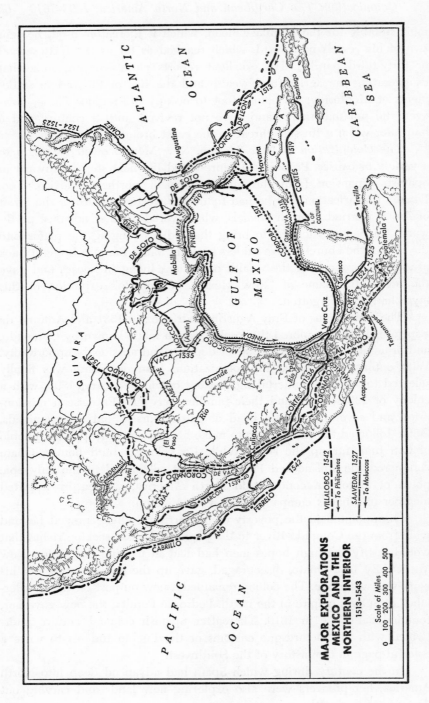

MAJOR EXPLORATIONS
MEXICO AND THE
NORTHERN INTERIOR
1513–1543

Scale of Miles

0 100 200 300 400 500

VILLALOBOS 1542
→ To Philippines

SAAVEDRA 1527
→ To Moluccas

Chapter IV

THE CONQUEST AND COLONIZATION OF SOUTH AMERICA, 1520-1580

Part I. THE OCCUPATION OF NORTHERN SOUTH AMERICA

Colonization of Venezuela and New Granada. Paralleling the colonization of the northern continent was the occupation of South America. Valuable pearl fisheries along the coast and the need for slaves on the island plantations encouraged profitable ventures along the Spanish Main. The Indian soul interested the missionaries. Las Casas, who had gone to Spain to protest the inhumane treatment of the island Indians, secured permission to colonize Cumaná on the eastern Venezuelan coast. But slave raiders had so antagonized the Indians that his experiment ended in failure in 1520.

The Germans in Venezuela. In 1527 Juan de Ampués founded Coro on the western Venezuelan coast to exploit the pearl beds. But this normal expansion was cut short by Charles V, who in 1528 mortgaged the northern shore line to the German banking house, the Welsers, in return for funds for meeting his debts. The Welsers sent out Enrique de Alfinger and Jerónimo Sailler with 300 Spaniards, fifty German miners, and other nationalities to Coro. With great cruelty, Alfinger enslaved the Indians as guides to lead him to rich cities believed to be in the interior and known as Meta and Omagua. He found no cities but he explored the Orinoco basin. After his death, George Speyer and Nicholas Federmann arrived to govern, but they, too, fell to searching for the mythical cities. Federmann, traveling through western Venezuela, crossed the Andes Mountains and descended into the valley of the Magdalena River in 1539.

The Conquest of New Granada. Farther west, slave raiders, following coastal explorations of Ojeda and others, began the history of New Granada. Rodrigo Bastidas founded Santa Marta in 1525, but, dying shortly, was succeeded by Pedro de Heredia. After founding Cartagena in 1533, he pushed into the interior where he, too, heard of rich Indian cities beyond the mountains ruled over by a gilded man who became known as "El Dorado." Preparing for the search, he was replaced by Gonzalo Jimenez de Quesada, ordered to explore the Magdalena River. Setting aside this project, Quesada went in pursuit of "El Dorado." Overcoming with great difficulty the coastal range of the Andes, Quesada finally reached the plains of the Magdalena River, where, conquering the Chibcha Indians, he founded on August 6, 1538, the city of Santa Fé de Bogotá and named the country the New Kingdom of Granada.

Planning to leave for Spain to secure the governorship of this new territory, Quesada learned of other Spaniards approaching from the south. These, led by Sebastián de Benalcázar, governor of Quito, had crossed the mountains northward, explored the headwaters of the Magdalena, and pushed down the Cauca River Valley. Two years later in 1538, on turning east to invade the territory of the Chibchas, he learned of Quesada's conquest. A few months later in April, 1539, after the two Spanish forces had joined, Federmann arrived on the scene from the east.

The three conquerors avoided a civil war. Quesada and Benalcázar signed an agreement which recognized the latter's right to the territory of the Popayáns in the west, while Federmann withdrew after turning over his army to Quesada. The latter hurried to Spain only to find that the king had conferred the governorship upon Luis Alonzo de Lugo.

In Venezuela, where the Welsers had failed to make their grant productive and had ruthlessly enslaved the Indians, Charles V canceled the concession. Thereafter Spanish missionaries, settlers from the islands, slave raiders, and adventurers entered the country. In 1567 Diego de Losada founded Caracas, the future capital of the province. Four years afterward in 1571 Alonzo Pacheco founded Maracaibo, named after an Indian chief at the time of Ojeda's visit in 1499. Santo Thomé, established about 1592 on the Orinoco east of the mouth of the Caroní River, represented the southern and eastern limit of Spanish occupation. Into the region before the century ended, flowed the full tide of Spanish culture—the Spanish language, religion, customs, and laws. Economic life centered around sugar, cotton, and tobacco plantations as well as the cattle industry and agriculture. Sugar, cotton, and tobacco were largely confined to the coastal areas. The cattle spread into the Orinoco Valley and became the source of hide and tallow exports through Caracas and its seaport, La Guaira. Agriculture flourished principally in the western mountain valleys.

Part II. THE COLONIZATION OF PERU, ECUADOR, AND CHILE

Peru. In western South America the major movement of conquest and colonization led to Peru. Balboa had initiated the venture, but Pedrárias, treacherously removing him, sent Pascual de Andagoya in 1522 along the Colombian coast. Leadership next fell to Francisco Pizarro, the illegitimate son of a colonel in the Spanish army. A penniless swineherd in Trujillo, Spain, he left his home for Española. There he joined Ojeda's expedition, aided Balboa at Darién, and crossed the mountains with him to share in the discovery of the South Sea. Ever alert, he secured permission after Andagoya's return to lead the next expedition in search of Peru.

With Hernando de Luque, a priest, to finance his undertaking and Diego de Almagro, a soldier of fortune, to gather supplies, Pizarro sailed in November, 1524, on his first undertaking. Though they advanced down the coast to four degrees south latitude, warlike Indians along the coast forced Pizarro, after three months of exploration, to return to Panama for reinforcements. Almagro, meanwhile, who had followed in Pizarro's wake, experienced much the same hardships but brought back considerable gold.

The Discovery of Peru. Pizarro, after signing in Panama a new agreement with his partners, sailed again with 160 men. Adverse winds and currents forced the leader to halt on Gallo Island off the Ecuadorian coast and send Almagro for reinforcements. On Almagro's return the expedition moved along the coast to find prosperous Indian towns, but at the same moment they received orders from the new governor at Panama, Pedro de los Ríos, to return. Pizarro dramatically drew a line in the sand and invited his followers to join him or return to Panama. Thirteen hardy souls stepped across the line. The rest with Almagro returned to persuade the governor to provide supplies and grant permission for further exploration. After waiting seven long months, Pizarro and his handful of adventurers received their reward: permission to explore for an additional six months.

With renewed hope Pizarro and his men coasted southward along the coast and suddenly sailed into the spacious Gulf of Guayaquil in 1527. There they discovered the first Inca towns, whose inhabitants, friendly and curious, loaded Pizarro down with beautiful textiles and gold and silver ornaments. Back in Panama Pizarro, fearing the cupidity of the governor, sailed for Spain to appeal directly to the emperor for permission to conquer Peru.

The Conquest of Peru. Charles V, always impressed with results, readily made Pizarro captain-general and *adelantado* of Peru, a jurisdiction called New Castile that extended 600 miles south of Panama. Luque was made bishop of Túmbez at Guayaquil and Protector of the Indians, while Almagro was made a captain with hidalgo rank and commander of the fort on the Gulf of Guayaquil. The government at Panama was instructed to aid him in the gathering of supplies and a crew.

Back in Panama, accompanied by his four brothers, Pizarro organized his undertaking, which sailed in January, 1531, made up of 180 men and twenty-seven horses. Almagro remained to gather additional supplies. Landing north of the Gulf, they collected from the Indians treasures of gold, silver, and emeralds which Pizarro sent back to encourage volunteers to enlist. Continuing southward, they sailed into the Gulf, where Pizarro learned of the recently ended civil war between the Inca followers of Huascar and Atahualpa.

Here, with preparations complete, he began his invasion of the Inca empire in September, 1532. Crossing the first range of the Andes, he found Atahualpa encamped in the valley of Cajamarca. After establishing headquarters, Pizarro, accompanied by de Soto and a handful of officers, galloped to the Inca's camp, where Atahualpa cordially received him. On the following day, November 16, Atahualpa returned the visit.

The Capture of Atahualpa. With his plans laid to seize the Inca, Pizarro first asked Father Vicente de Valverde to explain to Atahualpa why the Incas should place themselves under the authority of the Spanish king. Atahualpa, politely listening until tiring of a language he had never heard, brushed the Bible from Valverde's hands. The ending of the padre's harangue was the prearranged signal for attack. With the battle cry of "Santiago," the Spaniards charged, while their artillery thundered death among the royal bodyguard. After a brief and bloody battle, Pizarro made Atahualpa his prisoner, an action which ended all Indian resistance.

With hopes of freedom, Atahualpa, promising to fill a room with gold, sent his carriers to the ends of the empire to bring back the yellow metal. The huge ransom filled one room and overflowed into another, a treasure estimated in modern terms at over $17,000,000. But Pizarro meanwhile had learned of Atahualpa's usurpation of the Inca title, ordered his trial for rebellion in the Spanish emperor's dominions, and executed him. To keep his symbol of authority before Inca eyes, Pizarro placed Huascar's brother, Manco Capac, in the Incaship. With these arrangements, Pizarro advanced to Cuzco after sending his own brother Hernando back to Spain to present to Charles V his royal fifth.

Constructive Work of Pizarro. The Spaniards entered Cuzco on November 15, 1533, unopposed. In this ancient and magnificent city with a population estimated at 200,000, Pizarro's men found in its palaces, vaults, underground caverns, and burial places new treasures of gold and silver ornaments, exquisite examples of Inca art. When the looting was over, Pizarro set up a government to establish Spanish authority. In March, 1534, he organized the municipal administration of Cuzco along the lines of a Spanish town. He appointed two *alcaldes* and eight *regidores* and invited his followers to take possession of houses and lands. He himself assumed the title of governor and granted *encomiendas*. Father Valverde selected a site for a cathedral, and began building the Monastery of St. Dominic upon the Inca palace which had housed the Temple of the Sun and a nunnery upon that of the Virgins of the Sun.

Because of Cuzco's inland location and the need of sea communications with Panama, Pizarro in January, 1535, founded Lima, which he called the City of the Kings in honor of the feast of Epiphany. Northward along the coast in the same year he established Trujillo. In the rich valley of the Rimac and elsewhere in the interior, he granted lands and *encomiendas* to his men. Thus began the effective occupation of Peru.

Conquest of Ecuador. Peru now became a base for the expansion of Spanish control into all parts of the Inca dominions. Pizarro, hearing that Cortés' lieutenant, Alvarado, planned to invade Ecuador, sent Sebastián de Benalcázar and Almagro to thwart him. Successful, they established the Spanish capital in the ancient Indian city of Quito on December 6, 1534, organized the *cabildo,* and appointed city officials. Ecuador thus began its history under Spain. Benalcázar, the governor, soon expanded the claims of Spain eastward toward the Amazon and northward into the territory of New Granada.

Rivalry of Almagro and Pizarro. On his return to Peru, Almagro learned that Charles V had granted him the title of marshal and a vast new territory called New Toledo, which extended 200 leagues to the south of Pizarro's New Castile. Almagro, loath to leave the riches of Cuzco, disputed Pizarro's right to the city. The latter, however, fearing his lieutenant's new importance, urged him to take possession of New Toledo. Persuaded, Almagro set out in 1535 with a large body of adventurers and hundreds of Incas enslaved as carriers.

Almagro's expedition to Chile was one of the most harrowing experiences any Spaniards met in their conquest of the New World, but as usual the Indians suffered the brunt of their disasters. Following Inca military roads through northern Argentina, Almagro crossed the Andes with heavy losses, only to find himself in the barren deserts of the north. Struggling through these against thirst and hunger, he eventually emerged on a stream later called Río Coquimbo. But Almagro soon found there were no great cities and wealth. On the contrary, the unconquerable Araucanian Indians blocked his way. Discouraged, the leader turned his expedition back along the coast to experience again the horrors of a passage over the Andes to reach Cuzco in the interior. There Almagro and his bitter veterans determined to make Pizarro surrender the city.

In the meantime, Manco Capac, resenting his puppet role, revolted after the departure of Almagro in January, 1536. Throughout Peru the Incas, following his lead, besieged Cuzco for seven long months. Only when the Indians withdrew some of their forces to plant their crops did Pizarro succeed in getting supplies to the beleaguered city. Knowing the bitterness between Almagro and Pizarro, Manco Capac hoped to secure the latter's aid on his return in 1537. But Almagro, brushing aside this offer, captured the city singlehanded, imprisoned the conqueror's brothers, and defeated an expedition sent by Pizarro against the Indians. This event brought civil war. But Almagro was no match for the old conqueror, who defeated him in the Battle of Salinas, fought with all the pomp and display of two medieval armies. Captured, Almagro was promptly executed. To Spain Pizarro sent his brother Hernando to report the news, but there Almagro's friends had the ear of the emperor, who imprisoned Hernando for twenty years and sent out Vaca de Castro to restore order in the royal dominions.

With Almagro out of the way, Pizarro next defeated the Incas and founded military posts in the heart of the rebellious area. He established Guamage between Cuzco and Lima, the Villa of La Plata in Charcas (Bolivia), a mining area now opened, while to the southeast of Lima he founded Arequipa in 1540. To occupy these and other sites, he directed the flow of immigration pouring in from Spain and the West Indies as news reached these centers of Peru's riches. To make the settlements a success, he encouraged agriculture with the importing of seed and grains from Spain.

The Exploration of the Amazon River. With stability assured in Peru, Pizarro dispatched as governor to Quito his brother Gonzalo with instructions to explore eastward across the Andes for a rumored land of cinnamon. Leaving Quito in February, 1541, Gonzalo led an expedition of 220

Spaniards, 4,000 Indians, and a large herd of cattle over the Andes as far as the Coca River, a headwater of the Amazon. Here on December 26, 1541, he sent Francisco de Orellana forward to search for food. But Orellana, possibly motivated by ambition, did not return but constructed a boat to explore the Amazon to the Atlantic Ocean. While Gonzalo returned to Quito, Orellana, after remarkable experiences among the savage natives, successfully floated down the length of the Amazon to its mouth, whence he made his way to Venezuela and on to Spain. To the monarch he told stories of wealthy cities in the interior and of a republic of Amazon women. Impressed, the king gave him a commission to explore New Andalucía, but the prevaricating explorer died after going a short distance into the mouth of the Amazon in 1544.

The Colonization of Chile. To the south of Peru, Pizarro next dispatched Pedro de Valdivia to conquer and colonize Chile. Valdivia, whose ability and uprightness remind one of Balboa, left Lima in 1540 at the head of 150 Spaniards and a large body of Indians. Profiting from Almagro's experiences, Valdivia marched southward along the coast until he reached the Mapocho River, a tributary of the Maipú. There, finding the land fertile and populated with Indians, he founded the city of Santiago on February 25, 1541. During the next ten years, constantly harassed by Indian attack, Valdivia colonized and explored. In 1544 he founded Valparaíso, a port for Santiago to link it with Peru. To the north he discovered a rich gold mine in the Coquimbo Valley, where he established the city of La Serena on the coast. To secure more colonists, he sent his lieutenant, Alonzo de Monroy, to Peru riding a horse with a silver stirrup. Attracted by this evidence of wealth, many returned with Monroy. With these reinforcements, Valdivia expanded his territory south of Santiago. Going to Peru himself for new recruits, he advanced colonization southward to found new towns, outstanding among which was Concepción in 1550 on the banks of the Bío Bío River. Between Santiago and Concepción, Valdivia gave out lands and Indians in *encomienda*. In so doing he laid the basis for the Chilean oligarchy which after independence dominated Chilean history until the twentieth century.

The Araucanian Wars. Beyond Concepción, Valdivia faced the powerful Araucanian Indians. With gold and silver discovered in their territory, Valdivia advanced to found Villa Imperial south of Concepción, and later in 1551 to provide an outlet for the mining region, Valdivia, at the head of an excellent bay. Rapidly the area grew with new mining settlements at Villa Rica and Frontera. But the Araucanians were determined not to surrender their lands so easily. Fighting every inch of the Spanish advance, they finally organized their forces under two famous leaders, Lautaro and Caupolicán. Valdivia, hastening to defend the settlements between Concepción and Valdivia, fell into a trap set by Caupolicán, who captured and executed the Spanish leader in 1554. But Valdivia's work was done. Spanish colonization was firmly implanted from La Serena to Valdivia in the south. The Araucanian Wars are important in the history of Chile. During this conflict, which continued throughout the colonial period, there was a steady intermixture of the races brought about by the practice of the Chilean landowners acquiring captive Araucanians as workers on their estates. These vigorous people seem to have given much of their remarkable physical stamina to the Chilean race. The wars, too, produced an unusual literary contribution, an epic poem, *La Araucana*, written by Alonzo de Ercilla y Zúñiga. While ostensibly celebrating the feats of Spanish arms, the poem reveals the heroic qualities of the Araucanians in defending their lands and liberty. As such, the name of the poem's principal Indian figure, Lautaro, has become symbolic in Latin America of the struggle for freedom.

Francisco de Villagrá succeeded Valdivia to continue the offensive against the Araucanians, but internal bickering led the viceroy in Lima to send García Hurtado de Mendoza in 1557 as captain-general of Chile. While Mendoza carried on the wars, he continued colonization, founding Osorno in the south in 1558. Beyond, he sent explorers into the Archipelago of Chiloé. To the east his expeditions crossed the Andes Mountains to found Mendoza, which later became attached to Argentina. Mendoza's work completed the conquest, and under him Chile began its government under royal officials.

Peru: Civil Wars and Administration, 1542–1581. While Valdivia was conquering Chile, Peru fell into a series of civil wars. Almagro's defeat left his followers leaderless and landless. In revenge, Almagro's son, Diego, and a handful of adventurers assassinated Pizarro. In Spain, meanwhile, the king appointed Blasco Núñez Vela viceroy of Peru and an *audiencia*, among whose members was the future historian of the conquest of Peru, Agustín de Zárate. At the same time, influenced by the heroic efforts of Father Las Casas, the Apostle of the Indians, to mitigate the abuses of the natives, the king's council in Valladolid promulgated on November 20, 1542, the New Laws. These prohibited new grants of *encomiendas* in the empire, outlawed other abuses of the Indians, and required all *encomiendas* to revert to the king upon the death of the holder. Other reforms included the suppression of the *audiencia* of Panama, the creation of the *audiencia* in Peru, and the establishment of the viceroyalty of Peru itself.

In Peru the news of the reform in the *encomienda* system and the ending of unpaid personal service by Indians heretofore enjoyed by landowners, produced a revolt led by Gonzalo Pizarro. When the conflict resulted in the execution of the new viceroy, Philip, acting as regent, sent to Peru in 1546 Pedro de la Gasca, a distinguished and learned churchman whose devotion to duty and personality had overcome the defects of a deformed body. In Panama, Pizarro's appointees bowed to the authority of Gasca, to whom they turned over the fleet anchored in the bay. On arrival in Peru, Gasca announced a modification of the New Laws which recognized *encomiendas* granted during the conquest and fixed conditions under which Indians and Negroes were to continue in bondage. At the same time he offered amnesty to those who laid down their arms. Satisfied, the landowners in large part deserted Gonzalo Pizarro, whom Gasca shortly defeated, captured, and executed. With order restored, Gasca returned to Spain, leaving the *audiencia* to rule until the arrival in 1551 of Antonio de Mendoza, whom Philip II appointed as viceroy in recognition of his remarkable services in establishing the viceroyalty of Mexico.

Royal Administration. The new viceroy, exhausted by his labors in Mexico, died within a year. His successors, until the great Toledo succeeded in 1569, continued exploration, colonization, and organization of administration. Between 1556 and 1558 Juan Fernández Ladrillero explored the Strait of Magellan, while at the other end of the viceroyalty, Pedro de Ursua began in 1560 a new search for fabled cities beyond the Andes. Following the Marañón River and the Amazon he advanced possibly as far as the Río Negro. There Lope de Aguirre, a gifted but probably insane character, murdered Ursua and assumed command for an exploration northward. Pushing his way through the jungles, he reached the Orinoco River to follow that stream to the Atlantic Ocean. On the coast Lope seized the island of Margarita, threw off allegiance to the Spanish king, and launched a mad attack upon the coasts of New Granada. Defeated, he was executed.

Search for silver and gold deposits brought a major discovery in 1545 when rich silver veins were found at Potosí in Charcas (Bolivia). Twenty years later in 1563 the Spaniards stumbled upon the remarkable mercury deposits at Huancavelica. Together Potosí and Huancavelica became the basis of Peru's future prosperity. Further explorations beyond Potosí carried the mining frontier into northern Argentina, where in 1565 Lope García de Castro directed the founding of the city of Tucumán. The growing volume of silver production brought the establishment of a mint, Casa de Moneda, in Lima in 1565. Four years later in 1569, when Toledo began his administration, Philip II ordered the Inquisition to begin work in Peru.

Reforms of Toledo. When Francisco de Toledo became viceroy in 1569–1581, royal institutions had been firmly established. To improve administration, the new viceroy began a thorough inspection of the vice-royalty. Outstanding were his efforts to protect the Indians from abuses grown up over the years. Most serious was the *mita* system, forced labor in the mines, and unpaid personal service exacted by landowners and government officials. Both had been productive of frequent revolts. Under Toledo's ordinances the *corregidor* in charge of Indian towns had to follow a fixed order for the distribution of Indians each month, pay them in advance, and see that they labored only for the purpose for which they were hired. In the mines the ordinances regulated their hours of work, provided periods of rest, and restricted excessive use of their labor. While these laws were frequently evaded even while Toledo ruled, and became in many cases a dead letter afterward, they nevertheless remained a model for similar legislation in the later colonial period.

For Peru as a whole Toledo legislated on a wide variety of subjects. His ordinances provided the first system of *corregidores* for the administration of Indian towns. He drew up a mining code to encourage search for silver deposits and made regulations for the government of provinces and municipalities. He promulgated ordinances for the administration of the hospital of San Andrés in Lima, brought about the founding of the University of San Marcos, and encouraged the writing of a history of the Incas. In his own office he improved financial administration, directed the construction of roads and bridges, and dispatched exploring and colonizing expeditions into the interior. Against Toledo, ranked as one of the ablest colonial administrators and who became known as the "Solon of Peru" for his reforms, was his heartless and arbitrary execution of the Inca, Tupac Amarú. This Indian leader, in fact, had offered no armed resistance to Spanish power, insisting only that he was a king among his people. Although Toledo's apologists have claimed that Tupac was a threat to Spain's control, this blot on the viceroy's reputation has remained.

Part III. THE COLONIZATION OF SOUTHERN SOUTH AMERICA, 1515–1580

La Plata. Solís' voyage of 1515–1516 had opened the way for exploration and conquest into the interior of La Plata. Myths and fables had carried forward the first movement. The survivors of Solís' expedition learned from the Indians of a country filled with precious metal governed by a "White King." Led by Alejo García, a small party explored for the first time the Paraná River and the lands of the Guaraní and entered eastern Bolivia. Seeking a strait became the next objective of the Spaniards. Sebastián Cabot, following Vespucci and Solís, arrived in 1525 to search for an opening through the continent to Cipango and other fabled islands of the Orient. But instead he, too, sought the "White King," exploring, in the effort, the Paraná. The king of Spain, disappointed in Cabot's failure to seek a strait, sent Diego García in 1530 to take possession.

Mendoza's Attempt at Colonization. Pizarro's success in Peru gave new life to La Plata activities. Don Pedro de Mendoza, with a grant to conquer and colonize, left Spain in September, 1535, with eleven ships filled with 2,500 settlers and equipment for a colony. Early in 1536 he attempted a settlement at Buenos Aires, but Indian attack forced him to transfer the colony up the river to Corpus Christi. Many, dissatisfied and wishing to go on to Peru, led Mendoza to send Juan de Ayolas and Domingo Martínez de Irala up the Paraná to search for a route. In their absence Mendoza, discouraged, returned to Spain and died en route.

Irala and the Founding of Paraguay. Meanwhile, Irala, halting in Paraguay, founded a post and invited the remnants of Mendoza's colony to join him there. Thus the first permanent colony, Asunción, was established in La Plata in 1539. Irala turned to the serious work of making his undertaking a success. Subjugating the Guaraní Indians, he encouraged intermarriage between his colonists and Indian women. At strategic points he founded new settlements. In the east along the Paraná he aided the founding of missions and fixed the future boundary between Paraguay and Brazil. In the midst of this constructive work, Irala found himself set aside by Alvar Núñez Cabeza de Vaca, who, after a shipwreck on the Brazilian coast and a long walk through the wilderness, displayed to Irala's suspicious eyes his royal appointment. But Peru, as in the case of so many others, attracted him. Leaving Irala in charge, he set off to win a fortune; but the jungles turned him back. This time, Irala appealed to the king for the governorship, sent him an account of his work, and dispatched Cabeza de Vaca back to Spain in irons. Confirmed in the appointment, Irala continued to govern until 1556 when he died.

The Refounding of Buenos Aires, 1580. The cattle which Mendoza had brought from Spain multiplied along the banks of the Paraguay. Slowly they moved southward along the Paraná River, tended by cowboys while the land fell into the hands of cattle barons. Outstanding among these was Juan de Garay, who in 1573 founded Santa Fé to provide a port for Paraguay. Steadily driving the Indians back into the pampas and holding off his competitors for territory, Garay moved southward. At the mouth of the Paraná he defeated the powerful tribes there and in 1580 founded the city of Buenos Aires. Spanish colonization, meanwhile, was moving along other routes into the interior. From Peru silver miners had pushed their way through Charcas to found Tucumán in 1565. Luis de Cabrera established Córdoba in 1573, while farther west the Chileans under Mendoza had colonized at Mendoza. Buenos Aires, however, did not fulfill its promise as a port. With the interior devoted to raising cattle for hides, which were of no immediate value to the Spanish government, the city's trade was restricted to Lima beyond the Andes, while the government remained dependent upon Asunción until 1617.

Part IV. PORTUGUESE COLONIZATION OF BRAZIL, 1500–1580

Spain and Portugal: a Contrast. Portugal's colonization of Brazil presents a striking contrast with the work of Spain in the same century. With a vigorous sweep and restless energy, Spain colonized a continent and a half. Portugal's string of disjoined settlements along the Atlantic seaboard of Brazil presented no comparable picture. The reasons for the difference are many. Portugal spent its strength exploiting its possessions in Africa and in the Orient. These poured into the homeland a wealth comparable to that which Spain extracted from its American colonies. Neglect of Brazil was natural. Moreover, Brazil held no significant Indian civilizations, the main incentive to the Spanish advance into the interior of both continents.

The close control of the Spanish monarchs over their colonies sharply contrasts with the lack of centralized direction in Brazil. This weak supervision facilitated the growth in Brazil of a powerful, intrenched, feudal-patriarchal group based on slave labor and sugar-produced wealth. They controlled their own affairs. The Spanish colonies had the same group, based on Indian labor, but it was generally excluded from participation in government. Significantly, the church in Brazil, lacking the support given the church in the Spanish colonies, fell under the domination of the native Brazilian oligarchy. This fact contributed to the growth of a spirit of tolerance on the part of the Brazilian church unknown in the Spanish colonies.

Cabral and the Early Neglect of Brazil, 1500–1532. The casual manner in which Portugal regarded Brazil is seen in the fact that she made no immediate effort to take possession of any lands in the west after the signing of the Treaty of Tordesillas in 1494. Individual Portuguese doubtless traded along the coast, but not until Columbus in 1498 discovered South America and Pinzón coasted the northern Brazilian shore line did Portugal claim the land. In 1500 Pedro Alvares Cabral, bound for India with a fleet of thirteen vessels, reached the coast of Brazil near Mt. Pascual and landed to take possession in a bay he called Porto Seguro, about forty miles north. Much controversy attends the question as to whether Cabral had orders to find land in the west. The best opinion is that by following Gama's sailing instructions he came upon the coast of Brazil. However, the fact that King Manoel I was concerned about the Spanish voyages in the region and that Cabral sent a ship back announcing possession may indicate that he really had instructions to find land. Vespucci, as noted, followed Cabral and coasted the Brazilian shores southward.

By 1503 Portuguese traders, many of them Jews suffering persecution, emigrated to Brazil, where some were exporting dyewoods under royal concession. Others, *degredados* (criminals), were left behind by Cabral; shipwrecked sailors and castaways found haven along its coasts. The latter took wives among the Indians and some became chiefs of tribes with many concubines. Outstanding was Caramarú, who was venerated by the Indians in the region of later Bahia. A similar figure, João Ramalho, had an identical influence farther south and aided, as did Caramarú, Portuguese colonization in these areas.

Portuguese traders did not long enjoy a monopoly of the export of red Brazil wood. Frenchmen, chiefly from Normandy, built up a logwood trade and bartered with the coastal natives. Soon French pirates appeared to raid Portuguese shipping en route to India. In defense King Manoel sent Christovão Jacques in 1516 with a fleet, who, having driven the French temporarily from the coast, discovered the possibilities of sugar cultivation and is believed to have established the earliest sugar plantation in Brazil near Pernambuco. Spain renewed her interest in the region when Solís rediscovered the Río de La Plata and when she sent Sebastián Cabot who explored far into the interior and planned colonization there.

Colonization of Brazil: São Paulo. Dom João, faced with this foreign intrusion, determined to occupy Brazil. In 1531 Martin Affonso da Souza led out the first colony. After capturing French ships and examining the coast for a location, he stopped momentarily at Pernambuco and Bahia. Moving southward, he built a temporary fort at Rio de Janeiro, but one of his lieutenants, returning from coastal exploration to the La Plata, decided Souza to establish a permanent colony at São Vicente in January, 1532, on the coast near present-day São Paulo.

With land distributed among the Portuguese, São Vicente soon became a flourishing center for the production of sugar, wheat, barley, and grapes, from which wine and marmalade were made, as well as the cultivation of native maize and manioc. Shortage of labor led at once to Indian slavery and expansion into the interior. In 1534 Souza established Piratininga on the plateau north of São Vicente.

Near-by the Jesuit mission called São Paulo superseded Piratininga in 1554. Colonists received land grants, called *sesmarias,* some of which were enormous in extent, and cultivated crops of wheat, manioc, and the vine. On the surrounding plains cattle, pigs, and horses flourished. Too, São Paulo quickly became a slave mart for the coastal plantations at São Vicente. Father Pedro Manoel Nobrega established a Jesuit college in São Paulo, headed by Father José de Anchieta, for the children of Portuguese as well as the offspring of Portuguese and Indians, called *Mamelucos.* From São Paulo the Paulistas, as the inhabitants there were called, drove westward in a ruthless search for Indian slaves. Others expanded the cattle ranges to the south. Before the end of the century the Paulistas or *Mamelucos,* had became powerful, aggressive slavers, cattlemen, and soldiers who gave southern Brazil a macabre if picturesque character.

The slave raids of the Paulistas stirred the church to protect the natives. Outstanding were the efforts of Nobrega and Anchieta. The latter, traveling alone into the interior, won many converts. But he is more widely remembered for his school for Indians at São Paulo and his extensive accounts of Tupí-Guaraní civilization. In spite of the best efforts of the Jesuits, the inhumane practice went on until the Paulistas reached the Paraná River, where Irala in Paraguay threw up a line of posts to halt this westward Brazilian expansion.

The Capitanias: Bahia and Pernambuco. The Portuguese king soon realized that to ward off French piracy and trade a single colony would not be sufficient. He accordingly divided the coast of Brazil into fifteen administrative districts, called hereditary *capitanias,* to extend westward to the Spanish dominions. These he offered to the Portuguese aristocracy under terms which bestowed broad powers of almost unlimited civil and criminal jurisdiction, including the right to levy and collect taxes and extend trading rights even to foreigners who carried on commerce between Brazil and Portugal. Those who received these grants were called *donatários.* This system fixed the feudal pattern in Brazil. Not all of those who accepted had the resources to establish colonies, so that only a small number—seven—of *capitanias* were established. Affonso da Souza, who became a *donatário,* succeeded, as we have seen, at São Vicente and São Paulo. Farther north Francisco Pereira colonized Bahia.

Outstanding was the work of Duarte Coelho at Pernambuco, who established his capital at Olinda. This colony prospered from the advantageous position it enjoyed on the most eastern point of Brazil, where shipping to and from Portugal passed. More important, however, was the sugar cultivation of the region. Its rapid expansion developed a lucrative trade with Portugal on its own. To carry on operations, the Portuguese introduced Negro slavery into the colony, a commerce also contributing to the economic prosperity of Pernambuco.

Bahia. The fact that some *capitanias* failed and others did not meet royal expectations in protecting Brazil from foreigners led the Portuguese king to attempt centralization in colonial government. To reduce the powers of the *donatários* and centralize control, the king appointed Thomé da Souza, who, as an administrator, had extensive experience in Portugal's Asian and African colonies as governor-general. In Portugal he established a collector of finance to supervise the taxation system of the colony. Souza, with authority to coordinate the *capitanias* in a common defense, established his capital at Bahia in 1549–1550 with a large colony, created a coastal patrol, and colonized up and down the coast as far as Rio de Janeiro.

The Founding of Rio de Janeiro. Souza's vigorous administration found no counterpart in his successor, Duarte da Costa. French interest along the coast grew rapidly. Not only did transient French traders take out increasing quantities of brazilwood, but Vice-Admiral Nicolás Villegagnon projected a permanent Huguenot settlement at Rio de Janeiro, named "Antarctic France." In 1555 he placed a small fort, Coligny, on the bay at Rio, already the scene of French logging and trading activities. Soon three boatloads of French and Swiss Calvinistic

Huguenots arrived to establish the first European settlement on the bay.

The Portuguese king acted promptly. To succeed da Costa he sent Mem da Sá, an able military man who captured Fort Coligny and drove the settlers into the interior. There, befriended by the Indians, the French organized a force to attack the Portuguese slave mart at São Paulo. Three years of fighting closed with a temporary truce in 1564. Eustacio da Sá, who now came to Brazil, ended the French danger. From a base located on Sugar Loaf Island in the harbor, Eustacio in 1567 attacked successfully the strong Indian and French positions on the mainland. The French evacuées settled for a while in Pernambuco, but eventually returned to France. On the site of the former French colony, Portugal now founded Rio de Janeiro in 1570.

Though the land was free of the French, at sea they continued their attack on Portuguese shipping. To provide a better defense, the king created in 1572 two colonial governments, one with its capital at Bahia to protect the north, the other at Rio de Janeiro to include all settlements in the south. Luis de Brito de Almeida became the governor-general at Bahia, while Don Antonio Salema governed at Rio. Both maintained coastal defenses against the French. Possibly of more importance, they began warfare against the Indians to open the way into the interior. Discovery of mines and slave raids to supply the coastal plantations gave impetus to this movement. The church at the same time divided Brazil into separate provinces, with a bishop at Bahia and another at Rio. Politically, however, the experiment of dual governments failed, and Portugal restored Bahia as the sole capital in 1576 with Brito as governor-general.

Brazil under Spain: Governmental Changes. Dynastic turmoil in Portugal gave Spain control of that country in 1580. Two years before, in 1578, the death of Don Sebastián without heirs left the country in the hands of Cardinal Don Enrique. Among the candidates for the throne was Philip II of Spain, favored by the cardinal. Though opposition existed, the Duke of Alba quickly extinguished it by a vigorous campaign. An agreement drawn up in 1580 united the two crowns. Under it Portugal gave up Brazil to Spain and recognized the Philippine Islands as within the Spanish sphere in the Orient, although the line of demarcation had given those islands to Portugal. Also in the east Portugal retained the right to trade with Japan.

Brazil as a colony under Spain was little affected in the main lines of its development. Over the vigorous Paulistas in the south Spain had no control. In the north, she temporarily lost the Amazonian coast to

Holland; Brazilian effort later won it back. However, in administration she made some changes. To govern Brazil, Spain established in Lisbon a central body, the Transmarine Council, although the real decisions were made in Madrid, and a Council of Finance *(Conseho da Fazenda)* to replace the Inspector of Finance under Portuguese rule. In Brazil itself, Philip II replaced the original colonial law of Portugal with a code *(Ordenações Philippinas).* The code not only recognized an existing fact, namely, the power wielded by the *câmaras* or city councils, but it defined more clearly the authority of the governor-general. To improve the administration of justice, Philip II established a supreme court *(Relaçao)* with power to settle cases in Brazil. The most important change in local government was that of making the captaincy of Marañho directly responsible to Lisbon. Ocean currents on this Brazilian coast made communication easier between Marañho and the mother country than with Bahia, the capital.

The End of the Century. By the end of the sixteenth century, Spain and Portugal had firmly established their empires in the New World. The work of these two powers, which embraced the occupation of an entire continent and a half, posed problems of political administration. The arrival of colonizers who mixed with the native populations produced a new American society. For the exploitation of the natural riches of this vast area and to direct the productive labor of its colonial population, an economic system had to be devised. To these problems, we now turn our attention.

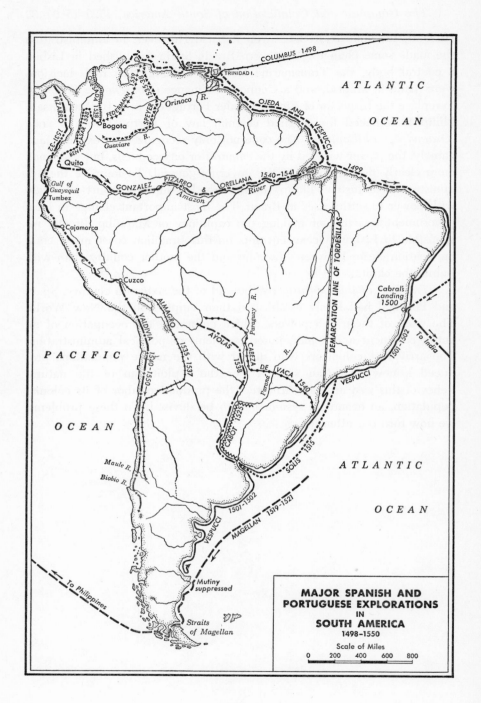

**MAJOR SPANISH AND
PORTUGUESE EXPLORATIONS
IN
SOUTH AMERICA
1498-1550**

Scale of Miles

0   200   400   600   800

Chapter V

THE POLITICAL AND
ECONOMIC ORGANIZATION
OF THE SPANISH COLONIES

Part I. THE POLITICAL SYSTEM

Introduction. By the year 1600 Spain had conquered, colonized, explored, and taken possession of almost a continent and a third. By 1574 she had built more than 200 towns and cities, with a total Spanish population living in them of about 150,000. Since the population of Spain itself in the sixteenth century reached barely 4,000,000, her achievement finds no equal in the history of colonization. Over this vast area of the New World and the Philippine Islands, the Spanish monarchs organized a colonial government, planned colonization, economic development, and conversion of millions of Indians to Christianity. Out of these broad measures colonial Latin America evolved (1) a political system, (2) an economical organization, (3) a social structure and a cultural life, a blend of Spanish and age-old Indian civilizations.

The Political System. The political administration of the colonies rested upon two sets of institutions: those created in Spain and those established in the colonies. The institutions in both places expressed the basic concept that the colonies were the sole possession of the Spanish rulers. For this reason the strong monarchy itself was the ranking institution. It functioned through two organizations in Spain: the Council of the Indies and the House of Trade *(Casa de Contratación).*

The Council of the Indies. The Council had its origin in the appointment of Juan Rodríguez de Fonseca in 1493, an archdeacon of the Sevilla cathedral. His duties consisted in aiding Columbus to outfit his second expedition and reporting to the king the events of the occupation of the West Indies. By 1524 the Council was formally organized as one separate from that of Castile and bore the title of Royal Council and Committee of War of the Indies, commonly called the Council of the Indies. By

1542 the Council had assumed permanent form, resided in Madrid, and consisted of a president, assisted by a grand chancellor, eight councilors, an attorney-general, two secretaries, a cosmographer, a mathematician, and an historian. Lesser officials were secretaries and various administrative appointees.

The Council exercised the power of the king himself, who frequently attended its meetings. As the supreme policy-making body, it exercised executive, judicial, and legislative authority. It appointed officials, both civil and ecclesiastical, the latter under the authority of the royal patronage *(real patronato)*, to posts in America. It directed the conversion of the Indians, a power which was described as its principal duty, superintended the expenditures and receipts of the royal treasury in colonial undertakings, authorized the preparation and dispatch of all sea and land expeditions, merchant and naval fleets, and all colonizing ventures. As the supreme judicial tribunal, it heard appeals from any of the superior colonial courts, *audiencias,* consular courts, and the court of the House of Trade. It also served as a court of original jurisdiction.

As the supreme legislative authority, it made laws and regulations affecting all aspects of colonial life. It laid down the rules which governed all activities of the church in the colonies and those which guided the conduct of all officials in colonial offices, even including the duties of the porter at the door of the *audiencias.* It drew up regulations for all colonizing expeditions, even the ordinances for the laying out of streets in colonial towns. Its rules called for diaries and reports of all exploring expeditions. It laid down the conditions upon which travelers, including foreigners, might go to the Indies, those governing trade and commerce in all their aspects, and the regulations for the guidance of ships and naval escorts and operations. Its vast body of legislation became so unwieldy by 1680 that its laws were codified in that year in a monumental publication, *The Digest of the Laws of the Indies (Recopilación de las Leyes de Indias).* Pervaded by a humanitarian spirit, this code, the most significant produced by any colonizing power, became the model for later French, British, and Dutch colonial legislation.

Early Political Development in the Colonies. In the New World, Spain established a hierarchy of centralized political offices to carry out the policies of the Council. These organs, however, grew slowly. Columbus did have the rank of admiral, governor-general and viceroy, but of these titles he was early relieved. The first royal official to govern in the Indies was Francisco de Bobadilla, governor and judge of Española in 1499. The office of governor was held by his successor, Nicolás de

Ovando, 1502–1509. Diego Columbus, who followed him, as governor-general and admiral. To share the powers of the governor, after 1509 the king appointed in 1511 three royal judges to sit in Santo Domingo. Their office became the forerunner of the *audiencia* of Santo Domingo, formally established in 1524, with authority over all the Spanish West Indies and Spanish Florida.

As colonization reached the mainland, the rank of *adelantado* or captain-general, besides that of governor, was frequently conferred upon the conquerors. The rank of *adelantado,* more associated with conquest than with government, had its origin in the Moslem wars. It implied the necessary authority of a commander to conquer and organize a government of a military character. For his conquest of Peru, Pizarro had such a title as well as that of captain-general; De Soto was *adelantado* of Florida and governor of Cuba, as was Menéndez, who undertook its conquest and colonization.

The Viceroy. When Cortés made his great discoveries of wealth in Mexico, the king saw the hazard in conferring such extensive powers upon individuals so far from Spain. Consequently in 1529 Charles V began to model the government of the colonies upon the centralized pattern of royal control in Castile. A hierarchy of offices thus evolved directly dependent upon the monarch himself.

Ranking first in importance was the office of the viceroy. Wishing to impress Spaniards and Indians alike, Charles V gave this office the authority of his own. For the position the monarchs chose men high in the councils of the government in Castile, of proven ability and loyalty to the crown. Eventually four viceroyalties were created: New Spain in 1536; Peru in 1542; New Granada in 1718, abolished in 1723, and recreated in 1739; La Plata in 1776. On arrival in America viceroys were received with ceremonies befitting a monarch. In their capitals they established courts which frequently rivaled in splendor those of Europe.

The primary function of the viceroy was to protect the colony from Indian revolt and foreign invasion. For this reason he exercised supreme military authority on land and the seas adjoining his command. To assist him he had a Spanish army, whose commanding officer sat on the viceroy's council, an inspector-general of the army and a number of subinspectors distributed throughout the viceroyalty. He could in times of war command the services of the captain-general who ruled neighboring administrative areas with powers and duties slightly less viceregal.

The viceroy's civil functions embraced every aspect of government. He enjoyed the right to appoint officials who were not directly appointed by the king in Spain. In the case of the church he exercised vice-patronal powers, that is, the appointment of churchmen to office and control over all papal communications to the colony. Since his chief civil duty was to increase the wealth of the viceroyalty, he supervised the collection of taxes through the office of superintendent of the *hacienda* (treasury). This office kept account of all expenditures and income of the viceroyalty. He appointed visitors or inspectors to look into specific matters, such as mining inspectors. These, for example, had the authority to administer the mining industry, enforce mining laws, encourage discoveries, and develop new mines.

The viceroy was specifically empowered to act as the Protector of the Indians. He appointed Protectors of the Indians who resided in various provinces, and he heard petitions directly at the viceregal palace. Other important duties included his functions as Protector of the Church and the founding of schools, universities, hospitals, and other charitable institutions. Upon leaving office, the viceroy was required to submit a detailed account of his administration, an *Instruction (Instrucción)* for the benefit of his successor.

Because of the viceroy's high powers, the king placed restrictions upon him, all, however, subject to exceptions, in order to discourage corruption and revolt. During his term of office, usually limited to three years, the viceroy could not marry, or if married, could not take his family with him. He was prohibited from engaging in trade or acquiring property in the viceroyalty. At the end of his term the viceroy had to submit to a *residencia,* that is, a court of inquiry of three judges sent from Spain to inquire into his administration. Complaints of injustice or corruption could be submitted against him, but he was allowed a rebuttal. If convicted, though this rarely happened, the viceroy was subject to fine, loss of property, and even imprisonment.

The Audiencia. The vast size of the viceroyalties made necessary smaller territorial divisions. The most important of these were the *audiencias,* composed of three to fifteen individuals, whose chief member was the president. They acted as political advisers to the viceroys, executed the orders of the viceroy in their district, kept the viceroy informed of local conditions, assumed military authority where necessary, and in the capital of the viceroyalty, acted as the supreme governing authority in the absence, death, or delay of a viceroy of captain-general.

In judicial affairs, the *audiencias* set as courts. They were the supreme courts in the colonies. Since only cases involving sums of 10,000 or more gold pesos could be appealed to the Council of the Indies, the *audiencias* heard the great majority of suits. They could bring viceroys and captains-general to trial, examine the proceedings of a *visita*, that is, an inspection ordered by the viceroy, take charge of the possessions of an individual who died without a will, and guard the interests of the Indians. The viceroy could not impose his power in judicial affairs; the *audiencias* enjoyed the right of corresponding directly with the king.

As in the case of the viceroy, the king placed restrictions upon the judges of the *audiencias*. They could not marry in the colonies except by royal permission, engage in business, attend social affairs such as weddings and christenings, or own real estate. Governing smaller areas than the viceroy, the members of the *audiencias* exercised in fact a greater day-to-day influence over affairs than did the viceroy.

Standing apart from the royal courts but nevertheless an aspect of the administration of justice were the consular, church, and military courts. These operated according to practices that had developed in Spain. The administration of justice for their special affairs was a privilege *(fuero)* granted by the king to set them apart from the jurisdiction of the royal courts.

The first *audiencia* created in the New World was that of Santo Domingo in 1524. Its jurisdiction included the Caribbean and the coast of the mainland from Venezuela to southern Mexico. Later it lost much of its coastal jurisdiction to mainland *audiencias,* but retained it over Florida. The *audiencia* of Mexico, the second, established in 1527, embraced central and southern Mexico and the Gulf coast as far as Florida. In northern Mexico the *audiencia* of New Galcia was created in 1548 with four *alcalde mayores.* In 1550, however, it became the *audiencia* of Guadalajara, with its seat in that city. This *audiencia* had a special significance for the history of the southwestern part of the United States, since Spanish colonization in northern Mexico and the American Southwest fell under its direction. In Central America and dependent on the viceroy of New Spain was the *audiencia* of Guatemala. Established in 1542 under the presidency of the captain-general, it exercised authority throughout Central America. In the far-off Philippine Islands was the *audiencia* of Manila, created in 1583, dependent upon the viceroyalty of New Spain but little influenced by it. Panama, because of its strategic location, was made into an *audiencia* in 1535, lost it temporarily, but received it back in 1563–1564.

In South America the *audiencia* of Lima came in with the other changes in the New Laws of 1542. Expansion from Lima soon required *audiencias* in the remote areas. The *audiencia* of Bogotá, dependent upon

Peru, was created in 1549; that of Charcas (Bolivia) in 1559; that of Quito in Ecuador, usually referred to as the Presidency, in 1563. The *audiencia* of Santiago was instituted in 1565, discontinued shortly after, and restored in 1609.

Provinces. Viceroyalties and *audiencias,* to facilitate administration, were divided into smaller units—provinces or *gobiernos.* On the frontiers military men usually held the office of governor to fend off Indian attack and foreign invasion. Governors held their position for five years. Their primary duties were to collect taxes, guard against revolt by the subjugated Indians, and aid the church in its work of conversion. Others involved the execution of superior orders, taking a census of the province, encouraging agriculture, mining, and trade, and presiding over emergency meetings of the leading settlers, caused by Indian invasions, revolts, or royal orders vitally affecting the province. The governor also appointed officials usually called *alcaldes* to represent him in the lesser divisions of the province, known variously as *aldeas,* or *alcaldías mayores.*

The cupidity of some governors and the strictures necessary to prevent Indian revolt frequently brought them into conflict with the provincial church officials. The latter opposed the customary practice of governors enriching themselves by the sale of Indians to the mines. On the other hand, governors, to avoid Indian revolt, frequently opposed the churchmen bent upon destroying Indian religious practices. The close touch that governors maintained with all elements of the population probably gave them the most direct influence upon the government of the colonial empire.

Residencia. To keep himself informed of the activities of his administrative officials and to prevent as far as possible corruption and failure of justice, the king required all major officials, viceroys, captains-general, governors, *corregidores,* and others to submit to a *residencia,* an investigation of an official's term of office. Such an individual was required to remain in the territory he governed until his trial was completed. To carry out the investigation in the case of the viceroy and higher officials, the king appointed three judges, usually from Spain, to whom complaints of injured parties could be submitted, with the officeholder enjoying the right of rebuttal. The *residencia* undoubtedly restrained officials from the abuse of their power. Too, it gave the crown an insight into the state of affairs prevailing throughout his dominions. Most officials feared the *residencia,* for it could be used by bribery as an engine of persecution.

Visitor-General (Visita). An equally effective instrument by which the king increased his royal authority and kept himself informed of the condition of the colonies was the *visita* or inspection conducted by a visitor-general. This individual, sent infrequently and usually without warning, had broad authority. Upon his arrival in a viceroyalty he superseded the viceroy while he carried out his inspection. Not only could he pry into the affairs of all officeholders, but he carried authority to make changes, if necessary, in taxation, the administration of justice, and military and financial affairs. Moreover, he could put such changes into effect. In this manner the crown was provided with a comprehensive view of its colonies, their weaknesses, abuses, strength, and the efficiency or lack of it among its administrative officials.

Local Government. Local government in the colonies derived from various sources. Spanish town government, long established, had won many important privileges, although in the sixteenth century the centralized monarchy deprived it of the right of sending representatives to court. Into the New World the towns carried with them many of the institutions developed in Spain, but added new characteristics. Affecting local government, too, was the influence of powerful landowners who held Indians in *encomienda*, frequently entire towns. Likewise the needs of royal administration made use of Indian town government, as did the church.

At the time of the founding of a colonial Spanish town, the site was marked off and lots distributed to the settlers after provision was made for the public buildings including the church and cathedral about the central plaza. At its founding, too, the town declared ownership of the immediately adjoining territory, which became known as common land; other lands beyond were called *los baldios*, a kind of public domain. Some common lands were devoted to pasture, others to timber with tracts set aside for the use of the town, and still others furnished space for fairs, recreational activities, and territory for expansion.

The property owners who organized the town government, the key institution of which was the *cabildo*, elected its officials. These, usually numbering between six and twelve, included the councilmen, *regidores*, who selected from among themselves the mayor, *alcalde* or *alcalde mayor*, judges (*alcaldes ordinarios*), a treasurer (*mayordomo*), and a constable (*alguacil mayor*). These officials appointed the officers necessary to carry on the town business. In time these offices were regularly bought and sold except those which the leading families succeeded in making hereditary.

The power of the *cabildo* varied, largely depending upon its distance from the metropolitan centers where the king had his highest officials, viceroys, captains-general, and the officers of the *audiencia*. Generally speaking, towns located in the interior away from these centers wielded much power. Within them the *cabildo* had authority to levy taxes; provide for public works; build roads, bridges, government buildings, and hospitals; supervise sanitation, meat markets, jails, and shops; regulate trade; police the common lands; supervise the forests; promulgate orders received from superior governments; in short, to take all measures necessary for administration of a town or city. In times of great emergency—Indian attack, pirate raid, or epidemic—the property owners met in a general assembly, called a *cabildo abierto*, to discuss whatever measures were necessary to take.

In the early sixteenth century, particularly in Española, towns for twenty-five years sent representatives, *procuradores*, to the king's court. Charles V, however, discouraged the practice and eventually ended it. Nevertheless, towns continued to have the right of appeal to the higher authorities, and submit petitions for redress in cases where the municipality believed itself injured by a higher command. Equally important, by procrastination and seeking clarification of royal orders, towns frequently were able to nullify completely the king's wishes.

A second aspect of local government arose from the use of the *corregidor* in the Spanish colonies as the representative of royal power in local areas. The territory of this official was called a *corregimiento*, which, when including Spanish towns, made the *corregidor* a power in the local *cabildo*. But he wielded his greatest authority in the regions designated as *corregimientos* of Indians. Within such territory his civil obligations included instruction of Indians in agriculture, exploitation of the wealth of his jurisdiction, and construction of public works, bridges, roads, public buildings, granaries, and other edifices. His most important duty, however, was the collection of taxes. He controlled Indian trade, frequently forcing the natives to buy goods totally useless to them, such as spectacles; allotted Indians for work in mines and on other projects; appointed officials, usually Indian chiefs; and often expoited Indian labor for his own enrichment. Eventually the corruption and abuses associated with the *corregidor's* office became so great as to bring its virtual abolition in the eighteenth century.

Indian chiefs as governors of Indian towns were not only made use of by the *corregidor*, but by wealthy holders of *encomiendas* and by the royal government. In the latter case the individuals of the Indian nobility, for they were recognized as such a social group, were appointed by viceroys, captains-general, and governors. Universally holders of Indians in *encomienda*, the Indian chiefs or *caciques* utilized their office, the *cacicazgo*, to enrich themselves and often abused their charges as cruelly as did some of the Spanish *encomenderos*. The use of this powerful office of Indian government, the *cacicazgo*, was in fact an important agency enabling Spain to control the millions of Indians in her empire. The church, in its policy of founding Indian towns, called *congregados* in the settled areas and reductions in the missionary regions, usually appointed Indian chiefs to act as the intermediary between the Indians and the missionary authorities.

Local government in the Spanish colonies had a decisive influence in the development of Latin America. The colonial *cabildos* were essentially undemocratic in nature, since they excluded the bulk of the population of towns and cities from participation in government. At the same time the few who enjoyed the privileged positions of power in the *cabildos* developed great political skill. They not only managed *cabildo* affairs, particularly away from the metropolitan centers, for some three centuries, but developed techniques for evading royal laws conflicting with their interests. In the latter respect the *cabildos* represented a developing nationalistic spirit and a civil tradition. Thus when the time came to launch the movement for independence, the *cabildos* took the lead.

Part II. THE ECONOMIC ADMINISTRATION OF THE SPANISH COLONIES

The Spanish Mercantile System. Economically, Spain's colonies rested upon a body of ideas developed by royal experience in Spain itself. The basic concept was the exclusive ownership of the overseas possessions by the Spanish monarchs. Practically, the ideas found expression in royal monopolies, royal taxes, and royal regulations imposed to provide the maximum profit for the monarchy itself, not for Spain. The system evolved was the mercantile system. Under it the colonies were to furnish raw materials for home industry and a market for manufactured goods. Until the eighteenth century the crown, to control trade and collect taxes, restricted commerce to Sevilla in Spain and to certain designated ports in America, particularly Nombre de Dios, transferred after 1584 to Porto Bello, Vera Cruz, Acapulco, Lima, Havana, and certain Spanish business houses within these ports.

The House of Trade. The central administrative agency for the economic development of the colonies was the House of Trade, established in Sevilla. Like the Council of the Indies, under whose authority it operated, the House of Trade had its origin in the powers of Bishop Fonseca in 1493. Formal organization took place in 1503, made necessary by the increase of trade with the West Indies. Its officials then consisted of a president, a treasurer, an attorney-general, three chancellors, three councilors, a pilot major, and a postmaster-general, together with various lesser officials and clerks. Attached to the House was a representative of the Inquisition, whose duties were to examine books destined for the Indies, primarily to exclude Protestant literature. The primary function of the House of Trade was to superintend all trade and commerce between Spain and its colonies; make the necessary regulations governing this trade and the sailing of ships, merchantmen, and warships; direct the gathering of economic and geographical data concerning winds, ocean currents, and the land of the New World; and see to the construction of maps and charts.

In detail, its officials at Sevilla arranged for the dispatching of merchant fleets and their naval convoys, the inspection of all goods from the colony, taking custody of the king's share, and ordering the distribution of the remaining cargoes to their owners. Its judges heard cases arising from violations of regulations and took possession of the property of all persons who died en route to the colonies until their heirs were located. The treasurer superintended the expenditures authorized by the Council of the Indies and received bullion and other wealth destined for the king. The postmaster-general was responsible for the organization of the mails, both official and private, en route by sea and for fixing routes of distribution in the colonies. A major addition in 1552 was the creation of a chair of cosmography. The law governing this office required all pilots and captains to keep detailed diaries of navigation. On the basis of these, delivered to the pilot major, the cosmographer's office constructed the House's huge collection of maps, charts, and geographical works, which became one of Spain's greatest contributions to the history and geography of the New World.

Both the Council of the Indies and the House of Trade carried on their work until late in the colonial period. The Council ended as an official body on April 7, 1812, set side by the *Cortes* of Cádiz. It was re-established by Ferdinand VII, but went out of existence finally in 1834. The House of Trade suffered a decline earlier. Transferred to Cádiz in 1717, it began to lose its importance after that date. With the reforms of Charles III and his use of Special Secretaries to direct colonial trade, the House lost all importance. A royal decree ended its career on July 18, 1790.

Sea and Land Routes. During the first half of the century, that is, until 1543, ships sailing alone to and from the Indies found themselves attacked by French and Moslem pirates. But as the rich cargoes from Mexico and Peru mounted in value, Spain organized in 1543 a fleet system to protect its shipping.

Sea Routes: the Fleet System. At Sevilla merchant ships and warships were organized into a convoy known as the Fleet, *la flota.* The *flota* sailed in the spring for the Caribbean with its principal port as Vera Cruz. A second fleet, the galleons, destined for *Tierra Firme,* that is, the mainland of South America, left late in the summer. The cargoes carried by the merchantmen consisted of wheat and other cereals, olive oil, liquor, wines, textiles including clothing, and stocks of arms and powder. As the colonies grew and produced some of the imported agricultural products, the cargoes changed to include a great variety of goods, shoes, linens, cottons, silks (though much of the latter came from the Philippine Islands to Mexico), hats, capes, woolens, books, high grade textiles, household utensils except furniture, porcelain ware, soap, vinegar, olive oil, and spices. Bulkier goods included machinery for mining, bricks and roofing tiles, quicksilver, iron, steel, wine, and wax. The passenger lists included emigrants, royal officials, churchmen, and adventurers.

The *flota* sailed, varying in the number of ships from seventy to one hundred, in convoy formation. A vanguard preceded, led by the commanding admiral, the merchant ships following, while a rear guard kept watch for pirates against flank attack. The voyage required from sixty to eighty days by way of the Canary Islands. Arrived at Santo Domingo, the *flota* discharged cargo destined for that port, continued to Vera Cruz, dispatching ships, en route, for Cuba and Campeche.

The second fleet, the galleons, after stopping at Santo Domingo for repairs, turned southward across the Caribbean to *Tierra Firme.* In the seventeenth century, when pirates and buccaneers flocked into this sea, Spain established the Windward Fleet (*Armada de Barlovento*) to patrol the northern coast of South America and escort the galleons to their various destinations. The first principal stop was at Cartagena, where the fleet remained usually about a month, a delay necessary to inform the viceroy of Peru at Lima of its arrival. So informed, the viceroy immediately sent orders for the fleet at Callao, which had already gathered its cargoes from ports on the Pacific coast, to set sail for Panama. This

fleet, called the *Armada del Pacifico* or Peruvian *Armada,* consisted also
of merchantmen and naval vessels for protection.

While waiting at Cartagena, the galleons received from the *Tierra
Firme* ports of Margarita, Río de la Hacha, Santa Marta, and Cartagena
itself a variety of precious cargoes. Venezuela contributed gold, cotton,
tobacco, cocoa, coffee, sugar, hides, and indigo. New Granada sent out
cargoes principally of gold, estimated at over 4,000,000 ounces in the
sixteenth century and more than 16,000,000 in the eighteenth. New
Granada also was a source for diamonds, emeralds, and other precious
and semiprecious stones. From its coastal areas came coffee, sugar,
indigo, and hides.

From Cartagena the fleet sailed to Porto Bello, the terminus of the
most important land route, that across Panama, for South America. The
occasion of the arrival of the galleons was a famous fair at Porto Bello
which lasted for forty days. While the merchants laid out the goods
brought by the ships in the public square, officials agreed upon prices.
Buyers came from other ports of the New World, Lima, Acapulco, and
Vera Cruz to buy and receive goods shipped them. At the same time
long lines of mules, sometimes as many as 200 in a caravan, wound their
way into Porto Bello from Panama. These, transporting the goods brought
by the Peruvian *Armada,* delivered on the wharves for shipment to Spain
or in the plaza for sale, chests of gold and silver, cocoa, wine, chinchona
bark, the source of quinine, vicuña wool, and precious stones. During
the height of the fair the streets were filled with traders, their clerks,
royal officials, representatives of the *consulados,* women, sailors, and
mule drivers. Gambling, cockfighting, and drinking houses flourished.
Lodgings rented for extremely high prices, as did temporary shelters put
up around the trading mart. When the fair was over and cargoes were
loaded for Spain, Porto Bello became a dead city. Its climate, which
took a heavy toll of life during the fair, made the port a pesthole.

From Porto Bello the fleet continued along the Central American
coast, and when the occasion demanded, cast anchor in the mouth of the
San Juan River. From this point the ships sailed for Havana to await the
flota en route from Vera Cruz.

The *flota,* meanwhile, having arrived at Vera Cruz, took aboard a
great variety of products. Leading in value were gold and silver shipments. The latter, cast in long bars of bullion, were stacked like cordwood
at the point of deposit. Other exports were cochineal, chiefly from Oaxaca,
an insect valued for its dye, sugar, flour, indigo, salt meat, hides, sarsaparilla, vanilla, jalap, a root with medicinal properties, soap, Campeche

wood, and Tabascan pepper. The arrival of the fleet at Vera Cruz was the occasion, too, for a grand fair. Held at Jalapa in the interior, since Vera Cruz was not suitable, the fair was attended by thousands of Indians with their native products, so that in picturesqueness, size, and trading activity it almost equaled that of Porto Bello.

After loading operations were finished, the *flota* sailed for Havana where, after repairs, preparations were made for the long voyage back to Spain, again accompanied by the galleons. The route followed was northward through the channel along the coast of Florida, thence into the open ocean to the Azores. In Spain the fleet put in at either San Lucár or Sevilla.

The Manila Galleon. Operating in the Pacific Ocean, a part of the general system of fleets was the Manila galleon. The galleons plied between Acapulco and Manila approximately every two years, but their sailings were irregular. The sea route from Acapulco on the southern coast of Mexico to the Philippine Islands was not difficult to navigate, but the problem of a return route was not solved until Fray Andrés de Urdaneta discovered in 1565 the current which ran northward along the Japanese coast. Francisco de Gali and Sebastián Rodríguez Cermeño in 1595 continued the exploration of this route along the great circle to California and thence southward to Mexico.

From the Philippines the Spanish merchants developed an extensive trade with China and even India, in addition to their commerce with the natives of the islands themselves. Ready for shipment back to Mexico these products included Chinese silks, fine porcelains, Indian muslin, silks, spices, beeswax, and precious stones. On arrival of the fleet a great fair was held at Acapulco, attended by Indians with their native manufactures as well as Spanish merchants from Mexico City and Lima, Perú. Silks especially found a ready market in Mexico, where the wealthy Creoles dressed themselves in Oriental finery. In 1579 Spain authorized trade between Lima and Acapulco, but not Lima and Manila. After that date Oriental silks, spices, muslins, and calicos taken to Peru were sold up and down the coast from Panama to Chile as well as in the interior cities. On their return to Acapulco, Peruvian ships carried back quicksilver, cocoa, and pieces of eight.

The Land Routes. The fleet systems calling at the Atlantic and Pacific ports were in turn linked with land routes over which goods were transported to and from the interior. In New Spain four major land routes formed the basic pattern of transportation. Like spokes in a wheel, these fanned out from Mexico City. One ran northwest to

Durango, Chihuahua, El Paso, and on to Santa Fé in far-off New Mexico. A second connected San Luis Potosí, Saltillo, Monterrey, and, through dangerous Indian territory, San Antonio, Texas, with Mexico City. The third ran due west to Guadalajara, where it turned north to wind across the rough valleys of the west coast to Sonora and terminate in Tucson. The fourth connected Acapulco, via Mexico City, with Vera Cruz.

Since the mercantile system closed all ports on the Gulf except Vera Cruz, the inhabitants of the northern frontier had to lay in their yearly stock of goods at fairs held in Saltillo, Durango, Chihuahua, El Paso, and Santa Fé. Outstanding in color and interest were the fairs at Taos and Santa Fé, New Mexico. There Plains Indians brought in buffalo, deer, and antelope hides, and large quantities of tallow; Navajos from the northwest exhibited their silver work, while the Pueblos displayed their pottery, cotton blankets, and handicrafts.

Flowing southward over these three northern routes to Mexico City were the endless caravans of mules, donkeys, wagons, and armed escorts. They brought out silver bullion bars, hides, tallow, corn, wine, and chile, while on their return they carried mining stores, iron, steel, quicksilver, brandy, rough woolens, cotton clothing, arms and powder for the interior presidios, as well as manufactured goods, hats, capes, and shoes. Chinese silks, in spite of restrictions against their transport, reached the interior.

In Central America the most commonly used route was along the San Juan River into the interior. Over it passed for export mahogany and other valuable woods, sugar, and hides. Southward across Panama ran the land route already noted from Panama to Porto Bello. Originally this route crossed the isthmus between Nombre de Díos and the city of Panama. After 1600 it passed along the Chagres River to Porto Bello.

The port cities of South America, which enjoyed a monopoly of trade, were also connected with the interior by a group of overland routes. To the east of Panama a major outlet of New Granada was along the Magdalena River and thence to Cartagena. To the south of Panama goods arriving by ship at Guayaquil moved over a tortuous route to Quito high in the Andes. But the outstanding city to which trade routes converged was, of course, Lima, the capital of the viceroyalty of Peru. From that city a northward running route connected Quito with Lima; a southward one passing through western Argentina crossed the Andes to Santiago, Chile. An eastward route kept communications open between Lima and Charcas (Bolivia) across the Andes by way of Cuzco, La Paz, and Potosí. From here two routes branched off to reach Buenos Aires. One lay southeastward along the Pilcomayo River to

Asunción in Paraguay, thence down the Paraná to Buenos Aires. The other ran almost due south through Tucumán, thence to Córdoba, and across the plains to the port city.

The caravans carrying merchandise and treasure over these usually dangerous routes were carefully organized. The vanguard included mounted men to guard against Indian attack or, on the Isthmus of Panama, pirates who frequently lay in wait for the Peruvian bullion. Behind the advance guard came the mules and donkeys laden with bars of silver or chests of gold, in turn protected somewhat by other animals carrying bulkier goods. At the rear mounted horsemen guarded against surprise. The arrival of these caravans going to and from Lima were the occasion of great fairs on their arrival in the larger cities, Bogotá, Lima, Santiago, Potosí, Buenos Aires, and others.

Consulados. To regulate the trade and the fairs the institution of the *consulado* or merchant guild became the important agency. Established in 1543 as part of the House of Trade, it originally handled cases resulting from bankruptcy and settled commercial disputes before a judge and officials who dispensed with legal procedures. In the course of time cases set precedents which fixed rules and ordinances governing the work of the *consulado*. In general the *consulados* acted as courts to settle small claims, heard cases involving large amounts over 1,000 pesos with appeal to the *audiencias,* and served as agencies to represent and defend in Spain the privileges of merchants. Over the centuries the *consulados* developed a body of commercial law peculiar to the Spanish colonies.

Taxation. Upon the varied activities of colonial trade the king laid a number of taxes. Early in the sixteenth century an *avería,* a tax somewhat in the nature of insurance, was collected when the fleet left Spain from merchants who sent goods to America. This same tax was sometimes levied on goods transported in the colonies to build roads, such as that between Porto Bello and Panama. A duty, *almojarifazgo,* of 7½ per cent, lowered in 1543 to 5 per cent, was levied on all goods brought from the Indies. Moreover, colonial merchants sending goods to Spain also had to pay an import tax of 2½ per cent. Various changes in these rates were made until 1695. To end widespread fraud which had developed as a result of imposing these duties, the crown next established a system of paying taxes, both import and export in Spain, according to bulk, weight, and number of items shipped. Trade in the colonies, however, continued to pay the tax of 5 per cent on imports and 2½ per cent upon exports. The Philippine trade was an exception. Imports from China paid 10 per cent; exports, 3 per cent. In 1778 Charles III in his liberal reform program, discussed later, granted free trade and abolished duties on goods produced and manufactured in Spain and in the New World. The major exception to this policy was the continued tax of 7 per cent levied on goods originating in foreign countries.

Closely associated with the tax on merchandise, imported and exported, was a sales tax, the *alcabala,* imposed on these same goods. Levied in the late sixteenth century upon all colonies, this tax, amounting to 2 per cent, was collected on the sale of all articles no matter how many times they were sold. Merchants, auctioneers, landowners, manufacturers, in fact all who sold goods in any form paid the tax under a carefully organized system directed by tax officials responsible for various groups classified to facilitate collection. Peddlers had to report all sales within twenty-four hours; landowners, every four months. *Consulados* paid a lump sum for the merchants of the city. Other groups were subject to arrangements suitable to their businesses.

Foreign Attack on the Spanish Monopoly. Spain's rigid regulations govering the conduct of her sea-borne trade, restrictions to certain ports, high taxation, and her inability to provide sufficient merchandise for her colonies opened the door to smuggling. While this story is told in detail below, we may note here that the pirates and smugglers of her competitors, Britain, France, and Holland, carried on a flourishing contraband trade in the sixteenth century. In the seventeenth they founded colonies in the Caribbean which became bases for a constant expansion of illegal commercial activities along the Spanish coasts. Spain attempted to patrol her colonial waters, but her naval resources were never sufficient to prevent smuggling. They did, however, successfully ward off invasions frequently attempted by her enemies.

Part III. THE LAND SYSTEM: AGRICULTURE AND OTHER COLONIAL INDUSTRIES

The Land System. The king as sole owner of the colonies fixed colonial land policy. The first laws promulgated in Española provided, as noted, for grants to colonists: the *peonía* and the *caballeria.* With the disappearance of the Indian and the arrival of the Negro, landholding in the Caribbean took the form of large plantations. On the mainland the founding of towns carried forward the system of small landholding, but more important as economic factors in colonial development were the huge estates, granted originally to the conquerors. The grants set the pattern for the system of *latifundia* throughout Latin America. The title to these estates had a double character: outright grants of land and the conferring of *encomiendas* of Indians for labor on the land. In size the variation was great, ranging in general from 2,500 acres upward in the agricultural regions and 4,400 and above in the cattle regions.

While land titles remained intact, subject to inheritance and sale, the *encomienda* system had a different history. Originating, as we have seen, in 1503, Charles V between 1523 and 1536 made valiant efforts to end this essentially feudal system. The demands of the colonists for labor, however, were too great for even the emperor to overrule. When the New Laws of 1542 abolished perpetual *encomiendas*, revolt forced recognition of the institution so that *encomiendas* could be inherited. However, the Spanish monarchs always opposed the institution. To weed it out they encouraged *encomenderos* to exchange their holdings for an annual money payment. In the seventeenth century they enacted laws providing for the reversion of lapsed *encomiendas* to the crown. In the next century the reforms of Charles III, notably the Ordinance of the Intendants, virtually ended the system. The effect of the change simply relieved the Indian of compulsory labor but forced him into debt to the owners of the land. The basis accordingly was laid for the system of peonage when independence eliminated royal control from the colonies.

The right of Indians to own land was recognized under a number of Spanish laws. In 1551 Charles V confirmed the ownership of Indian towns of their communal lands. These included the town dwellings, garden plots, and communal lands devoted to crops. The latter became known in New Spain as *ejidos*. To protect communal villages, Spanish law prohibited Indian towns from selling their lands without prior consent of the *audiencia*. Spaniards on their part were forbidden to enter the towns or take any lands granted to Indians. Moreover, Spanish towns could not be established where their lands would impinge upon those of neighboring Indian villages. To enforce this isolation of the two, laws required Spanish and Indian town lands to be separated by an uncultivated strip.

In addition to communal lands, Indians as individuals received land grants and even purchased property. Laws also protected the natives from the sale of their lands unless they stood to profit. However, while these laws were admirable in their intent, powerful *hacendados* with friends at court found on many occasions ways and means of depriving Indians of their property and forcing the dispossessed to work.

Agriculture. Upon these estates colonial agriculture had its basis.

The Indians already had a long history of the use of the land at the time of the conquest and produced a variety of crops. Outstanding were maize, potatoes, chile peppers, beans, manioc, *yerba maté* (Paraguayan tea), tomatoes, cocoa, sage, squash, melons, yams, peanuts, and vanilla. They supplemented their diet with wild fruits and intoxicating liquors, *pulque* and *aguardiente,* made from the maguey plants and maize stalks. They were aware, too, of the medicinal properties of ipecac, cocoa, chinchona (quinine), tobacco, sarsaparilla, and jalap.

Spain introduced a whole range of new food plants: wheat, barley, oats, rye, sugar, olives, figs, bananas, rice, and coffee. She also brought to the New World deciduous fruits, peaches, plums, apples, the vine, apricots, pears, and others. The development of both native and Spanish crops was facilitated by the introduction of the horse, oxen, mules, donkeys. The wheel, too, had been unknown as a useful instrument to the Indian.

Significance of the Leading Crops. Throughout the history of Latin America maize has remained the principal food of the masses of the people. Everywhere it exhibited a remarkable fecundity, flourishing both in the hot lands and on the elevated plateaus. Indeed, so dominant in Peru and Mexico was this plant that both have been referred to as "maize cultures." Its stalk was a source of sugar and its juice a fermented drink. Wheat, its European counterpart, was cultivated in all the colonies, but with difficulty. A luxury food, it was enjoyed only by the wealthier urban classes, as it was also in most of Europe.

The Caribbean colonies replaced Brazil after the late seventeenth century as the sugar center of the New World. By the middle of the next century, Cuba had so increased its production that one authority (Diffie) estimates its increase at eighteenfold. New Spain, the second important region, saw sugar grown from the date of the conquest. By the end of the eighteenth century its best plantations produced for export about 2,250 pounds per acre. Its total reached annually some 35,000,000 pounds, about half of which remained for home consumption. Lesser amounts were produced in Ecuador, Venezuela, Peru, and Louisiana. In all regions rum and molasses were important by-products.

Cocoa or chocolate, originally made known by the Aztecs, was first introduced into Europe from New Spain. However, the superior quality of that grown in Ecuador, Guatemala, and Venezuela supplemented the production of Mexico. Vanilla, derived from a creeper plant growing profusely along the coast of Vera Cruz and Tabasco, was exported in quantities ranging from 900,000 to 2,000,000 pods, sufficient to supply not only Spain but all of Europe. Coffee reached the new colonies in the eighteenth century. Cuba was the chief exporter to Spain, although the bulk production of French Haiti was considerably greater. Venezuela produced much less than the island colonies. New Spain exported less than Cuba, but supplied her own market with considerable amounts. Two plantations in the valley of Cuautla alone had about 500,000 coffee trees.

Cotton in common use among the Indians was grown in practically all the Spanish colonies, except Uruguay, Argentina, and Upper Peru (Bolivia). In South America it was consumed locally in textile products. In the Caribbean, Venezuela rapidly forged ahead in the late eighteenth century along with New Spain as the principal producers. The latter's coastal plantations exported the crop, while those in the interior highlands supplied the needs of the spinners at Zacatecas and other manufacturing centers. One authority estimated the value of cotton manufactures produced in New Spain in the eighteenth century at $5,000,000 annually.

Tobacco was grown profitably in Cuba from the early sixteenth century. Its cultivation carried on in other colonies made Venezuela, Peru, New Granada, and New Spain important centers. Its obvious importance as a source of revenue led Charles III to establish royal monopolies in the tobacco-growing areas. In New Spain cultivation became confined principally to the Orizaba and Córdoba districts. The ruthless destruction of the private tobacco fields in the Socorro region of New Granada produced the Comunero revolt in 1782. In Venezuela the monopoly brought on tobacco smuggling from Brazil.

Indigo grown in the Caribbean and in New Spain was exported until the late eighteenth century, when competition from Guatemala and Venezuela brought on a decline of the earlier centers. Cochineal, providing a brilliant dye, was both used locally and exported. It was a favorite of smugglers who carried large amounts to Europe. Beeswax produced in most colonies was consumed principally in church ceremonies. Forest products, particularly logwood and mahogany, were exported from Campeche and both Spanish and British Honduras. The former produced a valuable dye in wide demand in Europe.

The Cattle Industry. The cattle industry had its beginnings on the island of Española with the arrival of the first colonists in 1493. The animals accompanied the progress of the conquest on the mainland. In South America the industry did not have the importance that characterized it in New Spain. Venezuela exported hides in considerable number, being the chief source for Spain itself. An estimated 1,000,000 head roamed the Orinoco plains by the end of the eighteenth century. In the La Plata region Mendoza brought the first livestock, which increased with phenomenal rapidity in the lush lands of the Paraná and Uruguay river valleys. However, running wild on the plains, these cattle had little value until the end of the colonial period. At that time the demand for tallow and hides in Europe and in the United States gave the Argentine industry an importance hitherto unknown. A similar history accompanied the cattle industry in Chile.

In New Spain the cattle industry took first rank among all the colonies. The opening of the mines in mountainous northern Mexico made imperative importation of cattle for food. Its innumerable valleys, unsuited to agriculture, provided, however, enough fodder for cattle, sheep, and horses. Thus by 1571 in New Vizcaya larger herds reached as high as 250,000 head; ranches with 30,000 to 40,000 were common. By the end of the colonial period the animals numbered in the millions. Indeed, the origin of the cattle industry in the American Southwest stemmed from northern New Spain. From Texas and New Spain a thriving export trade was carried on through New Orleans and Natchez with the new American states beyond the Mississippi River.

Early in the sixteenth century royal regulations fostered throughout the empire the growth of the industry. In 1533 laws made pasture ground free to Spaniards and Indians alike. At the same time the cattle owners organized the *Mesta*, a guild or league on a model long known in Spain, to defend their interests. The *Mesta* protected brands, punished thefts, settled property rights, and awarded damages. It also served to represent the cattle owners before the government.

Ordinarily, the great cattle ranges were managed by superintendents. Cowboys and sheepherders tended the livestock and were usually members of private militias organized by the owners to protect their herds from Indian attack. Called *vaqueros* in New Spain, they were gauchos in Venezuela and Argentina. In New Spain the cowboy altered his dress. The tall sombrero replaced the low-crowned Andalucian hat which persisted in South America. The mining country of northern Mexico and southern Peru besprinkled his costume with silver ornaments. Solid silver spurs and heavily decorated bridles and saddles were common. The cowboy's lonely vigils gave rise to his folklore and song, simple and melancholy.

The products of the industry served a variety of purposes. Meat was consumed locally. Tallow provided the thousands of candles used especially by the churches. Hides were manufactured into bridles, harness, whips, shoes, and boots and used in the carriage and furniture industry. New Spain and Venezuela were the principal sources of hides for the mother country. One fleet from New Spain in 1587 carried more than 64,000 hides, as well as a quantity of tallow.

The Mining Industry. The colonial institution of mining originated in Spain, where the laws of Castile governed its growth. These laws in turn derived from the Civil Law and the *Siete Partidas,* under which all subsoil riches belonged to the king. Title to the surface passed only with the transfer of ownership. Pressing financial needs of the monarchy led to modification of these laws in the colonies. The first in 1504 gave the privilege of searching for mines to any Spaniard. In 1524 legislation placed mining property on an equal status with other private holdings. Philip II in 1584, to encourage discovery, decreed that anyone could prospect for and develop mines even on lands belonging to others. His only restrictions were that the mineowner should pay the crown one-fifth, the *quinto,* of the value of the minerals produced, register his discovery before an *alcalde,* and carry on sufficient work to maintain title to the mine.

Disputes arose in time over the question whether the crown had surrendered its ownership in the subsoil. Late eighteenth century authorities, however, believed that the king had retained ownership and had merely conferred upon mineowners rights protected by laws. Further to stimulate the industry, the crown frequently reduced the royal fifth to a tenth and in some cases to a twentieth. These liberal laws gave the impetus which led to the great discoveries in New Spain and Peru.

Mining in New Spain. The Aztecs and Toltecs mined surface deposits by placer mining or using small canals into which they dumped the ore to separate it from the gold and silver. While Cortés is believed to have mined silver at Taxco, the first authenticated discovery occurred near Compostela, New Galicia, in 1543. By 1550 the large number of smelters, reduction works, and refineries testified to the exploitation of the area.

In 1548, aided by Indians, prospectors opened up the famous veins of silver at Zacatecas. The rush of miners and new searches soon revealed the equally rich mines of Guanajuato, where the *veta madre* or mother lode was found. Viceroy Mendoza encouraged prospectors nearer Mexico City, who in 1549 discovered silver deposits in the present state of Guerrero. Two years later one of the greatest discoveries in the history of Mexico took place at Pachuca and Real del Monte a short distance north of the capital. In the next decade, 1569, a carelessly started forest fire exposed important deposits near Sombrerete, north of Zacatecas. Others were opened near-by at Durango. Indian attacks upon silver caravans led pursuing Spanish expeditions northeast of Zacatecas to discoveries at San Luis Potosí. In 1591 major finds brought a rush of miners and settlements to that area. By that date four great centers, Zacatecas, Guanajuato, Potosí, and Pachuca-Real del Monte, were making Mexico the second great silver producer of the New World.

Besides liberal laws, new methods contributed to the growth of mining. Particularly important was the development of the amalgamation process which used mercury and other minerals to amalgamate the silver. The process, invented probably by Bartolomé de Medina in 1557, made possible the operation of small mines and the recovery of gold and silver from low grade ores. Early in the seventeenth century, 1613, blasting with black powder came into the industry to replace the use of drills and hammers previously used to break up rock formations.

The seventeenth century saw the steady expansion of mining northward. In western New Vizcaya deposits discovered were so pure that they could be cut with a chisel. Farther west in Sinaloa at Alamos and in Sonora new and rich veins were opened up. Besides silver on the northwest coast the Spaniards opened copper mines and pearl fisheries. An observer traveling there later noted that from Mazatlán to Guaymas pearls, while "mostly small in size, . . . are so common in Mexico that they are worn by the lowest orders in the streets."

Decline and Revival of Mexican Mining. By the end of the seventeenth century various factors retarded colonial mining. Serious was the failure to use connecting galleries between shafts for ventilation. Underground tunnels were unknown as a means of carrying the ore to the surface. On the contrary, Indians loaded with ore sacks toiled tediously up and down long beams notched for footholds. A greater handicap was the lack of machinery to drain off water beyond a certain depth when a mine flooded. The great Real del Monte, abandoned for this reason early in the eighteenth century, did not resume production until 1782. Adding its weight to the difficulties of mining was the royal monopoly on quicksilver and the restriction of its production in Mexico. Its high cost bankrupted many smaller miners.

The Mining Guild. The revival of mining in the late eighteenth century arose from various factors. Smuggling reduced the royal revenue, while at the same time the empire was demanding greater expenditures for its protection. Miners themselves were clamoring for reforms. To meet all these problems, Charles III commissioned José de Gálvez, his visitor-general to New Spain, to take the necessary measures to revive mining. In accordance with the visitor's recommendations, Viceroy Bucareli created the Mining Guild *(Cuerpo de Minería)*. This body in turn drew up the famous Mining Code *(Ordenanzas de Minería)*, which began to function in 1783. Its most important provisions reduced the price of mercury, gave wide authority to miners over their own affairs, recognized the crown's ownership of all subsoil deposits, and provided for the establishment of a School of Mines *(Colegio de Minería)*, which opened in Mexico City in 1792. The freedom given miners under the Code brought about a marked increase in production, which characterized the industry until the Wars for Independence interrupted the work of the Guild. Significantly, the Code, extended to the Philippine Islands, Guatemala, Peru, and areas within the present United States, became the basis of the modern mining laws of those regions.

Mining in South America: Potosí. After the stupendous looting of the Inca collections of gold and silver, mining in Peru settled down to the normal process of prospecting, discovery, and exploitation. The same liberal laws applied in Mexico obtained in Peru, so that small capital launched many enterprises. Under Viceroy Francisco de Toledo the first mining ordinances issued and the introduction of Medina's process gave new stimulation to the industry. Rapid expansion followed in Upper Peru (Bolivia) and north and south of Lima. Outstanding was the accidental discovery of the great silver deposit at Potosí in 1545. Its production, exceeding that of Real del Monte, was estimated at 395,619,000 pesos up to 1593. From 1545 to 1800 it produced silver valued at over 800,000,000 pesos, but of which the king derived as his share some 165,000,000 pesos.

Huancavelica. The other major mineral resource of Peru, mercury, was discovered at Huancavelica in 1563. Together, as Whitaker indicates, Potosí and Huancavelica were the pillars supporting Peruvian colonial economy. Its greatest period of production, during which it frequently supplied Mexico, was between the late sixteenth and early eighteenth centuries. Its estimated production over 245 years was some 100,000,000 pounds. This figure, which is conservative, naturally does not include unknown amounts smuggled out of the mine. From mercury the king derived a revenue estimated at about 65,000,000 pesos. The mining of this mineral had its tragic side in the sufferings of the Indians under the *mita* system, lack of safeguards against poisoning, cave-ins, and other accidents. Other centers of mining were at Oruro in Upper Peru and at

Arequipa, south of Lima. The latter was famous for its beautiful plate and for the manufacture of church bells with a high silver content and pleasing tones.

Mining in New Granada. Ranking next to Mexico and Peru in total value of metals and precious stones produced was New Granada. Gold first became known to the Spaniards in that region from the ceremonial practices of the Chibcha Indians. Pursuit of the metal led to its discovery in Antioquía, Chocó, and Cauca areas. In spite of the waste occasioned by the use of slave labor and placer mining, the Spaniards produced significant quantities of the metal, estimated at about 500,000 ounces during the period, 1493–1800. This figure represented about one-half of all the gold production of the Spanish colonies.

New Granada also was a center for precious and semiprecious stones, particularly emeralds. Platinum, unrecognized for decades, did not become a valuable export until late in the eighteenth century, when Antonio de Ulloa introduced it into Europe. Before this time it had been used, amusingly, as a smear on Spanish pennies to counterfeit pieces-of-eight. Other parts of southern South America produced little mineral. Chile had some silver and copper mines, but gold placers of more value existed in the north. In La Plata, except in the province of Tucumán, no mining existed.

Colonial Manufactures. Spanish colonial manufactures were in large part but an addition to the universal handicrafts of the Indians. The highly trained personnel of these native industries supplied much colonial skilled labor, both in factories and specialized enterprises, such as tile-making and wood and metalworking. However, Indian manufacturing continued without interruption to provide native wearing apparel, household utensils, personal adornments, and other items in daily use.

Various factors dictated a policy that gave crown approval to colonial Spanish industry. The import of American silver into Spain sent domestic prices skyrocketing. To control inflation the monarchy restricted exports of manufactured goods and encouraged colonial production. Again, the ordinary daily demands of her huge empire required goods in such quantities that Spain alone could not have supplied them. Indeed, without colonial industry the empire could not have existed. It is important to note that restrictive legislation touching colonial manufacturing stood on a different footing from that affecting trade. The latter was in the hands of a comparatively few Spanish merchants who enjoyed monopolies; colonial manufacturing, on the other hand, was widely distributed among small entrepreneurs.

The silk industry early assumed importance, beginning in New Spain possibly before 1530. For more than half a century cultivation of the silkworm provided resources for the manufacture of taffetas, silks, satins, and velvets. The industry declined after the colonization of the Philippine Islands (1571), when both the imported Oriental finer grades and cheaper varieties offered competition. Eventually by 1600 Spanish restrictions on the cultivation of the silkworm ended the local supply. Raw silk from China continued, however, to provide materials for the Mexican factories until well into the eighteenth century.

Cotton and wool were the chief raw materials for the colonial textile industry. In New Spain factories flourished in Guadalajara, Puebla, Querétaro, Texcoco, and Saltillo. Puebla was well known for the manufacture of hats of excellent quality, some of which were exported to Peru. Quito in Ecuador produced a variety of textiles. Factories spread to other cities, but in the eighteenth century Ecuadorian industry suffered from foreign competition, chiefly English. Peru had extensive cotton-weaving looms in Cajamarca and other towns where Indian labor was easily available. Chile produced almost all its own cotton and woolen goods, including huge quantities of colored cloth manufactured by the Indians in the south. In La Plata the missions, discussed elsewhere, were important textile centers. Quality and variety depended upon the market. In the higher elevations the coarser cloth found ready sale. The finer grades were purchased by the wealthy.

Metalworking thrived in all parts of the empire. Silversmiths and goldsmiths, organized into guilds in New Spain, Peru, and New Granada, turned out beautifully decorated plate and altar pieces, as well as rings, brooches, necklaces, and other personal jewelry. Saddles, bridles, and harness, heavily laden with silver, were commonly used in many parts of Peru and New Spain. New Granada was famous for its lapidary work in emeralds, diamonds, and rubies, while New Spain boasted the world's most beautiful pearl necklaces. The churches made heavy demands upon the metal industries for altar vessels, gold leaf, gold and silver thread for vestments, and gold and silver crowns inlaid with precious jewels for the carved wooden figures adorning churches and cathedrals. Arequipa's famous church bells had a high content of silver and gold, thrown in at the casting, in the belief that these metals produced a softer and more beautiful tone.

Equally important were the carriage and furniture industries. Carts with their heavy wooden wheels, made locally, were widely used in the caravan trade of the empire. Beautiful and elaborately made carriages

were demanded by the wealthy. Of them Friar Gage wrote that the
Creoles of New Spain "spare no silver, no gold, nor precious stones, nor
cloth of gold, nor the best silks of Chine to enrich them . . . and . . .
the pride of some doth add the cost of bridles and shoes of silver." The
furniture industry, too, met the universal demands of the church throughout the empire for both simple and elaborate pews, altars, confessionals,
and other pieces. The tastes of the wealthy Creoles for tables, chairs, fine
cabinets, and beds frequently produced minor masterpieces of the wood-
worker's art.

Shipbuilding grew rapidly in the colonies. The discovery of the riches
of Peru stimulated the industry on the Pacific coast of South and Central
America. The west coast of Nicaraugua was an active center in the sixteenth century. Later Guayaquil was the chief shipyard for vessels for the
Peruvian trade, while Chile produced hemp and flax for ship stores and
sails. In New Spain at Acapulco on the west coast was a shipbuilding
port for the Philippine trade. Later San Blas farther north supplied ships
for California. Havana led in shipbuilding in the Caribbean, although
vessels were constructed on the other larger islands as well as in Venezuela.

The leather industries thrived in all the important cattle regions:
Venezuela, New Spain, Chile, Peru, and La Plata. Tanning was extensively carried on in factories which prepared leather goods, such as
saddles, harness, whips, shoes, boots, leather-bound mattress bags, and
leather upholstery widely used in both the carriage and furniture industries. Other industries important in New Spain and Peru included
iron foundries, porcelain, and glass. Puebla in Mexico was particularly
famous for its tile manufacturing, a handicraft introduced by the Spaniards and carried on by Indian workmen.

Part IV.   THE ROYAL INCOME

The Taxation System. Besides the varieties of taxes collected by the
Spanish monarchs on trade and commerce, they derived a huge income
from those levied on colonial agriculture, cattle, mining, and manufacturing industries. In mining the king collected the royal fifth, the *quinto*,
on the value of silver, gold, mercury, pearls, emeralds, and other precious
and semiprecious stones. Far from being fixed, the king's share was frequently reduced at different places and in different times to encourage
the search for minerals. The bullion, collected by middlemen at the
mines, was taken to the government mint or smelter for assaying. It was

then stamped and the *quinto* paid. Unstamped bullion was illegal and subject to confiscation.

Reminiscent of feudal peasant taxes in Spain was the head tax on Indians. Originally paid to the king in fixed amounts of gold or silver, landowners, as the empire developed, secured the right to collect the head tax. Many *corregidores* abused this privilege, the chief attraction of the office, and a source of corruption.

Monopolies provided a major source of income for the king. The monopoly on quicksilver had the added advantage of enabling the king's officials to make an accurate estimate of the *quinto* tax. Salt widely used in the cattle industry, in mining, and in commerce was also a royal monopoly. Others producing a large income were on the production and sale of tobacco, tickets to amusements, bullfights and cockfights, the sale of playing cards, gunpowder used for hunting and celebrations, and the manufacture and sale of ink and paper. Forced loans and gifts extracted on such occasions as the crowning of a new monarch or royal marriages and the need for funds in an emergency such as a war formed a source of income. Funds from the empire were collected to wage war against England in 1776. Among the contributors was New Mexico, which donated several thousand pesos.

The king derived a considerable income from the sale of offices, both those affecting all aspects of administration and the offices of the church. Also, under the agreement with the papacy in 1508, the Spanish monarchs received all the tithes collected in the colonies. Politically the collection of these tithes strengthened the king's control over the church; financially, however, the monarchy benefited little. The king retained only one-ninth of the tithes collected. The remainder he returned to the bishops and other administrative officials to carry on the work of the church. This royal interest was the chief driving force behind the colonial missionary movement to spread Christianity. After independence missionary activity declined sharply in all parts of Latin America.

While the empire was the principal source of income for the monarchy, the expenses attending its administration were very great, especially after the sixteenth century. Peru and parts of New Spain alone showed an income above expenses. All other colonies, whether in the viceroyalty of New Spain, such as Texas, New Mexico, and California, those of the Caribbean and Florida, or all of South America outside of Peru, were a drain upon the treasury. As empire administration expanded in the seventeenth and eighteenth centuries, operating expenses mounted rapidly. Especially did the eighteenth century impose huge burdens, such as the enlargement of fleets, construction of stone forts around the Caribbean, and increases in the size of colonial armies.

From another point of view the empire paid handsomely. It created a large number of private fortunes. Not only did the bulk of those who held office enrich themselves, but many landowners, miners, and businessmen became enormously wealthy. Private fortunes among the mineowners of Potosí ranged from $3,000,000 to $5,000,000. The Count of Regla, the owner of the Pachuca mines, presented Charles II with a battleship costing $3,000,000. A wealthy Creole in Lima, on the occasion of the arrival of a viceroy, paved a street with silver blocks. Thomas Gage, noting the wealth of businessmen, remarked that in the street of La Platería, Silver Street, Mexico City, one could see in less than an hour many millions worth of gold, silver, pearls, and jewels.

This vast range of economic activities to which were linked the Spanish political administrators was the basis for the evolution of Spanish colonial society. To that aspect of colonial development we now turn our attention.

Chapter VI

SOCIAL ORGANIZATION AND COLONIAL CULTURE

Part I. THE SOCIAL STRUCTURE

The thorough character of Spanish colonization was reflected in the transfer of identical social elements from Spain to the colonies. The fact that millions of Indians and a completely new social group, the mixed blood, did not alter but rather were fitted into the social structure is testimony to the effectiveness of the Spanish imprint upon her American colonies.

The Peninsulars. At the peak of the social pyramid stood the royal officials sent by the king to govern the colonies, known variously as *peninsulares, chapetones, gachupines,* and *godos.* From their exalted positions they not only drew their salaries, but often engaged in extortion and graft, and added to their income with illegal investments in land, trade, and commerce. Normally they monopolized all the chief offices, those of viceroy, captain-general, president of *audiencias,* the leading military ranks down to that of captain, governor, *corregidor,* tax officials *(fiscales),* and port executives. Likewise in the church they held the offices of archbishop, bishop, canon, custodian, and others. It is estimated that of the 170 viceroys and 602 captains-general and presidents, only 18 were native-born Americans, that is, Creoles, during the 300 years of colonial history. In the church during the same period, barely 100 Creoles held the rank of bishop among the 769 appointed to office.

The viceroys maintained a court comparable to that of the king in Spain. Captains-general and other high officials as well as the dignitaries of the church had the trappings of royalty in the ceremonies attaching to their office. This policy by the king of excluding colonials and holding his officials aloof from the population was deliberate. Spanish monarchs of the sixteenth century recognized that the colonies were essentially frontiers where powerful landowning families had carved out their own great fortunes and observed little law and order. Entrusting power to them was to court disaster. The history of the turbulent Spanish nobility was too recent to place royal policy in the hands of other than trusted servants.

The Creoles. Ranking next in the social structure were the Creoles, or American-born Spaniards. Their economic base varied, but the dominant groups among them were landowners who received agricultural, mining, and cattle grants as rewards during the conquest. Many, too, received patents of nobility, while some derived directly from the aristocracy of Spain itself. Other Creoles of humbler station in life occupied minor positions in government, in the army, and in the church. Still others were members of professions—physicians, lawyers, engineers. Some were merchants and traders and industrialists. In the late eighteenth century Creoles were the principal military officers of the colonial militia, a role particularly significant in giving rise to militarism in later Latin-American history. In the same century, too, the class received new recruits from the mixed bloods who purchased from the royal authorities documents testifying to their Creole status. But the significant fact was its wealth and its privileges, which, maintained by law, set this Creole class off from the less favored groups.

The children of these wealthy and privileged Americans were reared usually by nurses and tutors and entered colleges and universities established for them. Frequently their education received an additional polish from tours in Europe, where family connections admitted them to courtly society. Sensitive to the contempt shown them by the *peninsulares,* they bitterly resented the Spaniards' monopoly of high government offices. In their homes and in their dress they made lavish display of their wealth. Some Creoles with scholarly inclinations amassed valuable libraries and made outstanding intellectual contributions to the life of the colonies. Their role in *cabildo* domination has already been referred to as a school for political training.

The Indian. Of greater numerical importance than any other group in Latin America, the Indian's fundamental role in society was that of a food producer. For this reason the Indian was not removed from the land. On the contrary, specific laws prohibited Spaniards, with the exception of the priest, from entering Indian towns. They continued to till the land under their historical communal practices. Under the *encomienda* system the Indian labored, cultivating the soil for the Spaniards, who were entitled to the product and also to the payment of the Indian poll tax. The abolition of the *encomienda* at the end of the eighteenth century had little effect upon the ownership of land by Indian towns in the *encomienda* area.[1] In this respect the ending of the *encomienda* had small influence upon the Indian. In fact, his status as a worker continued essentially the same, for he descended into debt slavery. Paid very low wages, estimated by some authorities as little as ten pesos a year, he was unable to earn sufficient to keep body and soul together without going into debt. And until that debt was paid, he was unable to escape, for the laws bound him to the land.

Besides this system of forced labor the Indian was also subject to employment under the *repartimiento,* a system under which the natives were distributed to public and church officials and to private individuals for specific work projects, construction of churches and public buildings, digging canals, work in mines, factories, and inns, domestic work, and a hundred other onerous burdens. One of the most unfortunate forms of forced labor was in the *obrages* or factories, to which Indians were sent for committing some trivial offense or failing to pay their taxes. Conditions within the factories were prison-like, with labor from dawn to dusk, low wages which kept the worker in debt, and frequent punishment for failing to fulfill quotas.

But the harshest system of forced labor was the *mita,* which rested upon agreements between mineowners and *corregidores,* governors of Indian districts, who provided from Indian villages through the Indian chiefs the quota of workers needed for the mines. To supply the mines of Potosí, Viceroy Toledo in Peru designated sixteen provinces near-by which provided over 13,000 laborers. The *mita* was very destructive of Indian life owing to long hours, overwork, poor food, lack of ventilation in the mines, explosions, and cave-ins. To escape these various forms of work, Indians often fled to take refuge in near-by river valleys, where they became known as *Cimarrones.* If captured, they could be sold into slavery; the search for *Cimarrones* was a lucrative business.

Royal laws from the beginning of the Spanish dominion attempted to protect the Indians in their possession of lands, from forced labor, and from unpaid services. Other legislation limited hours, improved wages, and put restrictions upon the use of the *repartimiento.* Charles V attempted to end the granting of *encomiendas,* but opposition from the colonies forced modification of his order. The New Laws promulgated in 1542 brought rebellion in Peru and quick modification so that *encomiendas* could be inherited. Royal ordinances attempted to regulate labor in mines and factories, but these in large measure proved ineffec-

[1] For a statement of the chief features of the *encomienda* system, see *supra,* p. 51.

tive. The viceroy himself was made protector of the Indians and when, in Mexico, the task became too burdensome, the work was assumed by a Court of Indians (*Juzgado de Indios*) created for the purpose. To it Indians could appeal against Creoles and Spaniards for mistreatment, seizure of land, and other abuses. The court generally favored Indians, and there are cases on record of the Protector of the Indians, through the court, forcing the return of Indian lands seized by local landowners. The wide range of humanitarian legislation enacted by the Spanish monarchs reflects credit upon their zeal to protect the Indians. However, enforcement fell far below the standards set by the laws.

Quite apart from the body of the Indian population was the status of the ruling caste of Indians recognized by Spain as a nobility. They were, for this reason, given education, lands, and *encomiendas,* and enjoyed a status equal to that of Creole landowners. Placed in office in Indian towns, they showed themselves as harsh masters of the Indians as the Spanish. In this capacity Indian *caciques* played an important role in controlling Spain's huge colonial Indian population.

Several factors explain why the *caciques* were such "poor defenders of the lowlier Indians." Extensive intermarriage of the Indian aristocracy with well-born Spanish families tended, with few exceptions, to instill in Indian leaders the ideas and outlook of the conquerors. More, the *caciques* were separated from their own people by the Spanish practice of permitting them to retain all the insignia of their rank and extending to them special privileges, such as exemption from tribute and personal service. Significant, too, was the Spanish policy of keeping Indian and Spanish communities apart. Diffie observes that this segregation "delivered the workers into the hands of their own employers, and favored Indian factories over those owned by Spaniards." [2] Thus, in fact, Spaniards exercised no restraint upon the cruelty and avariciousness of the *caciques,* long accustomed to obedience from their own people.

The Negro. Like the Indian, the Negro was an agricultural worker. While the Indian was held in virtual serfdom under the *encomienda* and other systems of forced labor, the Negro worked in slavery. The first Negroes were imported into the Spanish colonies shortly after 1500. Columbus had started the system of Negro slavery; Las Casas advocated its use as a substitute for Indian labor. The rapid extermination of the Indian on the islands of the West Indies created an increasing demand for Negroes. John Hawkins in 1562 delivered the first Negro slaves to Española to begin British interest in this business. After 1550 Negroes

[2] Diffie, *Latin-American Civilization, Colonial Period,* Harrisburg, 1945, p. 389.

arrived in the colonies under contracts, *asientos,* a source of income for the Spanish monarchy. In 1713 as a result of the War of the Spanish Succession, Britain secured the *asiento* to import Negro slaves into the Spanish colonies. In the Caribbean the Negroes worked on sugar, cotton, indigo, and tobacco plantations. They suffered severe and arbitrary punishments for misdemeanors, for their masters in the islands—Spanish, Dutch, French, and British—held the mistaken belief that such abuse lessened the danger of Negro revolt.

From the Caribbean the Negroes spread to the mainland. They and the mulattoes composed the bulk of the population on the coast of Venezuela and Colombia (New Granada). Panama received a large number of Negroes. They existed in small numbers in Central America. In Mexico they settled along the Gulf coast, where they mixed with the Spaniards and Indians.

In South America, omitting Brazil here for later consideration, Negroes lived in considerable numbers in Lima, Buenos Aires, Santiago, and Bogotá. In Buenos Aires they were primarily servants in households, as Indians were driven into the interior. They arrived in La Plata through British contraband trade at Colonia, a Portuguese settlement opposite Buenos Aires. Chile, it is estimated, had 3,000 to 4,000 by the middle of the seventeenth century, a population which increased with that of the mulattoes, to 10,000 or 12,000 by the end of the eighteenth century. They served in domestic occupations and became showpieces in the homes of the wealthy, though some became tradesmen and skilled laborers. In Peru they suffered an oppression equal to that of the Indians.

These three basic racial groups, Spaniards, that is, Creoles and *peninsulares,* Indians, and Negroes, intermixed during the colonial period to produce a variety of mixed bloods. Broadly speaking, the lower economic groups, Spanish colonists, skilled and unskilled laborers, and others, more frequently intermarried with the Indians. But it is also true that many Indian women and even Negresses bore the offspring of the Creole landowners. Of all these mixed bloods, the group that grew most rapidly in numbers in the colonies was the *mestizo,* the offspring of Spaniard and Indian.

The Mestizo. The *mestizo,* excluded from the rigid caste of Indian society and suffering the same disability in the Spanish, became a mercurial element in the population. Not rooted in agricultural occupations, he served in a variety of capacities. Gravitating toward towns and cities, *mestizos* of both sexes became servants in the households of *peninsulares* and Creoles. As laborers, construction and dock workers, the bearers of heavy burdens or *cargadores*, they did the unskilled work in the colonies. Many, however, went into various trades and became tailors, shoemakers, candlemakers, and factory employees in the silk, cotton, linen, leather, and other industries. On the frontier they served as common soldiers in militia organizations and in the colonial armies. In the mining industry they were minor bosses; on plantations, overseers; in the cattle industry, cowboys and sheepherders.

Some *mestizos* in all the colonies, because of ability, graduated into the ranks of small businessmen, prospered, and became wealthy. Some were vendors of trinkets on the streets or owners of small shops. *Mestizos* often acted as middlemen in purchasing the handiwork of Indians for sale in the cities. Cases were frequent of *mestizos*, successful in prospecting, becoming mineowners. In all these activities, essentially middle class as distinguished from agricultural labor, *mestizos* rubbed shoulders with Creole and even Indian businessmen. Creoles, for example, dominated the commercial activities of Buenos Aires. Indians became mineowners in Peru and moneylenders in Guatemala. Moreover, more often than not, wealthy *mestizos* purchased documents from the Spanish king called blood-cleansers *(limpieza de sangre)* which made them legally Creoles. The fundamental characteristic of the *mestizo* was not his mixed blood, but his economic category. Viewed in this manner, it is clear at once that the *mestizo* formed, with the Indian, the bulk of colonial labor; secondly, as a businessman, that he played an important role in creating the Latin-American middle class.

Mulatto and Other Groups. The mulatto, the offspring of European and Negro, had a position analogous to that of the *mestizo*. Escaping from slavery for a variety of reasons, the mulattoes became laborers in towns and cities, engaged in small businesses, became landowners, and frequently held Negroes in slavery. Besides the *mestizo* and mulatto, there were a variety of other mixed bloods resulting from union of Indians and Negroes, mulattoes and *mestizos*.

Significance of the Social Structure. Unfortunately, the terms used to denote the various blood mixtures in the Spanish colonies have become somewhat fixed. As a means of understanding the social structure of the colonies, they are both inadequate and unreal. Fundamentally the social structure revolved around three groups whose role in colonial evolution, when understood, gives a basis for grasping the composition of present-day Latin-American society. For this purpose we may set aside the *peninsulares* who, after independence, either returned to Spain or merged themselves with the population of their respective countries.

Remaining as the dominant social group were the wealthy and privileged classes. Broadly speaking, these were landowners, descendants of the conquerors, and others who had become wealthy and who had acquired *privileges,* guaranteed by law, from which the bulk of the population was excluded. Even though an individual lost his wealth, his standing as a Spaniard or of European or American birth guaranteed his privileges, such as admittance into the clergy, the judiciary, the militia, or public office.

There was a further division within the wealthy privileged classes between those who were born in Spain and those born in America. The latter were generally called Creoles. They exhibited the greatest jealousy toward the former because of the preferences given them in high public office or similar positions within the church. In any event, a sharp line of cleavage existed between what was essentially a privileged and in part aristocratic class and those without wealth and privilege. The former with their traditions of power have come down into the modern period of Latin-American history to form a group essentially antagonistic to the aspirations of the lower economic and social classes.

The latter, composed of Indians, Negroes, *mestizos,* mulattoes, and other mixed groups, are best understood as composing the bulk of colonial labor, agricultural and proletarian. With a long background of poverty and association with hard physical work, they entered the modern period as the materials for the present strong labor groups of Latin America.

Thirdly, growing up within the colonial social structure was a middle class. It derived from all groups, Spanish, Creole, Indian, *mestizo,* mulatto, and even Negro. It should be remarked that the legal trade of the colonies was in the hands of the privileged Spanish merchants who belonged to the wealthier classes. This exclusion of Americans forced them into smuggling, but, at the same time, they were able legally to establish themselves as retail merchants. The Wars for Independence split the middle class, with the Spaniards naturally opposing the movement and the native American commercial groups, long resentful of the Spanish trade monopoly, supporting it. Accordingly, after independence, the American element in the middle class, with a tradition of colonial revolt, became a source of support for democratic ideas and reforms in a society essentially feudal.

Part II. COLONIAL CULTURE

Colonial Education. Spain transferred to her colonies her own great cultural traditions. In education she founded institutions for the various levels of colonial society. For the wealthy classes she established universities and colleges. The earliest created by royal order in 1551 were the University of Mexico and that of San Marcos, the latter opened in a monastery in Lima and becoming a separate institution in 1578. Outstanding besides these were the University of Santo Domingo, 1538, confirmed in the rank of a royal and pontifical university in 1757; the University of Chuquisaca, 1624; the University of Bogotá, 1655; the Jesuit College of Córdoba, Argentina, 1622; and the University of Guatemala, 1681. In the eighteenth century other similar institutions were founded in Caracas, 1721–1722; Santiago, Chile, 1747; and Havana, 1728. Colleges for the sons of Indian noblemen existed in Cuzco and Lima, founded between 1578 and 1581. Before the end of the colonial period, twenty-three higher institutions of learning existed in the Spanish colonies.

Other and more specialized colleges and academies met the needs of the Creole population. In the College of Santa Cruz de Tlaltelalco, Mexico, Franciscans taught Indian languages, Latin, medicine, arithmetic, drawing, and music. The Jesuits alone had in various parts of Mexico by 1767 twenty-three colleges besides seminaries. In 1775 Charles III, who had a great interest in cultural development, directed the establishment of the Royal Academy of Noble Arts *(Real Academia de Nobles Artes).* It had magnificent examples of the art of Greece and Rome, more beautiful and complete, according to Humboldt, than were found in any museum in Germany. In 1783 the Academy of San Carlos in Mexico City taught painting, sculpture, and architecture. The College of Mining in the capital, opened to Creoles in 1792, not only had competent instructors under a distinguished scientist, Fausto de Elhuyar, but contained a valuable collection of mineralogical specimens.

The curricula of these universities and colleges, apart from the specialized institutions, provided courses in theology, Spanish, grammar, scholastic philosophy, canonical and civil law, and medicine. Chairs existed for the study of Indian languages in almost all universities. In the eighteenth century new subjects found their way into the curricula of the universities, such as the study of modern science, anatomy, Newton's ideas, and Cartesian philosophy. Students completing the work of the various curricula in the leading institutions became candidates for their respective degrees, of which there were four: bachelor, licentiate, master, and doctor.

Student life added color to the otherwise drab scholastic atmosphere. Severe regulations governing students' dress and decorum testified to the irrepressible conflict with the administration. As in Europe, all universities prohibited students from carrying firearms into the classrooms. Extra-curricular activities after dark, carousing, gambling, and others, were frowned upon, and jails were maintained by the universities for punishing infractions of regulations. But those who fell afoul of the authorities were the exceptions. Most students took their work seriously. It is estimated by Lanning that some 150,000 higher degrees were conferred by these universities during the colonial period.

The faculty, like its counterpart elsewhere, was among the first to respond to new ideas. The traditional dominance of Aristotle over European universities found reflection in those of the colonies. But by the beginning of the eighteenth century modern trends of thought in science, philosophy, and politics asserted themselves. Aristotle's monopoly was undermined, while followers of Locke, Descartes, and Newton forced the acceptance of the experimental method and the questioning of authority. In this manner colonial universities played an important role in training Latin-American leaders late in the eighteenth century for their revolutionary roles after 1800. Outstanding in this work was the Caroline Academy of the University of Chuquisaca, although some believe that in this respect Lima was equally important.

For *mestizos* and other groups Spain established schools corresponding to their needs. Children of Indians and *mestizos* received training in carpentry, tailoring, leatherwork, shoemaking, arithmetic, reading, writing, and the Christian religion. The best-known school of this character, that of Father Pedro de Gante in Mexico, had more than a thousand students by 1530. Nothing comparable existed in Peru, where teaching of Indians in Lima was largely instruction in doctrine and in the Spanish language. In the frontier missions the fathers provided schools for Indian children which taught, besides doctrine, choir-singing, instrumental music, wood carving, painting, Spanish, and, for the more promising students, reading and writing. Viewed as a whole, the character of the educational system in the upper levels of the Spanish colonies tended to be classical in common with its European counterpart in this period, and weighted in favor of the well-born and the church.

Historians and Scientists. New World historical writing began with the monumental histories of the sixteenth century. Written by Spanish historians, they recorded the vast process of discovery, exploration, and colonization of the two continents. In the sixteenth century taking high rank is the *General and Natural History of the Indies (Historia general y natural de las Indias)* of Gonzalo Fernández de Oviedo y Valdes (1478–1557). Oviedo spent almost a quarter of a century in the New World, so that his history reflects direct observation and contact with events. Much controversy attends the *History of the Indies (Historia de las Indias)* by Father Bartolomé de las Casas, who wrote the history of the New World up until 1520 in a work that has never been completely published. Modern opinion, however, holds the work as the most valuable one, in spite of errors, inconsistencies, and exaggerations, of all those which describe the first arrival of the white man in America. Continuing the history of the New World until 1555 was the comprehensive general history of Antonio de Herrera y Tordesillas (1549–1625). Based upon extensive use of documents from the official archives and making use of the work of previous historians, particularly that of Las Casas, Herrera's *General History of the Achievements of the Spaniards in the Islands and on the Mainland of the Ocean Sea (Historia general de los hechos de los Castellanos en las islas y tierra firme del mar océano),* stands unequaled for the period it covers. Its chronological arrangement, however, makes the use of the work difficult. In the following centuries a galaxy of historians wrote the history of every province in the Spanish empire as well as accounts of specialized subjects. The missionary fathers reduced innumerable Indian languages to grammars and dictionaries. Some wrote invaluable histories of the Aztecs, Mayas, and Incas. The most famous is that of Father Sahagún's description of Aztec civilization, *A General History of Matters of Substance of New Spain (Historia general de las cosas de Nueva España).*

In the field of science a similar range of achievement is found. Humboldt is the authority for the statement that the work of the Jesuit, Father Joseph Acosta, in his *Natural and Moral History of the Indies (Historia natural y moral de las Indias)* laid the groundwork for physical geography. Important studies were made in the field of metallurgy. Alvaro Alonso Barba in the seventeenth century in Peru wrote the *Art of Metals (Arte de los metales).* Scientific beginnings were made in the field of medicine. The University of San Marcos in Lima offered a course in anatomy in the eighteenth century. Juan de la Fuente attempted to discover the causes of disease by the study of cadavers in the Royal Hospital in Mexico City. Many herbs and plants with medicinal properties were discovered and used. Quinine became known as a relief for malaria when the governor of Loja in Peru, having learned of it from the Indians, gave some to the wife of the viceroy, the Countess of Chinchón, in 1638. The Jesuits in Peru regularly used the coca leaf as a dentifrice. Father Bernabé Cobo experimented with it as an anesthetic. However, the practice of medicine in the colonies was attended with more superstition than science.

Outstanding were the achievements of the botanists. Francisco Hernández traveled in the late sixteenth century for seven years throughout the colonies, but principally in Mexico where he wrote sixteen volumes on the natural history of the regions visited. Unfortunately, the originals were lost in a fire in a Madrid archive, but not before copies had been made of much of the data. The greatest of the naturalists, however, was José Celestino Mutis, who described the flora of New Granada. Humboldt, who visited him in 1800, wrote that his collection of some 3,000 sketches of flowers and plants together with his botanical library was second only to that of Banks, the largest in the world, in London.

In the mathematical sciences colonial thinkers attempted to keep informed of European advances. In Bogotá the first observatory was established in the New World early in the nineteenth century. In Mexico Don Carlos Sigüenza y Góngora stands out as the greatest scientist. He not only observed Haley's comet as it passed over Mexico, but gave scientific reasons for its appearance. His conclusions were attacked by Father Kino, a distinguished mathematician also, but who supported superstitious explanations. Floriano Cajori, the historian of the mathematical sciences, comments that this was the first conflict on scientific matters in the New World. Sigüenza, a many-sided man, produced a valuable map of Pensacola Bay, an historical account of the revolt of the Pueblo Indians, and a history of the Mexican Indians, now lost; and he interested himself in engineering, journalism, philology, poetry, and philosophy. His contemporary in Peru, Pedro Peralta Barnuevo, less original in his gifts, was an engineer of note who constructed the sea wall at Callao, wrote poetry, and collected the traditions of the Inca Indians.

Books and the Press. The writings of historians, government officials, missionaries, scholars, and scientists were frequently printed in the New World. The first book published apparently appeared in 1535, but the oldest extant, a religious tract, dates from 1539. In South America the first press was in Lima, established there by a printer from Mexico in 1584. By the end of the colonial regime presses operated at one time or another in many of the leading cities throughout the empire. By that date hundreds of books and pamphlets had been published in the colonies: the bulk were religious tracts, grammars, and dictionaries of Indian languages and other works connected with the work of the church. Over all books published was exercised a strict censorship.

With presses running, journalism had an early beginning in the colonies. Some things of a periodical nature are dated in the sixteenth century in Guatemala and in Peru. One hundred years later Sigüenza y Góngora published in Mexico in pamphlet form for distribution among his friends, letters he received from abroad concerning newsworthy events. His work is considered the forerunner of the first major journalistic attempt, the *Gaceta de Mexico,* begun in 1722. In the next half-century a number of periodicals appear in Mexico, including that of Antonio de Alzate, *Gazeta de Literatura de México* (1788) and the *Diario de México* (1805). In Guatemala a *Gazeta* began publication in 1794, but the government, disturbed by the growth of liberal ideas, ended its career in 1816. In Peru a *Gaceta* appeared in Lima in 1743. Better known, however, was the *Diario de Lima,* the first daily newspaper to be published in Latin America (1790). Of greater influence was the cultural review, *Mercurio Peruano* (1791). Other periodicals were published at different times in Bogotá, Havana, and Buenos Aires. Thus the New World kept pace with the Old.

Complementing the publication of books and journals in the colonies was the importation of books from Spain. Royal decrees of Charles V and Philip II in the sixteenth century had established a censorship over books going to the colonies and could have been interpreted as prohibiting the entry of literary productions generally. The ban on the latter, however, was not enforced. On the contrary, every fleet brought shipments of books to the colonies, including the novel in all its forms, picaresque, pastoral, and sentimental romances of chivalry. Indeed, the literatures of France, Italy, Greece, Rome, and even the Orient were, as Professor Irving A. Leonard states, "laid under contribution."

However, when in the eighteenth century colonial newspapers and journals concerned themselves with the revolutionary changes in science and politics in Europe, and published as well satires on colonial life, censorship and suppression of books and newspapers became active. The ban against foreign writers, Milton, Voltaire, Chesterfield, Condorcet, Rousseau, Diderot, and others of the same character, was rigorously enforced. Nevertheless, these works continued to be smuggled into the colonies, an underground influence on the movement for independence.

For the most part a conservative attitude against any political and economic change continued to dominate the scene. The effect upon colonial literature was to place that whole field almost entirely under the influence of the models of the homeland or foreign literary productions accepted in Spain itself.

Literature. Latin America opened limitless possibilities to imaginative souls. Surrounding them was a New World whose environment teemed with infinite variations; native to it were Indian civilizations, colorful, picturesque, and even dramatic. Spain herself poured into the colonies shiploads of books drawn from the world's literatures. But to little avail. Generally, colonial literature was insipid, imitative, almost totally without originality, and stylistically so obscure as to give point to Shakespeare's aphorism on sound and fury signifying nothing. But since the law of averages operates even in the field of literature, a half-dozen names light up this starless desert.

The explanation of this extraordinary aridity of intellect is found in the accumulated wealth of the Creole families, their dependence upon the Indians for all labor, their fawning obeisance in the courts of Mexico City, Lima, and Quito. "In them," writes John A. Crow, ". . . the society of the upper class entrenched their European culture and their class-conscious wealth in the fertile soil of Indian slavery and ignorance. . . . It ate cake, danced and played with metaphors. . . ."[3]

It was not necessarily so. The robust sixteenth century, when Spaniards themselves engaged in the conquest, produced vigorous writers who initiated a literary tradition of great promise. Here the chronicle and epic recorded heroic deeds. Among the greatest of these writers was Bernal Díaz del Castillo, a soldier in Cortés' army, whose *True History of the Conquest of New Spain* was written half in anger and half in pride. Incensed at the praise heaped on Cortés by Gómara, Bernal Díaz determined he would write the *true* history. He recorded in picturesque detail the characteristics of the men and even the horses of the famous conquest. He described their battles with such vividness that today, after more than four centuries, his book is alive and vibrant in the hands of the reader. Friends to whom he showed the manuscript criticized his frequent reference to himself and his comrades. His answer was: "If we did not speak well of ourselves, who would?"

This frank self-praise arose from the old soldier's deep conviction that not Cortés, but he and his 400 comrades had conquered the Aztecs. Thus throughout the work he tells of the hardships, hopes, fears, and

[3] John A. Crow, *The Epic of Latin America*, New York, 1946, p. 299.

battles of the common soldiers. While making no pretense as a craftsman, Bernal Díaz had a strong sense of the dramatic, which, combined with a prodigious memory, builds up his climaxes with a literary skill equaled by few writers in his own or any other century. The work, invaluable as a history of the conquest, ranks as a masterpiece in the Mexican literary tradition.

Far to the south in Chile another Spanish soldier, Alonzo de Ercilla, a well-born cavalier out of the courtly circle of Philip II, wrote the great epic in New World literature, *La Araucana*. Traveling to Chile to share in the conquest, he fought by day, and by night recorded in verse the savage, brutal war upon the Chilean Indians. Although Ercilla set out to celebrate the valor of the Spanish soldiers, his sensitive, poetic insight made him admire the spirit and courage of the Araucanians. His poem is divided into three parts, the first of which describes the country, native customs, and the beginning of the war. Part Two deals with the development of the struggle. The final stanzas record with driving force the climax of the war in an intensity and horror that equals the best in modern realistic writing. The epic of Ercilla, a Spaniard, ranks as the great epic in the Spanish language.

The stanzas of Pedro de Oña (1570–1643), a native-born Chilean who attempted an epic on the same theme as Ercilla's, show him as a poet in his own right. His *Aruco Tamed* reveals a great love for his native land which he expressed in verse with deep and lasting feeling. As such, his poetry is among the first to reflect the American environment.

The chronicle, too, found an exponent in a native American, the Inca Garcilaso de la Vega (1539–1615). This gifted writer was born of a Spanish captain and an Inca princess. From the priests in Cuczo he learned Latin grammar and became thoroughly imbued with the European literary tradition, particularly that of the ancients; from the family of his mother, he absorbed the legends and lore of the Inca people. His masterpiece, the *Royal Commentaries,* glorified Inca civilization, but preserved as no other source does the political and social customs, legends, and traditions of the Incas, along with the stories he gathered from the veterans of the conquest of Peru. Woven together with high literary merit, the *Commentaries* rank as a great chronicle and an invaluable historical storehouse.

With the end of the heroic conquests of the sixteenth century, the life of the seventeenth found no literature to express its complexities. The capital cities were centers of culture in which universities, printing presses, and literary societies reflected the imported culture of Europe, particularly that of Spain. At the moment there reigned in Spain the cult of gongorism, a style of writing named after Luis de Góngora y Argote, which combined sharpness of style with diffusion of thought. In the hands of its imitators in the colonies, who for the most part had no style and were equally lacking in thought, *gongorismo* descended into elaborate phrases, far-fetched comparisons, preposterous images, artificial inventions, and exaggerated types of conceits, popularized in other European metaphysicals of the century. So, too, the society of the upper classes exhibited itself in extravagance of dress, manners, and speech and an almost obscene display of wealth. In architecture the extreme of decoration known as baroque did have the merit, however, of giving Indian sculptors an opportunity to reveal their innate artistry.

Within this century, but four names in Spanish Latin America add to the literary tradition. The first of these, educated in the church, was an Indian, Juan Espinosa Medrano (1632–1688?), known as Mole-Face *(El Lunajero)* from his birthmarks. Possessing a gifted mind and as an exponent of *gongorismo,* like the master in Spain he was saved by a deep understanding of poetry. He became the New World's first literary critic. His remembered contribution was to point out for the first time the relationship between the Roman writers who flourished at Córdoba— Seneca was one—and the literary complexities of Góngora himself.

Fleeing the arid desert of metaphors and similes that palled upon him in Mexico City was the Creole jurist, Juan Ruiz de Alarcón y Mendoza. A hunchback, repellent in all his physical characteristics, Alarcón preferred the barbs of the Spanish masters (he was a contemporary of Lope de Vega) to the ridicule of the toadying poetasters of the viceregal court. In Spain Alarcón eventually won recognition with the perfection of his dramas, and became world-renowned for the originality of his comedies, his masterpiece *The Liar* inspiring Corneille in France. The state of colonial Latin American culture is thus epitomized in the career of Alarcón, the Creole who went to Spain to become a recognized Spaniard. So thoroughly had the colonies been dominated by European literary tradition of the mother country!

One who did not flee but stayed to jeer was Juan del Valle y Caviedes, a popular poet of Lima (1653–1692). Caviedes poured scorn on the social parasites of the viceregal court, the pretensions of the academicians, and the pseudoscientific quackeries of colonial doctors. Religion alone escaped his barbs. Although his style is commonplace, his learning was extensive and his feeling sincere. His bitterness has been attributed to a youth that wasted the substance of his wealth and health. His career, as Torres Ríoseco tells us, testified to a cultural substance beneath the "baroque elegance" of the seventeenth century.

Even more profoundly revealing the love of learning and the heights to which a gifted mind could soar in this century was the career of the greatest literary figure of colonial times—Sor Juana Inéz de la Cruz (1651–1695). A woman of beauty, intelligence, and disarming charm, her life threw into stark relief the artificiality of colonial Mexican court life. Learning to read at the age of three, at sixteen she begged her mother to dress her as a boy so that she could attend the university. Denial of this privilege—for education was only for boys—left a deep mark upon Juana Inéz. Years later when a bishop, little aware of the hornet's nest he was probing, challenged her to give up her studies and devote herself to religious matters, she replied in a letter that has become a classic in defense of the right of women to use their minds.

Taken to court at sixteen, she became a favorite of the viceroy and his wife. The former, to test her extraordinary intellect, assembled forty of New Spain's most learned scholars to question her. For hours she met the attacks of professors, theologians, humanists, and scientists in a display of learning that so impressed the viceroy that he compared her to a magnificent Spanish galleon beating off the raids of lesser boats. Her beauty attracted men, among whom was one whose love matched her own. Legend, however, says her lover died. In any event Juana Inéz suddenly entered a cloister to study and meditate. She soon had a library of more than 4,000 volumes, together with scientific and musical instruments. There viceroys and other leading figures paid her homage. Throughout the years she devoted herself to intellectual pursuits. Her lyrics and sonnets on love are of such purity that they have been compared to those of Petrarch and Shakespeare.

Her range of poetic expression seemed limitless; she won the respect of scientists—not the medievalists, but those familiar with Newton—for her empirical observations upon the laws of nature. In music she is credited with foreseeing the chromatic scale. Since her death—she died courageously ministering to the sick in an epidemic—her proud countrymen have called her the "Tenth Muse."

But spirits like Juana Inéz and Alarcón were rare in any age. The next hundred years failed to produce significant writers either in Spain or in the colonies. In the former not even the entrance of French neoclassicism could renew the vigor of Spanish writing. Overseas the Spanish tradition continuing to dominate literary circles brought on a decadence even greater than in the homeland. At the end of the century the revolutionary ideas of the French *philosophes* stirred thoughts anew in the Creole mind. But these were mere beginnings—the harbingers of the burst of nineteenth century romanticism rooted in ideas of independence.

Colonial Architecture. Colonial architecture reflected the changing life of the colonies. Early sixteenth century building showed the hurried efforts of the missionaries to provide churches for converted Indians and for defense. They follow a style simple in design, with plain exteriors, crenelated walls, high, small windows, and low towers with little attempt at decoration except at the entrances. The cathedral of Santa María in Ciudad Trujillo (Santo Domingo) reveals these characteristics.

By the middle of the century, when wealth had accumulated, Renaissance architecture appeared, directly due to the influence of Juan de Herrera, who built the Escorial for Philip II. The most famous example of this architecture is the great cathedral of Mexico City, begun in 1573 and completed in 1804. Its 177-foot façade is divided by massive buttresses, flanked by magnificent towers over 200 feet high. The interior, supported by severe Doric columns, culminates in a vast dome. Its great beauty, the elaborate decoration of its façade, and its vast size convey the impression of strength and power. The largest church in the New World, it is considered by many to be the most authentic existing Renaissance cathedral.

Almost at the same time Moslem influence, *Mudéjar* (Moorish-Christian) architecture, reached the colonies. This took the form of wall decoration, geometric in design and of definite Arabic character. The use of Indian workmen, it is believed, accounts for certain Aztec elements in these designs. The most widely known example of this architecture is the Royal Chapel *(Capilla Real)* in Cholula, Mexico. In Peru wooden balconies were a striking detail attached both to Renaissance buildings and *mudéjar* architecture.

In the seventeenth century, baroque entered Latin America. It coincided with the rapidly growing wealth of the colonies, which found expression in vast programs of government and private construction. Colonial viceroys ordered construction of bridges, roads, aqueducts, public buildings, forts, and palaces. Wealthy families reared imposing residences, virtually palaces. The church also built magnificent cathedrals, churches, chapels, and residences for its higher clergy. In architecture the style became baroque or Plateresque, characterized by lavish decoration of exteriors. By the end of the eighteenth century baroque had evolved, some think degenerated, into Churrigueresque, with its highly involved elaboration of detail. The convent of La Merced in Mexico illustrates the Plateresque, as does the better known House of Tiles in Mexico City. Probably the most striking example of baroque decoration appeared in the Church of the Third Order of St. Francis in Salvador (Bahia), Brazil. In Peru and Bolivia baroque embellishment fitted in well with the Indian craftsman's love of decoration and mastery of fine detail. Universally, Indian motifs and symbols, flowering crowns of maize, were interwoven with Christian figures and designs.

At the end of the colonial period a reaction stemming from Europe set in against the extremes of baroque and Churrigueresque. The new style was called academic or neoclassical. Throughout the colonial empire from Mexico to Argentina late eighteenth century public buildings show its severe and classical features. Outstanding is the Royal School of Mines, the *Minería,* in Mexico City, designed by Manuel Tolsa, considered the most distinguished architect of the American academic school.

Painting. With the church as the chief patron of artists, colonial Latin-American painting found its principal outlet in the portrayal of religious subjects. It imported copies of the great Spanish and Italian masters of the sixteenth century, which became models for Indian artists to copy. The Creoles, too, imported copies, sometimes originals, for the decoration of their homes. Rapid expansion of the colonies, however, in the sixteenth century demanded more and more the use of the Indian's talent. Inevitably, as in architecture, they wove into their paintings their own religious symbols. A striking example was in the Mission Church of Laguna, New Mexico, where an unknown Indian artist decorated the altar with Christian symbols, but painted on the ceiling the moon, the sun, and a rainbow, expressions of his own deities. An interesting variation of influences other than Spanish is found in Venezuela. There colonial families and the church frequently relied upon Negro slave artists. Their productions show untrained craftsmen but a striking use of color that gives their work a remarkable freshness. In Brazil, unfortunately, no use was made of the colonial Negro talent.

In the seventeenth century native Creole artists, influenced by European traditions, made significant contributions. Gregorio Vásquez de Arce y Ceballos of Bogotá among these is considered the master in the history of Colombian painting. His portraits in churches and private homes are striking for their use of color and unusual dignity. Among Mexican Creole painters, Miguel Cabrera in the middle of the eighteenth century established a school of painting. He himself contributed a large number of canvases to the Jesuit churches as well as to the homes of his wealthy clients. Venezuela gave opportunity for the artistic contributions of José Campeche, a Puerto Rican artist.

At the end of the century Venezuela produced its first outstanding painter, José Rodríguez Rendón, from Cumaná. Sent to Spain in 1784, he studied European art and brought back to his country its traditions. The outstanding example of native Creole art, however, came in the early nineteenth century with the work of Martín Tovar y Tovar. His most famous paintings, those of the stirring battles for freedom in the Wars for Independence, show a style curiously marked by the restraint almost delicate and an avoidance of violent contrast. Elsewhere in Latin America in this period Creole artists reflected the influence of Goya.

Sculpture. Sculpture was practically a monopoly of Indian craftsmen. In Ecuador, famous for the carved wooden figures throughout its churches, Manuel Caspicara turned out masterpieces that compare with the best work of the Renaissance masters. His best-known figure is a Stigmata of St. Francis in the Catuña church in Quito. Indian carvers and wood-workers left their statuary usually of very high quality in the cathedrals of Bolivia, Peru, Colombia, Ecuador, and Mexico. One of the remarkable examples of their skill and art is the decorative relief and devotional figures in La Merced Church in Cuzco.

Part III. THE CHURCH IN THE SPANISH COLONIES

Organization and Conversion. The church deeply influenced all aspects of colonial life. It was, however, at all times subordinate to the royal authority. The root of this power of Spain's rulers lay in the late fifteenth century, a result of concessions made by various Popes in support of the war against the Moslems. After the discovery of America the Spanish monarchs succeeded in having their control recognized over the colonial church. Beginning in 1493 and continuing to 1508, a series of papal bulls gave the Catholic monarchs the right to appoint and remove officials of the church, to control their movements in the Indies, to censor communications with the papacy, and to collect all tithes. Although the church had the privilege (*fuero eclesiástico*) of maintaining its own courts to hear cases involving tithes, marriages, gifts, legacies to the church, including land, and other matters having a bearing upon religious affairs, the ultimate decision in all important cases rested with the Council of the Indies.

Too much emphasis can be put upon the role of the church in the Indies. Its work, however, is best understood when it is seen as fundamentally carrying out the wishes of the monarchs. Defiance of royal power brought punishment upon a church organization as it did upon any other institution that resorted to this dangerous expedient. The most famous exhibition of royal prerogative was the order expelling the Jesuits from the Spanish colonies in the late eighteenth century. However, the church rarely found itself in serious opposition to the king; on the contrary, the state and the church worked together closely in forwarding the establishment of the empire and in Christianizing the natives.

The organization of the church that had developed in Spain was transferred to America. The empire was divided into archdioceses, headed by archbishops, and dioceses, headed by bishops. Before the colonial period ended, seven of the former had been established and thirty-five of the latter. Outstandingly important were the archbishoprics of Mexico, Lima, and Santo Domingo. The principal orders of the church arrived to take up their work of missionary activity, education, and establishment of hospitals and other charitable institutions. Important among them were the Franciscans, Dominicans, Jesuits, Carmelites, and Augustinians. The work of carrying on religion and extending conversion fell broadly into two main aspects. Parish priests looked after the spiritual needs of the Spanish towns and cities, while *doctrineros* instructed in the faith Indians already settled in towns and villages. Beyond the frontiers of settlement the work of conversion was carried on by missionaries among the barbarous tribes.

The work of the parish priests in the cities founded by Spaniards offered no particular difficulty, since the population was ardently Catholic. The laws, in fact, permitted only those who were Catholic to emigrate to the colonies. There were, of course, some exceptions to this rule. The chief problem was that of converting the settled Indian tribes from their old established religions to Christianity. At first the barrier of language was overcome by resort to the use of interpreters, pictures, pantomime, and dramas to tell the basic stories of the Bible. The churchmen also learned the Indian languages to reduce them to dictionaries and grammars. But most important was the training of children in the study of Latin and Spanish.

Facilitating conversion were the extraordinary resemblances among many of the Indian religions to aspects of Christian beliefs and practices. The Mexican, Mayan, and Inca religions had evolved the concept of a Supreme Being and a belief in immortality. Prayer was common among them. Communion was extensively practiced, as were baptism, confession, and penance. Fasting and holy days were widely observed. Some symbols were common both to the Indian and Christian religions. The Mayan cross sculptured on their monuments was identical with the Christian. Other similarities lay in the foundation of monasteries and nunneries, religious organization based upon a hierarchy, and the use of temples cared for by a body of officials not unlike those of the Christian church. The church also took advantage of shrines used by Indians for their own religion. The most notable case was the choice of the hill of Guadalupe outside of Mexico City for the construction of a church dedicated to the Virgin. To this rocky elevation multitudes of Indians had for centuries made yearly pilgrimages to worship their gods. The belief that the Virgin made a miraculous appearance on the hill in 1531 continued the use of this shrine under Christian auspices.

Modern studies of primitive and historic religions have established that such beliefs, practices, and customs resembling those of Christianity existed in ancient times and in many cultures throughout the world. But the Spanish churchmen, discovering these characteristics among the Indians of the New World, attributed them to the efforts of Satan to have himself worshiped. Shocked, moreover, by the custom of human sacrifice, common to many Indian religions, and firmly believing that they were casting out the devil, zealous churchmen in the sixteenth century destroyed temples, idols, books, and other valuable evidences of Indian religious development.

Toward the end of the sixteenth century the Inquisition was established in the colonies. Inquisitorial powers had been conferred upon certain church leaders early in the century; Bishop Zumárraga exercised these, for example, quite freely in New Spain after 1536. Other church officials did likewise, notably in Peru. In 1569 the Tribunal of the Inquisition for the colonies was formally established and began operations in Lima in 1570 and in Mexico in 1571. As in Spain, the colonial Inquisition received accusations anonymously, though apparently its officials exercised considerable discretion in wielding their power. It prosecuted particularly cases of bigamy, heresy, Judaism, blasphemy, witchcraft, and violation of sacerdotal vows. In some cases governors of provinces fell afoul of the Tribunal as a result of conflicts with local church officials. Punishment ranged from simple penance to confiscation of property, fines, imprisonment, exile, and burning at the stake. Of the latter, however, there were comparatively few cases.

Protestants who came to the Spanish colonies, refugees from shipwrecks, prisoners captured from foreign vessels raiding the coast, smug-

glers, and others—all these the Inquisition sought to convert. Indians
were normally not subject to the Tribunal. Considered as children with
weak minds, their falling away from the faith, after conversion, was not
regarded as heresy but a fault to be remedied by their guardians, the
priests and missionary fathers.

The Inquisition exercised a wide power of censorship. It examined
and gave or withheld its approval over all books published in the colonies
and all those imported. Of the latter, its officials were particularly careful
to exclude Protestant literature. Late in the colonial period it exercised
great vigilance in preventing the importation of liberal political literature
from England, revolutionary France, and the United States. Such books
and pamphlets, if smuggled in and found, were burned. On the other
hand, as we have seen, purely literary writings of a wide variety entered
the colonies without hindrance and in great numbers.

Missionary Work. Missionary work began in the Caribbean with the
arrival in 1493 of twelve friars accompanying Columbus on his second
voyage. Cortés sent for Franciscan missionaries as soon as the conquest
of Mexico City was complete. But the great work of the missionaries
was winning souls among the barbarous tribes beyond the frontiers of the
settled Indian areas. Missionaries accompanied every expedition of exploration into the interior of both continents. On their return they became
powerful advocates for advancing the frontier so that they could work
among the heathen. They even frequently invented mythical tales of rich
cities and great wealth among the aborigines to interest the royal authorities in financing their desired undertakings.

The outstanding missionary orders were the Dominicans, Franciscans, and Jesuits. In the Caribbean the Dominicans found the greatest
expression of their zeal for missionary work in Father Bartolomé de las
Casas. The Franciscans after their arrival in Mexico in the 1520's kept
pace with the expansion of the frontier northward through central Mexico
into New Mexico and Texas. Father Alonzo de Benavides did outstanding work in beginning the conversion of New Mexico, writing an invaluable account of the missions and the region. In Texas Father Antonio
Margil de Jesús played an important part in the founding of the missions
there.

In North America the Jesuits first took up their work in Florida,
brought there by Menéndez after the founding of St. Augustine. Abandoning this field, which the Franciscans took over, the Jesuits after 1590,
led by Father Gonzalo de Tapia, turned their attention to the western
coast of Mexico, where they propagated the faith. A century later, under

Father Eusebio de Kino and Father Juan María de Salvatierra, they established missions, colonies, indeed Spanish power in Sonora and Lower California. To the east in the Sierra Madre the Jesuits with great sacrifices and successes worked among the Tepehuanes and Tarahumaras. After their expulsion in 1767 their field was taken over by the Franciscans. Two years later Franciscan fathers joined the colonizing expeditions into California, where, under the leadership of Father Junípero Serra, they began the line of missions along the California coast.

In Central America both Franciscans and Dominicans led the way in missionary activity. After the conquest the Dominicans became the principal order in the work of conversion among the Mayan towns and in missionary activity among the mountain tribes. In South America Jesuit missionaries led in Christianizing the Araucanian tribes of Chile; in Peru they penetrated the interior highlands to work among the Quechuan tribes, as well as in the Ecuadorian Andes. In La Plata Franciscans carried on work among the Uruguayan Indians.

Pre-eminent in La Plata, however, were the Jesuits. In 1608 they began their labors among the Guaraní Indians of Paraguay. By the middle of the seventeenth century they had persuaded many tribes to settle in organized towns along the Paraná, Paraguay, and Uruguay rivers. However, Portuguese slave raiders from São Paulo forced the Jesuits to retreat with their charges from the upper Paraná southward below the bend of the river to establish their principal base at Candelaria. This region became a major missionary area which, by the middle of the eighteenth century, had some 30,000 Indians established in a large number of villages. Here, too, after their expulsion in 1767, the Franciscans, principally, took over the administration of their missions.

Life in the Missions. When the Indian took the vows of a convert, he was subject to the missionary fathers in a relationship essentially paternalistic. The life of the Indians about the missions involved a variety of duties and some pleasures. As a teaching center the mission instructed Indians in Christianity. In Franciscan missions children were taught the Spanish language; the Jesuits learned the native tongues. The mission was an industrial school, too, in which the converts were taught crafts, such as carpentry, masonry, weaving, horticulture, and other simple trades. Outside the mission, Indians labored in the cultivation of the land, the care of orchards, and construction of irrigation ditches and dams. For mission buildings they brought timber from near-by mountains. Other Indians on the lands that stretched away from the mission tended herds of cattle, sheep, horses, and goats.

Conditions varied widely in the areas in which the missions were established. In the arid lands of Peru, northern Mexico, New Mexico, and Arizona, food production was limited to the few crops the native Indians had already developed, namely, potatoes, maize, beans, and peppers, to which were added the Spanish imports of wheat, fruit trees, and the vine. In the lush lands of La Plata, Chile, central and southern Mexico, and California, where Jesuits, Dominicans, and Franciscans established their centers of conversion, the missions developed a wide variety of agricultural products and manufactured goods. Hemp, flax, cotton, tobacco, corn, rice, sugar cane, and wheat flourished, while mission gardens gave forth beans, peas, beets, cucumbers, onions, potatoes, and watercress. Orchards produced figs, lemons, limes, olives, oranges, peaches, pears, and other fruits. Too, the missions were rich in the possession of huge herds of cattle, horses, mules, and other animals.

These products with imports of others became the basis for extensive manufacturing actvities, including the weaving of cloth, the making of bricks, tiles, and pottery, the tanning of hides, iron work including farm implements, locks, keys, spurs, scissors, and bells, as well as the manufacture of tallow, butter, soap, wine, flour, and the preparation of hides and wool for sale. In the Paraguayan missions the Jesuit monopoly of the Indian trade caused resentment among the Spanish merchants and government officials. In California the missions provided many of the supplies for the presidios and towns, as well as expeditions along the coast.

The social life of the Indians revolved about the mission. At sunrise the mission bell summoned all to church. After the noon-day meal and a rest, the Angelus at sunset called the Indians to prayer. In the evening they relaxed. In the various schools established at the mission the fathers instructed the Indians in music, the chant, the playing of the violin, flute, horn, violoncello, drums, and other instruments, and in art and wood carving. The exceptionally intelligent ones were taught reading and writing and frequently prepared for a career in the church.

In addition to religious holidays, certain seasons of the year were celebrated, the gathering of the harvest being a particularly important festival. Indians, too, were frequently permitted to observe their own festivals and visit with their families. They were instructed on such occasions to impress upon their tribes and families the superiority of life in the mission over that of the savage state of existence. Rodeos, dances, bullfighting, and other forms of relaxation were an important part of mission life. Possibly there were missionary fathers who abused their charges. Some took advantage of their office to exploit Indian labor; others even engaged in the slave trade, particularly in Venezuela. These, however, were the exceptions.

The mission in the total picture of the Spanish colonies had an important role. It was a force in expanding the empire. The missionary fathers served as explorers and Indian agents, recorded the history and geography of the frontiers on which they worked, and constructed valuable maps, besides bringing the Indians into contact with Christianity. Once established, missions became valuable centers for refuge and defense against savage attack. Too, their agricultural and industrial activities attracted Spanish traders and settlers, thus becoming nuclei for permanent towns and cities. The Spanish language taught the Indians became an important force in the amalgamation of the two cultures.

The Colonial Church: an Estimate. The church as a whole significantly helped in transferring the culture of Spain to the colonies in the educational institutions established and in the introduction of Spanish customs and language among the Indians. Because it was so deeply involved in all aspects of colonization, it inevitably became a rich and powerful institution. In the cities and towns, lands granted to it for cathedrals, churches, monasteries, convents, hospitals, and residences made it a wealthy urban landowner. In the rural areas its mission lands and *encomiendas* of Indians added to its wealth. It derived extensive income from its various activities, fees, gifts, income from rural and urban property, as well as taxes and tithes it received from the king after the royal seventh had been set aside.

At the same time the church performed functions which no other agency of the Spanish government could undertake. It frequently acted as a protector of the Indians against the rapacity of landowners and royal officials. Its charitable work in schools, hospitals, asylums, and foundling institutions involved often great sacrifices of its personnel. Many missionaries heroically gave their lives seeking to convert barbarous tribes. As far as its religious work was concerned, it carried on the Catholic tradition effectively in the cities and towns where the population was predominantly Spanish. Among the settled Indian groups, Christianity became an accepted religion, but did not entirely displace the worship of primitive gods, whose existence in the Indian mind had the force of great antiquity. In its important function of supporting Spanish power in the empire it was paramount. Its effectiveness as a social force became apparent in the Wars for Independence, when the royal power itself was overthrown but the religious organization was left largely untouched.

Though we have paused here in our study of historical events to examine the political, economic, and social organization of the Spanish colonies, we must resume again the thread of colonial growth and expansion. A new element after 1600 comes into the picture: the colonizing by other European powers who attempt to force their way into the Spanish possessions.

Chapter VII

SPANISH EXPANSION AND INTERNATIONAL RIVALRY IN NORTH AMERICA, 1600-1763

Part I. INTERNATIONAL RIVALRY: CARIBBEAN AND FLORIDA TO 1680

Introduction. Her empire firmly founded by 1600, Spain in the next century rounded out her frontiers. In North America she advanced into northwest Mexico and southern Arizona. In New Mexico she suffered a temporary setback in the Pueblo revolt of 1680, but recovered the lost territory by 1700. In the Caribbean-Florida area she fought off attacks by British, French, and Dutch upon her holdings there. In South America she warded aside pirates, exploited mines, and guarded against Indian rebellion.

British, French, and Dutch in the Caribbean. The wealth of the Spanish colonies in the Caribbean early attracted the sea rovers of France, Britain, and Holland. Spain's rigorous restrictions on trade made smuggling inevitable. The wars of Spain against France, Holland, and England at the same time gave piracy an air of respectability.

Preceding the English were the French pirates. In 1523 Cortés lost two of his treasure ships beyond the Azores to Juan D'Ango, a French pirate of Dieppe. In 1537 other French raiders attacked Cuba and threatened Havana. At the mid-century Jacques Sores led French corsairs upon Cuba. In 1555 he captured Havana, looted and burned it to the ground. Similar outrages occurred in the next ten years. It is in this framework of piracy and looting that the Spanish king regarded the Huguenot settlement at Fort Caroline in 1562. Religious conflict played its part, but to Philip II Fort Caroline meant a permanent base for French raiders to attack the galleons laden with silver from Mexico. As a matter of fact, after 1565 French pirates attacked St. Augustine and traded with the Indians along the Savannah River as late as 1605.

English traders appeared in the Caribbean in 1527, not as pirates but to penetrate the Spanish trading monopoly. Until 1570, excepting one piratical raid in 1545, they smuggled along obscure coasts with the clandestine cooperation of Spanish colonial officials. In 1562 John Hawkins disposed in this manner of a small number of slaves and merchandise at Isabella and at other points on the island of Santo Domingo. Two years later he traded with the covert permission of Spanish officials along the Venezuelan coast. On his return to England he visited the French colony founded by Laudonnière. The Spanish government protested these violations, but, undaunted, Hawkins returned in 1568 with Francis Drake to Venezuela. Storms drove their ships into the harbor at Vera Cruz, where a strong Spanish naval force destroyed most of them, but both Hawkins and Drake escaped.

Drake and Cavendish. After 1570 English traders gave up their attempt to break the Spanish monopoly. They openly attacked Spanish merchant ships, raided coastal towns, tortured and sometimes murdered the inhabitants. In England, where they returned to sell their loot, they were naturally regarded as heroes. In 1572–1573 Drake attacked Nombre de Dios, Cartagena, raided shipping along the northern coast of South America, and narrowly missed capturing a Peruvian mule train carrying silver and gold from Panama to Nombre de Dios. Completing his venture with French pirates along the Nicaraguan coast, he returned to England with booty amounting to more than £40,000.

Five years later in 1577 Drake began his famous voyage around the world. After raiding Spanish and Portuguese shipping along the African coast, he sailed into the Pacific Ocean via the Strait of Megellan. At Valparaíso he captured a ship laden with gold, sacked the city, and escaped. Near Callao he seized a Peruvian vessel with 1,500,000 gold ducats aboard. North along the coast of Mexico he waylaid more treasure ships. On the shore of California he anchored in present-day Drake's Bay, took possession, and explored the region. Naming it New Albion, he sailed next across the Pacific to the East Indies, took on a cargo of spices and returned to England by way of the Cape of Good Hope. For his achievements and the enormous profits of the voyage, Queen Elizabeth knighted him. Among the Spaniards, however, Drake's name became synonymous with terror.

Practically, the success of Drake led the viceroy of Peru, Toledo, to send an expedition under Villalobos and Pedro Sarmiento de Gamboa to explore and fortify the Strait of Magellan. In 1579 Sarmiento persuaded Philip II to appoint him captain-general of the Strait with rights to colonize. Unfortunately, on the way over, a storm took the lives of 800 of the colonists and forced him to anchor at Rio de Janeiro, 1582, then under Spain. In 1584 he sailed again with 400 settlers to found the town of Nombre de Jesús on the Strait.

The story of this colony was one of sheer tragedy. In 1586 Sir Thomas Cavendish, as ruthless a buccaneer as ever sailed, reached the Strait of Magellan on his voyage around the world. There he found the remnants of Sarmiento's colony now reduced to but fifteen men and three women. After promising to carry them to Peru, he cruelly sailed when he had aboard their few weapons for defense against Indian attack. Helpless, the handful of survivors shortly perished. In the Pacific, Cavendish, defeated in his attack on Valparaíso, ravaged the coast and burned defenseless towns. Off the shores of Mexico he captured rich prizes, sailed to the coast of California and then turned westward across the Pacific to arrive in Plymouth in 1587.

Meanwhile, Drake had returned to the Caribbean in 1585. Capturing and sacking the city of Santo Domingo, he made off with booty valued at more than £25,000. He repeated his exploit at Cartagena, where he sacked and burned until the citzens paid him a ransom of 110,000 ducats. With his capture of St. Augustine on May 28, 1586, he arrived in England with loot estimated at £60,000. In the last decade of the century other English pirates in the Caribbean from Cumaná in Venezuela to Honduras captured Spanish and Portuguese ships, burned towns which refused ransom, and traded where opportunity offered. Outstanding was the exploit of the Earl of Cumberland, who captured San Juan, Puerto Rico in 1596, although the prize yielded only a small amount of spices.

English Attempts at Colonization, 1585–1616. Acquainted with the Caribbean by the end of the century, England took tentative steps to colonize on the fringes of the Spanish empire. In 1585–1587 Sir Walter Raleigh lost a colony on Roanoke Island. He followed this failure with others of greater magnitude in Guiana. Lured on by rumors, long exploded by the Welsers and Spaniards, he led an expedition in 1595 to find the rich cities of Manoa. Exploring the Orinoco River a short distance, he wrote a valuable book describing the land on his return to England. In 1596 he prepared to found a colony at the mouth of the Orinoco, but in the midst of his work, James I imprisoned him for conspiracy for twelve years. Emerging undaunted, he returned to his plans. When Raleigh landed at Trinidad in 1616 with a colony, the Spaniards drove him out two years later. The protests of Spain against this invasion were used by the vengeful James I as an excuse to execute Raleigh.

Of all the English figures who appeared in the Caribbean in the sixteenth century, Sir Walter Raleigh showed statesman-like qualities which set him apart from his fellows.

The Spanish Armada: Myth and Fact. Viewing this record of piracy and vandalism in the New World in the sixteenth century, a word needs to be said about the so-called British sea power. The defeat of the Spanish Armada in 1588, an event connected with Spanish European policies, is commonly believed to have given Britain control of the seas. Nothing could be further from the truth so far as the New World is concerned, with particular regard to the Spanish colonies. As we have noted above, English sea power in the New World before and after the Armada was largely a hit-and-run affair. Spain lost no colonies in the sixteenth century as a result of the defeat of the Armada; England gained none. Spanish sea power, on the other hand, maintained control of the seas between Spain and the waters around her colonies during the colonial period. The best that British sea power could show for three centuries of activity in Spanish-American waters was the possession of a few small islands, winning a toe hold in the Guianas and British Honduras and managing a fleeting occupation of Havana in 1762; and though she gained Florida by trade in 1763, she lost it to Spain in 1780–1781. Even as late as 1807, with Spain helpless in Europe, a handful of Creoles expelled a major British overseas force from Buenos Aires. The explosion of the myth of British control of the seas in all the colonial New World is long overdue.

British Caribbean Colonies in the Seventeenth Century. The international conflict between Spain and her enemies intensified in the seventeenth century. The newcomers launched a determined program of colonization on islands and mainlands claimed by Spain. These in turn, when successful, became bases for attacks on the Spanish empire. After the abortive efforts of Raleigh on Roanoke Island and in the Guianas, Britain founded Jamestown in 1607. This intrusion of Gaule threatened the Franciscan missions farther south. Philip III protested and even sent a ship which entered Chesapeake Bay. Contemporaneously with Jamestown Britain attempted the Guiana settlement. It failed, as did the effort in 1616.

The British next transferred their efforts to the Lesser Antilles. There in 1625 they established two colonies, one on St. Christophe, shared with the French, the other on Barbados. By 1639 they had occupied St. Nevis, Antigua, and Montserrat where 20,000 English settlers thrived on an expanding tobacco and sugar prosperity. Like the Spaniards, they wiped out the island Indian population and imported Negroes for plantation work. Farther west in 1630 Puritans occupied the island of Providence off the coast of Central America, but in 1641 were driven out by a Spanish force under Admiral Francisco Díaz de Pimienta. Five years later in 1646 a group of dissident Puritans, the Independents, colonized the Bahamas under Captain William Sayle. In retaliation for the loss of Providence Island, the Providence Company and the Earl of Warwick financed Captain William Jackson, who in 1642-1643 raided the Venezuelan coast, looting the Margarita Island pearl fisheries, and captured Jamaica, releasing it for a £7,000 ransom.

This colonization in the early seventeenth century bridges in a sense the British buccaneering activities of the sixteenth and the outright wars initiated by Cromwell upon Spain. His succession to power gave a new impetus to English colonization in all the New World. In 1654, using the loss of Providence Island as an excuse, he sent Admiral William Penn to capture Santo Domingo. Dallying too long in his preparations off the harbor's mouth, the admiral failed in his mission. Thereupon, fearing Cromwell's wrath, Penn sailed for Jamaica, where, catching the Spaniards unprepared, he captured and annexed the island to Britain in 1655.

The next invasion of Spanish-claimed territory was in the Carolinas. In 1663 Sir John Yeamans and other Barbadian landowners secured a sea-to-sea grant from Charles II between the thirty-first and thirty-sixth parallels. Their efforts at colonization became successful when William Sayle established Charlestown in 1670. Coincidentally with Charlestown other British colonizers established themselves at Belice on the Honduran coast, where they took out dyewoods and mahogany. So effective was this occupation and so unsuccessful were Spanish efforts to dislodge it, that Belice, along with Charlestown, was recognized by Spain in the treaty with England in 1670.

Panama, too, fell within the range of British attempts to capture critical centers of Spanish control. From Jamaica in 1668 Henry Morgan sacked Porto Bello, captured several ships, and extracted 100,000 pieces of eight as ransom. Three years later in 1671 he crossed the isthmus with a large force and burned the city of Panama. After slight punishment Morgan was rewarded with the lieutenant-governorship of Jamaica. In 1679 English buccaneers, among whom were William Dampier and Lionel Wafer, raided Porto Bello and ravaged the isthmus. They got little booty, but stirred great interest in England with their subsequent accounts. These contributed in part to the abortive efforts to colonize Darién with Scotchmen at the end of the seventeenth century in 1699.

The French Caribbean Colonies. French efforts to colonize in the New World in the sixteenth century, like those of the British, failed. Menéndez expelled Laudonnière's colony from Florida, while the Sá brothers were driving out other Huguenot colonizers from Rio de Janeiro in 1558–1567. With religious conflicts ended in France by the beginning of the seventeenth century, Minister Sully created a favorable métier for overseas expansion.

The first steps in French Caribbean colonization came from the piratical voyage of Pierre d'Esnambuc and Urbain de Roissey, the "pirate of Dieppe," who took refuge, after a battle with a Spanish galleon, on the island of St. Christophe. Back in France, d'Esnambuc organized the Company of St. Christophe with the support of Cardinal Richelieu. Landing on the island where some Frenchmen were already cultivating tobacco, d'Esnambuc allotted land to his 500 settlers. Spanish attacks drove the colonists out, some of whom fled to Santo Domingo, but the majority returned to share the island with the English.

Neither the company nor the colony prospered, so that in 1635 a new company received St. Christophe and occupied Guadalupe and Martinique as well. Tortuga, off the northwest shore of Santo Domingo, sprang directly from pirate colonization. According to Esquemeling, a French buccaneer turned trader and author, Tortuga began as an emporium for sea rovers, English, Dutch, French, and Portuguese. They exchanged goods and planned attacks on Spanish ships and islands. Some pirates, becoming agriculturists, raised crops with Indian slaves. Others raided the cattle ranges of Santo Domingo for food. Their preparation of the jerked beef *(bucan)* for the crews of roving ships gave history the name "buccaneer." Trade directly with France from Tortuga and the western end of Santo Domingo gave France her claim, validated in 1664, to the region which became known as Haiti or Saint Dominique.

By 1662 the French colonies in the islands were taken under royal control by Colbert, the great financial minister of Louis XIV. Two years later France chartered the West Indian Company, which enjoyed a monopoly on trade and the right to colonize. To govern, Alexander Prouville de Tracy came out as the first lieutenant-general of the French colonies in America. In the same year, 1664, a colony of 1,200 Frenchmen eliminated the Dutch from Cayenne in Guiana. There, in fact, a small French colony had settled in 1604 which included fifteen or twenty Jewish families who raised tobacco and had erected a fort in 1652. In 1660 the French expelled the small colony of English from St. Christophe and possessed themselves of other smaller islands. Thus when the Treaty of Nymwegen was signed in 1678, confirming her Caribbean titles, France had fourteen islands. All, particularly Haiti, were rich in sugar production.

The Dutch Colonies. The Dutch in the sixteenth century were pre-eminently traders and pirates. After 1590 the first Dutch sea rovers attacked Spanish coasts and Portuguese colonies, then under Spain, along the littoral of Africa. By 1598 they traded along the Guiana rivers, establishing a fort on the Corantijn River in 1613 and possibly at other points. When in 1621 Holland chartered the Dutch West Indian Company, it turned its efforts to Brazil, where it held control in the north until 1661.

In the Caribbean the Dutch traded and raided along the Spanish main as well as among the French and English islands. The most outstanding exploit was the success of Piet Heyn, the Sir Francis Drake of Holland, in capturing in 1627 along the coast of Cuba the Spanish silver fleet from Vera Cruz. The loot was estimated in Holland at some $15,000,000. In 1629 Admiral Pater ravaged the coasts of Cuba, Puerto Rico, and Santo Domingo. Jan Jansz of Hoorn attacked on the Orinoco and at Trinidad. In 1630 Dirck de Ruyter and Pieter Ita lay in wait for Spanish shipping along the Florida Channel and at the western end of Cuba. Pater meanwhile attacked Cartagena, while other Dutchmen ransacked the Central American coasts. Spanish shipping, except that escorted by armed convoys, fled the Caribbean, while the Dutch monopolized the illegal trade between the islands and Europe.

Brethren of the Caribbean Dutch, based at Recife, Brazil, turned their attention to the Pacific. Many successfully attacked the coasts of Chile and Peru. In 1624, however, L'Hermite, commander of a Dutch squadron, met repulse at Callao, Guayaquil, and Acapulco. Browner's expedition of 1643, after destroying the town of Castro in southern Chile, failed to take Valdivia. Other attacks forced the Spaniards to fortify Panama, Guayaquil, Arica, and Valparaíso.

The lowly commodity of salt was responsible for the first Dutch settlement in the Caribbean. Locating a supply in the salt pans of Aruba and Curaçao, Holland took possession of these islands and that of Buen Aire in 1634. They smuggled along the Spanish main, cultivated the land, and attracted the ships of all the freebooting nations to their door. In a few short years they were supplying the French islands with horses and donkeys. From their slave pens they furnished both the French islands and the Spanish plantations in Venezuela with Indian and Negro slaves. A flourishing Caribbean and European trade made Curaçao easily the busiest commercial center of the West Indies in the seventeenth century. Besides Curaçao the Dutch also colonized Tobago and St. Eustatius and made settlements along the Guiana coasts, Berbice, Pomeroon, and Essequibo.

The Spanish Reaction. The successful colonization by 1680 of many parts of the Caribbean by the British, French, and Dutch, as well as the British occupation of the South Atlantic seaboard south to Charleston and that of Belice in Honduras, was regarded by Spain as a menace to her own great empire. She lost no important colony. But most of her efforts to dislodge the foreigners failed. Only at Providence Island did she drive the English out in 1641. In the Lesser Antilles she temporarily expelled the French and English settlers from St. Christophe. British colonization of the Carolinas and logging camps at Belice were grudgingly recognized by her in the treaty of 1670.

However, while Spain licked her wounds, she prepared for the future. Around the Caribbean she erected powerful stone forts to protect her key cities of St. Augustine, Havana, Vera Cruz, Panama, and Cartagena, as well as her Pacific coastal cities. She had not long to wait, for after 1680 the expansive forces of England and France began anew their efforts at empire building. In the meantime she was pushing her way farther into the North American continent.

Part II. SPANISH EXPANSION IN NORTH AMERICA, 1600–1720

The Jesuits on the Pacific Coast. While Spain was fighting off her enemies in the Caribbean in the seventeenth century, she was expanding her empire in western North America. Guzmán and Cortés led the way to the west coast of Mexico early in the sixteenth century. Guzmán founded Culiacán in 1531, the future base for expansion northward. Late in the century Ibarra explored Sonora and Sinaloa on the Gulf of California. But actual leadership in colonization in this difficult terrain fell to the Jesuits. Father Gonzalo de Tapia led the work with a settlement at San Felipe, north of Culiacán. Though he met martyrdom in 1594, his short career saw missions along the Río de Sinaloa and Río Fuerte. Soon miners and cattlemen followed.

After 1600 the frontier moved forward under Father Martín Pérez, ably supported by Captain Diego Martínez de Hurdaide. By 1625 missions sprang up in the next two river valleys, the Mayo and the Yaqui. But these wild tribes, jealous of their lands, frequently revolted. Against them Hurdaide made constant campaigns. In the following quarter of a century the advance was steady. Beyond the Yaqui the fathers entered

Sonora. By 1650 missions at Cucurpe and Arispe had carried the Spanish vanguard almost to the present Arizona border. Silver mining, the cattle industry, and settlements sprang up in the wake of the missionaries. Trade along the rivers and coast nourished the growing population of Spaniards and *mestizos*. By 1679 Sinaloa and Sonora had a population of about 3,000 Spaniards and *mestizos*. Thirty-five missions from San Felipe to northern Sonora served an estimated 40,000 persons, Indians and Spanish colonizers.

Into this region came in 1681 an heroic figure, the Jesuit Father Eusebio Francisco Kino. A trained mathematician, he refused a chair at the University of Ingolstadt to Christianize Lower California. After six years of heartbreaking experiences, he fell back in 1686 to establish a base in Sonora for a return to the peninsula. Founding his mother mission, Dolores, in 1687, on the Altar River, Kino created singlehandedly the colony of Sonora in the next twenty-five years.

Among the Upper Pimas and other Indian groups, he established a number of missions around which the neophytes learned to cultivate the ground. His encouragement of prospecting led to the discovery of important silver deposits. He brought in the cattle industry to supplement the slender diet of the colony. But his settlements, constantly threatened by Apaches from the north, forced him to organize a defense and call for the founding of presidios. Never forgetting his original purpose to get back to Lower California, he personally led a large number of explorations along the Gila and Colorado rivers. When it became apparent that he would need a base far to the north of Altar, he founded the mission of San Javier del Bác, 1700, near present Tucson, Arizona.

When Father Kino died in 1711, he had not gotten back to Lower California, but the results of his work were far-reaching. His helper, Father Juan María Salvatierra, founded missions on the peninsula. Building on his exploratory activities, other Jesuits, Pfefferkorn and Sedelmeyer, continued his work in the north. But more important, Sonora, Kino's monument, became the base for the colonization of Upper California in the late eighteenth century.

New Mexico and the Northern Frontier, 1610–1700. After the founding of Santa Fé in 1610, New Mexico remained the principal outpost on the northern frontier. The Franciscan fathers engaged actively in conversion. By 1630 some ninety pueblos, housing an estimated 60,000 Indians, were ministered to by over fifty religious. Besides agriculture, the fathers instructed them in the manual arts, music, and painting. The non-Indian population of New Mexico, including Spaniards and mixed bloods, barely exceeded 2,500 in 1680. From New Mexico, explorers went eastward into Texas to search for pearls along the Conchos. Others went northeast to the Arkansas. Missionaries, anxious to begin conversion, accompanied the expeditions.

But all was not well within the province. The Pueblo Indians resented the efforts of the missionaries to stamp out their ancient religions. The governors antagonized the Indians by selling some into slavery in the north Mexican mines. Spanish settlers encroached upon Indian lands. Complicating the picture were conflicts between the governors and the father custodians of the province. Some governors, anxious to keep the Indians peaceful, supported their religious customs and restricted the efforts of the missionaries. The custodians condemned the traffic in Indian slaves. The most famous of the church-state conflicts came to a head in the decade between 1660 and 1670. After bitter conflict with the governor, Don Diego de Peñalosa, the Custodian of the Missions, Father Alonzo de Posadas, succeeded in hailing his enemy before the Inquisition. Found guilty by that body, the governor was deprived of his property and exiled from New Spain. In France Peñalosa proposed to lead an expedition for the conquest of northern Mexico. But the French government favored the project of La Salle, a native Frenchman, to colonize at the mouth of the Mississippi as a means of reaching the mines of Mexico.

The Pueblo Revolt, 1680. In 1680 the long-smoldering resentment of the Indians broke out in the Pueblo revolt. Well organized under Popé, their leader, at the pueblo of San Juan, all Indian towns rose at the same moment. They massacred over 400 Spaniards and drove the remaining 2,200 out of the province. For thirteen years the Pueblos remained independent. A significant result of the uprising was the firm establishment of El Paso, where the settlers took refuge. There they turned to cultivate the soil and raise a variety of crops, among which was the vine. In the next decade El Paso became a wine center supplying northern Mexico. The fathers exiled from the north turned eastward to carry on conversion among the Texas tribes.

After repeated failures to reconquer the Pueblos, the governorship of New Mexico went into the hands of Don Diego de Vargas, an able military figure. Aiding him, however, was a change of sentiment among the Pueblos themselves. With the Spaniards gone, they found themselves and their crops raided by the merciless Apaches from the plains. When Vargas arrived in 1692 to begin the reconquest, he experienced little difficulty, as pueblo after pueblo submitted to his rule. By 1696 Spanish power was again firmly established.

After 1700 Spanish expansion turned northeastward. Fear of the French, who had established themselves on the Mississippi, disturbed the Spanish authorities. In 1719 Governor Valverde led an expedition into eastern Colorado to find at El Cuartelejo evidence of French trade with the Indians there. In the following year, 1720, a more ambitious project carried a Spanish expedition under Pedro de Villasur to the junction of the Platte River in western Nebraska. There, unfortunately, they found the French, in alliance with the Pawnees, who massacred most of the expedition including the leader, Villasur.

The Colonization of Coahuila. While Spain was moving northward into Sonora and Arizona and winning back the far-flung province of New Mexico, she pushed her border northeast toward the Rio Grande River. Carabajal's work in founding New León in the late sixteenth century provided the base. Between New León and New Vizcaya, an unoccupied area, Indians swept in to raid both provinces. After 1670 missionaries entered the region, supported by soldiers and followed by miners. In 1674 the region was organized as Coahuila, a part of New Vizcaya, with Monclova as its chief settlement. Thirteen years later in 1687 Monclova, protected by a presidio, became the capital of the new province of Coahuila.

From Monclova and New León missionaries urged upon the Spanish authorities in Mexico an advance across the Rio Grande where they reported a mountain of silver! Both slave raiders and missionaries explored the Rio Grande along its lower reaches. The normal process of advance was in the making. But at this moment Spanish expansion northeastward received a new impetus—La Salle's project of 1684 to colonize at the mouth of the Mississippi River. Spanish expansion in North America now became involved in the long international conflict between Spain and her enemies, France and England, on the Gulf and along the south Atlantic seaboard.

Part III. INTERNATIONAL RIVALRY IN THE GULF REGION, 1680–1763

Spanish and French Rivalry on the Gulf of Mexico. The long history of French rivalry with Spain in the New World culminated in the project of La Salle to colonize Louisiana. While Colbert was establishing French power in the Caribbean (1661–1681), other Frenchmen from Canada were advancing into the Illinois country. Joliet and Marquette opened the Mississippi River to exploration; La Salle completed it to the mouth in 1680. His imaginative mind grasped the significance of uniting French Canada, the Illinois country, and the Caribbean colonies with a settlement at the mouth of the great river. This crescent-shaped empire would hem in the British colonies on the east and provide a base to capture the Spanish mines of northern Mexico.

La Salle. La Salle set out on his expedition in 1684, having been preceded by French buccaneers who raided Apalachee in the year before. Arrived in the French West Indies, he enlisted adventurers to join his colony of 400 settlers. In November, 1684, they entered the Gulf, but missed the mouth of the Mississippi River and landed on the Texas coast near present Matagorda Bay. To aid the founding, his lieutenant, Tonty of the Iron Hand, was to come southward from the Illinois country. When plans went awry, Tonty returned. La Salle, meanwhile, after building a fort on the Garcitas River, made plans to move eastward to the Mississippi but was murdered. Indians who attacked and burned the fort dispersed the colony.

Spain, deeply disturbed by this invasion of the Gulf, took comprehensive measures to nullify it. Unaware of the fate of La Salle, expeditions set out by land and sea to search for the French colony. Five sea expeditions searched the Gulf coast between 1686 and 1693 from Vera Cruz to Apalachee. By land the governor of Florida sent Marcos Delgado in 1686 to search among the Indians east of the Mississippi River. From the west Alonzo de León led three parties in 1686–1689 from Monterrey and Monclova. On the last he found the ruins of La Salle's fort, and brought back two Frenchmen wandering among the east Texas Indians.

Alarmed by Frenchmen on Spanish territory, the viceroy ordered the occupation of Texas. In 1690 Father Massenet and Captain de León established a small mission in eastern Texas along the Nechas River. Three years later in 1693, with no indication of other Frenchmen, but hostility among the Indians, Spain withdrew the mission. Thus ended the first attempt to colonize Texas.

The Founding of Louisiana. In 1689, when England forged the Grand Alliance which included Spain against Louis XIV, the French invaded the Caribbean to capture Cartegena. While the Treaty of Ryswick ended hostilities, 1697, Louis XIV returned to La Salle's idea of a colony on the Gulf of Mexico. Two brothers, Pierre le Moyne, Sieur d'Iberville, and Jean Batiste le Moyne, Sieur de Bienville, from a prominent Canadian family sailed in 1698 for Pensacola. But Spain, long planning to occupy that port of which Sigüenza y Góngora had drawn an excellent map in 1693, hastened to anticipate the French. Thus in December, 1698, Pensacola, founded by a small colony from Havana, warded off Iberville. Moving westward along the coast, the French settled at Biloxi in 1699. Exploration soon revealed a better site at the head of Mobile Bay, where Iberville transferred his colony to found St. Louis in 1702. Eight years later in 1710 he established Mobile.

New Orleans Founded. French traders and missionaries soon established friendly relations with the Chickasaws and Choctaws. As allies, the French used them to block English expansion westward from the Atlantic seaboard and to oppose the Spaniards at Pensacola. To the west the French moved at last toward Louisiana. In 1712 Antoine Cruzat received from the king a monopoly of trade from the Illinois country to the Gulf and agreed to take settlers to Louisiana. His experiment not succeeding, his grant fell to John Law, who organized the Company of the West to speculate in Louisiana lands. Bienville, governor under the company, founded New Orleans in 1718. The company gave land grants, brought out settlers, and introduced Negro slavery. Agriculture flourished, while trade with the Illinois country and France thrived.

San Antonio Founded. French traders soon crossed the Mississippi. In 1713 St. Denis, a picturesque figure, built a post on the Red River, whence he crossed Texas to trade with the north Mexican frontier towns. This was too much for the Spaniards. They sent out a small colony in 1716 which established a presidio in eastern Texas near the Angelina River to oppose the French on the Red River. But the need of a stronger colony nearer northern Mexico was soon felt. Thus in 1718 sixty-five persons under Martín de Alarcón, made governor of Texas, founded San Antonio with a mission, town, and presidio.

After this date French and Spanish rivalry west of the Mississippi River centered around a struggle for the control of Indian trade and allegiance of the tribes. The French advanced westward along the Red River, where La Harpe in 1719 had a post among the Cadodoches and explored to the mouth of the Canadian River. Two years later La Harpe advanced up the Arkansas near present-day Little Rock. At the same time on the Missouri River, Du Tisné visited the Pawnees, traded with the Osages, and explored the Missouri as far as the villages of the Missouri Indians. After the defeat of Villasur's expedition in 1720 at the forks of the Platte River, Bourgmont established Fort Orleans near the mouth of the Grand River in 1723. In the south French traders pushed into eastern Texas to establish a strong trading position by 1750

among the north Texas Indians as far as the Wichitas in the Red River
Valley.

These long steps to the west sharpened French hopes of opening
trade with the Spaniards in Santa Fé. However, until 1739 the Comanches
in the far western plains stood as a barrier. In that year the Mallet
brothers passed beyond them to reach New Mexico with a cargo of
merchandise and returned to New Orleans. Other French traders soon
followed, but their trading of guns to the Comanches for furs exposed
New Mexico to formidable attacks. After 1752 the governor of New
Mexico, arresting French traders and confiscating their goods, ended
the commerce.

Part IV. SPANISH AND ENGLISH RIVALRY ON THE ATLANTIC SEABOARD, 1680–1763

Rivalry on the Florida Frontier to 1702. In 1597 Spanish missionaries who
had established missions on the coast north of Florida retreated before
Indian revolt. Shortly thereafter fresh contingents of Franciscans created
another religious province called Guale, later known as Georgia. By 1634
four missions manned by thirty Franciscans worked among some 30,000
converts in Guale. In the west Spain founded a mission at San Luis,
near present-day Tallahassee among the Apalachee Indians. But in the
middle of the century they revolted and expelled the fathers. By 1670,
when the English colonized the Carolinas, Spanish missions along the
coast reached almost to the Savannah River among the Yamassee Indians.

The aggressive Carolina planters soon moved southward and westward to trade with the Indians and seize them as slaves. The coastal
Spanish missions at the same time suffered from piratical raids, particularly serious in 1683–1684. But the struggle between the English and the
Spaniards took a new turn in 1685, when the Yamassees, as English
allies, attacked the Spanish mission of Santa Catalina, west of St. Augustine. The Spanish governor, Juan Marqués Cabrera, struck back in the
next year with an attack which burned Carolina plantations and destroyed Port Royal. In the west, meanwhile, the English threatened when
Dr. Henry Woodward crossed Guale to trade among the Creeks and
Alabama Indians. To meet this invasion, Governor Marqués sent soldiers
and Indian allies to hold the Indians in line.

Disturbed by the arrival of La Salle in the Gulf on his flank, the
St. Augustine governor sent Delgado to investigate. While this threat
quickly evaporated, the English appeared in the north in growing num-

bers. Their abundant cheap goods which they traded for furs earned them a warm welcome among the Indians. To punish their allies, the Spaniards sent an expedition which burned Indian towns that had traded with the English. To strengthen their hold, Governor Cabrera founded in 1691, far to the northwest of St. Augustine, a mission and presidio at Caveta on the Chattahoochee River. But pirate threats and Indian revolts soon forced the withdrawal of the troops. The English promptly moved in again to trade beyond among the Alabama and Chickasaw Indians. But the trade was only a prelude to the capture of Indians for slaves on the coastal plantations.

The War of the Spanish Succession in the Southeast. While Spain placed a colony at Pensacola in 1698 to hold it from the French, events took a new turn in 1702 when France and Spain became allies in the War of the Spanish Succession, which broke out in that year. The war involved both the South Atlantic seaboard and the Caribbean. Governor Moore from Charleston led a devastating raid upon Florida down the coast, destroyed the missions of Guale, and captured St. Augustine, but failed to take the stone fortress ably defended by Governor Zuñiga. In the next year, Governor Moore returned to destroy thirteen of the fourteen Apalachee missions and take back to the Carolinas 1,400 Indians, some as slaves, others as allies. In reply the Spaniards sent a force in 1706 to attack Charleston, but succeeded only in raiding the coast. Satisfied that the settlements were safe from attack, the English turned westward to lead in 1708 Alabama Creeks and other tribes in an attack on Mobile and Pensacola. However, Bienville, on the alert, thwarted this move. In the Caribbean the English attacked the French part of the island of St. Christophe and raided Spanish shipping.

The Treaty of Utrecht which ended the war in 1713 left an uneasy peace on the Florida-Carolina border. In the Caribbean, the treaty awarded the British the island of St. Christophe. More important for the expanding British trade in the islands were the provisions which permitted Englishmen to send annually a ship of not more than 500 tons to trade at Spanish ports, particularly Porto Bello. A separate agreement called the *Asiento* gave the British the exclusive right to sell slaves in the Spanish colonies for thirty years.

The War of the Austrian Succession on the South Atlantic Seaboard and in the Caribbean. Hardly had the Treaty of Utrecht been signed when the English in 1717 pushed beyond the Carolina frontier with a fort on the Altahama River and an alliance with the Cherokees. Sixteen years later they delivered a devastating blow to Spain's claims north of

Florida with the founding of Georgia in 1733. While Oglethorpe built Savannah on the coast, his sea-to-sea grant included Spanish settlements and Pueblo Indian towns in New Mexico! Paralleling this territorial advance, English traders, far from satisfied with the privilege to trade at Porto Bello, smuggled in all the Caribbean ports. In retaliation Spain established a coastal patrol which captured between 1713 and 1739 fifty-eight English ships. Naturally they confiscated the merchandise. The English, angered, demanded reprisals. This commercial conflict came to a head in 1739 when a Spanish captain cut off the ears of a captured smuggler, Captain Jenkins. Outraged, the English opened hostilities, a struggle which became known as the War of Jenkins' Ear (1739).

This conflict merged in the next year into a world-wide struggle, the War of the Austrian Succession (1740–1748). While its basic causes arose in Europe, in the New World the struggle for the control of trade and commerce in the Caribbean and for naval bases and territorial expansion, represented by the English advance into Georgia, motivated the contestants, Britain on one side, the French and Spaniards on the other. Between Spain and England the historic pattern of British attack on Spanish colonies asserted itself. In the Caribbean, Admiral Vernon captured in 1739 Porto Bello and destroyed its defenses. His attack in 1740 upon Cartagena, however, failed in spite of his powerful fleet and strong supporting army. Bickerings between the admiral and General Wentworth, together with sickness among the troops, lost Britain a key prize. This event threw its shadow upon all subsequent operations. In 1741 a similar combined attack on Santiago collapsed when Wentworth failed in the land attack. Cuba, most desired by the British, eluded their grasp. Similar attacks along the Venezuela coast and an attempt to seize Panama in 1742 likewise came to grief.

On the Georgia-Florida frontier both English and Spanish attacks failed. In 1739–1740 Oglethorpe led an expedition by land and sea to the very doors of St. Augustine. Governor Montano defeated the land forces, while a small flotilla in the harbor frustrated British landing attempts. By this date, when England had exhausted herself in the Caribbean, Spain sent a large fleet and several thousand men to attack Oglethorpe's settlements in 1742–1743. But mismanagement brought failure at Frederica, and Oglethorpe himself saved the day at the Battle of the Bloody Marsh.

Turning from the Spanish Caribbean where little success attended their naval efforts, the British attacked French naval power in 1743. Near Martinique, Vice-Admiral William Bowles destroyed a strong

French fleet in 1745. Two years later off Cape Finisterre the British in 1747 won a resounding naval victory over the French, and destroyed France's hopes of recapturing Cape Breton and Acadia, lost when the British took Fort Louisburg in 1745. A second naval battle off Cape Finisterre in 1748, bringing a major defeat to the French navy, prepared the way for British success in capturing Canada in the Seven Years' War. The end of the War of the Austrian Succession saw nothing changed in the international struggle between Spain and England. Oglethorpe had vindicated the title to Georgia; Spain still held Florida. The Treaty of Aix-la-Chapelle in 1748 restored all conquests. But it was a lull before the storm—the greatest of all the eighteenth century conflicts, the Seven Years' War.

The Seven Years' War, 1756–1763. This war had these basic causes in the New World: struggle for territory, control of the seas, and commercial rivalry. England was trying to destroy the French empire in the New World and in India, as well as push her way into Spain's possessions in the Caribbean. The crisis came in 1753 when the French occupied the Ohio country. For three years the English and French conducted campaigns either to take or to hold strategic positions from Virginia to Lake Erie. In 1756 Old World conflicts made the war worldwide when Prussia and Austria began anew the struggle for Silesia. France joined Austria, while England allied herself with Prussia. By 1759 English campaigns had defeated the French in the Ohio valley and captured Quebec and Montreal in 1760.

In this state of affairs, with France on the brink of collapse, Spain under Charles III entered the war in the hope of preventing France's New World empire from falling into the hands of Britain. The British, immediately accepting the challenge, attacked in the Caribbean. In a short time Admiral Rodney captured the French islands of Martinique, Granada, Grenadines, and St. Lucia, but centered the main offensive on Cuba. Reinforced by a fleet of over fifty vessels under Admiral Pocock, Rodney attacked Havana in June, 1762. For more than two months the Spanish fleet in the harbor and Moro Castle held out. In August, when the city fell, the British took £3,000,000 in loot. Shortly thereafter in October a British fleet under Sir William Draper and Rear-Admiral Cornish captured Manila and garnered a $4,000,000 ransom to save the city from looting.

The Treaty of Paris, 1763: Results. The Treaty of Paris, February 11, 1763, ended the Seven Years' War. With France eliminated from the North American continent, her territory fell into the hands of her great rivals, Spain and England. England acquired French Canada and all territory claimed by France east of the Mississippi River. Spain inherited French claims to lands west of the great river and New Orleans, which lay to the east of that stream. In a separate agreement with England, Spain exchanged Havana for Florida. Manila was returned, but the British secured a foothold on the Falkland Islands off the coast of southern Argentina.

With Spain and England masters of almost the whole of the North American continent, it was inevitable that both should prepare for a new struggle. England, beginning with Jamestown in 1607, had pushed frontiers westward and south until she reached the Mississippi and had possession of Florida. Spain, having surrendered Florida, won back Havana, the key to the defenses of the mainland empire. In the west, Spain threw up a bulwark against British expansion when she acquired Louisiana and New Orleans. Both contestants launched far-ranging re-organization programs in preparation for the coming struggle. But both were unaware of a new force which manifested itself in the dramatic revolt of the English colonies in 1776. It ended British expansion in the New World, but out of its ashes rose a power which contributed to the overthrow of the Spanish empire.

During this century and a half, while Spain was holding at bay her enemies in North America, she faced on the southern continent other problems equally serious and which eventually brought her downfall there. To this aspect of her colonial history we now direct our attention.

Chapter VIII

THE SPANISH EMPIRE IN
SOUTH AMERICA, 1600-1800

Part I. PIRATES AND INDIAN REVOLTS

Spanish South America in the seventeenth and eighteenth centuries had no spectacular movements in her history such as the international struggle in the Caribbean and the colonization of California. The steady production of wealth from the mines of South America drew pirates to the west coast; exploitation of Indians provoked rebellion within. Eighteenth century rebellion among colonials produced belated administrative reforms.

Piracy. With the Dutch at war with Spain, the sea rovers from Holland after 1600 raided the west coast of South America from Chile to Ecuador. Olivier Van Noort and Simon de Cordes attacked Valdivia and Castro in 1600. Fifteen years later Joris van Spillbergen, a Dutch naval commander, attacked Spanish naval power in Peruvian waters to weaken Spain's offensive against Dutch possessions in the East Indian archipelago. Other Dutch seamen swarming through the Strait of Magellan temporarily drove Spanish shipping off the seas from Panama to Chile.

In defense Spain strengthened her naval forces and fortified the principal Pacific ports, Valparaíso, Callao, and Guayaquil in South America and Acapulco in Mexico. As the sea raids intensified after 1640, when both British and Dutch rovers invaded, Spain dug in more deeply with improved defenses at Callao, where a sea wall was built and Lima fortified. Along her coast her naval patrols searched the seas for enemies, whose power wilted in the face of a strong defense.

With the growth of British commercial power evidenced in the success of her smugglers along Spain's New World coasts, the mother country sought temporary respite by granting the English the right to trade at Porto Bello after the War of the Spanish Succession in 1713. However, the economic effects of this concession were almost as destructive as piracy itself. Soon the cheaper English goods were entering the markets from Panama southward. After 1715 their abundance brought on the decline of Lima as a commercial center.

Indian Revolt. Spain in South America in the late colonial period saw constant rebellion of Indian peoples from Ecuador to Chile. These were principally against the abuses practiced upon the natives, evils made possible by the framework of the government devised to control the Indians. Among the worst offenders were the officials, the *corregidores*, who governed the fifty-odd *corregimientos* into which the viceroyalty of Peru was organized. Exercising the right to exact Indian labor and control Indian trade, they utilized the *mita* system through which Indians were dealt out for personal service to Creoles and Spanish officeholders and sent to work in factories *(obrages)* or in the mines. At the same time the monopoly enjoyed by *corregidores* over Indian trade enabled them to force the natives to buy items often useless, such as silk stockings and hats. For these, exorbitant prices were demanded. Failure to pay led to confiscation of the Indians' simple possessions. Equally serious as a cause of Indian revolts was seizure of their lands.

The Araucanians of southern Chile were in constant rebellion. In 1598 they isolated and attacked Concepción, Villarica, Imperial, and other frontier towns. Only with severe loss did the Spaniards drive them off. In 1620, incensed over invasion of their lands, the Araucanians rose again, but were quickly crushed. In 1624 a rapacious governor at Santiago drove both the Spanish colonists and the Araucanians into an alliance and revolt. Throughout the rest of the century Araucanian uprisings were frequent. In 1723, driven to desperation by abuse, exploitation, and loss of lands, they made an heroic effort to drive the Spaniards completely out of southern Chile. But reinforcements from Peru quelled the uprising.

Within Peru itself, personal service drove Indians into frequent revolt. In 1597 the Jibaras in Ecuador, resenting the exactions of the governor at Quito, revolted. For months they carried on a general massacre of Spaniards in Ecuador and northern Peru. A few years later the Piajos in the Magdalena Valley, used as loggers under disgraceful conditions, rebelled violently. In the same year the Chiriguanes on the boundary between Charcas and Paraguay likewise rose at the loss of their lands to the Spaniards from Paraguay.

Some government officials made efforts to mitigate the evils. Viceroy Conde de Santisteban, late in the seventeenth century, drew up regulations to alleviate conditions of work for Indian laborers in factories. These, like the regulations of Toledo a century before, were soon disregarded. The worst sufferers were the Indians who labored in the silver and mercury mines. Between 1633 and 1689 harsh conditions of work reduced the number of Indian miners in central Peru from about 40,000 to some 10,500. Many had escaped to the mountains and freedom. So unbearable had the exploitation become in the early eighteenth century that a revolt at Oruro in 1736–1737 foreshadowed the later uprising of Tupac Amarú. Led by one Juan Santos, who claimed descent from the Incas, the Oruro Indians rebelled, slaughtered Spaniards and *mestizos,* and brought ruin to most of the convents and houses in that city. Fifteen years later at Huarochiri in a similar revolt, the Indians set up a king and called for the extermination of the entire white race in Peru. Spreading into Chile, the rebellion was put down with the greatest difficulty. This long history of exploitation and revolt formed the background to the great uprising of Tupac Amarú in 1780.

Natural Disasters. Contributing to Indian discontent and the decline of Spanish power in South America were a series of earthquakes and volcanic eruptions which destroyed lives and wealth. In 1644 an earthquake destroyed Pamplona in New Granada, while Pichincha in Ecuador erupted to destroy Quito and Riobamba. Two years later a quake shook the Andes from Cuzco to Santiago. Destroying the latter city, it severely damaged cities and towns from Valparaíso to Arequipa. Other violent seismic and volcanic disturbances occurred in Lima, 1655, Chile, 1657, and Ecuador, 1660. An earthquake in 1677 destroyed the Lima cathedral, while twenty years later a similar disturbance diverted the course of the Río Apurimac and wiped out an Indian town near the capital.

The eighteenth century saw earthquakes and tidal waves recurring with increasing force. In 1725 a quake destroyed parts of Lima. Five years later another in central and northern Chile threw down buildings and churches, while a tidal wave inundated Concepción. In 1736 a tidal wave reduced Valparaíso to shambles. But the most destructive of these seismic disturbances occurred on October 18, 1745. In Lima it took thousands of lives, destroyed 1,200 private homes, the University of San Marcos, two palaces, the *Casa de Moneda,* the *Cabildo,* the prisons, eighty churches, and forty convents. At Callao, Lima's seaport, the sea swept in to claim all but 500 lives of a population of some 5,000. Before the dead could be buried, an epidemic carried off another 10,000 persons in the coastal areas. The resulting suffering of Indians and the white population alike was intensified by marauding bands whose depredations brought the colony almost to the brink of ruin.

Part II. EIGHTEENTH CENTURY REVOLTS AND ADMINISTRATIVE REFORMS

The Ulloa Secret Report. The Spanish colonies in South America saw a constant history of revolt and discontent. A high army officer, Antonio de Ulloa, gave a picture of conditions about the middle of the century that fully accounted for the unrest manifest everywhere. Ulloa had accompanied La Condamine's scientific expedition to determine the location of the equator in Ecuador in 1736. After this tour of duty he traveled extensively in the viceroyalty of Peru, observing closely contemporary conditions and reporting secretly, as he had been ordered, to the king. He detailed the unconscionable exploitation of the Indians by the *corregidores* and churchmen in the Indian towns. Appalled by conditions of work in the mines and the system of forced labor, he gave sufficient insight into these abuses to explain Indian revolts in the past and why they eventually should have erupted in the most famous of Indian protests, that of Tupac Amarú.

On the relations of the Spaniards in the viceroyalty, he portrayed the unceasing conflicts between the *peninsulares* and Creoles, emphasizing particularly the corruptness of colonial officials and the antagonism aroused by monopolies. The report, however, had no effect; Ferdinand VI took no steps to improve conditions.

Illustrating the truth of Ulloa's account was a Creole uprising in Venezuela in 1749. Here, dissatisfied with the trading monopoly in the hands of the Caracas Company, conferred in 1728, the Venezuelans complained at first that the company did not bring sufficient Spanish products into the country, that it raised the price of those it did bring, and that it refused to pay adequately for goods purchased in Venezuela. In place of meeting the criticisms, the captain-general appointed a Spaniard, the agent of the company, to replace as judge the Creole, Juan Francisco de León. Rising in revolt León attempted to rally his countrymen in support. He failed and was eventually captured, but the event signalized the antagonism against Spain rapidly growing in this key province.

Far to the south in the same years, discontent with monopoly of trade led to defiance of royal authority. There, as we have noted, the Jesuits had established their power in the Paraguayan area in 1609. While they performed an effective service in organizing the Indians into settled missions and defending the territory against the marauding

Paulistas, their monopoly of the Indian trade offended the commercial Creoles of Asunción. The latter felt aggrieved, too, at the restrictions imposed upon them by the Lima monopoly. But the final straw that set them off on revolt was the invasion of Paraguay's commerce by Buenos Aires traders.

Led by Antonio Antequerra, the *cabildo* of Asunción rose in rebellion in 1721. Refusing to recognize a governor sent by the viceroy at Lima, they expelled the Jesuits and defeated a force in 1724 from Buenos Aires. With stronger reinforcements behind him in 1726 Governor Zabala of the port city invaded anew and captured Antequerra, who was later executed. But the Paraguayans continued defiant. They demanded the withdrawal of the Jesuits, confiscated their property, and closed the Jesuit college in Asunción. In 1735 Zabala, campaigning again, finally forced the rebels into submission, mercilessly punished the leaders, and reinstated the Jesuits. Adding further injury, the governor deprived the Paraguayan *cabildo* of their right to elect their own governor.

The War of the Seven Reductions, 1750–1761. The Jesuits, restored to control in the Paraguayan area, were soon, however, to find themselves opposing royal authority. In 1750 Spain, to accommodate her European interests, had agreed with Portugal under the treaty of that year to transfer the seven Jesuit missions east of the Uruguay River to the Portuguese king. In the missions' territory the terms of the treaty threw both Jesuits and Indians into consternation. There the more than 30,000 Guaraní Indians in the seven missions lived in terror of Portuguese slave raiders. Deeply attached to their homes and fields, they were loath to turn these over to their ancient enemy. The Jesuits, horrified at the prospect, gave the Indians strong moral support and resorted to delaying tactics.

Commissioners sent by both powers quickly realized that nothing less than military force could accomplish the transfer. Thus a combined Spanish-Portuguese army in 1754–1757 warred upon the missions or reductions, wiping out settlements, killing hundreds of men, women, and children, destroying crops, and eventually driving the Guaraní into the forests. At the moment when the region lay prostrate, the two powers reached a truce which rendered the whole military action meaningless. Thus in the treaty of 1761 Portugal returned to Spain the seven missions, while Spain ceded Colonia to Portugal.

The War of the Seven Reductions had considerable significance. By confirming Spain's title to the mission area, it ended Portugal's expansion along the upper Uruguay River. Of great importance was the fact that the resistance of the Indians marked the earliest example of American opposition by revolt to the dictation of Old World dynastic interests in New World affairs. Finally, the role of the Jesuits in antagonizing both powers prepared the way for their expulsion.

The Expulsion of the Jesuits, 1767. The reasons for this extraordinary measure have never become fully known. Charles III himself said that he kept the chief one "locked in his breast." Undoubtedly, however, of major importance was the need of funds for the royal treasury. Equally weighty was the great power of the Jesuits in both Spain and in the colonies. They controlled the best farm lands in large estates in Chile. They monopolized the government of the Indians in Paraguay. In Venezuela and New Granada they were active in trade and commerce. In Peru, Mexico, and Cuba they possessed much urban real estate. From all these sources the order derived a large income and exercised a correspondingly large political influence.

It must be said in fairness to the order, however, that it devoted a considerable part of its revenue, as did the church in general, to founding and maintaining hospitals, orphanages, mental institutions, and other worthy social undertakings. The immediate cause of their expulsion undoubtedly was the offense the Jesuits gave to the governments of both Spain and Portugal when they failed to cooperate whole-heartedly in carrying out the terms of the Treaty of Madrid (1750) applying to the Uruguayan mission area.

The uncompromising terms of the expulsion decree of February 27,. 1766, left the royal officials no alternative but immediate compliance. Summoned usually at four o'clock in the morning at their churches, colleges, monasteries, and missions, the Jesuits were hurriedly transported to designated coastal towns to await deportation to Europe. Eventually the bulk found a haven in the papal states of Italy. Their properties were inventoried and turned over to royal officials, or in some cases, notably in Sonora, Mexico, to the Franciscans. Nowhere was resistance encountered; the Jesuits submitted quietly and left. Rigid orders forbade the population from talking about or even watching the deportation.

The results of this action had a universally recognized bearing upon the later movement for independence. The Jesuits believed that Spain's loss of her colonies was divine punishment for their exile. It is certainly true that the end of Jesuit domination over colonial education displaced a major obstacle to the entry into the empire of democratic ideas, already fermenting in France and in the English colonies. Interestingly, the Jesuits themselves unwittingly cleared the ground for revolutionary thought within the colonies. Many professors in the colonial universities and colleges in the early eighteenth century were openly teaching the ideas of Descartes, the Prince of Doubt. Before the end of the century they had introduced the modern scientific and philosophic ideas of Newton, Locke, Lamarck, and others to their students, many of whom were future leaders in the Wars for Independence. In the universities of Méride (Venezuela), Caracas, Lima, San Carlos of Guatemala, and Mexico, as Lanning states, "the revolution [i.e., the attack on authoritarianism and the introduction of doubt] was thoroughly achieved in the last half of the eighteenth century . . ." and "the evolution of thought had eased over inexorably from the nature of essence to the nature of political justice. . . ."[1] Within such an environment the growth of democratic political ideas found a firm foothold.

The Revolt of Tupac Amarú, 1780–1781. Although docile and obedient, the Indians of the seven missions in La Plata had been victims of harsh military action. It is not surprising, accordingly, that across the continent in Peru the unrelieved exploitation of the native by both European and American Spaniards produced the most violent of colonial Indian uprisings. Numerous viceroys in the past had sought to lighten their burdens, and royal laws for this purpose existed. But Ulloa's confidential report to the king had shown that the Indians of Peru in the middle of the eighteenth century were not better off than they were before Toledo's reforms in the sixteenth. A humane viceroy, Manuel de Guirior, endeavored in 1777 to reduce somewhat the crushing burden of taxation when he ended the tribute paid by Indians in the form of a sales tax *(alcabala)*. This sensible action was promptly set aside by the new visitor-general, José Antonio de Areche. The latter, rigidly following royal orders, believed that the loss of income should be compensated for by direct taxes upon the natives. But he made matters infinitely worse when he not only imposed the direct taxes, but restored the *alcabala*. Areche's harshness brought to a head the long-standing antagonism of the Indians against evils of forced personal service, labor under the *mita* system in the mines, disregard of laws designed to protect them, interference with their communal properties, and abuses reflecting upon their dignity.

At this moment they found a leader, Tupac Amarú, baptized as José Gabriel Condorcanqui, a direct descendant of Tupac Amarú I, who was put to death by Viceroy Toledo in the late sixteenth century.

[1] John Tate Lanning, *Academic Culture in the Spanish Colonies*, New York, 1940, pp. 70, 84.

A man of wealth and culture, his ideas were at first simply to force the observance of laws made by the king of Spain for the protection of Indians. But the implacable attitude of Areche toward social reforms left Tupac with no alternative but to seek, in his own words, "independence or death."

Tupac began his revolt on November 4, 1780, by executing Antonio Aliaga, the *corregidor* of Tinta province near Cuzco, for violating the laws and oppressing the Indians. Securing funds, Tupac captured a supply of guns and ammunition and received from his followers the title of Inca. Near Cuzco they vented their wrath upon factories where Indian workers suffered abuses under the *mita* system. The news, spreading rapidly, brought revolts throughout Peru and Charcas until Tupac had a following of some 60,000 Indians. Many natives, however, feared or refused to join the rebellion. In November, near Cuzco, Tupac successfully defeated a large Spanish army. Aroused by this threat to royal power, Areche gathered a force of 17,000 men, many of whom were Indians forced to serve. Unfortunately, Tupac, lacking military ability and able advisers, suffered a shattering blow in May, 1781. Capturing him shortly afterward, the Spaniards sent Tupac to a horrible death and ordered every vestige of the royal Inca line extirpated.

The revolt did produce measures which temporarily relieved the worst conditions. Personal service and work in mines were limited. Only one-seventh of the population of a district could be used for labor at one time. Moreover, they could not be transported more than thirty miles from their homes. This measure was aimed at reducing the high mortality among Indians from lower altitudes formerly forced to work in mines high in the Andes. As previously, however, the natives could still be forced to work on roads, public buildings, and in agriculture, the principal source of wealth. When fears of revolt died away, Creoles and Spaniards alike ignored the reform measures. The Indians, returning again to suffer the old abuses, became an asset later when the movement for independence began.

The Comunero Revolt, 1781. The uprising of Tupac Amarú played a part in the revolt of the *Comuneros* in the next year, 1781, in New Granada. There, however, Creoles and *mestizos* took the lead, to be joined later by Indians seeking relief from oppression. As in Peru, a long background of exorbitant taxes, brutal methods of collection, and corruption in government prepared the ground. The immediate cause of the uprising was the establishment of a royal monopoly in tobacco. The authorities trebled the taxation on locally produced tobacco in the

Socorro area of New Granada and ruthlessly destroyed many privately owned fields to make the monopoly more effective.

Enraged, the *Comuneros,* meaning townsmen, in Socorro in March, 1781, attacked the public buildings and forced the *cabildo* to suspend the taxes. Organizing a committee with Juan Francisco Berbeo as chief, they collected an army of 4,000 and induced other towns, particularly Tunja, to revolt. Defeating a royal force sent against them, they proposed independence and planned a republic. In a short time their forces grew to some 20,000 men under arms recruited from sixty-six towns in the three important provinces of Boyacá, Cundinamarca, and Santander. On their approach to Bogotá the viceroy's regent, Juan Francisco Gutiérrez de Piñeros, fled, leaving the *audiencia* to mediate. At this point several thousand Indians, aroused by the success of Tupac in Peru, joined the rebels.

The *audiencia* accepted the demands of the *Comuneros* to abolish monopolies and reduce taxes, and appointed Berbeo *corregidor* and chief justice of Socorro. Satisfied, the *Comuneros* dispersed. When the *audiencia* failed to keep the agreement, José Antonio Galán led another revolt. But the viceroy's forces, reinforced with troops from Bernardo de Gálvez' army preparing to attack Jamaica, crushed the uprising and jailed and executed the leaders.

Administrative Reforms. The growing volume of Indian protest and revolt, the complaints of the American Spaniards against corruption, and abuse of monopoly privileges demanded but did not result in far-reaching reforms. Those advanced in South America were largely administrative changes designed simply to increase efficiency in government.

On the West Coast. The vast viceroyalty of Peru included La Plata as well as Charcas (Bolivia), Ecuador, and New Granada. The first step to reduce this area to more manageable proportions was in 1718 when New Granada was lopped off to be made a viceroyalty. Abolished in 1723, it was re-established in 1739 when the growing strength of English invasion of the Caribbean demanded a higher military officer nearer than Lima. The growth of population in Chile necessitated administrative changes there. In 1700 its inhabitants had reached about 80,000; by 1778 they numbered almost 200,000. To govern the area more effectively, Charles III in 1778 created the captaincy-general of Chile and reduced its territory by transferring Cuyo and Tucumán to Buenos Aires.

In La Plata. The most striking administrative reform, however, was the creation of the viceroyalty of Buenos Aires. In 1766 Charles III took the first steps toward this end when he authorized the governor of

Buenos Aires to alminister all the territory from Banda Oriental (Uruguay) southward to Cape Horn. When war broke out with Portugal in 1776, he ordered the establishment of the viceroyalty itself. To it he gave power to govern Paraguay, Santa Cruz de la Sierra, Potosí, Charcas, Tucumán, and Cuyo. Pedro Ceballos arrived as the first viceroy and captain-general as well as the president of the *audiencia* of La Plata. In the interior the viceroy organized the vast spaces of Argentina into provinces, made settlements on the Patagonian coast, and brought the Falkland Islands under his authority. Six years later in 1782, to make administration more effective, the king established the intendant system, with seven intendancies in La Plata. These changes came none too soon for the defense of the area. Portugal, threatening invasion of La Plata, found Ceballos more than a match. He became known as the "terror of the Portuguese."

Part III. RIVALRY OF SPAIN AND PORTUGAL IN LA PLATA, 1600–1777

Origin. The expansion of activity by the Portuguese slave raiders from São Paulo carried Portugal's power to the very borders of Spanish Paraguay by the end of the sixteenth century. After 1609 the Jesuits, who established their missions along the Paraná River and east of the Uruguay, took up the struggle against invasion. By 1642 their armed mission Indians had successfully stemmed the tide of Portuguese slave raiding. War in the area was succeeded by contraband trade with the Paulistas. Both Asunción and Buenos Aires, forbidden to use the Río de la Plata and forced to buy the high-priced goods from Lima, sought cheaper articles smuggled in from Brazil. This pattern of war and trade repeated itself farther south at the mouth of the Río de la Plata. There Portuguese traders sold their contraband directly to Creole merchants in Buenos Aires. To support this expansion, Portugal in 1680 founded a fort, Colonia do Sacramento, opposite Buenos Aires. This established Portugal's first claim to the east bank of the Río de la Plata (Banda Oriental).

Eighteenth Century Rivalry. Spanish reaction to this invasion was immediate. Governor José Garro attacked the post on order from Lima and quickly captured it. But in Europe, England brought pressure upon Spain to restore the settlement. Twenty years later the treaty of 1701 recognized Portuguese ownership of Colonia. In 1702, when the War of the Spanish Succession broke out, with Portugal allied to England, the governor of Buenos Aires again captured Colonia. By the Treaty of

Utrecht in 1713 England won valuable commercial concessions from Spain. Among these was the re-cession of Colonia to Portugal, for by that date England was supplying most of the merchandise carried by Portugal to her colonies. In return, however, Portugal recognized Spanish claims to the territory of the missions along the Uruguay River.

Founding of Montevideo. To offset her loss of Colonia, Spain founded in 1723–1726 Montevideo, where a small colony of Canary Islanders had already established themselves. To the new settlers Governor Bruno Zabala gave generous grants of land, together with 200 head of cattle and 100 head of sheep. Montevideo established its *cabildo* or town government. In the interior, gauchos, cattle and landowners infiltrated across the Uruguay River from the pampas to expand Spain's claims. They slowly exterminated the cannibalistic Churrúa Indians, established cattle ranges, and built their haciendas. Trade restrictions, however, slowed the growth of the colony.

Colonia, ideally situated between the new settlement and Buenos Aires, prospered on its contraband trade. In 1735, when war broke out anew between Spain and Portugal, Governor Miguel de Salcedo seized the Portuguese post. But once again England with France's aid interceded and saved the settlement for Portugal in the treaty of 1737.

Spanish Occupation of Banda Oriental. In the next twenty years La Plata had assumed vital strategic and economic significance for Spain. Smuggling operations from Colonia by both British and Portuguese traders had reduced drastically the royal income and stirred dissatisfaction among the Creoles of Buenos Aires. To meet this threat, as we have seen, Charles III created the viceroyalty of La Plata in 1776 and placed strong military forces there under Pedro Ceballos. In that same year war broke out between the two powers. Ceballos in 1777, with an army of 9,000 men, landed at Montevideo, whence he forced Colonia into surrender after a two months' siege. Portugal, recognizing the hopelessness of the struggle, agreed on October 1, 1777, to the Treaty of San Ildefonso. Its terms transferred Colonia to Spain, permitted Portuguese to remain there who wished to do so, provided for the drawing of boundaries between Brazil and Banda Oriental, and prohibited contraband trade. The latter provision was given effective force when in 1778 Spain opened Montevideo and Buenos Aires to free trade with Spain and her colonies.

Spain blocked Portugal from La Plata. Her opening of the ports to trade gave impetus to the growth of the two cities after decades of stagnation. In this new freedom sentiments of nationalism emerged which enabled Buenos Aires to resist English invasion in 1808 and prepared the colony for its later role in the movement for independence.

South America at the End of the Eighteenth Century. By the end of the eighteenth century the trend of events indicated clearly the decline of Spanish power. The exploitation of the Indians in the mines, factories, and fields had fixed among them a strong tradition of revolt. The monopoly of office and trade by Spaniards stirred revolutionary feelings among American-born Spaniards. Their reaction to trade restrictions was widespread smuggling of foreign goods along the west coast, in Venezuela, and in La Plata. The resulting loss of income to the monarchy forced the commercial reforms under Charles III. The Regulation of 1778, which opened both Montevideo and Buenos Aires, was followed in 1784 with a liberalized code permitting the entrance of foreign goods and the importation of Spanish wines and manufactures. Although the removal of these historic impediments promptly diverted the wealth of Upper Peru (Charcas) from Lima, the opening of the ports on the west coast rapidly increased Peru's trade with the homeland and the neighboring colonies. Between 1785 and 1789 imports from Spain exceeded $42,000,000, while exports to the peninsula reached almost $36,000,000. The colonies adjoining Peru sent her a variety of products. Chile exported wheat, hides, tallow, and copper; Paraguay, maté and tobacco; New Granada, cocoa and coffee. Peru returned textiles, rice, sugar, gold, and silver.

In spite of the obvious success of free trade, Spain continued many of her controls and monopolies which antagonized the colonies. Limitations upon agriculture in Peru prevented the cultivation of cocoa and the vine for the manufacture of wine. Wheat production suffered from a variety of restrictions. Royal monopolies governing the production of alcoholic liquors in Ecuador produced a serious revolt in the capital, Quito. There Creoles and *mestizos* alike demanded the expulsion of all Spaniards from the city. In 1785 resentment flared in Peru when Charles III granted a monopoly to the Philippine Company over trade with the East Indies. The effects were evident in the rapid growth of contraband after 1790. The Nootka Sound Convention of that year, permitting English ships to navigate within ten leagues of the Spanish coast, opened the door wide to smuggling. Travelers reported large amounts of foreign wares along the west coast. English products were in common usage; luxury goods came from France, Italy, and the German states as well as from Spain.

The reforms in trade introduced by Spain in South America but whetted the appetite for other freedoms. The American colonies were equally antagonized by restrictions on the mind. Free trade, in fact, had brought in contraband literature. Evidence of ferment appeared in the demands for political reform and even independence in the sentiments for a republic expressed in the *Comunero* revolt in New Granada. Similar ideas appeared in Chile, where in 1780–1781 a conspiracy reflected the opposition to increased taxation, the influence of the revolt of the English colonies in North America, and the ideas of French philosophers. There José Antonio Rojas and two Frenchmen, Antonio Barney and Antoine Gramuset, planned a liberal republic. Writing to the Spanish king, they politely informed him that Chile was to become an independent state. But a traitor in their midst betrayed them to the regent in Santiago, who quietly arrested the conspirators and sent them to Peru for trial.

The Spanish reaction after the Tupac and *Comunero* revolts was the banning of all political literature from entering the South American provinces and the suppression or burning of books believed to have revolutionary doctrines. In Peru, in accord with a royal order of 1785, Viceroy Teodoro de Croix collected and burned the works of French, English, and Italian philosophers, notably those of Montaigne, Machiavelli, Locke, Voltaire, the *Encyclopedia,* and others. Libraries, public and private, were searched for suspected literature, while the Inquisition was called upon to prevent the importation of books not previously approved.

This decline of Spanish power in South America had its parallel after 1789 in her North American colonies. There rivalry with England and France added their weight to the difficulties of internal discontent and administration.

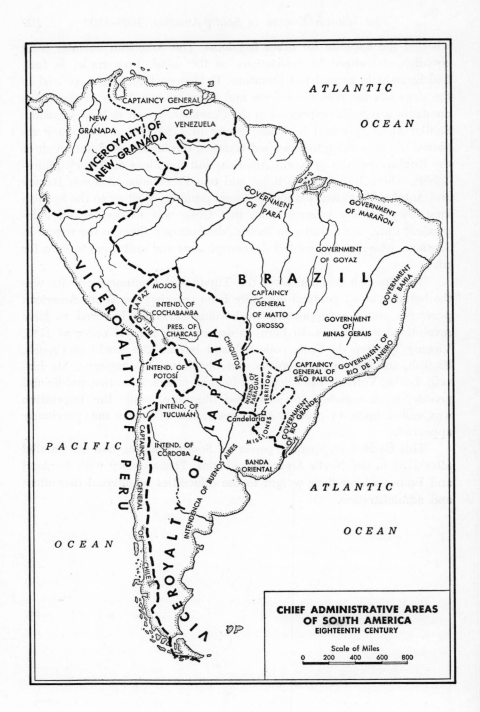

ATLANTIC

OCEAN

CAPTAINCY GENERAL
OF
VENEZUELA

NEW
GRANADA

VICEROYALTY OF
NEW GRANADA

GOVERNMENT
OF PARÁ

GOVERNMENT
OF MARAÑON

GOVERNMENT
OF GOYAZ

B R A Z I L

GOVERNMENT
OF BAHIA

MOJOS

LA PAZ

INTEND. OF
COCHABAMBA

CAPTAINCY
GENERAL
OF MATTO
GROSSO

GOVERNMENT
OF
MINAS GERAIS

PRES. OF
CHARCAS

VICEROYALTY

CHIQUITOS

OF

INTEND. OF
POTOSÍ

LA PLATA

CAPTAINCY
GENERAL OF
SÃO PAULO

GOVERNMENT OF
RIO DE JANEIRO

INTEND. OF
TUCUMÁN

INTEND. OF PARAGUAY

MISSIONES TERRITORY

GOVERNMENT
OF RIO GRANDE

Candelaria

PACIFIC

INTEND. OF
CÓRDOBA

VICEROYALTY

BANDA
ORIENTAL

ATLANTIC

CAPTAINCY GENERAL OF CHILE

INTENDENCIA OF BUENOS AIRES

OCEAN

OF PERU

OCEAN

OCEAN

**CHIEF ADMINISTRATIVE AREAS
OF SOUTH AMERICA**
EIGHTEENTH CENTURY

Scale of Miles

0   200   400   600   800

Chapter IX

THE SPANISH EMPIRE: REORGANIZATION, EXPANSION, AND DECLINE, 1763-1808

Part I. REORGANIZATION

Introduction. Between 1763 and 1789 the Spanish empire in North America expanded in territory and power. Various factors brought about this sudden growth. From the results of the Seven Years' War, Spain knew from her long rivalry with Britain that the latter, dissatisfied with acquiring only half of the French possessions, would soon threaten her own. For this reason the Spanish monarchy, in close cooperation with French advisers, launched an energetic program of expansion and reorganization of her empire, most particularly in North America where danger of British attack was greatest.

After 1789 the French Revolution in Europe, the rise of British industrialism, and the expansion of the United States toward Florida and the Gulf region weakened Spain's imperial power in the New World. Her career during the entire period, 1763–1808, can best be studied under three main phases: (1) the reorganization of the empire, with special emphasis upon North America; (2) the expansion of imperial frontiers; (3) the decline of the empire after 1789.

Reorganization and Reforms of Charles III. During the critical years of the Seven Years' War, Charles III ascended the throne in 1759 and ruled until 1788. Aware of the shortcomings of the empire, and advised by Frenchmen embittered by the losses of the Seven Years' War, Charles III began the overhauling of his empire, precedent for which was in the piecemeal reforms of his Bourbon predecessors. Pre-eminent in his considerations was the need of increasing the income of the royal treasury. Preparation for possible attack by the British demanded military reorganization. Administrative evils, threats of revolution, and declining trade dictated reforms. In carrying these out, he centralized his administration and created new institutions.

Reform in Trade Policy. To balance his budget Charles III opened the ports of the colonies to free trade with any of the ports of Spain. Begun first in the West Indies in 1765, the policy was extended to South America in 1775–1781, to Louisiana in 1768, and to Campeche in 1770. As the benefits became apparent, royal decrees in 1776–1777 included New Granada. In 1778 the famous *Reglamento* of that year threw open virtually the whole empire to freer trade with the leading ports of Spain. Important exceptions were Venezuela and New Spain, which were held under rigid control until 1789 when they, too, were opened.

The results were astounding. Exports from Spain increased in the thirteen years from 1765 to 1778 by some 300 per cent. By the beginning of the nineteenth century the yearly average revenues had almost doubled. Those of New Spain increased from 6,000,000 to 20,000,000 pesos in 1778–1798. All major aspects of the mercantile system disappeared. Fleet convoys by galleons had virtually ended by 1748, though irregular sailings continued until 1789. The House of Trade was abolished in 1790. On the other hand, the *Consulados* or merchant guilds assumed a new importance in local control over commercial affairs. One result the monarchy did not anticipate. The taste of freedom, implicit in free trade, nourished revolutionary aspirations for complete independence.

Military Reforms. A second major aspect of the reforms of Charles III was military reorganization. The plan here involved strengthening the fortifications of the leading colonial ports. These fixed defenses were in turn supported by the creation of colonial armies. The latter, composed of regular troops, were stationed permanently in the colonies, with some units sent back and forth from Spain on a rotation basis. But the greatest dependence was put upon the rehabilitation of the militia organizations in the colonies themselves. Something of a precedent had been set in 1761 by Viceroy Manuel de Amat y Junient of Peru, who created, when Spain entered the Seven Years' War, a militia troop in every major province of the viceroyalty. In addition he improved the defenses of Valparaíso, Valdivia, Chilöe, Guayaquil, and Panama. However, the plan after the war had its first application in Cuba, where Spain established the captaincy-general of Havana in 1764. She also increased the size of the army in Cuba, strengthened the defenses of Moro Castle, and enlarged the naval forces. In Mexico she sent a high army officer, Juan de Villalba y Angulo, who reorganized the army and militia system. These reforms were to pay off handsomely later in the war against England.

The Intendant System. A more general administrative reform was the intendant system. Set up under a series of decrees between 1764 and 1789 throughout the empire, it, too, began in Cuba in 1764. Its primary object was to do away with friction between officials and concentrate authority of the intendant principally in two departments, finance and war, although the Department of Justice and Police was also under his administration. Broadly, the intendant system was to assist the viceroy in the collection of revenues and administration of justice and relieve him of many details of administration. In operation it replaced the old system of tax collection through *alcalde mayores* and *corregidores* with subdelegates of the intendants. Specifically, this reform ended the *encomienda* system in the colonies. The viceroy, thus relieved, could concentrate his main efforts upon the military protection of the colonies. The intendants, however, did have certain military powers in their areas, providing funds, clothing, and shelter for troops, their transportation from one province to another, the holding of reviews, and making recommendations for promotions. The empire was eventually divided into these new administrative areas. New Spain had twelve intendancies; La Plata, seven, besides the three provinces and the presidency of Charcas; Peru, eight; and Chile, two.

José de Gálvez, Visitor-General of New Spain. To effect these reforms in New Spain, the richest and most exposed colony to British attack from Florida, Charles III dispatched José de Gálvez in 1765. Gálvez, one of the great figures Spain sent to the New World in the late eighteenth century, rose from the humble station of shepherd boy to the rank of Marqués through sheer ability and his achievements. Gálvez' chief economic and administrative measures for the rehabilitation of New Spain were the centralizatiton of the tax collection system, the establishment of a tobacco monopoly, and the improvement of administration in the lower ranks of the bureaucracy, particularly among tax collectors at the ports. Having significance as a means of increasing funds, effect was given by Gálvez to the order of Charles III to expel the Jesuits from New Spain.

The visitor-general's most far-reaching reforms, however, were in defense of the viceroyalty: the reorganization of the northern frontier to ward off Indian attack, the colonization of California, and the occupation of Louisiana.

The Defense of the Northern Frontier of New Spain. Indian attack on the frontier in the north from Texas to Sonora made reorganization of its defenses imperative after 1763. For more than fifty years the Apaches of the Plains had steadily increased the destructiveness of their attacks upon the Spanish frontier settlements. Being themselves driven from their lands by the Comanches pressing upon them from the rear, they had little alternative. After the middle of the century, the Spaniards found themselves abandoning mines, towns, cattle ranges, and highways to escape unending Apache raids. In New Vizcaya alone in a period of five years, over 1,800 persons were murdered or captured, 116 haciendas and ranches abandoned, and more than 68,000 head of livestock stolen. Spain faced either a complete collapse of her northern frontier or working out a comprehensive program of defense.

The acquisition of all the land west of the Mississippi as a result of the Seven Years' War carried with it all the Indian tribes previously allied with France. This new burden was added to the one the Spaniards already had in the north. Fortunately, Spain secured the services of the French Indian agents to win the allegiance of the new tribes to the Spanish crown. Outstanding in this work was Athanase de Meziérès, well known to the Indians in east Texas and along the Red River. Between 1768 and 1780 de Meziérès tied these Indians to Spain, made treaties with the Comanches on the Red River, reinforced the defenses of Louisiana, and prevented English traders from penetrating beyond the Mississippi, except in a few instances. The control of the Indians farther north fell under the direction of the governor of Louisiana and his representative in St. Louis.

The more immediate problem was defense against the Apache who spanned a vast area in the great arc from west Texas around to Arizona. The missions and settlements of Texas, New Mexico, Coahuila, New Vizcaya, and Sonora all came within range of their invasions. Gálvez, after examining this problem with the viceroy of Mexico, the Marqués de Croix, dispatched the Marqués de Rubí in 1766 to study the frontier and make recommendations for its defense.

Rubí made an intensive investigation from San Antonio in Texas to Tucson in Sonora during the next two years. His principal recommendations were to relocate the line of presidios across northern Mexico to block at strategic points the entry of the Plains Indians into the provinces, and to develop the local defenses of Texas and New Mexico which lay beyond the main line of the frontier. To carry out this work, Viceroy Antonio de Bucareli, who had succeeded Croix, sent Don Hugo

Oconor. For more than four years from 1772 to 1776, Oconor campaigned against the Indians and relocated a number of the presidios. But the Indians, too numerous for his limited forces, pulverized almost at will the frontier settlements.

Teodoro de Croix. Back in Spain as Minister of the Indies, Gálvez studied these reports from Oconor and Bucareli and recognized the need for more drastic measures. On his recommendation, accordingly, Charles III in 1776 authorized the division of the viceroyalty of New Spain into two administrative units. The viceroy was to continue in his office at Mexico City and govern New Spain with the exception of the northern provinces. These, including Sonora, New Vizcaya, Coahuila, New León, Texas, and New Mexico were made into a military command called the commandancy-general of New Spain, headed by an official with the rank of commander-general. To this office Charles III appointed another of his very able officials, Teodoro de Croix, who served as commander-general from 1776 to 1783.

Croix succeeded in stabilizing the frontier. Relocating the presidios at more strategic points than those selected by Oconor and backing them up with military settlements, he provided a line of effective defense. To control Apache attack upon this line, he sought next an alliance with the Comanches, who pressed upon the Apache rear. In line with this policy in Texas, de Meziéres negotiated a treaty of peace and alliance with the Comanches on the Red River. In New Mexico, Juan Bautista de Anza, governor of New Mexico, failing at first to win Comanche support, campaigned against them in 1779. In a brilliant encircling maneuver which took him north of Santa Fé around the peak, later "discovered" by Zebulon Montgomery Pike, he attacked the Comanches on the plains of eastern Colorado, near Pueblo of today. Finally, defeated and moved by admiration for the military force against them, the Comanche chiefs readily entered into an alliance with Anza against the Apaches. The success of this encirclement policy brought the Apaches from New Mexico to Coahuila to seek peace at Spanish settlements.

By 1781 the basis of an effective defense was laid. At that moment, however, several contingencies weakened and eventually destroyed the work of Croix by diverting emphasis from the frontier. He, himself, in recognition of his achievements, was promoted by the king to the office of viceroy of Peru. More seriously, Spain engaged in a war with England in the Caribbean, divested the north of troops for attack on the British possessions. Succeeding Croix were viceroys who won back the administration of the north, but, at cross-purposes, hampered the work of later commander-generals. By 1789 renewed Apache attack, now joined by the Comanches, once more brought destruction on the frontier settlements. After this the decline of this part of the empire was rapid.

Part II. THE EXPANSION OF THE EMPIRE IN NORTH AMERICA, 1769–1790

The Colonization of California, 1769–1790. The colonization of California culminated the process of Spanish expansion along the Pacific coast. Cortés took the initial step with his efforts to colonize Lower California and explore the Gulf of California. Late in the sixteenth century the needs of the Manila galleon for a stopping place on its return from the Philippines inspired plans for the occupation of the California coast. Father Kino established a base in Sonora and explored northward along the Colorado and Gila rivers. Later Jesuits continued this exploratory work in the early eighteenth century. The immediate cause that led to the colonization in 1769 was the fear of Russian occupation, a possibility that seemed implicit in the Czar's fur traders moving southward from Alaska.

Russian expansion across Siberia, initiated by Peter the Great after 1680, had reached the Pacific coast by the beginning of the eighteenth century. In 1728 Vitus Bering, a Swede in the employ of Russia, crossed the strait which bears his name to carry Russian claims into Alaska. Bering explored the Alaska coast and thus opened the way for Russian fur traders, who established stations to carry on seal hunting, fishing, and trade with the Indians. By 1763 in pursuit of seal furs Russian traders were operating off the coast of California. As Charles III studied the reports of his ambassadors in St. Petersburg and those coming from New Spain concerning Russian activities in the Pacific, he commissioned Gálvez to colonize California.

Founding of San Diego and Monterrey. In 1769 Gálvez, deciding that the time had come to head off possible Russian settlement, ordered the founding of San Diego. He himself organized the first expedition to colonize California with Captain Fernando Rivera y Moncada at the head, accompanied by the new governor, Gaspar de Portolá and Father Junípero Serra, famous later for the founding of the California coastal missions. Their objective was the occupation of San Diego Bay, whence they were to explore northward to establish a post on Monterrey Bay for the convenience of the Manila galleon. By sea two ships sailed from

Mexico with supplies. Late in June, 1769, Portolá and his small force founded San Diego, while Father Serra built the first mission.

Portolá next sought to discover a land route to Monterrey. His party, however, overshot its curving coast and accidentally discovered San Francisco bay in November, 1769. This remarkable body of water had remained hidden during the preceding centuries, for Spanish explorers had carefully avoided the rocky, fog-covered Farallone Islands that guarded its mouth. With this important news Portolá hurried back to San Diego, where he found discontent and suggestion that the whole project be abandoned. Father Serra remained adamant against retreat. Supply ships arriving at the critical moment saved the enterprise. Portolá then returned in 1770 to Monterrey, where he established a presidio, meanwhile sending the viceroy in Mexico news of the great discovery.

The Founding of San Francisco. In Mexico and in Spain the authorities recognized the importance of the discovery and immediately ordered the occupation of San Francisco bay. Far removed, almost a thousand miles, from the settled areas of New Spain, communication posed a problem. Coming forward at this critical moment were two frontier figures, Juan Bautista de Anza, a Sonora presidial captain, and Father Francisco Garcés, who offered to find a land route from Sonora to California. In Mexico City Viceroy Bucareli listened to their proposal and gave his consent. Setting out in 1774, Anza and Garcés with a small party successfully found their way around the great Mohave Desert, discovered a pass through the coastal range, and reached Monterrey.

Back in Mexico City, returned from his long trip but full of enthusiasm, Anza next proposed to lead a colony to found San Francisco. Again the viceroy, impressed with the achievement in exploration, consented. In 1774–1775, with a colony of about 250 persons, men, women, and children, together with a caravan of supplies, Anza led them over a 1,500-mile journey across deserts and mountains to deliver them safely at Monterrey. There the colony waited while Anza and others surveyed the bay region for a suitable site. On July 4, 1776, Spain founded on the tip of the peninsula the city of San Francisco with a presidio and a mission, Dolores.

With bases at San Diego and San Francisco, colonization went steadily forward. To connect these widely separated posts, Father Serra began building missions a day's journey apart. Neve, the new governor, gave aid to Father Serra and founded towns. Santa Clara was begun in 1777; San Gabriel and the pueblo of Los Angeles in 1781; a group on the Santa Barbara channel, San Buenaventura, and the presidio and mission of Santa Barbara, in 1782. Eventually twenty-one missions dotted the coast between San Diego and San Francisco.

Around the missions and towns colonists and converted Indians cultivated the land. Herds of cattle and sheep supplied tallow, candles, soap, hides, and other products. Farms produced grains in abundance; orchards of fruit trees, vineyards, and gardens thrived. By 1824 almost 90,000 Indians had been baptized and worked in and about the missions and towns of California.

Expansion Northward: the Nootka Sound Controversy. From this new base on the Pacific coast, Spanish expansion, drawn on by fear of foreign invasion, moved northward. The Russians were still a threat, but more serious from the Spanish point of view were the English invaders of the north Pacific. To ward these off Viceroy Bucareli dispatched in 1774 a sea expedition under Juan Pérez to plant Spanish claims at sixty degrees north latitude. Pérez discovered and claimed Nootka Sound at fifty degrees north, whence he returned. Bucareli immediately sent Bruno de Heceta and Juan Bodega y Quadra on a second exploring expedition. On this journey they discovered the mouth of the Columbia River in 1776, ten years before Captain Robert Gray sailed into that stream. Three years later Bodega sailed as far as sixty-one degrees north, and sighted Mount St. Elias, whose glaciers were first described on this expedition by the Italian scientist, Malaspina.

Spain's competitors under the lead of Captain James Cook invaded the northwest Pacific after 1776. In that year Cook visited the Hawaiian Islands, which he named for Lord Sandwich, and sailed for Nootka Sound. There his men traded with the Indians. A sixpenny knife in one case purchased furs which later sold in China for about $100. After Cook came Captain Robert Mears, who explored the waters of Vancouver Island. Almost at the same time New England traders, learning from John Ledyard, who had accompanied Cook, of the rich fur regions of the northwest, sent Captain John Hallet in 1784 from Boston to trade. In 1787 Robert Gray and John Kendrick explored the Oregon coast and entered the Columbia River.

Regarding these activities as violations of Spanish territory, Viceroy Conde de Revilla Gigedo in 1789 ordered the occupation and fortification of Nootka Sound. There the Spanish commander seized several British merchant ships sent to trade with the Indians and hunt seals. When the news reached England, she promptly delivered an ultimatum in May, 1790, to Spain either to release the ships or face war. At that moment Spain, in a controversy with the United States over the control of the Mississippi River, feared a British-American alliance. She accordingly agreed in 1790 to the Nootka Convention, which recognized equality of opportunity for both powers to trade with the Indians and navigate and fish in Pacific waters. English ships, however, were not to navigate within ten leagues of Spanish coasts in the New World. This event ended the expansion of Spain in the northwest and marked the beginning of her decline on the Pacific.

The Occupation of Louisiana: Antonio de Ulloa, First Governor. The acquisition of Louisiana by Spain in 1763 was a deliberate move to create a barrier against English expansion westward. France on her part ceded the territory to persuade Spain to make peace and accept the British proposal to exchange Florida for Havana. Reforms and reorganization of her empire elsewhere delayed Spain's taking possession of Louisiana immediately. When restlessness among the French Creoles warned of difficulties, she sent out Antonio de Ulloa, more famous as a scientist than as an administrator, to govern. Arrived at New Orleans on March 5, 1766, Ulloa's cold treatment of the Louisiana French stirred discontent smoldering over the transfer of the colony from France to Spain. Ulloa's restriction of trade to Spanish ports strained relations further. Believing his principal task was to strengthen the colony against the English, Ulloa garrisoned forts at Balize on the Mississippi below New Orleans and on the Red and Iberville rivers. Suddenly in 1768 the French, through their governing body, the Superior Council, expelled Ulloa without warning.

Spain, sensitive to the importance of the colony as a buffer against the English, sent out at once General Alejandro O'Reilley, who arrived on August 18, 1769. He continued Ulloa's measures to protect the colony, but won French support by using Creoles in office and observing French customs. He added to the line of forts begun by Ulloa, entrusted the control of the Indians west of the river to de Meziérès, and directed the Spanish commandant at St. Louis to license British trade in that area as a means of controlling it. The British on their part, noting the growing strength of Louisiana, dispatched 1,000 men to garrison Pensacola in 1770. Spain, disturbed by this action which England took as a result of a dispute over the Falkland Islands, ordered Governor Unzaga, who succeeded O'Reilley, to hasten the colony's defenses.

Spanish Aid to the American Revolution. When war broke out on the North American continent as a result of the revolt of the English colonies in 1776, Spain sent to Louisiana as the next governor one of the ablest figures of this period, Bernardo de Gálvez. Spain, seeing in this revolt the possible elimination of her ancient rival in the New World, directed Gálvez to give all aid to the American patriots. He ousted all English traders from Louisiana and turned the slave trade, a British monopoly, over to the French. He welcomed American privateers at New Orleans and rejected British protests. Unzaga had secretly supplied American forces which successfully held off the British at Fort Pitt and Wheeling. Gálvez continued this policy in cooperation with Oliver Pollock, the American agent at New Orleans. He made available more than $70,000 worth of arms and provisions, part of which enabled General George Rogers Clark to conquer the British posts in the Illinois country.

The British defeat at Saratoga in 1777, which brought French aid to the colonies, also influenced Spanish policy. She feared that with the defeat of England, France might resume her place as an imperial power and secure those British possessions which did not become independent. Chief among these was Florida. Consequently in 1779 Spain declared war on England for the purpose of expelling the British from the Gulf of Mexico and from the banks of the Mississippi River. To Gálvez in Louisiana fell the task of driving the British out. In 1779 he captured five English forts in the lower Mississippi area, while another Spanish expedition against St. Joseph on Lake Michigan destroyed British stores there and forced British Indian allies to remain neutral.

The Reconquest of Florida: Bernardo de Gálvez. But the main Spanish objective was the reconquest of Florida. With ample supplies pouring in from Mexico, Gálvez launched in January, 1780, a campaign to capture Mobile. With a force of 754 men and a fleet he advanced upon the British garrison. After short resistance the city fell in March, 1780. With additional reinforcements from Mexico and Havana, Gálvez next marched upon Pensacola. Here the British, aided by Indian allies, resisted longer, but in May, 1781, surrendered their entire garrison of 800 soldiers. With West Florida safely in their hands, the Spaniards now turned the flank of East Florida by the capture of New Providence in the Bahamas in 1782. Simultaneously, they sent a relief expedition to defend Central America against a planned British attack. Gálvez was now in a position to direct his main attack upon the principal base of the British in the Caribbean, Jamaica. However, in the midst of preparations for this campaign, he was forced to divert a considerable part of his army to New Granada, where the *Comunero* revolt threatened the loss of that colony. Before this action ended, an armistice terminated hostilities between Britain and Spain.

Spain's participation in the revolt of the English colonies had significant results. Her supplies aided the American conquest of the Mississippi territory held by the British; her conquest of Florida destroyed any possibility of its use as a British base against the southern colonies. However, with Britain out of North America as a competitor of Spain, the new American states were to contribute to the decline of Spanish power. Equally damaging to Spain's empire was the example of a successful revolution against a colonial power. Spain's aid in that success was to stimulate revolutionary thought in her own colonies.

Part III. THE DECLINE OF THE SPANISH EMPIRE IN NORTH AMERICA, 1798–1808

Rivalry of Spain and the United States in the Southeast. After 1783 Spain fought a losing battle in the southeast against the expanding power of the United States. The Treaty of Paris in 1783, ending the Revolutionary War, created a conflict with Spain in two realms: the navigation of the Mississippi River and the boundary of West Florida. The Paris treaty with England guaranteed forever to both Britain and the United States free and open navigation of the Mississippi River. On the question of boundaries, however, Spain's treaty with England gave Spain East Florida and recognized Spanish claims to West Florida, whose boundary had been placed at thirty-two degrees and thirty minutes north latitude. The Paris treaty between the United States and England, on the other hand, agreed that the boundary of the United States should be at thirty-one degrees, assuming England maintained possession of Florida.

While the legality of the Paris treaty was questionable on this point, the frontiersmen moved westward and southward regardless of it, as they had done in the colonial period. They gave the United States the kind of support which Spain found difficult to combat. Spain, on her part, turned to win the Indians of the southeast and use them as a buffer to the expanding Americans who coveted both Spanish and Indian lands. To give effect to her policy, Spain employed Alexander McGillivray, who commanded the support of a loose Creek confederacy. An offspring of a Scotsman and a Creek woman, McGillivray achieved his position through his mother's clan. He had served the British and went over to the Spanish because of Georgian claims to Creek lands. McGillivray wanted to form a confederacy of all the tribes with Spanish support to oppose the United States.

Spanish policy, however, had a more limited objective, simply a treaty between Spain and the Creek Nation, which Governor Miró at New Orleans achieved in the Treaty of Pensacola in 1780. Spain followed this with a commercial agreement with the Chickasaws and Choctaws, a success resulting from Creek dissatisfaction with Georgia's treaty with a small group of Creeks at Augusta, May 31, 1783, which ceded Creek lands to Georgia. The Creeks were further angered in 1785 when Georgia commissioners extracted another cession of Creek lands. Governor Miró, fearing war with the United States, refused to aid McGillivray, who planned to attack the Georgia settlers on Creek lands.

McGillivray's successful attack induced the United States to take over the ceded Creek lands from Georgia. This action won McGillivray's support, who went to New York in 1790 to sign a treaty with the United States. Under its terms Creek lands within the United States were guaranteed to the Creek Nation, McGillivray was made a brigadier-general in the United States army, and Creek trade was opened to Americans. Miró regarded this treaty with satisfaction, for in his opinion it recognized the Creek Nation in effect as a buffer between the Americans in Georgia and the Spaniards in Louisiana. However, in 1792 when Hector, Baron de Carondelet, replaced Miró, Spain adopted a new policy, namely, McGillivray's original plan of organizing the Indians into a confederacy and supplying them with arms to wage war against the United States. But this policy failed largely as a result of President Washington's energetic action in preventing speculation in Indian lands and thereby removing a cause of discontent with the United States.

Spain and the United States on the Mississippi River. Paralleling the conflict between the United States and Spain over the control of the southeastern Indians was the struggle over the navigation of the Mississippi River. Here Spain's policy was to use the control of navigation of the river as a means of strangling American expansion below the Ohio. She hoped that the settlers moving into Kentucky and Tennessee would be attracted to Spanish allegiance. To implement this policy Spain announced to the American government in 1784 her claim to exclusive rights to navigate the Mississippi and to the territory west of the Allegheny Mountains northward to the Ohio River and thence up the Mississippi River to its source. Economic interest on the Atlantic seaboard adverse to the development of the west were at the moment antagonizing the trans-Allegheny settlers. Both the Spanish edict and the eastern opposition stirred the westerners, particularly Kentuckians, to anger.

James Wilkinson, a frontier merchant with military ambitions, attempted to exploit this feeling of separatism. To Miró in New Orleans he suggested that Spain should build a Spanish party in Kentucky, stir up a revolution against the United States, and unite the new state to herself. As an alternative to that plan, he proposed that Spain encourage American immigration into Louisiana as a means of depopulating Kentucky. Spain accepted neither suggestion, but in 1788 adopted a policy of allowing American frontiersmen to use the river to New Orleans by paying a 15 per cent duty and encouraging them to immigrate by offering free land.

The new convention of 1787, which produced the Constitution of the United States, gave pause to Kentucky separatists. After the new American government was set up, Washington appointed western leaders to responsible positions. Even Wilkinson became a brigadier-general. Thus with McGillivray won over to the American side and the westerners placated by recognition, the position of Spain in the southeast weakened.

Decline of the Empire in the Southeast, 1789–1803. At this critical moment Spain found herself being driven from pillar to post by events beyond her control. In the Nootka Sound controversy in 1790, she feared a British-American alliance. At the same time the progress of the French Revolution had ruined her hopes of a renewal of the compact between the royal houses of France and Spain. Profoundly disturbed by the spread of revolutionary ideas in her colonies, she turned in desperation to make an alliance in 1793 with her historic enemy, England, against republican France. This pact opened Louisiana to British trade. The French Republic, angered by the new agreement, sent Citizen Genêt in 1793 to the United States to undermine Spain's control in Florida. His agents in Charleston soon revived the interest of the Georgians, who planned attacks on Florida and invaded Creek lands.

As she reviewed the results of her policy, Spain abandoned the English alliance and made a separate peace at Basle with the French Republic in 1795. To ward off the rage of the British, Spain hurried to negotiate with the American envoy in Madrid, Thomas Pinckney, and thus avoid a possible British-American alliance. The resulting Treaty of San Lorenzo in 1795 conceded the two main points for which the United States had contended. First, Spain recognized the boundary of West Florida at thirty-one degrees; secondly, she opened the Mississippi River to American navigation.

Practically prostrate in this part of her empire, Spain could offer no serious defense when Napoleon struck at her possession of the Mississippi Valley in 1800 and forced her to sign the Treaty of San Ildefonso.

Equally helpless three years later in 1803, she could do no more than protest when Napoleon ceded the Louisiana Territory to the United States. Florida alone remained, but that, too, fell (1821) in the path of American expansion when the movement for independence in all of her colonies ended her empire in the New World.

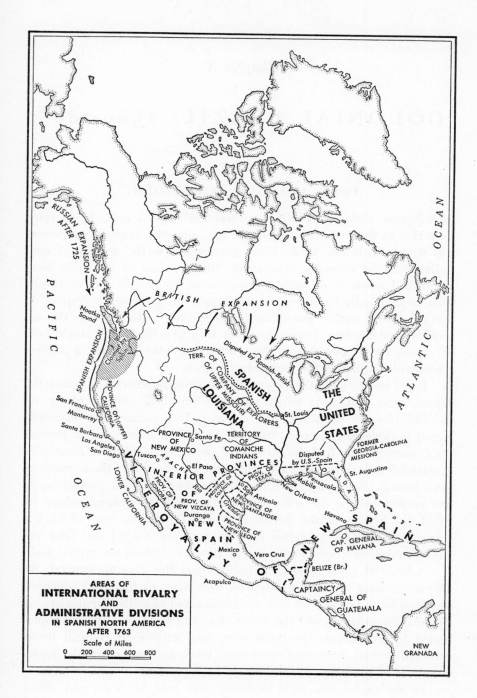

RUSSIAN EXPANSION AFTER 1725

PACIFIC OCEAN

Nootka Sound

SPANISH EXPANSION

PROVINCE OF (UPPER) CALIFORNIA

San Francisco
Monterrey
Santa Barbara
Los Angeles
San Diego

Tuscon

APACHE

VICEROYALTY

LOWER CALIFORNIA

PROV. OF SONORA

INTERIOR PROVINCES

PROV. OF NEW VIZCAYA
Durango

NEW

Mexico

Acapulco

Vera Cruz

BRITISH   EXPANSION

Disputed by Spanish-British

TERR. OF COMPANY OF UPPER MISSOURI EXPLORERS

SPANISH

LOUISIANA

St. Louis

THE UNITED STATES

PROVINCE OF NEW MEXICO   Santa Fe

TERRITORY OF COMANCHE INDIANS

El Paso

Rio Grande

PROVINCE OF COAHUILA

PROV. OF TEXAS

San Antonio

PROVINCE OF NEW SANTANDER

PROVINCE OF NEW LEON

OF

SPAIN

Disputed by U.S.-Spain

FLORIDA

Pensacola
Mobile
New Orleans
St. Augustine

FORMER GEORGIA-CAROLINA MISSIONS

Havana

NEW   SPAIN

CAP. GENERAL OF HAVANA

BELIZE (Br.)

CAPTAINCY GENERAL OF GUATEMALA

ATLANTIC OCEAN

NEW GRANADA

AREAS OF
INTERNATIONAL RIVALRY
AND
ADMINISTRATIVE DIVISIONS
IN SPANISH NORTH AMERICA
AFTER 1763

Scale of Miles
0   200   400   600   800

Chapter X

COLONIAL BRAZIL: 1580-1808

Part I. COLONIAL GOVERNMENT

Introduction. Colonial Brazilian government differed radically in spirit from that in the Spanish colonies. In the latter the central government was strong; in Brazil, weak. Local government in the absence of centralized control naturally dominated. This freedom of action in local affairs had much to do with a comparative absence of violent revolts such as frequently characterized the history of the Spanish empire. At the same time native Brazilians had opportunity to develop the resources of the colony largely for their own benefit. In the single field of mining development did the Portuguese king exercise a control comparable to that of the monarchs of Spain.

Royal Institutions. The powers of the governor-general at Bahia, the capital, were ample—on paper. He was the chief military officer responsible for the defense of the colonies. This authority he exercised largely in protecting the coast from pirates and smugglers. In the interior the captain-general had the theoretical power to require the *donatários* to establish militia organizations and aid in the defense of the captaincies from Indian attack and slave revolt. His principal civil powers made him responsible for the collection of taxes and for curbing, where he could, the actions of the governors of the captaincies into which the colony was divided. In actual fact the governor-general and later the viceroys rarely exercised any important power outside of the capital itself.

A body of royal officials at Bahia aided the governor-general. An attorney-general *(ouvidor geral)* took over most of the legal functions exercised by the *donatários* and was empowered to settle disputes arising between the colonists and the *donatários*. The royal treasury was represented by a treasurer *(provedor mor)* who supervised colonial trade, collected custom duties and other royal taxes, and supervised the representatives of the office established in the captaincies.

In the captaincies royal authority was held by a judicial officer *(ouvidor)* with wide powers over civil, criminal, and military affairs. As such he organized a royal police to maintain order in the districts of the captaincies.

Municipalities. While these royal institutions existed, Portugal's early neglect of the colony, the powers granted to the original *donatários*, and the vast unconnected spaces of Brazil made captaincies and municipalities the governing force. The royal officials in the captaincies fell under the domination of the Brazilian *capitão môr*, captain-major, while the municipalities exercised authority over vast areas. The municipalities had their center of authority in a town council called the *senado da câmara*. This institution was far from a democratic one. Usually the officials in it were selected from the wealthy families, landowners, merchants, and rich traders. Its members were either elected, appointed to office for life, or held office as a hereditary right. The *câmaras* exercised legislative and executive authority. The latter functioned through the office of the *capitão môr*, whose powers will be discussed below.

The *câmaras* legislated to protect the interests of its members. They levied taxes and custom duties; directed the construction of roads, public buildings, and bridges; raised militia; along the coast provided for naval defense; and fixed regulations for ports and shipping and for governing guilds of workers in towns and cities. Unlike the Spanish municipalities, the Brazilian towns maintained the right to keep a representative in Lisbon who effectively protected their interests. Upon the municipality, too, rather than upon the king of Portugal, the church depended for its principal support. Municipalities contributed to the establishment of hospitals, orphanages, churches, cathedrals, and monasteries. In this arrangement the lower clergy suffered and were often reduced to begging in the streets for a living. Inevitably, the bishops in the cities became powerful figures and a source of occasional conflict between the church and the municipalities.

The Capitão Môr. The governors of the captaincies appointed as their aides an official, the *capitão môr* or captain-major, a term which descended from the title of the *donatário* conferred with the founding of the *capitania* system in the sixteenth century. This official became the most powerful figure in colonial local government. Usually the *capitão môr* was selected from one of the leading families in the district, whether a captaincy or a municipality. Over the population he exercised a despotic power from which there was usually no appeal. The *capitão môr* enforced laws, organized militias, intervened in judicial processes, and with this semimilitary authority he frequently abused and oppressed his enemies. Many of these officials took advantage of their position to enlarge their landed properties, or, if merchants, to extend their monopoly on trade, or secure lucrative posts in the governments of the captaincies. After 1750, when Portugal relied upon its own colonials in her struggle with Spain in La Plata, the office of *capitão môr* was held by more Brazilians than Portuguese. For this reason the institution became firmly imbedded among the wealthy families who later dominated Brazilian national history.

Though the *capitão môr* has been condemned by some authorities in Brazilian history as a tyrant, not all were of that character. Mawe describes the *capitão môr* at St. José (São Paulo province) as one "who lives in a princely style, and possesses a very considerable property, which he diffuses with great public spirit and liberality."

This dominance of local colonial government by Brazilians allowed a freedom of action in Brazil more parallel to that enjoyed by the English colonists in North American than that of the regimented life of the neighboring Spanish colonies. It is certain, in any event, that rugged, individualistic Brazilians led the colony's expansion into the interior.

Part II.   THE EXPANSION OF BRAZIL: 1580–1750

Expansion in the North, 1580–1713. The transfer of Brazil to Spain in 1580 exposed the colony to renewed foreign attack. The French, with a century of interest in Brazil, seized upon the northern coast to colonize. Previous to this date French corsairs raided in these northern waters and carried on trade between the Amazonian coast and France. To ward them off Portugal sent expeditions northward after 1584 which fixed its power in Ceará, Rio Grande do Norte, and Parahyba. But, hampered at home by the Spanish occupation, the Portuguese saw in 1610 the French government grant to Sieur de la Ravadière a strip of territory along the coast south of the Amazon. In 1612 Ravadière settled his colony on the island of Marajó at the mouth of the Amazon and explored for better lands in the interior. However, the Portuguese, aided by Brazilians and Indians, promptly attacked the settlement, which, receiving no reinforcements, withdrew in 1614. Opposite the island the Portuguese then founded Santa Maria da Belém in 1616. Five years later in 1621 Portugal created the captaincy-general of Maranhão, directly dependent upon Lisbon rather than Bahia.

These steps marked the beginning of Portugal's claim to the Amazon

Valley and the process of pushing back the line of demarcation. The Portuguese thereafter turned inland along the Amazon itself, took possession, and explored the rivers flowing into that great stream. In 1637 Pedro Teixeira pushed up the Amazon all the way to Quito and returned with valuable information that stirred hopes of finding silver and gold in the interior. While this vision did not materialize, the Portuguese and Brazilians soon found among the Indians valuable products, such as cocoa, vanilla, and cinnamon. New interests quickly grew. Slavers raided Indian towns to supply coastal plantations. Jesuits followed to protect the natives and to found missions.

The Dutch Occupation, 1621–1661. Portuguese expansion toward the north suffered an interruption when the Dutch seized the coastline from Bahia northward to their possessions in the Guianas. The origin of this interest in Brazil stemmed from Dutch antagonism to Spain and visions of profits comparable to those Holland derived from her Oriental ventures. There the Dutch East India Company had successfully raided the Portuguese African posts and laid the basis for Holland's empire in the East Indies. After 1600 the Dutch turned their eyes to the New World to send Henry Hudson to explore and take possession of what became New Amsterdam on the Hudson River. Other Dutch traders and buccaneers invaded Spain's possessions in the Caribbean and had a post on the Guiana coast as early as 1613. Encouraged by these events, the Estates-General authorized in 1621 the formation of the Dutch West India Company to operate in the New World. With broad powers to build forts, make treaties with the natives, develop trade with South America, and raid Spanish shipping, the company fixed upon the bulge of Brazil as the most suitable base to carry on the work.

The Dutch opened their attack in 1624 with the capture of Bahia, but lost it in the next year. In 1627 they recaptured Bahia and paved the way for the occupation of Pernambuco in 1630. When at the end of a seven years' war the Dutch had firmly established themselves, Holland sent over Prince Maurice of Nassau to govern (1637). Maurice soon broadened the Dutch power to extend from Bahia to the Marañon River. In this territory he made trade free, encouraged agricultural development, restored Brazilian families to the possession of their properties, permitted freedom of religion, and even attempted to set up a representative government. These sensible efforts fell athwart the greedy interests of the company, the ambitions of Portugal to free itself from Spain, and those of the native Brazilians to oust the Dutch from their homeland.

Juan Fernández de Vieira. In 1640 when a nationalist movement in Portugal overthrew Spanish control, the new monarch of the Braganza line, Dom João IV, agreed by treaty as a means of strengthening home defenses to recognize Holland's conquests in Brazil. This disregard of Brazil's rights, combined with antagonism to Dutch Protestantism and the native Brazilian merchants' resentment toward the Dutch monopoly of trade and commerce, sparked a revolution under the leadership of Juan Fernández de Vieira in Pernambuco. The Dutch in turn were weakened by the resignation of Prince Maurice, who opposed the home policy of unrelieved exploitation of the colony in favor of high profits. For the next fourteen years, Vieira carried on incessant guerrilla warfare. By 1654 Holland, prostrated by its larger conflict with Britain under Cromwell, gave way in Brazil before the attacks of Vieira and withdrew from most of Pernambuco. Assuming the governorship, Vieira and his followers resisted all Dutch efforts to dislodge him. By 1661 Holland, in a new treaty with Portugal, agreed to withdraw all Dutch claims to Brazil. The success of the native Brazilians against the Dutch intensified local patriotism in the north. Henceforward they continued to show their aggressive and independent spirit.

The Palmares Republic, 1633–1695. Having warded off the Dutch danger to their trade and won back their lands, the Brazilians of Pernambuco returned with greater energy to develop their sugar plantations. However, the planters discovered that in the confusion attendant upon the Dutch occupation, many Negroes had escaped from the plantations into the interior of Pernambuco. There by 1633 several thousand slaves had established settlements, attracted their fellows in slavery, and raided Portuguese towns. In 1650 they had organized themselves into a loose confederation called the Palmares Republic. The Negroes elected a head of the state, set up a judicial system, and allotted lands. Between raids they carried on trade with neighboring Indian settlements and the Portuguese along the coast.

By 1675 the Portuguese launched a series of campaigns to destroy this republic now considered a threat to their safety. In defense the Negroes erected fortifications, trained an army of some 10,000 men, and defeated the initial steps to oust them. But the wars were so profitable from the capture and sale of slaves that the Portuguese dragged them out for more than twenty years. Finally, in 1695 an army of 6,000 men, reinforced with Paulistas from southern Brazil, ended this interesting Negro experiment in government. At the collapse thousands of Negroes preferred suicide rather than return to slavery.

Monopolies, Revolts, and Expansion in the North, 1678–1718. Meanwhile, in the midst of this struggle to destroy the republic, the chief industry, sugar, in the north rapidly declined, replaced by the growing exports of the European colonies in the Caribbean. To rehabilitate her weakened economy, Portugal had recourse to a device already well tested by her competitors—the monopoly company. The first of these, chartered in 1649 under the influence of Father Antonio Vieira, a Jesuit, was the Brazil Company (Companhia do Brasil). Its objective was to end the advantages secured by the Dutch in northern Brazil during their occupation. The company enjoyed a monopoly on fish, wine, oil, lumber, brazilwood, and flour. The only foreign merchandise to go to the colony had to be carried in the company's two fleets which sailed each year. British goods under a commercial agreement soon replaced those of the Dutch.

In Brazil the decline of sugar production in the face of Caribbean competition produced growing discontent. The home government added to Brazil's declining prosperity when it authorized a group of Portuguese capitalists to organize the Company of Maranhão. Its monopoly over the trade of Maranhão struck a blow at local control and raised the price of slaves, 500 of whom it had the right to import annually. Discontent increased when the Jesuits, who monopolized Indian labor on the mission lands, further reduced the supply of slaves. In desperation the planters, led by Manoel Beckman, rose against the monopoly in 1684. Although Beckman was captured and executed, the event forced the abolition of the company. Ten years later in 1694, with conditions still unimproved in the north, the *câmaras* there joined with those in the south to protest and eventually force the Portuguese government to take over the Company of Brazil in 1694. It remained a government enterprise until 1720 and greatly increased the revenues of the crown.

The War of the Mascates. The continued decline of sugar exports, Portuguese monopoly on trade, high prices for imported goods, and the collection of taxes in the northern captaincies produced a repetition of the Beckman revolt in 1710. In that year the native Brazilians of Olinda, the original capital of Pernambuco, made desperate by their growing bankruptcy, their indebtedness to the Portuguese merchants of Recife, and resentful of the latter's prosperity, resisted the efforts of the home government to elevate Recife to the rank of Villa. Their action plunged the entire province into a civil war, the War of the Mascates, 1710–1711, in which the Brazilian planters were defeated a second time. Thereafter Recife, with a more solid economic base in her coastal trade, replaced the decaying sugar capital at Olinda.

Portugal in the Amazon Basin. Trade and opposition to Jesuit control of the Indians gave impetus to Portuguese expansion into the Amazonian basin and northward to the territory claimed by France as Guiana. Attacks upon the Jesuits after the Beckman revolt forced them deeper into the Amazonian territory. Strengthening Portugal's claims there was the establishment in Pernambuco in 1676 of a new bishopric which supported the Amazonian missions. Indicative also of this growth in the valley was the founding of Manaus on the great river in the late seventeenth century as the result of trading activity. South of the river another advance took place after the War of the Mascates in 1711, when Pernambuco plantation owners, abandoning their holdings because of declining prices, moved into the interior. Preceded by slave raiders the planters and other settlers established Piauhy in 1718. Trade, colonization, and Jesuit missions in the Amazon region had provided by 1715 a firm basis for Portugal's hold on the great river valley. Her claims received their first international recognition and carried the expansion of Brazil northward beyond the Amazon in 1715 when, in the Treaty of Utrecht, France and Portugal fixed on the Oyapoc River as the boundary between French Guiana and Brazil.

Part III.　EXPANSION IN THE SOUTH, 1580–1763

Paulista Expansion. In the seventeenth century, Brazilians and Portuguese, driving both the French and Dutch out of the north, had begun the advance into the Amazon Valley. In the same years in the south they carried on aggression from São Paulo against the neighboring Spanish colonies of La Plata. The Paulistas who became the leaders of this expansion were known under a variety of names—Paulistas, *mamelucos*, and Bandeirantes. Their striking characteristics made them easily the most dynamic group in colonial Brazil. Like their counterparts, the North American frontiersmen, the Paulistas moved westward in groups, carrying banners (whence the name Bandeirantes), accompanied by their families. Frequently they paused in their wanderings to cultivate the ground and search near-by streams for gold. Some donned Jesuit robes to lure Indians into captivity.

　　Their contributions to Brazil's development were many. As explorers they opened up trails into the interior to the headwaters of the great São Francisco River. They discovered the rich gold deposits of Minas Gerais, Goiás, and Matto Grosso. Everywhere they took with them cattle and horses to southern Brazil. Making known the good lands of the interior, some turned to agriculture to pave the way for settlers in the vast region from São Paulo to Uruguay. Politically, their expansion enabled Portugal to claim lands successfully in the south and west beyond the line of demarcation awarded to Spain.

Toward the Paraná. Spanish Jesuits, as we have seen, had built missions after 1609 among the Guaraní in the spaces east of the Paraná and Uruguay rivers. Even earlier, Portuguese Jesuits moving westward from São Paulo had begun to Christianize the Indians. Keeping step with the latter were the Paulista slave raiders. They found the missions convenient centers for capturing the helpless natives. Afterward they sold their victims to the owners of the growing coastal sugar plantations which in early days lacked sufficient labor.

By the opening of the seventeenth century the Paulistas had carried their attacks against the Spanish Jesuit reductions along the Paraná River. Between 1580 and 1640, even while Portugal and Brazil were under Spain, the Paulistas raided the Paraguayan missions. In the process whole tribes were exterminated or forced back into savagery in the forests. In 1640 the Jesuits had begun a retreat with their charges to new reductions in southeastern Paraguay. Here, armed by the Paraguayan authorities, the mission Indians in 1642 decisively defeated the Paulistas. Halted, the Bandeirantes turned to smuggling, an activity welcomed by the Jesuits and the Indians suffering from the high prices of Spanish goods imported from Lima.

Toward La Plata. South of São Paulo the Bandeirantes pushed into the wide open spaces of the Paraná pine forests and across the rolling prairies of Rio Grande do Sul. There they established permanent homes and built their great country houses in the midst of their growing cattle herds. Their hides and tallow they sent to coastal towns for export. South of São Paulo along the coast, fine lands offered easy cultivation of sugar, fruits, manioc, olive, and orange orchards. Towns sprang up which exported the tall Paraná pine for shipbuilding; cattle, hides, and tallow from the interior; and fish from whaling stations. Santa Catharina, settled in 1651, was enlarged by a colony from the Azores in 1693. Laguna was founded in 1654; Porto Alegre in 1743; and far to the south, Rio Grande in 1737.

Commercial expansion by sea carried Portuguese traders southward to the La Plata River. By 1580 they were trading at Buenos Aires when Spain took over the Portuguese empire. In the next century contraband trade thrived on the Río de la Plata, nourished by the Spanish mercantile restrictions on the trade of Buenos Aires. By 1680 the various Portuguese trading posts along the east bank of the Río de la Plata coalesced into a colony, Colonia do Sacramento, recognized formally by Portugal in that year. In this region, the East Bank (Banda Oriental), the Spaniards, as we have seen, carried on a counteroccupation with the founding of Montevideo in 1723–1726 and an infiltration across the Uruguay River into the interior. While Spain won both Colonia and the mission area along the Uruguay River, Paulista expansion had delivered to Portugal the vast areas of present-day Santa Catharina and Rio Grande do Sul.

Governmental Changes. In recognition of the importance of this southern area, Portugal made São Paulo a captaincy-general in 1709. In 1712 the city gained the right to a *senado da câmara* to control its own municipal affairs and superseded São Vicente as the center of government. In 1739 Santa Catharina, separated from São Paulo, became a captaincy. Rio Grande do Sul likewise in 1760 was elevated from a military district into a separate state. In 1763 the Treaty of San Ildefonso returned the island of Santa Catharina off the coast of Santa Catharina to Portugal.

Part IV. EXPANSION INTO CENTRAL BRAZIL, 1580–1763

The Founding of Minas Gerais. The restless Paulistas searched for gold as well as for slaves. They made their first discovery some twenty-four miles south of São Paulo at Jaragua early in the sixteenth century. As entire tribes of Indians disappeared, slave raiding became less profitable. More and more after the middle of the seventeenth century the Paulistas turned to wash the sands of westward-flowing rivers for gold. Entering the region later known as Minas Gerais, they made their great discovery in 1693 along the Rio das Velhas, a headwater of the São Francisco River.

News of the discovery spread quickly to São Paulo, Rio de Janeiro, and northward to Bahia. A spectacular rush of Bahia prospectors, Negroes, bankrupt plantation owners, and immigrants from the coastal areas and even Portugal poured westward through the mountain passes into the valley of the São Francisco and thence southward to the gold fields. Against these invaders the Bandeirantes waged a ceaseless struggle. During the next ten years the new arrivals, or *emboabas,* as they were called, growing in numbers, dispossessed the Paulistas of their richest fields. In desperation the Paulistas declared open war in 1708. Their enemies, led by Manoel Nunna Vianna, defeated the luckless Bandeirantes and drove them out. Licking their wounds, they moved westward over the mountains to find new gold deposits in Goiás and in far-off Matto Grosso.

Diamonds. In the midst of the gold rush into Minas Gerais, the even more startling discovery of diamond fields occurred in 1725. At first their value went unnoticed. One report stated that the "pretty pebbles" found their way to Portugal, where the Dutch minister, suspecting their character, sent them to lapidaries in Holland. Another and more picturesque legend has it that these sparkling stones, used by miners in card games as counters, were recognized as diamonds by a wandering cleric who had lived in the Orient. In any event their value, soon known, launched a new rush into Minas Gerais. But the government acted quickly, declared a monopoly over the district, fenced it off, and founded Diamantina in 1730.

The Portuguese carried on gold and diamond mining with extreme inefficiency. Carts, wagons, and even wheelbarrows were unknown. Sharpened stakes and iron bars were used in place of picks, while stones served as hammers to break up the ore. All work was done by Negro and Indian slaves by hand. Their wages went to their owners, who congregated in the neighborhood of the diamond fields and lived in idleness. Naturally many of the slave owners encouraged Negroes to smuggle out the precious stones. The Negroes, hiding the stones in their curly hair, behind their ears, and between their toes, succeeded in carrying out such large numbers that one authority reports that diamonds were the most common medium of exchange in Tezuco (Diamantina). To discourage the practice, eventually the crown officials carefully supervised the diamond washings, imposed harsh punishments on Negroes detected in theft, and offered large rewards for smugglers captured at check points *(registros)* set up about the district. Smuggling of both gold and diamonds was, in fact, so extensive that in 1806 it was estimated that diamonds alone, valued at more than $2,000,000, had found their way illegally into Europe.

In spite of the losses suffered by the government, the Portuguese monarchy enjoyed a large income from the diamond and gold mines. The latter in Minas Gerais alone yielded a royal fifth from 1715 to 1771 of almost $1,000,000 annually; over the century down to 1812 the royal income from this province reached almost $69,000,000. Lesser amounts came from Matto Grosso and Goiás.

Development of Central Brazil. The discoveries of gold and diamonds had their greatest importance, however, for Brazil rather than for Portugal. Minas Gerais, Goiás, and Matto Grosso had been regions of Paulista wanderers, explorers, and Jesuit missionaries. In the wake of gold and diamond rushes cities sprang up. Ouro Preto in the vicinity of the first discoveries appeared in 1698. Villa Rica, already settled by gold hunters, was organized in 1711 as a town. Villa do Principe appeared on the map in 1715. In Matto Grosso, Cuiabá was founded in 1720. Its rich deposits by 1726 had attracted hundreds of Paulistas, who drove their cattle and slaves westward from São Paulo, a journey of more than a thousand miles. The steady production of the mines created in time the great family fortunes of the leaders of these new states.

As the population of these interior provinces continued to grow, the settlers sought outlets for exports and imports. By 1725 explorers moving northward found routes into the Amazon Valley by way of the Tapajós, Xingu, and Tocantins rivers. Supplies brought in by way of Belém over these avenues reached the settlements of Goiás and Matto Grosso. For most of Minas Gerais, however, the São Francisco became the principal highway of travel. In addition, a well-trod route ran north from Rio de Janeiro to Barbacena, where it branched off to Cuiabá far to the west and Minas Novas, founded in 1727, and other gold fields of Minas Gerais in the north.

To support the large population that poured into Minas Gerais and in smaller volume into Goiás and Matto Grosso, agriculture and cattle raising thrived. A visitor to the interior of Minas Gerais early in the nineteenth century, although he deplored the bad husbandry, noted everywhere crops of cotton, tobacco, coffee, flax, wheat, maize, grapes, vanilla, artichokes, spinach, cabbage, kidney beans, and potatoes. Keeping pace with agriculture was the phenomenal growth of the cattle industry. Along the banks of the São Francisco River grazed herds numbered in the hundreds of thousands of head. Thus when mining failed, agriculture and cattle remained the pillars of the economy of the area.

Government. Over this new rich region Portugal soon established governments. São Paulo lost its jurisdiction there in 1710 when Minas Gerais was organized in that year. Within Minas Gerais a separate jurisdiction at Diamantina was erected, placed in the late eighteenth century under an intendant with judicial authority. Other officials were an *ouvidor,* treasurer, and a *capitão môr* who commanded the troops. An administrator-general, with a number of lesser officials, looked after the recovery of the diamonds from the various deposits. Matto Grosso and Goiás were separated from São Paulo and made into new captaincies in 1744 and 1748 respectively.

Part V. THE REFORMS OF POMBAL, 1750–1777

Conditions in Portugal. By the middle of the eighteenth century the institutions of government and the main lines of Brazil's development were fixed. The discovery of the mines hastened the occupation of the interior, but did not alter the basic pattern of Brazil's colonial development. It did, however, have a revolutionary effect upon Portugal. In the early part of the century the greatly increased revenues from Brazil fell to a wastrel, John V (1706–1750). He spent them lavishly upon mistresses and the building of a palace in imitation of that of Versailles. The frivolities of his forty-odd years of government permitted the nobles and the church to reduce Portugal to a condition of feudalism.

At the same time the Portuguese merchants, suffering from the decline of the empire in Africa and the Orient, did not share in the wealth of the mines. They received a further blow to their prosperity when the Treaty of Methuen in 1703 opened Portuguese and Brazilian ports to British goods. Brazil itself paid a high price for the incapacity of its monarch. The Treaty of Methuen, allying England and Portugal, opened Portugal's colonies to French attack. In 1710 Jean Duclerc attempted to capture Rio de Janeiro. While he failed, Duquay Trouin in 1711 succeeded, sacked the capital, and held it up for ransom estimated at 20,000,000 cruzados.

When, at long last, Joseph I ascended the throne in 1750 he was determined to restore royal power. Supported by the bankrupt and discontented Portuguese middle class, he turned to the Marquis of Pombal to carry out his policy. Influenced by the ideas of the French philosophers of the Enlightenment, but ruthless in his methods, Pombal governed Portugal in effect for the entire reign of Joseph I (1750–1777). Directing his efforts first to restoring the power of the monarchy, he attacked both the nobility and the church. The most striking measure affecting the latter was the expulsion of the Jesuits both from Portugal and Brazil. For the middle class he launched a constructive program to revive Portuguese trade, eliminate the British as far as possible in Portugal's commerce, and encourage industry, agriculture, and education, particularly the founding of technical schools.

Pombal's Reforms in Brazil. The reform program in Portugal had its counterpart in Brazil under three main aspects: (1) governmental, (2) commercial, (3) social reforms.

Governmental Reforms. In a series of measures aimed at centralizing royal authority and increasing colonial revenues, Pombal made several drastic changes in Brazil's government. To reduce inefficiency and corruption he ended the practice of appointing officials for a term of three years. Previously most officials used the short term to exploit the office for personal gain; frequently at the end of three years the crown lost able men devoted to their work. Pombal established Councils of Justice to reduce through these law courts the importance of church courts and to settle local civil actions with greater speed. Two supreme judicial tribunals were set up in the colony, one in Bahia in 1757, the other in Rio de Janeiro, from which appeals could be taken to Lisbon. To reduce confusion in government, Pombal extinguished nine feudal *donatários* either by outright purchase or confiscation. Maranhão, made dependent upon Lisbon under the Spanish regime, was reincorporated into Brazil's administration. When danger of war threatened in La Plata, Rio Grande do Sul became a captaincy.

Rio de Janeiro, the Capital. In 1763 Pombal's centralizing measures culminated in the establishment of the Brazilian viceroyalty and the transfer of the capital from historic Bahia to Rio de Janeiro. In this action he was undoubtedly influenced by the success of the viceregal system in the neighboring Spanish colonies. But of more significance was the growth of population and the importance of the southern and central areas of Brazil. Minas Gerais, Rio de Janeiro, São Paulo, and Espíritu Santo were the wealthiest provinces in the export of minerals, tobacco, cattle products, lumber, and other raw materials. Bahia and the sugar areas of the north, on the other hand, declined after the middle of the seventeenth century in the face of competition from European sugar-producing colonies in the Caribbean. Equally important, the growing interests of Portugal in La Plata, in conflict with those of Spain, demanded the center of government closer to the scene of action than Bahia, far removed in the north.

When the first viceroy, Count Cunha, chief of the royal armies, arrived, Rio de Janeiro presented a sorry picture, for "in spite of the glorious beauty of its hills, the sparkling waters of its bay . . . the city was an offensive humiliation to the senses." Narrow, dirty streets, ugly houses, and evil smells, its population crowded close to the bay, the city was anything but an attractive capital. It was, in fact, a bustling commercial center with none of the aristocratic traditions of Bahia. Its merchants were shop owners: "small shops, metal and gold beating shops, grain shops, weavers' shops, barber shops, hat shops, tap houses, drug shops," [1] together with a variety of clothing and food stores, were all

[1] The above quotations are from Costa, *Rio in the Time of the Viceroys*, pp. 6–7.

owned by Portuguese merchants whose monopoly on trade made them great fortunes. Throughout the city, slaves performed all manner of menial tasks. Unlike Lima, Mexico City, and Bogotá, it was not a city of culture, but one nourished by the interior mining regions and the sugar plantations along the near-by coast.

Commercial Reforms. In commerce and trade Pombal's aim was to increase Portugal's revenues and reduce the British domination of Portuguese trade in Europe. To achieve this objective he established trading companies. Outstanding was the General Company of Grand Pará and Maranhão (1755), headed by Pombal's brother. It received a monopoly over the Brazilian trade along the Amazonian coast. A second company, the Pernambuco and Bahia Company, organized in 1759, was less successful. But both brought new capital to Brazil, reduced the influence of British trade, and gave an impetus to the expansion of cotton, rice, and slave trading. Both companies were abolished after Pombal left office, because of local opposition to Portuguese monopolies.

Social Reform. The social legislation of Pombal affected all Brazilian classes. Motivated by the ideas of the French Enlightenment, Pombal ended the political inequalities of the Brazilians and Indians. In São Paulo particularly this reform had extensive effects. Under it São Paulo families established their control over militias through the office of the *capitão môr.* Pombal's most drastic action was the expulsion of the Jesuits from Brazil and Portugal in 1759. While this move seemed social, the roots were fundamentally economic. The great wealth of the Jesuits in Brazil, as in the Spanish colonies, had given them considerable political power. They had had control over the export from their properties of lumber, hides, and sugar and over the trade with the Indians through their missions, a most sensitive point in the dispute. Both of these monopolies had long caused native Brazilians to protest to the mother country through their *câmaras* in São Paulo, Maranhão, and Pará. At times they had revolted against Jesuit control. From the first, Jesuit policy had protected the Indians from slave raiders out of humane motives, but had themselves exacted labor from their charges. Many of their plantations used Indians in place of Negroes as workers. The incident, however, that was seized upon to justify their expulsion was the refusal of the Jesuits to cooperate with the Portuguese government in carrying out the terms of the Treaty of Madrid in 1750 applying to the seven missions. This opposition gave Pombal the opportunity to order out of Brazil the powerful order which blocked his campaign to limit the influence of the church in secular affairs.

The crown sent administrators to take over the Jesuit holdings. While the expulsion undoubtedly increased the centralization of royal power, the Jesuits' missions of the interior were thus left vacant and the Indians turned back to savagery. More serious, Indians without the protection of the Jesuit fathers fell victims to the raids of slavers, although Pombal tried to avert this calamity.

Indeed, Pombal's Indian policy became the next major aspect of his social reforms. In 1758 he decreed through a royal order the abolition of all forms of Indian slavery, a step preceded by liberation of the Indians in Maranhão two years before. In an effort to enforce colonial recognition of "equality" of Brazilians and Indians, he appointed directors over Indian towns and settlements, many of which that year had been taken from the Jesuits. These overseers were to place Indians in local offices of government. However, the reform was vitiated by the decree itself, for it permitted the allotment of Indians for employment for wages and the enslavement of Indians if they rebelled. Ways and means were naturally found by employers to avoid payment of wages so that peonage resulted; when Indians rose up, slavery ensued. To offset the shortage of labor caused by the freeing of the Indians, Pombal encouraged immigration of Portuguese workers. But these crowded into the coastal cities, went to the mining areas, or became agriculturists rather than manual laborers.

While this statesman-like attempt at reform failed, abolition of Indian slavery left its mark on Brazil in her growth toward nationhood. As Nash points out, Pombal's social measures originated the "great Brazilian idea: to incorporate all castes and colors in one body politic on a footing of absolute equality." Pombal's reforms ended with the death of the king, his own removal from office, and his exile. Queen Maria I, under pressure of the church, returned it to power in both Portugal and Brazil and replaced colonial Brazilian officeholders with Portuguese. Nevertheless, though defeated and out-maneuvered by his enemies, because of Pombal's sincere interest in the well-being of the colony, Brazilians have continued to hold him in high regard.

Part VI.   THE LAST YEARS, 1778–1808

Decline of the Economy. The effect of Pombal's measures continued to benefit Portugal for a decade after his death. But the reactionary government of the mother country resorted more and more to repressive measures against the colony. To rehabilitate the rapidly declining sugar production, Portugal closed all factories in Brazil in 1785 to provide more laborers for the sugar plantations. Gold mining declined; the diamond market became glutted. With a fall in prices, many miners left Minas Gerais for other parts of Brazil; abandoned towns became a common sight. Agriculture fell into ruin. Those who remained became embittered at the crown's blind insistence upon tax collection.

The Tiradentes Revolt. Within this framework of discontent Brazilian students, writers, poets, and others, who had formed under the influence of French ideas, academies, literary circles, and scientific groups, became leaders demanding more liberty for the colony. Some even wanted independence. In 1789 Minas Gerais, suffering from the decline of mining, became a center for plots. Influential intellectuals organized the "Conspiracy of Minas," composed, among others, of Claudio da Costa and José da Silva Xavier, a dentist, called Tiradentes. They planned, with independence achieved, a republic, to free the Negroes, establish factories, introduce printing presses, and found a university. Badly organized and lacking general support, the conspiracy was quickly snuffed out, Tiradentes was executed; other leaders were jailed or exiled. Its immediate effect, however, was to end the government's monopoly on the production of salt and to reduce taxes. More significant, the "Conspiracy of Minas" marked the beginning of a movement to make Brazil a republic—achieved just a century later.

Chapter XI

COLONIAL BRAZIL: ECONOMIC AND SOCIAL LIFE, 1580-1808

Part I. ECONOMIC LIFE

Agriculture. The Amazonian north, the great plains of the south, and the mining areas of central Brazil, combined with rich soils of the coastal regions, produced a rich and varied agriculture. Sugar from the beginning was the chief colonial crop. All the northern coastal provinces, Maranhão, Pernambuco, Bahia, Pará, and even Santa Catharina and São Vicente, had sugar plantations. Other crops commonly grown were rice, Indian corn, tobacco, and indigo. Late in the colonial period Pará exported fine cocoa, coffee, sarsaparilla, gums, and wood products. Cotton, important in the south, spread into the interior of Minas Gerais.

The Cattle Industry. The cattle industry began with the founding of São Paulo. It spread rapidly into the interior and branched north and south along the river valleys. By the middle of the seventeenth century the industry had shifted its center of gravity to the banks of the Rio Grande do São Francisco. Along that stream in Pernambuco, one authority estimated 800,000 head. Later the herds moved slowly into the Amazonian states. Settlement westward through the state of Bahia carried cattle along the southern and eastern banks of the São Francisco to the Rio das Velhas. There they numbered some 500,000 head. Significantly, when the mines of Minas Gerais declined, the cattle industry and agriculture remained the chief features of the economy.

Trade: Exports. By the middle of the seventeenth century the exports of Brazil were extremely varied. Brazilwood, pre-eminent in the early sixteenth century, was secured principally from Rio de Janeiro northward to Pernambuco, which produced the highest quality. Sugar soon superseded brazilwood in value, and far exceeded other plantation crops, such as tobacco, cotton, and indigo. Other exports varying in value were rice, hides, tallow, wax, horse and cow hair, horns, fur, skins, feathers, molasses, rum, and forest products, which besides brazilwood, included chiefly pine, for shipbuilding, and coffee, important after 1770. Exports from Minas Gerais after the gold and diamond discoveries included gold in chains, topazes, amethysts, tourmalines, aquamarines, and various manufactured ornaments.

Imports. The principal imports into Brazil came from Portugal. Outstanding were vinegar, hardware, linens, cottons, silks, oil, hats, and wine. At the same time valuable products came in the late eighteenth century from the United States: salt provisions, flour, household furniture, turpentine, pitch, and tar. From Africa arrived wax, oil, elephant's teeth, sulfur, ivory, ebony, drugs, and gums. At the end of the colonial period, England provided iron—though Swedish iron was in greater demand—boots, silks and cotton hosiery, shoes, brassware, lead, tinplate, wine, cheese, gunpowder, drugs, salt provisions, ham, tongue, pork, and a variety of luxury goods.

Industries. The demands of the plantation and mining centers as well as the growth of small businesses in the colony created widespread local industries. On the plantation a variety of skilled workers manufactured the necessities, clothing, building materials, tools for cultivating the land. Heavy goods, such as the *engheno,* a machine used for the making of sugar, were imported, although simple handmade *enghenos* were produced for the smaller plantations.

In the cities on the coast and in the mining areas, a considerable variety of small industries developed. Probably the most important was the textile. It manufactured coarse cotton cloth in great quantities, most of which was consumed locally, but some exported to the Spanish possessions in La Plata. Other industries were those manufacturing iron tools, copperware, gold and silver products, wrought jewelry, shoes, and leather. So much leather was used in the colony that one Brazilian historian termed the colonial period the age of leather.

In the south from São Paulo to Uruguay along the coast the fishing industry, mostly whaling, manufactured its own fishing lines, nets, and cordage from flax growing in the areas, and blankets and sheets from cotton. The southern coast also was a center for the making of pottery, including jars, culinary vessels, and large waterpots. An important shipbuilding industry centered at São Francisco do Sul, where large and small vessels were made from Paraná pine by the merchants of Bahia, Rio de Janeiro, and Pernambuco. Sorocabá had a small iron industry, employing many smiths in the manufacture of horseshoes.

Part II. SOCIAL CONDITIONS IN COLONIAL BRAZIL

Population. The population of Brazil by 1808 has been estimated at between 2,000,000 and 4,000,000, one-third of whom were Negro slaves and possibly two-fifths mulatto. Walsh, writing in 1828 shortly after the colonial regime ended, reported that the estimates of slaves and mulatto offspring were 2,500,000, while the white population was but 850,000. Another calculation just before the end of the colonial era in 1798 placed the population at 3,250,000, of which about 2,000,000 were Negro slaves and freedmen. A modern authority, generally accepted, Dr. J. F. Oliviera Vianna, has estimated the total population at 2,419,406.

Estimates of various areas and municipalities confirm that the population was under 3,000,000. The four provinces of Santo Espíritu Santo, Rio de Janeiro, Santa Catharina, and São Paulo had about 800,000 people. Minas Gerais was estimated at the end of the colonial period at about 360,000. Individual cities have had their colonial population placed at figures probably too low. Careful observers reported Rio de Janeiro in 1648 at 2,500; in 1700, at 25,000; and in 1811, at 100,000. However, the latter figure should be revised upward, as slaves were not counted. A Brazilian writing in 1802 noted that many families had as many as sixty, seventy, or more "unnecessary persons," a circumstance not unusual, he commented, in the country, but remarkable in the cities. Walsh confirmed this practice of omitting slaves. He estimated from his own observation in 1828 that Rio de Janeiro had a population of 150,000, but that in the official estimate Negroes were not included. He noted that in the city in all houses lived in by whites, each householder had three or four slaves; some maintained as many as twenty. In one case he reported a family which gave shelter to fifty Negroes. Rio Grande in the far south was estimated to have about 100,000 people in and about the city; Bahia, 70,000; Cuiabá, 30,000; Pernambuco, 25,000; Ceará, 20,000; and Pará, 10,000. São Paulo had compiled in 1811 what are believed to be accurate statistics, namely, a total of almost 23,500 composed of 11,538 whites, 4,734 Negroes, and 7,314 mulattoes.

Social Structure. As in the Spanish colonies, officeholding and land-ownership were the distinguishing characteristics of the ruling classes of colonial Brazil. For the rest of the population, except the commercial class, labor was the chief occupation, whether it was work on the plantations by Negroes and Indians or mulattoes; in the mines by the same groups; agriculture, mostly by Portuguese immigrants; or employment of workers and artisans in the cities. However, because of the predominant number of Negroes in the colony and extensive intermingling of the races, Negro blood became unremarked among all classes. Pombal's freeing of the Indians from slavery and making them citizens did not shock prevailing mores. Thus in the schools, children of whites, mulattoes, and Negroes were received and treated alike. No distinction of color was made in training priests for the church. Traditions of race assimilation distinguished colonial Brazil to a degree unknown in any other European colony in the New World.

The Colonial Aristocracy. The colonial period saw the establishment of Brazil's landowning aristocracy. It had its origin in the grants to the *donatários* in the sixteenth century. In the main, the aristocracy had its greatest numbers in the northern states, where sugar was the basis of their great fortunes. Other aristocratic groups grew up among the cattle landowners of Bahia, Minas Gerais, São Paulo, Santa Catharina, and Rio Grande do Sul. In the eighteenth century other families became prominent as a result of wealth gained from the mines of Minas Gerais, Goiás, and Matto Grosso.

Since the royal government exercised little or no supervision over the owner or *fazendeiro* of the coastal sugar estates, a social structure developed within these that was distinctly feudal in character and of great influence throughout Brazil. The owner was at once a feudal lord, a patriarch, and a dominant political force in local government. His domain or *fazenda* was practically self-sustaining. Artisans and craftsmen, usually mulattoes and free Negroes, made all tools, furniture, clothing, and other handicraft products needed to maintain life on the plantations. The *fazendeiro* usually imported fine clothing and certain foods from Portugal for himself and his family.

So all-pervading was the influence of the sugar aristocracy that it affected all aspects of Brazilian colonial life. The *fazendeiro* had complete authority, extending to life and death, over his family, artisans, and slaves on his estates. He exercised military power in the militias he organized to protect his property from Indian raids, slave rebellions, and even piratical incursions. His local power revealed the weakness of the central government, which was rarely able to collect taxes in his domain. The plantation reduced the cities and towns of Brazil to a subordinate role. The rural towns were under the thumb of the *fazendeiros*, while the large cities were but centers from which they purchased supplies needed for their plantations. The importance of the cities came late in the colonial period when their own population, becoming sufficiently large, provided a market to rival that of the rural regions. Indeed as in Olinda, plantation owners who fell into debt to Portuguese merchants in Recife, cancelled their obligations by armed revolt against urban mercantile power.

The plantation subordinated the church to its customs. The *fazendeiro* customarily required one of his sons to enter the priesthood and, when ordained, remain on the great estate itself. As was common custom, the priests took concubines, and reared and recognized their children as openly as did the patriarchs. Moreover, the churches had pictures and images of the landowner's ancestors placed along with those of the saints in the plantation church. This lack of independence of the church, of familial Christianity, as Freyre describes it, had a profound effect upon the history of Brazil. The church became tolerant, never acquired the wealth and power it had in the Spanish colonies, and hence was no obstacle in the political development of Brazil after independence.

With long traditions of aristocratic life, huge estates, great wealth, practical independence, and local political power, the Brazilian aristocracy was in fact a feudal society. But within this society the patriarch recognized the principle of racial mixture, enmeshed the church in the homogeneous culture of the plantation, and contributed to the idea of Brazilianization.

The Middle Class. As in the Spanish colonies, Brazil also saw the colonial beginnings of a middle class. The Portuguese had well-established institutions of capitalism at the time Cabral took possession of Brazil. During the succeeding centuries, trade and commerce, while theoretically in control of the mother country, saw native Brazilians smuggling along the coast and among the Jesuit missions along the Uruguay River. Later, when mining developed, native traders, capitalists, and small landowners appeared in the gold and diamond fields. Mawe, writing in 1808 of the early gold discoveries, noted that "the first settlers might have prevented the exposure of their good fortune, had they been able to moderate their joy, and consented to act in concert; but as gold was in such great abundance, every individual appropriated a lot of ground, and thus became a capitalist."

The colonial middle class made its presence known by frequent protests and even revolts when its commercial interests were endangered. They forced the reduction of the powers of the Company of Brazil and its eventual abolition in 1720. They played a part in the Beckman revolt and that of the Mascates over the commercial privileges accorded the Portuguese monopolists in Recife. They welcomed most of

Pombal's reforms, except that of granting monopolies to Portuguese companies. When in 1808 the king of Portugal established his government in Brazil, they became strong supporters of the monarchy precisely because he opened the ports to free trade.

The Negro in Colonial Brazil. The Negro arrived in Brazil as a slave. In that capacity he replaced the disappearing Indian, the first to be enslaved, as he was in the Spanish and English settlements. Although the slave raiders pursued the natives into the interior, the catch was inadequate to meet the needs of the rapidly expanding sugar plantations. The precise time of the arrival of the first Negroes in Brazil is unknown, but the earliest recorded shipment was in 1538, possibly to Bahia.

As the sugar economy expanded north and south along the coast, the Negro followed. The extremities, Maranhão in the north and São Vicente in the south, had fewer Negroes than the predominantly sugar-growing regions of Bahia and Pernambuco. However, after the Dutch took possession, they imported greater numbers along the Amazonian coast. In the south, on the other hand, as São Paulo became less important as a sugar center and turned to pastoral industries, the Negro declined in numbers. When gold and diamonds were discovered in the interior, the transfer of Negroes was rapid from Bahia, Pernambuco, and Rio de Janeiro.

Statistics on the Negro population, like those on the colonial population as a whole, vary greatly. Father Anchieta stated that in 1585, of the 57,000 people in Brazil, 14,000 were Negro, 10,000 of whom were in Pernambuco and 3,000 in Bahia. After 1600, however, the colored people were imported in constantly growing numbers. Some authorities state that the annual average for the colonial period was between 50,000 and 60,000 or 5,000,000 or 6,000,000 by the opening of the nineteenth century. Other equally respected students believe that this figure is too high and reduce it almost by half. In 1798 it was estimated that there were 2,000,000 slave and free Negroes in the colony. Mawe in 1808 placed the Negro and mulatto populatiton of Minas Gerais at 200,000.

The Brazilian Negro came from different parts of Africa, chief of which were the Sudan, Nigeria, the Gold Coast, Gambia, Sierra Leone, Liberia (today), the Ivory Coast, northern Nigeria, Angola, the Congo, and Mozambique on the east coast of the continent. The accounts of slave voyages across the Atlantic still produce a shudder of horror. At the ports, principally Rio de Janeiro, Bahia, Pernambuco, and Maranhão, and in the interior at Villa Rica and Minas Gerais, were the principal slave marts. There the helpless creatures were sold to plantation and mine owners who examined them and haggled over the prices as they did over the purchase of cattle.

Contributions of the Negro. The lowly status of the Negro should not conceal the fact that he played an important part in the production of Brazil's colonial wealth. His other contributions were many and varied. The African herdsmen, long acquainted with the raising of cattle and sheep, probably knew as much in their way of this industry as did the Portuguese. As transplanted farm laborers, the Negroes, accustomed to long hours of work in the sun of equatorial Africa, proved a priceless asset to the Brazilian planter whose Indian slaves withered and died.

Equally important, the Negroes brought a knowledge of the manual arts. Their understanding, very old, of the use and manufacture of iron was invaluable in the development of the mineral areas of Minas Gerais. In the towns and cities and on the plantations they became excellent artisans in the handicraft industries. Thus in the basic economy of Brazil, agriculture, mining, and cattle raising, the Negroes, to quote Nash, "carried upon their well-muscled backs the full weight of the [American] Portuguese empire in the eighteenth century," and he might have added the seventeenth as well.

Besides their economic contributions, the Negroes had much to add to Brazilian cultural development. In costume Bahian women copied that of the Moslem Negresses from the Sudan. Music and the dance, especially group dancing, such as the *macumba,* which was derived from the Negroes' African background, provided valuable themes for modern Brazilian music. So, too, they brought into Brazil the use of a large number of wind instruments, remnants of their religious cults, an art in the preparation of food, and a wealth of folklore.

Mixed Groups. With Negroes plentiful as slaves and the Portuguese landowners knowing no law but their own, it was inevitable that inter-mixture of the races should occur. The mulattoes soon emerged as a distinct element in the population. These frequently became artisans rather than workers in the field. Both on occasion escaped from the plantations to the forests in the interior. There they mixed with the Indians and gave rise to a group called the *cafuso.* As intermingling took place among all these various strains, their offspring, where no one characteristic was identifiable, were called *pardos.* Many of this group are found in the Amazon valley today where they are also known as *caboclos.* The latter term, however, is frequently applied to Indian-white offspring in the Amazon, whereas in the south such a mixture is known as *mameluco.*

Part III. THE CHURCH IN COLONIAL BRAZIL

The Jesuits. The church as a whole in colonial Brazil from the beginning remained weak and poverty-stricken. The one order, the Jesuit, that accumulated wealth and power was exiled. Around it the church had its most important history in the colony. The Jesuits upon their arrival in Brazil with Thomé da Souza in 1549 began a campaign to convert the natives. Their work was distinguished in the sixteenth century by the efforts, among others, of Fathers Manuel da Nobrega and José de Anchieta. Nobrega worked among the natives of São Paulo, where he established a school in 1553 of which Anchieta became the head. Both played a part in winning the support of the Indian confederation, which aided the Portuguese to expel the French from Rio de Janeiro.

The most important work of the Jesuits was encouraging and establishing missions in the interior of São Paulo. This very success, however, had two unfortunate effects. Congregating the Indians made slave raiding easy for the Paulistas, who eventually exterminated most of the Indian tribes in the southern region. Secondly, the effort of the Jesuits to protect their charges led to a conflict between them and the Paulistas. This struggle broke out violently in 1639 when the Jesuits through their influence secured renewed papal condemnation of Indian slavery. In reply the Paulistas expelled them from the province for fifteen years. They were readmitted only upon the pledge not to concern themselves with the Paulista slave expeditions among the Indians.

In other parts of Brazil the Jesuits likewise had established their missions and attempted to block the Brazilian slave raiders and plantation owners. Outstanding in the seventeenth century was the work of Father Antonio Vieira who came to Brazil in 1653, having persuaded the government to establish the Brazil Company. In Brazil he had royal authority to improve the status of the Indians. After arrival in the colony he reported to the king in vivid descriptive phrases the horrible condition in which Indians were held in slavery, particularly in the Amazonian provinces of Maranhão and Pará. Returning to Portugal in his enthusiasm to improve the lot of the natives, he succeeded in persuading the king to place the Indians under the exclusive control of the Jesuit order.

Thus armed, Vieira effectively carried out the royal order and secured widespread emancipation of the Indians. Enraged, the Brazilians revolted in Maranhão and expelled the order in 1661. As in São Paulo in the previous decades, the Jesuits were allowed to return (1663) only after they had surrendered much of their authority over the Indians. However, they immediately set about to restore their control. By 1684 they had become so successful in blocking the raids of the slavers from the coast that their activities were a cause of the Beckman revolt of that year. After that date they turned to carry on missionary activity deeper in the Amazonian territory.

However, it should not be inferred that the Jesuits played a disinterested role. Besides their practically complete monopoly of Indian trade and labor, they branched out into every aspect of Brazil's colonial development. Eventually, as we have seen, these varied activities and conflicts with Brazilian and royal authority brought their expulsion in 1759.

Other Orders. Other orders, too, established missions, particularly the Franciscans, Dominicans, Mercedarians, Carmelites, and Capuchins. In the cities all had their churches and cathedrals, convents and monasteries. Though not so powerful as the Jesuits, the Benedictines owned several hundred houses in Rio de Janeiro at the end of the colonial period. Almost equally wealthy were the Carmelites. All orders performed important social services in maintaining hospitals, orphanages, and other similar charities.

Character of the Colonial Priesthood. The expulsion of the Jesuits removed the most aggressive force from the Brazilian church. Most of the other orders had settled down into the deeply eroded pattern marked out by the culture of the *casa grande,* that is, the plantation. There it became far removed in spirit from the influence of Rome and resembled little the discipline of the church in the Spanish colonies. This integration into Brazilian culture reflected itself in various ways in the eighteenth century.

One of the commonest practices in the church was the general disregard of the priestly vow of celibacy. Since so many clerics had families, a demand grew up in the late eighteenth century that the church should modify its "unnatural" rules and relieve the clergy of the penalty attached to marriage. Some writers, noting this violation of the vows, have charged the colonial clergy with laxity of morals. However, Walsh, the chaplain of the first British embassy in Brazil and a careful observer, wrote in 1828, shortly after the colonial regime ended:

I cannot find they deserve the character imputed to them. From what I have seen myself and heard from others, they are, generally speaking, temperate in their diet; observant of the rules of the church, assiduous in attending the sick and charitable as far as their limited means permit them. There is one serious charge, however, of which I cannot acquit them . . . the too frequent violation of the vows of celibacy. . . . Their attachments, however, are constant. . . . The thing is not regarded with the same degree of scandal . . . as it is in other places.[1]

The church in Brazil also admitted Negroes to the priesthood. Doubtless the practice on the plantations of the priest of recognizing his own children paved the way for the entry of the mulattoes and Negroes into the offices of the church. The poverty of the church left it, furthermore, with little choice but to select from its schools promising students irrespective of their color. "To this cause," wrote Chaplain Walsh, "perhaps may be attributed, in some measure, the admission of Negroes to holy orders. . . . I have seen myself three clergymen in the same church at the same time; one of whom was white, another a mulatto, and the third a black. . . . In Brazil a black is seen as the officiating minister, and whites receiving it [the sacrament] from his hands." [2]

That Roman conservatism little influenced the Brazilian church is apparent in the widespread sympathy among bishops and other leaders of the church for the revolutionary doctrines of the late eighteenth century. These ideas the Inquisition and the church leaders of the Spanish colonies suppressed. In Brazil the priest was ". . . one of the few educated persons in the colony . . . [who] read the books of French philosophers, of Montesquieu or Voltaire. He was liberal or revolutionary, and as he was bound to the great families of the land he worked for the political and economic independence of the country." [3]

Ownership of volumes prohibited by the Index was common. In 1808 Mawe was impressed by the liberal outlook of the clergy of São Paulo and commended the interest of the bishop there in the sciences. Walsh commented on the library of the bishop of Rio de Janeiro, which contained 4,000 volumes, with a large proportion of French and English authors. Out of this liberal tradition and lack of an effective hand from Rome, came in the early nineteenth century a remarkable Brazilian toleration of Protestantism. The bishop of Rio de Janeiro was even anxious to have Protestantism introduced into Brazil. A few years later the bishop of São Paulo offered to introduce into the state legislature a proposal of a Protestant missionary to place a dozen copies of the New Testament in the library of every primary school in the provinces!

[1] Rev. R. Walsh, *Notices of Brazil*, 2 vols., London, 1830, Vol. I, p. 374.
[2] *Ibid.*, p. 366.
[3] Smith and Marchant, *Brazil: Portrait of Half a Continent*, New York, p. 539.

Part IV.　LEARNING AND THE ARTS

Learning: Father Anchieta. Colonial Brazil, from the nature of its material history, produced little of original native contribution to the arts and sciences. Given an environment in which slavery predominated, combined with a cattle and mining frontier, the arts made little progress. The Jesuit father, Anchieta, at São Paulo is the first important figure in the record of Brazil's literary career. To carry out the Christianization of the Indians he composed poetry in the Tupí language, which he mastered. So, too, he wrote religious dramas and songs in Portuguese and Latin and delivered sermons in Indian languages, besides leaving valuable descriptive accounts of the conditions of the colony. Outstanding is his 3,000-stanza poem to the Virgin. All of his writings have not yet come to light and his figure may bulk larger in future literary history.

A second important writer in the sixteenth century was Gabriel Soares da Souza. In 1587 he wrote a *Tratado descriptivo do Brazil (A descriptive Treatise on Brazil)*, a valuable history and description of the new colony, lauding the mineral riches of the land. Although he saw more than actually existed, his accounts of the people and early Brazilian industries and resources make his treatise significant. A contemporary of Soares was Pero de Magalhãez de Gandavo, who wrote in 1570 two books, one a history and the other a description of the colony which supplements Soares' work.

In the seventeenth century four figures add to the literary tradition. One was Father Vicente do Salvador, whose *History of Brazil*, published in 1627, gives him rank as an able historian. Father Antonio Vieira, referred to above, a Portuguese and not a Brazilian, nevertheless left famous sermons which have a significant content in dramatic description of social conditions. Contemporary with Vieira was the Jesuit Simão de Vasconcellos, whose book, the *Chronicles of the Company of Jesus in the Province of Brazil*, which appeared in Lisbon in 1663, has remained the standard authority on the Order. However, this work has been greatly supplemented recently by a seven-volume history of the Jesuits in Brazil as a whole, and a more specialized work in three volumes on the Jesuits in São Paulo.

But the most outstanding figure of the seventeenth century was the native Brazilian, Gregório de Mattos Guerra, 1633–1696, a satiric and lyric poet of considerable stature. From a wealthy Bahian family, he was educated at the University of Coimbra where, though studying law, he indulged his taste in the poets. His own verse has its chief significance in its unvarnished criticism and burning satire on the vices (in which he heartily participated), corruption, dishonesty, and immoral practices of his wealthy neighbors in Pernambuco, where he spent his declining years. As such, his poetry, like Father Vieira's sermons, revealed Brazilian social life in the colony.

Antonil. At the turn of the century, when Portugal itself was suffering from the decline of the sugar trade but just beginning to feel the effects of the new wealth from the mines, an amazing work appeared to detail the extraordinary resources of Brazil. This study by an Italian Jesuit, João Antonil, was entitled *Cultura e opulencia do Brazil por sus drogas y minas (Culture and Wealth of Brazil Derived from Its Forests and Mines)* and appeared in 1711. It gave such a dramatic and detailed account of Brazil's wealth that the Portuguese government immediately suppressed it. They feared its effects would awaken both the cupidity of foreigners and the nationalistic pride of the Brazilians. It recounted the "fabulous" production of gold mines, just beginning; the extent of the cattle industry; the number of sugar mills; the wealth they produced; together with similar data on other industries, as well as the changing social picture effected by the discovery of mines and the flocking of people into the interior.

In the eighteenth century native Brazilians left a few important accounts. Outstanding was the work of Sebastião Rocha Pitta, whose *Historia de America Portuguesa,* published in 1730, gave him high standing as a scholar and historian. Local history found its student. In São Paulo, Pedro Taques de Almeida Paez Leme provided especially valuable sketches of the leading families of the south. In Bahia, José Antonio Caldas wrote a report for the king of Portugal in 1759 entitled *Noticia geral de toda esta capitania da Bahia desde o seu descobrimento até o presente ano de 1759 (A General Survey of All Parts of This Captaincy of Bahia from the Time of Its Discovery to the Present Year of 1759),* which, after the work of Antonil, became the most important source for the study of Bahia's economic history until the early nineteenth century.

In Minas Gerais were a number of literary figures who interpreted the evolution of Brazil for their countrymen. Among the better known were two epic poets. José de Santa Rita Durão presented, in imitation of Camões' style, the story of Caramarú at Bahia. Even more nationalistic and patriotic was the epic, *O Uruguay,* by José Basilio da Gama, not only because he escaped the influence of Camões, but because he revealed the intense love of the Brazilians for their homeland. Other poets of the

Mineiro school reflected a Brazilian outlook and eschewed the style of Camões. Prominent among these was Claudio Manoel da Costa, who displayed a talent for such elegant verse that he has been called the Petrarch of Brazil. It is interesting to note that these and other poets, notably Thomas Antonio Gonzaga and Alvarenga Peixoto, were among the leaders of the "conspiracy of Minas"—a sufficient testimony to their Brazilianization.

Architecture. Unlike the Spanish colonies, which reflected a variety of architectural styles, Brazil was dominated by baroque. In the south were some examples of Renaissance. However, the interiors of churches and cathedrals were lavishly decorated by painters, wood carvers, and sculptors. The most remarkable example of church architecture is the magnificent Church of the Third Order of Saint Francis in Bahia, which reflected the great wealth of the coastal families. Built with Lisbon stone, its façade is covered with sculptured figures of saints, volutes, coats of arms, and arabesque decoration. The interior, the altar and massive walls, covered with carved and gilded woods, Brazilian cedar, and jacaranda, is overpowering in its richness. As an achievement in baroque, it is probably without equal either in the New or the Old World. The most famous of native Brazilian architects was Francisco Antônio Lisboa, nicknamed "O Aleijadinho" ("the Little Cripple"), whose beautiful baroque churches in Minas Gerais are minor masterpieces.

Lack of Institutions of Learning. Brazil's limited colonial culture, when thought of in relation to the vast range of refinements in the Spanish colonies, is also apparent in the virtual absence of schools. The church did train Indians and the children of the poorer classes in trades, manual skills, and agriculture. Other schools that the church established in the larger cities provided for the advancement of talented children into secondary schools for entrance into the work of the church. Pombal made an effort to remedy the deficiency of schools by placing responsibility for primary institutions upon the *câmaras* after the expulsion of the Jesuits. But the lack of teachers rendered the change useless. Highly restrictive in character were the tutorial colleges maintained for the sons of the wealthier families, from which students and those trained in church schools could advance to the University of Coimbra in Portugal.

The Importance of Brazilian Colonial Culture. In contrast with the Spanish colonies, Brazil had no universities or other institutions of higher learning. Characteristic of the cultural lag was the absence of any printing press in the colony. The first press arrived with the court of the king of Portugal, João VI, in 1808. But for three centuries not a book or pamphlet was published in Brazil. In favorable contrast with the Spanish colonies, however, there was no censorship over the importation of books. Paradoxically, in Brazil there was greater freedom to read and discuss ideas than in the Spanish colonies, which boasted universities and printing presses. Doubtless toleration of races and ideas, which is such an impressive characteristic of the Brazilians, stems from the happy absence in the colonial period of a powerful church and a strong, centralized government.

THE WARS
FOR INDEPENDENCE

Chapter XII

THE WARS FOR
INDEPENDENCE: NORTHERN
SOUTH AMERICA

Part I.   GENERAL CAUSES

Introduction. The Wars for Independence (1808–1826) in Latin America present a vast panorama of revolt against Spain and Portugal. The movement had unity in Creole leadership, common in all colonies. Its most striking characteristic, however, was the current of democratic ideas which partly inspired the struggle and produced, with the exception of Brazil, a galaxy of new republics in the New World.

The great distances spanned by the Spanish empire made a single military undertaking impossible. The wars fell into five separate movements: (1) in northern South America, which included Venezuela, Colombia, and Ecuador; (2) in southern South America, which included the Platine colonies of Argentina, Uruguay, and Paraguay; (3) in western South America, Chile and Peru; (4) and in Spanish North America, comprising Mexico and Central America. (5) Brazil carried through its movement for independence in the brief space of two years, 1821–1822.

Causes: Exclusion from Office. Since under the theory of royal ownership of the colonies, the king appointed all officeholders, the native-born Spaniards were normally excluded from holding any important office in the colonies. The Spaniards from Spain, moreover, held the Americans as socially inferior and mentally incompetent to govern. The wealthy Americans on their part, educated and frequently of aristocratic origin, bitterly resented their exclusion. Their wealth had made them dominant in *cabildo* affairs, skilled in political maneuvering, and prepared to provide the leadership for the struggle for independence.

Exclusion from Trade. The Spanish mercantile system also excluded the native colonial middle class from its benefits. Restriction of trade to certain cities and to favored Spaniards within the cities inevitably aroused the resentment of colonial merchants, traders, and businessmen. While the Creoles could find no way to break the monopoly of office-holding, the middle class did undermine the commercial monopoly by smuggling. In this activity they had the cooperation of British and American traders, whose influence in every port gave the Latin-American traders encouragement to throw off the restrictions. This successful flaunting of the Spanish law, combined with corruption in office, lessened respect for the royal authority. From disrespect for the law it was but a step to demanding the ending of the mercantile system and the opening of the colonies to free trade. Of this forbidden fruit, the commercial groups had had in fact a taste in the reforms of Charles III. The restoration of restrictions on trade after his rule intensified the antagonism of the colonial middle class against the royal government.

Taxation. Upon all Americans fell the full weight of arbitrary taxation. Export-import taxes, sales taxes, taxes on paper and on mineral production, land taxes, Indian head taxes, and a multitude of others touched every aspect of colonial life. Equally burdensome were the royal monopolies in land, mercury, salt, amusements, and tobacco.

Tradition of Revolt. From the sixteenth century, Indians had revolted at one time or another in all parts of the empire. The Incas had a long history of insurrection until the royal Inca line was extirpated in 1781 upon the defeat of Tupac Amarú. The Araucanians in Chile likewise rose up against Spanish power on many occasions. In the eighteenth century the Indians of the seven missions, as we have seen, revolted against both Portuguese and Spanish authorities. In North America, Indians in Mexico from the time of Cortés frequently rebelled. The revolt of the Indians in the Mixton region in the middle of the sixteenth century had its counterpart in those of the Yaqui, Seri, Pueblo, and Yucatan uprisings in the seventeenth and eighteenth centuries. These are but a few instances of the untold story of Indian efforts to regain their land and resist oppression.

Democratic Ideas. Ideas stirred by the late eighteenth century revolts in France, in the English colonies, and in French Santo Domingo spread the democratic faith in Latin America. Wealthy Creoles, accustomed to travel in Europe and familiar with the writings of English and French political philosophers, prepared the ground. They embraced these ideas, however, as a means of achieving independence from Spain; they had, in fact, no fundamental interests, with few exceptions, in the principles of democratic government *per se.* But once democratic ideas—those of representative government, freedom of speech, press, and religion, and the protection of individual rights—entered the Spanish colonies, they attracted an ever-increasing following, namely, the commercial classes interested in free trade and participation in government, intellectuals passionately devoted to the very principles themselves, and Indian leaders.

Rousseau's ideas of sovereignty residing in the people and the American doctrine that all men are created equal were justification for Creole attack upon the inferior position to which the *peninsulares* had condemned them. The American slogan, too, "no taxation without representation," fell upon willing ears. The hierarchy and the wealthy repudiated Voltaire, but many of the lower clergy, incensed by the crushing burdens upon the Indians, seized upon the Frenchman's writings. The books of the French philosophers, the revolutionary documents of the American independence movement, and those of the French Revolution were smuggled into the colonies. Antonio de Nariño in Colombia translated the French *Declaration of the Rights of Man* and distributed copies to his friends. Bernard Monteagudo in Buenos Aires cried out that it was an insult to ask Americans if they should be free. The Caroline Academy in Bolivia taught French revolutionary ideas and sent its students into Chile, Peru, and Argentina. Father Hidalgo in Mexico had Voltaire's writings in his library. British traders at Buenos Aires brought in copies of Adam Smith's *Wealth of Nations* as well as the writings of Jeremy Bentham and other British economists.

Examples of Successful Revolutions. Stimulating to revolutionary thought in the Spanish colonies were three successful revolts. The first, that of the English colonies from Britain, not only was a success, but Spain's aid to those colonies awakened ideas of independence in her own empire. Aware of this possibility, the Count of Aranda in 1783 suggested to Charles III putting three kings, one in Mexico and two in South America (while reserving for Charles himself the position of emperor), on American thrones to preserve the empire. Two years before, in fact, a conspiracy in Chile in 1781, as we have noted, reflected the influence of the revolt of the English colonies.

The French Revolution reverberated throughout the Spanish empire. For Latin America it signified the overthrow of a monarchical system of government and the weakening of Spain, associated with the French royal house in a family compact. As an example of successful revolution, however, the revolt of French Santo Domingo (Haiti) against the efforts of

Napoleon to put it down had the most important immediate effect upon the Spanish colonies. Once free, Haiti became for a moment a base for Bolívar in his campaign to liberate northern South America.

Part II.   PRELIMINARY MOVEMENTS FOR INDEPENDENCE

Haiti, 1789–1804. The movement for independence in Haiti stemmed directly from the French Revolution. The events of 1789 produced deep conflicts within the colony. The Negro, composing the bulk of the population, lived in slavery. The mulatto, the next most numerous group, and mostly free, looked down upon the enslaved blacks. A step above were the Little Whites, Frenchmen engaged in business pursuits or small-scale farming. The Big Whites, the wealthy planters and chief slaveowners, topped the social scale.

French colonial administrators, recognizing this social organization, maintained rigid control, but the Big Whites were antagonistic to the officeholders sent to govern. When in August, 1789, the National Assembly promulgated the Declaration of the Rights of Man, the planters claimed the right to share in the government of the island. The mulattoes on their part, imbued with ideas of equality and supported by their society in Paris, The Friends of the Negroes, petitioned the National Assembly for equal status with the whites.

The planters took the first revolutionary step when they called assemblies, one in the north, another in the south, and a third in the west, to enforce their rights to participation in the government. These, all rejecting mulatto petitions to join them, called a general assembly at Saint-Marc for April, 1790. There, after deliberations, they published a constitution, virtually a declaration of independence. However, the Little Whites, fearing the power of the planters, supported the French colonial officials against the assembly. Colonel Maduit of the French army marched on Saint-Marc, seized the assembly hall, and, after throwing the delegates through the windows, dissolved the body. The surviving members thereupon took ship for France, where they were jailed.

Meanwhile, the mulattoes, incensed by the rejection of their petitions, revolted in October, 1789, under Jacques Vicente Ogé, who stirred his followers to fight for their rights. Big and Little Whites instantly dropped their differences to crush the uprising. This event, reported to the National Assembly in Paris, led that body to declare in May, 1790, that mulattoes were entitled to participate in colonial assemblies. The news of the Assembly's action incited the jubilant mulattoes and the first Negro revolt in 1791. In the north large numbers of slaves plundered plantations and murdered the whites. In hope of strengthening their position, the mulattoes joined the whites in putting down the slaves. After the revolt the mulattoes settled down near Port-au-Prince in the hope of sharing the government with the whites. But in Paris the planters had prevailed upon the government to set aside the May decree. Assuming they now had blanket authority, the whites proceeded to slaughter the mulattoes near Port-au-Prince. In terror the latter fled under Petión, their leader, and called upon the slaves to revolt.

At this juncture Saint Léger at the head of a French commission arrived, shortly reinforced by 6,000 French troops. After order was restored, Léger announced that the government recognized but two classes in the island, free, including whites and mulattoes, and slave, that is, the Negroes. However, a new commission headed by Santhonax replaced that of Léger and showed sympathy with the Negroes. When the whites refused to accept the mulattoes in their assembly and defied the home authority, Santhonax recruited the Negroes, who destroyed Port-au-Prince. Santhonax next issued in August, 1792, a declaration of freedom for all slaves. Enraged by this turn of events, the planters sent a mission to Jamaica to invite British intervention.

Toussaint L'Ouverture. Toussaint, who lated added L'Ouverture to his name as a symbol of his mission to open the way to freedom, had, under a gentle master, Bayou de Libertas, learned to read and write, acquired a knowledge of mathematics, and an understanding of the medicinal properties of herbs. Santhonax, respecting Toussaint's intellect, invited him to join the French forces as a doctor, sought his advice, and by 1795 had raised the talented Negro to the rank of a general of a brigade. In turn, Toussaint had influenced Santhonax to issue the Negroes' declaration of freedom. Toussaint soon showed marked military abilities. Operating in the north he drove the invading Spaniards from that part of the island. In the south he successfully put down an uprising of the mulattoes jealous of his position.

In the meantime, the British, long envious of French ownership of Haiti, sent a fleet with troops in answer to the planters' call for aid. Colonel Whitelock with little resistance occupied Môle St. Nicolas, while another fleet seized Port-au-Prince. Against this new invader Toussaint now led his forces and captured Port-au-Prince. The rest of the English withdrew from the north in 1797–1798. Three years later in 1801 he forced the Spaniards to observe the terms of the Treaty of Bâsle, which had turned Santo Domingo over to France.

During these years of campaigns against foreign invaders, Toussaint, virtually head of the government, revived the prosperity of the island. But by 1801 he realized that if his people were to remain free, he must seek independence. Accordingly, in that year he proclaimed a constitution which left France with merely nominal authority in the island. This event, however, coincided with Napoleon's assumption of power as First Consul and conflicted with his plans for the coming conflict with England. Totally disregarding the Haitian Negroes' struggle for freedom, he projected a new French empire in the New World of which Santo Domingo was to be the anchor in the Caribbean, and Louisiana, forced from Spain under the second Treaty of San Ildefonso in 1800, the bulwark on the continent. With the peace of Amiens signed, Napoleon sent General Le Clerc in 1802 with a huge fleet and an army of over 30,000 troops to re-establish slavery in Santo Domingo.

Toussaint prepared to defend his precious island. In the north he placed Henri Christophe, who burned Cap-Haitien to ward off General Rochambeau. Dessalines at the same time reduced Saint-Marc to ashes and retired to the hills. Frustrated by these measures, Le Clerc corrupted Christophe and Dessalines with promises of high rank in the French army. Toussaint, deprived of the bulk of his forces, agreed to halt hostilities upon guarantees of freedom for his Negroes and for himself and the continuation of his supporters in the government and in military offices. Le Clerc accepted these terms and Toussaint retired to his estate in the western part of the island. However, Le Clerc's officers shortly afterward treacherously seized the great Negro and sent him to France, where he died in prison in April, 1803.

Independence, 1804. But Toussaint had done his work well. Having tasted freedom, his people were in no mood to return to slavery. Accordingly, late in 1802 when Napoleon decreed the restoration of slavery in the colonies recognized as French by the Treaty of Amiens, Dessalines revolted. Soon Christophe joined him. From all parts of the island Negroes trooped to fight anew. The struggle opened with cruel excesses committed by both sides. But yellow fever had taken a frightful toll of French lives. One by one the principal interior strongholds fell to the blacks. General Rochambeau, who had taken command after Le Clerc died of yellow fever, finally surrendered when the British blockaded the island in November, 1803. With the French expelled from Santo Domingo by January 1, 1804, Dessalines and Christophe proclaimed independence and gave Saint Dominique its aboriginal name, Haiti. At the same time Dessalines, made governor-general for life by the army, opened the national history of Haiti.

   The Creole Defense of Buenos Aires: Forerunner of Independence. In La Plata, Spain's restrictive commercial policy not only stirred resentment, but lured British, Portuguese, and American smugglers into the La Plata River. Moreover, in Buenos Aires the Porteños were intensely nationalistic, a feeling nurtured by their long rivalry with the Portuguese for the control of the river trade. They readily embraced the teachings of the French political writers, absorbed British economic tracts, and admired the republic in North America. Later their chief spokesman, Manuel Moreno, demanded complete freedom of trade, and his speeches and writings stirred enthusiasm for political independence.

   In this frame of mind the Porteños endorsed the plans of Francisco de Miranda and Admiral Popham in 1803 to free Spanish America. Admiral Popham himself in 1804 submitted his own project for occupying Buenos Aires, but Pitt, eyeing Napoleon on the continent, rejected an undertaking so far away. When, however, in 1805 the battle of Trafalgar exposed both Dutch and Spanish colonies to British seizure, the way was open for an attempt to conquer La Plata. Britain's first objective, however, was the Dutch colonies athwart the British route around Africa to Indian. With Cape Colony safely in their hands, the British turned next to Buenos Aires.

   Admiral Popham, in command of the British naval forces, secured permission of the military commander at the Cape to take a force of 1,650 men under General Beresford and six naval vessels and transports to South America. When the force arrived in La Plata, Viceroy Sobremonte's defense was so weak that the British quickly occupied Buenos Aires, seized a treasure of almost $1,500,000, opened trade with Britain and her colonies, and guaranteed the inhabitants their Catholic religion.

   The Porteños were no more satisfied to see the trade monopoly in British hands than in those of Spain. The Spanish traders naturally opposed the change. Led by Martín Alzaga, a Spanish merchant, the Porteños plotted with Santiago de Liniers, a Frenchman in Spanish employ, who secured some 1,100 troops from the Spanish garrison in Banda Oriental and attacked the city. With cooperation from within, Liniers was able to force the British to withdraw. When free, the Porteños, resenting the cowardly actions of Sobremonte, in a *cabildo* meeting of the leading citizens made Liniers viceroy, an action approved by the Spanish government.

The British government, which had not authorized Popham's actions, promptly removed him, but to efface the defeat sent General Whitelocke in 1807 with 12,000 men. Whitelocke easily captured Montevideo, whence he planned his attack upon Buenos Aires. Meanwhile, Manuel Belgrano and other Creoles had hastily drilled and trained a militia force to resist the invasion. Whitelocke on his part gave an example of military incompetence which has few equals. Dividing his overwhelming force into columns to enter the city by the principal streets, his troops fell victim to the deadly fire directed upon their heads from the housetops where Belgrano had distributed his forces. Totally unprepared for such an attack, the British commander lost a third of his army in two days. Seeing no way to regain the initiative, he surrendered. In the treaty Whitlocke not only agreed to leave Buenos Aires immediately, but to evacuate Montevideo in sixty days. Few times in British history has incompetence been so costly. Britain lost, in Argentina, the counterpart of Canada in the northern hemisphere.

The successful defense of their city filled the Creoles with pride. Thus began the well-known spirit of Argentine nationalism. They had succeeded where Spain had failed. When in the next year, 1808, the Spanish monarchy itself gave final evidence of incapacity in collapsing without a struggle before Napoleon, Buenos Aires was prepared to lead the movement for independence in southern South America.

Miranda the Precursor in Venezuela. Following upon the heels of revolt and independence in Haiti, Francisco de Miranda, affectionately known as the Precursor, led an attempt in 1805–1806 to win freedom in Venezuela. Venezuela had long resented Spain's monopoly of trade and government. The center of dissatisfaction was in eastern Venezuela, where the Caracas and coastal middle class had linked their interests with the cattle barons of the interior plains. In the valleys of the mountainous west were the landowning Creoles, known as Andinos. These, depending upon agriculture for wealth, had long reduced the Indians and *mestizos* to the usual colonial serfdom. Except for hatred of the Spaniards, the Andinos had little in common with the more progressive-minded middle class and cattle barons in eastern Venezuela.

Sebastián Francisco de Miranda, born in a family of traders in Caracas on March 28, 1750, entered the Spanish army at an early age. He served with Gálvez at Pensacola and under Cagigal in the capture of New Providence in the Bahamas. Accused of smuggling, he left the army and journeyed to the United States during 1783 and 1784, where he met many of the leaders of the Revolutionary War, just ended. After travel in Prussia and Russia, he joined the armies of the first French Republic. At the battle of Neerwinden in 1793 he fought with the rank of general, second in command. Imprisoned for a year after this battle which his superior lost, he successfully cleared himself of negligence. During these years he had become obsessed with his great idea—the freeing of Latin America from Spain. In 1798 he went to England to lay his plans before Pitt. There he met Admiral Popham, an enthusiastic supporter of his ideas, but Pitt, in need of Spain's support on the continent, turned a deaf ear to the Venezuelan's pleadings.

In London, Miranda had met Rufus King, the American minister, who showed great interest in his plans. When convinced that the British government would not give him aid, Miranda sailed for the United States, where President Jefferson received him. Returing to New York from Washington, Miranda, asserting that he had the sympathy of the American government, quickly gathered a volunteer force of almost 200 Americans, with promises of army ranks and land as rewards for their service. He sailed in April, 1806, with the *Leander*, his flagship, and two other vessels. Gaining more recruits and ships in Santo Domingo, he set out for Venezuela. The Spanish authorities, alert to the danger, drove him off. But Admiral Thomas Alexander Cochrane of the British naval station at Barbados escorted the *Leander* to Coro, where Miranda finally landed in August. However, he did not find the support he expected among the Venezuelan Creoles, who were dubious, possibly, of a leader who had been away from his homeland for so long. Recognizing his failure, Miranda returned to England to plan another expedition. But in 1808 in the midst of his preparations, the tremendous news of Napoleon's invasion of Spain reached London. The English government at once dropped Miranda to send its aid to the Spanish people struggling against Napoleon. Venezuela nevertheless sent for her great son to lead the revolution in the homeland.

Part III. THE WARS FOR INDEPENDENCE IN NORTHERN SOUTH AMERICA

Immediate Cause. Napoleon's invasion of Spain in 1808 was the immediate cause of the movement for independence in Latin America. The colonists contended that since Ferdinand VII was the sole owner of the colonies, his removal from the throne broke the connection with the homeland. They refused to recognize the authority of Joseph Bonaparte, the brother of Napoleon, made king of Spain by French power. At the

same time the Creoles denied the authority of the Central Junta formed
in Spain to resist the French. Dominated by middle-class Spaniards,
this Junta proposed to transfer the king's monopoly of trade to itself
and to give the colonies representation in the Spanish government in
Spain. The Americans found these reforms distasteful. The commercial
class wanted free trade, whereas the wealthy were not satisfied with the
provisions for elections of representatives from all classes in the colonies.
Under the circumstances the Americans, refusing both Spanish governments, marched to revolution under the slogan of "the old king or none."

The First Venezuelan Republic, 1812. The arrival of the news of
the Central Junta's reforms, made in 1809, and the overrunning of the
peninsula in the next year, called the Disaster of 1810, were sufficient to
launch the revolutionary movement in Venezuela. On April 18 and 19 the
Caracas Creoles called an open meeting of the *cabildo*, forced the resignation of Captain-General Vicente de Emperán, and established a committee or junta to defend the rights of Ferdinand VII. Supported by the
provinces, the *cabildo* sent a commission to Britain headed by Bolívar
to secure arms and urge the return of Miranda to lead the struggle.

Based upon the seven eastern provinces, the Venezuelan junta converted itself into a national congress. It declared the independence of
the country on July 5, 1811, and drew up a federal constitution. Thus was
established the first Venezuelan republic. Miranda, having returned with
Bolívar from England, was made military commander. Its strong, well-
organized forces attracted the allegiance of other provinces, but an
earthquake on March 26, 1812, brought its downfall. Killing more than
20,000 people and destroying Caracas, it caused serious damage in other
cities and towns of the eastern provinces. Western Venezuela escaped
the ravages of the disaster, a fact which led the archbishop of Caracas
to proclaim the event a divine punishment for the people of the seven
provinces in defying the authority of Ferdinand VII. Many people fled
from the eastern provinces to the territory controlled by the Spanish
forces; others, influenced by the church, deserted the patriot cause.

In spite of these defections, Miranda successfully resisted Domingo
de Monteverde, the Spanish commanding general, who launched attacks
in the midst of the disaster. However, a second blow, the betrayal by
a traitor of Puerto Cabello, the principal depot of the patriots' supplies,
forced Miranda to seek an armistice. On July 25, 1812, Miranda and
Monteverde drew up the Capitulations of San Mateo under which the
Venezuelans surrendered their arms in return for amnesty for past
offenses against the royal authority.

These Capitulations produced one of the most hotly debated questions of the war. Miranda's supporters claimed that he, an experienced general, was salvaging what he could to renew the struggle later under more advantageous conditions. His critics insisted that he not only acted without consulting the government, but that the military situation was not so serious as to justify surrender. Lecuna, the great Venezuelan historian, considered that Miranda's action arose from a defect in his character, namely, a lack of military perseverance in the face of obstacles. His bitterest critics virtually charged him with treason, claiming that Miranda's surrender suited Britain, offering at the moment to mediate between Spain and her colonies in return for free trade in colonial ports. In any event, the surrender ended Miranda's career. While Miranda was waiting at La Guaira to board a British ship, Bolívar and others threw the old veteran into prison, where Monteverde captured him when he attacked the city. Sent to Spain, Miranda died in a dungeon in Cádiz in 1816.

Meanwhile, Monteverde, the Spanish commander, did not keep his word to respect the persons and property of the patriots guaranteed in the Capitulations. On the contrary, he seized, exiled, and imprisoned leading citizens and confiscated their possessions, while his soldiers barbarously persecuted civilians. The inevitable effect was to drive the Venezuelans again into revolt, now led by Páez, whose cowboy cavalry drove Monteverde back into the capital, Caracas.

Simón Bolívar, the Liberator. In these tragic circumstances the Venezuelans turned to a man destined to become one of the two greatest leaders of the Wars for Independence in South America—Simón Bolívar. Bolívar's ancestors, migrating to America in the sixteenth century, had become great landowners in Venezuela. Born in Caracas on July 24, 1783, he became heir to a large fortune and aristocratic traditions. Fortunately tutored in his youth by a man of broad interests, Simón Rodríguez, and endowed with great intellectual gifts, he completed his education by a long sojourn in Spain, Italy, and France. Of greatest influence upon his subsequent career was his first-hand observation of the reforms of the French Revolution and the rising star of Napoleon Bonaparte, whom he saw crowned in Berlin.

Back in Venezuela in 1807 at the age of twenty-four, he soon plunged into the growing revolutionary movement. His abilities quickly recognized, he was sent to England to bring back Miranda. In 1810 Miranda gave him command of Puerto Cabello, which in spite of Bolívar's best efforts at defense, was treacherously betrayed to the enemy. Deeply disappointed in having no part in the field operations against the Spaniards, Bolívar was among those who criticized Miranda harshly for his surrender to Monteverde.

The Second Venezuelan Republic, 1814. To secure aid against Monteverde at Caracas, Bolívar fell back to New Granada. There the revolutionary movement was handicapped by rivalries among the patriots. But Bolívar's arrival gave new life to the uprising. Made a citizen of New Granada and commissioned a brigadier, Bolívar executed a series of campaigns which cleared the Spaniards from the coastal area. He next recrossed the mountains to attack Monteverde in Venezuela. At Trujillo Bolívar issued his famous decree of "war to the death" on June 15, 1813, for which he has been both praised and condemned. Lecuna, the Venezuelan historian and authority on Bolívar, citing the Spanish decree of January 11, 1813, anticipating Bolívar's by several months, justifies the latter's extreme action. Other historians have pointed to the savagery of the war as a sufficient explanation. Bolívar's critics, however, past and present, show him little quarter.

His attack drove Monteverde back into Puerto Cabello and opened the way for a patriot occupation of Caracas in August, 1813. In January, 1814, the Venezuelans restored their republic with Bolívar at the head, with the title of Liberator. Bolívar, attempting to strengthen his position along the coast, neglected the interior. There the Spaniards recruited the services of José Tomás Boves, a brutal, half-civilized leader of the *llaneros,* southeast of Caracas. Capturing Ocumare near Caracas, Boves barbarously beheaded the bulk of the population. Bolívar, giving way to popular indignation over the crime, retaliated by beheading Spanish prisoners in Caracas and La Guaira. In July, 1814, Boves, reinforced with loot-crazed *llaneros* from the interior, drove Bolívar from Caracas back to New Granada.

Defeat in New Granada, 1814–1815. In New Granada after Bolívar's departure for Venezuela, Antonio de Nariño had driven the Spaniards south to Pasto. Overconfident, he was trapped and captured. In the north, rivalries between Bogotá and Cartagena blocked unified action. When Bolívar arrived a second time in New Granada, he was received with honors and given command of the patriot forces by a congress assembled at Tunja to bring about a union of the divided provinces. He forced Bogotá to enter the confederation and then turned to attack Cartagena to achieve the same end. But in the midst of these operations, he learned that General Pablo Morillo had arrived with strong reinforcements from Spain. Unable to face the superior forces that Morillo brought to bear upon Cartagena, Bolívar resigned his command and departed for Jamaica to organize a new effort.

This moment was one of the darkest in the history of the struggle for independence, for Napoleon's defeat had freed large Spanish armies for service in the colonies. In New Granada Morillo advanced with 10,000 men upon Cartagena, capturing it after a long siege from the defenders, who died by the thousands of hunger. From Cartagena, Morillo sent forces to reconquer Venezuela, while he himself advanced upon Bogotá. With false promises of amnesty he took possession of the capital, May, 1816, and bloodily executed many of its leading citizens. Others he imprisoned. In the provinces his troops carried out his shockingly cruel orders, destroying many prominent families one after another.

Bolívar's Campaigns, 1816–1819. In this dark hour Bolívar proclaimed in his famous letter to a Jamaica resident on September 6, 1815, his faith in ultimate success and his ideas for the kind of governments to follow independence. Therein he portrayed the virtues of the republican form over the monarchical, and made the astonishing prediction that America could well "tolerate" seventeen republics. With Haiti already independent, Bolívar missed the number by only two! From Jamaica, where he had taken refuge, Bolívar moved on to Haiti. There, joined by his principal supporters, he secured aid from President Pétion upon a promise to free the Negroes in Venezuela when independence was achieved.

Receiving news of a successful revolt led by Santiago Mariño on the island of Margarita off the eastern coast of Venezuela, he landed on the island in May, 1816. With a government established under Bolívar as supreme chief, the patriot forces advanced to the mainland. General Gregor McGregor won victories near Barcelona, but Bolívar found it impracticable to attack the capital, Caracas. Instead he pushed into the interior of Venezuela to establish his capital at Angostura on the Orinoco River in 1817. In the meantime in 1816 he had sent commissioners to England to enlist volunteers. These had little difficulty, for unemployment after the Napoleonic wars plagued England. Some 6,000 Scotch and Irish officers and men flocked to join the patriot army.

Angostura on the Orinoco proved the base from which Bolívar conducted the campaigns for independence of both New Granada and Venezuela to a successful conclusion. There a congress that he assembled established a government and made Bolívar the president of Venezuela and its commander-in-chief. Before this assembly he delivered his memorable address in which he applauded the virtues of a limited democracy, scorned the relics of Spain's domination, and advocated a government after independence modeled upon republican elements of the British constitution.

However, the road to victory was not an easy one. Continued reinforcements arrived to strengthen Morillo at Caracas. Within the patriot army insubordination was rife. Manuel de Piar, who had kept the revolution alive in eastern Venezuela when Bolívar retreated to Haiti, planned with Mariño, who had captured the island of Margarita, to replace the Liberator. Informed of the intrigue, Bolívar court-martialed and shot Piar to restore discipline. Leadership of the guerrilla forces operating against Caracas now fell to José Antonio Páez, of unswerving loyalty to Bolívar.

The Orinoco Campaign, 1819. Leaving Páez in command in Venezuela, Bolívar began his famous march in June, 1819, through the swamps of the Orinoco and across the Andes Mountains. His army suffered the torments of the jungle and the icy blasts of the high mountain passes. More than 100 of the 2,500 men froze to death, others deserted, and many became ill. Heavy baggage had to be abandoned and most of the horses perished. When early in July, 1819, Bolívar arrived at the foot of the Andes in New Granada, his forces were in the last stages of exhaustion. The Spaniards in Bogotá found it impossible to believe the stories of the passage, for the Andes had never been crossed before in these high and rugged regions. The slowness of Spanish reaction gave Bolívar time to recoup his strength, rouse the patriots, secure mounts, and launch his attack upon the capital.

In New Granada, Francisco de Paula Santander had kept alive guerrilla resistance and now proved an invaluable ally. Joining Bolívar, the combined armies marched upon the capital. Too late the Spaniards at the capital sent into the interior for the principal forces. At the bridge at Boyacá near Bogotá, Bolívar intercepted the main Spanish army and defeated it. This proved to be the decisive battle and opened the way for the capture of Bogotá.

The Independence of New Granada and Venezuela, 1819–1821. The winning of New Granada marked the turning point in the struggle for independence in northern South America. Morillo found it impossible to send aid to the Granadine loyalists; everywhere patriot hopes revived. Taking full advantage of this enthusiasm, Bolívar united the vast territories from the Pacific Ocean to the Orinoco into the Republic of Colombia. Santander became vice-president in Bogotá, while the congress at Angostura endorsed the new state. Bolívar now prepared for the freeing of Venezuela.

At this favorable moment the patriots received assistance from an unexpected quarter. In 1820 in Spain a revolt broke out in Cádiz within an army preparing to embark for the colonies. The successful Spanish liberal leaders forced the king to reaffirm the constitution of 1812, overthrown after his returning to the kingship in that year. The new Spanish government, hoping to end the revolt in the colonies, sent peremptory orders to Morillo to make peace, put the constitution into effect, hold elections, and send representatives from the colonies to the new Spanish *Cortes.* Unable to accept the changed situation, Morillo returned to Spain, leaving in command General Miguel de la Torre.

In the meantime, Bolívar was energetically raising new forces. In Maracaibo the inhabitants revolted and joined the new republic. Fully prepared for the final attack early in 1821, Bolívar crossed the Andes again to invade Venezuela in the north. La Torre with but 9,000 men now faced a patriot army grown to more than 20,000. The two forces came together on the plains of Carabobo.

Carabobo. The new Spanish commander, La Torre, soon found himself hemmed in by Bolívar on the west and the guerrillas under Páez on the south. Though outmaneuvered, La Torre fought so well that only a hard-charging British battalion supported by Páez' cavalry saved the day for the patriots. After Carabobo the road to Caracas was open. In a short time Páez had cleared Venezuela of the remaining enemy forces. For the third time a republic was established in Venezuela, now called the Republic of Colombia. Its constitution was drawn up at Cúcuta in 1821. In October of that year Bolívar became president and commander of its military forces.

The Freeing of Ecuador. The news of the overthrow of Ferdinand VII provoked in Ecuador, as it did elsewhere, a revolutionary movement (August, 1809). There Creoles set aside the president of the *audiencia* of Quito, Conde Ruíz de Castilla, and called a meeting of the *cabildo* which recognized Juan de Montúfar to govern the country. The uprising was shortly put down and Castilla again assumed the presidency. The overrunning of Spain in 1810 by French troops produced the second revolutionary uprising among the Ecuadorian Creoles. The Central Junta of Spain, however, dispatched Joaquín de Molina, supported by a Spanish army, which ended the revolt and placed General Toríbio Morites in office as president of the *audiencia.* Until 1820 when the revolt in Cádiz occurred there were no further uprisings in Ecuador. In that year on October 9 the Creoles rose in Guayaquil. While they were eventually put down, they effectively tied up royal forces at the moment when San Martín was landing on the southern coast of Peru.

Pichincha, 1822. In 1821 Bolívar turned his attention to this last stronghold of Spanish power in northern South America. With the Colombians already marching toward Quito, the Liberator sent General Antonio José de Sucre to Guayaquil to direct the campaign. Young, able, and the favorite general of Bolívar, Sucre blocked reinforcements sent from Peru and pinned the Spanish army against the slopes of the volcano of Pichincha. Here, awaiting aid from San Martín, Sucre held off his attack upon Aymerich, the Spanish general. The latter, hoping to defeat his young opponent before reinforcements arrived, opened the battle on May 22, 1822, but shortly found himself routed by the brilliant strategy of Sucre.

The victory of Pichincha placed Quito and soon afterward all of Ecuador in the hands of the patriots. Bolívar arrived in the capital in June and annexed Ecuador to the Republic of Colombia, somewhat against the wishes of the inhabitants of Guayaquil. Bolívar next turned his eyes toward Peru, where San Martín had been operating for two years. In November, 1822, San Martín arrived in Guayaquil to confer with Bolívar for the final effort to overthrow Spanish power in South America.

Chapter XIII

THE WARS FOR INDEPEND-
ENCE: SOUTHERN SOUTH
AMERICA AND BRAZIL

Part I. THE INDEPENDENCE OF LA PLATA

Argentina. The Argentines, as noted, defeated in 1807 the efforts of Britain to conquer La Plata. But once the British threat had passed, the inhabitants were torn by internal dissension. The Creoles of Buenos Aires, eager to overthrow Spanish power everywhere, sent delegations, notably to Chile, to stir up revolt. But in the next year, 1808, when news of Napoleon's invasion of Spain arrived, the Spanish merchants opposed Creole proposals for independence. Liniers, a Frenchman elevated to be viceroy after the defeat of the English, favored allegiance to Joseph Bonaparte. This suggestion, however, both Spanish royalists and the Porteños opposed. The *cabildo* of the city, determined that no such recognition should occur, removed Liniers. To replace him the Central Junta of Spain sent out Baltásar Hidalgo de Cisneros y Latorre.

The attempt of the Spanish Junta to hold the colonies in the mercantile system drove the Buenos Aires Creoles to oppose the action in an open *cabildo* meeting on May 25, 1810. The viceroy promptly resigned and the *cabildo* assumed powers of government, thus beginning in fact Argentina's career as an independent nation. The actual declaration of that independence, however, did not come until 1816. The principal leader, at the moment the secretary of the junta of Buenos Aires, was Mariano Moreno, advocate of middle class reforms, particularly free trade.

Steps to Independence, 1810–1816. In the junta, conflict quickly broke out. The Spanish merchants insisted upon loyalty to the Cádiz government, while the Porteños demanded outright independence. Complicating this internal struggle was the effort of the junta as a whole to establish its authority over the interior provinces of Argentina as well as over those areas formerly governed by the viceroy, namely, Charcas, Paraguay, and Uruguay. In the struggle to control the junta, the Spanish residents succeeded in investing the head, Cornelio de Saavedra, with viceregal powers. The latter got rid of his principal opponent, Moreno, by sending him on a mission to England. Too, Saavedra won support from provincial leaders who feared the domination of the port city. In this struggle, however, Saavedra lost, with a triumvirate of Porteños winning control in 1811.

The junta next summoned two congresses, one in 1812 and the second in 1813, voiced vigorous opposition to federalism, and proclaimed its absolute power over the United Provinces of the Río de la Plata. To strengthen their position they placed power in the hands of a supreme director, Gervais Posadas, advised by a council. The work of the two congresses is significant in making reforms to end colonial restrictions. Among their chief measures they reduced the power of the church, abolished the Inquisition and compulsory tithing, prohibited anyone from entering the church service as a priest or nun before the age of thirty, set aside the oath swearing obedience to the Spanish king, and required all officials and employees, military, religious, and civil, to become Argentine citizens. Significant reforms included freedom of children of slaves and of Indians from forced labor, measures for the education of both groups, ending the importation of slaves and the Indian head tax, and provision for the freedom of the press. Reorganizing the administration of justice, the congresses abolished judicial torture and cut the last legal tie with Spain. The government's proposal to adopt a constitution, however, was set aside by the congress, which decided that the country should first rid itself of the Spaniards' power.

Declaration of Independence, 1816. The congresses of 1812 and 1813 represented a victory for the centralist forces in Buenos Aires. But the interior provinces, dominated by powerful landowners favoring a federal form of government, refused to accept the aspirations of the port city. As the conflict intensified after 1815, a variety of proposals appeared. Some suggested a monarchy; Belgrano wanted to place an heir of the Incas on an Argentine throne; others favored a Spanish Bourbon prince; still others wanted to make Argentina part of the Portuguese empire. Their counterparts suggested, because of the great popularity of France, a ruler from the French royal family.

A foreign threat, the Portuguese invasion of Uruguay, hastened the decision to form a government. To this end the centralist faction of Buenos Aires conceded the principle of federalism. To give point to their offer they selected the interior city of Tucumán for the meeting place of the national assembly. Some provinces sent no delegates, but enough appeared to present a picture of unity as a warning to the Portuguese. No agreement could be reached concerning a constitution, but the assembly did draw up, as its most important achievement, a declaration of independence and chose the name, the United Provinces of the Río de la Plata, for the new nation on July 11, 1816. To head the new state the convention selected Juan Martín de Pueyrredón as supreme director.

Buenos Aires and the Provinces, 1810–1816. During these years, 1810–1816, in the midst of efforts to establish a united nation, the junta of 1810 and later governments sent out expeditions to bring the provinces of the former viceroyalty under control. Don Francisco Antonio Ortiz de Ocampo, "to enforce the mandates of the people at the point of the bayonet," departed for the interior and Charcas at the head of 1,100 volunteers. The expedition suffocated opposition to Buenos Aires in the Pampas provinces, and under Don Antonio González Balcarce, who replaced Ocampo at Córdoba, continued its advance into Charcas. There the Porteño invaders occupied all strategic points as far as the frontier of Peru itself, after a victory at Suipacha, November 1, 1810. Everywhere in Charcas patriots rose to greet the liberators.

To consolidate the hold of Buenos Aires upon this valuable area, the junta sent Dr. Juan José Castelli. Devoting too much energy to political activities, the invading army had neglected elementary measures to protect its military position. Taking advantage of the opening, Goyeneche, president of the *audiencia* of Charcas attacked and defeated the Porteños at Hiaqui near Lake Titicaca. By September, 1811, Goyeneche had driven all the Argentine troops from Upper Peru and turned upon the Charcas republicans to inflict punishment.

Goyeneche next planned to conquer Buenos Aires itself and marched toward Tucumán. But Manuel Belgrano, sent hastily to replace the defeated Argentine commanders, threw back Goyeneche and pursued him into Charcas. The tide turned again when General Joaquín de Pezuela, with reinforcements recently arrived from Spain, decisively defeated Belgrano in two battles, at Vilapugio and Ayohuma, in October–November, 1813. Thus ended the hopes of Buenos Aires to establish its authority in Charcas.

The Independence of Paraguay. Paraguay had experienced a major revolt against Spanish authority in the early eighteenth century. When the French overthrew Ferdinand VII, the Paraguayans refused to recognize either Joseph Bonaparte or the Central Junta at Cádiz. The governor at the moment, Bernardo de Velazco, declared for the dethroned Spanish king and also refused to submit to Buenos Aires. The junta in the port city thereupon despatched Belgrano with an army to take Asunción. Crossing the Paraná River at Candelaria, he met Velazco with an estimated force of 7,000 at Paraguarí. There the invaders were decisively defeated on January 19, 1811. Under the armistice Belgrano agreed to leave the province, but Paraguay opened its borders to free trade with Buenos Aires.

With subjection to Buenos Aires warded off, Velazco lost power in an internal conflict. The victors organized themselves into a junta and drew up a constitution, adopted on October 12, 1813. Emerging as the leader of this movement was José Gaspar Tomás Rodríguez Francia, better known as Dr. Francia, who shortly established a dictatorship, but maintained the independence of Paraguay.

The Struggle for Independence in Uruguay. The struggle for freedom in Uruguay between 1810 and 1821 centered around her great national hero, José Gervasio Artigas. When Napoleon conquered Spain in 1808, Uruguay set up a junta in Montevideo, recognized the Central Junta of Cádiz, and refused admittance of Napoleon's envoys. Cisneros, the viceroy in Buenos Aires and the appointee of the Cádiz Junta, opened Montevideo to Spanish trade. In 1810 after the *cabildo* of Buenos Aires assumed power, the new viceroy who succeeded Cisneros, Francisco Xavier de Elío, established his residence in Montevideo. From there he planned an attack upon Buenos Aires. But the action of the Buenos Aires leaders set an example the Uruguayans were not slow to follow. Opposing Elío's plans, they rose in revolt on February 28, 1811.

Leading the uprising was Artigas. Born in the northern part of Uruguay in 1764, a descendant of one of the families which founded Montevideo, little is known of his youth. As a smuggler he became so prominent that the Spaniards, to aid their control of the interior, made him the guardian-general of the rural regions. He participated in the defense of Montevideo and Buenos Aires against British attack and fled to Argentina when Elío arrived at Montevideo. There, joined by other Uruguayan patriots, he raised an army of 1,000 men to lay siege to Elío's capital. The junta in Buenos Aires, hoping to bring Uruguay into its jurisdiction, sent reinforcements under General José Rondeau.

With no aid forthcoming from Spain and seeing himself unable to hold out against the combined armies, Elío turned to King João VI, who had fled to Rio de Janeiro in 1808. The king immediately sent a strong force over the protests of the British resident minister, Viscount Strang-ford. The action saved Elío. Buenos Aires, seeing the impossibility of holding Uruguay against the Brazilians, agreed to the armistice proposed by Elío. Under its terms Spanish authority was to be recognized in Uruguay, while the Argentine and Brazilian armies were to depart in October, 1811.

Artigas, angered by the agreement, called a general meeting of the leading Uruguayan families. They consented to follow him in a great migration. More than 13,000 inhabitants, including 3,000 soldiers and hundreds of Indians, crossed the Uruguay River into Argentina. Meanwhile, in Rio de Janeiro, Viscount Strangford, the English minister, forced the return of the Portuguese troops from Uruguay where they had remained in violation of the armistice. This event opened the way for Argentina to renew the attack upon Montevideo.

Artigas in Montevideo. A second siege of Montevideo lasting two years began in October, 1812. The irritations attending the siege brought discord between Artigas and Buenos Aires. In 1813 Artigas called a national congress of Uruguayans, which made him president and military commander of the country and sent a delegation to the assembly in Buenos Aires. That body, strongly centralist in character, refused to seat the Uruguayans, who favored federalism. In protest, Artigas withdrew from the siege, an action which led Buenos Aires to declare him an outlaw. Using his great influence in the northern Argentine provinces, he stirred up a revolt in Corrientes, Entre Ríos, and Córdoba as well as in Uruguay itself against the authority of the assembly.

In the midst of this conflict Gervasio Antonio Posadas, the supreme director in Buenos Aires, sent William Brown, an Irish-American who had volunteered his services to Buenos Aires, with a fleet to blockade Montevideo. Cooperating with the land forces, Brown contributed to the fall of the city on June 20, 1814. Brazil, meantime, observing Artigas' revolutionary activity among a large block of provinces, massed troops on her Brazilian-Uruguayan border. The combined threat of a Brazilian invasion and the success of Artigas forced Buenos Aires to turn Montevideo over to the Uruguayan leader early in 1815.

Artigas at once established authority throughout Banda Oriental. He included in his jurisdiction the territory of the seven Jesuit missions which Spain had transferred to Portugal in 1750, but which had been returned to Spanish control in 1757. Over this territory Portugal had never given up hope of extending her power. King João VI in Rio de Janeiro saw in Artigas' action an opportunity to recover not only the seven missions, but extend Brazil to the Río de la Plata. Declaring Artigas a "disturbing influence," he invaded in 1816 by land and by sea.

Annexation of Uruguay to Brazil. Although greatly outnumbered, Artigas and his men fought valiantly. He himself and José Fructuoso Rivera surrendered Montevideo in 1817. Early in 1818 his ablest general, Juan Antonio Lavalleja, was captured, and Rivera forced to surrender his army before the year was out. Artigas kept up the unequal struggle for another year. When, finally, in 1820 he lost the support of the Argentine provinces and suffered devastating defeat at Tacuarembó, he fled to take refuge in Paraguay under Dr. Francia. There he died in 1826. In 1821 a Uruguayan congress, subservient to Brazil, voted, with the British minister in Rio de Janeiro approving, the annexation of Uruguay to Brazil as the Cisplatine Province. Seven years later, as we shall see, Uruguay finally won its independence.

Part II.   THE LIBERATION OF WESTERN SOUTH AMERICA: CHILE AND PERU

San Martín and the Freedom of Chile. By 1816 the patriots of Buenos Aires became gravely concerned with the seeming failure of the independence movement. Morillo had re-established royal authority in Colombia and Venezuela. In neighboring Chile, Spanish troops had crushed the revolutionary movement. Nearer at hand Portugal had moved down to the very doorstep of Argentina into Uruguay. While many liberty-loving Argentines regretted the welter of their politics, one man emerged able to rise above civil conflict and hold to the idea of driving Spain from all of South America—José San Martín.

Born in 1778 in the little mission town of Yapetú along the middle course of the Uruguay River, San Martín was the son of a lieutenant-governor of that region. At an early age after his father's death he returned with his mother to Spain. There he entered a military school from which he joined the Spanish army and fought in Africa and against the armies of the French Republic in 1793. In Cádiz, where he was stationed for a time, he met liberal leaders from South America, notably his fellow countryman, Carlos Alvear, who apparently influenced him to enlist in the struggle for freedom. Others explain his action in leaving the Spanish army by his belief that Spain could never recover from the double blow of Napoleon's invasion and the revolt of her colonies. Certain it is that San Martín never accepted republican principles, but remained to the end a monarchist in outlook.

Arriving in Argentina early in 1812, San Martín served with distinction in the siege of Montevideo which began in that year. Later he brilliantly defeated a royalist invasion directed at Buenos Aires in 1813. After Belgrano's disaster in Upper Peru, San Martín relieved him at Tucumán and threw back with inferior forces the invading royalist army. While the loss of Montevideo in 1814 discouraged further Spanish plans to take Buenos Aires from Peru, the crushing of the revolt in Chile in October of that year warned Buenos Aires of possible invasion from that quarter. It was at this point that San Martín, stepping aside from the violent political battles of the capital, sought the governorship of the western province of Cuyo, to create there an army to attack Spain in Chile.

With an energy that equaled Bolívar's, San Martín stirred the patriotism of the inhabitants of Cuyo for sacrifices they little dreamed possible. At Mendoza, the capital, he organized the citizens into beehives of industry, turning out clothing, military supplies, food, and equipment needed to mount the high passes of the Andes. With little aid from Buenos Aires he whipped into shape a cavalry out of the rough, hard-riding, individualistic gauchos and trained an army of volunteers. When ready to march early in 1817, San Martín commanded an army of over 4,000 men. Inspired by his leadership, it became one of the most formidable fighting forces of the Wars for Independence.

O'Higgins and the Early Struggle for Independence, 1810–1814. In Chile a vigorous sentiment existed for independence long before Napoleon invaded Spain in 1808. Inspired by the American revolution, conspirators had made an early attempt in 1781. The spirit was kept alive in Concepción, where liberal thinkers organized themselves into "literary," in fact, revolutionary clubs. Outstanding among the ardent advocates of freedom was Bernardo O'Higgins, the natural son of a governor of Chile, Ambrosio O'Higgins, later viceroy of Peru in 1796–1801. At the age of twenty, when he arrived in Europe, he immersed himself in the revolutionary literature of the time and met many of the South American revolutionary leaders including Francisco de Miranda. On his return to Chile in 1801 he inherited his father's rich estates in southern Chile and immediately assumed leadership in the Concepción club.

When news of Napoleon's invasion of Spain reached Chile, Don Juan Martínez de Rozas, an Argentine liberal residing in Concepción, stirred up sentiment for revolt. Supporting him against the measures of Captain-General Carrasco was O'Higgins. In 1810 O'Higgins and Rozas won a dominating influence in the city council of Santiago, where they nourished the revolutionary movement. They succeeded next in organizing a junta which declared freedom of trade. But divisions within the patriots' ranks and opposition of Spanish traders slowed their efforts to organize a revolt. Unable to secure control of a congress called in Santiago in 1811, O'Higgins and Rozas withdrew with a sprinkling of followers to Concepción, where they set up a junta.

In Concepción, José Miguel Carrera, fleeing from revolutionary activity in Spain, joined Rozas and O'Higgins. Fiery, able, and ambitious, Carrera soon assumed leadership, and on September 11, 1811, overthrew the congress in Santiago. In the following year, 1812, he promulgated the 1812 Spanish constitution, reorganized the *cabildo* in the capital on the basis of the population, and prepared a constitution for the country. In the midst of these changes the army of the viceroy of Peru, Fernando Abascal, invaded the south, where General Antonio Pareja captured Valdivia and finally Concepción.

Carrera fell from power to be succeeded by O'Higgins, who, however, did not have full patriot support. Viceroy Abascal sent reinforcements under General Mariano Osorio, who defeated O'Higgins on October 2, 1814, at Rancagua. This victory seemed to end the hopes of the Chileans for independence. The liberal leaders were seized, some executed, and others sent to prison. Carrera and O'Higgins escaped across the Andes Mountains to Mendoza, where O'Higgins united his veterans to those of San Martín. Carrera, however, continued to Buenos Aires.

San Martín and the Independence of Chile. By January, 1817, San Martín was ready to mount the Andes. His basic strategy was to cross the two passes, Uspallata and Los Patos, cut through the center of the enemy forces, and capture Santiago. As part of an elaborate deception, he dispatched General Juan de las Heras with a small force through the principal and shorter pass, Uspallata, to Santa Rosa where he was to draw if possible the principal fire of the enemy. In the meantime, San Martín with the bulk of the main forces, accompanied by O'Higgins, took the longer northern pass, Los Patos. The whole movement was covered with propaganda and the dissemination of false reports by spies sent ahead of the armies.

The maneuver was a complete success. Both armies met at their rendezvous, San Felipe, at the appointed time. The commander of the Spanish forces in Chile, Marcó del Pont, because of the strong liberal strongholds in the south had maintained the bulk of his forces there. Consequently, San Martín had time to rest his men, replenish his supplies from the enthusiastic population, and prepare for his next step, the march on Santiago. What forces Marcó was able to summon from the south were hardly half the number in San Martín's army. The two met at a little town of Chacabuco north of Santiago, where San Martín won the first decisive battle for Chile's independence on February 1, 1817.

After Chacabuco, Santiago fell quickly. San Martín and O'Higgins were received with joy and honors. Refusing to become head of the state, San Martín urged that the people confer the office of supreme director upon O'Higgins, which was done. Meantime, the new viceroy in Peru, Pezuela, who as a general had defeated Belgrano, sent a new army under General Osorio to southern Chile. Advancing to meet this threat, San Martín and O'Higgins to their surprise were overwhelmingly defeated. But Osorio made the error of not following up his success. San Martín took the breathing space to reorganize his forces and fall back to Maipú on the River Maule, outside of Santiago. There on April 5, 1818, with the two armies evenly matched at about 6,000 men each, the bloodiest battle of the Wars for Independence was fought. Osorio went down to defeat so complete that nothing remained of Spanish power in Chile except the coastal city of Valdivia. Following this battle O'Higgins returned to Santiago and shortly called a constitutional convention which declared the independence of Chile on February 12, 1819.

San Martín in Peru, 1820–1822. San Martín, who had long studied the problem of expelling the Spaniards from South America, had four years before in 1816 worked out a simple plan. First was the freeing of Chile; secondly, the acquisition of a navy to transport his forces to Peru; and lastly the capture of Lima. After the final defeat of the Spaniards at Maipú, he planned the details of his invasion, including the acquisition of a naval force. O'Higgins attacked this problem and soon had acquired by purchase and capture four small ships. These, under Chile's first admiral, Blanca Encalada, quickly distinguished themselves in defeating Spanish ships on the coast of Chile. But they were not enough for the Peruvian expedition. Fortunately, in England Chilean agents secured the services of a great British seaman, Thomas Alexander Cochrane, the same who had aided Miranda years before in his effort to free Venezuela.

Arrived in Chile, Cochrane took command of the Chilean navy with the rank of vice-admiral, a post graciously surrendered by Blanca Encalada. After a sortie of bombing the coast of Peru, which drove the Spanish fleet into Callao harbor, he captured Valdivia and turned over to San Martín its valuable military stores.

On August 20, 1820, San Martín launched his long-planned invasion of Peru from Valparaíso. His force consisted of 4,430 men carried in sixteen transports and escorted by eight men-of-war under command of Admiral Cochrane. San Martín knew from the beginning that his tactics would have to be Fabian, for Spain had 23,000 trained soldiers distributed throughout Peru, as well as overwhelming supplies to maintain these. Landing on the coast at Pisco, about eighty miles south of Lima, he spread revolutionary pamphlets far and wide calling the population to arms against their Spanish oppressors.

Peru in the colonial period had a history of Indian revolt. The material for revolution lay about on every hand, but the powerful forces maintained by the king of Spain in his richest South American possession effectively suppressed all uprisings. Nevertheless, with the invasion of Spain by Napoleon, Antonio María Pardo attempted in 1809 to establish a junta in imitation of the Central Junta of Spain. The movement was quickly suppressed. In 1810 José Riva Agüero organized secret meetings which included representatives from all classes. When these meetings were discovered, some of those who attended were imprisoned, but Riva Agüero escaped to the interior. Between 1811 and 1814 violent uprisings took place in the provinces—at Huánuco, in the far south at Tacna in 1811–1813, and in Cuzco in 1814. In the latter the rebels established a constitutional *cabildo*, secured the support of the garrison, and placed at the head of the government an Inca Indian who had previously fought against Tupac Amarú. Before the uprising was put down on March 11, 1815, it had the support of more than 20,000 men. Representatives of these defeated movements welcomed San Martín to Peru.

The Spanish Revolt of 1820 and Peru. At the moment of San Martín's landing, two events occurred which greatly aided his plans. In Spain the revolt of 1820 found reflection in an uprising in Guayaquil on October 9. There the patriots, on learning of San Martín's arrival, rose and seized the city. Not only did their action tie up Spanish forces in Ecuador, but, more important, the rebels held for a time the only important shipyard on the South American coast. The second event gave San Martín control of the sea along the Pacific coast. It arose from the daring action of Admiral Cochrane, who, tiring of patrolling Callao to hold the Spanish fleet there, daringly slipped into the harbor and captured the *Esmeralda*, Spain's best warship on the coast. San Martín immediately moved his base northward to Huacho, about 100 miles beyond Lima to attack that city.

These events had a demoralizing effect upon the Spaniards. Viceroy Pezuela, with much larger forces, vacillated, for he did not know how effective the revolutionary propaganda was upon the people. The news of the constitution of 1812, proclaimed in Cádiz, split the Spaniards in Peru into two camps, and divided both from the rich, landowning Creoles. Those who still supported the king were the Absolutists; those who favored the new Spanish government, the Constitutionalists. Finally, the Creoles and the hierarchy of the church, fearing both the effect of the 1820 constitution if promulgated in Peru and the influence of San Martín's revolutionary propaganda upon the Indians, became sympathetic to the idea of revolt from Spain. Like the Creoles in Mexico under Iturbide at this precise time, they preferred a revolution they could control to reforms imposed by the Cádiz constitution. The fact that San Martín himself was known to hold monarchist views made them view him somewhat in the light of a savior.

Thus in Lima a small clique of Creoles and high churchmen forced Viceroy Pezuela to resign and replaced him with General José de la Serna, who opened negotiations with San Martín. When negotiations, however, finally broke down, San Martín advanced and captured Lima on July 6, 1821. La Serna, after strengthening Callao, retreated to the high Andes to gather reinforcements from Upper Peru. At this point San Martín discovered that the capture of Lima did not mean the independence of Peru. Moreover, his zeal for a republican Peru seemed to have cooled. In place of continuing the attack upon La Serna, he turned to political maneuver.

Hardly had he established himself in the capital when he called an assembly of notables, presided over by the archbishop, which declared the independence of Peru on July 14, 1821. For several months thereafter, San Martín, now Protector of Peru, remained inactive, while the viceroy prepared his forces in the mountains. The patriots' domination of Callao's port through the blockade and capture of the capital proved a stumbling block to the viceroy's plans for attack. General José Cantarac, after trying vainly to relieve the garrison at Callao, retreated to the mountains in a maneuver which challenged San Martín to battle. Surprisingly, the Protector let him escape unmolested. However, on September 21 San Martín captured Callao, filled with stores of armaments and supplies.

In the following months the Peruvian Creoles attempted to interest San Martín in accepting a crown, a matter which he seriously considered. But his Chilean soldiers strongly petitioned against any such action. At the same time Admiral Cochrane, displeased with the general's inaction, left with the fleet. These events seemed to have deterred the Argentine, but possibly of more importance was his projected visit with Bolívar.

The Guayaquil Conference, July 26–27, 1822. The two leaders of the independence movement in South America met in Guayaquil, Ecuador. In a series of conferences they sharply disagreed over most of the important matters they discussed. These cannot be identified with complete accuracy, since the men met in private. While San Martín remained silent, Bolívar wrote several accounts. From these it is apparent that the latter could not accept San Martín's monarchical ideas regarding the future governments of the liberated states, particularly Peru. It is evident also that San Martín offended Bolívar in not asking for Colombian troops to conquer Peru. Bolívar, however, felt that the conquest would require greater forces than those at San Martín's disposal. Sharper light is thrown on the extent of the disagreement between the two leaders by San Martín's action in leaving immediately after the conference for Argentina, whence he ultimately departed for Europe to die there in 1850. One result of the Guayaquil conference, certainly, was that it launched the most famous controversy in Latin-American history.

The Independence of Peru. When San Martín departed for Guayaquil, Viceroy La Serna in Peru attacked Lima. The crisis brought the expulsion of San Martín's lieutenants and raised Colonel José Riva Agüero, the popular liberal leader, to command the Peruvian patriot armies, aided by Andrés Santa Cruz, an ambitious general. Riva Agüero energetically reorganized the defense of Lima and Callao, and sought reinforcements that Bolívar had offered to San Martín. The Liberator promptly dispatched Colombian troops under General Sucre, whom the Peruvian congress elevated to the command of its armies.

But for a moment the war seemed to turn in favor of the Spanish armies. Santa Cruz, operating in the south, had attempted to defeat La Serna by attacking the viceroy's forces near Cuzco. But La Serna, cutting his opponent's line of communication, forced the patriot army back with serious losses. Sucre, meanwhile, who had occupied Arequipa in the south, was forced also to retreat to Callao when Santa Cruz refused cooperation. In the midst of this danger Bolívar himself arrived in Lima on September 1, 1823. The Peruvian congress at once conferred dictatorial powers upon him to stem the tide. But the ardent republican troops of Argentina and Chile resented this action, as they did the offering of a crown to San Martín. When their discontent reached the proportions of a revolt, General Cantarac attacked Lima with 7,000 men. Unable to defend the city, Bolívar fell back all the way to Guayaquil.

Junín. This reverse only inspired Bolívar to greater efforts. Gathering a powerful army of 10,000 men, well drilled and equipped, he advanced again into Peru to occupy the territory north of Lima. Sucre, aided by guerrillas, opened the way to Pasco where Bolívar arrived in full force. At the opposite end of this valley high in the Andes was Cantarac with his army and base at Junín. In a brilliant maneuver which enticed Cantarac to attack under unfavorable conditions, Bolívar defeated his enemy with inferior forces at Junín in one of the two final and decisive battles in Peru, August 6, 1824.

With the coast and central Peru now in the hands of Bolívar, Cantarac fell back upon Cuzco in the interior. Bolívar, believing that the year was too far advanced for the Spaniards to continue the war, ordered Sucre into winter quarters southwest of Cuzco. Sucre, however, supported by his generals and advised by his guerrilla leaders, believed that the Liberator had miscalculated. He had learned that Cantarac, preparing a new attack, had sent for reinforcements to Upper Peru. Fortunately for the patriots, the royalist army suffered at the moment from divided counsels. The overthrow of the Cádiz constitution and the restoration of Ferdinand VII to absolute power in Spain in August, 1823, had led General Olañeta, an Absolutist, to believe he might replace La Serna, the Constitutionalist. He therefore refused reinforcements to La Serna for the coming struggle with Sucre.

Ayacucho, December 9, 1824. La Serna nevertheless went ahead with his plans. For eighteen days the two armies maneuvered for advantage in the mountains near Cuzco. La Serna hoped to cut Sucre's communication line, while Sucre sought a favorable field for battle. Finally, on December 9, 1824, on the plains of Ayachuco the two armies met, La Serna's numbering over 9,000, Sucre's some 3,000. La Serna, abandoning his advantageous position on the heights above the plain, descended to attack. When he carelessly exposed his center upon charging Sucre's right, the latter sent his hardened Venezuelan cavalry against this weak spot. Its devastating attack threw the whole royalist army into confusion and rout. The viceroy himself fell into Sucre's hands. Ayacucho proved to be the decisive victory of the Wars for Independence in Spanish South America.

Sucre followed up his advantage and pressed into Upper Peru (Bolivia). There early in January, 1825, Olañeta died in a mutiny of his troops who joined the revolution. Three months later in March, 1825, Sucre entered Potosí and ended the last Spanish resistance in Peru, with the exception of a desperate band of loyalists who held out in Callao until early in 1826.

Part III. THE INDEPENDENCE OF BRAZIL, 1808–1822

Causes. The struggle for independence in Brazil lacked the violence of the movements in the Spanish colonies. The underlying causes were identical. Portuguese colonial administration was corrupt; office holders waxed wealthy. Excessive taxes imposed on the population of the mining province of Minas Gerais led to the first movement for independence in 1789. Royal monopolies restricting commerce to Portuguese companies blocked the growth of native Brazilian traders and encouraged smuggling. While Pombal's reforms gave Brazilians a larger part in high civil offices and in the army, this taste of freedom, like the reforms of Charles III in the Spanish colonies, only whetted their appetite for power. Their subsequent exclusion by Maria I, the return of the Jesuits to power, and the reimposition of trading monopolies intensified Brazilian antagonism toward the mother country.

International Influences. After 1780 discussion and literary circles grew rapidly in the larger cities where the Brazilian Creoles debated the ideas of French political writers. In an effort to halt the entrance of French political literature, the government forbade the importation of books and printing presses and installed censorship. Revolutionary secret societies took the place of discussion circles. In France Thomas Jefferson gave encouragement to Brazilian leaders, notably through José Joaquim da Maia in 1787. In the next year José Alvez Macial, recently arrived from France, forced a circle in Ouro Preto to organize the Minas conspiracy, which was led by Tiradentes in 1789. While it failed, it firmly established the idea of republicanism in Brazil.

The Flight of Dom João VI to Brazil. The flight of Dom João VI to Brazil when Napoleon invaded Portugal in November, 1807, began a train of events which led directly to the independence of Brazil. The idea of transferring the monarchy to the colony had been suggested first in 1580 when Spain occupied Portugal. Pombal proposed it again after the earthquake which devastated Lisbon in 1755. In 1808 several factors contributed to the royal decision to migrate. Most important was the fact that Brazil had a cushion of wealth to meet the needs of the royal house. Moreover, Brazil was out of reach of Napoleon. Influencing greatly the discussion of the move was the British offer to transport the royal family and its aristocracy. British interest arose not only because both had a common enemy in Napoleon, but also because England saw an opportunity to open Brazil's ports to her trade.

Reforms of Dom João. After a short stop in Bahia, Dom João made Rio de Janeiro his capital on March 8, 1808. He immediately launched a series of measures which in fact converted Brazil from her colonial status to one more in keeping with the position of the king, the head of the Portuguese empire. He ended at once the Portuguese monopoly on the trade of Brazil. In 1810 he signed the Anglo-Portuguese treaty of that year which gave British subjects involved in lawsuits trial before a special judge, and imposed a lower tariff on British goods than those imported from Portugal. The effects of this treaty by 1816 were to place more than one-half of Brazil's trade in British hands.

He levied new taxes to support the royal house, and, to increase the royal income, repealed laws and regulations restricting mining operations and those hampering the development of native Brazilian industries. He established the first bank of Brazil, and societies to study ways of improving agriculture. He founded military and naval academies, a national museum, a school of fine arts, and colleges of medicine and surgery. Designed to provide a base to support the monarchy, these reforms launched Brazil in the following years on its career as a nation.

Foreign Affairs. With Napoleon occupied in Europe and Spain's colonies in revolt, Dom João saw opportunities to extend his Brazilian empire. In 1809 he declared war on Napoleon and seized French Guiana. In the next year when Viceroy Elío, besieged at Montevideo, asked aid, he sent a strong force over the protest of the British minister, Viscount Strangford. Once the siege was raised, the Portuguese troops remained. The British, however, who opposed both Brazil's and Argentina's designs on Uruguay, were in a position at the moment to force Dom João to withdraw from Banda Oriental, for they had occupied Portugal in the Peninsular War.

But Dom João was not so easily turned aside. He saw in the continued conflict in Uruguay possibilities for intervention. His next opportunity came in 1815–1816 when Artigas, in control of Montevideo, extended his administration over the seven missions' area in the north, which Portugal once had a claim to under the treaty of 1750. Using this claim as an excuse and fearful of Artigas building a strong state, he invaded in 1816. Within a few years, as we have seen, he had defeated the armies of the Uruguayan leader and annexed Uruguay to Brazil as the Cisplatine Province (1821).

Steps to Independence, 1816–1822. Dom João's reforms and acquisition of territory benefited his position as a monarch, but laid the basis for discontent among the Brazilians. His arbitrary imposition of taxes, replacing native Brazilians with his favorites in office, and utilizing Brazilian resources for conquering Uruguay flew in the face of the rising movement both in Brazil and Portugal for more responsible government. The Spanish constitution of 1812 found supporters in Portugal for a similar fundamental law. Moreover, when Dom João in 1815 gave Brazil equality in the empire with Portugal and Algarve, the Portuguese, fearing that this was a step in their descent into colonial status, called for both the return of the king, and more representative government. These demands took the form of a revolt in Oporto in 1817.

In Brazil local conditions in Pernambuco, corruption in government, sale of justice, economic decline, and opposition to the war in Uruguay led to the proclamation of a republic under the slogan of the "Spirit of 1817." Led by Domingo José Martins and supported by merchants and clergy, the movement won over the Brazilian soldiers sent to put it down. Expelling the governor, they formed, in imitation of the French Revolution, a committee of public safety, freed the press, and launched propaganda in neighboring provinces to join the revolt. Although Dom João crushed the uprising with Portuguese and mercenary troops, the event cast its shadow.

After 1817 Dom João was constantly caught in the cross fire of republican movements in Portugal and Brazil. In 1820 the successful revolt in Cádiz, which restored the Spanish constitution of 1812, found immediate reflection in Portugal. In August, 1820, the regency Dom João had left to govern in Lisbon was overthrown by juntas formed in Oporto and Lisbon itself, which, adopting the Spanish constitution, called a *Côrtes,* that is, a parliament. The *Côrtes* gave immediate effect to the constitution, which provided for the election of representatives in the colony to sit in the Portuguese parliament, and virtually ordered the king to return to Portugal.

In Brazil the Portuguese example found ready followers. Most of the captaincies elected juntas; Minas Gerais went further and demanded a republic. The king, disturbed by these events, approved the Portuguese constitution and permitted the election of Brazilian representatives to the *Côrtes* in Lisbon. To return to Portugal under the new constitution was a bitter pill for the king, an Absolutist. Moreover, he had fallen in love with Brazil and was loath to return for this reason. His wife, Queen Carlota, who missed the brilliant social life of a European court, held Brazil in low esteem. The British, needing the Portuguese monarchy in Europe to support their policy *vis-à-vis* France on the continent, urged his return. This period of vacillation ended on April 26, 1821, when the dispirited king returned to Portugal. However, he left his son Dom Pedro as regent and urged him, in case of a revolt in Brazil, to put himself at the head of the movement.

The Independence of Brazil. With the king back in Portugal, the conflict between Brazil and the mother country broke out into an open struggle. The Portuguese *Côrtes,* determined to reduce the colony to its former status, ended free trade, reimposed the mercantile laws, and deprived Brazil of all the advantages enjoyed under the monarchy. To take over the government of the colony, the *Côrtes* ordered Dom Pedro to return home. At first Dom Pedro played a dubious role, alternately begging his father to order him home and refusing orders to return. As the *Côrtes* became more insistent upon Dom Pedro abandoning his post, Brazilians rallied to his support with petitions to remain. Playing a leading part in this growth of Brazilian nationalism was José Bonifacio de Andrada e Silva, later known as the Father of Brazilian Independence. On January 9, 1822, Dom Pedro took the decisive step when he announced to the people of Brazil: "I will remain." Portuguese military leaders in the colony attempted to force his return, but Dom Pedro, with Brazilian help, drove the royal garrison out of Rio de Janeiro and prevented reinforcements from landing.

Portugal, hoping to regain control of the country, attempted to divide Brazil into captaincies, each directly dependent upon the mother country, and sought to stir animosity between one captaincy and another. More practically, they sent General Madeira to occupy Bahia in March, 1822. To drive him out the Brazilians organized an army and employed Admiral Cochrane to command a Brazilian navy provided by the confiscation of Portuguese battleships in Brazilian ports. The land army succeeded in bottling Madeira up on a narrow neck of land in much the same way that Washington trapped Cornwallis at Yorktown, while Cochrane sailed into the bay. Cochrane's reputation did more damage to the Portuguese than his guns. The Brazilian army, showing remarkable ingenuity in equipping itself from odds and ends, made the siege a success. Finally in July, 1822, cut off from food supplies, Madeira left the city.

Having abandoned Portugal in fact, Dom Pedro organized a ministry with José Bonifacio as prime minister, called a congress, and refused to give effect to laws passed by the Portuguese *Côrtes* concerning Brazil. Brazil at the moment was far from presenting a unified picture. The northern provinces were strongly against separation from Portugal; São Paulo in the south had a powerful Portuguese party. Minas Gerais not only demanded independence but wished to establish a republic. To determine the state of opinion in the two most important provinces, Minas Gerais and São Paulo, Dom Pedro in April visited Villa Rica, the capital of the former, where Juiz da Fora had headed a revolt and refused to recognize the authority of Dom Pedro himself. In the city Dom Pedro congratulated the rebels on their spirit and promised them to free Brazil. Back in Rio de Janeiro, he called a constitutional convention. This action the *Côrtes* considered rebellion, of which it demanded an immediate disavowal. Meanwhile, Dom Pedro had visited São Paulo where he found in fact strong sentiment for independence.

Ypiranga, September 7, 1822. The message of the *Côrtes* reached Dom Pedro at Ypiranga outside the city of São Paulo. Recognizing its import, he determined to end all connection with the mother country. Stepping out of his carriage and drawing his sword he cried, "Independence or Death!" Known as the "Cry of Ypiranga," this event marked the winning of independence for Brazil on September 7, 1822.

Chapter XIV

THE WARS FOR
INDEPENDENCE: SPANISH
NORTH AMERICA

Part I. MEXICO

The Abortive Revolt of 1808. Napoleon's invasion of Spain in 1808 launched New Spain on its struggle for independence. When the news reached Mexico, the city council, made up primarily of Creoles and the Spaniards who composed the *audiencia,* split on the question of recognizing the Central Junta of Spain. The Creoles declared for Ferdinand VII, while the Spaniards insisted upon the recognition of the authority of the Cádiz Junta. The viceroy, José de Iturrigaray, ambitious to succeed to the head of the government in the colony, joined with the Mexicans. He immediately summoned a congress made up of representatives of the provinces to convene in Mexico City. The *audiencia,* recognizing this action as virtual rebellion, organized a volunteer corps of Spaniards, who arrested the viceroy and sent him in chains to Spain. They then selected an elderly general, Pedro de Garibay, who suppressed demonstrations in Mexico City while the *audiencia* uncovered and arrested Mexican conspirators in Valladolid and Guanajuato.

Garibay, although successful in raising large sums for the Spanish Junta to fight against the French, failed, in the *audiencia's* opinion, to put down disloyalty to the Cádiz Junta. He surrendered his office in 1809, to be succeeded by the Mexican archbishop, Lizana y Beaumont, who strongly disapproved of popular government. Like Garibay, he was too old to be effective. The *audiencia* assumed control again until Viceroy Francisco Xavier Venegas arrived in August, 1810, appointed by the Cádiz Junta.

Hidalgo, the Father of Mexican Independence. While the Creole uprising of 1808 was futile, it bespoke the restlessness in the country augmented by the agitation for freedom carried on by the agents of

Napoleon. However, these revolutionary ideas did not interest the wealthy landowning Creoles, who feared their effect upon the lower classes, the Indian and the *mestizo*. After the arrival of Venegas in 1810 the viceregal government resumed the pattern of colonial oppression. Liberals formed secret organizations and discussion groups. Outstanding were the "Guadalupes" in Mexico City, who aided the gathering of revolutionary forces in various parts of Mexico. The most significant of the discussion circles was in Querétaro, organized by Ignacio Allende, the *corregidor,* and his wife, famous later as *La Corregidora.* Among others who joined the group was the parish priest of the little town of Dolores, Father Miguel Hidalgo y Costilla. Hidalgo had read deeply in the French political classics and looked upon revolt as a means to a more humanitarian form of government for his beloved Mexico.

In Dolores he had long shown a deep regard for the Indians under his care. He sought to improve their crops, introduced new ones, and by his unwonted energy had incurred the displeasure of both the government and the Inquisition. Hidalgo's vigorous personality gave the Querétaro circle a new enthusiasm. They expanded their efforts and sought to win army officers to the cause of expelling the Spaniards, but traitors revealed their plans. When orders for the arrest of the conspirators were issued, Allende's wife, *La Corregidora,* gave warning, while Allende hastened to inform Hidalgo.

Father Hidalgo acted at once. On September 16, 1810, he called his Indians together, and told them the time had come to fight for their freedom. Taking a banner inscribed with a picture of the Virgin of Guadalupe, as their protector, Hidalgo led his charges down the road toward Mexico City. Indians arose on all sides. Slaughtering the inhabitants of the Creole rural haciendas, they bore down on Celaya. There, some 50,000 strong, they sacked the city and made Hidalgo commander-in-chief. Marching next upon Guanajuato they captured it and executed unmercifully the Spanish defenders who took refuge in the public granary. More important for the revolution, they seized a large supply of money and military equipment. By this time the movement had revealed its fundamental character: a revolt against *both* the Mexican landowners and the Spaniards. Hidalgo, sensing the direction of the movement, abolished the head tax, returned the land to the Indians, and began the organization of a new government.

By the end of September, Viceroy Venegas, believing he was faced with a simple Indian revolt, sent out General Calleja to crush the uprising. Hidalgo moved to Valladolid to meet the danger. Mistakenly he opened negotiations with Calleja, who treacherously attacked him. Rejecting Allende's advice to make an immediate march on Mexico City, Hidalgo fell back to Guadalajara, a strong center of revolutionary sentiment. There he organized the first government of the revolution, became its head, and associated with himself an uncompromising liberal, Father Morelos, and an able general, Ignacio Rayón.

When Calleja's army of some 6,000 trained men reached the outskirts of Guadalajara in January, the patriots, about 80,000 strong, assembled to meet the Spaniards. The battle centered around a small bridge across a stream, the Lerma, where success first attended the patriots' attack. However, an unlucky shot, exploding in Hidalgo's ammunition train, set fire to the dry grass which swept through the patriot forces and threw them into confusion. Calleja's well-trained veterans attacked and routed the panic-stricken Indians. Still hopeful of reorganizing their scattered forces, Hidalgo and Allende fell back toward northern Mexico. Rayón and Morelos retreated to the south.

With the defeat of the main army of Hidalgo, the revolution collapsed in the north in one province after another. Retreating toward the United States, where Aldama had been sent to get aid, Hidalgo and Allende were both captured, having been betrayed by a follower who hoped for royal preferment. Taken to Monclova, Allende was shot out of hand, but Hidalgo, already excommunicated and charged with heresy, largely because of the works of Voltaire found in his study, was first tried by a church court. It unfrocked him and turned him over to the military for execution on July 30, 1811.

Morelos: Hero of the South. New leaders arose to take up the work of Hidalgo. Rayón in the south joined Morelos, who had already planted the seeds of rebellion. Before a year had passed, Rayón had kindled centers of revolt in eight provinces, including Puebla, Jalisco, Michoacán on the west coast, and Vera Cruz on the east. Zitácuaro, Michoacán, he made his headquarters where, before Calleja drove him out in January, 1812, he had manufactured a large supply of armaments and clothing for his troops. There, too, Morelos took the first tentative steps to organize a second revolutionary government.

Hardly had Rayón's forces been dispersed when the king of Spain ordered Viceroy Venegas to give effect in Mexico to the 1812 constitution. It was a bitter pill for the royalists, for many of the provisions of that document called for reforms for which the patriots were fighting. When Viceroy Venegas withheld the clauses providing for freedom of speech and press, the Mexican representative at the *Côrtes* in Spain,

Miguel Ramos Arizpe, forced him to grant it. At once a great revolutionary fervor, abetted by the aggressive "Guadalupes," sprang into life in newspapers, magazines, and public harangues. The writers and speakers dinned unceasingly upon Mexico's right under the constitution to equality in government, elections in which all could participate for municipal office, and the ending of the special privileges of the church and military courts.

Emboldened by the freedom now enjoyed, a small but courageous group demanded complete independence. The bulk of the Mexicans, however, still considerably influenced by conservative thought, acted in moderation. But the viceroy, unable to stomach the discussions of liberty and freedom, soon withdrew the constitution, an action which, while approved in Spain, intensified the struggle in Mexico.

Morelos, in control of the south and west, had little confidence in a paper constitution from Spain. He continued to extend his power until it reached in a semicircle from Vera Cruz to the coast of Michoacán. Many patriots advised an attack upon the capital when the viceroy withdrew the constitution, but Morelos, possibly mistaken, attacked and captured Acapulco early in 1813. With a large part of southern Mexico now under control, he called the dispersed Junta of Zitácuaro together and held new elections for a national congress.

This body met at Chilpancingo in September, 1813. Besides providing for a temporary government, with Morelos at the head, the congress declared the independence of Mexico on November 6, 1813. Before adjourning, the congress set the date for another meeting in 1814 to draw up a constitution. This document, issued on October 22, 1814, while ineffective, has significance in revealing Mexican political ideas and the mature thinking of the men who prepared it.

It provided for an executive, a president and vice-president, a congress of two houses, and a national judiciary system headed by a supreme court. Suffrage was exercised by all individuals over eighteen years of age, but voting was for electors who were to choose officials. The Catholic religion was declared the sole religion of the state, not surprising since interest in Protestantism and the demands for freedom of conscience did not appear in Mexico until a decade later. Besides promulgating the constitution, the congress adopted laws passed in the preceding year. Slavery was abolished; many colonial taxes ended, as well as the distinctions surviving between the races. Education was provided for, to be administered by Jesuits for lack of any other personnel.

The promulgation of this constitution brought quick attack by the viceregal government. The royal army drove toward Querétaro and Vera Cruz, while the church turned its fire upon the congress. In the west Rayón suffered defeat, while Agustín Iturbide pursued the congress southward. On the point of capture, the congress, escorted by the troops of Nicolás Bravo, was saved by the heroic action of Morelos who permitted himself to be taken prisoner. After a farcical trial the second great leader of the movement for independence went to his death on December 22, 1815.

Decline of the Revolution, 1816–1819. Although Viceroy Calleja reported to Spain after the execution of Morelos that only bandits roamed the hills, the revolt was far from being crushed. It is true that in these four years the insurgents were unable to establish a central authority to direct their efforts, such as had existed under Hidalgo and Morelos. They dissolved, consequently, into bands, varying in number from 700 or 800 to more than 2,000, in all totaling about 9,000. Outstanding and destined to be the next great figure in the revolution was Vicente Guerrero. Commanding about 1,000 devoted veterans, Guerrero harried incessantly the Spanish convoy trains passing between Vera Cruz and Mexico City. Elsewhere the revolution flickered but never died. Nicolás Bravo, Mier y Terán, Guadalupe Victoria, and others, who were later to launch Mexico on its republican career, raided Spanish garrisons, captured valuable treasure, and bided their time.

While these liberal leaders frequently quarreled among themselves, more serious to the cause was the ending of the Napoleonic wars, which permitted Spain to send reinforcements to Mexico. Against the 9,000 patriots, the viceroy had at his command after 1816 some 30,000 troops, more than half of whom were of the regular Spanish army. In August, 1816, the king sent out a new viceroy to replace Calleja, Juan Ruíz de Apodaca. His vigorously directed campaigns brought the liberal cause to its lowest ebb.

Among the unhappy events of this dark period was the failure of the Mina expedition of 1816–1818. Francisco Xavier Mina, a young Spaniard and refugee from the reactionary policy of Ferdinand VII, had fled to England, whence he found his way to the Gulf coast of Mexico. There, with American volunteers and a fleet gathered among the Gulf pirates, he launched what he described as the Relief Expedition of the Mexican Revolution. In Mexico his agents sought to win support of some Spaniards by announcing that the Expedition favored restoration of the constitution of 1812. This constitution had deprived the king of his monopoly over trade and had temporarily benefited many colonial Spanish businessmen. Arriving at Matamoros, he pushed on toward Guanajuato, the original stronghold of Hidalgo where liberal sentiment was strong. Here he enjoyed some successes against the viceroy's troops. But these in the end proved too strong. Dissension within the ranks of his motley followers led to his capture in a surprise attack and execution. Most of the remnants, fleeing back toward the United States, were captured and hanged.

By 1818 Guerrero practically alone among the various band chieftains still maintained his forces intact. Mier y Terán had retired from the struggle; Guadalupe Victoria fled alone from place to place, but never surrendering his hope of ultimate victory. Viceroy Apodaca, viewing with satisfaction his work in crushing the revolution, informed the king he had no need of further reinforcements.

Mexico and the Spanish Revolt of 1820. In March, 1820, came the revolt of the Spanish army in Cádiz under liberal leaders who forced the king to swear allegiance to the constitution of 1812. Some of its provisions for reform were in advance of those demanded by the Mexican liberals. The new government in Spain abolished the Inquisition, took over the church's tithes, granted freedom of speech and press, and ordered elections held in the colonies to select delegates to sit in the Spanish *Côrtes*. In Mexico the arrival of the news threw the wealthy Creoles and church officials into consternation. Unable to disobey, the viceroy held the required elections and Mexican representatives sailed for Spain. There they joined the Spanish liberals in restoring the church to its purely spiritual functions. They suppressed the Jesuits, ended the church's special courts, and expropriated church property to help pay for the establishment of educational programs.

It was clear to the wealthy Creoles and church officials in Mexico that these and other reforms would be insisted upon by the Mexican representatives for their homeland. In the face of this threat to their ancient privileges, the hierarchy took the lead in advocating union with Guerrero to win independence. With their objective achieved, namely, avoiding the application of the 1812 constitution to Mexico, the conservative groups were confident of their ability later to eliminate the liberals from the future government of Mexico.

Led by a canon of the Mexican cathedral, Dr. Juan Monteagudo, the head of the Inquisition, leading lay members among the Spaniards settled upon a plan for revolt. For their military leader they selected Agustín de Iturbide, whose services were known to be available to the highest bidder. Viceroy Apodaca, believed by some to have been sympathetic to the idea of his own selection as the future ruler of Mexico, gave permission to Iturbide to contact Guerrero.

The Plan of Iguala, February 24, 1821. Having been pursued by Iturbide before, Guerrero at first was wary of the purposes of the royalist Creole. Convinced eventually, however, that Iturbide was seeking cooperation against Spain, Guerrero agreed to meet him in the little town of Iguala in southern Mexico. There, after a series of conferences, the two leaders reached an agreement, which became the program for winning the revolution, the "Plan of Iguala." This plan centered around three guarantees: (1) a guarantee of personal rights, property rights, and the privileges of the church; (2) a union of forces to fight for independence; (3) recognition of equal rights of all races, Europeans, Africans, and Indians, to hold political office. Iturbide's and Guerrero's armies, united under this plan, became known as the "Army of the Three Guarantees." Their battle cry, superseding the *Grito de Dolores,* became "Religion, Union, and Independence."

Back in Mexico City, Iturbide tried to interest the viceroy in supporting the movement, but Apodaca declared Iturbide an outlaw. Rejoining Guerrero, the Creole leader formed a plan of campaign under which Guerrero advanced from the south and Iturbide from Guanajuato invaded from the west. The turning point in the struggle against Apodaca came when a powerful Creole general in the Spanish army, Anastasio Bustamante, joined Iturbide with a large force. A revolt in Mexico City organized by the Masonic lodges and the "Guadalupes" forced the resignation of Apodaca. This event virtually ended the struggle for Mexican independence on July 6, 1821.

Meanwhile, in Spain the liberal Spanish government, influenced by the Mexican representative, made a desperate last-minute effort to save the colony for Spain. To replace Apodaca Madrid sent over Juan O'Donojú, who proved to be the last viceroy of New Spain, to reach an understanding with Iturbide. Without troops, O'Donojú remained at Vera Cruz and entered into negotiations with the Mexican leader. In August the two met at Córdoba, a short distance inland, where they drew up the Treaty of Córdoba on August 24, 1821. Its most important provision recognized the independence of Mexico and called for the withdrawal of all Spanish troops from New Spain. Other clauses incorporated the chief provisions of the Plan of Iguala. The effort to save Mexico for Spain was found in the clause which provided for a Bourbon prince to become the monarch of Mexico. Iturbide's fine hand was evident in a further clause providing a royal Mexican house in case a Bourbon aspirant was not available. Thus the movement for independence, begun by Hidalgo in 1810, had after extraordinary vicissitudes achieved success by 1821.

The Empire of Iturbide. To this significant event, independence, was attached an incubus, the empire of Iturbide, 1821–1823. This empire had its roots in the fears of the privileged classes of republican institutions advocated by Guerrero and other liberals. After the Córdoba treaty was signed, Iturbide set up a regency composed of conservatives, but excluded Guerrero. He next called a congress to draw up a constitution for the new state. However, the elections, in spite of his efforts to control them, brought a large contingent of supporters of a republican form of government. Those liberals who suspected Iturbide's monarchical designs proposed to undermine his power by reducing the size of the army, replacing his wealthy supporters in the regency with congressional appointees, and reducing the high salaries Iturbide had allotted to the officers of the regency and military leaders.

Blocked by congress on his road to the throne, Iturbide resorted to a *coup d'état* followed by a dictatorship. At the same time leading members of the congress were arrested or fled from the city. On May 19, 1822, he called together what was left of the congress, principally his supporters, who voted the establishment of an empire with himself as Emperor Agustín I. On October 31 he dissolved the congress and appointed a committee to draw up a constitution at his direction.

Iturbide's rule was short. Finding popular sympathy turning to the old heroes of the independence movement, he crushed manifestations of what he considered disloyalty. In an attempt to win popular support he dispatched an army into Central America to annex that territory to Mexico. But as the liberals organized their forces under Guerrero, Bravo, and Guadalupe Victoria, they won province after province to their side. The conflict came to a head in the actions of an opportunist in Vera Cruz, Antonio López de Santa Anna. This figure, sensing unerringly, as he did many times later, the drift of public opinion, declared, as commander of the port of Vera Cruz, against Iturbide.

The revolt took a turn that neither Santa Anna nor Iturbide anticipated. The republican leaders throughout Mexico in the preceding months had prepared a careful statement for the reorganization of the Mexican government. This document, circulated among the officers of Iturbide's army, appealed to them, and even Iturbide himself, as a solution to the conflict. Known as the "Plan of Casa Mata," its chief provisions recognized the sovereignty of the people, called for the assembling of a new congress, and significantly placed power meanwhile in the hands of the provincial deputations, an institution that represented the conception of federalism then emerging in Mexico. Issued on February 1, 1823, the plan was in full force by March. It meant in effect Iturbide's loss of control of the provinces, an event which automatically forced his abdication. His end thereafter came speedily. Exiled by the new congress, he was forbidden to return on the penalty of death. He returned and was executed in July, 1824. The liberal leaders of the movement resumed their normal course, already opened by the Plan of Casa Mata, for the establishment of a republic in 1824. This event began the national history of Mexico.

Part II. THE INDEPENDENCE OF CENTRAL AMERICA

·Of the five regions which made up the captaincy-general of Guatemala, the smallest, El Salvador, assumed leadership in the struggle for independence. Under Nicolás Aguilar and José Matías Delgado they led the first revolt in 1811. It was shortly snuffed out. But almost at once Nicaraguan liberals followed with an uprising in December, 1811, and another in April, 1812. These forced the Spanish officials temporarily out of office. Meanwhile, in Guatemala, the capital, conspiracies and discussion groups headed by Dr. Pedro Molina and José Cecilio del Valle kept rebellion alive. Late in 1812 the promulgation of the Spanish constitution of that year split the country into two groups: Spaniards loyal to the mother country and an independence party composed in part of wealthy landowners who feared the liberalizing tendencies of the 1812 constitution. With them the liberals accepted as a program the Plan of Iguala promulgated in Mexico.

In September the independence party, inspired by Father José Simeón Cañas, forced the captain-general, Gavino Gainza, to call a meeting of all the citizens, a *cabildo abierto,* to debate what should be done. Bitter arguments characterized the discussions. When the supporters of the movement to separate from Spain won, they issued on September 15, 1821, a Declaration of Independence, and prepared for an election of a national assembly. Immediately liberals and the conservatives divided over the question of the form of government for the new state. Dr. Molina, the liberal leader, called for a democratic constitution. The conservatives on their part sought union with Iturbide's reactionary empire. Against such a move the strong liberal centers in Granada, El Salvador, and Honduras held out.

In the midst of this conflict Iturbide sent an army in November, 1821, to annex Central America to Mexico. The news of this action led the junta set up in Guatemala City to query the councils of the various provinces making up the captaincy-general. When a majority of these replied in favor of the union, the junta declared the captaincy-general annexed to Mexico. El Salvador stoutly refused to accept this decision, and attacked and drove out the Guatemalan troops stationed in the country. The junta turned to General Vicente Filisola, who had led the Mexican army into Guatemala.

Filisola, attempting to negotiate with El Salvador, was overruled by Iturbide, who ordered war upon the small state. Invading El Salvador, Filisola captured the capital after desperate resistance. But this victory was short-lived, for in the field he received news of Iturbide's overthrow in Mexico. Returning at once to Guatemala City, he called an assembly together which reissued the Declaration of Independence of September 21, 1821, and ended the union with Mexico on July 1, 1823. This Act of Independence also united the former five provinces of the captaincy-general into the new state, the "United Provinces of Central America." Under these conditions Central American countries began their career as independent nations.

Part III. THE WARS FOR INDEPENDENCE: CONSEQUENCES

The American Revolution. If one regards the two continents of North and South America as the stage of American history, the Wars for Independence concluded what Herbert E. Bolton correctly described as the American Revolution. The thirteen English colonies had the honor of initiating the revolt in 1776; Santo Domingo continued it in 1789–1804; the colonies of Spain and Portugal completed it by 1824. The unity of this half-century of revolution is readily apparent in the fact that in 1776 all the New World was in a colonial status. By 1824 the New World was independent, made up of free nations, with a few exceptions, the most notable ones of which were Canada and Cuba. If we say that the French Revolution in Europe laid the basis for the growth of democratic institutions on that continent, then we also may state that the American Revolution from 1776 to 1824 created a similar base in the New World.

Political Effects of the Wars for Independence. The Wars for Independence politically resulted in establishing the republican form of government in all Latin-American countries except Brazil. These initial republics were far from being democratic. But their form of government provided the framework in which a struggle for democratic institutions could be carried forward. Because of the structure of Latin-American society, this battle resembled that fought in Europe in the nineteenth century rather than the story of the comparatively unobstructed evolution of democracy in the United States. In common with Europe, Latin America had a landowning aristocracy linked with a single powerful church and a tradition of militarism. These three elements in the population represented the chief obstacles to democratic growth throughout Latin America. With a background of colonial privileges, conservatives were determined to maintain these when the Wars for Independence overthrew Spanish control and brought them to power.

Conservative Parties. In most of the newly freed countries, the traditional landowning and wealthier groups expressed their ideas through political parties called in the main conservative. The principles of these parties varied little from country to country. They favored restrictions on suffrage and property qualifications for holding office. Accustomed as they were to Indians as serfs on their estates, and having a low regard for mixed bloods, the wealthy class felt that government was the prerogative of the elite. They favored union of church and state, and education as a function of the former.

Although during the struggle for independence, the conservatives willingly adopted the democratic slogans of the American and French Revolutions, they thought of these in terms of freeing themselves from Spanish subjection. It was not their purpose to apply democratic principles to benefit the less favored economic groups, the middle class, the mixed bloods composing rural and urban labor, and the Indians. They accordingly opposed after independence the basic principles of freedom of speech, press, and religion. Because they were few in number and had a privileged position, they favored a strong standing army. It is through this institution that militarism became fixed in the political evolution of Latin America.

Liberal Parties. The Wars for Independence gave opportunity for democratic ideas to flourish. The liberal forces embracing these ideas represented no such integrated group as did the conservative. From the privileged class itself frequently came liberal thinkers who grasped the validity of democratic ideas. As leaders who, though few, were highly literate, they exercised an influence upon public opinion out of proportion to their numbers. By far the most compact group among the liberals was the commercial class, solidly based upon trade, commerce, and industry. In general opposed to the economic power of the church, businessmen saw in the latter's extensive properties, rural and urban, and in its money-lending activities a block to their own expansion. For this reason they recognized in the liberal parties a vehicle for their own programs entirely lacking in the conservative. A third group, which found leadership in Mexico alone during the Wars for Independence, was the Indian. Practically voiceless until the middle of the nineteenth century, Indian leaders supported the liberal parties usually favorable to their comprehensive plans for land reform and relief from colonial abuses.

These groups expressed their ideas in liberal parties whose principles included extension of the suffrage, separation of church and state, and a system of state-supported education. Liberal doctrine, too, embraced the principles of freedom of speech, of press, and soon after independence, of religion. Regarding a large standing army as a threat to their liberties, liberals favored a small national army. Efforts to solve the problem of what was essentially militarism presented the liberals with their greatest dilemma. The common soldiers, *mestizos* and other mixed bloods, whose position in society liberal principles sought to elevate, were generally illiterate. They were easily led into support of conservative revolts against liberal reform programs. This problem could only be solved by universal education, but this reform in turn was usually blocked by the overthrow of liberal regimes.

Character of the Early Constitutions. Without entering upon a discussion of constitutional developments, reserved for the individual surveys of the states, it is possible to point out a significant contrast in the early groups of constitutions which represent the liberal-conservative conflict. Generally speaking, those immediately following the Wars for Independence represented attempts of the liberal forces to incorporate their principles into fundamental law. Thus the Constitution of the United States, of Spain of 1812, and of the French Republic in 1793 were drawn upon in making the constitutions of Mexico, Argentina, Venezuela, and Central America, both for the form of government and statement of liberal principles.

Overthrown in the 1830's, conservative constitutions took their places characterized by restrictions on suffrage, high property qualification for voting and holding office, and an absence of the basic freedoms. Moreover, the new documents usually contained political monstrosities under various names set up to guard the state, such as the "Conserving Power" of the Mexican constitution of 1836 and the "Chamber of Censors" of the Bolivian constitution of 1831.

Growth of Democratic Ideas. The basic conflict between the conservatives and liberals became the principal dynamic factor in nineteenth century Latin-American history. But out of the welter of that struggle one fundamental fact emerged, namely, the steady growth of the ideas of democracy. These ideas expressed in constitutions and in the writings of nineteenth century liberals find lodgment in the institutions of the various Latin-American nations. By the end of the century, the struggle had hammered out the fundamental positions of both groups. The dictatorships of the twentieth century frequently represent the last-ditch stand of the conservative forces to prevent the flowering of liberal ideas into legislation effectively establishing the institutions of democracy.

Economic Effects of the Wars. The economic effects of the independence movement naturally lay at the base of the political conflicts. One significant result was the freeing of the landowners from the burdens of royal taxation and in many cases from mortgages held on their estates by Spanish businessmen. They also enjoyed without restriction the products of the labor of their Indian serfs formerly diverted to the king in the form of taxes in kind and head taxes. The economic base was thus laid for their huge fortunes and their success in dominating the government. This preoccupation with agriculture gave the economy an essentially feudal aspect, emphasized by the decline of roads, land routes, sea ports, mining and manufacturing.

However, the new life gained by the coastal cities from the collapse of the mercantile system compensated somewhat for the rural retrogression. The commercial classes free from restrictions increased their wealth. But lacking national merchant marines, they became dependent upon foreign shipping, primarily British, and, to a lesser extent, American. Moreover, British pre-eminence in trade opened the way for loans to the new republican governments. Mexico, Central America, Colombia, Venezuela, Peru, Chile, Argentina, and Brazil all negotiated loans in varying amounts in the British market before 1826. Trade and loans paved the way for British and American recognition. Recognition in turn opened Latin America to British concession-hunters, who, securing ownership in Mexico, Peru, and Brazil of mines formerly Spanish and Portuguese, began the build-up of the huge British investment in Latin-American mineral resources.

Social Effects of the Wars. The changed economic and political conditions in Latin America after the wars had their counterpart in altered social relationships. Obviously with the disappearance of the *peninsulares*, the Spanish officeholders, the wealthy American classes stepped up to the commanding position in the social structure. The commercial class, with its increased wealth, created a social position for itself sufficiently strong to permit frequent intermarriage with the old landowning element. A merging of these two groups began after the Wars for Independence, but this alliance did not assume significance until after the opening of the twentieth century.

The *mestizos* and other mixed bloods whose position in the social structure was that of rural and urban labor did not fare so well. Those who made up the previous colonial militias and served in the armies of liberation, became the troops of the *Caudillos* in the national period. In the cities the status of the urban labor class did not alter. They remained exploited, hardworking, and underpaid and became, when foreign investment entered, workers in the extractive and transportation industries. Late in the nineteenth century they provided the material for the emerging labor movement in Latin America.

The movement for independence worsened the condition of the Indians. During the colonial regime the Spanish monarchs maintained the office of Protector of the Indians. The church, particularly the missionary fathers and lower clergy, recognized in many cases their obligations to improve the material well-being of the Indians as well as serve his spiritual life. When, however, the Spanish king lost the colonies, the Indian faced the landowner with no protection. His descent into peonage had already begun with the abolition of forced labor in the late eighteenth century. After independence the Indian had no rights recognized in any court. In addition, with the decline of missionary work of the church, the Indians descended in many parts of Latin America into barbarism.

Effects of the Wars upon the Church. The Wars for Independence both strengthened and weakened the position of the church in Latin America. Possessing as it did large landholdings in all the new nations, the church was no longer subject to royal supervision. The monarchs' control was exercised through the *real patronato* (royal patronage), which gave the Spanish kings the authority to appoint all officials in the colonial church, collect the tithes, and supervise all communications between the hierarchy in the colonies and the papacy. Released by the wars from this control, the church looked toward the Vatican as the source of appointments and collected the tithes, which were compulsory, for itself, as well as the various fees, burial, marriage, death, and others, established by long colonial custom. Its rural properties and urban real estate brought it a large income subject to no taxation. At the same time its accumulation of money placed it in an enviable position as a money-lender. In the early constitutions clauses guaranteeing the privileges of the church protected its new and strengthened position.

Economically, the church benefited by the ending of the expensive missionary work of the colonial period. At that time the king under the royal patronage financed missionary activity from sources of income derived by the church itself. After independence, while these same sources continued to produce their usual income, practically nothing was expended in missionary work. In fact, one of the striking phenomena of the national period is the decline of missionary activity, a condition which, before the middle of the century, furnished an opening for Protestant missionary work in Latin America.

These various changes strengthened the church in a number of respects, but the entrance of democratic ideas during the wars weakened its political and eventually its economic position. With independence came the end of the Inquisition. Books concerning Protestant literature could be imported, while freedom of speech and press permitted the discussion of religious questions. One of these affecting the position of the church, raised early by the liberals, concerned the power of appointment. The church, supported by the conservatives, believed that appointment was a function of the church, and insisted that the patronage, lost to the Spanish kings, be returned to the papacy. The liberals, on the other hand, believed that the church's immense property holdings made it such a decisive economic influence in the life of the state that appointments should be recommended by the state so that citizens and not foreigners should hold church office.

The magnitude of this change, the entrance of new ideas, religious, political, and economic, is better appreciated when it is recalled that for the preceding 300 years, the growth of Protestantism and the development of democratic political institutions were unknown pages of history to the majority of the people of the Spanish colonies. The Wars for Independence, beginning the liberation of minds as well as people, has enabled Latin America to become abreast of these new aspects of Western civilization. The elaboration of these ideas by Latin-American liberal writers in their own nineteenth century literatures became one of the significant aspects of democratic development throughout Latin America.

International Effects of the Wars for Independence. Out of the Wars for Independence emerged by 1839 sixteen independent republics and the empire of Brazil. In the process of the wars, particularly at their end, Bolívar in northern South America, Iturbide in Mexico, and the leaders of Argentina attempted to create large political units out of the former administrative areas of the Spanish viceroyalties. However, these efforts failed, largely owing to difficulties of communications and local jealousies and patriotisms. By 1830, with the exception of the Union of Central America which dissolved in 1839, the area of Latin America embraced, in South America, the empire of Brazil and nine republics; in North America, five Central American republics, independent after 1839, and Mexico. Panama was still part of Colombia, while Cuba did not win her independence until the end of the nineteenth century.

The emergence of these independent new states upon the world stage was in itself a significant fact in international affairs. With each of them the United States and the European countries had to develop new policies. Within Latin America each of the new republics developed its own set of relations with the others.

The Wars and the United States. The Wars for Independence officially gave the United States an opportunity to extend its boundaries. Unofficially, American citizens gave their services to aid the success of the movement for independence. Officially, the United States in 1810–1812 annexed West Florida as part of the Louisiana Purchase. An uprising there accompanied this action. After December 19, 1815, when the Spanish government accredited Luis de Onís as its minister, the American government negotiated for the cession of East Florida and for a definition of the western boundary of the Louisiana Purchase. Not wishing to endanger the negotiations and aware of factional disputes between the patriots, the United States refrained from recognizing the Latin-American revolutionary governments until after the treaty with Spain was ratified.

Because public opinion favored the independence of Latin America, many Americans successfully violated the neutrality laws of the country. The Magee-Gutiérrez expedition of 1812–1813, which attempted to free Texas, was organized in Louisiana. The Mina expedition of 1817 recruited most of its forces from the Gulf region of the United States. Moreover, many Americans enlisted their ships in the aid of the revolting colonies, flew their flags, and raided Spanish commerce. Frequently these privateers, such as the La Fitte brothers of New Orleans, disposed of their captures in American ports. Galveston and Amelia Island off the

Florida coast were centers of privateering. Louis Aury, a well-known privateer of Amelia Island, joined the Mina expedition and later, serving as commodore in the Colombian navy, raided the Central American coast in 1820.

Against these violations of neutrality, Minister Onís protested violently. To halt them, the armed forces of the American government drove out the privateers from Amelia Island in 1817. In the same year and in 1818 Congress enacted new neutrality laws. That of 1818, which amended earlier legislation, prohibited aid to the Spanish colonies and was effective in ending violations of American neutrality. Henry Clay, who fought against the enactment of this law, after its passage turned his great oratorical gifts to secure recognition for the rebellious Spanish colonies.

While during these years the United States refused to entertain petitions of the agents of the revolutionary states seeking recognition, American special commissions investigated the status of the Latin American states which claimed to be independent. Among these was Joel R. Poinsett who as consul-general represented the United States in Buenos Aires and in Chile and Peru. When in 1821 the success of the revolution in most parts of Latin America was apparent, and the Adams-Onís treaty had been signed by the Spanish king, the way was open for recognition. Thus in 1822 the Congress of the United States enacted legislation providing for recognition and exchange of representatives with most of the new independent states.

The Wars and Great Britain. The Latin-American revolutionary governments also sought recognition in Europe, particularly from Great Britain. However, between 1808 and 1814, while England was at war with Napoleon on the continent, she needed the aid of Spain too greatly to give aid to the Spanish colonies by way of recognition. While, as in the United States, the government maintained a rigid neutrality policy, many British volunteers after the Napoleonic wars joined the army of Bolívar in the campaigns to free northern South America.

More important, British traders took advantage of the Wars for Independence to expand their trade, long desired with the Spanish colonies, and began investments in South America. Several British commercial firms established themselves at La Guaira shortly after 1810. Between 1817 and 1820 British merchants outfitted largely on credit numerous expeditions to Venezuela to aid in the independence movement. After the success in northern South America the new Colombian government in 1820 agreed to recognize claims of British merchants in England to the extent of some £500,000. Similar expansion of trade and investment took place in other South American colonies. When the Wars for Independence ended, the merchants of Glasgow, Manchester, and other cities petitioned the British government repeatedly to recognize the new states.

This heavy British investment and trade in the Latin American states decisively affected British policy toward Europe and the United States. It was the principal reason why the British withdrew from the Congress of Verona of 1822, whose purpose was to restore Spain's colonies and obviously ruin British economic interests there. At the same time Canning, fearing the growing economic interests, particularly the trade of the United States in Latin America, attempted to restrict this expansion by proposing that the two countries act jointly against any attempt at restoring Spain's colonies.[1] Adams fortunately succeeded in persuading Monroe to reject this proposal. A year later in December, 1824, the English government took the first steps toward recognition by granting it to the two states in which British trade and investment were the heaviest, Colombia and Mexico.

Implicit in the British policy of attempting to join the United States in a program *vis-à-vis* Europe and equally clear in the American rejection of it, were the beginnings of British-American rivalry over trade, acquisition of raw materials, and strategic areas in Texas, Cuba, and Central America.

The Wars and Latin-American Boundary Conflicts. The independence of the Latin American states precipitated at once conflicting boundary claims. At first the various countries adopted as a principle *uti possidetis*, meaning, broadly speaking, that the boundaries of the new states would be those they had as colonies of Spain. However, Spain had not in fact drawn accurate boundaries between her major administrative areas of the empire. Neither had Spain and Portugal defined the boundaries between their respective empires. Yet the Latin-American republics in the national period settled the majority of these thorny questions without resort to arms. Considering that boundary disputes in Europe had produced innumerable conflicts, Spain could not have left a more explosive heritage. The success of the Latin Americans in settling their mutual boundary difficulties without war, with few exceptions, is part of their present strong tradition of international cooperation.

The Monroe Doctrine and the Pan-American Movement. In the wider field of world affairs the Wars for Independence produced two doctrines of international significance. The United States, viewing the

[1] See p. 699 for elaboration of Britain's policy.

possibility of European intervention in Latin America as a result of the actions of the Congress of Verona of 1822, promulgated in December, 1823, the Monroe Doctrine to warn Europe not to interfere in American affairs. Simón Bolívar, equally concerned over possible European intervention or Spain's use of Cuba as a springboard for invasion, called the first Pan-American congress in 1826. This body began the definition of the principles of inter-American cooperation. These two doctrines, discussed elsewhere in detail, have thus a common origin, namely, in the successful winning of independence by the Latin-American states.

MODERN LATIN AMERICA

SECTION I

The Atlantic Republics

*Argentina, Uruguay,
Paraguay, and Brazil*

Chapter XV

ARGENTINA

Part I. BUENOS AIRES AND THE PROVINCES, 1819–1890

Character of Argentine History. Argentine history between 1819 and 1890 was a struggle for power between the capital city, Buenos Aires, and the provinces in the interior. Viceregal rule had fixed centralistic tendencies in the capital. Moreover, the Argentine business classes, disturbed by the feudal outlook of the provincial leaders, feared their domination. Against the Porteños the landed oligarchy offered stubborn and effective resistance. While the capital sought a centralized form of government, the oligarchy supported federalism.

After 1880, having federalized the capital, the provincial leaders succeeded in establishing control over the country. By that date, too, modernization of the agricultural and cattle industries increased their wealth and political power.

However, by 1890 immigrant laborers and small businessmen were demanding a share in government. Organizing the Radical party, they forced by 1916 the beginnings of democratic development symbolized in the Sáenz Peña law. Between 1916 and 1930 their reform program was making headway in planting democratic institutions in Argentina.

In 1930, taking advantage of the depression, the conservative elements revolted to establish a dictatorship. Blocking the growth of democracy, the dictatorship began the industrialization of the country, extended minimum benefits to labor, and maintained intact the oligarchical control of land.

The Constitution of 1819 and Dissolution. When in 1816 Pueyrredón became dictator after the Tucumán declaration of independence, no compromise sufficed to bring together a constitutional convention until 1819. In that year the Buenos Aires *Unitarios,* as they were called, succeeded in getting one adopted. Providing for a republic, an executive called a director, a congress, and a supreme court, it placed power in the central government while allowing little autonomy to the provinces.

Thoroughly unacceptable to the interior leaders, one province after another revolted. In the face of the anarchy, Pueyrredón resigned. Buenos Aires made peace, while the country dissolved into practically independent feudal states.

Reforms of Rivadavia. Buenos Aires in those troubled times turned to its own affairs. In 1821 the state of Buenos Aires, of which the city of Buenos Aires was the capital, elected Martín Rodríguez governor. Under Bernardino Rivadavia, the most able man in the cabinet, reforms went forward which touched no other part of the country. Rivadavia established schools, notably the University of Buenos Aires, reformed and reduced the army, deprived the church of its monastic lands, exiled the Jesuits, and encouraged women to organize a charitable society, the *Sociedad de Beneficia.* Thus in the first effort in Latin America to emancipate women from the Spanish tradition of inferiority, he hoped to replace with public-spirited women the nuns of the church who administered hospitals, schools, asylums, and other benevolent institutions.

In 1824 Gregorio Las Heras, who followed Rodríguez, called a congress to draw up another constitution, under which Rivadavia was elected president. At once a division between the *Unitarios,* led by the president, and the Federalists of the state of Buenos Aires, headed by Manuel Dorrego, appeared. For three years the new government functioned, held together largely by fears of the expansion of Brazil which in 1821 had conquered Uruguay. Rivadavia made valiant efforts to unite the country. He secured a law which, nationalizing the province of Buenos Aires, brought it under the control of the capital and ended its local government. He also gave haven to Uruguayans fleeing Brazil's control and aided their struggle for independence. This action led to war between Brazil and Argentina, which lasted until 1828 when Uruguay achieved its independence. From Great Britain, Rivadavia won recognition for Argentina with the signing of a treaty providing for a favorable trade exchange and extending religious freedom to diplomatic representatives.

However, the opposition to Rivadavia, based on fear of the extension of his reforms to the rest of the country, led to revolts. The state of Buenos Aires, resenting the loss of its independent status, joined the Federalist opposition under Manuel Dorrego. Discouraged, Rivadavia resigned in July, 1827. With Rivadavia's retirement the efforts to introduce liberal reforms in Argentina's economy collapsed. Congress was dissolved, Buenos Aires was restored to its status as a state, with Dorrego as governor, and Argentine troops were recalled from Uruguay. Confusion was further confounded when an officer of the returning army, Juan Lavalle, a *Unitario,* assassinated Dorrego and plunged the country into civil war.

Juan Manuel Rosas. Out of the conflict emerged Juan Manuel Rosas, elected governor of Buenos Aires in 1829–1832. Rosas, a Creole and a man of considerable education, had won financial success in establishing meat-salting plants on his estates in the province of Buenos Aires. This activity gave him an interest in foreign trade, but he remained a Federalist in politics. He had constantly enlarged his landholding by successful wars against the Indians. In doing so he not only gained valuable grazing lands, but surrounded himself with a devoted army of gauchos whom he later used to establish his dictatorship.

Rosas' first administration is chiefly significant for his nationalistic endeavors to establish Argentina's claims to the Falkland Islands off her southeastern coast. When in 1831 he seized some Americans fishing off the islands, the United States government promptly sent the *U.S.S. Lexington,* whose commander ended the Argentine colony there. Great Britain, attracted up the uproar, immediately occupied the islands on the basis of claims recognized by Spain in the late eighteenth century. While Rosas' appeal to Washington to apply the Monroe Doctrine and end British control failed, his defiance of both foreign countries greatly increased his popularity and stirred Argentine nationalist feelings.

At home his struggle with the *Unitarios,* who fought against his autocratic measures, disgusted him with politics and led him to retire in 1832 to his estates. With Rosas out, liberal reform came to the fore. The conservative groups in the city, unable to stop this movement themselves, again appealed to Rosas in 1835. Their convention, which invited him to assume the reins of government, conferred upon him dictatorial power.

The Rosas Dictatorship. In 1835 he established a government of Draconian severity. Throughout the provinces, with the exception of Corrientes, he hounded the *Unitarios* to death and exile. His organized bands, called the *Mazorca* or "Ear of Corn Society," terrorized the population in the interior. Many distinguished conservatives, unable to approve the murders and denials of liberty, fled the country. With his appointees governing the provinces and his gauchos bludgeoning the civilian population, he achieved a dictator's peace. The business classes, won by his encouragement of foreign trade, closed their eyes to the brutalities of the regime. The church, recovering the privileges lost under Rivadavia, blessed the regime, although the Jesuits preferred exile to placing Rosas' picture above the altar in their churches. Throughout he had the support of a cunning and ruthless woman, Encarnación Rosas.

Foreign Affairs. In foreign affairs Rosas continued the imperialistic trends of the independence period. He fought to put a puppet in Montevideo and thus end the commercial threat of Uruguay to Buenos Aires. His policy found support among the Uruguayan *Blancos*, the large landowners, fearful alike of Brazil on the north and the liberal-minded *Colorados* along the coast. His opportunity came in 1839 when Rivera, the *Colorado* president from 1835 to 1839, exiled Oribe, the *Blanco* leader. Rosas provided the latter with military support, while he himself besieged Montevideo by land and sea. His plans, however, ran athwart the commercial activities of the French and British, who disregarded his blockade to support Rivera. Equally serious for Rosas was the antagonism of the up-river provinces, Entre Ríos and Corrientes, injured by the dictator's control of river shipping.

These conflicts set the stage for Rosas' overthrow. Justo José Urquiza, a typical *caudillo* of Entre Ríos, resenting the loss of income from the decline of the river trade, turned against the dictator. In 1851 he reached an understanding with the *Colorado* forces and with Brazil, disturbed on her part by Argentine designs on Uruguay. After raising the siege of Montevideo, Urquiza led a combined force into Argentina. Ferried across the Paraná River by a Brazilian fleet, the allies, 24,000 strong, defeated Rosas at Monte Caseros in February, 1852. Fleeing abroad, the dictator lived in southern England until his death in 1877.

Rosas' dictatorship deeply affected Argentine history. Constructively, his regime saw the first tentative steps toward modernizing the country. He stimulated the growth of trade on the Paraná, began a banking system, and initiated moves toward railroad construction. His censorship, attacks on schools, and the University of Buenos Aires deadened the cultural life of the country. His defiance of foreign powers gave an impetus to Argentine nationalism unfortunately colored by imperialism. Politically, his overthrow opened the way for the assumption of power by the landowning oligarchy, which consolidated its position in a new constitution in 1853.

The Domination of the Oligarchy, 1853–1890. The first step in the process by which the oligarchy established its power was the creation of a federation of the provinces. In each of these the great families held the political machinery in their own hands. This provincial control was the political basis for the establishment of a confederation, achieved in the constitution of 1853. Buenos Aires did not participate with the other thirteen provinces in the convention which met at Santa Fé in 1852–1853. Characteristically, its most important ideas came from a leading thinker of the oligarchy itself, Juan Bautista Alberdi, of Tucumán, who wrote *Bases y puntos de partida para la organización política de la República Argentina (Bases and Points of Departure for the Political Organization of the Argentine Republic).* While Alberdi and the fathers of the document were influenced by the Constitution of the United States, they favored the southern interpretation of the nature of the American union.

The constitution provided for a federal republic, with a president and vice-president, chosen by an electoral college, to serve six years. The legislature was bicameral, with two senators elected by the provincial legislatures for nine years. The members of the House of Deputies, elected on the basis of population, served for four years. This body could initiate tax legislation and impeach members of the government before the senate. Qualifications for voting were left to the states to fix. The president appointed members of the superior and inferior courts which the congress created. Catholicism was made the state religion.

But the most significant provision was that which empowered the president to intervene in provincial affairs to preserve the republican form of government. This apparent contradiction within a constitution which provided for a confederation and yet conferred upon the president broad powers of intervention in provincial affairs has a simple explanation. The provincial oligarchies dictated the elections of the local legislatures, the election of delegates to the electoral college, and hence the selection of the president. The presidential power of intervention was but an additional guarantee of the political structure. This fact became amply manifested between 1891 and 1910 in presidential interference to prevent political parties, opposed to the provincial oligarchies, from winning control of local legislatures, governorships, and even the presidency.

Conflict with Buenos Aires. The Confederation established its capital at Paraná, the capital of Entre Ríos, over which Urquiza ruled as dictator. The rest of the states drew up constitutions along the lines laid down at Santa Fé. Urquiza, as first president, immediately signed trade treaties with several European nations and the United States to open the Paraná and Uruguay rivers to foreign commerce.

These events stirred uneasy feelings in Buenos Aires. Its natural monopoly at the mouth of the Paraná was threatened. To attack further the position of Buenos Aires, the Confederation established Rosario in 1856 as its principal port and promulgated a tariff whose differentials on European imports forced foreign ships to by-pass Buenos Aires. The

latter accordingly declared war, but was defeated. The peace treaty required Buenos Aires to join the Confederation. Unable to accept the
loss of her commercial supremacy, she prepared to renew the war by
making an alliance with the *Colorado* party in Uruguay, likewise incensed at the action of the Confederation. At the same time she violated
the law governing the selection of her delegates to the new constitutional
convention called to include her in the Confederation. When the convention rejected the Buenos Aires delegates, she resorted to war.

In the new conflict the Porteños were aided by internal conflicts
within the Confederation itself, particularly between Urquiza and his
rival in Entre Ríos, Santiago Derqui. Too, in her own leader, Bartolomé
Mitre, she had a figure of unusual military ability. When the forces of
the two met in the battle of Pavón, September 7, 1861, the result was
indecisive. Politically, Buenos Aires won when Derqui's refusal to support Urquiza led the latter to withdraw from political life.

The Confederation, now without able leadership, reached an understanding with Mitre, who assumed command of Confederation affairs.
The compromise further provided for the transfer of the capital to
Buenos Aires for five years and support of Mitre by the provinces for
the presidency in the election of 1862. While this agreement ended the
war, the fundamental question of the control of Argentina was not
settled. That conflict next emerged in Argentine history as the "Capital
Question."

The Administration of Mitre. As president (1862–1868), Mitre carried
forward a vigorous policy to improve the economic life of the nation.
Railroad construction began when a British company, with a right of
way six miles wide and a guarantee of 7 per cent on its investment,
opened work on a line from Buenos Aires to Rosario. At the same time
the company encouraged immigrants to settle on its lands. This opening
of the interior was accompanied by the enactment of a commercial code
and a revision of tariffs to stimulate European imports, especially British.
In foreign affairs Mitre took the field in the Paraguayan war, a conflict
which greatly stimulated the city's commercial growth.

The election of 1868 saw the next step in the advance of the oligarchy to control of Argentina. Mitre, undoubtedly influenced by the
frightful slaughter of the Paraguayan War, had no desire to see a revival
of the civil wars in Argentina over the question of the presidency. At
the same time the oligarchy, centered at Córdoba, determined to break
the hold of Buenos Aires on the office and threw its support behind
Urquiza. Buenos Aires' candidate, Adolfo Alsina, governor of the state

of Buenos Aires, commanded only partial support in the country, mostly in the capital city. Urquiza on his part faced opposition in his own province. Thus when it became apparent that neither candidate would have a majority in the electoral college, Mitre, to avoid a civil war, declared he would use his office simply to guarantee a fair election. This decision, known as the "Testament of Mitre," led the oligarchy to withdraw its support of Urquiza and turn to Domingo Faustino Sarmiento, who hailed from Córdoba itself. At the same time they offered the vice-presidency to Alsina. This combination of Buenos Aires with the leading interior states of Córdoba, Jujuy, Mendoza, Rioja, San Luis, and San Juan gave Sarmiento the victory.

The Administration of Sarmiento, 1868–1874. Sarmiento easily takes rank as one of the greatest nineteenth century figures in Latin America. His reputation rests not only upon his achievements as president, but upon his contributions to literature and the political thinking of the time. A man of vast range of thought, he wrote a masterpiece in *Facundo*, a social document, which depicts the institution of the *caudillo* as opposed to civilization. In politics he translated parts of the *Federalist* and other writings of American jurists. In the press he wrote on a great variety of subjects, urging his countrymen to educate themselves. Unerringly he recommended to them the great figures of his time, Buckle, Humboldt, Motley, Macaulay, Prescott, Horace Mann, and others. He traveled widely in Europe, Africa, and the United States, and admired the vigorous frontier spirit of the latter nation. Unlike the majority of Latin-American intellectuals, he turned from Europe to the United States for inspiration. He felt that the remedy for *caudilloism*, which he equated with barbarism, lay in education. As president he therefore launched an offensive against ignorance, and imitating American educational patterns, founded public primary and normal schools.

As president, gripped by an intense desire to modernize Argentina— his friends called him the "crazy man"—Sarmiento carried forward a program of internal improvements. Not only did he see the completion of the railroad from Rosario to Córdoba, he pushed it beyond to Tucumán to tap the northwest mineral resources. He encouraged European immigration into the newly opened lands, greatly extended telegraphic communication, favored the development of scientific stock raising and wheat farming, and took the first reliable census of the country in 1869.

In foreign affairs he was aggressive and nationalistic. Not satisfied after the Paraguayan War with annexing the Missions Territory and a slice of land between the Río Bermejo and the Río Pilcomayo, he was prevented only by Brazil from seizing more territory northward as far as the Río Verde. To defend Argentine interests in the Missions Territory, he sent Mitre to negotiate an Argentine-Brazil boundary line. Argentine claims were too much for the Brazilians, who later appealed to President Cleveland to settle the dispute. With Chile he agreed to a treaty which fixed the boundary of the two countries, inconclusively it turned out, along the Andes. At home, intent upon making the authority of the president respected and detesting *caudilloism,* he made war upon the *caudillo* of Entre Ríos, one López Jordán, who had murdered Urquiza.

When the question of a successor came up, Sarmiento supported Nicolas Avellaneda, also from Córdoba. The Porteños, feeling that the next president should come from Buenos Aires, nominated Mitre. While Sarmiento reiterated Mitre's pledge to remain out of the contest, he did not restrain Avellaneda from using his position as minister of justice to influence the voting. Mitre, aroused by what he considered a violation of the constitution, revolted. Sarmiento using his full powers crushed the uprising and thus assured the election of Avellaneda.

The Administration of Avellaneda, 1874–1880. The internal improvements of Sarmiento brought steadily increasing wealth to the provincial landowners of the interior. Under Avellaneda they lost no time in seizing additional lands opened up in the west by campaigns against the Indians. The most striking event illustrating their power was the land legislation of 1876 under which individuals could buy as high as 80,000 hectares, some 200,000 acres, of the national domain. At the same time the administration sponsored a new immigration law which successfully attracted large numbers of immigrants from Europe to labor on the interior estates. The significance of these two measures is seen in the contrast they offered to the land policy of the United States in the nineteenth century. Immigrants from Europe arriving in the United States and purchasing land in small lots became landowners and automatically a pillar in American democracy. In Argentina, however, immigrants found no opportunity to become landowners, but only the bleak prospect of fitting themselves into a feudal system of large estates practically identical with that they had sought to escape from in Europe.

The Capital Question. The success of the government in winning lands from the Indians led Avellaneda's Secretary of War, Julio Roca, to drive the aborigines from northern Patagonia. His success left the Indians with a miserable existence on the wind-swept plains of the south, but precipitated the final conflict between Buenos Aires and the provinces. The state of Buenos Aires, anxious to expand its territory as a counterweight to the dominance of the oligarchical landowners of the interior provinces, demanded all the lands conquered by Roca. Avellaneda's government set aside the proposal and organized the region into territories. Fearing the reaction of the state of Buenos Aires, the government next proposed to weaken it by federalizing its capital city, Buenos Aires.

However, the Porteños refused to accept this solution. They organized a military force, the *Tiro Nacional,* set up a revolutionary government when Avellaneda abandoned the capital, raised money for a city militia, won the support of Corrientes, and nominated Carlos Tejeda, the governor of the state, for the presidency in the 1880 presidential campaign. The results of the election found Roca, the administration candidate, with a majority in the electoral college. With his veterans behind him he promptly marched into the city, where a bloody battle on July 20 and 21 saw the defeat of the Porteños. Avellaneda's congress immediately followed the victory with new elections, declared the delegates from the state of Buenos Aires ineligible, and used force to expel the Buenos Aires revolutionary legislature. With the ground thus prepared, the national congress enacted legislation on September 21, 1880, which separated Buenos Aires from the state of that name and made it the federal capital. La Plata became the new capital of the state of Buenos Aires. The control now passed completely into the hands of the great landowners of the interior. From the federal capital they dictated fundamental national policy until 1916.

The Administration of Roca, 1880–1886. Roca continued the program of internal improvements. Railroads and telegraph lines were extended; the tide of immigration rose rapidly to provide labor for the expanding economy of the nation. Naturally, the oligarchy, having little interest in public education, abandoned Sarmiento's program of public schools. Thus the new immigrants added to the large number of illiterates in the country. Westward and southward expansion and opening up of the recently conquered lands forced the government into a program of foreign borrowing, made more dangerous by the issuance of inconvertible paper money. In this way Roca contributed to the unstable administration of his successor.

The Presidencies of Juárez Celman and Carlos Pellegrini: 1886–1890; 1890–1892. With no serious opposition from Buenos Aires, Roca's brother-in-law, Miguel Juárez Celman, became president. Under him the floodgates of corruption opened. He filled public offices with his supporters who used their official connections to graft and speculate in public lands. The president himself added to the instability of the regime by new issues of inconvertible paper and large-scale, reckless borrowing abroad. This speculative fever in Argentina was indeed a faithful reflection of the world-wide boom which in France, Britain, and the United States also rested upon similar conditions. Consequently, when in 1889 the Crédit Mobilier in France collapsed and involved important British banks, particularly Barclay's, the effect in Argentina was immediate. The fall of land values and failure of banks and stock companies in which many Argentines had invested their savings produced the first major political revolution in Argentine history. In 1890 a revolt in Buenos Aires forced the resignation of Juárez Celman, who was succeeded by his vice-president, Carlos Pellegrini, who served the remainder of the term. These events, however, were but surface indications of deep economic and social changes, operating since 1860, which gave rise to the democratic movement in Argentina.

Part II. ECONOMIC CHANGES AND THE GROWTH OF THE DEMOCRATIC MOVEMENT TO 1930

The Argentine Economic Revolution, 1860–1914. The driving force behind the changes in Argentina's economy after 1860 was the demand for food by the industrial countries of Europe, particularly Britain. In 1860 Argentina imported wheat and other cereals, while her cattle industry was still colonial. In the following decades Argentines, under the influence of British advisers, developed scientific methods in agriculture. The results were phenomenal. By 1914, with little more than 800,000 acres under cultivation in 1860, Argentina had expanded her acreage to some 60,000,000. The export of wheat amounted to 190,000,000 bushels; corn rose from some 300,000 bushels to over 263,000,000; linseed production grew in exports from 1,000 tons in the 1870's to over 1,000,000 tons; sugar from 3,000 tons to over 200,000; wine from 57,500,000 liters to over 500,000,000.

Agricultural growth was paralleled by an equally significant change in the cattle industry. Historically, Argentine cattle were valuable simply for their hides and tallow. But under the influence of British needs, scientific cattle breeding changed the tough, wild pampas animals into beef cattle, a metamorphosis contributed to by the importation of blooded stock, fine horses, fairs, rodeos, and exhibitions. By 1914 over 23,000,000 head of cattle and 43,000,000 head of sheep were the foundation for this vast industry. The export of meat, with the invention of refrigeration in transportation, poured enormous wealth into the hands of Argentine landowners. In 1894 the export value of frozen meat equaled some $11,000,000; by 1914 it had risen to over $90,000,000. A corresponding value attached to the export of mutton.

Technical changes came on the heels of these expanding industries. The steel windmill provided water for both herds and crops. Barbed wire, fencing valuable lands, put an end to the free-running cattle of the gaucho era. The thresher and reaper, which transformed the American West, found a huge market in Argentina. Sheep-dipping, veterinary science, mechanical wool clippers, and a variety of other devices played their part in the growth of the cattle industry.

Accompanying these changes in the cattle and agricultural industries were others equally far-reaching. Railroad construction, which in 1870 amounted to a bare 500 miles, had reached by 1914 almost 21,000. The lines fanned out from Buenos Aires in a vast network to the north, west, and south, so that all the main centers were connected with the capital. Beyond Argentina's borders one line ran to Santiago, Chile, another to Asunción, and a third reached the frontier of Bolivia.

At the great ports of Buenos Aires, Santa Fé, and Rosario huge dock systems grew up to receive the flood of raw materials from the interior. In 1920 more than 30,000 craft, steam and sail, went in and out of Buenos Aires alone. In the littoral cities, too, rose huge refrigeration plants, principally British and American. Other businesses flourished. British banks, insurance houses, and export and import firms grew rich upon the growing volume of Argentine exports. This expanding urban economy required modern transportation systems, tramways, buses, public utilities, light, heat and water, improved streets, sewage disposal systems, and other necessities of modern cities.

These extensive economic changes were nourished by a huge stream of foreign investment, principally British. The latter owned most of the railroads, though French investors had significant holdings. Argentine landowners invested their funds in land and improvements of their cattle and agricultural possessions. By 1914 the national wealth was estimated at fifteen billion dollars, of which foreigners owned almost a fourth. The national income, it is estimated, increased between 1880 and 1914 fifteen times over. But this wealth was unevenly distributed. While Argentina had more millionaires per capita than any country in the world, almost 90 per cent of the population earned less than $1,200 annually; the great majority of these had, in fact, an income of less than $500 a year.

While the economy of the country attracted attention by its spectacular growth, the most important element was the human. Before 1860 Argentina's population numbered barely 1,500,000. Largely through immigration it had reached by 1900 some 4,000,000; by 1913 it had doubled to 8,000,000. These immigrants worked the crops of the pampas and the mesopotamian areas of Corrientes and Entre Ríos. Farther north they labored in cotton plantations and in the forests of the Gran Chaco, felling quebracho trees for their tannin and gathering *yerba maté*. To the west they cultivated the vineyards of Mendoza. In the south on the bleak plains of Patagonia and even in Tierra del Fuego they tended millions of head of sheep. Other millions of immigrants found work on the docks and in other unskilled occupations in cities and towns. Their labor throughout Argentina produced the wealth that brought that country to such high rank among Latin-American nations.

Another wealth-producing group, too, had its roots in the immigrants arriving from Europe—the Argentine middle class. The bulk of these were small businessmen or white-collar workers in the industries connected with the country's vast export trade. Some amassed fortunes and invested their money in Argentine industry, to become later a driving force in modern Argentine nationalism.

These vast economic and social changes made the political framework of Argentina totally inadequate to meet the new needs of the country. Neither labor nor the growing middle class enjoyed representation in the government. The constitution of 1853, drawn up by representatives of the landowning families of the interior provinces, fixed the pattern of political control. Among themselves they struggled within each state for the control of the governorship. The governor designated candidates for local office, controlled the elections, and frequently used military force to dictate his successor. The governor generally looked forward to becoming a senator in the national congress; in any event, he used his office to place his friends or relatives in that body. Moreover, the governors played a leading part in the selection of a president, for, controlling the state's political machinery, they selected the delegates to the electoral college.

The struggle for the office of president usually reduced itself to a competition between the more powerful families in the various states. While, in theory, the constitution gave the president the power to intervene in the states to protect representative government, he frequently fomented revolts himself in those states which his enemies controlled. With an excuse to intervene he was thus enabled to dictate a new election of a governor and the representatives in the electoral college. Finally, in combination with friendly governors in other states, the president was able to dictate the nomination, which was equivalent to election, of his successor.

However, between 1860 and 1890 the new labor and middle class elements were demanding participation in the government. Labor suffered from low wages, inadequate housing, lack of education for their children, and many other abuses. The middle class resented the corruption in government, excessive public borrowing, the flood of inconvertible paper money, and taxation. Within this framework of monopoly of government of a small group and widespread discontent among the majority of the people in Argentina, the panic of 1889 precipitated a crisis out of which emerged new political parties and new leaders.

New Political Parties. When the panic was at its height in 1890, ten thousand people assembled in a public square in Buenos Aires to demand reform in government. Their leader was Leandro Alem, ably supported by his nephew, Hipólito Irigoyen, destined to become one of the great figures of modern Argentina. Alem formed a revolutionary committee, won the support of the underpaid younger naval officers, and seized the arsenal in the capital. After two days the revolt was crushed. Alem next proceeded to form the Civic Union party, which had as its platform reform in government administration, elimination of corruption, and extension of the suffrage. In the midst of these events Juárez Celman resigned. Vice-President Pellegrini, as chief executive, immediately began to salvage the fortunes of the oligarchy. He recovered for the nation much of the land illegally sold under Juárez Celman, expelled the worst offenders from government service, halted unnecessary expenditures, suspended, in agreement with the British bondholders, service on the national debt, and founded the National Bank of Argentina.

Fully aroused by the force of Alem's and Irigoyen's demand for an extension of the suffrage to all classes, Pellegrini and his supporters sought to split the Civic Union party. In this maneuver they had the support of the wealthier coastal landowning families who, as former supporters of Buenos Aires, were deprived by the settlement of 1880 of any participation in the government. On the littoral, too, were many new families, who derived their wealth from business. Neither of these two groups had sympathy with the democratic program of Irigoyen, the chief spokesman of Argentine labor. This understanding between the traditional conservative oligarchy and the equally conservative wealthy groups on the coast became known as the *Acuerdo* or "Accord," and had as its objective the exclusion of Irigoyen's reform group from the government. For the presidential election of 1892, after setting aside Mitre who was a candidate, the *Acuerdo* combination settled upon Luis Sáenz Peña.

The Radical Party. Alem and Irigoyen, denouncing the *Acuerdo* as a betrayal, formed what subsequently became the major democratic party of Argentina, the Radical Civic Union party, known today as the Radical party. It derived its name from its espousal of the principle of separation of church and state, that is, a *radical* change in the relation of these two institutions. It also demanded universal suffrage, fair elections, labor reforms, and a system of state-supported public schools. The principal supporters of the new party came from the ranks of labor, which had been demanding reforms in the preceding twenty years. In 1882 German workers in Argentina founded a club, Vorwärts, modeled upon the German Social Democratic party. In 1889 the International Workers, supporting the Club Vorwärts, petitioned the Argentine congress to adopt laws recommended by the Workers' Congress of Paris, namely, an eight-hour day, prohibition of child labor in factories, one day a week rest, and other similar reforms. In 1890 the next significant development took place when the Workers' Federation of the Argentine Republic, shortly renamed the International Committee of Argentine Workers' Federation, organized and petitioned Pellegrini to relieve their distress caused by the panic of 1889–1890. The refusal of their petitions threw labor into Irigoyen's new Radical party. When in October, 1891, the presidential election took place with Alem and Sáenz Peña as candidates, the administration, fearing the strength of the new party, declared a state of siege, arrested Alem and his lieutenants, who were later exiled, and elected Sáenz Peña president.

The Administration of Luís Sáenz Peña, 1892–1895. The administration of Sáenz Peña was filled with struggles characteristic of the new forces emerging in Argentina. While Alem was exiled, Radical deputies elected to Congress demanded his return, acceded to by the president, an upright man. For this action he was attacked by his own supporters. At the same time Alem and the Radical party, supported by the rapidly multiplying labor organizations along the littoral, pushed their demands for reform. When these were not forthcoming, revolts and riots occurred in Buenos Aires, Tucumán, Santa Fé, and San Luis. General Roca crushed the uprisings and drove Alem and his leading supporters into exile. Sáenz Peña, refusing to take the blame for these actions, resigned in 1895 to be succeeded by Vice-President José Uriburu. When Alem returned in the next year, 1896, he found the spectacle of an uncompromising government so depressing that, like his great contemporary in Chile, Balmaceda, he committed suicide. Irigoyen now succeeded to full leadership of the Radical party.

After 1895 the *Acuerdo* was formally organized into a new political party composed of the two conservative groups and called the National Autonomist party. It nominated Roca as its candidate in the 1897 election, while the Civil Union put forward Mitre. The Radical party, recognizing that the election would be a controlled one, abstained, as a protest, from participating. Roca won with ease. However, testifying to the seriousness of the internal political conflict was Roca's action in the next year, 1898, in submitting to the Chilean ultimatum over the Andean boundary dispute.

The Administration of Roca, 1898–1904: Foreign Affairs. While political conflicts seethed within the state, Argentina's constantly expanding economy brought recovery from the 1889–1890 crisis. By 1898 she had renewed service upon her foreign debt and reduced the amount of inconvertible paper money. In foreign affairs her growing strength revealed itself in demands upon her neighbors and her assumption of leadership in inter-American conflicts. To the Missions Territory in dispute between herself and Brazil, Argentina entered a claim for the bulk of the land despite the fact that the population included almost no Argentinians compared with more than 5,800 Brazilians. A treaty in 1889 between the two countries referred the question to the United States for arbitration. In 1895 President Cleveland awarded the entire region to Brazil.

A more important question was the boundary dispute with Chile. Chile, whose territorial expansion antedated that of Argentina, had as early as 1847 founded a town on the Strait of Magellan and pushed her claims to both sides of the Strait. In a series of negotiations culminating in a treaty in 1881, Argentina recognized Chile's claims. In a second treaty in 1884, both agreed that the boundary between the two nations along the Andes would reach northward from fifty-two degrees south latitude to "pass along the highest crests of the Cordillera which divide the waters." Joint exploration of this line led to disputes. The Chileans interpreted the treaty to mean that the division line was the watershed; Argentina claimed that the crest or the highest peaks determined the line. This dispute was complicated further by a conflict between the two countries over the boundary of the Atacama *Puno* in the north.

The struggle reached a climax in Roca's administration in 1898, when Chile sent an ultimatum demanding arbitration. The matter was referred to the United States for settlement, and the American minister to Bolivia, Buchanan, was appointed to preside over a commission which included besides himself a representative from each of the two countries. Buchanan hit upon a simple device, namely, dividing the entire area into sections and voting with the country which seemed to have the best case in each section. In this way the commission reached agreement covering the Andean area from Bolivia to fifty-two degrees south in three days. In the far south, beyond fifty-two degrees, the boundary question between the two countries was submitted to Queen Victoria as arbiter. Her commission fixed the boundary in 1902, which established Chile's claim to the Strait, and divided Tierra del Fuego between the two nations.

In commemoration of the peaceful outcome the two nations melted down the cannon they had collected for the war that many had thought inevitable to erect high in the mountains a statute known as the "Christ of the Andes"—one of the many examples Latin America has set for a world thus far too blind to follow. An amusing sequel occurred. When the statue was discovered to be facing Argentina with its back to Chile, an acrimonious exchange between the two countries began anew. Amenities were restored shortly, however, when a Chilean wit pointed out that the Argentines needed watching.

In the broader field of inter-American affairs, Argentina also took a hand when Roca's foreign minister, Luis Drago, promulgated in 1903 the Drago Doctrine. In essence the Doctrine stated that the principle Argentina would like to see recognized was "that the public debt cannot occasion armed intervention, nor even the actual occupation of the territory of American nations by a European power." Various interpretations have been attached to Argentina's action. One is that the protest, while directed at European powers, was, in fact, a criticism of United States use of military force in the Caribbean countries. Argentina was thus announcing her leadership of the growing opposition in Latin America to the United States policy of intervention in Hispanic-American affairs.

The Election of 1904. The expanding economy of Argentina continued to draw ever larger numbers of immigrants from Europe. These in turn joined labor unions and added their voices to the demand for reforms. In 1901 the first national union was created when the Workers' Regional Federation of Argentina (FORA) established itself. To combat its rising power, the government secured the passage of a "law of residence," the effect of which was to make noncitizens ineligible for membership in unions. Its provisions further made possible the exile of foreigners, a technicality used to exile many prominent labor leaders. However, these measures were ineffective in blocking the growth of Argentine labor. In 1902 the salaried employees organized the General Union of Workers, the UGT, which soon after included a variety of unions. They demanded the reforms called for in the previous decade, an eight-hour day, organization of cooperatives, one day's rest in seven, and arbitration of industrial disputes. The Roca government, hoping to anticipate labor reform, enacted a labor code; but this proved to be unacceptable to labor. In the growing number of immigrants from Europe, too, came influential socialist groups which shortly before 1900 organized the Socialist party under the leadership of Alfredo Palacios.

The continued refusal of the government to enact legislation extending the suffrage embittered the political conflict, so that when the election of 1904 arrived, the Radical party in protest again boycotted the polls. Manuel Quintana of the National Autonomist party easily won the election, with José Figueroa Alcorta as vice-president. Irigoyen, charging fraud, attempted to lead a revolt, with widespread support in Buenos Aires, Santa Fé, Córdoba, and Mendoza. The attempt failed and Irigoyen was again exiled. The event, however, did produce two significant results. One was a labor law providing for reforms in the nation's capital, Buenos Aires. The other was the administration's loss of control in the House of Deputies in the 1906 congressional elections. To head off reforms implicit in this victory, Alcorta, who had succeeded Quintana upon the latter's death in 1906, forcibly dispersed the lower house and intervened in the various provinces to break up the obvious power of the Radical party.

The Radical Reform Movement and the Election of 1910. By 1909, the year of the next presidential race, fully 4,000,000 workers, practically the bulk of the laboring population, was excluded from the suffrage. Between 1906 and 1910, by petition, public meetings, and strikes, they campaigned incessantly under Irigoyen's leadership for a law extending the suffrage. At the same time there was a growing split in the National Autonomist party's ranks. Many of the liberal business groups were anxious to meet the demands for electoral reform, fearing that the alternative would be revolution. Thus the moderate wing of the conservative party succeeded in nominating Roque Sáenz Peña, who campaigned on a pledge to extend the suffrage. Elected overwhelmingly, Sáenz Peña, an upright man like his father, submitted to the national congress in August, 1911, what was to become the famous Sáenz Peña law. This law provided for secret and compulsory male suffrage. Its enactment had great significance. In Argentina it paved the way for the triumph of the Radical party in 1916. Elsewhere in Latin America it was copied as a model for making democratic government effective.

The Administration of Sáenz Peña, 1910–1916. With the Sáenz Peña law on the books, the Radical party prepared for the congressional elections of 1912. In this it had the support of the labor unions. By that year three national organizations existed, the General Union of Labor, the Argentine Regional Workers' Federation, and the Agricultural Regional Federation. These in turn had established powerful locals in the leading cities of the interior, a political force which stood ready to support the legislative program of the Radical party. Thus in the congressional election of 1912, with voting secret and compulsory, the Radical party won complete control of the House of Deputies in the national congress, gained a considerable number of the senatorial seats, and elected governors in the states of Santa Fé, Córdoba, the historic center of conservatism, and Entre Ríos.

Democratic Reforms. The congress of 1912 began immediately to enact legislation making reforms advocated since 1890. It passed laws prohibiting creditors from attaching workers' wages and providing for employers' liability for accidents, one-day rest out of seven for workers, a low-cost housing program, pensions for railroad workers, a sanitation program for the city of Buenos Aires, the creation of a department of labor, free labor exchanges, and a postal savings bank.

World War I and Argentina. World War I had the effect of strengthening the reform movement in Argentina. Its immediate effect upon the country was to produce widespread unemployment. The British blockade of the Central Powers cut off Argentina's European markets; the German submarine blockade of Britain made Argentine shipping hazardous. As a consequence, huge stocks of beef, mutton, wheat, and other cereals piled up along the docks. A similar glutting took place in the interior. Corn, wheat, barley, and oats withered in the fields; the grape crop rotted on the vines in Mendoza; thousands of older cattle and sheep were slaughtered on the ranges. Dock laborers, railroad employees, farm hands, and workers in the vast network of export industries found themselves without employment. The financial condition of the government approached bankruptcy.

The war also involved Argentina in a struggle between the great powers to win her support. Upon the outbreak of the conflict, President

Plaza, who succeeded Sáenz Peña upon the latter's death in 1914, declared Argentine neutrality. At once the British, with heavy investments and strong influence among the wealthy middle class, campaigned to win Argentina to the allied side. France on her part exercised a powerful influence upon the intellectuals, who were shocked at the German invasion of Belgium and France. When in 1915 Italy joined the Allies, the several hundred thousand Italians became supporters of the Allied cause.

Supporting neutrality were the Germans, who, though much less influential than the British and French, nevertheless had the backing of the Argentine army leaders, admirers of German military efficiency. Joining the military were other conservative groups, who, afraid of the democratic implications of World War I, hoped for a German victory. But of most significance in keeping Argentina neutral was the Radical party, which saw in the war a danger to the continued progress of the reform program fought for since 1890.

The Administration of Irigoyen, 1916–1922. Under these circumstances the 1916 presidential campaign saw Irigoyen and the Radical party, strengthened by thousands of new voters who were enfranchised by the Sáenz Peña law, advocating neutrality, while the conservative candidate, supporting the Allied cause, demanded Argentina's entry into the war. The election resulted in a victory for Irigoyen.

German violations of Argentina's neutrality made Irigoyen's policy hard to maintain. On two occasions German submarines sank Argentine ships carrying food to Europe. The third sinking became known when the United States published some intercepted dispatches of Count von Luxburg, the German ambassador to Argentina. It was apparent that Irigoyen had agreed with the ambassador to prevent Argentine ships from sailing and that, in case any did, the Germans were to let them through. However, Luxburg wryly advised his government to define the policy: either to permit their passage or to "sink them without a trace." On the third occasion Luxburg, speaking on a different subject, implied that his government should use strong measures, since the South Americans were but Indians under a thin veneer of civilization, and that it was possible to use the large number of Germans in South America to establish a German state. The publication of these dispatches marked the high point in the effort to bring Argentina into the war. Irigoyen met the storm by expelling Luxburg and seizing the files of the German embassy. These measures, he insisted, in the face of strong opposition, were sufficient to satisfy Argentine honor.

While Irigoyen continued to maintain neutrality, he nevertheless favored the Allied cause. He condemned German propaganda that Britain and the United States were trying to dominate South America, and vigorously supported Uruguay, whose government believed, without foundation, that the Germans of southern Brazil were plotting an invasion. In January, 1918, Irigoyen further strengthened his position with the Allies by agreeing to furnish Britain and France with 2,500,000 tons of wheat, declaring his sympathy for the Belgium people and the objectives of the Allies, then being stated by President Wilson. At home Irigoyen's position was strengthened by workers' mass meetings supporting his neutrality policy, but more important was the success of the Radical party in the congressional elections of 1918 which they won with huge majorities.

The achievements of the Irigoyen administration in the six-year period, 1916–1922, have been obscured by the more spectacular events of the war. But they recorded the next major advance in Argentine democracy. Among the major measures were laws for the protection of women and children employed in factories, minimum wages, and measures to eliminate "sweatshops." The Radical congress required foreign-owned utilities to grant pensions to its workers. Applying to all labor was a law requiring arbitration of industrial disputes and a reduction in the penalties for strikes. Outstanding was the first measure in Argentine history to regulate the drug traffic. For the country at large the Radical congress also enacted laws aimed to bring fresh water and adequate sewage systems to all towns of the republic in an effort to reduce the ravages of typhoid and other similar diseases.

In the field of education Irigoyen's administration supported the establishment of the University of the Littoral, an institution which provided for schooling under one system from the kindergarten to adult education. Not confined to Buenos Aires, this institution had its branches in Corrientes, Santa Fé, Paraná, and Rosario.

Upon the end of the war Argentina, in common with many other nations, suffered a depression. An expansion of her traditional industries, wheat and other cereals and beef, stimulated by the war, suddenly collapsed with its end, as markets disappeared. As at the beginning of the conflict, warehouses filled up, railroad transportation ground to a halt, and food was left to rot in the fields. (This serious situation, however, was alleviated somewhat by the fact that Argentina, by remaining out of the war, had incurred no war debt.) Inevitably, unemployment grew and bankruptcies became common. In 1920 thousands of the unemployed in the larger cities advocated a general strike, urging socialist proposals to relieve their condition. Resulting riots and disorders forced Irigoyen to break the strike with troops, an action the conservatives hoped would split the Radical party. However, the record of reforms under Irigoyen was sufficient to maintain the support of labor in the 1922 elections.

The Administration of Alvear, 1922–1928. In the 1922 election, with Irigoyen barred from a second term by the constitution, the party turned to Marcelo Alvear, an outstanding figure and long identified with the Radical party. Elected by large majorities, Alvear and his congress continued the program of reform. Under Alvear came rapid advances in labor organization, which supported the Radical party's program. In 1922 a new labor union, the Argentine Syndical Union (USA), was created including 397 organizations. In effect it succeeded the General Union of Labor, the UGT. The next year, 1923, saw the creation of the Argentine Workers' Confederation, the COA, which had as its object the union of all labor organizations under a single union. With almost 100,000 members it included within it the country's largest single union, the Argentine Railroad Workers. Created in 1920 after the failure of the general strike, its organization, drawn from a large number of fraternal societies, had about 75,000 members in 1926. At the same time the older organization, the Argentine Federation of Regional Workers (FORA), became nation-wide in the 1920's with 598 unions and a membership of some 130,000.

Reforms in the States. Based upon this solid core of organized workers, the Radical party supported reform measures in state legislatures. A law providing for an eight-hour working day was enacted in Córdoba, San Juan, Tucumán, and Mendoza. In the latter state, in addition, was a minimum wage law. Old age pensions were provided in Córdoba and Mendoza, while Tucumán and Salta in the far northwest took the lead in requiring medical care for sugar workers and a program of comprehensive social legislation. Much of this legislation was the work of state administrations put into office by Irigoyen's use of the power of intervention.

Alvear and Reform. Under Alvear the national program of reform went forward. Bakeries in Buenos Aires, of which there were thousands, were forced to improve conditions of work and establish regular hours for their employees. Agricultural labor unions secured laws requiring accident-prevention devices installed on machinery used on the large estates. Pension laws were extended to include workers in financial houses, a tribute to the influence of the USA. A decree extending the industrial arbitration law required railroads to submit disputes with their workers to arbitration. Other legislation extended further protection to women and children in factories.

The first attempt at a comprehensive workers' pension law failed when, after a three-year trial, the legislation was repealed in 1926. Fabulously wealthy Argentines found themselves forced to contribute to the general welfare by the first inheritance tax and a tax upon real estate, the latter to provide funds for a public school program. Touching the land, the Alvear administration, too, enacted the first legislation when railroads were required to encourage colonization on the lands so generously granted them in the nineteenth century. This law became, in fact, the first attempt to attack the problem of *latifundia* in Argentina. Thereafter all the democratic parties included in their programs proposals for the breaking up of large estates.

Foreign Affairs. In international affairs the Alvear administration reflected its democratic outlook. Argentina, which joined the League of Nations, led in demanding the admission of all states including Germany. Its position rested upon its sympathy with the newly established German republic, which, under the Weimar constitution, was attempting reforms identical in many ways with those in progress in Argentina. That constitution, with its bill of rights and comprehensive labor provisions, reflected many of the ideas of Argentine political leaders. Upon the League's refusal to consider her proposals, the Argentine delegation withdrew.

Inevitably, the question of church and state arose under the Alvear administration, since the Radical party advocated separation. The problem first presented itself when the Argentine government refused to recognize the bishop of Santa Fé for failure to present his credentials and attempting to take office in defiance of the government. When the papacy retaliated by refusing to ratify an earlier appointment to the archbishopric of Buenos Aires, the Alvear government severed relations with the Holy See in 1926.

Division within the Radical Party. While the Radical party maintained its record of reforms, a serious conflict within its ranks divided its supporters into *Alvearistas* and *Irigoyenistas*. One reason was the inexperience of many members of parliament and key figures in the administration. The oligarchy, thoroughly skilled in political maneuver, had excluded from government all but members of its own class. But the men that Irigoyen and Alvear had to depend upon were new to politics. Many were blind followers of Irigoyen, who could commit no wrong. Others, more conservative businessmen and powerful party workers offended at one time or another by Irigoyen, supported Alvear. The relations of Alvear and Irigoyen, too, were reminiscent of those between Theodore Roosevelt and President Taft after the latter had assumed office. Irigoyen, who had headed the party since 1896, naturally thought of himself as indispensable. Alvear, an able man, meant to be president in fact as well as in name. Adding to the discord were the conservatives, who naturally magnified the mistakes of the Alvear administration, particularly the compulsory contribution, opposed by labor, of 5 per cent of the workers' wages to a pension fund.

But the most important issue which split the party arose over the question of reviving Argentine foreign trade, depressed since the end of World War I. Before that conflict Argentina had practically a monopoly of European markets in wheat and beef. But World War I stimulated the cultivation of wheat in the western part of the United States and Canada. In the case of beef Australia became an important exporter. These competitors cut into the Argentine export trade. In 1922 Argentina lost her American market with the passage of the Fordney-McCumber tariff of that year. So vital to her prosperity did she consider this market that the Argentine delegate left the Pan-American conference in Havana in 1928 and her ambassador resigned his Washington post in protest to the refusal of the United States to discuss tariff reform.

In these circumstances of growing unemployment, loss of markets, and conflict within the party, the 1928 election arrived. Alvear, afraid of a conservative victory, took the lead in calling upon the party to close ranks and support Irigoyen for the presidency. Such was the magic of the great man's name that he considered it unnecessary to wage a campaign. Entirely justified in his estimate, he was elected by an overwhelming majority, 269 electoral votes to 138 for his opponent.

The Administration of Irigoyen, 1928–1930. Irigoyen began his second administration an old man, suspicious and disappointed by the criticism directed against him by some of Alvear's followers. He attempted to run the Argentine government single-handed. Important offices went unfilled, loyal party workers unrewarded. His followers frequently blocked needed legislation proposed by either *Alvearistas* or the conservatives. The declining income of the government in the face of shrinking markets led him to defer payments on debts. He antagonized both the dock workers and the powerful railroad union by breaking a strike when he took office. Businessmen, bewildered by delays in payment of bills owed them by the government, joined the growing chorus of criticism. Irigoyen did nothing to counteract the attack. Having given his fortune to the party and charitable institutions, he lived in a small apartment, unable to afford the upkeep of the presidential mansion. His absence from the center of affairs gave unscrupulous followers opportunity to line their pockets with graft. Into this paralysis of government, the world depression of 1929 struck with full force.

The Revolt of 1930. The cycle of events that occurred in 1914 and again in 1920 repeated itself. Argentine markets collapsed, unemployment grew, the government income fell to new lows. Discontent, riots, strikes, and frantic appeals to the government to take action added to the confusion already clogging Irigoyen's administration. The opportunity for the conservative groups was golden. In Mussolini's Italy, of which the landowners were admirers, they had an example of a successful *coup d'état* halting democratic reforms. To them continued control by the Radical party meant more reforms in education, land, and industry and the growth of labor power. The results would inevitably transform Argentine society. Moreover, the wealthy middle class, impatient of their country's one-crop economy, was anxious to support a government with a program to industrialize Argentina.

The leadership of the revolt naturally came from the army, led by José Evaristo Uriburu, General Agustín B. Justo, and a host of generals and colonels. In the interior states the commanders of military departments had their instructions in hand when word should come from Buenos Aires to act. An incident in the capital provided the moment for striking—a parade in protest over the death of a university student killed in a demonstration before the presidential mansion. The cadets of the Argentine Military Academy in Buenos Aires, led by Juan D. Perón, joined the parade. At a given signal they seized the government buildings. The navy, brought into the harbor, refused to protect the government. Irigoyen, arrested, was placed aboard a naval vessel after he had delegated his power to Vice-President Martínez. In the meantime a military junta gave the prearranged orders to the military leaders in the interior. They immediately took over all communications and police headquarters, dissolved legislatures, arrested all governors who had been elected by the Radical party, and established censorship of all newspapers. Two days, September 4–5, 1930, sufficed for the success of the revolt.

This event arrested the reform movement in Argentina aimed at broadening the base of its democracy to keep step with the economic changes which were making Argentina into a modern state. In this period of more than 100 years, Argentine literature had reflected in part the struggle for liberty and concerned itself with the influence of the pampas on the national development. After 1930 most of the leading Argentine writers took refuge in escapist literature.

Argentine Literary Development. Argentine literature of the national period had its roots in literary societies, largely of French political persuasion, organized to gain independence. After freedom from Spain, writers, influenced by the romantic movement of the period, recognized the challenge offered by the barbaric life on the vast plains to cultured society. Giving most perfect expression to this conflict was Sarmiento in his famous work, *Civilization and Barbarism: The Life of Juan Facundo Quiroga* (1845). This extraordinary work deals with the primitivism of the landowners and the *mestizo* gauchos, the plainsmen, whose total lack of cultural background and animal-like savagery opposed them to all semblance of law and order. This barbarian power threatened the very existence of civilization in Argentina. In developing this theme, Sarmiento portrayed every aspect of Argentine life of the period. Indeed, his insight into Argentine culture was so deep and his skill so great in exposing the anatomy of tyranny that the book, defying classification, still stands as the most powerful work ever written by a Latin American.

Though Rosas was overthrown (1852) and power passed into more civilized hands, the gaucho on the plains continued his sway over Argentine literature. He himself was a maker of verses, the product of his lonely vigil on the vast spaces and fear of nature's manifestations. As such he early attracted the attention of writers, of whom the great Argentine poet, José Hernández (1834–1886), succeeded in catching the spirit of his primitive culture. His poem, *The Gaucho Martín Fierro,* has become the gaucho epic, one of the classics of the Spanish language and Argentine literature. Its greatness lies in the fact that Hernández, literally and intellectually, placing himself in the gaucho's boots, saw that the "civilization" which Sarmiento gloried in was, in fact, a threat to the gaucho love of freedom. Thus the work became a classic expression of the age-long struggle of man's fight for justice and liberty. The poem, too, symbolized the disappearance of the gaucho as a group.

After Hernández Argentine literature surrounded the gaucho with halos, the hero of dramas and novels. This romancing reached its height in the third masterpiece of Argentine literature, Ricardo Güiraldes' *Don Segundo Sombra.* Therein the gaucho became a symbol. Ennobled into a "historic national character . . . the shadowy figure of Don Segundo will forever stretch across the pampas, not as a picture drawn from life, but as a legendary symbol of a heroic type that was." (Torres Rioseco).

With the twentieth century the great social questions of the nation forced themselves upon the attention of Argentine writers. Converted by this date from a wild gaucho country, Argentina was a nation of scientific agriculture and cattle raising. Streams of immigrants poured through its great port of Buenos Aires. The middle class and labor became new social forces which created new cities of huge dimension. Voicing the new ideas that accompanied these changes is Manuel Gálvez (1882–   ). Writing on a great variety of subjects—education, poverty and crime, capitalism and labor, the drawing rooms of the wealthy, jails and convents—he covered in his novels every major aspect of Argentine society. His most widely known work, *Nacha Regules,* dealt with prostitution in Buenos Aires. Others of lasting merit described the struggle of a country school teacher with the provincialism of the interior, and the conflict between intrenched religion and the new liberal ideas taking hold of the imagination of the young.

José Ingenieros (1877–1925), Gálvez' contemporary, while not a novelist, yet commanded such an influence over young writers that he affected the course of Argentine literature. From humble beginnings among the poor, Ingenieros' extraordinary intellect early won him honors in the field of medicine; eventually he became internationally known for his contributions to experimental psychology. One of his studies on criminal madness has been classed in the field of literature. However, his work having the greatest influence upon Argentine writers was *The Mediocre Man.* Therein he advanced the thesis that since the bulk of humanity is mediocre, ideals should be set for them to imitate. Democracy, of which he was a fervent advocate, should be made to function in such a manner that it would bring to the fore individuals whose concepts, constructive in nature, the masses could follow.

For a brief moment Alfonsina Storni (1892–1938), a woman poet of extraordinary power, crystallized in verse the varied life of the metropolis, Buenos Aires. Her works, arising from her own suffering as a struggling school teacher, caught the spirit of the city streets and the city's pitiless power to crush the individual. The dictatorship after 1930 made even blacker the "spiritual poverty" which so oppressed her, and she took her own life. Other Argentine novelists and poets, notably Leopoldo Lugones, a poet (1874–1938), and Eduardo Mallea, a novelist (1903–   ), have eschewed social problems and sought the literature of escape. Some of the works of the latter, however, have won praise for their philosophical content.

Part III. THE RETURN OF THE DICTATORSHIP, 1930–1955

The Dictatorship of Uriburu, 1930–1932. Once in power, with Uriburu acting as head, a provisional government began a systematic rooting out of Irigoyen's supporters. It intervened in twelve of the fourteen states to bring into office its own appointees, and postponed, in violation of the constitution, a national election until November, 1931. Only those parties which had the permission of the government were allowed to present candidates. Naturally, the Radical party was excluded. For that election the various conservative groups combined to form a new political party which they called, significantly, the National Democratic party. With the opposition silenced, this party elected Agustín B. Justo president, who took office in 1932.

Administration of Justo, 1932–1938. The Justo administration was characterized by a sharp political struggle in which the democratic parties attempted to restore their control, but failed, and secondly, by economic measures to overcome the depression of the 1930's. Coincidentally with the dictatorship of Uriburu, the Spanish Falange, which was later successful in putting Franco into power in Spain, established its New World headquarters in Buenos Aires. When Hitler in 1933 assumed power in Germany, the German embassy became the center for the establishment of a powerful Nazi organization in Buenos Aires. Strongly supported in its domestic policies by these totalitarian groups, the Justo government continued to harry the Radicals, although it did permit Irigoyen to return to Argentina to die in 1933. The vast outpouring that attended the old warrior's funeral dramatically reminded the dictatorship of Radical sentiment. But the Justo government, undeterred, intervened in all fourteen provinces to maintain its power. Its outstanding disregard of democratic processes occurred in Entre Ríos, where the Radicals, having won with a large majority, were forcibly driven from office by the interventor's troops and a government was installed that was favorable to Justo.

The Radical and other democratic parties, confronted with a military government supported by the Falange and Nazi organizations, attempted on two occasions to revolt in 1934. These attempts failing, the Radical party formed a National Civil Militia, while the Socialist party set up a Red Guard. More significant in the struggle against the growth of a rightist state was the organization of a new labor union in 1930, the General Confederation of Labor (CGT). While the new organization declared against political action, it took a forthright stand on economic matters. Against the proposals of powerful business groups, the CGT declared that protectionism to favor national industry is wrong and persons and goods should circulate freely. This policy of the Confederation coincided with the Hull program of reciprocal trade agreements soon being urged as a solution of the world depression. Deeply afraid of Fascism, the Confederation launched a movement to unify the labor movement. Its president, José Domenech, succeeded in bringing into the Confederation in March, 1936, the aggressive Maritime Federation of Labor and the Federation of Telephone Employees. By that date the Confederation represented 550 unions with some 250,000 members. As such it became one of the most powerful labor unions in Latin America.

While the CGT did not directly participate in politics, its members became the core of the opposition to the establishment of a Fascist dictatorship advocated by the Falange, certain Argentine conservatives, and the Nazis. Thus with labor support in the congressional elections of 1934, the Radical party, again legalized and headed by Alvear, the Socialist party, the Communists, and the Progressive Democrats won control of the House of Deputies. When a year and a half later the Franco rebellion occurred in Spain, the Argentine democratic parties immediately formed a United Front to block a similar movement in Argentina.

The issue, all knew, would be fought out in the 1937 presidential elections. The United Front nominated Alvear. The conservatives, rightly judging the power of the democratic parties, organized on their part a National Front of conservative parties and put forward Roberto M. Ortiz, a wealthy businessman, but with decidedly liberal views. His running mate was Ramón Castillo, staunchly conservative, but of mediocre ability. With Ortiz the conservatives hoped to attract the votes of the small businessmen deeply disturbed by the growth of the Communist party. The election resulted in the selection of Ortiz as president, although many contended that Alvear had won and pointed to electoral frauds in nine of the fourteen states.

Economic Policies of Justo, 1932–1938. While the political battle waxed hot, the Justo government took measures to bring the nation out of the depression. To cut down expenses, Justo restricted many of the social programs of the Radical regime. Teachers' salaries, public school appropriations, and health programs were greatly reduced. New taxes were imposed, particularly a sales tax, while the inheritance tax was broadened. To take care of the widespread unemployment in the larger cities, the government instituted a public works program and encouraged the unemployed to colonize on lands in the interior. To open such lands, railroads were extended into Patagonia and extensive port improvements were made at Bahía Blanca.

Financially, the government followed the advice of a British monetary commission to reorganize the banking system and establish the Central Bank of Argentina. The wealthy middle class, which had cast its lot with the 1930 revolution, saw its hopes fulfilled with the enactment of tariffs to protect Argentine industries from foreign competition. Ortiz in his administration particularly threw his influence behind the middle class demand for industrialization. However, since the economy of Argentina still rested upon the export of basic foods, the Justo government sought outlets for the surplus products piling up as the depression deepened.

The most significant success of the Justo government was the conclusion of the Roca-Runciman agreement of 1933. This trade treaty arose from Argentina's protest against Britain's new economic policy of Empire preferences adopted at Ottawa in 1932. Until that date Britain was the principal purchaser of Argentine food products, but the depression forced the British to placate the members of the Commonwealth at the Ottawa meetings. They agreed there to erect tariff walls around the Empire and exchange goods within. One effect was to exclude Argentine products and to favor Canadian and Australian exports. Argentina's threat, however, to open its markets to the United States forced the British to include Argentina within the circle of Empire preferences. The resulting Roca-Runciman agreement did provide Argentina an outlet for her beef and wheat, but it also effectively blocked the negotiation of a reciprocal trade agreement with the United States. In the following year, 1934, in pursuit of the same objective, the Argentine government negotiated a barter agreement with Germany which accepted large amounts of food supplies in return for markets for her electrical and chemical goods. These varieties of economic measures had by 1937 largely mitigated the worst effects of the depression. Less than two years later Argentina was to capitalize upon her improved economy when World War II broke out.

World War II and Argentina, 1939–1945. World War II had the same immediate effects upon Argentina as had World War I and the depressions of 1921 and 1929. Its foreign markets collapsed. Foreign shipping, from a high of 150 ships a day entering the harbor at Buenos Aires before September, 1939, hardly averaged in the next few months twenty-six ships a week. As in the previous crises, surplus beef, wheat, and other cereals piled up on the docks and in the warehouses while the transportation system slowed to a halt. In Patagonia thousands of sheep were slaughtered on the range to save the rest from starvation. Unemployment mounted in the cities, while the finances of the government headed toward bankruptcy.

The Ortiz government, knowing that drastic political effects would follow continued unemployment, hastened to stabilize the economy. From the British the government obtained an order of 400,000 tons of meat. Ortiz sent a mission to the United States which secured two loans amounting to $110,000,000. With these funds Argentina could extend credits to the British and the French, while the British in turn established an Argentine credit in sterling in London. These events, significantly, began the process which ultimately ended British financial control of Argentina. Other measures set in motion were control of currency exchange, a public works program, low-cost housing, subsidies for farmers, and government purchase of surplus raw materials, such as the wool crop in Patagonia.

While Argentina refused new efforts of the United States to negotiate a reciprocal trade agreement, she did enter into such arrangements with Japan. In return for beef, mutton, wool, linseed oil, and other products, Japan shipped industrial goods. Finally, to absorb the growing unemployment, the government launched a huge military program. By the end of 1940 these measures had blunted the edge of the worst effects of the loss of markets in Europe and had given a new spurt to the growing demand for industrialization.

The War and Argentine Political Conflicts. As World War II progressed it produced deep conflicts between the conservative and democratic groups. The former saw in the war an opportunity, by remaining neutral, to amass vast wealth by the sale of Argentine products to any buyer. This policy paralleled the interests of the Nazis, who were anxious to use Argentina as a base for infiltrating neighboring South American republics. Their objective here, too, was to cripple the production of raw materials which would inevitably be sought by the democratic nations. In opposition the democratic parties called for strong support of the nations opposing the Axis, and condemned the ruthless German attack upon the smaller nations, the invasion of France, and the bombing of Britain.

Unfortunately for the revival of the democratic movement in Argentina, President Ortiz became seriously ill in 1940. He had pursued a policy of insisting upon fair elections—all that was needed to bring back the Radical and other democratic parties into control of the national congress. Thus Alvear, elected to congress, took the lead in organizing movements in behalf of the Allies. With Ortiz virtually out of office after September, 1940, the National Democratic party resorted to widespread fraud in 1941 to win control of Mendoza and Santa Fé. In retaliation the democratic parties in congress launched an investigation of Nazi activities in Argentina. These soon revealed their influence in schools, newspapers, radio, the armed forces, and even plots to overthrow the Uruguayan and Bolivian governments. Castillo, acting president in Ortiz' absence, resorted to ruling by decree. The senate on its part defied the government and ratified the Havana agreements of 1940. The congress found support in mass meetings of the citizens, who demanded Argentine support of Britain and France.

In the midst of this conflict came news of the Japanese attack on Pearl Harbor on December 7, 1941. This dramatic event produced universal reaction in Latin America in favor of the United States. The Argentine House of Deputies immediately voted to adopt the recommendations of the Rio Conference, January, 1942. At the same time it passed a resolution requesting the government to break relations with Germany and Japan. The United States, in hopes of strengthening the democratic groups in Chile and Argentina, charged through Sumner Welles that those two countries were hotbeds of Nazi spies, who, in telephonic contact with German agents in the United States, were responsible for the sinking of American ships in the Gulf, the Caribbean, and the Atlantic Ocean. In Argentina the effect was to stir a strong public demand that the government submit its "neutrality" policy to a plebiscite.

Meanwhile the United States, determined that the Nazi groups and their Argentine supporters would not interfere in the North Arfica campaign by giving bases to German submarines, secured from Uruguay air and naval bases to patrol South Atlantic waters. When the campaign in North Africa had succeeded in the following spring, forcing Rommel to fall back and eventually surrender Tunis, Castillo weakened and sent congratulations to the American government. The United States, however, still distrustful of the Argentine government for its failure to ratify the Rio agreements, cut off all negotiations for further military supplies.

The democratic parties in Argentina, quick to note the weakening of Castillo, again demanded that Argentine policy be submitted to a plebiscite and that she join the hemispheric defense program. The fact that the country had returned the Socialists and Radicals to the control of the House of Deputies in March, 1942, strengthened the force of their appeal. Finally, with the resounding defeat of the Nazis in North Africa followed by a second major defeat at Stalingrad, in March, 1943, Castillo felt himself obliged to submit to the demand for a plebiscite.

The Revolt of June 4, 1943, and Perón. The threat of a plebiscite produced a crisis which proved to be a turning point toward totalitarianism in Argentina. The Nazis, the Falange, the military, and the wealthy middle class, enjoying great benefits from the high prices obtained by Argentina under war conditions, organized a revolt against the Castillo government to prevent the holding of the plebiscite. Successfully carried out on June 4, 1943, the core of the attack was the United Officer Group, GOU, whose moving spirit was Juan D. Perón. General Arturo Rawson served briefly for two days, to be succeeded by General Pedro Ramírez, who immediately dissolved congress, all political parties, and the huge General Confederation of Labor. He followed these actions with a ruthless campaign to stamp out freedom of the press and speech, break up protesting mass meetings, establish a censorship of the press, and arrest labor leaders and prominent figures in the Socialist and Radical parties. Attack on the University of Buenos Aires and the public schools ensued when educational leaders signed a document demanding Argentine support of the American nations against the Axis.

The Argentine revolt disturbed the United States greatly since the connections of the United Officer Group with German espionage agents were known. When Ramírez became president, Washington recognized his government, misled by certain statements which seemed to indicate an end to Argentine neutrality. When, however, it became obvious that Ramírez was destroying the Argentine supporters of the hemispheric defense program, the American government hastened to adopt defensive measures. An opportunity came when the Ramírez government appealed to the United States for military supplies under a lend-lease agreement. Secretary Hull sharply rejected the request and pointed out that the purpose of lend-lease was to put weapons in the hands of friends and not enemies of the United States government.

The correctness of Hull's position was almost immediately verified when the British arrested an Argentine consul serving as a Nazi spy. At the same time Argentina gave support to a Nazi-inspired revolt in Bolivia in December, 1943. These disclosures, published and circulated in Argentina in spite of censorship, forced the resignation of Ramírez in February, 1944. He was succeeded by General Edelmiro Farrell with Perón as vice-president. This government the United States refused to recognize, as did the British. The continued repressive measures of the Farrell regime included the suspension of the famous Argentine daily, *La Prensa,* and attacks on other democratic papers. The United States next recalled its ambassador, condemned the Farrell government for not rooting out Nazi spies, and finally, in August, 1944, applied sanctions by cutting of all gold shipments to Argentina.

Argentina and the Chapultepec Congress, 1945. The successful landing on the Normandy beaches in June, 1944, followed by the rapid retreat of the German army from France, produced the next change in Argentine relations with the Allies. When the collapse of Germany was certain after the Battle of the Bulge, the United States called a meeting of the American nations at Chapultepec, Mexico, in February, 1945, to plan for the postwar world in America. There Mexico and the United States sponsored a resolution inviting Argentina to rejoin the family of American states. Two qualifications were attached to the invitation: one was to declare war on the Axis and the second to root out Nazi spies. In March, 1945, when Germany was stumbling to defeat and the whole force of Allied power could be loosed on Japan, Argentina declared war on the Axis. Later in 1945 the American government declared it was satisfied that Argentina had eliminated its Axis spies. Under these circumstances Argentina became a member in good standing in the inter-American system. This fact in turn provided the basis for the United States to sponsor Argentina's entrance into the United Nations when that organization was formed in San Francisco in May, 1945.

The Perón Dictatorship, 1946–1955. While world-wide events affected the international position of Argentina, the traditional pattern of power asserted itself within the country. Juan Domingo Perón, an army leader and Secretary of Labor under Ramírez, was one of the few figures to recognize that control of labor had to be continued if the dictatorship of the right were to remain in power. Labor itself at the moment was handicapped by internal conflicts. Moreover, its principal political weapons, the Socialist and Radical parties, persecuted and long excluded from government, were weak. Perón stepped into this vacuum. As Secretary he extended wage increases and put pressure upon employers to grant increases in wages, shorten hours, extend vacations with pay, and provide labor with other of its minimum demands. His immense popularity became apparent in October, 1945, when, after the conservative government exiled him, a workers' demonstration forced his return within a few days.

He became in 1946 the logical candidate of the rightists for the presidency. Winning in an election characterized by fraud and violence, he set about establishing an iron control over Argentine labor. In this work he had the assistance of his wife, Eva Perón, a former radio performer. Combining a flair for the theatrical with a ruthless determination and vaulting ambition, she eliminated old labor leaders, seized union funds, captured key positions, and appointed Perón's supporters to the principal union offices including that of the powerful Argentine Confederation of Labor.

Her power rested principally upon the control of the Eva Duarte de Perón Foundation, an agency created by law which gave her direction of all welfare organizations in Argentina. Its financial support came from levies on workers' wages, pressure on employers for "gifts," and contributions from municipal and state bodies as well as from the national government. The Foundation, too, was the beneficiary of properties confiscated from enemies of the regime, the most outstanding example of which was the Bemberg estate of some thirty-one corporations valued at $200,000,000.

There is no doubt that considerable funds of the Foundation went into the building of housing projects for labor, establishment of hospitals, recreation centers, and other needed facilities. Eva Perón also continued the policy of extending benefits in wage increases, insurance programs, better working hours, and improved health conditions in factories, department stores, and other businesses. A significant and lasting effect of her work was to instill Argentine women with a feeling of equality. She secured for them political rights within the framework of a Peronista Women's party organized in 1949 and gave them full status with the Peronista party in 1950.

She herself became immensely popular. When, however, her ambitions soared beyond the position of labor leader and she sought the vice-presidency in 1951, the army—the real power in the nation—stepped in and forced her withdrawal. The shock of this defeat undoubtedly contributed to her early death in 1952.

The Argentine army acted as the principal base of Perón's power. Traditionally it was linked with the landowning oligarchy, but under Perón sons of the middle class entered the higher ranks so that the army leadership lost its former homogeneity. Perón fostered the army's military power by re-equipping it with modern weapons and beginning its mechanization. He also extended generous increases in pay to both officers and enlisted personnel. Distributed throughout the nation the army performed the important function of maintaining in power the interventors and other officials of the Perón regime. The Argentine navy did not fare so well under Perón. It did receive some destroyers, submarines, and other smaller vessels and also benefited from increased pay. However, its higher echelons continued to be drawn from the landowning families. The air force, greatly expanded, was equipped with some jet planes.

Upon becoming president in 1946, Perón did not neglect the church. His most significant concession to it was a law in 1946 granting church control of education. The support of big business and the wealthy middle class was maintained by Perón through his program of industrialization, discussed below. By these varied measures Perón kept labor at the service of the dictatorship and held intact until 1955 the traditional Argentine pattern of power: the army, landowners, church, and big business.

The dynamics of Perón's dictatorship was the drive to industrialize. His first Five Year Plan was launched in 1946, buttressed by a huge gold and credit reserve accumulated during World War II. The Plan laid the basis for beginning steel, chemical, electrical, and other heavy industries. Communications of all kinds—air, highways, railroads, and water routes—were extended. Characteristic was the purchase of British and French railroad holdings in 1947. To these Perón added a trans-Andean line to connect Salta and Antofagasta to import Chile's copper and nitrates. To provide additional fuel for Buenos Aires' industries, a thousand-mile pipe line was begun from the Comodoro Rivadavia fields in the south.

Perón maintained a rigid control over agriculture to take advantage of high prices caused by food shortages after World War II. The government set import quotas and issued exchange rates to direct purchases abroad in favor of the industrial program. All these varied activities involving trade were directed by a powerful government corporation, the Argentine Institute for Trade Promotion.

By 1950 various factors produced a major crisis in Argentina and threatened Perón's position as dictator. Industrialization, carried forward at the expense of agriculture, had cut down the latter's production. Many farmers, incensed at low prices, refused to plant crops. By that date, too, the world shortages in food had eased, so that Argentina's foreign trade declined. But most serious was a drouth extending over almost two years which became so devastating that Perón had to resort to meatless days and even plan to import wheat. The resulting discontent forced him to take a series of ruthless measures to maintain control.

The first to suffer was the free press, which published the facts of the agricultural collapse, widespread strikes, and arbitrary denial of citizens' rights. Outstanding was the confiscation of the famous newspaper, *La Prensa.* In 1950, after various measures had failed to silence this paper, Perón charged it with being a tool of foreign interests. A government-controlled news vendors' union next demanded the suspension of *La Prensa's* subscription list. This "dispute" Perón referred to a congressional investigating committee, which seized the paper. Finally in April, 1951, Perón expropriated it for its "un-Argentine" and "unpatriotic" policy of using foreign news services in place of those of the Argentine state. Hundreds of other newspapers were likewise closed by the committee on various pretexts.

Paralleling the attack in 1950–1951 upon *La Prensa* as a foreign tool, Perón launched a violent offensive upon the "imperialism" of the United States in Latin America and upon Britain. Against the United States he directed his fire for its policy of negotiating mutual defense agreements with various Latin-American nations. Britain he attacked for her claims to ownership of the Falkland Islands, which Argentina had insisted had been hers since independence from Spain. In 1950 Perón spectacularly seized possession of Deception Island. Britain removed the Argentines but was eventually constrained to share possession pending a final settlement. Argentina also extended her claims to include the South Orkney Islands and, reaching farther south, established a post on Graham Land in conflict with both Chilean and British claims to this region. Ultimately by 1954 Argentina had seven bases beyond the Antarctic Circle.

Perón's violent attacks during 1950–1951 upon *La Prensa* and upon the "imperialism" of the United States and Britain did much to divert public attention in Argentina from the internal economic crisis. This offensive also paved the way for his re-election to the presidency. To this end he amended the Argentine constitution to permit re-election, and, hoping to buttress his position further, he put his wife on the ticket as the vice-presidential candidate. The army, however, as noted above, forced her withdrawal. As election time neared, he moved up the date to the fall of 1951. Finally, when the campaign was at its height, Perón arrested his principal opponent, Ricardo Balbín, the Radical party nominee, and utilized a "state of internal war" decree to prevent the opposition from campaigning. At the last moment he freed political prisoners and held what was described as "a free and honest election." With these various measures, the destruction of a free press, intimidation of the political opposition, and appeals to nationalism, Perón weathered the two-year crisis.

Perón's Second Administration, 1952–1955. In office Perón was favored by a break in the drouth and bumper crops. However, the effects of the collapse of agriculture and the near exhaustion of gold and credit reserves on the first Five Year Plan forced him to seek new sources of wealth. He unhesitatingly reversed his policy toward foreigners at this point to attract capital for investment in Argentine industries and raw materials. Thus he had enacted in 1953 legislation under which investors after two years could transfer abroad profits up to 8 per cent annually. After ten years the capital itself could be repatriated at the rate of between 10 and 20 per cent each year.

World conditions favored this change of policy. The revival of Europe's economy found industrialists of West Germany, Italy, France, and Switzerland investing heavily in Argentina and establishing new industries. At this moment, too, the cordiality of the reception of Milton Eisenhower in Buenos Aires during his visit to Latin America for the President of the United States established a basis for good will between United States businessmen and Perón's government. In 1954 United States capital began moving south, with the Kaiser Corporation building a factory to manufacture automobiles at Córdoba for the Argentine market. Other corporations sought concessions. In 1955 the Export-Import Bank extended a $60,000,000 loan to Argentina.

Paralleling this effort to attract capital, Perón also sought agreements of various kinds with his neighbors to secure raw materials for Argentina's growing industries. The first agreement was negotiated with Chile in 1953 after the failure of various efforts dating from 1947. This pact provided for free ports, improvement of sea, land, and air contact and other communications, and a study of methods to make the economies of the two countries more complementary. With Bolivia a treaty provided for the exchange of wheat for oil and other minerals; with Peru, wheat for iron ore; with Ecuador, various agricultural products for sulphur; and with Paraguay, quebracho wood (tanning extract), for Argentine cattle and food. These treaties hardly supported Perón's claim of an economic union, but they do clearly show the beginnings among South American nations of an exchange of raw materials for their nascent industries. In the future these industries undoubtedly will reduce more and more Latin America's dependence upon goods imported from the traditional industrial nations.

Because these various measures to meet the shortage of funds to continue industrialization did not fully do so, Perón in 1954 for the first time denied labor's demands for increases in wages to meet the mounting cost of living. The resulting discontent of labor gave the church an opportunity to organize an essentially Catholic labor party, which, supporting the workers' demands, offered competition to Perón's control of labor. In answer to this challenge, Perón attacked the church, not upon the issue, but accusing it of misusing state funds for education. The ire of the church was further aroused by legislation in 1955 granting divorce, the first in Argentine history, extending rights to illegitimate children, and threats to separate church and state.

This conflict with the church culminated in June, 1955, in a revolt against Perón. The incident opened with an attempt of the church and its supporters to hold a procession celebrating Corpus Christi Day in opposition to a government ban. After the procession was held, Perón charged the demonstrators with attacking public buildings and foreign embassies. He then arrested and deported high church officials, for which he and his government were promptly excommunicated by the Vatican. Almost immediately thereafter, Argentine naval planes bombed the Argentine White House (Casa Rosada) and other government buildings. Perón thereupon directed the army to crush the revolt. However, by September the rebels had organized a new resistance under army leadership. Centered in Córdoba under General Eduardo Lonardi, they captured that city and were quickly joined by units of the air force. Meanwhile, to close the ring on Perón, naval cruisers stood by in the Río de la Plata ready to bombard Buenos Aires itself. Faced with this formidable array the dictator sought asylum in Paraguay. A military junta in temporary command surrendered to Lonardi, who was sworn in as provisional president on September 23, 1955.

The Lonardi regime lasted a bare seven weeks before it was overthrown in a bloodless coup on November 13. The new regime under General Pedro Eugenio Aramburu claimed totalitarian influences had dominated the Lonardi government and that the time had come to return Argentina to "true democracy." By the early part of 1956 Aramburu had dissolved the Peronista parties, cleaned out Peronista influences from the principal labor unions, notably the General Confederation of Labor, ended laws making criticism of the government a crime, and early in

February returned *La Prensa* to its owners. Basic problems, however, remain: continued industrialization, land reform, and inflation.

The effectiveness of the Aramburu government in re-establishing democracy in Argentina will hinge on recognizing religious liberty, on holding early elections with full effect given to the Sáenz Peña law, which makes voting universal and compulsory, and on its policy toward the press when free newspapers again criticize government actions. Thus far the new government has given some indication it will resume the democratic development initiated under Irigoyen and the Radical party in 1916.

Chapter XVI

URUGUAY

Part I. THE *BLANCO-COLORADO* STRUGGLE FOR POWER, 1828–1870

Character of Uruguayan History. Uruguay owes its origin to the rivalry of Spain and Portugal in the colonial period. Its struggle for independence was carried on within the framework of Argentine and Brazilian rivalry over the Río de la Plata. After independence Uruguay's unique position between these two great powers guaranteed its continued existence as an independent nation. Its two political parties, the *Blanco* and *Colorado,* struggled for control until after the middle of the nineteenth century. By that date the steady influx of European immigrants seeking land, the introduction of scientific agriculture and cattle raising, and the growth of a progressive middle class turned the scales in favor of the more enlightened *Colorado* party.

With the opening of the twentieth century the *Colorado* party launched its great experiments to modernize the nation. Its new political concepts and its social and economic reforms resulted in making Uruguay completely self-governing in the next fifty years under firmly established democratic institutions.

The Independence of Uruguay, 1828. After Brazil had annexed and re-named Uruguay the Cisplatine province in 1821, her lenient policy reconciled some Uruguayans to her control, among them José Fructuoso Rivera, who held a military command. Other Uruguayans preferred exile in Argentina. In 1825 these patriots, under leaders called the "Thirty-three Immortals" and aided by Rivadavia in Buenos Aires, invaded their native land. Led by Juan Antonio Lavalleja and joined by Rivera, they won the support of the people and defeated the Brazilian army sent against them at Sarandí in October, 1825.

When, in accord with earlier promises to Buenos Aires, Uruguay joined the United Provinces of La Plata, Dom Pedro I, emperor of Brazil, declared war on Argentina. The conflict, thus continued for another two years, ended in 1828 when the Uruguayans overcame the inefficiently led Brazilian armies. After that event Dom Pedro I, urged by British minister Viscount Strangford, for commercial reasons to make peace, signed the treaty of August 25, 1828, which established Uruguay's independence guaranteed by both Argentina and Brazil.

Struggle between the Blancos and Colorados. With a constitution drawn up in 1829, elections were held in the following year which made Rivera president, an office he owed to his brilliant military record against the Brazilians. Lavalleja, disappointed in the outcome, revolted and plunged the country into a civil war. Out of this conflict Manuel Oribe emerged as president in 1835. Soon Oribe broke with Rivera, a fact which had the interesting result of giving birth to two political parties which thereafter dominated Uruguayan history. These parties, the *Blanco* and the *Colorado,* rested upon definite principles which separated them. The *Blanco* party had its basis in the conservative landowning oligarchy of the interior. At the same time they looked upon Argentina as a counter-weight to Brazil, whose domination they feared. The *Colorado* party, on the other hand, while including the coastal oligarchy, did find room for a progressive middle class and liberal intellectuals. Its strength was principally in the river towns and coastal cities. Because this region was associated with the trade and commerce of La Plata, the *Colorados* feared Argentine domination and were consequently pro-Brazilian in their outlook.

Rosas and Uruguay. The civil war between the *Blancos* and *Colorados,* the former led by Oribe and the latter by Rivera, gave Rosas in Argentina an opportunity to extend Argentine domination into Uruguay. Oribe, expelled from the country, secured Rosas' support. At the moment, however, the Argentine dictator made the error of abusing French residents in Buenos Aires, an action which led the French government to blockade the Argentine capital and, by aiding Rivera, drove Oribe from power in 1838. Rivera, now president, foresaw further Argentine aid to his rival and sought reinforcements from France. That country obligingly sent 1,000 troops and stationed battleships on the Río de la Plata. Rivera also secured an alliance against Rosas with Colonel Genaro Beron de Astrada, the dictator of Corrientes. When he received news of Oribe's agreement to bring Uruguay into Rosas' Argentine Confederation, Rivera declared war and drove both Rosas and Oribe from Uruguay.

Rosas, not easily thwarted, returned in 1843 to conquer Uruguay. In February he laid siege to Montevideo, an operation successfully maintained for eight years. At the same time Oribe led his *Blanco* sup-

porters and an Argentine force against the beleaguered nation. The fatal
drawback to Rosas' operations, however, was his inability to prevent
British and French vessels from running his blockade. When he attacked
this shipping, the two foreign powers blockaded Buenos Aires itself in
1845. Their action opened the Paraná and Uruguay rivers and correspondingly strengthened the defenders of Uruguay.

Rosas' campaign to get control of the Paraná and succeed in conquering Uruguay raised the fears of Brazil, already greatly disturbed
by a revolt, the Farrapos, in its most southern province, Rio Grande do
Sul. Likewise, Rosas' restrictions on river traffic antagonized the dictator
of Corrientes, Justo José Urquiza. By 1851 these three powers, Brazil,
the *Colorados* of Uruguay, and Corrientes under Urquiza agreed to an
alliance against Rosas. The Brazilian fleet overcame the blockade of
Montevideo, while Urquiza and the *Colorados* operated to raise the siege
on land. With the city freed, the Brazilian fleet transported the allied
army across the Paraná to defeat Rosas at the battle of Monte Caseros in
February, 1852. Thus ended the most serious threat to Uruguay's independence in the nineteenth century.

The war had significant effects upon Uruguay. The Uruguay River,
freed from Buenos Aires control, guaranteed this important outlet to
Uruguay. Less happy were the demands of the Brazilians: compensation
for injuries to her nationals in early conflicts and a settlement of the
boundary between the two nations. Agreed to in the treaty of alliance,
Uruguay was left with no choice but to surrender an important region
in the north. The boundary settlement fixed the line along the Cuareim
and Ilucú rivers, granted Brazil the largest part of the control over
Lake Mirim and the Yaguarón River, and finally recognized the Cuareim
River as the boundary between the two countries in the northwest. The
long war intensified the antagonisms of the *Blancos* and *Colorados* and
caused one or the other to turn to Argentina or Brazil in their internal
struggles. Thus on these terms for the next ten years the two parties
struggled for power.

Uruguay and the Paraguayan War. In 1863 the interminable struggle
between the two parties in Uruguay was deflected from its usual channels by the sudden emergence of Paraguay as a military power. In that
year the *Blancos,* led by President Bernardo Berro, a ruthless persecutor
of the *Colorados,* found themselves faced with an invasion by the *Colorado*
leader, Venancio Flores, supported by both Argentina and Brazil. Argentine backing was explained by the antagonism of Mitre toward the
barbarous actions of the *Blancos* in battle. Brazil was disturbed by the

injury to her nationals from the guerrilla warfare across her border. More-over, although the *Blanco* government was unable to maintain internal peace, it rejected Brazilian demands for compensation.

With both Argentina and Brazil recognizing Flores, President Berro appealed in August, 1864, to the dictator of Paraguay, Francisco López, for support against Brazilian threats of invasion. López agreed to Berro's proposals and warned Brazil that an attack upon Uruguay would be a cause for war. The Brazilians, underestimating the danger in Paraguay, sent in October, 1864, battleships by sea and an army overland to sup-port the *Colorados*. López, true to his promise, declared war on Brazil. But the *Colorados*, having overthrown Berro, assumed power and re-pudiated the *Blanco* agreements with López. Uruguay then joined Brazil in the war against Paraguay. The war, dealt with elsewhere, found little contribution coming from Uruguay. However, the peace treaty in 1872 between Paraguay and Brazil guaranteed that the Uruguay River, along with the Paraná and Paraguay, should be free to the commerce of all nations. Thus an additional bulwark to Uruguay's future economic growth was assured.

Part II. ECONOMIC AND SOCIAL CHANGES: GROWTH OF DEMOCRATIC INSTITUTIONS, 1870 TO THE PRESENT

Economic and Social Changes, 1870–1900. As in Argentina, the demands of European industrial cities for La Plata food products, cereals, beef, and mutton began to transform the economy of Uruguay after 1870. Its primitive agricultural and cattle areas responded to modern scientific methods. Sheep increased seven fold in numbers between 1860 and 1900 to reach by the latter date more than 14,000,000 head. Cattle not so numerous as sheep increased in value by modern methods of breeding and care. The export of these products and cereals made mandatory an improved transportation system. Railroad construction began in the administration of Flores. In 1884 British capital laid out a well-integrated system of lines which fanned out from Montevideo into the interior. A vast expansion of shipping and docking facilities complemented the transportation system.

This expanding economy of Uruguay drew increasingly large num-bers of immigrants. Soon after the abolition of slavery in 1842, Spaniards, Italians, French, Swiss, British, and Germans began arriving to take advantage of generous land grants. Brazilians came in along the northern frontier, while a considerable number of Argentinians—refugees and some businessmen—settled in southern Uruguay. In 1869 with a population of barely 200,000, the country by 1900 had almost 1,500,000 inhabitants. These vigorous elements played a leading part in transforming Uruguay from an essentially feudal state into a modern one. An early effect appeared in demands for a better educational system to meet the needs of these heterogeneous stocks and their varied occupations. Under the influence of Sarmiento's writing on education, the great Uruguayan educator, José Pedro Varela, visited the United States, studied the American school system, and in 1877 founded the first public schools in the country.

But the most significant force in ending the feudal character of the country was the political struggle, given a new meaning by virtue of the influence of the rising tide of immigrants. The *Colorado* party of Flores and later *Colorado* leaders, strengthened by the economic changes, contended against violent outbreaks of the *Blancos* after 1870. Succeeding Flores was Colonel Latorre, who ruthlessly crushed the *Blanco* opposition under a dictatorship which lasted until 1880. Máximo Santos of modest background and talents succeeded to the control of the country, but retired in 1886 to make way for a progressive-minded president, General Máximo Tajes. With wise decrees he supported the expanding economy, reduced the size of the army, and prepared the way for a free election of his successor, Julio Herrera y Obes.

Herrera, however, and his successor, Idiarto Borda, were wasteful and extravagant with public funds. The long domination of the *Colorado* party had corrupted its bureaucracy and leaders. When the election of 1896 took place under fraudulent conditions, the *Blancos* won power in a revolt which shook the financial standing of the country. Led by Aparicio Saravia, they achieved a political compromise under which the *Blancos* secured control of six of the nineteen departments of the country and the presidency. Far from bringing reforms hoped for, however, the agreement had the effect of reviving the bloody warfare between the two historic parties.

The Rise of José Batlle y Ordóñez. The *Blancos* under Saravia ruled despotically in their domain, while street fights and riots went on in the cities. Thinking Uruguayans, deeply disappointed by the turn of events, again embraced the *Colorado* party. Chastened by defeat, it had sought new leadership which held out promise of ending political corruption and civil war. Prominent among the groups seeking a solution were the immigrants who had little interest in the battles between the oligarchies of either the *Blanco* or *Colorado* party. Their ideas found expression in José Batlle y Ordóñez. Batlle, thoroughly experienced in

Uruguayan politics, had founded his famous newspaper, *El Dia,* in the 1870's, in which he carried on a campaign for social justice. His political thinking won support among the new citizens of Uruguay, who had come from European countries where they were familiar with democratic and socialist ideas. Within Uruguay, too, as early as 1905, after a long career of activity, the labor movement organized its first unions. Supporting them, Batlle contributed to making Uruguay the first Latin-American country to adopt the eight-hour law and launch a program of social legislation.

After the *Blanco* fiasco under Saravia, Batlle was elected president of Uruguay in 1903 the leader of a rejuvenated *Colorado* party. In this, his first administration, he had to divert valuable time and funds to crushing a *Blanco* revolt under Saravia. Even so, he extended the educational program and secured legislation to improve the condition of workers in factories. Batlle's successor in 1907, Claudio Williman, carried on the program of reform and initiated the extensive dock system of Montevideo.

Meanwhile, Batlle traveled in Europe to study forms of government for the purpose of proposing a constitution which would forever end the ceaseless civil conflicts between the *Blancos* and *Colorados.* His efforts resulted in a significant contribution to political thinking in Latin America. He believed that the root of the evil in Uruguayan politics was the presidential system. The president, he stated, dictated the election of his successor, with the opposition left with no alternative but revolution. To break this vicious circle, he proposed a substitute which he called the collegiate executive. Elected to the presidency again on his return from Europe in 1911, Batlle launched a battle to abolish the office he held and establish the collegiate executive. The struggle split the *Colorado* party, with the younger and more progressive forces led by Baltasar Brum. Under his successor, Feliciano Viera, elected in 1915, the issue was finally submitted to the people when congress enacted legislation calling for a constituent assembly, elected by universal, secret suffrage under proportional representation. The country, supporting Batlle's proposal, returned a majority favoring the reform. Thus a new constitution embodying Batlle's ideas, drawn up in 1917, became effective in 1919.

The Constitution of 1919. The new document provided for a president elected by popular vote for four years, with powers over foreign affairs, army, navy, and the interior. The president also had some authority in preparing the budget. However, the innovation, not called a collegiate executive, but a National Council of Administration, was incorporated into the constitution. This Council, with one-third of its members elected every two years by universal suffrage, shared executive power and had powers not reserved to the presidency. These included complete jurisdiction over public instruction, finance, public works, commerce, and industry. The significance of this division of powers was the control given the Council over internal administration. To carry out its policies the Council appointed four of the seven ministers in the cabinet. All conflicts between the Council and the president were to be settled by congress.

The constitution further provided for a bicameral legislature with one member from each department elected by an electoral college. The members of the House of Representatives were chosen by direct vote for a term of three years. Between sessions a permanent committee of seven members sat. The judiciary of both superior and inferior courts was appointed by congress. For the departments and municipalities a large degree of autonomy was provided. The suffrage, the unvarying key to the status of democracy in a nation, was universal and secret for all males over eighteen years of age. The separation of church and state likewise emphasized the democratic character of the document. This constitution successfully solved the basic problem of conflict over the executive by the elimination of patronage from the hands of the president. At the same time the powers of the Council enabled it to launch a broad program of internal improvements in the next fourteen years.

Democratic Reforms under the Constitution, 1919–1934. Fortunately, the constitution went into effect in the hands of its friends. Baltasar Brum served from 1919 to 1923, José Serrato from 1923 to 1927, and Juan Campísteguy from 1927 to 1931, all *Colorados.* With her finances in excellent shape from the high prices for which she sold her products during World War I, Uruguay between 1919 and 1931 reformed her economy to become the most stable state in South America. Legislation included a minimum wage for agricultural workers, old age pensions, indemnity for accidents in industry, abolition of the death penalty, legal rights for illegitimate children, and divorce at the demand of the wife. The period saw a rapid expansion of public ownership of utilities, the establishment of a state mortgage bank, state ownership of the electrical industries, railroads, and other transportation, and the establishment of a national refrigeration plant. The government also greatly extended educational facilities in an effort to reach every child in the country. By 1928 the illiteracy rate, 40 per cent, was the lowest in Latin America.

The program included as well health clinics, adult education, hygiene laboratories, and playgrounds.

Attempt at Dictatorship: Gabriel Terra 1931–1938. In the election of 1931 Gabriel Terra, the head of the conservative faction of the *Colorado* party, was elected to the presidency. When the depression brought on the loss of Uruguay's world markets, with resulting unemployment, the government launched an offensive to destroy the constitution of 1919, declaring it was an obstacle to recovery. Hoping to secure the support of a considerable body of new conservative votes, Terra secured legislation in 1932 which extended suffrage to women both in national and municipal elections for the first time in any Latin-American country. In March of 1933 Terra, to avoid impeachment, suddenly dissolved, with military forces, congress and imprisoned and exiled the leaders of the opposition. Among these was former president Baltasar Brum, who committed suicide, despondent over what seemed to him a breakdown in the democratic process in his beloved Uruguay.

With a dictatorship established, a junta of nine men with himself at the head, Terra governed until the constituent congress which he called had prepared a new constitution. The congress re-elected Terra for a term of four years, and in May, 1934, promulgated a new constitution after it had been approved in a controlled plebiscite. The new instrument abolished the Council of Administration, concentrated power in the hands of the president, reduced legal opposition to his action by requiring a two-thirds majority of both houses to force the resignation of the chief executive, and finally buttressed the president's office in its dictatorial character by requiring that the seats in the senate be equally divided between the two parties which received the highest number of votes cast in the preceding national election. Finally, the constitution incorporated the legislation extending suffrage to women.

In power, Terra attempted to cope with the depression by revaluing the national gold supply, which provided almost 50,000,000 pesos for financing government undertakings; launching a program of highway construction and a public works program including low-cost housing and port works; completing an oil refinery capable of meeting the nation's needs; and beginning a power project on the Río Negro for the electrification of the interior of the republic. To revive foreign trade Uruguay negotiated bilateral treaties or conventions with England, France, Germany, Italy, Spain, and Sweden.

The Administration of Alfredo Baldomir, 1938–1942. When Terra's term drew to a close he decided against becoming a candidate. By that date the liberal parties, particularly the Batllistas and National Independents, who had attempted a revolt in 1935 against the destruction of the 1919 constitution, had the support of Uruguay's two powerful labor organizations, the General Union of Uruguayan Workers and the General Federation of Uruguayan Labor, established in 1930–1931. Thus when the liberal wing of the *Colorado* party nominated Alfredo Baldomir, well known in public life for his probity and uprightness, the bulk of the members of the anti-Terra parties returned to the *Colorado* fold and elected him.

In the following year, the outbreak of World War II adversely affected Uruguay. The markets for her wool clip, cereals, and beef disappeared. Unemployment mounted; the government's income declined precipitately. But the social programs installed in the 1920's and broadened in the depression acted as a cushion. Aid to the jobless was readily found in pushing forward the public works programs begun in the depression. The war itself was brought home to the Uruguayans when in December, 1939, the *Graf Spee* sought refuge from attack of British cruisers in the harbor of Montevideo. While both the British and the Germans violated the Panama Declaration on this occasion, the former contended that Uruguay permitted the war vessel to remain in harbor too long. When finally the *Graf Spee* sailed, her commander thwarted the hopes of the British by sinking his vessel in the Río de la Plata.

In spite of the war and the strain put upon the government, Baldomir, in response to widespread demand, restored the National Council of Administration. Likewise he encouraged the growth of labor unions, which in 1942 met in Montevideo to create a single union for the country, the General Union of Workers of Uruguay. The government also gave refuge to victims of fascist persecution in Argentina, while Foreign Minister Alberto Guani exposed the activities of German espionage agents in Argentina, Bolivia, Peru, and elsewhere. In Uruguay herself the government launched an investigation which rooted out a Nazi fifth column, for which she was attacked by both the Argentine and German governments. Opposing the attack on the Uruguayan Nazis and Argentine sympathizers was Luis Alberto de Herrera, the leader of the *Blanco* opposition. His party sought aid from Argentina and led the opposition to the United States' hemisphere defense policy.

With such an obvious ally against Argentine and Nazi activities, the United States in November, 1940, reached an agreement under which Uruguay provided air and naval bases for all American countries, except Argentina. A year later when the Japanese attacked the United States at Pearl Harbor, Uruguay at once shaped her foreign policy to support the United States. Axis resources were seized, known Nazis arrested, and in January, 1942, she ratified the Rio agreements and broke relations with the Axis. The United States on its part extended to Uruguay a lend-lease agreement and purchased her huge wool clip which had mounted yearly since 1939.

In the same year Uruguay continued her policy of supporting the Allied nations by breaking relations with the Vichy government, recognizing the Free French Committee of De Gaulle, and re-establishing relations with the Soviet Union, discontinued by Terra in 1935. On February 21, 1945, she declared war on the Axis.

In internal affairs President Baldomir took decisive steps to restore democratic practices interrupted by Terra's constitution of 1934. His action was provoked by the *Blanco* opposition led by Herrera. The latter not only sought Argentine aid to impede the nation's support of the war, but blocked in congress measures to improve the internal economy. Herrera was able to succeed by virtue of the constitution which provided that his party should have three members in the cabinet and one-half of the senate. With no alternative, Baldomir boldly dissolved congress in February, 1942, and appointed a council to aid him in governing. Meanwhile, the constitution was amended to provide for the election of senators on a proportional basis and for the elimination of the National Council of Administration. The latter Herrera had made useless. In the election on November 29, 1942, Juan José Amézaga defeated Herrera, while his party, the *Colorado*, captured control of both houses of parliament.

Under Amézaga (1942–1946) Uruguay, as we have seen, supported the Allied war effort. At the same time the president pushed a reform program. From the Export-Import Bank, Uruguay secured a $20,000,000 loan with which to carry on the public works program and begin the construction of a steel plant. But probably the most important constructive event of the administration was the completion of the first unit of the great Rincón del Bonete power plant on the Río Negro. Begun in 1937, it went into operation in December, 1945. Financed by a loan of $12,000,000 from the Export-Import Bank, the plant sends power 150 miles away to Montevideo and near-by towns, as well as to central and western Uruguay. It was fathered by Victor B. Sudriers, a Uruguayan engineer, whom the government has appointed vice-president of its administrative board.

The labor program of the Amézaga administration made advances, including the creation of wage boards, increased pay for piece workers, minimum wages for construction workers, unemployment insurance for packing and wool workers, low-cost housing projects in Montevideo and Artigas, and family allowances and paid vacations for workers in commerce and industry. Somewhat to balance urban labor's gains, Amézaga secured legislation granting social security to agricultural workers in 1943. To encourage farming in the interior, the government established scholarships for sons of farmers and agricultural workers in forestry, orcharding, and the raising of poultry, pigs, and bees.

Benefiting the population as a whole was a reforestation program, improved sanitation in cities and towns, public health programs, and the establishment of specialized schools, a school of liberal arts, one of library science, and an oceanic and fishing service. All aspects of these varied undertakings were financed in part by a tax imposed on all profits over 12 per cent. Among the final acts of the administration was legislation guaranteeing to women civil rights and equality with men in work and family relations, such as control over their own property, equal control over children, and the right to dissolve marriage on request. Equally important was military reform to weed out Peronista sympathizers. The chief features were a 30 per cent increase in salaries for lower ranking officers and obligatory retirement at fifty for top ranking officers.

The Administration of Batlle Berres, 1947–1950. In spite of the strong efforts of the conservative *Blanco* party, Tomás Berreta, the candidate of the *Colorados,* won. Upon Berreta's sudden death, Vice-President Luis Batlle Berres was inaugurated on March 1, 1947, to complete the four-year term, expiring March 1, 1951. Batlle's chief problem was to find markets for the cattle products of Uruguay, which by 1950 had an estimated 8,000,000 head of cattle and 25,000,000 head of sheep. Around the dominating role of this industry, all other economic activities centered.

Seeking trade agreements, the government successfully negotiated with Britain, which, sorely pressed by Argentina for higher prices, agreed in 1951 to buy 12,000 tons of meat for a period of twelve years, while in the year before the United States had taken 5,000,000 pounds for its armed forces. Throughout this period the United States continued to be a heavy buyer, particularly after the outbreak of the Korean War, of wool and hides. Other treaties negotiated during the regime, but signed in 1952 and 1953, were with Japan in return for machinery and textiles, with Italy in exchange for manufactured goods, and with Brazil for maté, coffee, tobacco, and cocoa.

With the very considerable income derived from the export trade, the Batlle government continued the industrial and agricultural development of the nation. This program involved extending government ownership over many new aspects of the economy, but the political stability of the nation was so assured and free enterprise so well guaranteed that foreign and native capital continued to pour into the development of the resources of Uruguay. It was estimated that in the latter half of 1950 more than $300,000,000 entered. The four-year public works program begun by Amézaga went forward with the purchase of 100,000,000 pesos' worth of United States machinery for use in hydroelectric projects, roads, bridges, oil drilling, farms, and irrigation.

Communications were extended. In 1948 a large new airport was opened at Carrasco near Montevideo for the use of both civilian and military planes. On March 2 of the same year Uruguay purchased the existing British railroads for $28,814,500 and added them to the state-controlled railways. Improvement of both began immediately with the issuance of a 7,000,000 peso bond issue to modernize facilities with the use of Diesel engines and cars, of which seventy-six had been purchased by 1951 from Austria and other countries.

Highway construction was pushed in all parts of the nation to facilitate movement of cattle to port cities and open up unused agricultural lands. Outstanding was the completion of roads which connected Paysandú and Salta on the Uruguay River, later extended to Bella Unión near the Brazilian border. In the interior, highways connected Durazno and Treinta y Tres; Florida and Minas in the south; and Melo in the far northeast with Paysandú and Salta.

Much emphasis was put upon improving the capital, Montevideo. Late in 1947 the government completed a vast hospital project begun in 1931 which, besides the hospital itself, includes a variety of research institutes, making this medical center one of the most modern in South America. In the same year the city began the acquisition of all transportation lines to modernize them. Important was the purchase of the British-owned network of tramways for $6,201,000 paid for by sterling held in London at Uruguay's account. In 1948 the city approved another large project for the construction and improvement of roads, bridges, wharves, and sports arenas to supplement the ten-year port improvement program to modernize and extend the city's piers, jetties, docks, warehouses, and loading facilities. Also in the same year the Departmental Council set aside $2,622,000 for a public works program to construct low-cost housing, public buildings, and parks.

To improve the diet of the Uruguayan people and reduce imports of food by expanding its own agricultural possibilities, the government in 1950 invited the United Nations Food Administration Organization to make recommendations. Their report, submitted in 1951, called for measures to control animal diseases, improve arable land by utilizing high-yielding legumes and creating feed reserves, better rotation of crops, control of plant diseases and pests, and improvement of grading, transportation, storage, and marketing of agricultural commodities. The commission further advised the reorganization of research, advisory, and other technical services for agriculture.

While the country in 1949 and again in 1951 had to import sugar and potatoes, the national production of milk, some 951,000,000 pounds, owed its increase to subsidization policies carried out for reasons of national health, so that consumers paid low prices for this essential food. Wheat and corn were in ample supply, while the production of wine from vineyards had revealed over the years an astounding growth from 8,920 acres cultivated for the purpose in 1896 to about 42,000 acres producing in 1943 over 20,400,000 gallons of wine. Another valuable addition to the food supply came from the planting of some 41,000 olive trees, which came into production in 1951. Another 30,000 planted immediately, it was estimated, would meet the national demand. Similarly, the production of rice has gone through a rapid expansion. National production doubled in the decade, 1941–1951, to 45,000 tons produced in the latter year.

In this expanding economy of Uruguay, organized labor has played a significant role. The first major large scale unions, the General Union of Uruguayan Workers, appeared in 1930 and the General Federation of Uruguayan Labor in 1931. In 1942 the General Union allied itself with the Latin-American Labor Confederation (CTAL). During World War II both confederations and other unions played an important role in combating Nazi activity in Uruguay and especially in forming the strongest centers of resistance to Peronista influences. After the war the issue of Communism divided the labor movement. By 1951 Communist strength in the powerful General Union had declined rapidly. In the same year the non-Communist unions formed a new organization, the Confederation of Uruguayan Trade Unions, which in 1952 joined the Inter-American Regional Organization of Labor (ORIT) which, broadly speaking, opposed the CTAL on the Communist issue.

While the unions disagreed on the question of Communism within labor's ranks, they voted as a unit to support the program of the liberal *Colorado* party. At the same time the unions took a leading part in bringing about measures to improve Uruguay's school system and in beginning the movement to improve the status of rural labor, one-third of which as late as 1952 was outside the range of most social legislation accorded the other major elements in Uruguay's society. The greatest obstacle to the improvement in rural areas arose from the opposition of the large landholders, who thwarted all efforts to increase rural wages and establish rural schools. Particularly was the school program impaired by the necessity of poorly paid parents of taking their children out of school to supplement the family income. In this double aspect—low-paid, unorganized rural labor and the poor quality of rural schools—Uruguay has been backward.

Trueba and the Abolition of the Presidency, 1950 to the Present. In view of the almost universal labor support of the *Colorado* party when the time came for the presidential elections of November 26, 1950, its candidate, Andrés Martínez Trueba, was easily elected to the presidency, a record of successes for the party uninterrupted since 1865. Interestingly, in contrast, but inevitable where native reform parties meet the needs of a nation, the Communist party lost its only senator and saw its representation in the House of Deputies reduced from five to two.

In office, Trueba devoted himself in the next two years to a campaign to abolish the office he held, believing, as José Batlle had earlier, that the presidency lent itself to the establishment in Latin America of tyrannical governments. He and his supporters advocated a nine-man council to replace the executive. A committee appointed from parliament reported a plan favorable for such a council, in essence to be composed of six members from the party winning the largest number of votes and three from the principal opposition parties.

In the following months the proposal, which had to secure two-thirds of both houses to agree to a national plebiscite, was vigorously debated throughout the land. Some unions in the urban centers, which were against any participation of the *Blanco* Herrerista party in government, opposed with strikes the change which would automatically guarantee the *Blancos'* key positions. On December 16, 1951, the Uruguayans voted to settle the issue favorably, agreeing to amend the constitution to abolish the presidency and replace it with a Federal Executive Council. While still in an experimental stage, the change has been hailed as a significant advance in the development of Uruguay's democratic institutions. Weighing heavily in this interpretation was the belief, with Peronista Argentina as an object lesson, that the existence of an executive council rather than a president at the head of the government reduced the possibilities of a dictator seizing control of the country.

Equally strong was the belief that the guarantee of political participation of all major parties in the government strengthened democratic institutions. On March 1, 1952, the Federal Executive Council, as it came to be called, was inaugurated, with former president Trueba chosen as chairman of the nine-man council.

The administration of national affairs proceeded smoothly after the change was made, but the effectiveness of the Council as an executive was challenged on two international issues. From both, however, the Council emerged with increased prestige. The first arose over the action of Argentina in banning its nationals from Uruguay as tourists, whose spending provided an important source of income. The Perón government in this case exerted pressure upon Uruguay to abandon the agreements she had made with Britain which had given her rights to carry on trade via flying boats with the Falkland Islands. Argentina, claiming jurisdiction over the islands, questioned Uruguay's right to make such agreements. The Argentine attitude was further motivated by her anger at Uruguay's granting refuge to exiles and other Argentines fleeing political persecution. The Council stood firm on both points even to the point of withdrawing her ambassador, an action which eventually brought Argentine recognition of Uruguay's position.

The Council, too, found itself supported in its proposal to accept the military mutual aid pact offered by the United States. Though proposed in 1952, strong opposition from many quarters delayed ratification until June, 1953, after the Council had urged it for more than a year. Again the congress had supported the Council on a vital issue which strengthened the effectiveness of the latter. Under the agreement the United States is given access to Uruguay's strategic resources and provides in return military aid and equipment.

In November, 1954, Uruguayan voters gave overwhelming approval to the council system when elections were held to fill the offices of the Council, the senate, the House of Deputies, and all departmental (state) and municipal councils. In the election the *Colorado* party won control throughout the nation. The results put that party again in possession of six of the nine seats in the Federal Council. Heading the Council was the former president, Luis Batlle Berres.

Uruguay, with its long development of democratic institutions is, with Costa Rica, in the vanguard of Latin-American nations in this respect. Costa Rica, which has abolished the army, and Uruguay, with its replacement of the presidency by a council, give promise of continuing the role of pioneers in the creation of new forms of human cooperation.

Chapter XVII

PARAGUAY

Part I. INDEPENDENCE AND DICTATORSHIP, 1814–1920

The Character of Paraguayan History. The influences dominating the history of Paraguay have been four: (1) its isolated geographical position in the interior of the continent; (2) its overwhelming Indian population; (3) its battle against the encroachments of its neighbors, and (4) its efforts to establish in recent times democratic institutions.

The Dictatorship of Dr. Francia. Paraguay for 300 years was largely one Spanish city, Asunción, surrounded by a million or more Guaraní Indians. When the Wars for Independence freed this region from Spanish control José Gaspar Tomás Rodríguez Francia established a dictatorship on May 11, 1814. For the next twenty-six years Dr. Francia kept Paraguay virtually isolated, an achievement unique in American history. From the first he recognized the danger of Argentine aggression and feared equally the expansion of Brazil. He ruled the Guaraní Indians with a benevolent hand, cooped up ambitious Creoles in their homes who might with outside aid seek his overthrow, and sealed Paraguay's borders against foreigners and even foreign trade except to secure the absolute necessities.

Francia did not neglect the building of an army. Exploiting Guaraní superstitions, he surrounded himself with such mystery and exercised such pervading authority that the Indians called him *El Supremo,* "the Supreme One." For his officer personnel he depended largely upon *mestizos,* from whom he secured blind obedience. Ruthless and sudden death was the lot of one whose loyalty he doubted. With his troops he fortified the borders of the country at strategic spots. He moved about in secrecy, ordered all persons off the streets while he drove through at a furious pace. To avoid assassination he slept in different rooms in the spacious governor's mansion. His orders to his army commanders, when delivered and executed, were returned and destroyed.

Regarding the church as a competitor, he struck at its influence and control. He appointed its officials, repudiated the claims of the papacy, and abolished feast days, religious orders, and all outward manifestations of the church's power, such as celebrations of saint's days and processions. Education he looked upon as a disturbing influence among the Indians and he would have none of it. But the everyday life of the Guaraní Indians was his prime concern. He encouraged agriculture, hand industries, and activities of all kinds that contributed to the Indians' well-being. He introduced new crops besides the traditional yucca and *yerba maté*. He revived the Jesuit emphasis upon wheat production as well as maize and cotton. The last he particularly fostered to release Paraguay from its dependence upon imported supplies.

To the cattle and sheep industry he also gave his attention. He even seized cattle lands of the Creoles and converted their ranges to state-owned farms to provide food and leather products for the state. His policies produced results. With leather and cotton available for clothing, food abundant, and work required of everyone, Paraguay presented a strong contrast with the saber-rattling republics on its borders. It is true that it enjoyed an uninterrupted peace for almost thirty years. But it is also true that neither the Indians nor anyone else enjoyed freedom.

Toward his neighbors, Brazil and Argentina, Francia maintained the greatest reserve. He exchanged no representatives with their governments or any other after Brazil's minister was asked to withdraw in 1825. He defied the effectiveness of Argentina's control of the Paraná River by turning the principal item of import to cotton production and opening and closing the port at Asunción as the needs of the country demanded. He refrained from involving himself in the disputes among Argentina, Uruguay, and Brazil, although he did give haven to Artigas and other refugees from these struggles. Francia's rule did not in the last analysis benefit Paraguay. His policy of isolation and maintenance of ignorance and blind obedience on the part of the Indians prepared them for the slaughter of the Paraguayan War twenty years later.

The López Dynasty, 1840–1870. When Francia died in 1840 the handful of Creoles in Asunción came out to look about them. A small military junta assumed power. Doubless impressed with the fear of one man's power, they set up two consuls as the executive head of the government. But the effort was unavailing, for one of the consuls, Carlos Antonio López, through superior ability dominated the office and soon controlled the government. Elected under a constitution largely of his own devising in 1844, he served a ten-year term. Re-elected he held the office of president until his death in 1862.

López reversed the policy of isolation followed by Francia, although he maintained the internal dictatorship intact. He encouraged education. He opened the port at Asunción to foreign trade, negotiated commercial treaties, exchanged ministers, and fostered immigration into the country. He carried out a program of internal improvements with the construction of roads, the building of a railroad between Asunción and Paraguarí, establishment of telegraph communication, and, under government control, the exploitation of timber, hides and tallow, and *yerba maté.* He treated the Indians justly and ended some of the cruel punishments instituted by Francia. While he freed the few Negroes in the country from slavery, he used forced labor on state lands whose products the government monopolized.

While López was anxious to restore Paraguay to normal relations with the outside world, he proudly defended what he considered the rights of his country. He defied Rosas in 1849 by making an alliance with the dictator of Entre Rios, whom the Argentine dictator was trying to crush. On the other hand, he refrained from joining the alliance which overthrew Rosas. Against Brazil he vigorously defended Paraguay's claim to territory in the north where the Paraguay River had its headwaters. To strengthen the country's defenses he constructed forts, the principal one of which was at Humaitá, strategically located at the confluence of the Paraguay and Paraná rivers.

On his death in 1862 his son, Francisco Solano López, succeeded to power. The younger López did not have the compensating qualities of his father to offset an overbearing ego. With misgivings, but, where important positions were at stake, unwilling to go outside of his family, his father in 1855 made him head of the army and minister of war at the youthful age of twenty-eight. Four years later, hoping that foreign travel would modify his son's self-importance, he sent him as Paraguayan minister to Paris. Unfortunately, here the son came in contact with the glittering court of Napoleon III, possessed, too, of overweening ambitions. The rising military power of Germany also attracted his attention. Thus upon his return to Asunción in 1862 to succeed his father, López' legitimate ambition to make Paraguay great and respected was tarnished by Napoleonic ideas of glory. In all this he was encouraged by a beautiful but ambitious wench, Madame Lynch, his mistress.

The Paraguayan War, 1864–1870. For the Paraguayan army built by Dr. Francia and the elder López, the ambitious son provided European weapons and German officers to organize it along modern lines. From López' point of view, Argentina's attempts to conquer Paraguay during the Wars for Independence and the later danger of Rosas justified his measures. To the east, Brazil, with a record of aggression against Uruguay, cast a shadow of domination over the La Plata river system. More, Brazil claimed in the north territory that López insisted was Paraguayan. These countries on their part believed that López intended to add territory to Paraguay, a belief reinforced by López' insistence upon a voice in affairs affecting the Paraguay, Uruguay, and Paraná rivers.

The immediate cause of the Paraguayan War arose from the efforts of Brazil to force compensation from Uruguay for damages done Brazilian nationals during Uruguayan civil wars. In 1863 President Berro was faced with an invasion of *Colorados* under General Flores with Brazilian and Argentine support, and he appealed to López for assistance in August, 1864. López' demands upon Brazil and Argentina for a statement of their purposes were ignored. The Paraguayan dictator thereupon followed his request with an ultimatum to Brazil. He warned that country not to invade Uruguay and thus endanger the security of the La Plata nations. Upon Brazil's refusal to consider the ultimatum, López attacked.

After seizing a Brazilian vessel on the Paraguay River, he sent troops to take over Matto Grosso in the north. When Mitre, president of Argentina, learned of these events, he refused López permission to send troops across the Missions Territory into Brazil's Rio Grande do Sul. At the same time Argentine and Brazilian troops put Flores in power in Montevideo. When Argentina next declared war on López, she joined Brazil and the new Uruguayan government in an offensive-defensive alliance. This treaty revealed the correctness of López' fears that Paraguay was the objective of Brazilian and Argentine imperialism. One provision called for the annexation of Paraguayan territory claimed by Brazil in the north, while regions on the east and west of Paraguay were to go to Argentina. Other terms, in contradiction, stated that the objective of the allies was to overthrow the López regime and guarantee the integrity of Paraguayan territory.

The war at first sight showed that Paraguay's position was not hopeless. López had an army of some 70,000 to 80,000 men, fairly well trained, though armed with old-fashioned muskets. Moreover, Paraguay fought behind lines with communications guaranteed. Argentina had no army, barely 6,000 men; Uruguay sent only a token force. Both had to operate from bases far removed from the front. The same was true of Brazil, which provided the largest army. She had, however, the additional support of a fleet capable of operating along the Paraná. Counting most heavily against López was his own incompetence as a commander. He used up valuable troops on hopeless undertakings and failed to provide a commissariat commensurate with the size of his forces.

The war soon settled down into one of attrition, with cholera exacting a heavier toll from the armies than bullets. The turning point in the struggle came in 1868 when Brazilian ironclads fought their way past the powerful fort at Humaitá. Landing troops behind the fort, the Brazilians starved out the defenders, who surrendered in August. After that success the allies, principally Brazilians, poured troops into the interior. López by this date, having used up his best forces, recruited women and children to fight off the invaders. His armies, now regarding him as a hero defending the fatherland, fought doggedly at his commands. The Brazilians overcame one defense line after another and finally forced López to flee. Pursued, he was trapped in a swamp and killed in March, 1870. The war was formally ended by treaty on January 9, 1872.

The results of the Paraguayan War were far-reaching. Paraguay itself lost, it is estimated, two-thirds of its population. This disaster included almost all able-bodied men; a nation of women and children remained. The land itself was devastated; cattle and sheep herds declined; communications were destroyed; and many towns were wiped out. A provisional government set up by Brazil surrendered a strip of the northern territory to the latter beyond the Apa River extending east and west from the Paraguay to the Paraná. To Argentina, Paraguay lost the Missions Territory between the Paraná and Uruguay rivers. In the west she further surrendered to Argentina the region between the Pilcomayo and the Río Bermejo. Argentine attempts to extend her claims beyond to the Río Verde were opposed by Brazil and failed when President Hayes of the United States, after an arbitration agreement, awarded the region to Paraguay in 1878.

Upon Brazil the war had significant effects. The conflict did achieve López' fundamental objective in a treaty clause which declared that the Paraná, Paraguay, and Uruguay rivers were to be free to the commerce of all nations. This settlement, while it provided an outlet for Brazil, at the same time blocked her efforts to dominate the region. The war affected Uruguay and Argentina but little, but cost Brazil an estimated 50,000 casualties. Through the acquisition of the territory north of the Apa River, the war opened the way for Brazilian expansion here toward

Bolivia. Internally, as noted elsewhere, the Brazilian army entered political affairs at home. The war also emancipated from slavery Brazilian Negroes who served in the conflict.

Continued Dictatorship, 1870–1920. After the war Paraguayan exiles returned to the country to begin once more the endless struggle for the control of the presidency. Economically, recovery was slow. In time the herds of cattle and sheep revived. The richness of the Paraguayan soil soon erased the worst effects of devastated farm lands. Foreign capital came in before the end of the century to exploit quebracho for its tanin, while *yerba maté* resumed its importance as an export crop.

Politically, the war produced a new constitution, that of 1870. The provisional government in power in that year called an assembly which met the demands of the small minority until its overthrow in 1940. Under this document of 1870 the president was elected by a body of electors, a fact which threw the presidency into a continuous struggle between the wealthy families of the state. The document had a number of democratic provisions, but rarely were they observed in practice. One provided for the direct popular election of senators for a term of six years, while the members in the House of Deputies served for four years. Too, the document provided for universal suffrage for males over eighteen, a bill of rights, and freedom of worship. Under the operation of the constitution two political parties emerged. The Radicals, favoring separation of church and state, had liberal tendencies; the Civic party later known as the *Colorado* party, composed mostly of large landowners and the military, represented the traditional conservative position. Until the end of World War I the political history of the country was marked by frequent palace revolutions, mainly struggles between the leading families for the presidency.

Part II. DICTATORSHIPS AND GROWING LIBERAL MOVEMENTS, 1920–1955

Paraguay and World War I. World War I gave a stimulus to Paraguay's economic development. The economy saw an expanded export of timber, quebracho, *yerbe maté,* sugar, and cotton. At the same time the increased labor force required for these industries brought the normal demand for improvements in labor conditions. More significant as an immediate influence was the student movement at the University of Asunción, which demanded the modernization of the nation. The depression of 1929 brought on the collapse of Paraguay's foreign markets. Unemployment, bankruptcies, and decline of government income resulted. With political agitation growing among labor and intellectuals, the government was glad to take advantage of the dispute over the Chaco territory to halt the reform movement.

The Chaco War and Paraguayan Reform Movements. The Chaco War, as noted in the survey of Bolivia, resulted in Paraguay securing two-thirds of the territory in dispute, although Bolivia acquired an outlet, Puerto Suárez, on the Paraguay River. Politically, reform groups, after the truce was signed in 1935, organized a new party, the National Revolutionary Union, under Colonel Rafael Franco. The latter, using dictatorial methods, attempted to introduce socialist measures, including distribution of lands to returning veterans. To pay for expropriated land, the government issued bonds. For labor Franco declared an eight-hour day and a forty-eight-hour week. For the first time in Paraguay's history, the government created a Ministry of Labor and a Department of Public Health to combat hookworm, malaria, and other parasitical diseases common in the country. Other aspects of reform included the nationalization of the industrial and raw material resources of the country. Supporting the government were labor organizations which coalesced in 1936 at a labor congress in Asunción into the National Confederation of Workers of Paraguay. Its body was made up of sixty-six unions and 55,000 members of unions organized among industrial and farm workers as well as seamen and intellectual groups.

This first attempt to modernize the Paraguayan state failed. The army, seizing upon an agreement which Franco made to settle the peace with Bolivia, organized a *coup d'état* and drove Franco into exile. In the next three years, however, revolts led by students and labor forced the drawing up of a new constitution. At the same time the second liberal leader in the post-Chaco War period came to power in José Félix Estigarribia, who won the presidency in 1939. The new constitution, promulgated in 1940, had a corporate character. Under it the president divided the executive authority with a council composed of representatives of economic groups. The congress had extensive power which enabled it to support labor reforms. The new constitution recognized in part the land reforms of Franco, where homes already built on expropriated lands were to remain in the possession of the owner. The document also broadened the suffrage to include women. The election of Estigarribia saw further support in labor's effort to extend unionization.

Morínigo's Dictatorship. Unfortunately, President Estigarribia, killed in September, 1940, in an airplane accident, was succeeded by General Higinio Morínigo. The new president, disregarding the constitution, postponed the holding of elections until 1943. During this time he established a censorship of the press, set aside the civil liberties guaranteed by the constitution, jailed and exiled the leaders of the Liberal party, and put in power the traditional reactionary leaders of the *Colorado* party. With the opposition destroyed, Morínigo held an election in 1943 in which he was not only the only candidate, but permitted no registration of voters. With the army controlling the polls, Morínigo was easily elected to the executive office and inaugurated on August 15, 1943.

In the next four years he ruled with an iron hand, but to his credit he took measures designed to develop the resources of Paraguay. With Bolivia he signed a commercial and oil agreement in November, 1943, under which Bolivia was to use Puerto Casada as an outlet for her products. A year later in August, 1944, Paraguay, and Brazil signed a convention under which the latter was to supply capital to construct a railroad from the port of Concepción to the towns of Pedro Juan Cabellero and Ponta Porã in Matto Grosso. In the south, Paraguay and Argentina on June 1, 1945, fixed the boundary line along the Pilcomayo River and agreed to share its waters for irrigation projects in both countries.

In an effort to develop the resources of the Chaco, whose estimated area was some 88,000 square miles, he interested an American oil company to explore for oil, but the latter withdrew in 1950 after five years of fruitless search. World War II stimulated the industrial development of the country so that by 1945 Paraguay had metal industries, rayon factories, industries of leather, glass, textiles, paper, and oils, and some chemical and pharmaceutical plants, besides its agricultural production of *maté*, rubber, tobacco, and forest products, notably quebracho. These providing a base for export led Morínigo in 1945 to found a state merchant marine with the modest beginning of one ship. However, growth was rapid. By 1953 the merchant marine operated a small fleet of ships between her ports and those of Argentina, Uruguay, and Brazil.

To stimulate food production, the Morínigo government extended technical aid to farmers through agricultural regional offices equipped to provide advice on soil problems, methods of cultivation, and utilization of new crops. It also made loans to aid stockbreeders, and established for the benefit of farm wives model home economic centers at Yaguarón. Its success served as an experience to plan others. Outstanding in agricultural aid, however, was the work of STICA (the Inter-

American Technical and Cooperative Service for Agriculture) under the direction of an American expert. Launched in 1942, STICA influenced agriculture throughout the country. Significant projects were a model dairy farm; a 25,000-acre ranch in the eastern Missions region to develop new grasses and new types of beef cattle; and a 5,000-acre experimental seed farm near Asunción to breed a large number of different varieties of new crops. More than 6,000 Paraguayan farms adopted the new methods, abandoning the wooden plow common, when the undertaking started, to utilize modern agricultural equipment. Contributing directly to improvement of the diet of Paraguayans, STICA advised on the construction of storage and refrigeration plants and dairying, and introduced an understanding of the importance of milk and green vegetables in the Paraguayan diet of corn, beans, and manioc. Beginning in a small way the agricultural reclamation of the Chaco were Mennonite settlers, who arrived in considerable numbers between 1926 and 1930. After World War II over 4,000 more moved to Paraguay from Germany, aided by the International Refugee Organization.

In spite of efforts to improve the food supply and develop an export trade, the cost of food remained high in urban centers, the result of land monopoly by Paraguay's weathy oligarchy. Adversely affecting labor, the principal food consumer in the cities, whose wages were the lowest on the continent, were inadequate housing and poor working conditions in the factories. Although a minimum wage law for all workers over eighteen years of age was granted in 1943, the law was not enforced. Labor unrest joined that of university students, professors, editors, and other intellectuals, all suffering from various repressive measures of the dictatorship. So, too, the outlawed political parties resented the Morínigo monopoly of power. Warning of the widespread discontent was a general strike in April, 1944, which paralyzed the capital. Before the strike ended, Morínigo had jailed several hundred labor leaders, while in the heat of the struggle railroad workers had destroyed a considerable number of bridges.

In the next three years the growth of opposition to Morínigo was steady. To suppress it, the dictator took harsh measures: persecution, suppression of the press, and exile to concentration camps. Significant of the distress was the claim of the Communist party that it had 4,000 members in transportation and communication unions. By the end of the year the army was called out to put down attempted revolts. Morínigo's seeming concession, agreeing to call a constitutional convention, was regarded as insincere since the *Colorado* party, the dictator's own organization, permitted no representation to the *Febreristas,* a powerful left-wing party with wide labor support.

The long record of opposition to the dictatorship finally culminated in a major revolt against Morínigo in March, 1947. Centered in Concepción in the northern part of the country, about one-third of the army joined the uprising. From the beginning the non-Communist character of the revolt was clear, composed as it was of the leaders of the *Febrerista,* other liberal parties, and a considerable number of army officers. For the next four months the rebels tried vainly to capture Asunción, the capital, while the government dispatched its forces against the rebel stronghold at Concepción. Late in July the rebels, launching a major offensive, succeeded in besieging Asunción while government armies swung around the enemy to capture their capital. By the middle of August, however, the siege of Asunción had failed. With their own center of resistance gone, the rebels disbanded their forces, while Morínigo granted amnesty to the enlisted men who joined the uprising, but purged about thirty officers and some of the political leaders, liberals, *Febreristas,* and Communists who had made common cause with the revolt. However, most of the leaders sought for arrest escaped into exile or into hiding.

The revolt caused a split in the *Colorado* forces, the more reactionary of the *Colorados* holding out for exemplary punishment of the rebels, in opposition to the more moderate course followed by Morínigo. Thus when the presidential elections were scheduled for February 15, 1948, the wing supporting the president selected J. Natalicio González as president for a five-year term starting on August 15. No other party, of course, was allowed to present a candidate. For the next year and a half the turmoil within the *Colorado* party continued. In that period González was overturned after a six-months' turbulent rule, leaving Raimundo Rolón in office. But hardly had he occupied the chair when another revolt placed Dr. Felipe Molas López in the office, who was inaugurated in May, 1949, to finish González' term. However, López' unwillingness to make concessions to the opposition led to his overthrow on September 12, 1949, when congress chose Federico Chávez as provisional president.

In Chávez Paraguay found another dictator the equal of Morínigo. He successfully prevented opposition parties, liberal and *Febrerista,* from undertaking rebellions and held an iron control over the *Colorado* party until his overthrow in May, 1954, by the head of the armed forces, General Alfredo Stroessner.

Social and Economic Conditions since 1949. During these years from Morínigo to Stroessner the basic economy of Paraguay remained unchanged. The country was dominated by landowners who exported the principal wealth in forest products, especially quebracho, cotton, sugar, rice, tobacco, and maté or Paraguayan tea. Because the government collected practically no export tax and imposed no income tax, it had insufficient funds to meet the needs of the Paraguayan people. STICA, discussed above, is just beginning to teach Paraguayans the importance of diversified agriculture. Wheat is imported, although the land is excellent for its cultivation. Roads are in the most primitive condition. Only in 1955 had the government begun any program of road building worthy of the name. As a result all goods imported into Paraguay are expensive. The cost of living for the ordinary person is the highest in any Latin-American country.

Social conditions present a woeful picture. Out of a population of an estimated 1,400,000, there are barely 400 doctors in the entire country, with over 300 of those living in the capital. The first significant steps to improve health conditions came under Chávez, with the establishment of a Joint Commission for Economic Development under Point Four. Its original objectives were to provide technical knowledge, skills, and techniques for the investment of capital. But in 1953 its program was broadened to give aid in health, sanitation, and educational projects. The dire need of such measures was apparent in that until 1955 Paraguay's capital, Asunción, was the only one in Latin America without a public water system.

The condition of education is correspondingly low. Only 15 per cent of the national budget goes for education; the military absorbs over 50 per cent. But apparently few of the allotted funds reach the schools. It is estimated that 42 per cent of the children of Paraguay between seven and fourteen years of age are without any schools. Illiteracy as a whole is estimated at about 80 per cent. The bulk of the people are workers on the plantations or make up the small labor groups in the capital and in the few other cities. Rural and urban labor thus far has been able to do little to improve its status in the face of the power of the *Colorado* party, the instrument of the large landholders. To meet unrest the government resorts to periodic salary increases for government workers and army personnel.

With Paraguay depending so completely upon exports which must go out by way of the Paraguay and Paraná Rivers, it has fallen under Argentine domination. This dependence was partially revealed in the treaty negotiated in 1953. That document, following the lines of the

Chilean agreement, has in addition more specific provisions calling for Argentine exploitation of Paraguay's mineral deposits, control of communications between the countries, and, above all, import of Argentine food. Recent developments, however, indicate that Argentine domination may be modified in the future. Paraguayan labor in 1951 in its Second Labor Congress rejected association with Perón's "international" labor organization, ATLAS. Further, it organized a new Confederation of Paraguayan Workers and declared its support of the principles expressed in the Charter of the United Nations and the labor agreements reached at the Chapultepec inter-American meeting of 1945.

Possibly of more immediate importance in counteracting Argentine influence in Paraguay are developments in neighboring Brazil and Bolivia. The recently completed railroad line crossing the Paraguay River at Corumbá on the Brazilian-Bolivian border offers an alternative outlet to the Paraguayan River for Paraguayan travelers and products. Moreover, the growth of the Brazilian west in this area is already providing a base for Paraguayan development in the north. Bolivia's interest in her eastern lands has been reflected in commercial treaties with Paraguay, under which border settlements of the two countries exchange products unhindered by tariffs.

Viewing the turbulent recent history of Paraguay, in which eleven presidents have served in office since 1936, only three of whom were elected with any semblance of legality, it is apparent that the social, economic, and cultural condition of the nation is nearer a feudal than a modern one. However, established labor unions and a small but growing middle class are struggling to make real the democratic ideas that entered Paraguay after World War I and received new stimulus after the second world war. Possibly the influence of Brazil and Bolivia will counteract Argentina's long standing dominance. In any event, Paraguay, located strategically between three states, in all of which fundamental changes are rapidly taking place, is destined to play a more important role than hitherto in South American affairs.

Chapter XVIII

BRAZIL

Part I. BRAZIL UNDER THE EMPIRE, 1822–1889

Character of Brazilian History. Brazil has followed steady growth in the development of democratic institutions. In the colonial period tolerant attitudes among her population laid the basis for this evolution. The Brazilian church, so different from that in the Spanish colonies, tolerated and even supported liberal ideas of the late eighteenth century. Racial toleration became a characteristic of her colonial development. The first Brazilian constitution allowed the widest latitude in freedom of speech and press and even favored religious freedom. Later in the century the Brazilians abolished the institution of slavery, not by violent conflict, but by the legislative process.

With the overthrow of the empire the Brazilians established a republic influenced in form by that of the United States. In more recent times the dictatorship of Vargas (1930–1945) paradoxically strengthened democratic institutions. Strong labor unions emerged. A vigorous middle class assumed its place in government. A new constitution, that of 1946, guaranteed the fundamental freedoms. Elections are held in peace. Brazil has become a power in inter-American cooperation and a bulwark in the democratic struggle in the United Nations.

The Empire of Dom Pedro I, 1822–1831. Brazil's national history opened with a conflict between the native Brazilians and Dom Pedro I, who represented a remnant of Portuguese control. While Brazilians accepted the empire that he established after independence, they were determined to participate in the government. At the same time the Brazilians were divided into groups with different economic and political interests. The most influential was the Brazilian aristocracy, which was, in fact, a feudal, landholding social element, of which in the northeast the slaveowning plantation owners were the oldest and probably the wealthiest. In the center in Minas Gerais were the mining barons. In the south the Paulistas, extending their holdings south and westward, had enslaved Indians and raised agricultural crops and herds of cattle.

In all these areas the landowners commanded military forces under a system of compulsory service which entrenched their power. They exercised political control of the *câmaras,* the town councils. The viceroy at Rio de Janeiro, hampered by inadequate communication, had little power in the interior. Thus land, slaves, military power, and political control had firmly fixed the base of the Brazilian aristocracy long before independence.

The second group was the middle class, the product of the migration of Portuguese traders, merchants, and settlers who had established themselves in the port cities. Portuguese laxity over trade encouraged their growth. Pombal's reforms favored them. In the south they smuggled along the Río de la Plata and gave support to the crown's imperial interests in Banda Oriental. In the north they made huge profits from the slave trade and even smuggled along the coast of Brazil itself. When Dom João VI opened Brazil's ports to trade in 1808, Brazilian merchants prospered and became strong supporters of the monarchy. When Portugal later threatened to restore Brazil's colonial status, the middle class became leaders in the movement for independence.

A third group having economic and social roots among both the middle class and the landowners were the liberals. They supported in general the principles of a republican form of government. Outstanding during the reign of Dom Pedro I were the Andrada brothers, particularly José Bonifacio. Educated in Europe and Portugal, he returned to Brazil after the Portuguese revolution of 1820. There in 1823 he took a leading part in framing the proposed constitution of 1823. This document limited the power of the monarchy, gave suffrage to Catholics and non-Catholics alike, and made the lower house the most powerful branch of the national government.

Dom Pedro I, intent upon maintaining exclusive power, dissolved the constituent assembly in 1823, banished its leaders including the Andrada brothers, and appointed ten men to draw up a new fundamental law. This document, promulgated in 1824, conferred practically absolute power upon the monarchy. Under it the emperor could dissolve parliament, restrict suffrage to Catholics, and make extensive appointments. But his most important power rested in the "moderative" clause, which enabled him to keep in balance the "independence, harmony, and equilibrium" of the political powers created by the constitution itself. A concession to the liberal influence of the time, however, was in the recognition of the principles of freedom of speech and press.

Under the appointive clause Dom Pedro ran head-on into the Brazilian aristocracy. Traditionally the landowners had dominated the *câmaras,* the provincial and municipal councils. In the colony the presidents of the provinces, too, had been little more than figureheads. But under the new constitution Dom Pedro I appointed presidents who, backed by the royal army, dominated the local and provincial assemblies. Particularly galling to the powerful landowners of the interior were the emperor's mercenary troops, Prussian, Swiss, and Irish, who supplemented the royal army of Portuguese soldiers.

Even before the emperor had promulgated his constitution, he had installed by force a president in the wealthy sugar province of Pernambuco. The local *câmaras* refused to recognize this official and chose Manoel de Carvalho. Carvalho organized a revolt with support in Ceará, Rio Grande do Norte, Parahyba, and Maranhão, the latter a strong center of republicanism. Hoping to take advantage of republican opposition to the monarchy, Carvalho proposed a Confederation of the Equator in 1825. In such a state, power would automatically revert to the component states and thus the traditional authority could be established. But Dom Pedro I sent Lord Cochrane, now in the employ of Brazil and admiral of the navy, to put down the uprising. Cochrane succeeded, ruthlessly executing the republican leaders, but permitting Carvalho to escape.

While the aristocracy remained the core of the opposition, the commercial class withdrew its support over the British debt and the loss of Uruguay. The issue of the debt came up over the question of recognition. When Dom Pedro sought recognition in the United States, that government, after some debate over the propriety of recognizing an empire in America, extended the courtesy. But Great Britain, anxious to protect its economic interests, forced concessions in return for recognition. Upon Portugal Britain first brought pressure to secure recognition of Brazil's independence. In return Dom Pedro I agreed to assume for Brazil a Portuguese debt to Britain of some £1,000,000 and to reimburse Dom João VI to the extent of £600,000 for his property in Brazil. British recognition then followed in 1825, but with two strings attached. By the first Britain secured the guarantee of the debt from Portugal; secondly, on threat of withholding recognition, she forced Dom Pedro to agree to the terms of a treaty negotiated with Portugal in 1817. This treaty called for the abolition of the slave trade and gave both countries the right of search for slaves on merchant vessels. In pursuance of the 1827 treaty Brazil enacted legislation in March, 1831, to end the slave trade.

The commercial classes, antagonized by Brazil's assumption of the

Portuguese debt and the blow to their lucrative slave trade, were turned against the monarchy by the loss of Uruguay. After its annexation to Brazil in 1821 as the Cisplatine Province, Brazilian traders flocked to the Río de la Plata. The patriotic Uruguayans, however, continued the struggle with the aid of Argentina, averse to the extension of Brazil's power to La Plata. Thus in 1825 when Lavelleja launched the fight for freedom, Rivadavia in Buenos Aires sent Argentine forces with the liberating army. The action resulted in a war between Brazil and Argentina.

Various factors contributed to the defeat of Dom Pedro's army. In 1825 the Confederation of the Equator, threatening disintegration of his state, seemed more important than the revolt in the far south. On the Río de la Plata the Brazilian fleet could not make effective its blockade of Buenos Aires against British and French shipping. On the other hand, Admiral Brown, in the service of Buenos Aires, thwarted efforts to reduce the city. On land a major battle at Ituzaingó in February, 1827, proving indecisive for the Brazilians, paved the way for peace. Contributing to this end was Viscount Strangford, British minister to Brazil, who urged an armistice. Thus in 1828 Dom Pedro signed a treaty in which Brazil and Argentina in effect guaranteed the independence of Uruguay. With the loss of the Cisplatine Province the monarchy alienated the support of the commercial groups.

Dom Pedro's conduct of the government and his private life offended all Brazilians. While his empress, Leopoldina, was greatly respected, Dom Pedro fell completely under the influence of his mistress, the Marchioness of Santos, a beautiful and ambitious woman. Besides his own frequent disregard of the wishes of congress, he permitted the marchioness to select his advisers and dismiss capriciously his ministers. By 1831, despised by the Brazilians and subject to ridicule and harsh criticism, he seized an opportunity to abdicate when his daughter asked his help to save her Portuguese throne. On April 7, deserted by his army, his last bulwark, he stepped down in favor of his five-year-old son, destined to become one of Brazil's greatest figures, Dom Pedro II.

Dom Pedro I lacked any vision of Brazil as a great independent state. His Portuguese background had nothing in common with Brazilians rooted in their native soil. In foreign affairs he was influenced by the British; in domestic, by his mistress. His most important contributions to Brazil were his leadership in the independence movement and the abolition of the slave trade.

It is a tribute to the Brazilian's love of freedom that the period was outstanding in developing democratic traditions. The debates of the constituent assembly of 1823 centered around the establishment of schools and universities, the abolition of slavery, and humanitarian proposals to aid Indians and Negroes, as well as informed discussion of the principles and government of the United States. The press thrived. By 1828 there were twenty-five newspapers and periodicals published in Brazil; fifteen in Rio de Janeiro, three at Bahia, and others in Pernambuco, Villa Rica, São Paulo, and St. João del Rey. The periodical of the Andrada brothers, *O Tamoyo*, provided trenchant arguments against the monarchy. *Republica*, founded during these years, led the attack for a republican form of government. The *Aurora*, however, of Evaristo da Veiga, who believed in a limited monarchy, was the most formidable critic of Dom Pedro's administration. The *Imperio do Brazil* defended the emperor. Public libraries and schools were established. The imperial library of some 60,000 volumes on a wide variety of subjects was kept open to the public at all times with free access to its books. Democratic ideas flourished in this environment.

The Regency, 1831–1840. The abdication of Dom Pedro I released the economic and political forces implicit in the struggle for independence, but held in check by Dom Pedro. For the first time Brazilians assumed the control of their government. A regency of three governed during the minority of Dom Pedro II, but congress became the power in the state. Political parties emerged, conservative and liberal in character. The former included the Liberal Monarchists, who demanded the return of control of local government to the provinces. The Liberals, divided into two parties, were the Moderates, who advocated a limited monarchy, and the Exalted Liberals, who favored a federal republic.

At once the Brazilian aristocracy sought to restore its power in provincial and local government. It succeeded in 1834 with an amendment to the constitution, the Additional Act *(Ato Adicional)*. According to its provisions each province gained the right to select its own assembly, levy taxes, and govern itself. The only exception was the naming of Provincial governors by the central authority. These officials, though little more than figureheads, were important symbols of national unity. These concessions to the provincial aristocracies paved the way for the growth of the Liberal Monarchist party headed by Evaristo da Veiga and Father Diogo Antonio Feijó, a priest strongly influenced by the writings of the Positivists. As minister of justice, Feijó became the leading figure of the regency and an ardent advocate of Brazilian unity. In 1835 he became the sole regent with wide powers to maintain the integrity of the nation threatened by revolts in many areas.

These revolts stemmed from a variety of causes. In Rio Grande do Sul, Pará, Maranhão, Minas Gerais, and Ceará the populace rose to drive out the Portuguese holdovers from Dom Pedro's reign. In Pernambuco, where the fighting was bitter, the unpaid mercenaries sacked the city several times. Thus unable to rely upon the military forces from the empire, the regency created a National Guard. In other states attempts were made to set up liberal republics, the most significant of which was in Rio Grande do Sul.

In that state the arbitrary rule of Dom Pedro I stimulated revolutionary movements. Republican ideas in the neighboring states of Uruguay and Argentina seemed to have influenced local leaders. When Uruguay won its independence from Brazil in 1828, the movement grew rapidly, culminating in 1836 in the revolt of the Farrapos and the establishment of the Republic of Piratinim. Feijó's attempts to put down the new state were thwarted when the Farrapos general, Benito Gonçalves, resorted to guerrilla warfare. Following Fabian tactics, the insurgents were able to maintain themselves until 1846. Significantly, both sides to win Negro support offered emancipation, the net effect of which was to free slaves in this part of Brazil.

The Farrapos war, together with violent opposition to his policies in parliament, forced Feijó to resign in 1838. In this crisis Brazil was saved from disintegration when the Liberal party proposed to elevate Dom Pedro, barely sixteen, to the office of emperor. Accepted in parliament, the new emperor, Dom Pedro II, assumed office by act of congress on July 23, 1840. The regency made important contributions to Brazil. Brazilians received training in parliamentary government. Freedom, after the restrictive policies of Dom Pedro I ended, found full reign in political discussion. The regency also facilitated economic growth. Coffee became an export crop of growing importance. Favorable laws encouraged European immigration.

The Reign of Dom Pedro II, 1840–1889. Dom Pedro II was mature far beyond his years when he became emperor. Modest, preferring simplicity in dress and manner, he avoided pomp and circumstance. To his gifts of mind he added a strong sense of justice; democratic in outlook, he tolerated criticism of his person unequaled by any other nineteenth century monarch. The emperor's regard for law, his interest in education, and his respect for parliamentary institutions aided the growth of the democratic tradition in Brazil. However, because of his conservative, slaveholding associations he failed to grasp the need of supporting middle class financial reforms aimed at developing Brazil along capitalistic lines then current in Britain, France, and the United States.

Dom Pedro governed under the constitution of 1824. It provided for a two-house legislature, with the lower house elected every four years, while the senate was composed of royal appointees from a list prepared by electors. The ministry or cabinet had begun to emerge under Dom Pedro I; the regency increased its importance, and Dom Pedro added to its strength by appointing men of ability and intellectual power. Aiding him was a council of state, a body also composed of eminent men. In his zeal to strengthen Brazil, however, he constantly increased his hold on the provinces through his power to appoint the presidents of the states. In national affairs he controlled through the use of the "moderative power" conferred by the constitution.

The emperor early demonstrated his capacity to govern by ending the republican revolutions inherited from the regency. Through persuasion and military action he snuffed out the republican movement in Minas Gerais under Theophilo Ottoni. In Pernambuco, an historic center of republican disaffection, Dom Pedro ended the revolt with tact and military pressure. Several factors aided his stamping out the Farrapos revolt. Rosas' brutal crushing of the *Unitarios* in Argentina and attack on Uruguay repelled the republic's leaders. At the same time they sensed the democratic cast of mind in the emperor. Dom Pedro encouraged this sympathy by extending amnesty to all who had revolted. The Duke of Caxias, an able military figure, defeated the irreconcilables in battle.

The Expansion of Brazil. Dom Pedro II made important additions to the territory of Brazil. With the Farrapos revolt ended, he was determined to protect the southern outlet of Brazil along the Paraná River, threatened by Rosas' invasion of Uruguay. As noted elsewhere, Dom Pedro joined Rivera and Urquiza to defeat Rosas at Monte Caseros in 1852. However, under the treaty between Brazil and Uruguay negotiated for this purpose in 1851, the latter agreed to transfer a large area between the Ibicui and Cuareim Rivers and to recognize Brazil's domination of Lake Mirim and the Yaguarón. This advance marked the high-water mark of Brazilian expansion southward.

A second major territorial addition to Brazil coming from the war with Paraguay in 1864–1870 carried her frontiers westward. Because Brazil had borne the brunt of the Paraguayan War, she planned, in fact, to annex the entire country. Protest by other Latin-American nations, however, thwarted this ambition. But under the treaty which closed the war in 1872, she did annex a large part of the territory claimed by Paraguay in the north, roughly between the Río Apa and the Río Blanco with extension southeast to the Paraná River.

Even while the Paraguayan War was in progress, Brazilian expansion was moving westward to the boundaries of Bolivia. With that country in 1867 Count Rio Branco negotiated a treaty under which Brazil acquired a large region between the headwaters of the Paraguay River and the Madeira, subsequently added to the state of Matto Grosso. The treaty also fixed the boundary line which divided the Acre territory of Bolivia between the two countries. This laid the basis for later Brazilian advance westward when in the next ten years Brazilian rubber workers poured into the Acre region of Bolivia.

An important part of Brazilian westward expansion, too, was the opening of the Amazon River to world trade in 1867. In the basin itself Brazil's own commercial classes had long recognized a possible source of wealth. Moreover, after 1850 Brazilian rubber interests, seeking foreign capital to develop western Matto Grosso and the Acre territory, added to the demand for the opening of the great river. This Brazilian interest received, too, an unexpected impetus from the fervor of an American, Lieutenant Matthew F. Maury of the United States navy, who succeeded in sending the Herndon-Gibbon expedition to explore the important headwaters of the Amazon as well as the river itself. British and American scientists, particularly Louis Agassiz of Harvard, studying the flora and fauna of the basin, did much to stimulate interest in Brazil itself in the possibilities of the river as a trade route. Brazilian leaders, notably Tavares Bastos, hammered on the theme of undeveloped wealth and pointed out the inconsistency of Brazil's war in Paraguay to guarantee an outlet to the south while the government prohibited foreigners from entering the Amazon. After long agitation Brazil in September, 1867, formally opened the great river to the commerce of the world.

Economic Growth of Brazil under the Empire. The expansionist activities in the south, west, and north had their counterpart in the growing economic life of the people. Industrialization in Europe and in the United States, which changed Argentine economy, gave an impetus to economic expansion in Brazil. In Minas Gerais British investment in gold and diamond mines increased the output of these minerals. Coffee, after a slow growth in the early part of the century, took a spurt after 1855 when several million trees came into bearing. In the next thirty years its rate of growth steadily accelerated until the decade 1880–1890 saw the greatest period of coffee planting in the history of Brazil. To transport coffee and minerals, railroads were built. In 1852 plans were launched to construct lines from Rio de Janeiro to São Paulo and also to Minas Gerais. The railroad from the capital to São Paulo was completed in 1876–1877. In the next thirty-five years almost 7,000 miles of railroads connected the principal ports and cities in the south, besides short lines between Rio de Janeiro and Petropolis, the emperor's summer capital, and between the capitals of Bahia and Pernambuco and the interior.

Responding to the opportunities and needs of Brazil was a steadily increasing flow of immigrants. Some, notably German, had entered Brazil during the rule of Dom Pedro I. By 1859 more than 20,000 Germans had settled on agricultural lands in Rio Grande do Sul and in Santa Catharina. After the Civil War in the United States, a considerable number of Southerners migrated to Brazil. The need of trained orchardists for the coffee plantations drew Italian, Portuguese, Spanish, and other Mediterranean immigrants after 1870. From some 4,400,000, estimated in 1819, Brazil's population had reached 10,000,000 by 1870. The growth of Brazil's industries and the productivity of her labor were reflected in an increased export and import trade. Thus between 1840 and 1890 her trade increased tenfold over the 57,000,000 milreis of the former year.

Economic changes and an increasing population began to alter the pattern of education, confined largely to the wealthy. A middle class and skilled and semiskilled workers made clear the need for more schools. The emperor himself took a leading part in expanding the system. Thus from some 3,000 public schools in 1860 the number had increased to more than 6,000 by 1888. Higher education found expression in the traditional universities, normal schools, and a mining academy in Minas Gerais. The universities provided instruction in law, astronomy, medicine, and agriculture. The emperor himself patronized schools of music, fine arts, and painting in Rio de Janeiro.

Political Conflicts and the Abolition of Slavery. The political events of Dom Pedro's reign had their origin in the differing economic and social interests of the population. The sugar aristocracy in the north and lesser agricultural landowners throughout Brazil dominated the Conservative party. The Liberal party drew its support in part from the commercial classes, the coffee barons in the south, and the mineral landowners in the interior. Throughout the history of the period the

Conservative party usually controlled. The Liberals took the lead in demanding freedom of trade and industry and the ending of monopolies held by the state, holdovers from the colonial mercantile system. An outstanding figure representing the Liberal point of view was Viscount Mauá, a self-made man, railroad builder, banker, and industrialist. He fought a losing battle trying to persuade the government to use specie as a basis for issuing paper money and thus facilitate Brazil's development. The Liberals, besides this financial outlook, advocated greater self-government for provinces, cities, and towns and state-supported schools in opposition to subsidized church institutions. They stood, too, for full freedom of conscience.

In practical politics the Liberals advocated the reduction of the army in peacetime. Watchful of the emperor's actions, they called for the ending of the political power of the Council of State. They insisted that the prime minister be held accountable for the emperor's exercise of the "moderative" power in the constitution. They also sought to reform the senate and to end the authority of the emperor to appoint senators for life. They demanded electoral reforms to give greater self-government in the states. Finally, they advocated the abolition of slavery.

Gaining strength throughout the century was a third party, the Republican. While not so important as the other two, its ideas could be traced back before independence to the Tiradentes revolt of 1789. Intellectuals and many members of the Brazilian middle class hoped for a republic after independence and pointed to the success of the United States. After the overthrow of Dom Pedro I, they attempted to establish republican governments, as we have seen, in northern, central, and southern Brazil. Republican ideas, in fact, continued to flourish in the south. Thus it was in São Paulo in December, 1871, that the Republican party was first organized.

The strength of the new party grew rapidly after 1871. Not only did it attract many leading intellectuals everywhere and political leaders in Rio Grande do Sul, Minas Gerais, and São Paulo, but it also had the support of the growing numbers of immigrants, already schooled in European philosophies of democracy and socialism. Within the army, too, a large number of men, influenced by Benjamin Constant, a Positivist, enrolled in the Republican party. Others joined when Dom Pedro II, fearing military power after the Paraguayan War, resisted the efforts of soldiers to participate in politics.

The combined strength of the Liberal and Republican parties after 1871 forced political and social reforms. The first was the Rio Branco law of 1871, better known as the "Law of Free Birth," which freed all children born in slavery. Later the great Liberal leader, Joaquim Nabuco, labeled it a palliative, but it was nevertheless sufficient to split the Conservative party and antagonize the slaveholding sugar aristocracy.

Two years later an equally serious political problem confronted the emperor when he found his authority challenged by the church. The issue arose out of the promulgation by the papacy of the *Syllabus of Errors* in 1864, condemning as errors liberal economic and political philosophies of various groups including Freemasons. Its enforcement in Brazil violated the constitution, under which no papal communication could be published without prior imperial sanction. In pursuit of papal orders the bishops of Olinda and Pará in 1873 commanded Catholic brotherhoods to expel Masons from their membership. When the bishops closed the lodges and refused to desist upon imperial command, the emperor ordered them arrested and tried for violating the laws of the empire. Found guilty, they were sentenced to prison, from which the emperor pardoned them two years later. The event turned the powerful hierarchy against the monarchy and contributed to the growing volume of opposition led by Republicans, Liberals, and the slaveholding conservatives dissatisfied with the Rio Branco law of 1871.

In the meantime, Liberals and Republicans alike were agitating for electoral reforms. In 1877, in response to the growing pressure in the states and municipalities for local control and better representation in the central government, the emperor proposed reforms. Because these threatened the position of the Conservative party, the Conservative ministry resigned. However, the work of reform was carried through in 1881 under Prime Minister José Antônio Saraiva, whose electoral law provided direct elections governed by property and literacy qualifications. The most important demand for reform was not met, namely, local self-government for municipalities and states. Failure to do so became one of the important reasons for the overthrow of the empire in 1889.

The Abolition of Slavery. The growth of Liberal power, essentially middle class, the spread of its ideas by the Republican party among intellectuals, the army, and the new immigrants, and the antagonism of the church after the bishops' case contributed to the overthrow of the empire. But the most decisive factor was the abolition of slavery. The leadership that brought both events, abolition and overthrow, to fruition came from São Paulo, where the powerful coffee planters resented the emperor's power over the state through his appointment of the president. Less strongly objected to were the taxes imposed by the central government on the export of coffee. But, unable to secure national legislation protecting what they considered their interests, the coffee growers fought for the abolition of slavery as a means of weakening the Conservative party. On the other hand, a variety of events conspired to weaken the sugar oligarchy itself. Sugar production, notably in Cuba and in the beet sugar fields of western Europe, proved less costly than the inefficient slave labor of the Brazilian planters. Their economic position, in fact, was already undermined before the final blow of abolition struck them.

The first significant step taken to end the institution was the abolition of the slave trade. Under Dom Pedro I the British forced the ending of the trade by threatening to withhold recognition. Although the necessary legislation was enacted in March, 1831, New Englanders, British, and Portuguese smuggled Negroes into the country in increasing numbers. When the British government attempted to bring pressure on Brazil, the latter resentfully refused to renew the treaty of 1827. Britain thereupon passed the Aberdeen law, which transferred all cases of captured slavers to Admiralty courts for trial in place of presenting them to the mixed commission which had hitherto sat in Sierra Leone and Rio de Janeiro.

With Brazilian restrictions off after 1837, the slave trade saw annually an average of more than 50,000 Negroes entering the country. To end the horror, the British sent their ships into Brazilian territorial waters to seize offenders. Brazil protested these violations, but mounting criticism at home and abroad tempered her attitude. Significant, too, was the fact that Brazil herself profited little from the trade. Portuguese merchants controlled the gathering of Negroes in Africa and their sale in Brazil, while foreign ships, largely American, carried the cargo. In these circumstances in September, 1850, Minister of Justice Eusebio de Queiroz secured a new law which effectively ended the trade. One provision declared slave traders pirates, while another required all ships clearing for Africa to post a bond for the total value of ship and cargo. Under this law British and Brazilian navies brought a complete cessation of the trade by 1852.

After this date Brazilian abolition leaders redoubled their efforts. The fearful Civil War in the United States in the next decade greatly strengthened their appeal. In 1871 the Rio Branco law of "free birth" had halted effective legislation until the next decade. In 1880 the movement received new life from the vigorous leadership of Joaquim Nabuco. Although from the ranks of the slaveholders, he led the fight uncompromisingly for outright abolition. But the institution by them was collapsing of its own weight. Bankrupt sugar planters supported local legislation in Ceará in 1883 and in Amazonas in 1885 to emancipate slaves in those territories. In the next year, 1886, the national legislature freed all slaves over sixty years of age. By this time, too, the Negroes were emancipating themselves.

The Golden Law, 1888. With public opinion voiced in press and parliament, the demand for emancipation could no longer be delayed. Thus in 1888 Brazil enacted the "Golden Law" under which all slaves in Brazil were declared free with no compensation to their owners. Dom Pedro's daughter, Isabella, serving as regent and herself an ardent abolitionist, signed the bill on May 13, 1888. Seven hundred and fifty thousand slaves stepped from serfdom to freedom. Their value reached almost $250,000,000. This extraordinary act not only freed the slaves; it also ended the Brazilian empire.

The Collapse of the Empire. The fundamental cause of the collapse of the Brazilian empire rested in the basic change in the economy of Brazil itself. The growth of the coffee industry led powerful and wealthy families in the south to demand control of local government and participation in the national legislature to foster their interests. Supporting them were the emerging industrial groups connected with railroads, steamship lines, banks, and the rubber industry and financial figures engaged in opening up the Brazilian west. But Dom Pedro gave his support to the politically dominant sugar planters represented in the Conservative party. However, the sugar economy itself was collapsing in the face of foreign competition in world markets. The Conservative party, too, split over the issue of emancipating the slaves. Thus when the "Golden Law" struck at the foundation of the sugar economy, the planters withdrew their support from the empire, for they received no compensation. Adding to the forces antagonistic to the empire were the Republican party and the hierarchy of the church, discontented over the bishops' case.

The immediate cause of the overthrow of the empire was the revolution of 1889. The last cabinet under Ouro Preto made valiant efforts to stave off the event. It proposed reform bills to extend more power to the states, to end the moderative powers of the emperor, and other similar measures. But the conspiracy to replace Dom Pedro was already under way, led by Marshal Deodoro da Fonseca from Rio Grande do Sul and Benjamin Constant, whose Positivist teachings in the military academy had done much to inspire republican ideas in the army itself.

In the government itself Floriano Peixoto, a member of the cabinet, allayed fears by assuring the prime minister that rumors of revolt had no foundation. When the moment for the *coup d'état* came, with the government off guard, Fonseca led the troops through the city to seize the government buildings, imprison Dom Pedro, and order his exile. Dom Pedro, unwilling to plunge his beloved country into civil war, accepted his fate. Thus with practically no bloodshed and little fanfare, the quietest revolution in American history was over on November 15, 1889.

Part II.   THE REPUBLIC, 1890–1930

The Constitution of 1891. The revolution of 1889 unleashed the forces of Brazil's economic expansion. Under the provisional government, headed by Deodoro da Fonseca, the vigorous industrial and coffee groups received immediate assistance. Ruy Barbosa, the minister of finance, established a banking system with the power to issue paper money. With little gold to back up the script, the government relied upon the issuance of bonds purchased by the newly created banks. The Bank of Brazil itself engaged in a wide variety of activities, providing funds for financial undertakings, agricultural expansion, railroad construction, and other similar ventures. At the same time the sudden availability of money led to a wild orgy of speculation characteristic at the moment of similar booms in France, the United States, and Argentina. The government, essentially a dictatorship under Fonseca, winked at corruption. In 1892 the bubble burst, leaving the early republic with heavy debts at its outset.

In the meantime, the constituent assembly, drawing up a constitution, largely the work of Ruy Barbosa, finished its deliberations early in 1891. Promulgated on February 24, 1891, it established the United States of Brazil. It provided an executive, a president and vice-president, both serving for four years elected by direct vote of males over twenty-one. The president appointed his own cabinet. A bicameral legislature was composed of a senate, whose members, three from each state, were elected for a term of nine years, and a House of Deputies, elected every three years by direct vote on the basis of population. The judiciary consisted of a national supreme court and inferior courts with judges appointed by the president for life. Indicative of the growth of democracy was a bill of rights including a provision for freedom of worship.

Of outstanding significance was an economic provision which enabled each state to levy and collect export taxes. This provision, as later history revealed, automatically threw the control of Brazil's development into the states of São Paulo and Minas Gerais, most important export states. Rapidly building up strong state treasuries, they were able to dominate the presidency and congress and through them establish political control in the other states until 1930.

Fonseca, who appointed military men as governors of the states, greatly enlarged the army and permitted military personnel to engage in politics, facilitating his own selection as the first president under the constitution with Floriano Peixoto as vice-president. Fonseca and his advisers, unable to grasp the fundamental change in Brazil's economy, had, in fact, no program for the development of the country. Inevitably, the powerful coffee planters and other business groups criticized the government, which in turn led the president to suppress freedom of speech and support the dictatorial rule of his appointees. Congress, retaliating by refusing to pass legislation designed to enlarge the army, found itself dissolved while Fonseca established a dictatorship in November, 1891.

Revolts broke out, but were particularly effective in São Paulo, Rio Grande do Sul, and Minas Gerais. The navy under Admiral José de Mello joined the uprising in the south as well as some army leaders. Unable to crush the revolt there, Fonseca resigned on November 23 to be succeeded by Vice-President Peixoto. A military man, younger and of sterner stuff, Peixoto took steps to solidify the dictatorship instead of returning to constitutional government. Using military force to overthrow presidents and governors in the states, he forced congress to ratify his acts.

For a few months there was peace, but uprisings again flared up in September, 1893, in a serious revolt. Again Rio Grande do Sul, São Paulo, and Minas Gerais took the lead, to be joined by Admiral de Mello. Sailing into the bay of Rio de Janeiro, he turned his guns on the city to force Peixoto to resign. The president, acting swiftly, jailed all sympathizers, trained the guns of the fort on the fleet, and prepared to shoot it out. At this juncture the commanders of naval units of the United States, Great Britain, Italy, France, and Portugal warned Mello that they would not tolerate a bombardment of the city. More serious, the American admiral, Benham, gave protection to American merchantmen landing their cargoes. Recognizing the hopelessness of the situation, Mello fled southward to join the rebel forces when the land batteries, opening fire, sank his ships. In the south, too, Peixoto's forces defeated the insurgents piecemeal before they could unite. By the end of a year's fighting, except for a few recalcitrant bands, peace was again restored. To the surprise of everyone, when Peixoto's term expired in November, 1894, he stepped down from the presidency.

While Peixoto's decision to leave the office and his action in putting down the revolts are usually acclaimed as nipping in the bud a cycle of military governments, such an explanation is hardly adequate. It is probably true that he was insisting on respect for the office of president, but equally decisive was a national treasury depleted by the economic collapse of 1892 and the expense of suppressing the subsequent revolts. Significant, too, was the fact that São Paulo, Minas Gerais, and Rio Grande do Sul, with rich state treasuries, were girding for a new effort if military repression continued. Thus with the barren dictatorships of Fonseca and Peixoto out of the way, Brazil under its new constitution elected civilian presidents who began Brazil's modern development.

The Administration of Moraes Barros, 1894–1898. Dr. Prudente José de Moraes Barros of São Paulo, who followed Peixoto, immediately removed the military governors of the states to aid the return of civilian officials, and appointed a civilian cabinet of whose members Rodrígues Alves, minister of finance, was the most able. The new president faced pressing problems. In the south, Brazil vigorously resisted Argentina's claim to all the Missions Territory in dispute after the Paraguayan War. When finally brought to arbitration, the commission appointed by President Cleveland awarded the bulk of the territory to Brazil. In the north the government, conscious of the growing importance of rubber in the Amazon, combated with equal vigor the claims of France and Britain that their Guiana territories extended to the great river.

The expansion of the rubber industry itself in Brazil produced, too, a serious revolt in the northeast. This region, called the *sertão*, was a semiarid territory in the interior of Bahia. Its mixed society of Portuguese, escaped Negro slaves, and Indians were suspicious of intruders and fanatically devoted to their lands. The attempt by Brazilian rubber companies to invade the region and enslave its dwellers brought to the fore a remarkable leader, Antonio Maciel, called the "Councilor," a refugee from Ceará.

Under his leadership the *sertanejos* in turn defeated the military forces sent against them by the state and later federal reinforcements. To put them down, Moraes Barros himself led a federal army into the region. Months of campaigning finally brought defeat to Maciel and opened the way for the rubber companies to resume their march. The brutality attending the destruction of this primitive culture, however, stands in strong contrast with the pride which Brazilians take in the work of Euclydes da Cunha, *The Sertões,* a description of these primitive people and their customs, considered one of Brazil's literary masterpieces.

The Administration of Campos Salles, 1898–1902. Manuel Campos Salles, a fellow Paulista, succeeded Moraes Barros in 1898. The collapse of 1892 and the succession of revolts culminating in the Canudos uprising had brought Brazil by 1898 to the verge of bankruptcy. Adding to the financial difficulties was a coffee surplus which the government had purchased to save growers from bankruptcy. Unable to meet its payments on the foreign debt, Moraes Barros had sent Campos Salles to Britain where he secured a funding loan from the House of Rothschild with import duties as security, and won a suspension of specie payments for three years. His success elevated him to the presidency. During his administration he rescued Brazil from its financial morass. A rise in import duties, a stamp tax on common necessities, and a drastic reduction of government expenses enabled Brazil by 1901 to meet her foreign obligations.

In foreign affairs Campos Salles had similar success. Brazil's rubber companies, advancing rapidly into the Amazon, brought on boundary disputes with Bolivia, France, and Great Britain. France claimed that her Guiana territory extended to the Amazon. Annexation was stopped in 1895 by Francisco Xavier de Viega Cabral. When the question was arbitrated before the Swiss Federal Council, Brazil established her interpretation of the boundaries fixed by the Treaty of Utrecht in 1713 along the crest of the Guiana Highlands. Britain, too, was held back. While the United States blocked her aggressive expansion to the mouth of the Orinoco in 1895, she pushed her claims into the Amazonian basin. Once again, with the dispute submitted to arbitration by Victor Emmanuel III of Italy, Brazil, represented by Joaquim Nabuco, won in 1904 her claims protecting the great river, although Britain secured 73,000 square miles of territory against the 5,400 awarded to Brazil.

With Bolivia, whose eastern boundaries were poorly defined in the treaty of 1867, Brazil had her greatest success. The conflict arose over the territory of Acre, into which thousands of rubber workers had entered, while other Brazilians fled there from drouths in the Ceará *sertão.* Bolivia, which was disturbed, established her authority with a custom house at Porto Alonzo in 1899. The new arrivals, resenting the action, revolted, set up an independent state, and asked Brazil for protection. Bolivia promptly sent military forces, but the Brazilian government cooperated with the frontiersmen by refusing the use of the Amazon for supplies for the Bolivian army. Complicating the dispute was Bolivia's lease of the rubber area to an Anglo-American syndicate, whose holdings were bought out by Count Rio Branco, the Brazilian foreign minister. With no alternative, Bolivia agreed to a treaty settlement, that of Petropolis on November 17, 1903. Under it Bolivia ceded the territory of Acre, in return for which Brazil paid $10,000,000 in cash, agreed to build a railroad around the falls on the great Madeira River, and construct roads to connect the two countries. The line later built, known as the Madeira-Marmoré railroad, was to provide an outlet for Bolivia's trans-Andean territories, although, in fact, it did not prove practicable.

Campos Salles left Brazil with a stabilized treasury and territorial additions that make his administration memorable, although his successor, Rodríguez Alves, whose government completed the negotiations, is usually credited with the diplomatic successes.

The Administration of Rodríguez Alves, 1902–1906. The next president, Francisco de Paula Rodríguez Alves, also came from São Paulo. His outstanding achievement was the re-construction of Rio de Janeiro. The actual direction of the building program fell to the mayor of the city, Dr. Francisco Pereira Passos. Around the beautiful bay Pereira cut a grand boulevard, appropriately named after the Count of Rio Branco, and opened up broad avenues leading into the city and others along the ocean beaches. The docks, reconstructed on a vast scale, took rank with the world's largest.

To stamp out yellow fever, worsening as the population grew, the president turned to Dr. Oswaldo Cruz, a student of Pasteur, who had studied the methods of the United States in Cuba and Panama. Believing that the stegomyia mosquito and unsanitary conditions were the principal sources of infection, Cruz, supported by the president, relentlessly drove his campaign forward in spite of opposition. Between 1903 and 1909, with deaths from yellow fever dropping from an annual toll of almost a thousand to zero and the rebuilding program taking form, Rio de Janeiro became both the most beautiful and healthful of South American capitals. Brazil gratefully recognized the work of Cruz in the Oswald Cruz Institute established for the study of tropical diseases.

In the field of foreign affairs Rodríguez Alvez' administration completed the negotiations with Bolivia, France, and Great Britain which fixed the boundary of much of her Amazonian territory. Inter-American relations took on significance when at the Third Pan-American Conference, held in Rio in 1906, Foreign Minister Count Rio Branco emphasized that the Monroe Doctrine should have the collective support of all American states, foreshadowing thus inter-American cooperation adopted twenty-five years later at Montevideo. At the moment Brazil gave effective expression of her Pan-American spirit by voluntarily sharing with Uruguay joint control over Juguarón River and Lake Mirim. The conference also tightened United-States–Brazilian relations when Secretary of State Elihu Root, who attended the conference, persuaded Brazil to reduce her tariff on American goods 20 per cent by virtue of the fact that the United States purchased the bulk of her coffee.

The Administrations of Moreira Penna and Nilo Peçanha, 1906–1910. In 1906 Affonso Augusto Moreira Penna, a native of Minas Gerais, became president, but died in 1909 to be succeeded by Nilo Peçanha, vice-president. While Rodríguez Alves did much to meet the needs of Brazil's expanding economy, the country's reliance upon coffee as its principal source of income brought disaster in 1907. Producing 16,000,000 bags in 1901 to supply four-fifths of the world's markets, Brazil's crop of more than 20,000,000 in 1906, together with 3,000,000 bags marketed by the Caribbean and Central American nations, left her with a surplus of 11,000,000. This huge carry-over, with an even greater production forecast for 1907, broke the world price and brought São Paulo growers to the verge of bankruptcy.

Complicating the crisis were huge quantities of unsupported paper. The administration attempted to reduce the paper by establishing a central bank of conversion with a gold reserve and power to issue new paper redeemable in gold. However, the loss of income from coffee forced her to seek large loans abroad with which she salvaged the planters under a plan called valorization, that is, government purchase of surplus coffee. Attempting to withhold coffee stored in New York warehouses, Brazil ran afoul of the antitrust laws of the United States. For a moment an acrid dispute marred friendly relations, but as valorization at home succeeded, good feelings were restored. The most important effect of valorization, however, was to add to a growing discontent in Brazil, since foreign loans placed heavy tax burdens upon states not benefiting from the program.

The Administration of Hermes da Fonseca, 1910–1914. The success of Hermes in winning the presidency, based on discontent with the São Paulo-Minas Gerais control of the presidency since 1894, was aided by a split in the heretofore dominant Liberal party. Penna, who died in

June, 1909, had already selected his successor, but during the next year
and a half Nilo Peçanha's congress, setting up a nominating convention,
put aside Penna's choice. Marshal Hermes da Fonseca from Rio Grande
do Sul was chosen, while Ruy Barbosa of São Paulo opposed him. When
Hermes was declared elected, many believed that the Paulista had lost
through election frauds.

Hermes' administration unquestionably suffered from the decline
of income caused by the crisis in the coffee market and from considerable corruption. However, his government did much for the economic
development of the country. Railroads almost doubled their mileage.
Many native Brazilian industries came into existence. More than 500,000
immigrants arrived in the country. But Brazil suffered a blow during
these years from an unexpected quarter, the collapse of her rubber industry. Entirely Brazilian controlled, from an export in 1890 of some
16,000 tons, it had reached by 1910 about 40,000 tons. But some enterprising British, foreseeing the great future of this important raw material, had smuggled out of the country seeds of the rubber tree, which
they grew scientifically on plantations in the Malay peninsula. When
in 1910 these trees came into production, British ships in the Brazilian
trade were transferred to that of the Malaya, while the price of rubber
was cut on the world market. Overnight the rubber industry in Brazil
collapsed. Large cities in the interior, of which Manaus on the Amazon
was a striking example, became ghost towns, unemployment grew,
wealthy Brazilians were swept into bankruptcy, and the government income declined.

This blow and the necessity of purchasing the yearly coffee surplus
forced Hermes to resort once more to the issuance of quantities of inconvertible paper money. Taking advantage of the widespread economic
disasters, the traditional coalition, Minas Gerais and São Paulo, were
able to win back the presidency in 1914 with the election of Wenceslau
Braz Pereira Gomes, a native of Minas Gerais.

Brazil and World War I. World War I initiated some of the country's most important modern movements: industrial development, an
organized labor movement, and a vigorous but not aggressive nationalism. The immediate effects of the war were devastating. Brazil, with
its economy weakened by valorization, the collapse of the rubber industry, and the burden of large quantities of unredeemable paper, lost,
in addition, her coffee markets in central Europe through the British
blockade. Her currency collapsed, unemployment grew in the great

cities, vast supplies of coffee and other export goods piled high in the fields, and Brazil was again forced to seek a new foreign loan in October, 1914. Until 1917 these conditions prevailed, when the United States, entering the war in that year, immediately purchased huge quantities of coffee and other valuable raw materials. Brazil's economy responded quickly and by 1918 was enjoying boom conditions.

With her economy integrated into that of the Allies, various forces carried Brazil into the war in 1917. The Allies waged a vigorous propaganda campaign to this end, with Britain, whose huge investment amounted to $1,161,500,000 and annual trade some $650,000,000, wielding the greatest influence. France, almost a second homeland to Brazilian intellectuals, won powerful support when Germany invaded. Brazilians themselves, under the lead of Ruy Barbosa, formed a League for the Allies, and endorsed the democratic ideals of the war. Italy's entrance into the war threw Brazil's large Italian population to the Allied side.

Against these forces, Germany could offer no comparable influence. While Germans had emigrated to Brazil during the preceding one hundred years, they were culturally isolated as much from Germany as from Brazil in the interior of the southern states of São Paulo, Santa Catharina, and Paraná. Estimated in 1914 at over half a million souls who maintained their language, customs, and religion, the majority, many of whom had a Social Democratic background, declared their loyalty to Brazil. Clumsy German propaganda in Uruguay and Argentina, referred to elsewhere, alerted the Brazilian government, which jailed a number of individuals and placed certain German business houses under restraint.

The immediate causes of Brazil's entry into World War I, however, were the sinking of some of her ships by German submarines and the entry of the United States into the war in 1917. After her experience of losing her rubber markets from lack of shipping, Brazilians were highly indignant when German submarines sank the *Paraná,* a merchant ship, in April, 1917. On April 11 she severed diplomatic relations. In the following month, June, she seized forty-six German vessels in her ports, and finally, on October 26 declared war when Germany sank another of her precious ships.

Brazil gave significant aid to the Allies. She put her products and vast natural resources at their disposal, coffee, sugar, cocoa, rubber, timber, beef, mutton, and huge quantities of minerals. Too, she patrolled the South Atlantic, a service which relieved allied fleets to concentrate upon the submarine menace in the North Atlantic. In addition, her supervision of pro-Germans in the southern states lessened Allied leaders' concern over sabotage and possible submarine bases there.

Upon Brazil the war had far-reaching effects. Foreign capital flowed into the country, largely American. Electric light companies, of which there were but three in 1889, had reached 320 by 1920, the greatest increase occurring between 1914 and 1918. This development in turn gave Brazil a new interest in the possibilities of her innumerable water-falls as a future source of power. New native industries grew rapidly while older ones expanded. Scientific advances in the cattle industry were made, while refrigeration plants established at Porto Alegre began shipping chilled beef for the first time. Shortage of Paris footwear led to the investment in leather-manufacturing industries, of which by 1920 more than 1,300 were making shoes. The greatest stimulus was given, however, to the textile industry, which from eighty-seven factories before 1914 had expanded to more than 300 by 1920, mostly in São Paulo. A wide variety of other industries sprang up during the war, so that by 1920 more than 6,000 factories of various kinds were in operation. Significant in aiding the growth of her foreign trade were the German ships confiscated during the war.

Of decisive importance in the later history of Brazil was the growth of labor organization. Before World War I the labor movement had its origin in mutual societies whose members contributed funds to aid one another in time of crisis. Such a society, the Beneficent Association of Workers in carbon minerals, had been organized in 1905. An organization of workers based upon the principle of union appeared in 1903 when the United Society of Stokers and Stevedores established itself in Rio de Janeiro. Others followed. The growth of the textile industry brought the next important union into existence, that of the Union of Operators in 1917. By 1919 the Transport Workers' Union had an almost national basis.

The Nature of Political Conflicts, 1918–1930. These new forces appearing in Brazilian history, industrial growth and labor development, produced political and economic conflicts which led directly to the revolution of 1930. The continued dominance of São Paulo, the coffee state, hampered the growth of both industry and labor, as well as other raw material industries stimulated by the war, such as cattle, cocoa and sugar. The revolts and the policies of the various administrations between 1918 and 1930 are best understood in this light.

The Administrations of Rodríguez Alves and Epitacio Pessôa, 1918–

1922. In 1918 Wenceslau Braz was followed by Rodríguez Alves of São Paulo, but upon the latter's death in 1919 a new election was held. The Republican party, dominated by the states of São Paulo and Minas Gerais, supported Dr. Epitacio da Silva Pessôa from Paraíba, who had held important judicial and political posts. As president, he initiated a program of water conservation and hydroelectric development to benefit Paraíba, Ceará, and Rio Grande do Norte. He modernized the army, nationalized fishing, and began a general census of Brazil. However, during his administration the war boom suffered a collapse in 1920. Overproduction of coffee and high prices for other Brazilian raw materials led to an unwise expansion, which, combined with speculation, brought a severe depression during 1920–1922.

As the time for the election of the next president drew near, the depression stirred all the opposing groups to action. Widespread unemployment of labor gave a foothold to the Communist party, led by Carlos Prestes. Many businesses went into bankruptcy, while the new industrialists, angry at the government for giving them no relief, demanded a change. To meet the crisis, the government, concerned primarily with maintaining coffee prices, issued huge quantities of unsecured paper, an action which automatically increased the prices of common necessities. With coffee threatened by the continuing depression, the conservative Republican party, supported by the president, dictated the election of the candidate from Minas Gerais, Arturo Bernardes. This action precipitated the revolt of 1922, which Hermes da Fonseca with militarists behind him opportunistically headed. The government, after seizing Copacabana fortress and bombarding the city, crushed the uprising.

The Administration of Bernardes, 1922–1926. Bernardes, safely in office, took energetic steps to save the coffee industry. His principal remedy was to reduce expenses by sharply cutting appropriations for health, schools, and public service programs, as well as abandoning Epitacio's flood-control undertaking in the northeastern states. Aiding his retrenchment policies were the recommendations of a British financial commission which advised stimulating foreign investment by reduction of state taxes. This measure, of course, struck a blow at those native Brazilian industries trying to protect themselves from powerful foreign competition. The commission also recommended the stimulation of national industry, that is, coffee and minerals. These policies revealed a lack of understanding of the needs of labor and the new industrial groups. They also prepared the way for the next uprising, that of 1924.

In this revolt a combination of labor, São Paulo industrialists, and the underpaid lower ranking officers of the Brazilian army captured São Paulo and organized the city for defense. But the influence of the Communists, led by Carlos Prestes, disturbed the more conservative groups, who at the end of three weeks surrendered to the federal forces. Throughout the rest of Bernardes' term suppression of the press and of freedom of speech and assembly became a common occurrence, factors which conditioned the later success of the 1930 revolt. Moreover, with the recommendations of the British commission given effect, native industries continued to be adversely affected, while, on the other hand, competition from the Caribbean area in the coffee markets held the world price of that commodity at a low figure.

In international affairs, Bernardes' administration was marked by Brazil's withdrawal from the League of Nations. In the absence of the United States she coveted a permanent seat on the Council by virtue of her prominence as an American country and a participant in the war. When Germany was admitted after Locarno and her own petition was refused she withdrew. Much speculation attends Brazil's motives on this occasion. One suggestion has been that the effort of the League's commission, apportioning German ships among the Allies according to their losses, involved Brazil's surrendering forty-six ships and receiving back four. Possibly, too, the internal political situation still disturbed in 1926, led the Bernardes' government to take spectacular action in the international field to aid the election of Washington Luis Pereira da Souza, the administration candidate from São Paulo.

The Administration of Washington Luis Pereira da Souza, 1926– 1930. Martial law and a subservient congress enabled Bernardes to dictate the election of his successor, Washington Luis. Luis continued the traditional policy of favoring the coffee growers by levying taxes that the whole of Brazil had to pay and by providing through the Coffee Institute, a government agency, the subsidization of the planters and the purchase of the coffee surplus. Mounting discontent in turn led to the reimposition of martial law in a number of the states. But in spite of the usual economies practiced by Luis, the growing coffee surplus and the funds necessary for the conduct of government forced the president to resort to the usual remedy, namely, new loans abroad. This practice by the central government had its parallel in the state governments, which under the national constitution enjoyed the power of levying export taxes and contracting foreign loans. Thus by 1929 states, municipalities, and the federal government had outstanding foreign obligations to the amount of $1,800,000,000. The annual service on this debt reached a figure between $175,000,000 and $200,000,000.

In this precarious financial situation, Brazil was struck with the full force of the 1929 depression. The government, negotiating for a foreign loan, found even that avenue blocked when the stock market crashed in October of that year. Worse, the depression drastically reduced the purchase of coffee, from which the government received 70 per cent of its revenues. A vast surplus accumulated. Bankruptcies and unemployment spread rapidly. This national calamity brought Getulio Vargas to the head of the Brazilian state.

The assumption of power by Vargas in 1930 opened a new era in the history of Brazil. The event was the turning point at which Brazilians began to free themselves from dependence upon a one-crop economy. The cultural life of Brazil, too, had been undergoing a similar change. New writers and artists, throwing off their dependence upon foreign forms and themes, were seeking to express their native Brazilian culture.

Brazilian Culture, 1822–1954. Brazilian culture drew its inspiration from the tropical luxuriance of the land and the mixture of its races, Portuguese, Indian, and Negro. With independence came a new force, romanticism, the influence of French, British, and Spanish experimentalists in ideas and forms. Stimulated by their extravagant praises of nature and the freedom of man, Brazilian romantics adopted exaggerated forms, both in poetry and prose. Little of their writing had any permanence. But among them Antônio Gonçalves Dias (1823–1864), who boasted white, Negro, and Indian blood, took high rank as a poet. His descriptions of Brazil's natural wonders and his songs of the Indian race made him the national poet of Brazil.

Novelists, too, responded strongly to the romantic influence. Brazilian love of nature, combined with the political yeast of the new freedom from Portugal, opened the floodgates of their prose. Giving the highest expression to the intense feeling for the land and its primitive inhabitants was José de Alencar (1829–1877). Of him one well-known Brazilian critic wrote that he ranked among the greatest of Brazil's novelists: "Many believe that he still is, as the most typical, original and most representative of the country's landscape, customs, and languages." (Alceu Amoroso Lima). His masterpiece, *Iracema*, symbolically portrays the crossing of the races in the love of an Indian girl, Iracema, for one of the Portuguese conquerors.

Toward the end of the century Brazilian writers assumed a more critical spirit in their productions. Exemplifying the trend was Alfred d'Escragnolle, Viscount Taunay (1843–1899), whose *Innocence* bespoke a concern for national problems, although the scene of the novel, a story of love and vengeance, was in the wilds of Matto Grosso. Standing out above all of Brazil's great writers, past and present, is Joaquim Maria Machado de Assis (1839–1908). This mulatto, who suffered all his life from epilepsy, left the only record of his inner thoughts in his novels and poems. He distinguished himself by shifting the emphasis in his novels from landscape to man. The man he described was not necessarily a Brazilian; it could be any man. His most important works, among which are *Quincas Borba, Dom Casmurro,* and *Memórias pósthumas de Braz Cubas,* the latter translated into English under the title, *Epitaph of a Small Winner,* mark him as a profound psychological novelist.

His impartial judgment and independence of thought have made some call him a cynic. But throughout his works in his portrayal of men's actions, seemingly unconcerned whether they are good or evil, runs a deep feeling for humanity. As a poet, he avoided the extremes of romanticism and gave Brazil its first example of modernism. His elegant style, philosophical content, and perfection of form make him the acknowledged genius of Brazilian literature.

Comparable to the contribution of Machado de Assis as a realist was Euclydes da Cunha (1866–1909). This writer, neither novelist nor poet but an engineer, wrote *The Sertões,* a study of the psychology of the dwellers in the northeastern part of Brazil. In delineating the extraordinary life of these people, forever at the mercy of natural forces which capriciously changed rich, exuberant valleys into sterile deserts, he shows the individual as a man of powerful physique governed by a fatalistic mind. To this hopeless outlook was added over the centuries a strange amalgam of religious beliefs, superstitions, and social customs derived from the mixed population of Indians, Negroes, and Portuguese. So conditioned, these people became fanatical followers of freak religions and insane messiahs, such as Maciel, the "Councilor."

Cunha prefaced his study of their culture with a scientific (for the time) investigation of the *sertões* region and the relation of its primitive inhabitants to their environment. He also provided an historical account of the attempt of the Brazilian army to crush these highly individualistic people. Because of its style and the poetical descriptions of the land, together with the author's remarkable gift of penetrating the mind of the people, the book has been justly acclaimed as one of the finest works produced by a Brazilian.

In the twentieth century Brazilian writers, in common with their counterparts elsewhere in Latin America, awoke to the great social and economic forces drawing Brazil closer to the modern world: the emergence of a middle class, an organized labor movement, and a vigorous nationalism. In literature Graça Aranha initiated a new trend, the social. Strongly nationalistic and anti-European, Aranha became the spokesman of Brazilian modernism. Contemporary Brazilian writers, responding to this new influence, have in the main sought themes for their novels in the nation's varied regions and in social problems.

Outstanding is José Lins do Rego (1901–   ), who has brought the rural plantation life of the northeast into sharp focus. Jorge Amado (1912–   ), a novelist, portrays the life of Bahia with a strong feeling for the lower classes of his native state. Graciliano Ramos' (1892–   ) profound introspective novels, concerned with the lives of the underprivileged, have reminded some of his readers of Machado de Assis. Erico Verissimo (1905–   ), although strongly influenced in his early writing by foreign authors, European and those of the United States, has produced moving novels of the life of Brazilian cities. More recently he has turned with marked success to produce a monumental novel portraying in all its varied aspects the cultural history of the state of Río Grande do Sul.

In this modern tradition is Gilberto Freyre (1900–   ), not a novelist but a social historian. His studies of the evolution of Brazilian society, *Casa grande e senzala,* translated into English under the title of *Masters and Slaves,* have made him internationally famous. The central idea he has advanced in his works is that the defects attributed by some to Negroes are not in reality defects of character in the colored race but are the characteristics of a slave society which burdened Brazil for so long. This hopeful outlook, together with his profound studies of the process of the fusion of Negro, Indian, and European in Brazil, has given that nation new dimensions in the eyes of the world and new insights into the problems of racial mixture.

In music Brazil produced in the nineteenth century some distinguished composers. Outstanding was Antônio de Carlos Gomes, who won fame outside of his native country. A composer of lyrics and operas, his best known work in the latter field is "Il Guarany." In the twentieth century Heitor Villa-Lobos (1889–   ) has become widely appreciated for his compositions based upon Brazilian folk and popular music. Extremely inventive, his compositions number in the thousands and include five symphonies and numerous operas. His greatest work, honoring the memory of Bach, is the "Bachiana Braziliera No. 1," a fusing of the spirit of the famous German with that of Brazilian folk music.

Brazil has given the world a great artist in Cândido Portinari (1903–   ). Like Villa-Lobos, Portinari has drawn his inspiration primarily from his native, exotic homeland and its heterogeneous people. His works, produced in immense volume, ranging from the primitive to the classic in style, and utilizing every form, depict all aspects of Brazilian life. Strongly evident is an emphasis upon the harsh realities of the life of the underprivileged. One of his greatest paintings, "Coffee," powerfully depicts stevedores and reveals his feeling for rugged, full-bodied form. Monumental and original, "Portinari is one of the most gifted of living artists." (Robert C. Smith).

Part III. GETULIO VARGAS AND THE DEVELOPMENT OF DEMOCRATIC INSTITUTIONS, 1930 TO THE PRESENT

The Revolt of 1930. The fundamental cause of the revolt of 1930 was the determination of the new industrial leaders, cattle barons, cocoa and sugar plantation growers, and organized labor to end the domination of the São Paulo-Minas Gerais coalition. The industrialists clearly understood that Brazil itself, if developed internally, offered a national market for goods manufactured in Brazil. But this avenue was closed by the dependence upon the export principally of coffee and minerals which, permitting the influx of foreign goods, blocked the expansion of native manufacturers. Lack of participation in the government in turn denied Brazilian industrialists legislation to foster their own growth by tariffs against foreign goods.

Labor received even less consideration at the hands of the government. Receiving low wages in the textile industry, on the docks, in the transportation system, and in all industries, urban and rural, they were denied even the necessities by the high prices of imported manufactures. As a recourse during the 1920's they turned to organize labor unions and form political parties. In 1929 the workers in Porto Alegre, where Getulio Vargas was governor, founded the Brazilian Labor party. In the same year workers in various industries in São Paulo and Rio de Janeiro established the General Confederation of Brazilian Labor and the National Confederation of Labor made up of unions not included in the former. A Labor party congress held in July, 1930, in Rio de Janeiro represented 614 different labor organizations with a membership of almost 340,000. Outstanding were the commercial employees' union of

86,000, the textile workers' union of 70,000, and thirty-eight other unions with some 40,000.

With these powerful forces running strongly against the coalition, a split in the official party facilitated the success of the revolution. Minas Gerais, whose choice was Dr. Antonio Carlos da Andrada, had by this date become dissatisfied with São Paulo's domination of the coalition. Accordingly, when Dr. Julio Prestes (not to be confused with Carlos Prestes, the Communist leader), the president of São Paulo, was selected by the administration party, Minas Gerais withdrew from the convention.

The opposition, composed of many political figures representing industry, cattle, sugar, cocoa, and other industries, gathered in Rio de Janeiro in July, 1930, to organize a new party, the Liberal Alliance. As their candidate they selected Dr. Getulio Vargas, who had made an outstanding record as governor of the state of Rio Grande do Sul. The platform of the Liberal Alliance stated clearly the objectives of the new groups who had emerged from the economic changes during and after World War I. Among other things their program called for the right of the people to choose their own president with no dictation from the party in power. The document held that not only coffee but agriculture should receive assistance and that industry should be protected to encourage the production of native manufactured goods. In the financial field the ideas of the industrial leaders found expression in the demand for stabilizing the currency and balancing the budget by increasing domestic production. Labor's influence was sought in the proposals for a compulsory voting system, the secret ballot, extensive public education and medical services, and amnesty for labor leaders exiled by Bernardes and Luis.

When the election was held in March, 1930, the official government count gave Prestes 1,089,949 votes to Vargas' 735,032. Oswaldo Aranha, Vargas' campaign manager, promptly denounced the government figures as fraudulent. Vargas at the state capital, Porto Alegre, Rio Grande do Sul, left by train for Rio de Janeiro. On the way in every town, large and small, crowds hailed him. Meanwhile, in Rio de Janeiro itself General Goes Monteiro, heading a military group, forced Washington Luis to resign. Under these circumstances Vargas was made provisional president in November, 1930.

The Vargas Dictatorship, 1930–1945. The fundamental objective of the Vargas regime was to broaden the economic and political basis of Brazil. Achieved paradoxically under a dictatorship, the reforms established Brazil's present-day democratic government. For the first four years, until 1934, when Vargas' congress promulgated a constitution, the government was provisional. During this period Vargas made a series of basic reforms by decrees, later incorporated into law. The most significant ended the power of the states to levy internal tariffs and export taxes, thus providing the central government with a source of income commensurate with its obligations. Ranking next in importance were decrees restricting the planting of coffee trees and destroying rather than purchasing the vast surplus piled up in the previous years. Thus by 1934 over 29,000,000 bags of coffee, mostly inferior grades, had been burned or dumped into the ocean. Other decrees reduced the production of sugar, revived by World War I.

Paralleling these restrictive measures were others designed to stimulate, by the granting of subsidies, such industries as those of cattle, silk production, lumber, cocoa, and cotton. The manufacturing industries were aided by protection from foreign competition and benefited also from stringent laws requiring foreign corporations to use Brazilian raw materials and employ more Brazilians in their industries.

Politically, Vargas governed Brazil with interventors, who, replacing the former state executives, prevented the old political machines from organizing a counterrevolution, and who put into effect the government's measures outlined above. In the central government he relied heavily upon industrial and political leaders who represented the various economic groups with the exception of labor.

In São Paulo the first attempt to revolt against the new regime occurred in 1932. There the powerful coffee oligarchy were bitter over their loss of both the control of the government and the right to levy an export tax, the principal source of the state's income. As former rulers of Brazil, they deeply resented the interventor who governed the state and whose principal duty was to reduce the production of coffee. Joining them, but for altogether different reasons, was labor, which, suffering from depression conditions, was disappointed at Vargas' neglect to provide remedies. The São Paulo leaders made alliances with similar elements in Minas Gerais and Rio Grande do Sul, but these fell through at the last moment when Vargas made concessions to them. When the federal army invaded the state, more than 200,000 factory workers and their families volunteered for the quickly organized São Paulo army and, as workers in industries, converted to munition-making. For eighty-three days São Paulo held off Vargas' forces, but as the well-organized unions more and more took over the control of the rebellion, the wealthier supporters lost their enthusiasm. This split in the rebel ranks facilitated Vargas' defeat of the state's forces and brought an end to the uprising.

Probably the most important result of the São Paulo revolt was the decision of Vargas to call a constituent assembly to draw up a new constitution. Fifty political parties participated in the election of the delegates with women voting for the first time in Brazil's history. The constitution drawn up by this assembly and promulgated in 1934 has its chief importance in that it met the objectives of the 1930 revolt, excepting labor's, that is, the extension of representation to other economic groups in Brazil besides the traditional coffee and mineral industries.

It provided for a federal republic, with a president elected every four years for a single term only, and with the right to appoint his ministers of state. The legislature was bicameral, elected for four years. The franchise was universal for registered literate men and women, a test which in fact eliminated about 80 per cent of the population.

The constitution showed also that Vargas' power as a dictator was very far from complete. Several provisions limited his authority. One was the restriction to a single term. A second required the president to secure authority from the federal supreme court to intervene in states suffering from financial difficulties. Another required him to secure the support of the Chamber of Deputies to appoint interventors. Under the constitution, moreover, the interventor had to respect local laws or but temporarily suspend them. Restrictions also surrounded his power to declare a state of siege. Finally, in the election of the president, secret, compulsory, and direct, probably a reflection of the Argentine Sáenz Peña law, a special body apart from congress, presided over by the vice-president of the supreme court, counted the votes.

The economic provisions of the document particularly reveal the influence of the new groups, notably the industrialists. It provided that concessions for the development of mines and hydroelectric energy had to be acquired from federal authorities, not state, and could only be granted to Brazilians or companies organized under Brazilian law. Further, all foreign concerns in Brazil had to become Brazilian.

While this constitution was set aside by Vargas in 1937 and another substituted, this instrument is significant in marking a step in the economic emancipation of Brazil from the restrictive policies of the Minas Gerais-São Paulo groups and from foreign control previously exercised as a result of Brazil's need for foreign loans. The document also shows that, with the restrictions put upon the president and the powers given to the states, the power of the state political oligarchies was far from broken. This fact was one reason for Vargas' action in setting aside the constitution in 1937, for Vargas himself hinted at such action when the document was submittted to him.

After the document was promulgated, Vargas became president under it on July 17, 1934. During the next three years he carried forward his program to develop the resources of Brazil on the broad basis made possible by the document. In so doing, however, he still showed himself unaware of the pressing need for relief on the part of labor so adversely affected by the depression. As conditions grew worse, revolts broke out in the north at Natal. Powerful labor unions in the capital and in São Paulo, notably the Stevedores' Union, joined the movement which saw the Communists led by Carlos Prestes assume a prominent position. The uprising, too, had other international aspects, namely, a protest, joined by many liberal political leaders against the government's toleration of a native Fascist movement called *Integralismo*. In answer to the uprising, Vargas declared a state of siege, crushed the revolts with considerable ruthlessness, and sentenced Prestes, who was captured, to virtual life imprisonment.

In putting down this labor revolt, the Brazilian *Integralistas,* led by Plinio Salgado, a dangerous mystic, played an important part. Immediately thereafter, with support from the German embassy and other Nazi organizations, Salgado became a candidate for president in the forthcoming elections. At the same time, many liberals, who were sincerely concerned about the danger of a Nazi movement in Brazil, joined labor to form the Democratic Union party. Vargas put forward José América de Ameida, minister of transport, as the official government candidate. In São Paulo the Democratic Union party threw its support behind Amando Salles, who had the backing of the governor of Rio Grande do Sul, General Flores da Cunha.

José América, proving to be an impractical politician, soon became an obvious failure. General Flores, the most formidable political force behind Salles, was forced to flee to Montevideo when Vargas dispatched troops to garrison Rio Grande do Sul. With Plinio Salgado the only candidate left, Vargas took drastic action to prevent such an obvious pro-Axis leader from winning the election. He set aside the elections and proclaimed a new constitution! Much debate has centered about Vargas' motives for this action. Some believe he was loath to relinquish power. Others insist that he was sincere in his antagonism toward Fascism as a form of government. Certainly his later career gives foundation for such a belief. In any event, Vargas' action marked a profound ,change in his own outlook. In the remaining years of his control of Brazil, that is, until 1945, he gave Brazil increasingly an orientation toward democratic government.

The Constitution of 1937. The constitution of 1937 differed from that of 1934 in centering more authority in the hands of the federal government. Its form was that of a federal republic. The legislature was bicameral, with a Chamber of Deputies chosen indirectly. In place of a senate was a Federal Council selected from each state by the Chamber of Deputies. An additional ten members of the Council were appointed by the president. The document provided further for a Council of National Economy of employers and labor to advise the president. Centralization of power was evident in the agency that the constitution provided to coordinate purchases and direct funds into projects beneficial to the state. Organized as the Department of Public Service or DASP, this agency had other powers which gave it authority subject to the president over practically all administrative functions of the government. Another function transferred to the central government by the document was control over elementary education.

The corporate character of the new government was apparent in the provisions under which syndicates could form, organize federations, and thus secure representation in the national government. Fifteen national federations so formed included seven each for employers and labor and one for the liberal professions in industry, commerce, land transport, maritime and air transportation, communications, credit institutions, educational and agricultural agencies, and the liberal professions. Thus within this framework of government in which a large number of social and economic groups before 1930 had no voice, Vargas was able to launch programs to develop the potentialities of his vast country.

At the outset of his new administration, however, he faced an attempt to overthrow him. His quick action in setting aside the elections to head off Plinio Salgado infuriated the *Integralistas,* who in May, 1938, essayed a daring *coup d'état* and the assassination of Vargas himself. The president, acting promptly, broke up the organization's headquarters and local centers, seized its records, exiled Plinio Salgado, and severed relations with Nazi Germany. To his surprise labor, which he had so ruthlessly crushed in 1936, hailed his action, for the working class had a genuine fear of a Nazi state.

Industrialization under Vargas. In the short period before World War II broke out in 1939, Vargas did much to launch Brazil on a program of broad industrialization. Laws required all foreign business concerns to have a majority of Brazilians in their employ. To stimulate national consumption, the government sponsored an educational program to "buy Brazilian." But of greater significance in giving Brazil a better-balanced economy, Vargas ordered a comprehensive survey of the country's resources. The investigation revealed minerals in quantities little known, although nineteenth century scientists had reported their existence. In Minas Gerais, the historic mineral state, and among neighboring states millions of tons of bauxite, the source of aluminum, were found. Minas Gerais, too, contained iron ore with a content as high as 70 per cent. Other iron deposits, not so rich, were found in São Paulo, Santa Catharina, Espírito Santo, Goiás, and Rio Grande do Sul. In all, Brazil's iron deposits were estimated to amount to one-fourth of the world's total. Bahia and São Paulo revealed valuable deposits of nickel and mica pyrites from which sulfuric acid is manufactured. Minas Gerais showed even greater deposits of mica, as well as a rare mineral, zircon, used in the making of steel. Of greater importance, possibly, in Minas Gerais was the discovery of huge beds of manganese, duplicated to a considerable extent in the neighboring states of Matto Grosso, Bahia, and Goiás. In Minas Gerais, also, the mining of industrial diamonds, the principal source of the world's supply, received new impetus from the survey.

Elsewhere in Brazil gold was found in São Paulo and Goiás, while coal was revealed in vast quantities, athough of a low grade, in São Paulo and other southern states, notably Rio Grande do Sul. Oil and oil shales, but in insignificant quantities, were encountered in Bahia, with indications of other deposits in Ceará, Matto Grosso, and states bordering the Amazon River on the south. Diatomite, used in making explosives, was found in northern Brazil, while in São Paulo, primarily an agricultural area, apatite, valuable for its phosphates, was disclosed in large quantities.

When the survey had been finished and digested, it became the basis for a comprehensive Five Year Plan launched in 1940 for the development of Brazil. Of greatest importance in this program was the proposal to build a steel mill to utilize the fabulously rich iron ores of Minas Gerais. This objective became a reality in September, 1940, when Brazil negotiated a $20,000,000 loan from the United States which she more than matched with an appropriation of $25,000,000. The Export-Import Bank supervised the administration of the purchase of the materials, while the Bethlehem Steel Company undertook to build the mill of which Brazil was ultimately to become the sole owner. The site finally selected at Volta Redonda, some ninety miles west of Rio de Janeiro, was able to draw on the huge iron deposits at Itabira. By 1946 it began the production of steel.

Throughout the whole of Brazil the total value of all industrial production by 1943 amounted to $1.5 billion. Producing this wealth were an estimated 60,000 manufacturing concerns. The number of employees was estimated in 1940 at 1,412,000, whereas they numbered barely 500,000 in 1930. The estimated minimum wage was 270 cruzieros ($13.50) a month down to one-third of this amount, depending upon the standard of living in the particular locality. Among the foreign companies operating in Brazil were sixteen leading American firms, including General Motors, Ford, Armour, Wilson, Swift, Johnson and Johnson, Bates' Valve, Presto-lite, Goodyear, General Electric, Firestone, Hobart-Dayton, Du-Pont, Esso, International Harvester, and Ferroenamel, besides such department stores as Woolworth's.

While Vargas' policies opened the way for the development of industries, he gave proof of his concern for the well-being of the Brazilian working classes by enacting in 1943 a labor code, a charter which ranks among the most enlightened codes in the world. It provided for an eight-hour day, equal pay for equal work for both sexes, a minimum wage program, and laws facilitating and legalizing the formation of unions. It set up a system of social insurance covering workers in industry, transportation, commerce, and finance, which, among other provisions, established thirty-two different pension funds for the various categories of workers. It included regulations governing conditions under which children could work, while women employed in industry were entitled where necessary to maternity leave with full pay, six weeks before and after confinement. This charter, together with the provisions in the constitution granting labor recognition in the government, gave the basis for the whole-hearted cooperation of Brazilian workers in the war against the Axis.

Forest Products and Agriculture. The Vargas regime also stimulated the expansion and use of Brazil's vast forest resources. Revival of the rubber industry was demanded by the industrialization program. New uses were found for her widespread pine forests, as well as the hardwoods and perfumed woods. The famous carnauba palm, called by Humboldt the "tree of life," provided an ever-widening supply of products, chief among which were fibers for cordage, bags, hammocks, blankets, brooms, bridge girders, and fence posts, while its wax furnished the chief ingredients for floor waxes, unguents, ointments, oils, soap, picric acid, and materials for the manufacture of moving picture film. In agriculture, besides extending the cultivation of maté and manioc, the latter the staff of life for most Brazilians, the regime aided the expansion of the fruit industry, bananas, pineapples, and grapes; the development of the wine industry, of which the grapes of Caxias in Rio Grande do Sul were the most famous in Brazil; and tea, tobacco, and cocoa plantations, the latter of which in southern Bahia by 1945 were producing 100,000 tons annually.

The historic crops remained, however, the leaders in agriculture, sugar, cotton, and coffee. While Vargas' measures had restricted the production of coffee, so that from representing 71 per cent of Brazil's exports in 1931, it had fallen to 45 per cent by 1940, the market had become stabilized by the coffee agreement of November 28, 1940. Under this international arrangement, including the United States as the principal consumer, together with the Central American countries, the Caribbean, and Mexico, Venezuela, Colombia, and Peru, Brazil had a guaranteed market for 9,300,000 bags annually.

Education. The intense drive to industrialize Brazil demanded a more comprehensive educational program. The beginning dates from Vargas' first year in office, 1930, when there were but 27,000 elementary schools in the country. By 1945 these had almost doubled, reaching about 50,000. Most of this increase came after the central government set up a national system of education in 1934. High schools increased, while vocational schools more than doubled, until they numbered in all over 2,000. The total school population likewise increased from 2,500,000 in 1920 to almost 4,500,000 in 1945.

To give the work direction, the government organized a variety of educational agencies. Outstanding was the National Council of Education, with members from public and private institutions to advise the ministry of education, which secured legislation making education free and compulsory. The federal government was given the authority to determine objectives, namely, the physical, intellectual, and moral training of children, while the states, aided with federal funds, directed elementary education. Provision, too, was made for normal schools in all states and a number of agricultural colleges.

Included in the educational effort and affecting, in fact, all citizens was a vast program called "Brazilianization." Its objective was to convey to the diverse elements of Brazil's population an understanding of the country's culture and the resources of the homeland. Chief among its specific aims was the teaching of the Portuguese language in all Brazilian schools.

Secondary and higher education were also organized to meet the demands of Brazil's expanding economy. In 1942 a decree made secondary education uniform throughout the country, with the purposes of developing the abilities of the students, inspiring them with patriotism and humanitarianism, and providing those qualified with a curriculum leading to specialized studies in higher education. While physical culture and guidance programs were required of all students, religious education was to be in accord with their beliefs.

Higher education was not neglected. In 1930–1931 various professional schools in Rio de Janeiro were organized in the first Brazilian university, that of Rio de Janeiro. In 1937 a federal law broadened this institution to include all major branches of the sciences and arts to become the University of Brazil. In addition state universities expanded to meet Brazil's growing modernization by adding faculties in agriculture, veterinary medicine, dentistry, pharmacology, and polytechnical education to the older faculties of law, medicine, and engineering.

Foreign Trade. The efforts of the Vargas administration to lift Brazil by its bootstraps, to break the one-crop economy, and to create a vast industrialization program brought a rapid expansion of her foreign trade. Germany, hastening war preparations, became a temporary beneficiary of Brazil's appetite for machinery, manufactured goods, and tools; in exchange, under the commercial agreement of 1934, the Nazis received raw materials, cocoa, coffee, sugar, rubber, and agricultural and timber products, as well as minerals and beef. Germany led in providing railroad equipment for Brazil, while the former's chemical industry displaced competitors. However, the thorn in this arrangement was its barter character. Brazil received no gold for her goods to enable her to purchase needed equipment in other markets. The British declined in Brazilian foreign trade. The United States under the Roosevelt administration secured a new foothold with the Reciprocal Trade Agreement of 1934. It enabled Brazil to sell her products, particularly coffee, for gold. By 1938 the United States trade with Brazil advanced to almost $80,000,000, about equal to that of Germany's. When in the next year World War II broke out, German trade rapidly declined in the face of the British blockade, while that of the United States correspondingly increased.

World War II and Brazil. Probably the most significant effect of World War II upon Brazil was to give added impetus to her industrialization program. As already noted, she succeeded in constructing her first steel plant during the war. While the loss of markets in central Europe due to the British blockade temporarily affected her adversely, the

United States, through the Export-Import Bank, came to her rescue with a $19,000,000 loan. This event signalized the beginning of increasingly friendly relations.

In cooperation with the American program of hemisphere defense, Brazil played a leading part. Before the war she had strongly supported the agreements of previous inter-American conferences directed toward that end. Thus when Japan attacked the United States on December 7, 1941, Brazil invited the various American foreign ministers who met at Rio de Janeiro in January, 1942, to lay down basic policy for the protection of the continent. Brazil set an example in carrying out the principal resolution of the Rio conference, the breaking of relations or declaring war on the Axis powers, when, before the conference adjourned, she had severed relations with Germany. What was equally important, as Japanese conquests took over the raw materials of the Southwest Pacific, Brazil in a series of agreements with the United States made her rubber, copra, essential fats, nut oils, cocoa, cuffee, sugar, cotton, timber products, and minerals—beryllium, quartz crystals, mica, and others—available to the Allies. When this aid and the granting of bases led Germany to retaliate by sinking Brazilian ships, Brazil declared war on Germany in November, 1942.

In preparing Brazil for a part in the war, Vargas won the highest praise from the Allied powers. In March, 1942, he created the air base at Natal which, built in cooperation with the United States, became the largest in the world in the transport of air freight and personnel. Air bases were also constructed at Recife, Belem, Fortaleza, and Bahia. These bases were not only decisive in the defeat of Rommel in North Africa, but all through the war the Allies transported via Natal and Recife troops and vital war materials, the latter of which in the last six months of 1944 amounted to 22,000,000 pounds. In addition she rapidly built up her own military power so that by 1943 she had two battleships, two cruisers, ten destroyers, six torpedo boats, and four submarines, together with a large and efficient air force. Her army consisted of about 100,000 troops with 300,000 reserves.

With this force Brazil carried out valuable operations. Her navy patrolled the South Atlantic sea lanes and convoyed merchant ships. In October, 1944, the Brazilian fleet and air force took over the complete patrol of the South Atlantic to release American fighting units for service in the Pacific against Japan. Her coastal patrol rescued victims of torpedoed ships, while her air force sank and damaged a number of German submarines. Outstanding was her organization of a division for service in Europe. The Germans ridiculed the undertaking with the comment that when Brazilian soldiers fought in Europe, a snake would smoke a pipe. When a completely equipped Brazilian division, 25,000 strong, with doctors, nurses, and hospital equipment landed in Italy in July, 1944, the Brazilians had the satisfaction of displaying to the surprised Germans their divisional emblem—a snake smoking a pipe! At the front the Brazilians not only fought bravely but captured over 20,000 of the enemy, a number almost equal to the size of the division itself.

The Overthrow of Vargas, October, 1945. As the war drew to a close, Vargas faced a growing demand for an end to his long dictatorship and the restoration of democratic government. Labor was anxious to have the essentials of its hard-won code incorporated into a national constitution. Thus in February, 1945, Vargas declared his intention to resign and fixed December 2 as the day for the presidential election. This announcement at once brought Brazil's political parties into action to select candidates. Within the Vargas group itself the conservative wing named Gaspar Eurico Dutra as the official candidate of the Social Democratic party. The opposition organized the National Democratic Union and nominated Eduardo Gómes, who had made a brilliant record as organizer of the Brazilian air force during the war. Both of these parties, essentially conservative, supported programs about the same as that of Vargas, namely, expansion of educational facilities, reduction of taxes on necessities, development of Brazilian resources with the assistance of foreign capital, increasing tariffs to protect Brazilian industry, and insistence upon the recognition of Brazil in the United Nations as a great power.

When the European war ended in May, 1945, the conflicts between the Vargas supporters and the conservatives behind Dutra became increasingly sharp over policies to be followed as unemployment developed, widespread bankruptcies occurred, and labor demanded new reforms. On the point of more reforms affecting the laboring classes, Vargas was known to be sympathetic. In this critical situation Vargas proposed postponing the election. At the same time he legalized the Communist party and freed Carlos Prestes from prison, who promptly supported Vargas for the presidency, although the latter was not a candidate. Fearing a possible understanding between Vargas' powerful labor support and the Communist forces, a small group of conservatives, mostly military men led by General Pedro Goes Monteiro, organized on October 29 a *coup d'état* which removed Vargas from the presidency and placed José Linhares, the president of the supreme court, at the head of the government until an election could be held on December 2.

Linhares swept out of office Vargas' key supporters including the interventors in the states and the mayors and chiefs of police in the principal cities. He selected judges to count the votes in the municipalities in place of the regular officials. Under these circumstances the election, generally considered one of the most honest ever known in Brazil, was held. Dutra, to the surprise of many, won with a substantial majority of 1,000,000 out of 8,000,000 votes cast. The Communist candidate polled over 600,000 votes, a surprising revelation that the Brazilian Communist party was the largest in the Western Hemisphere.

The Vargas regime made many significant contributions to the development of modern Brazil. In breaking down the monopoly of office held by São Paulo and Minas Gerais since 1894, it opened the way for wider participation in government by all Brazilians. Its economic policies, notably the development of industry including a steel plant, began to free Brazil from dependence upon foreign nations and launch her on a career of broad national development. Probably of greatest significance in Vargas' contribution to the development of Brazilian democracy was extending the suffrage to all, including women, and supporting necessary labor reforms which gave the bulk of the Brazilian people a stake in their own country, previously lacking. To his credit, when removed from office by force, Vargas bowed to the event and made no effort to resort to military power. Accepting the change with dignity, he promptly became a candidate for office under the new constitution of 1946.

The Administration of Dutra, 1946–1950. Dutra assumed the presidency on January 31, 1946. His congress at once went to work to draw up a new constitution. This document was in line with the developing democracy of Brazil. It provided for the usual separation of powers, legislative, judicial, and executive. The president was to hold office for four years, elected by direct vote of the people, men and women, and could not succeed himself. Congressmen were to serve three years, and senators nine. The document provided for social reform programs; gave labor the right to organize and bargain collectively; permitted expropriation of uncultivated lands for redistribution; contained liberal provisions for participation of foreign capital in industry, mining, banks, hydroelectric power, and insurance companies; and liberalized tariff policies, but prohibited monopolies. Based in many aspects upon that of the United States, it contained a bill of rights, provisions for freedom of press, speech, conscience, and from arbitrary arrest, and guarantees of the right of property. However, it prohibited political parties in opposition to the democratic form of government. Strongly Brazilian in outlook, the constitution gave the government the right to monopolize any industry, regulate the use of property, and take measures against abuse of economic power. Finally, the document limited sharply the power of the president in time of a state of siege.

The impetus to industrialization given Brazil by Vargas was carried forward by Dutra. In 1946 Dutra opened the great Volta Redonda steel plant begun in 1940. With the war at an end, Brazil, starved for manufactured goods, launched under Dutra a huge program of constructing new industries. Benefiting from the $650,000,000 in gold and credits accumulated during the war, Dutra gave full play to the purchase of food, oil, and machinery for factories, steel industries, electric power development, agriculture, and construction of railroads and highways.

Outstanding was the completion of a through highway connection between Uruguay and Salvador on the coast. From there the plans projected the highway northward to Natal. Dutra's government also purchased the British railways, the Leopoldina line and the Great Western. In the west was begun the construction of a railroad from Santos westward to Corumbá and thence to Santa Cruz in Bolivia, envisaging eventually a continuous line to Arica on the Chilean coast via Cochabamba. The chief significance of this undertaking is that it is aimed to tap Bolivian oil for São Paulo's industries and open up the Brazilian Matto Grosso frontier.

Politically, the Dutra administration concerned itself chiefly with measures, such as industrialization, favorable tariffs, loans, and the like, to support middle class interests to the neglect of labor. The latter suffered severely from the high cost of living, shortages, frequently of food, and inadequate housing. Labor's discontent gave the Communist party a foothold to extend its influence. This became particularly apparent in the January, 1947, elections, congressional, state, and municipal. In these elections the Communists polled some 800,000 votes to the intense surprise of everyone, electing two senators, fourteen deputies, a large number of legislators, and almost winning control of the city council in Rio de Janeiro, besides establishing strong positions in many other municipal offices.

This was a threat not to be overlooked. The party was hailed before the Supreme Electoral Tribunal, which after considerable debate declared it illegal on the ground that it was subservient to a foreign government. The president thereupon closed down, by police and military action, all Communist centers. At first congress refused to expel the duly elected Communists in the 1947 election, but eventually did so early in 1948. Prestes, their leader, went into hiding.

By 1950 Brazil had reached a crisis. The lavish spending of her reserves accumulated during the war threatened her currency. Hastily the Dutra government installed restrictions upon all but vital imports and negotiated bilateral treaties to open new markets for Brazilian production. When, however, the Korean War broke out in the middle of 1950, prices for her raw materials again rose. In this year the presidential election was held.

The Administration of Vargas, 1950–1954. Vargas' election in 1950 was overwhelming, carrying sixteen of the nineteen states as well as the Federal District and the territory of Amapá. However, the Brazilian people elected a Congress dominated by opposition parties. Recognizing the impossibility of ruling except through a coalition government, Vargas assigned only one post in his cabinet to his own Labor party; four went to Dutra's Social Democratic party, which held the largest number of seats in congress. Other parties, particularly the National Democratic Union received fewer posts.

Vargas' policies for his administration were in the main two: continuation of the program of industrialization, the most cherished dream of Brazilians, and second, an insistence that labor be given due recognition in Brazil's development. Outlining his ideas in his early speeches he called on Brazilians to invest their capital in native industry. He promised to seek loans from the Export-Import Bank, the World Bank, and Point Four funds. Noting Brazil's dependence upon coffee, cotton, and cocoa, he planned continuation of bilateral treaties with other nations, diversification of exports, the discovery of new markets, the broadening of old ones, and an expansion of the internal market. Not pleasing to the wealthier elements in Brazil, he promised new taxes on their huge profits derived from speculation in the black market and booming urban real estate. For labor he insisted on the extension of the labor code to rural workers, provision for medical aid, large-scale housing programs, elementary education, and encouragement of home ownership. To aid him in his program, he called upon labor to join unions immediately, and promised to permit the unions to elect their own leaders, appoint heads of their various welfare organizations, and select their labor court representatives.

Vargas' demands for labor were sensible. The 1950 census in Brazil showed a rural exodus and rapid growth of cities. São Paulo, now with a population of over 2,250,000, increased over the 1940 census by some 73 per cent; Rio de Janeiro, larger in size, by 35 per cent; Recife, by 55 per cent. All other cities showed similar gains. The rural northeastern hinterland was being drained; agriculture was in consequence declining; and population pressure in the cities was producing slum conditions favoring the growth of Communism.

In carrying forward his industrialization program, Vargas drew up a Five Year Plan which, besides using government funds and securing local capital, he proposed to finance by securing loans from the United States while facilitating her acquisition of raw materials. The plan called for an investment of one billion dollars. The United States responded, having sent the Abbink Commission to survey Brazil's resources, and formed with Brazil the Brazilian-United States Joint Commission for Economic Development. Its objectives were to balance Brazil's industry, transportation, power, mining, and farming as essential both to Brazil's future and the security of the United States. The latter had in mind that food shortages, inflation, and neglect of labor would encourage the growth of Communism. The commission, after making a series of surveys to discover important needs, arranged for the financing of the proposed projects with Brazilian-United States capital, the latter through the Export-Import Bank and the International Bank for Development and Reconstruction (the World Bank).

To expand the steel production of Volta Redonda, producing in 1952 some 500,000 tons yearly, Vargas matched a $25,000,000 loan from the Export-Import Bank. Other steel mills were planned at Santos, São Paulo, Vitória, capital of Espíritu Santo, and Laguna, Santa Catharina. Eventually these expect to meet Brazil's internal needs and save at the same time the huge sums spent for purchase of such imported products.

Under the impetus of the government's program, industries and development of resources continued advancing in all parts of Brazil. An aluminum plant was established in Ouro Preto, the first in South America, and an alkali plant in Rio de Janeiro; also, there were cement plants, railroad and passenger car factories, using largely Brazilian-made steel, and a host of other industries, among them penicillin plants, automobile factories making tires (from Brazilian rubber) and spare parts, Diesel and machine tool industries, and fertilizer factories. An index to the extraordinary growth of industry is seen in the census of 1949, which showed that 29,000 factories in São Paulo had grown by 1952 to over 40,000, employing almost 1,000,000 workers and producing goods valued at almost four billion dollars.

Industrialization has demanded improved docks and harbors, extension of railroads, and a huge expansion of highway construction. It has also required, because of the low heating power of coal, the development of hydroelectric plants. Outstanding among the latter and ranking seventh in the world in size is the São Paulo Light and Power Company. A second, almost as large, was completed in 1954 at Paulo Affonso Falls on the São Francisco River to furnish water to irrigate and provide power to some 264,000 square miles of territory within Bahia. In Minas Gerais other numerous hydroelectric plants are being constructed, while Rio Grande do Sul is electrifying practically the entire state.

The expanding need for raw materials has added impetus to the production of iron from the Rio Doce Valley, 80 per cent of which is now exported to the United States. Explorations have revealed other rich iron deposits as well as tin, bauxite, and manganese deposits. Important is the exploitation of the latter in the Amapá territory by the Bethlehem Steel Company and Brazil with Export-Import Bank funds. A more recent discovery of manganese has occurred near Corumbá on the Paraguay River.

In view of the lack of adequate coal and still lagging hydroelectric power, the possibilities of atomic energy have fired Brazilian imagination. Thus at the new University Research Center in Rio de Janeiro, scientists have recently installed a cyclotron, provided by the United States, to launch this new industry. Active search for uranium deposits have revealed beds in Minas Gerais, export of which is forbidden along with thorium and other atomic ores.

This vast industrialization of modern Brazil suffers from a serious impediment—the lack of adequate oil resources. Forced to import almost 99 per cent of her needs, Brazil has resorted to building refineries in coastal cities to reduce the cost of importing petroleum products. Significant are the huge refineries at Mataripe, Bahia, and Cubatão at São Paulo. Politically, the oil question has stirred Brazilians deeply, with strong nationalist groups, including high army officers, rejecting all foreign participation in its search and exploitation. Vargas acceded to this nationalistic demand, securing legislation which placed all exploration, production, refining, sale, and distribution of oil in a government-controlled corporation, *Petroleo Brazileiro* (Petrobras). Simple statistics indicate the seriousness of the lack of oil: in 1945 Brazil consumed 11,000,000 barrels; in 1955, over 40,000,000, costing $250,000,000.

Finally, plaguing the Vargas administration was the financial problem of meeting the costs of industrialization and basic requirements of food and housing for Brazil's 58,000,000 population. With many of her imports of heavy industrial equipment, oil, and other essentials purchased on credit, Brazil found herself early in 1953 facing widespread demands of her foreign suppliers for payment of bills. To meet this condition, Vargas in March, 1953, secured a loan from the Eisenhower government for $300,000,000. The loan met the immediate needs of the foreign creditors, but the difficulties attendant upon industrialization continued. In an effort to find a solution Vargas appointed Oswaldo Aranha as finance minister in the middle of 1953. By the end of the year his program of austerity had made some progress toward paying off past debts, but brought down on his head the intense antagonism of those adversely affected by restrictions on imports.

The year 1954 produced a profound crisis in Brazil's modern history. Vargas' policies to carry forward industrialization and at the same time to extend social benefits to labor required vast sums. Corruption in high places undoubtedly added to the runaway inflation arising from the basic policies toward industry and labor. As the cost of living rose, Vargas insisted upon wage increases. The crisis produced violent political attacks upon him and eventually a demand for his resignation. Riots and strikes broke out in various cities. In the midst of the mounting tension an effort to assassinate an anti-Vargas newspaperman resulted in the death of an air force officer. New demands for the president's resignation followed. Finally, on August 24, facing forcible removal from office, Vargas committed suicide. All the reasons surrounding this action are still hidden. In any case, one of the most remarkable men in Brazil's history passed from the scene. He had maintained democratic government since his election; he had undercut Communist growth; and over the years he had given labor a protection it was entitled to by its role in a state becoming increasingly industrialized.

Brazil since 1954. Vice-President João Café Filho became president to finish Vargas' term. He continued the emphasis upon industrialization and sought new loans abroad to meet the mounting cost of government. But by the end of 1955 he had found no solution for the frightening problem of inflation. In this continuing crisis, sharpened by the suicide of Vargas, Brazil faced the election of a new president in 1955. Some Brazilians, possibly influenced by the success of the revolution in neighboring Argentina, talked even publicly of a military dictatorship. But normal maneuvering of the parties went forward. Candidates were properly nominated, and they conducted a spirited campaign for the high office of president. The peaceful election held in October gave new testimony to the strength of Brazilian democracy. Chosen for the presidency was Juscelino Kubitschek, the nominee of the Social Democratic party and the governor of the state of Minas Gerais. João Goulart, the head of the Brazilian Labor party, succeeded to the office of vice-president. Both men reflected the basic philosophy of Vargas.

In spite of the clear victory of Kubitschek, a small minority in congress and in the army, abetted by influential newspapers, began a campaign to prevent the successful candidates from assuming office. The situation reached a crisis early in November when Café Filho took a leave of absence after a heart attack, and one of their number, Carlos Coimba da Luz, succeeded as provisional president. When he proved unwilling to move against the plotters, the army, led by General Henrique Teizeira Lott, with naval support drove Luz from office. The House of Deputies thereupon named Nereu Ramos, president of the Senate, provisional president. Without further incident Kubitschek and Goulart were inaugurated on January 31, 1956. Kutibschek's highly successful record as governor of Minas Gerais has inspired high hopes that he will successfully meet the overwhelming problems of present-day Brazil. United States confidence in the new government was apparent in the prompt granting of a $31,000,000 loan to enlarge the Volta Redonda steel mill.

Today Brazil is a huge underdeveloped country struggling to maintain democratic government in the face of great difficulties. Indeed, her efforts to industrialize herself, combat illiteracy, improve transportation and agriculture to feed her almost 60,000,000 people, halt inflation, reduce the cost of living, and ward off violent political strife, all intensified by the unceasing agitation of the outlawed Communist party, make her future precarious. Happily, her recent orderly and peaceful election, involving millions of her citizens, gives genuine hope that she will remain one of the world's great democratic powers.

MODERN LATIN AMERICA

SECTION II

The Pacific Republics

Chile, Bolivia,
Peru, and Ecuador

Chapter XIX

CHILE

Part I. THE REPUBLIC OF THE OLIGARCHY, 1821–1925

The Character of Chilean History. While Chilean history up until 1925 saw the dominance of its landowning oligarchy, strong liberal trends appeared early in the nineteenth century. These made notable advances in movements for education, separation of the church and state, and laying the groundwork for a wider participation in government. The stresses resulting from World War I prepared the way for a major political revolution beginning in 1920 and ending with the constitution of 1925. After that date Chile launched political, economic, and social reforms which by 1956 have placed her in the forefront of democratic countries in Latin America.

The Social Organization of Chile. At the beginning of her national independence, Chile found herself divided into rather sharply defined groups. The rich central valley lying between the Andes and the coastal range provided a base upon which colonial landowners firmly fixed themselves on great estates. Tilling the land were peasants called *inquilinos,* whose status differed little from that of the peasant in the late Middle Ages in Europe. Along the coast of Chile and in the capital, Santiago, towns of considerable size, Valdivia, Concepción, Valparaíso and others, saw the beginnings of the Chilean middle class. The long coastline of the country facilitated their growth, for it offered one of the chief means of communications and trade. After the opening of the seventeenth century *inquilinos* constantly escaped from the landed estates to the capital and coast cities where they became known as *rotos,* the urban laboring classes. The Wars for Independence had the strong support of the coastal middle class, for they wished to end the restrictions of the Spanish mercantile system. At the same time the common soldiers in these wars were largely drawn from the *rotos* of the cities and towns.

O'Higgins and the First Struggle for Reform, 1818–1833. While Bernardo O'Higgins was a wealthy landowner in the southern part of Chile, he had received these lands from his father, a self-made man whose sheer ability had won for himself appointment as viceroy of Peru. Bernardo, sent to England at an early age for his education, was deeply influenced by the French revolutionary writers and Spanish patriots. Later in England he became acquainted with Miranda and others planning revolts for the independence of the Spanish colonies.

As the head of the government (1818–1823), O'Higgins initiated liberal reforms. He attempted to abolish entailed estates and establish a class of small landowners. To stimulate trade and native industry, he eliminated colonial taxes. Through agents he negotiated in England a loan for $5,000,000 to bolster the treasury burdened with the costs of the War for Independence. His social reforms included prohibitions on the use of titles and the sale of offices, as well as restrictions on bullfighting, cockfighting, and other amusements which were a source of constant brawls and drunkenness. He established, too, the first police systems in Santiago and Valparaíso. In education he founded public primary schools supplemented by the Lancastrian system of teaching. In defiance of the church, he encouraged the importation of foreign books and magazines, the establishment of public libraries, provisions for burial grounds of Protestants, and restrictions on the number of saint days.

O'Higgins' reforms stirred up bitter resentment among the traditional conservative groups, the landowners and the church. At the same time lack of funds to pay the troops led to revolts in the south, headed by Ramón Freire, the governor of Concepción. In Santiago the oligarchy succeeded in ousting O'Higgins in January, 1823, who went into exile. Freire thereupon assumed control.

While Freire did not subscribe to the doctrinaire liberalism of O'Higgins, he nevertheless favored reforms benefiting the middle class. To secure money for the new government, he granted a monopoly over tobacco, tea, and liquor to a private company headed by Diego Portales, in return for which the government was to receive funds to pay the interest on the London loan. To add to the state's income, he seized property belonging to the church. He continued O'Higgins' policy of attempting to reduce the church's influence by refusing to accept a Vatican accord offered by a representative of the Pope. At the same time he removed from office the bishop of Santiago, who had a strong influence over political activities in Santiago.

Freire succeeded in having a new constitution drawn up in 1826 to establish a federal government, but a revolt overthrew him. The elections held under the new constitution, however, brought in a congress in sympathy with Freire's ideas as well as a president, General Francisco Pinto. Almost at once a split appeared in the liberal forces. The wealthier middle class, led by Manuel Rengifo and Diego Portales, the latter being influential through his control of the tobacco monopoly, was anxious to establish stable conditions to permit trade and industry to flourish, and joined the conservatives in their effort to overthrow the government. The two forces met in a decisive battle at Lircay in 1830. General Joaquín Prieto, the victor, rapidly crushed the remaining liberal groups, while Portales seized control in Santiago. Prieto assumed the presidency in 1831, with Portales as vice-president. In the next eighteen months, with the country under a dictatorship, the Conservative party called a constituent congress which drew up a constitution, written largely by Manuel Egaña.

The Constitution of 1833. The constitution of 1833 became the citadel of conservative control of Chile for almost a century. The document provided for a president chosen indirectly, no vice-president, a bicameral congress in which senators, elected indirectly, served for six years, and a Chamber of Deputies with members from each province, elected directly to serve for three years. The president was advised by a Council of State and a cabinet of seven ministers, members of both of which could hold seats as senators. Other provisions established a supreme court and inferior courts and gave the franchise to all literate males of twenty-one years of age who were registered and recognized the Roman Catholic as the state religion.

The operation of the constitution had the effect of placing the control of government in the senate, which had the power to initiate money bills. Equally important, cliques within the senate dictated the election of the president, who in turn selected his cabinet from his supporters in the senate. The senators, through their power to control appropriations, dictated to the president the nomination of heads of provinces, mayors, judges, and other figures of local importance. Under the circumstances the struggle for the control of the Chilean government was largely one carried on between the powerful provincial families to elect senators to represent their interests. Out of this struggle developed the pernicious practice of purchasing votes, providing liquor during elections, and controlling the list of registered voters.

The Administration of Prieto, 1836–1841. Prieto, president in 1831, was again elected to the office in 1836 for a term of five years. Rengifo, his able head of the treasury, improved the economy of Chile. Valparaíso's port was expanded to become the principal outlet of Chilean trade. An enterprising American, William Wheelwright, started a steamship line, the first in South America, which plied between Valparaíso and Callao, Peru. Burdensome colonial excise and sales taxes *(alcabala)* were ended and custom duties imposed to stimulate agriculture, industry, and the cattle business. Rengifo's reorganization of tax collections assured the country of larger revenues, while his success in renegotiating the English loan established Chile's credit abroad. This domestic stability was accompanied by a normal political growth: the emergence of Chile's historic parties, Liberal and Conservative, although at the time the former were known as *Pipiolos* and the latter as *Pelucones* or big-wigs.

In foreign affairs Prieto joined with Argentina to make war in 1836 upon Santa Cruz, dictator in Bolivia, who had fashioned that state with Peru into a huge confederation. Successful, the allies defeated Santa Cruz in 1838 at Yungay and forced the dissolution of the large northern state.

The Administrations of Bulnes, 1841–1851. Bulnes' two administrations, although conservative, continued the progressive economic development of Chile and gave an impetus to a broad educational program. Rengifo, who was retained as head of the treasury, fostered new methods in agriculture, the building of roads, and removal of restrictions upon commerce and foreign investment. The copper industry began under this administration, although in foreign hands. Commercial treaties with the British and the United States opened new markets for Chile's goods. Interestingly, the discovery of gold in California and Australia impelled those regions to seek Chilean wheat for the thousands of new arrivals in the mining regions. Almost at the same time in the later 1840's Chilean economy received new impetus from the arrival of German refugees fleeing the collapse of the Revolution of 1848. Their settlement in southern Chile became, too, a part of the southward expansion of the country toward the Strait of Magellan, where before 1850 Chilean colonists established Punta Arenas on the Strait.

Bulnes distinguished his administrations by his aid to education and toleration of political discussion. Giving impetus to both was the famous Venezuelan, Andrés Bello, who had arrived in Chile in 1829. There, early in the 1830's, he established a literary circle and carried on in the columns of the periodical, *El Mercurio,* a healthy discussion of Chile's domestic problems. By 1841 Bello's biting criticisms of Chilean culture stirred Chilean leaders to seek a remedy in education. At the invitation of Bulnes, Bello, an authority on the Spanish language and international law and an interpreter of nineteenth century science, drew up a plan for a state university. His ideas were adopted with practically no change by the Chilean congress in 1842 to establish the national university. As rector, Bello invited two of his brilliant protégés, José Victorino Lastarria and Francisco Bilbao, to become professors in the new institution. Their uncompromising analyses of the country's culture stimulated widespread discussion and contributed to the progressive ideas of the time. The Argentine, Domingo Faustino Sarmiento established and headed the first normal school in Santiago as part of Bulnes' idea for a nation-wide school system.

By the end of Bulnes' second administration Chilean educational progress was represented by a university, a National Institute, advanced secondary schools, fifty public schools, schools of architecture, painting, and music, and scientific institutions. While small in comparison with present-day systems, Chile's achievements at this date shone like a star in comparison with the rest of Spanish America.

The Administrations of Montt, 1851–1861. Manuel Montt, also conservative, continued the main trend of Chilean economic expansion. But the liberal growth under Bulnes suffered a setback. Montt's candidacy, feared by the Liberals, was attacked notably by Francisco Bilbao, who had a large following in the cities. Fearing armed uprising, Bulnes declared martial law to ensure Montt's election. But that event did not come about until more than 2,000 people were killed in a Liberal uprising and Bilbao and Lastarria were exiled.

With the treasury still benefiting from the sale of wheat to California, Montt's regime saw the building of the first railroad line from Valparaíso to Santiago, completed in 1863. Later other lines were built southward through the interior of Talca and northward to connect the rich silver deposits at Copiapó with the coast. Telegraphic communication linked the principal cities. Montt's encouragement of German immigration saw the expansion of farming areas and the cattle industries and the establishment of breweries in the south. With these developments went a corresponding increase of Chile's southern coastal trade, accompanied by internal improvements, such as highway construction, bridge building, and better policing of cities. A census taken in 1854 revealed Chile with more than 1,500,000 inhabitants. The growth of cities was striking, with almost one-tenth of the population in Santiago, while Valparaíso had 60,000. In these cities the small but vigorous middle class prospered and many individuals became extremely wealthy. But the bulk of the population, largely poverty-stricken, suffered from unsanitary conditions, a source of the contagious diseases which frequently ravaged Chilean cities in the nineteenth century.

The needs of the growing middle class made ever more evident the continued expansion of educational facilities. Montt supported these, but came into violent conflict with the church. During his administrations some 500 public schools were established, alongside an equal number of existing private and religious schools. Normal schools increased in number, as did technical institutions and libraries. The hierarchy, resenting the invasion of their control of education, opposed the government's actions. Montt in turn supported legislation which established the principle of civil marriage, extended the power of the government over the activities of parish priests, and ended compulsory tithing along with the abolition of entailed estates, first attemped by O'Higgins.

Montt's conflict with the church had important results. It stimulated the movement which eventually led to separation of church and state in Chile and it split the Conservative party. Those who supported Montt came to be known as Nationalists, while the opposition organized the Clerical party, supported in considerable measure by the landowners of the interior, who were antagonized by Montt's legislation against entailed estates.

Montt's regime closed with a bloody conflict. The various democratic groups in Chile had frequently opposed Montt's efforts at autocratic power, but his attempt to dictate the election of his successor brought open revolt. The Liberals, headed by a distinguished writer and historian, Benjamín Vicuña Mackenna, were supported in this case by the disgruntled Clerical-Conservative party and threw themselves against Montt's Nationalist party choice, Antonio Vara. The Liberals, opposed to the two-term arrangement, advocated constitutional reforms and various measures to reduce the power of the president. When Montt resorted to martial law to control the election, revolts flared in Santiago and in the north. Bloody fighting forced the Liberals to give up their opposition, but Montt withdrew his support of Vara, known to be of dictatorial temperament, in favor of José Joaquín Pérez, a man of more moderate views.

The Administrations of Pérez, 1861–1871. Under the Pérez administrations Chile made rapid advances in the expansion of her economy. The growing volume of mineral and agricultural exports demanded new additions to her railroad system. At the moment Henry Meiggs, an American refugee from the sheriff in San Francisco but of the same heroic mold as the "Robber Barons," undertook the construction of Chilean railroads. Eminently successful, he began the system which eventually linked the great interior valley from end to end. In the north Chileans rapidly developed the nitrate areas of the Atacama Desert to meet the demands of modern agriculture in Europe and the United States. To the south they utilized the Strait of Magellan for their European shipping. In the south, too, new agricultural and cattle lands were opened over the stubborn opposition of the Araucanian Indians. Fighting bravely for their homes, after their outbreak in 1859 the Araucanians held off final defeat until 1885, when the government's incessant war against them brought submission.

In foreign affairs the Pérez administrations became involved in a war with Spain. The latter country, hoping to bolster its shaky monarchy, invaded Peru in 1864. Chile's vigorous protest against the action, seconded by independent aid to Peru by some of her citizens, brought a Spanish blockade of her ports and the bombardment of Valparaíso on March 31, 1866. Damage was estimated in the millions, but more important, the event brought home to Chile the need of a naval building program to defend her exposed coasts.

Politically, the Pérez period also saw new advances in the growth of liberalism. A new party, the Radical, appeared, advocating a radical separation of state and church and a state-supported public school system. One of its leaders, Diego Barros Arana, a great Chilean historian and a student of Comte, was intensely interested in modern science and in the need of making his country more progressive in outlook. In 1865 the Liberals and Radicals pooled their strength in congress to secure a constitutional amendment enabling Protestants and others to found their own schools and places of worship. Three years later they won a second amendment which ended the power of the president to dictate his successor, limiting the chief executive to one term in office. In 1876 further legislation provided for Protestant burial grounds in public cemeteries and had removed the civil and criminal jurisdiction of the church over cases involving the clergy.

The Administrations of Errázuriz and Pinto, 1871–1881. The contribution of Frederico Errázuriz Zañartu to Chile was to begin the beautification of the capital, Santiago. However, his somewhat extravagant spending on public improvements left Chile, in spite of increased revenues from nitrates, in a weak position to meet the world-wide depression of 1876–1879. His successor, Francisco Pinto, elected in 1876, bore the brunt of the collapse. England, Chile's chief customer, virtually halted all purchases. Bankruptcies, unemployment, and widespread suffering, made worse by a crop failure, left the country prostrate.

The government, faced with an empty treasury, resorted for the first time to issuing inconvertible paper money. For decades the device adversely affected the working class. Paid in this practically worthless currency, they suffered a continuous decline in their living standards. The landed oligarchy, on the contrary, profited, for their wealth in land remained untouched. At the same time the cheap currency enabled them to pay off their debts. Within this framework of discontent and rising protest, Pinto used his influence to bring to the presidency a Liberal with strong anticlerical views, Domingo Santa María. However, reforms suffered delay with the outbreak of the War of the Pacific in 1879.

The War of the Pacific, 1879–1883. The fundamental cause of this war was the expansion of Chile into the rich nitrate areas of the Atacama Desert. An important contributory cause was a conflict over boundaries, undefined by Spain in this region in the colonial period. In Atacama, Chile rested its case upon the assertion in the constitution of 1833 that its northern boundary was the Atacama Desert. Bolivia stated its claim when Sucre assumed administrative authority over the desert as part of the territory inherited from the colonial period. Peru based her title to the region upon a similar background, namely, that viceregal administration included the province of Tarapacá. Disputes before 1866 were largely academic. But in that year Chile and Bolivia agreed upon a boundary along the twenty-fourth parallel, an arrangement clouded by Argentina's claim to an Andean frontier in the area of this parallel.

Almost immediately after the treaty was signed, nitrate discoveries at Antofagasta in the Bolivian area and silver at Caracoles drew mining groups, mostly British, into the region. At the same moment French and American mining companies supported Peru's expansion into her province of Tarapacá to exploit its nitrate beds. Near Antofagasta the Chilean Nitrate Company had already secured concessions under a contract with the Bolivian government in 1876. Under it Bolivia had guaranteed that the tax on each hundredweight of nitrates would not be increased during the life of the contract. Two years later the irresponsible dictator of Bolivia, Hilarión Daza, needing funds and inspired by the successful example of Peru in seizing Chilean properties in Tarapacá, levied an increase of ten centavos upon each hundredweight of nitrates taken out by the Chilean company. The company, of which the Chilean government was a part owner, regarded the action as a violation of the original contract and refused to pay the additional tax. Daza thereupon seized the Chilean properties at Antofagasta, expelled the Chilean forces, and declared war, calling upon Peru to honor the treaty of 1873, an offensive and defensive alliance signed with Bolivia in that year. At the same time both Peru and Bolivia sought Argentine support against Chile. But the skill of the Chilean ambassador in Buenos Aires and the approaching Argentine crisis of 1880 dashed their hopes. When Peru at Chile's request refused to denounce the 1873 treaty, the latter declared war upon both countries in April, 1879.

The combatants were unevenly matched. Chile, smarting under the Spanish bombardment of Valparaíso, had built an efficient navy, while her army, mostly of veterans, was fresh from the Araucanian wars. Peru had but two naval vessels, while Bolivia had none. Moreover, the Bolivian army was too far from the scene of the conflict to overcome transportation difficulties necessary to reach the fighting front. During the first year of the war Peru's *Huascar*, commanded by Miguel Grau, rammed the Chilean *Esmeralda*, while the latter's sister ship, the *Independence*, wrecked herself on a reef. Later the *Huascar* terrorized the Chilean coast, but was eventually run down by the *Almirante Cochrane*. With control of the sea, Chile landed troops on Peruvian territory, captured Iquique, and took possession of Arica. After an American attempt at mediation failed, Chile carried the war into Peru. With a fleet and a force of 30,000 men, the Chilean general, Baqueano, landed near Lima and captured the capital in January, 1882. The Peruvian collapse, except for guerrilla bands which fought on until 1883, was complete. Peruvians looted the capital while their military forces fell upon one another. The Chileans sacking the city left Peru no alternative but to sign a hard peace, the Treaty of Ancón, in October, 1883.

The treaty ceded Tarapacá to Chile and provided for Chilean control over the Peruvian provinces of both Tacna and Arica for a period of ten years. At the end of that time a plebiscite was to determine final allegiance of the provinces, with the understanding that the winner was pledged to pay the loser 10,000,000 pesos. In 1884 Chile and Bolivia signed a truce under which Bolivia recognized Chile's sovereignty over Antofagasta. The effect of the war on Peru was to plunge that country into bankruptcy. Also, it became the object of Bolivia's antagonism for signing a separate peace. Bolivia on her part lost her frontage on the Pacific Ocean and eventually turned to seek an outlet through the Chaco to the east.

Upon Chile the war had far-reaching effects. Her vigorous military actions stamped her as a major military power of South America. The acquisition of the valuable nitrate territory added great natural wealth to the country's resources. Moreover, the rapid expansion of nitrate exports from the newly acquired territories filled the coffers of the treasury. Finally, the war prepared the way for a major political crisis in the traditional struggle between the Liberals and Conservatives.

The Administration of Santa María, 1881–1886. When the War of the Pacific, which had covered the last two years of Pinto's regime and the first two years of Santa María's, ended, the Liberal program to which Santa María was sympathetic continued to win successes. Under Santa María all restrictions upon the use of cemeteries for burials were removed; civil registration of births and deaths was required; and in 1883 civil marriage was legalized. The intensity of this conflict appeared in the action of the archbishop of Santiago, who excommunicated the president, cabinet members, and congressmen who had supported the civil marriage law. Another aspect of the Liberal-Conservative struggle arose over the question of the use of the increased revenues derived from the tax on nitrate exports. The issue became the chief one in the 1886 election. Conservatives had little interest in devoting the revenues to modernize Chile's economy. But the wealthy middle class, the bulk of the Liberal party, favored a program of currency reform, internal improvements, extension of roads, highways, and railroad lines, and dock and port construction. The Radical party supported them, but also wanted a continuation of political and social reforms fought for in the preceding years. In this latter field labor joined forces with the Radical party, having but recently formed the Labor party under a talented lawyer, Malaquais Concha. The result of the election placed in office the candidate of the Liberal parties, José Manuel Balmaceda, a distinguished anticlerical.

The Administration of Balmaceda, 1886–1891. Balmaceda in office used the powers of the president, with the support of the congress elected with him, to expand Chile's economy. Financially, he reorganized the treasury, installed an accounting bureau to keep track of expenditures, ended the last of the colonial taxes, and increased taxes on real estate. He raised the low salaries of government workers and carried out a reorganization of the military forces. Answering the need for internal improvements, he launched a program of public construction of needed government buildings and constructed highways, railroads, and bridges in various regions of Chile. In the field of education he founded a Pedagogic Institute to train teachers. By 1890 Chile provided education in the *liceos,* secondary schools for both boys and girls, for some 80,000 students. Supplementing the educational program, Balmaceda fostered the founding of libraries, museums, and other centers of public enlightenment. He began for the first time in the history of Chile a health program for the benefit of the working class, the need of which was evident in the fact that Chile at that time had the world's highest tuberculosis rate.

These reforms, covering the first five years of Balmaceda's administration, stirred the antagonism of the traditional Conservative-Clerical party. Too, Balmaceda, somewhat high-handed in his methods, alienated many of his Radical supporters. The Liberal and Nationalist parties on their part, made up of businessmen, opposed the benefits extended to the laboring classes. By 1890 Balmaceda had lost his majority in congress, while his supporters were principally those he had appointed to office and the voiceless working classes. His antagonistic congress attempted to force ministers of its choice upon him, whom he accepted for a time. But eventually he appointed his own cabinet without reference to congress, an action which was denounced as unconstitutional, but which in reality only violated a custom hallowed by time. Defeated at this point, congress in 1890 took a more serious step, a refusal to pass the budget submitted for the year 1891 until Balmaceda removed his principal appointees, particularly the intendants of the provinces. In reply Balmaceda, by a decree issued in January, 1891, declared the budget of 1890 in force for the collection of taxes. This action, clearly unconstitutional, provided the senatorial party the excuse it needed to launch a revolution.

The Revolution of 1891. On January 7 on its own initiative Congress declared the president deposed and organized a junta to govern, at the head of which they placed Jorge Montt, a naval officer. Uncertain of the army, for too many of the soldiers' families had benefited by Balmaceda's reforms, the leaders of the Congressional party, as it now called itself, sailed with the navy to the north to seize control of the nitrate fields, the principal source of income of the government. Landing at Iquíque, they established their capital, negotiated credits through British bankers in return for concessions to nitrate deposits, and sent a ship to the United States for military supplies. The mission of this vessel, the *Itata*, proved fruitless, but provoked an incident in the relations of the United States and Chile.

Lacking an army to conduct the war, the Congressional party relied upon Chilean sailors in the coming struggle with Balmaceda. The latter, badly handicapped from lack of funds, raised volunteer militia organizations and secured some support from the Chilean army. In August, 1891, after long, bitterly fought battles between the two forces, Balmaceda's generals suffered defeat. With the country thrown open to the Congressional army, Valparaíso and Santiago, citadels of Balmaceda support, were ruthlessly sacked. Elsewhere the president's followers were quickly driven from power. He himself, despondent over the loss of life and the defeat of his program, took refuge in the Argentine embassy where he committed suicide, but left a moving message that bespoke his faith in the ultimate triumph in Chile of the ideals he held.

The Revolution of 1891 ended for almost thirty years any effective democratic reforms in Chile. While the Congressional party claimed they had ended a threat to parliamentary government, they had, in fact, but preserved the autocratic power of an oligarchy, guaranteed under the constitution of 1833. Congress, once in control of the country, immediately enacted legislation to make impossible in the future independent action on the part of a president such as had characterized Balmaceda's. This legislation divided Chile for electoral purposes into a large number of small jurisdictions within which communal councils exercised control over voting lists and the naming of candidates for communal, provincial, and national offices. Such jurisdictions were called autonomous communes. The significance of this reorganization was simply that the majority of the communes fell within the rural areas, so that the more progressive urban populations could never elect more than a small percentage of the members of the national congress. The effect of this legislation was theoretically to give the communes certain duties, such as the extension of education, beautification of towns, support of police forces, and the encouragement of industry based upon congressional appropriations. In actual fact the members of the communal councils were political representatives of senators and deputies who used the power of the communes to control voting lists to ensure their own election and that of their candidates to local offices.

As a result of this legislation political struggles between 1891 and 1920 became contests between members of the wealthier families, whose principal weapon to win office was to bribe the electorate and secure control of the communal voting lists. Thus the cost of being elected to the Chilean lower house ranged as high as 100,000 pesos; that of senator required several times that amount. This practice of purchasing votes had pernicious effects. In most communes those who got on the voting lists had such a low standard of living that the sale of the vote became an important addition to their incomes. Many necessities for the family could be purchased at such times. When some thirty years later labor unions took the lead in the political education of the Chilean people, this practice of selling one's vote and the distribution of free liquor on election day were among the most serious obstacles to making democracy work in Chile.

Under this new organization of the Chilean political system, the upper level, broadly speaking, fell into two political groups. One was conservative, made up of landowners and the wealthier members of the middle class, the Liberal-Conservative alliance; the other, composed of Radical and doctrinaire liberals, included the remnants of the democratic groups of the earlier period. Since no one party could command a majority, the government was carried on by combinations of parties working together. Thus by bargaining they selected a president who was naturally but a figurehead. As before 1891, the president made a practice of selecting his cabinet from the senatorial cliques which had brought about his election. Thus between 1891 and 1920 there were no presidents of outstanding importance; one president so selected was so aged that he invariably slept through all cabinet meetings.

Expansion of Chile: Economic and Territorial, 1891–1910. With political control again safely lodged in the hands of the traditional conservative groups, Chile's exports grew by leaps and bounds, an expansion entirely due to the demand of foreign countries' needs for minerals, principally nitrates. By 1891 the bulk of the one hundred companies engaged in nitrate mining were foreign-owned, principally British, whose capital invested reached some $100,000,000. In 1892 a trifle more than 300,000 tons of nitrates were exported; 1896 saw a total of slightly more than 1,000,000 tons. Ten years later nitrate exports passed 11,600,000 tons. In addition to the nitrate production, there were about 12,000 mines producing copper, gold, silver, lead, iron, coal, and manganese. This prosperous state was reflected in Chile's foreign trade, which amounted to 29,000,000 pesos in 1891, reached over 140,000,000 by 1896, and rose to about 580,000,000 by 1906. Upon this trade the Chilean government levied an export tax, its principal source of revenue. This wealth found some productive use in the construction of harbor facilities and the building of railroads. Two of the most important lines completed by 1914 were the north-south system, some 1,400 miles, through the interior valley from the Atacama Desert to Osorno at the head of the archipelago in the south, and the Trans-Andean railway across the mountains to connect with the Argentine railway system at Mendoza.

Foreign Affairs, 1891–1902. As the valuable copper and other mineral deposits poured forth their wealth, Chile naturally became interested in settling the Andean boundary with her neighbor, Argentina. In these same years, too, Argentina, rapidly expanding westward, was concerned with the vast territory on her western frontier from Bolivia to the Strait of Magellan. Moreover, Argentina's interest was heightened by Chile's success in the War of the Pacific, for the territory gained by the latter from Bolivia in the Atacama region impinged on regions Argentina claimed. Immediately after the signing of the Treaty of Ancón, Chile and Argentina reached an agreement in 1884 which paved the way for a final settlement of the Andean boundary disputes.[1]

Growth of Chilean Labor, 1891–1915. The copper and nitrates areas drew growing numbers of laborers into the mining industry. Wages usually paid in company stores' scrip failed to meet the workers' needs. Mines, moreover, lacked safety devices: workers were exposed to dust, underground explosions, and similar hazards. Around the mines the workers and their families lived in the rudest huts. For labor in the cities conditions were little better, where low wages, inadequate housing, and unsanitary conditions gave rise to periodic epidemics. On the great estates in the interior the *inquilinos* still lived in the squalor characteristic of medieval times. Because of the fantastically high cost of imported manufactured goods, the workers of Chile had no means of purchasing them. Their clothing was of the cheapest quality and shoes were practically unknown among them, while their diet in most parts of the country was beans. Drunkenness was the common escape from their lot.

Out of this environment a labor movement emerged, first given life to by leading nineteenth century liberals, Bilbao, Lastarria, Santiago, Arcos, and others. Bilbao and Arcos sensed the importance of improving the standards of the bulk of the Chilean people, and founded in 1850 the first workers' society, called *La Igualdad* (Equality). Three years later the first workers' mutual benefit society was formed. By 1870 thirteen such groups existed. By 1900 their number had increased to 150, when their status was legalized. The purpose of these early societies was simply to provide, through tiny contributions from their meager wages, a common fund for the members in times of crisis, sickness, and funeral expenses. More important in the long run were the educational programs of the societies, which demanded public libraries, lecturers, night schools, and theaters for the workers. From these germinal centers sprang the movement to organize Chilean labor.

---

[1] For a discussion, see pages 289–290.

Between 1900 and 1915 Labor made rapid headway. Its principal organizing centers were in Valparaíso among the dock workers, in Santiago in various urban industries, and in Antofagasta, the heart of the nitrate area, among the miners. Their demands at first consisted in calling for higher wages and cheaper food. In Santiago in 1905 a major event in the history of unionization was the formation of a committee to protest the high cost of meat in particular, and to petition the government against a proposed tariff on Argentine beef, a law proposed by Chilean cattle growers to maintain high prices. This was one of the first steps taken by labor to enter into the discussion of political questions. When in 1906 the great earthquake of that year brought widespread suffering, especially in Valparaíso, where more than 60,000 people had to flee the city, new attempts to form unions made rapid progress, but strikes were put down with severe reprisals. In this same year the movement to form unions in the nitrate region and call strikes to raise wages and improve housing likewise met with harsh suppression. Out of the bitterness engendered among labor the unions tended to become more and more Marxian in outlook, a fact that had significance in Chile's later history.

By 1909 the labor movement had a sufficiently broad national basis to organize a central union, called the Workers' Federation of Chile (FOCh). The Federation, combining many separate organizations throughout the country, popularized the idea of unionization. Out of its work came powerful and influential leaders, among whom was Luis Emilio Recabarren, who spread socialist and democratic ideas throughout Chile by means of the Socialist Workers' party, which was founded largely through his influence in 1912. By this date the Federation had greatly broadened its demands for the improvement of working conditions in Chile. It called for laws providing compensation for workers in case of sickness; life and unemployment insurance; a fund for widows and orphans; the establishment of consumers' and producers' cooperatives; and a savings and credit bank. In addition the Federation carried on a vigorous temperance campaign among the workers to educate them to the importance of their vote and to avoid the consumption of alcoholic drinks, particularly during elections. The Federation also fought against the establishment of saloons in mining towns, which absorbed the hard-earned wages of the workers. It was unending in its demands for schools for the workers' children. This early action of the Federation, carried on consistently in the succeeding years, was one of the important reasons for the political revolution in the early 1920's.

World War I. World War I arrived in Chile amidst its rapidly expanding mineral production and the growing restlessness of its labor. The war stimulated to even greater heights the production of minerals, and also brought increasing demands for political reforms. The events of the war that touched Chile had, of course, their contemporary significance, but simultaneously were harbingers of future closer associations of Chile with world affairs. As in all other Latin-American countries, the war forced Chile to declare its position, which in her case was a prompt neutrality. The Chilean navy was strongly pro-British, for it had been trained by distinguished British seamen in the nineteenth century. The Chilean landowners had long admired British institutions and felt that their national government had a kinship with British parliamentary practices. Chilean labor and its leaders, already conditioned to accept the values of democracy, were strongly pro-Ally. Among all the groups only the German settlers, who had nostalgic feelings for the Fatherland, harbored anti-British sentiments, but were in the main loyal Chileans with traditions of the democratic, revolutionary background of 1848.

Chile's neutrality, however, was early violated. When Japan declared war on Germany in August, 1914, Admiral Count von Spee, commanding the German Asiatic fleet, left for the southern Chilean coast with the cruisers *Nürnburg, Gneisenau,* and *Scharnhorst,* bombarding en route British naval installations in the Southwest Pacific. Joined by the *Dresden* and the *Leipzig* at Easter Island, whose Chilean authorities were still uninformed of the outbreak of the war, von Spee secured needed supplies and continued to his destination, southern Chilean waters, where he hoped to secure supplies of coal. The British, foreseeing this maneuver, ordered Sir Christopher Craddock to pursue the German fleet. His force of three ships proved inadequate and met defeat in the succeeding battle on November 1, 1914, off the coast of Chile. The British thereupon dispatched a much stronger squadron under Admiral Sir Frederick Sturdee. Meanwhile, von Spee, hoping to reach Germany before the arrival of the British, fell into a trap off the Falkland Islands, where he lost all of his cruisers except the *Dresden* and met his death on December 8, 1914. On the following March 14 the British finally drove the *Dresden* ashore on the Chilean island of Juan Fernández, where her crew destroyed her. Chile protested these various violations of her neutrality not only to Germany but to Britain, whose ships had also disregarded her rights.

Of great significance to Chile's future was the opening of the Panama Canal in 1915. This union of the two oceans reduced by more than half the sailing distance between Chile and the Atlantic ports of the United States. This more rapid communication gave new stimulus to Chilean nitrate production, for the United States at that time (1915) was being called upon by the Allies for the production of explosives in which nitrate was an important ingredient. When in 1917 the United States declared war upon Germany, the flow of nitrates increased. So vital to the winning of the war were Chilean nitrates that Bernard Baruch, chairman of the War Industries Board, stated after the war that had the Germans concentrated their submarine attack on nitrate ships on the west coast of South America, both the United States and Britain would have been forced to give up the production of explosives within two weeks.

The opening of the canal also facilitated the growth of American investment in Chilean nitrates and other minerals, for both Britain and Germany were handicapped in meeting the needs of the Chileans for the development of their resources. Outstanding in this expansion of American capital was the $20,000,000 investment of the DuPont chemical industry in the nitrate area. The occasion for this interest arose from the failure of the German government to return, on Chile's request, $20,-000,000 in gold on deposit in Berlin, a refusal which impelled the Chilean government to seize the German nitrate holdings. These in turn were then taken over by the DuPont Company for the amount owed Chile by the German government. The copper mining industry likewise received an impetus in production during the war from the investment of American capital.

The war, with its high demand for minerals, the creation of great wealth for the few, and the continued low standard of living for the workers, inevitably produced demands for reform. Leading the protest in the Chilean senate was Arturo Alessandri, of Italian descent, elected from the nitrate province of Tarapacá. However, movements and demonstrations by workers were suppressed ruthlessly by the president, Juan Luis San Fuentes, elected in 1915 by a conservative coalition. The end of the war in 1918 produced disastrous conditions among the bulk of the Chilean people. With the abnormal demand for nitrates and copper cut off by the armistice in November, 1918, the mining industries immediately closed their plants in Chile. The miners, suddenly thrown out of work and left to their own resources, had no alternative but to find their way back, with their wives and children, to the cities of the central valley and coast. But there, too, the unemployed filled the streets. In this crisis the government had no plans except to discharge thousands of employees who joined the ranks of the idle. The picture was further darkened by numerous bankruptcies among the small business houses which depended upon the export trade. Thus the terrible winter of 1918–1919 passed with suffering among the masses of the Chileans sufficient to alter the nation's history. But this change had long been presaged by Chile's writers.

Chilean Literary Development. The first outstanding figure was Andrés Bello, the classicist, who, we have noted, was instrumental in founding the University of Santiago in 1842. The rigid scientific discipline to which he subjected his students turned their minds to a study of Chile's native culture. Later influenced by British and French writers, they became fervent romanticists in the literary vogue sweeping Europe at the time. Fortunately, at the moment the greatest Latin-American romanticist, Sarmiento, was then in exile in Chile. In a famous intellectual battle with Bello, carried on in Santiago's two leading newspapers, Sarmiento attacked his opponent's classicism with ringing demands for liberty, the acceptance of new ideas, and a new literature emancipated from eighteenth century formula.

Sarmiento's most important convert was José Victorino Lastarria (1817–1888). Lastarria opposed the colonial traditions of Chile and the contributions of the Spaniards, whom he characterized as exploiters, their universities as centers of imbecility designed to perpetuate ignorance, and their legal institutions as engines of tyranny. From this sort of heritage Lastarria urged the Chileans to free themselves, adopt forms of government which would guarantee a minimum of interference of the state in the affairs of the individual, forgo the worship of Europe, and recognize that the new teachings of democracy in America would emancipate the spirit of man.

This emphasis upon the importance of the American environment, a characteristic of romanticism in Latin America, found even more emphatic treatment in the work of Lastarria's contemporary, Francisco Bilbao (1823–1865). In his famous essay, "The Nature of Chilean Society," Bilbao concentrated his fire upon the church, but his cry was always for liberty. Elsewhere in his writings, contrasting Latin America with the great republic in the north, he called the former the Disunited Spanish States while the latter was properly named the United States of America. She deserved such a title, Bilbao insisted, because her traditions had been those of freedom. The United States, he stated, was not only rich and progressive, it was a great creative nation, testified to by its political thought and its literature. That Bilbao was touching a chord of sympathy among many contemporaries was apparent later in the extraordinary influence of Walt Whitman upon Latin-American literature.

By the end of the century the romantic movement had produced Chilean poets, writers, and thinkers who had thoroughly explored their native scene. The movement in this respect opened the way for realistic writers who probed the depths of Chilean society. The greatest Chilean realist in the field of the novel was Alberto Blest Gana (1830–1920). Of him one authority wrote: ". . . to understand the formation of the aristocracy, the middle class, and the lower class in Chile, to observe how the government functioned . . . to witness popular action and popular speech at close range, one need only turn to the novels of this conscientious realist. . ." (Torres-Rioseco). His masterpiece, *Martín Rivas*, portrays the society of Chile from every conceivable point of view, the liberal-conservative struggle, political corruption, the *rotos* (urban proletariat), the middle and upper classes. On a smaller scale a contemporary writer, Joaquín Edwards Bello, in his novel *El Roto*, has continued the portrayal of life in Chile's cities, emphasizing especially the degradation and suffering of the poorer classes. In so doing he has contributed to the growth of social consciousness among Chileans expressed in their modern programs of reform.

But outstanding in the galaxy of poets and writers after World War I is a woman, a poet, Gabriela Mistral (1889–   ). Today she is acclaimed by all Latin Americans, and, indeed, by the world, as evidenced by Sweden awarding her the Nobel Prize for Literature in 1945. Born in humble circumstances, she knew sorrow from an early age and saw deeply into the unhappy life of her people. She early plunged into a great educational work, made possible by the political revolution after 1920. Her own country recognized her merit and favored her with high position, as did the League of Nations and later the United Nations. Her poetry reflects her own sorrow welded with that of her fellow man. Her deep compassion for humanity gives her poems a universal appeal, whether she voices hope for a corrupt world, sympathy for the unwed mother, or pity for the victims of tyrannies preceding this century's second holocaust. She played an active part in Chile's political struggles after 1920 and had much to do with establishing its modern educational system and winning recognition for the rights of women and children.

Part II. GROWTH OF DEMOCRATIC INSTITUTIONS AND INDUSTRIAL EXPANSION, 1925–1956

The Campaign of 1920. With the campaign of 1920 a basic change in Chile's political evolution began which culminated in the constitution of 1925. The severity of the depression after World War I brought labor, intellectuals, and small businessmen behind the candidacy of Alessandri. Supported by the Socialist, Liberal, and other parties advocating change, they nominated him under the banner of the Liberal Alliance party created in the stress of the struggle. Seemingly unaware of the fundamental changes produced by World War I upon the economy of Chile, the conservative parties grouped themselves into a National Union to name in the traditional manner Luis Barros Borgoño. In control of the election machinery, the conservative government seemed confident of the outcome.

Alessandri, however, launched for the first time in Chilean history a campaign tour that took him into every part of the nation. A remarkable orator, he made real the need of electoral reform and the nature of the fundamental issues of the election: a more representative government, land reform, establishment of native manufacturing industries, improvement of labor's condition, and a national health program. His fiery and passionate appeal stirred even for the Liberal Alliance an unexpected response. The returns after the election showed that Alessandri had a bare majority of the electoral vote. To protect the victory which the conservatives proposed to set aside, Alessandri's supporters organized protest meetings in cities and towns and called strikes in the principal industries. At the same time thousands of workers began a march on Santiago. A Tribunal of Honor, used to decide presidential elections in the past, found fraud on both sides, but with vast throngs menacing the capital city, the Tribunal wisely decided that Alessandri had won the election.

The Administration of Alessandri, 1920–1925. When Alessandri took office in 1920, several factors contributed to the temporary defeat of his reform program. He began his administration under conditions of depression following World War I. At the same time the conservative groups were confident they could block in the senate, still under their control, the administration's first reform legislation, a labor code. This bill provided for reducing working hours, legalized unions and their right to organize, provided for cooperatives and collective bargaining, forbade child labor, established regulations governing working conditions in factories for women, called for safety devices in mines and other industries, and furnished insurance for old age and against accidents and sickness. To block its enactment, the conservatives proposed a general labor law in which compulsory industrial unions were to be formed, directed by employers but containing other provisions more liberal than those proposed by the government. The two bills split the supporters of Alessandri's program, for the representatives of the lower middle class tended to support the senatorial proposal.

The failure of his legislation impelled Alessandri to campaign again throughout the country in the congressional elections of 1924 to get a congress to support him. While he found widespread support, he was forced to recognize that the bulk of the autonomous communes located in the interior rural areas were still in control of the senatorial oligarchy. Taking a leaf from their book, he used force to win the election. His followers broke up political meetings of the opposition, while the army and police patrolled the booths to ensure the election of his candidates.

The 1924 congress was pro-Alessandri, but composed of men largely inexperienced in politics, a natural state of affairs since the bulk of the Chileans had always been excluded from participation in government. Many had given up their work to become candidates for congress, so that, when elected, one of their first acts was to pass legislation providing salaries for members of congress. The action was immediately attacked by the conservatives in their newspapers, whose arguments seemed to be logical since the government was behind in its payment of salaries to the army, schoolteachers, and other public servants.

A second piece of proposed legislation, presented by petition, also came under fire, namely, a reform in the army providing for higher salaries for officers in the lower ranks and for a better system of promotion. Violently opposed by the conservatives and the higher-ranking officers of the armed forces, Alessandri sought to win their support by inviting a military leader, General Luis Altamirano, to form a cabinet composed of military officers. When his cabinet refused to support the proposed reforms, Alessandri resorted to a drastic expedient, common in Latin-American countries to draw national attention to a basic problem. He tendered his resignation as president and went into voluntary exile in September, 1924.

The Constitution of 1925. Upon Alessandri's departure the government passed into the hands of a military junta, headed by General Altamirano, one of two generals, and an admiral. It immediately began to destroy the political basis of Alessandri's support by turning out of office his appointees and overthrowing the municipal assembles controlled by Alessandri's party. On the other hand, it failed to meet the demands of the younger officers for pay increases and liberalizing promotions. The latter thereupon, led by Major Carlos Ibáñez and Major Marmaduke Grove, sought an understanding with the followers of Alessandri, who at the moment were about to launch a series of strikes, demonstrations, and political meetings against the government. The two groups combined, with Grove and Ibáñez at their head, overthrew the junta by military force, and established a new junta with themselves in control. Their first action was to invite Alessandri to return to Chile.

Promptly accepting the invitation, Alessandri was received upon his arrival by vast, cheering crowds. Upon again assuming the presidency on March 20, 1925, he took vigorous measures to prevent a counter-revolution. Outstanding was his banishment of conservative political leaders and the retirement of twenty-six generals and nineteen colonels. This action opened the way for the promotion of the younger army officers including Ibáñez and Grove. He also decreed an increase in the pay of the army as well as that for civil employees of the government.

But the most important step taken by Alessandri was to call for the writing of a new constitution, a task in which representatives of the major political parties, business, and labor participated. This document ended the power of the conservative-clerical oligarchy which had dominated Chilean history since 1833, and prepared the way for a fuller development of democratic institutions. The most important provision altering the seat of power was the transfer from the senate to the House of Deputies of the control over the budget. In effect the president had the authority to prepare the budget, which had to become law after four months, but during this time Congress could make changes. Another provision of the document forbade the use of appropriations for the support of political machines in the provinces. The constitution gave the provincial assemblies the power by majority vote to govern the provinces, a provision which, taken together with that guaranteeing universal manhood suffrage for all literate Chileans over twenty-one years of age, gave the basis for the development of democratic practices in the provinces. Although the vote was not extended to women at this time, later provisions have since enfranchised them, as the normal growth of democratic attitudes demanded.

The presidential office under the constitution was strengthened. As already noted, the president had the authority to prepare the budget, likewise to appoint his own cabinet and the provincial governors, but these were limited by the grant of power to the provincial assemblies. A limitation on his power existed in the provision restricting the president to one term with no immediate re-election. In the provisions establishing the congress, the entire process of democratic procedures was strengthened. Both the members of the house and the senate were directly elected; the former every four years on the basis of the population; half of the latter, five from each province, every eight years. Thus for two-thirds of the congress, elections were mandatory every four years. Besides its power to pass on the budget, congress could impeach ministers and the president and enact legislation. Under the constitution a supreme court and inferior courts were provided whose members the president appointed.

Other provisions of the constitution that were of democratic significance were those providing for a progressive income tax, the first in the history of Chile, the separation of the state and church, the absolute guarantee of freedom of religion, and all individual liberties and rights. The provision separating church and state enabled the state to establish a public school system, for which purpose it took over church school properties, but with generous compensation which included the right of the church to maintain its other properties, exemption from taxation on land and structures used for religious purposes, and a subsidy for five years to cover the period of transition. Finally, the constitution included a provision which placed a restriction upon the ownership of property, the latter being made subject to the "progress of the social order." Thus far the provision has never been enforced or interpreted, but it is believed that it derives from the ideas concerning property in the Mexican constitution of 1917.

The revolution in the political organization of Chile between 1920 and 1925 was essentially a middle class one with the strong support of labor organizations, the majority of which espoused socialist ideas. In this period, too, out of the desperation of a number of workers during the economic collapse following World War I, the Communist party made its appearance in Chile. Thus when the major step in the revolution was completed with the constitution of 1925, the middle class were anxious to revive markets, develop the resources of the nation, and escape from the continued depression. In this environment emerged, as their spokesman, Carlos Ibáñez, a man with a military background and dictatorial tendencies. After the nation had adopted the constitution by plebiscite, the presidential elections were held with Ibáñez, minister of war in Alessandri's cabinet, a candidate. Upon Alessandri's request to resign from his cabinet position, Ibáñez refused. Rather than risk a civil war and the possible loss of the hard-won gains, Alessandri himself resigned and turned the government over to his minister of the interior, Barros Borgoño, the man he had defeated in 1920. The conservatives put forward as their candidate Emiliano Figueroa Larraín, while Alessandri's supporters, principally labor, turned to Dr. José Santos Salas. Figueroa won easily, with Alessandri's supporters hopelessly split over Ibáñez, to whom labor was antagonistic but whom many small businessmen supported, fearing the growth of labor's influence in the government.

The Dictatorship of Ibáñez, 1925–1931. Figueroa, who became president on December 25, 1925, served until May 4, 1927. Responding to the demands of the middle class now dominant in congress, he launched a program of improving the administration of the government. The principal problem was that of funds, which he attacked by the dubious method of reducing salaries, but he balanced this action by increased taxation on foreign corporations. Too, he secured legislation necessary to overhaul the entire administrative apparatus. While he himself did little in this direction, his successor, Ibáñez, used the law both to make economic reforms and to consolidate his own position as dictator.

As Figueroa's program did not include any measures for advancing the interests of labor, he came under violent attack. Incompetent to meet the assault, he turned to Ibáñez, whom he appointed minister of the interior, virtually premier, who lost no time in accepting the challenge. To crush opposition to his program, Ibáñez, now supported by the army, which was contented with higher pay, jailed and drove into exile intellectuals and leaders of the Socialist and democratic parties and even threatened Alessandri, who, however, refused to leave the country. Ibáñez likewise exiled political leaders and editors of conservative newspapers, representatives of the oligarchy which hoped to work itself back into power, including even the chief justice of the supreme court, the brother of President Figueroa.

With the ground cleared, Ibáñez made reforms in the judiciary and in the ministry of finance, to both of which he brought more efficient administration. To control congress he utilized a provision of the constitution permitting the head of the state to appoint members of that body. Figueroa, having no capacity to resist these measures, quietly resigned. In an election in the nature of a plebiscite, Ibáñez was almost unanimously elected on May 22, 1927. However, the main problem was still ahead of him, that of rescuing Chile from the continued depression. One of the principal reasons for this condition was the steady decline of copper and nitrate exports, the chief source, some 80 per cent, of the government's income and the prosperity of the middle class, whose businesses were linked with the export trade. The loss of markets largely stemmed from the successful development of synthetic nitrates by both Germany and England during World War I. Thus from supplying 55 per cent of the world nitrate demand in 1923, the figure stood at 23 per cent by 1929. Four years later, with the added effects of the 1929 depression, the figure fell to an all-time low of 4 per cent. The unemployment attaching to the collapse of the nitrate industry steadily increased to become a major problem facing Ibáñez.

To meet the problem, Ibáñez launched a comprehensive program of public works. The cities of Chile secured an American loan of some $15,000,000 to inaugurate municipal improvements. Under the impetus of this expansion, harbors and docks were improved, railroads built, dams and canals constructed, to aid agriculture. These did much to absorb the unemployed. More significant in the long run, however, were the colonization law and educational law of 1928. Under the former the Ibáñez government endeavored to reduce the number of unemployed and to encourage the growth of small landholding. How serious the lack of the latter was is seen in the fact that some 548 families held more than 62 per cent of the land. The government had no intention of breaking up these old estates; rather the colonization law provided for the purchase of estates where the owner was willing to sell and for carving out of the national domain small parcels of land for those willing to farm. The legislation further provided aid to farmers in the form of rural agricultural cooperatives, credit banks, tools, warehouses, and a rural school system.

The educational law of 1928 was a landmark in the development of Chilean democracy. It expressed the need both of the expanding middle class for a trained personnel necessary for businessmen and of labor for the education of its children. Under this law the University of Santiago received autonomy and separation from politics by conferring the power to govern that institution upon the faculty and administrators. Too, the law decentralized higher education so that other universities were not hampered in their growth by restrictions put upon them by a single national institution. Secondary and primary schools were so organized under the law that their programs would have some relation to one another. Moreover, the curricula of the lower schools were broadened to provide a wide basis for technological and trade schools as well as training in the arts and crafts. Certain schools continued to provide the necessary courses leading to study in the higher institutions. The law provided specifically, too, for vocational and technical schools and professional institutes, such as those for engineering, public health, nursing, music, and the fine arts. Running through the whole system was provision for the training of teachers abroad, particularly in the United States. At this time, 1928 and in subsequent years, many Chileans, studying under John Dewey, who was revolutionizing American educational methods, introduced his ideas into the Chilean educational system.

While not organically connected with the school program, the educational law and the colonization law of 1928 provided for a broad system of rural schools. The laws took note of the fact that the high rate of illiteracy and lack of knowledge concerning health, agricultural techniques, and modern methods of cattle raising required rural schools to provide the elementary basis in these practical matters as well as attacking illiteracy.

The Overthrow of the Ibáñez Dictatorship, 1931. The Ibáñez dictatorship began to crumble as the effects of the 1929 depression took hold in Chile. The loans upon which the dictatorship rested were no longer available after the New York stock market crash of October, 1929. The collapse of nitrate and other mineral exports became catastrophic. British and American nitrate companies proposed in the crisis to pool their production with that of the Chilean-controlled fields, hoping in this way to compete with the German I. G. Farben monopoly of synthetic nitrates. A company, *Cosach,* formed for this purpose, failed, however, to bring I. G. Farben to terms and collapsed. This event was the deciding factor in the overthrow of the dictatorship.

Faced by widespread unemployment, the populace in the larger cities demonstrated against Ibáñez, who adopted autocratic measures to suppress the criticism. Forced to economize, he discharged thousands of government employees, an action which added to the unemployed ranks, and tried to raise money by increased taxation. The crisis came in July, 1931, when students of the University of Santiago revolted. The uprising had popular support, not only of unemployed labor through its unions, but of doctors, engineers, lawyers, and other white-collar groups. In other cities similar outbreaks took place. On July 25 Ibáñez bowed to the inevitable, resigned, and fled to Buenos Aires.

The Dávila Regime, June–September, 1931. Between Ibáñez' flight and Alessandri's election to the presidency for a second time in October, 1932, Chile was plunged into violent civil conflict. A naval revolt, in which army airplanes bombed the fleet at Valparaíso, was put down early in September, 1931. Against the election of an archconservative to the presidency, Montero Rodríguez, in October, city riots in which the Communist party took a leading part occurred. In April, 1932, the president's declaration of martial law led to a successful revolt which overthrew the government. Leading this movement was Carlos G. Dávila, who assumed the office of president until elections could be held. Behind Dávila were the Chilean labor unions, the Socialist party, and liberal groups toward whom he turned to give a socialist basis to his government.

Dávila encountered strong opposition and after a few months was ousted from the presidency, but he succeeded in creating a group of corporations out of which emerged one of great significance for the future of Chile. This organization, later called the Chilean Development Corporation, envisaged a broad program for the development of Chilean resources with government support. Dávila, overthrown by a conservative revolt, had no time to put his plans into operation. However, when elections were held on December 24, 1932, Arturo Alessandri was again chosen as president with promises to effect reforms, some socialist and others, economic and financial, demanded by his lower middle class supporters.

The Administration of Alessandri, 1932–1938. Alessandri faced the same fundamental problems which had overthrown Ibáñez, namely, unemployment, loss of foreign markets, decline of government income, and rising political movements, which were both radical and ultraconservative. The new president vigorously attacked these problems. Recognizing that foreign loans were impossible to negotiate, the government turned to Chilean businessmen. From the *Banco Central*, Alessandri secured a large loan, reduced the emission of government paper money except that necessary to stimulate native industries, and used the funds to subsidize native business undertakings. Confident in the government's monetary policies, Chilean industrialists and financiers responded to this effort to help themselves. Complementing these economic measures, Alessandri's government negotiated commercial treaties with foreign countries to open up markets for Chile's products. Thus between 1932 and 1937, while imports doubled in value, exports expanded more than fourfold. Foreign investors, particularly American, encouraged by the stability of the country, increased their own investments. By 1936 direct American investments in Chile in manufacturing concerns, distribution agencies, mining and smelting, public utilities, transportation, and various miscellaneous industries totaled about $484,000,000, with four-fifths in copper and nitrates.

Naturally, Alessandri did not neglect to encourage the growth of labor unions and to protect them in such matters as schooling and health. He launched a vast school building program for rural and urban elementary schools, low cost housing construction, and extension of water and sewerage services, so that all towns of 5,000 inhabitants had drinking water and towns of 10,000 had both drinking water and sewerage. This work was supplemented by the Social Welfare Bureau of the Ministry of Public Health, which directed thirty-nine different funds whose total assets amounted to approximately 1,740,000 pesos. These agencies engaged in a variety of activities, such as increasing milk production by preventing the export of milch cows, inspecting canning factories and food stores, supporting campaigns of the brucellosis and cancer commissions, providing in 1937 almost 2,000,000 medical treatments paid for by low cost insurance, and insuring through the Workers' Social Security Fund all children under two years of age. Employment for workers was found in the various building programs noted above, as well as in the construction of highways, bridges, and municipal buildings, extension of the railroad system, and various constructive activities in rural areas and in both native Chilean industries and those foreign companies engaged principally in mining. Other workers and immigrants who wished to farm were supported by the Agrarian Colonization Fund, which by 1938 had divided and established some 2,000 families upon more than 1,000,000 acres in the various provinces of Chile.

While these admirable measures were going forward to place a sound economic base under Chile's developing democracy, the political struggle assumed a violent character. The traditional conservative groups looked upon Alessandri's measures as nothing short of socialism, while the more aggressive labor groups were dissatisfied that not more was being done. But this more or less normal difference of political opinion was sharpened by world events. With Hitler's rise to power in Germany in 1933, German embassies and consulates throughout the world became centers for the distribution of Nazi propaganda and organizing activities. In Chile under a native leader, González von Marees, a National Socialist movement was founded. It followed all the techniques of Germany in attacking democratic parties in Chile. But Chilean democratic leaders, intellectuals, and labor unions, treasuring highly their hard-won victories since 1920, did not hesitate to meet the challenge. At the same time the Communist party, established in Chile in the early 1920's, followed its line at that time and associated itself with the democratic groups.

Under the impetus of the growing menace of the Chilean Nazi

movement, Chilean labor organizations supported demands for strengthening her democratic tradition. Chief among those enacted into law in 1937 was the extension of municipal suffrage to women, many of whom were active members of the unions. Of more importance in meeting the direct attack of the Nazis was the decision of the three most powerful labor organizations to combine into one. This objective, achieved in a labor congress in 1936, brought about the Confederation of Workers of Chile, which has become one of the most powerful independent labor groups in South America. By 1940 it had affiliated with it some 1,200 unions with a total membership of about 400,000.

The labor unions and the various democratic parties, sensing the possibility of a Nazi putsch, organized a Popular Front in 1936. This new political group, however, had more than just the negative purpose of defeating the Nazi element; it proposed a continuation of the reform program which had been launched with the enactment of the Constitution of 1925. Its platform consisted of higher taxation upon foreign corporations and church properties to lessen Chile's dependence upon the unstable mineral exports. The more radical groups within the front secured a plank calling for the nationalization of Chile's mineral deposits. The program included further minimum wage legislation, requiring foreign corporations to employ Chilean labor, skilled, unskilled, and technical, to the extent of 95 per cent of its personnel. It also supported the extension of the public school system and the continuation of the government's health program into the rural areas. For its leader it nominated the head of the Radical party, a member of the Front, Dr. Pedro Aguirre Cerda, long interested in public health questions. The conservative forces chose Gustavo Ross, minister of finance in Alessandri's cabinet. In spite of disturbances preceding the election, it was carried out peaceably with Aguirre Cerda the successful candidate.

Alessandri's administration until the following December 5, 1938, when Aguirre Cerda was inaugurated, stands out not only for its program of improving schools, health, and the economic life of Chile, but resisting successfully the antidemocratic trends that manifested themselves as a result of the 1929 depression. The election of 1938 had its significance in establishing that Chile, like Brazil, but unlike Argentina, had a definite orientation in the direction of democratic development on the eve of World War II. The succeeding administration and that war strengthened this trend.

The Administration of Aguirre Cerda, 1938–1941. Hardly had Aguirre Cerda assumed office when Chile suffered a devastating earthquake damaging Concepción and almost leveling Chillán in the south. Dead and wounded ran into the thousands, with almost 100,000 left homeless, while property damage reached some $50,000,000. Straining the resources of the country to meet the emergency, Aguirre Cerda revived the idea of Carlos Dávila to create, with the cooperation of all groups, the Chilean Development Corporation. Set up in April, 1939, its rapid mobilization of funds, supplies, and medicine did much to relieve the earthquake sufferers. Thereafter it became a major agency of the government designed to promote projects too large for the limited capital of native investors in mining, agriculture, industrial development, and electrification. Organized on a broad basis, its council included representatives of the president, congress, organized labor, and private and semiprivate bodies.

The Aguirre Cerda program for Chile was stated simply by the president himself to include directing the government's activities toward those matters considered fundamental for national progress. In domestic affairs the president's policies envisaged a vast internal development. He secured legislation to protect industry from foreign competition and to develop agriculture, the cattle industry, and the production of wine. His administration gave aid to large and small cooperatives, launched a program of low-cost housing, and instituted a system of credit for purchasers. In the field of public health the administration began a chain of state-supported people's restaurants in leading cities where low-paid salaried workers and laborers could secure well-balanced meals at minimum prices. Other social measures included facilities for the care of poor mothers and children, offering them the necessary food and medical treatment as well as instruction to secure a healthy development of the children.

For agriculture the government established a Farm Credit Bank, which extended long-term, low interest loans to aid farmers in buying tools and livestock and planting fruit trees and stands of timber. Other assistance included aid for control of insect diseases, experiment stations, and information regarding new varieties of cereals suitable for various soils. In the urban areas the administration supported the formation of unions, industrial and professional, out of which came a remarkable growth: some 888 unions in two years, a number that almost equaled the 925 established in the years between 1925 and 1938. Located in urban centers, the labor organizations took the lead in demanding similar rights for rural workers in an effort to raise their standard of living.

Aguirre Cerda did much to expand the public school system. Between 1921 and 1938 the population of Chile grew by 22 per cent, while school facilities increased only 12 per cent. Between 1939 and 1942 the administration began an extensive school building program, primary and industrial in particular. Primary attendance reached 415,624, the greatest in the history of the country, but more than 300,000 children of school age still failed to attend for reasons of poverty, isolation, lack of buildings, and lack of teachers. Significant for breadth of view was the government program to use the schools as means of combating the high death rate among children under sixteen years of age—about 55,000 died in 1937 in this age group out of 109,000. To meet the problem, the state provided free medical and dental care, furnished clothing, and in 1941 provided 15,000,000 breakfasts and 11,000,000 lunches.

In an effort to aid the economy as a whole, the Aguirre Cerda administration began bridge and highway construction to extend Chile's 24,855 miles of roads and develop her inland waterways. In the far south in Aysén province the government launched a colonization program to settle families on an estimated 10,000,000 acres. Beyond Aysén in Magallanes province more than 500,000 acres were surveyed for colonization and in a search for oil deposits believed to exist there. Aiding all these aspects of Chilean growth were the activities of the Chilean Development Corporation. In these years it spent 66,000,000 pesos on low-cost urban housing, and invested funds to aid national production of automobile tires and electrical goods as well as to import raw materials for medicinal preparations. To support these projects and others connected with industry and agriculture, the Export-Import Bank of the United States extended a loan of $12,000,000.

The Administration of Ríos and World War II, 1941–1946. Overwork and ill health brought a lamentably early death to Aguirre Cerda on November 25, 1941. By this date the Popular Front which had elected him had dissolved from internal conflicts, out of which emerged the Radical party as the most powerful single political group. After a spirited contest between Juan Antonio Ríos and Gabriel González Videla, the former won the presidential nomination to be elected president in February, 1942. When Ríos took over the office, Chile had already been adversely affected by her loss of markets. But the sturdy democracy of the country demanded whole-hearted cooperation with the Allies. In January, 1942, she broke relations with the Axis and on February 12, 1945, declared a state of belligerency which culminated in her policy of extending every assistance to the United Nations' war struggle. Characteristic were her actions in placing her copper and nitrate reserves at the disposal of the United States, expropriation of Axis nationals' property, and extension of nonbelligerent status to all American powers at war with the Axis.

The loss of her markets forced upon Chile a comprehensive internal program to cushion the shock of the war, essentially a continuation of the Aguirre Cerda expansion. To open new markets between 1940 and 1943, Chile negotiated commercial agreements and treaties with Peru, Bolivia, Brazil, Colombia, the United States, and others designed to strengthen the security of the continent. Significant was the opening of negotiations to reach a customs union with Argentina to serve as a model for similar agreements with Peru and Bolivia.

Internally, to offset the declining export market, the Ríos government began diversifying the economy with a Five Year Plan to expand fisheries, survey forests, and add to the industrial potential. In the latter respect the Chilean Development Corporation had made possible by 1944 the beginning of electrification in rural and industrial areas and the expansion of steel industries at Concepción and Valdivia, and aided the increase of production of coal, copper, and cement plants. A six-year public works program included aid to railroads, highway construction, inland waterway projects, and harbor improvements, financed largely by taxes on copper production. Buttressing these varied undertakings was a $5,000,000 loan from the United States devoted also to building sewage disposal plants, water systems, low-cost housing, hospital construction, and sanatoriums.

For agriculture the government drew up an agrarian plan, the first in the country's history, with 500,000,000 pesos to support it. It envisaged cultivating more than 1,000,000 new acres for small farms, irrigation works, expansion of rural road systems, wide use of farm machinery, and aid in meat packing, milling, truck gardening, vineyards, and construction of warehouses and elevators. By 1945 the plan was showing results in increased wheat, rice, barley, and oat production. An important feature of the work was in Aysén, where colonists, largely native Indians, were settling on lands provided under the previous administration.

The social side of the economy was not forgotten. The government continued expanding the school system, so that primary attendance had reached by 1945 almost 500,000 children; secondary schools enrolled, however, but 55,000. Significantly for the future progress of Chile, the bulk of the increase took place in the rural areas, while new emphasis was given to reducing adult illiteracy in urban centers with night schools, civic programs, and individual efforts.

The Administration of González Videla, 1946–1952. Like Aguirre Cerda, the burdens of office were too much for the frail health of Ríos who, becoming ill, died in 1945, leaving Alfredo Duhalde as acting president. The shortages caused by the war, inflation, and the funds expended in the heavy construction program brought on a huge national deficit. Efforts by the Ríos administration to meet new costs by imposing taxes were avoided by the wealthy, so that the burden fell upon the lower income groups, particularly labor. These issues dominated when the campaign for the presidency arrived. Gabriel González Videla stood out among all the candidates, with the support of the traditional Radical party as well as the Authentic Socialist and the Communist parties. Splits among the conservative groups assured his election and he took office on November 4, 1946. Recognizing the varied groups who supported him, the president began his administration with a fusion government of Radicals, Liberals, Independents, and Communists, the latter holding, in fact, three of the cabinet positions.

The González Videla administration was characterized by continuation of industrialization and by sharp political conflicts. The latter arose from the struggles of labor to improve its condition and from the policies of the Communist party in the face of the cold war and the Korean conflict. The program of industrialization, supported by loans from the Chilean Development Corporation, was further buttressed by the considerable accumulation of wealth from World War II in the hands of the middle class. It envisaged a huge electrification plan, oil exploration, construction of refineries, farm mechanization, improvement of livestock, reforestation, expansion of the fishing industries, and, capping the whole effort, new steel mills.

An ambitious feature was the expansion of the steel industry. With aid from the Export-Import Bank, the government itself, and patriotic citizens, Chile built an integrated steel plant at Huachipato, near Concepción. Its production of pig iron, ingot steel, and finished steel by 1950 was meeting the bulk of Chile's needs. The plant, too, became the basis for establishing other industries near-by. With their steel mill in operation, Chileans believed that their industrial revolution was well under way. The truth of this outlook seemed supported by the building of the El Abanico hydroelectric plant in 1948, one of the largest in South America, and the construction that was begun to link the Argentine-Chilean railroads near Temuco with the Argentine line crossing the latter country to Bahía Blanca. Similarly, port improvements at Valparaíso and Arica, as well as expanding San Vicente, a port to serve as an outlet for the steel of Huachipato, went forward. In the far south oil discoveries in 1946 gave Tierra del Fuego a new importance expressed in a nationalistic proposal in Congress in 1950 to reserve all Chilean oil deposits to the government. In this picture of basic raw materials, coal deposits recently opened near Aruco in the south indicate that Chile has the largest deposits of this mineral in South America.

Seeking new sources of raw materials, particularly oil and uranium, Chile advanced her claims to Antarctica. There she took possession of an area reaching to the South Pole and extending from fifty degrees to ninety degrees west longitude. Her claims, however, sharply conflicted with both those of Argentina and Britain to the same region. Nevertheless, in 1948 she established a base on Palmer peninsula, renaming it O'Higgins Land.

The expanding economy of Chile demanded, too, new markets for her goods and new sources of supplies. While refusing to entertain the idea of a Latin-American economic bloc, González Videla did propose that Chile negotiate treaties with other Latin-American countries "that would reflect a Pan-American thought of economic unity in hemisphere coordination of the Americas' economic well-being, each nation helping others while helping itself" to attain economic interdependence. To this end Chile exchanged wheat and rice for Peruvian sugar; with Brazil she traded nitrates and copper for coffee and *yerba maté*. The president met opposition, however, when he proposed to give Bolivia a corridor ten kilometers wide through the deserts of Antofagasta in exchange for use of the waters of Lake Titicaca, Poopó, and Coypasa for desert irrigation and development of hydroelectric power. With Argentina, González Videla also began negotiations for trade agreements which came to fruition in the administration of his successor, Ibáñez. Other commercial treaties were concluded with West Germany, Japan, Britain, and Portugal. With the United States, her most important customer and source of loans, Chile signed the Mutual Assistance Pact in April, 1952, under which she received military supplies and equipment.

The dynamic quality of Chile's expanding economy found reflection in an active political life. The essentially democratic elements, the middle class and labor, had long established their parties: Radical, Socialist Liberal, and Democratic, with the Radical party dominant in numbers. Carlos Ibáñez created in 1949 an Agrarian-Labor party; and in the following year the Falangist party, radical in outlook and in no way related to the Spanish Falange, appeared. The Communist party, in existence since the 1920's but weak in numbers, was outlawed in 1948. The traditional landed oligarchy, the church, and the upper echelons of the military found representation in the Conservative party.

The political struggles of the González Videla administration arose from conflicts sharpened by the efforts to industrialize Chile in the face of declining employment resulting from the ending of World War II. The spending of huge sums for launching steel and other industries while imposing restrictions upon foreign imported goods contributed to a serious inflation. The resulting high cost of living adversely affected labor and white-collar workers. The Conservative party was opposed to the program of industrialization and feared too the growing power of labor, which actively campaigned for the unionization of rural workers on the estates of the oligarchy.

Reflecting the wide dissatisfaction arising from inflation and consequent suffering, the Communists in 1947 elected a large number of aldermen in many Chilean cities, four governors, four senators, and fifteen deputies to the national congress. Also, Chilean labor launched strikes in nitrate, coal, and copper mines, in the ports, and on the bus lines of Santiago. In many of the unions Communists were strong. In congress the Communist representatives tried to secure legislation to unionize the rural workers, and in this effort had the support of other representatives from urban areas. Congress did enact such a law, but the president vetoed it.

In the following year, 1948, with the major strikes temporarily settled, Congress enacted legislation outlawing the Communist party. Other legislation met urgent needs of the industrialists and workers. That the country approved was apparent in the success of the Radical, Liberal, Moderate Democratic, and Socialist parties in the congressional campaigns in winning the bulk of the senate and Chamber of Deputies. Significantly, from Santiago Carlos Ibáñez was elected senator while his Agrarian-Labor party elected fourteen members to the lower house. In the face of this showing González Videla reorganized his cabinet to eliminate the Communist members and include only Radicals and Moderate Liberals.

Congress shortly thereafter attacked the problem of Communism with legislation, passing in April, 1950, a Law for the Defense of Democracy. More significant in meeting social problems was the action of Congress enfranchising women for the first time in Chilean history to participate in national elections.

New difficulties appeared, however, with the end of the Korean War when a decline in the prices of copper and nitrates set in. The weakening of the foreign market for these minerals, still accounting for 80 per cent of the government's income, immediately produced discontent. Thus when the presidential election of 1952 shortly approached, the Socialist and Feminist parties consolidated their support behind the candidate of the Popular Socialists, Carlos Ibáñez, who promised relief. On a platform calling for repeal of the Law for the Defense of Democracy, re-establishment of relations with Russia, stronger economic association with Argentina, and revision of copper agreements with American companies to secure greater benefits for Chile, Ibáñez won and was inaugurated on November 3, 1952.

Chile since 1952. In office, however, Ibáñez refused to repeal the Democracy Defense Law. He put the emphasis of his policies upon reviving Chile's main sources of income, copper and nitrates, finding new markets for her products, and expanding oil resources. In 1953 legislation gave the Central Bank of Chile exclusive control over all sales of Chilean copper. To stimulate national production, as distinguished from that of American-owned companies, a National Copper Corporation aided owners of small and medium-sized mines to sell their product on the world market. That market brought a higher price than the one offered by the United States, to which Chile shipped annually about 300,000 tons of copper at approximately thirty cents a pound.

However, since the American mines at Chuquicamata and Potrerillos, owned by the Anaconda Copper Company, and *El Teniente,* owned by the Kennecott Corporation, produced fully 90 per cent of Chilean copper, the Ibáñez government enacted legislation reducing taxes to encourage a greater production. Favorable results followed immediately in an increase in the price of copper in the United States and in the expansion of mining operations in Chile. The urgency of these measures was apparent in the growing demand, stimulated by the country's serious inflation, of some powerful political and labor groups for the nationalization of foreign-owned copper companies.

Attempting to find new outlets for Chilean products and secure raw materials for her industries, the government sought loans from the Export-Import Bank and economic agreements with her neighbors. To this end Ibáñez negotiated a treaty with Argentina on July 8, 1953, which called for better cooperation between these states. Under it a national council of Argentines and Chileans, composed of five men, began studying ways and means of complementing the two economies. The treaty proposed to reduce excess taxes and duties, modify exchange rules to aid easy payments, ease restrictions on exchange of goods along the mutual frontiers, improve transportation and communication, establish free ports, aid tourism, and fix rules governing exchange of products.

With Bolivia, Ibáñez returned to González Videla's program of economic exchange. Meeting early in 1955, the two presidents prepared a treaty to facilitate trade by revision of taxes, duties, and regulations, to encourage capital investment in industrial production, and to exchange Chilean iron and steel for Bolivian oil. The two countries also made plans for a petroleum pipeline from Oruro to Arica and a new highway from Oruro to Iquique. These measures to increase oil needed by Chilean industry complemented the efforts of the government to expand its own oil production in the far south, which by the beginning of 1956 was almost 1,300,000 barrels annually.

Chile by the middle of the twentieth century presented to the world a picture of encouraging economic development and political growth. Freed from an earlier dependence upon nitrates, she is, by diversifying her industrial production, trying to avoid a too great dependence upon her other great raw material, copper. Politically, she freed herself by the 1925 constitution from the dominance of an oligarchy. Since that date she has given convincing proof of a capacity to maintain her democratic institutions while converting her raw material economy and colonial society into a modern state. The chief shadow on the Chilean horizon is inflation. The spiral derives from her entirely understandable efforts to industrialize herself and her attempt to maintain wages for her working population necessary to meet the constantly rising cost of living.

Chapter XX

BOLIVIA

Part I. DOMINATION OF FEUDAL INSTITUTIONS, 1824–1936

The Character of Bolivian History. The history of Bolivia strikingly reflects the evils of the colonial period. When the campaigns of Bolívar and Sucre had swept away Spanish power, Bolivia revealed all the elements of a feudal society. The large body of Indians remained serfs on the estates of the Bolivian landowners. The *mestizos* became the miserable soldiers of generals who fought one another for the presidency. The nineteenth century saw but the bare beginnings of a middle class. Perpetuating this frozen structure into the twentieth century was the isolated geographical location of the country which afforded but little contact with the outside world. Thus Bolivia's history has revealed three clearly marked trends. One was the constant succession of militarist presidents in the nineteenth century. They plunged the country into bloody civil war and sacrificed territory of the fatherland. After the middle of that century, foreign economic interests grew steadily, nourished by the rich mineral resources of the nation. Finally, in the twentieth century, denial of political rights, lack of education, and extreme poverty among the majority of Bolivia's people nurtured a strong socialist movement which, after the Chaco War, plunged Bolivia into its present efforts to reconstitute its society.

Sucre, 1825–1828. With independence established in 1825, Bolívar, after whom the country was named, gave it its boundaries, its constitution, and its first president, General Antonio José de Sucre. The constitution recognized the main features of the country's feudal character. The president was to serve for life; its congress had three bodies, in which the Chamber of Censors exercised the power to see that the laws were obeyed. The Catholic religion was to be the sole religion of the state. Suffrage restricted to property owners eliminated fully 90 per cent of the population. In his short administration Sucre organized the new state and significantly laid claim to Bolivia's title to the Pacific seaboard provinces which the *audiencia* of the colonial period had administered.

Santa Cruz, 1831–1839. But neither the constitution nor Sucre lasted, for in less than two years the Colombian troops left in Bolivia mutinied. Taking advantage of this discontent, General Santa Cruz and General Gamarra invaded from Peru and drove Sucre out in 1828. Elevated to the presidency, Santa Cruz handed down a constitution in 1831 which differed little in its fundamentals from that of Bolívar's. While the president was committed to a four-year term, the Creole oligarchy found protection in a Council of State, the successor to the Chamber of Censors. The new body exercised control over both the president and the two-chamber legislature. Suffrage restrictions, differently worded, also excluded the bulk of the people.

Santa Cruz, leaving the oligarchy to its role of exploitation of the Indian serfs, turned in 1835 to conquer Peru. Successful in this project, he organized that country and Bolivia into three large administrative districts over which he ruled as Protector, while puppets governed the three divisions. This arrangement disturbed both Chile and Argentina, which sent armies to overthrow Santa Cruz. Acting independently, the forces of the two countries ousted him at the battle of Yungay in January, 1839.

Ballivián: the First Liberal Program, 1841–1847. José Ballivián, the successor of Santa Cruz, alone in the nineteenth century revealed an understanding of Bolivia's needs. His constitution of 1843 reduced the power of the oligarchy, provided for development of the nation's resources, and emancipated Negro slaves. His administration encouraged foreign investment and made an effort to develop Bolivia's trade by way of the Amazon River. Internally he began a program of road and bridge building, construction of hospitals, and other public works. He even dared to defy the power of the church by encouraging public education, scientific discussion in literate circles of the capital, and support of other cultural activities. Unable at this early date to alter the fundamental structure of the society, he found himself driven into exile by an infuriated oligarchy in 1847.

Belzú, 1849–1851. Other men not so high-minded as Ballivián sensed the power and yearning latent in the masses. Among the first was General Manuel Isidoro Belzú, whose demagoguery stirred uprisings that for the first time in the nation's history directed themselves at the wealthy and powerful. On one occasion Belzú cried out to his followers: "Know that all, as far as you can see, belongs to you, because it is the fruit of your work. The riches of those who say they are nobles, is what they have stolen from you." His rule was filled with popular uprisings, exile of conservatives, and the sacking of towns, all of which he defended as the impartial acts of the people. By 1851 Belzú retired in favor of his son, and handed down a constitution undistinguished by any political thought. Until 1858 civil wars tore the country asunder and resulted in the victory of the conservatives. In their efforts to blot out the memory of Ballivián and Belzú among the people, they resorted to such extreme measures as to pave the way once more for the rise to power of the worst of the demagogues, General Mariano Melgarejo.

Melgarejo, 1865–1870. Once in power, Melgarejo converted the president's mansion into a barracks. His roitous living, as one author characterized it, of "women, liquor, gambling, and gluttony," was varied with cruel persecution of his enemies. When funds were needed he sold Indian communal lands at auction. But probably the most unfortunate effect of his rule was his sacrifice of Bolivian territory. In 1866 he negotiated a treaty with Chile which surrendered Bolivia's claim to the territory south of the twenty-fourth parallel and gave that country joint jurisdiction over Bolivian lands north of this line. He further granted the Chilean Nitrate Company a concession to exploit for fifteen years, soon extended to twenty-five, the nitrate and guano deposits for a fixed tax per hundredweight taken out. He got additional funds from Brazil by negotiating with that country the treaty of 1867 which surrendered Bolivian claims to the Acre territory in the east. Moreover, this treaty, drawn loosely, enabled Brazil later to secure additional lands at Bolivia's expense. In 1871 a revolt drove him from the country to exile in Peru, where he met a violent death in Lima.

The War of the Pacific, 1879–1883. From the wreckage of Melgarejo's rule, Bolivia moved into the disaster of the War of the Pacific. Until 1878 a succession of military figures fought for the presidency after the dictator's overthrow. In this period Bolivia signed the secret treaty (1873) with Peru, impelled by fear of Chile. In 1876 Hilarión Daza, who came to power, proved himself the equal of Melgarejo in looting the public treasury. But his action in 1877, in violating the agreements with the Chilean Nitrate Company by levying an additional ten-centavo tax upon each hundredweight of nitrates extracted, became the immediate cause of Bolivia's greatest loss. The refusal of Chile to pay the tax led him to seize the company's holdings at Antofagasta and put them up for auction. Chile, retaliating, captured the nitrate town itself and precipitated the war. Daza was soon overthrown, the Bolivian army defeated, and the country stood helplessly by while Peru and Chile signed a separate peace which divided the territory, although unequally, between them.

The treaty provision which left Chile with occupation of both Tacna and Arica subject to later plebiscites was a calamity for Bolivia. Arica, by arrangement with Peru up until the war, was, in fact, her principal Pacific outlet. Bolivia was left with no alternative but to negotiate directly with Chile, as a result of which in 1884 she recognized by a temporary agreement Chile's control above the twenty-fourth parallel. She also consented to turn over the tariff duties in the region due her to pay her debts to Chile, particularly that which she incurred by her seizure of Antofagasta.

Thus by 1890 Bolivia, looted and despoiled of territory by her militarists, like her neighbor Peru, had taken no steps to implement the freedom implicit in the movement for independence. On the contrary, the conservative forces, led by Narciso Campero, ousted Daza during the war and succeeded in drawing up a new constitution in 1880 which consolidated their grip on Bolivia until 1936. The 1880 document, restricting suffrage to males of twenty-one years of age who were both literate and property holders, enabled the aristocracy to control the election of officials to the central government. The president and vice-president served four years. The senate was composed of two members from each department, into which the country was divided, elected for terms of six years. The members of the Chamber of Deputies were elected for terms of four years. The membership of the supreme court, composed of seven judges who were selected from a list prepared by the senate, were chosen by the lower house. The Roman Catholic was the state religion.

Growth of Foreign Interest, 1890–1920. The growth of foreign interest in Bolivia, which became significant after 1890, had its beginnings in the middle of the century. After independence various British companies received concessions to the abandoned Spanish mines. In the 1850's the United States, interested in opening the Amazon River, sent Lieutenant William Herndon and Lardner Gibbon to explore Peru's and Bolivia's rivers leading to the Amazon. While Herndon entered through Peru, Gibbon made explorations to the Madeira-Mamoré river system.

Little mining beyond that of silver characterized Bolivia until 1880. In the following decade, while restrictions were taken off the production of silver, the state's income from that source steadily declined as European countries moved toward a gold standard. Compensating somewhat for this decline, however, was an increase in the production of rubber and a new mineral for Bolivia, tin, the latter first appearing in her export records of 1884. By 1900 this metal was assuming a leading place in Bolivian exports, largely due to energetic native Bolivians, among whom

Simón Patiño was to be the most remarkable. Rubber began to be exported after 1900 in growing volume and became a major source of revenue to the state. However, when British rubber from the Malay peninsula reached the world's markets after 1910, the Bolivian industry collapsed.

This expansion of the Bolivian economy had important international effects. The need for an outlet for her raw materials led Bolivia to put pressure upon Chile to secure port facilities on the Pacific coast. In pursuit of this aim, too, she made a treaty with Argentina in 1891 agreeing to consider joining the Argentine Confederation in return for aid against Chile. To head off such a move, Chile agreed in 1895 to compensate Bolivia for the loss of the Atacama region by providing port facilities and a corridor. But it was fully ten years before the two countries reached a definitive treaty. Under it in 1904 Bolivia secured a port outlet at Arica, while Chile paid her $1,500,000 for the territory of Atacama, assumed all Bolivia's debts to Chileans, and agreed to build a railroad to the port of Arica, completed in 1913.

To the east in her search for an outlet, Bolivia protested the terms of the Paraguay-Argentine treaty of 1878, which recognized Paraguay's rights to the region north of the Pilcomayo River. Thereafter until 1913 Paraguay and Bolivia made a series of treaties in efforts to settle their claims to the disputed territory. With Brazil, Bolivia was more fortunate in securing an outlet, although at the loss of more territory in Acre. The agreement with Brazil in 1867 had fixed a temporary boundary line. Two years later in 1869 an American company attempted to build a railroad around the cataract of the Madeira River, but failed. A second American venture, after completing four miles of track, gave up the project in 1876, for the cost in human lives proved too high.

By this date Brazilian rubber companies had carried their workers across this 1867 line. In 1899 friction led to the revolt of these Brazilians against Bolivia's authority. Although the latter dispatched military expeditions, she was unsuccessful in putting down the uprising. Two years later in 1903 at Petropolis, Bolivia ceded the Acre territory in return for $10,000,000 and Brazil's promise to build the Madeira-Marmoré Railroad around the cataract. This project, completed by the Farquahar American syndicate in 1912, shortly proved useless when the Bolivian rubber industry collapsed.

The growing income of the state, her expanding exports, and foreign investments brought internal improvements in their train. With the $10,000,000 available from Brazil, Bolivia launched railroad construction to connect her important mining centers. The Oruro-La Paz line was completed in 1910. In 1908 the line from La Paz to the southern end of Lake Titicaca linked Bolivia with Peru's Southern Railway and thus gave access to the port of Mollendo. Of greater importance was the continuation of the railroad from Oruro southeast, begun in 1912, to link that mining center with Argentina and southwest with Antofagasta. These, combined with the completion in 1913 of the Chilean-built railroad from Arica to La Paz, provided Bolivia with outlets which, when the early crisis of World War I was passed, enabled her to profit from the demands for her tin and other minerals on the high plateau.

The condition of her finances by 1912 was such that the actual income of the state exceeded the budget estimates by 3,000,000 bolivianos, about $1,200,000. This circumstance enabled Bolivia to go on the gold standard and to establish in 1911 a national bank, the *Banco de Nación Boliviana*. Symbolic of the economic growth along modern lines was the success of the Liberal party in 1899, whose election of José Manuel Pando brought about the transfer of the capital from its historic conservative stronghold at Sucre to the more progressive city of La Paz. Pando was succeeded in 1904 by an outstanding Liberal leader, Ismael Montes, who was largely responsible for initiating the financial policy which freed Bolivia of debt. He was succeeded in the elections of 1909 by Eleodoro Villazón, who continued the liberal policies. Montes returned to the presidency in 1913, but his plans for continued program of essentially middle class economic reforms was interrupted by World War I.

World War I and American Loans, 1914–1931. The advent of World War I threw Bolivia into the hands of foreign investors who in the succeeding three decades dictated the country's development. The first impact of the war sent the cost of living soaring as the combatants cut off vital imports. At the same time loss of revenues rose to more than five billion bolivianos. In 1915 conditions began to improve with the opening of the Panama Canal. That quick route to American ports, together with Bolivia's new outlets at Mollendo and Arica, facilitated the rapid growth of her mineral exports. The resulting inflow of foreign capital brought a prosperity to mineowners hitherto unknown in Bolivia's history. The helpless mining workers and defenseless Indian serfs remained, however, at their low standard of living, made worse by the high cost of imports. Tin, copper, wolfram, bismuth, and antimony steadily rose in production and price. Bolivia, unable without great difficulty to secure imports, saw the sale of minerals and foreign investment bring huge capital gains into the country, estimated in 1919 at 148,000,000 bolivianos.

The ending of the war brought to Bolivia the collapse of her foreign trade and widespread suffering among the bulk of her people. Politically, it brought dissatisfaction with the dominance of the Liberal party in power since 1899. Growing opposition to it during the war saw a new political force, the Republican party, rise to dispute the Liberal control. José Gutiérrez Guerra, elected in 1917 to succeed Montes, was overthrown in 1920 by the Republican leader, Bautista Saavedra, who became president. To meet the economic crisis, he imposed indirect taxes, raised the government's royalty and share of the profits in oil production, and negotiated new loans in New York City. The most outstanding of these was that of 1922 under which American banks secured, among other things, control over Bolivian customs and the national bank and supervision over the collection and disbursement of taxes derived from the alcohol and tobacco monopoly. However, part of the 1922 loan was constructively used to complete by 1925 the long-planned railroad to connect Oruro with Antofagasta and thus provide Bolivia with a southern outlet from her rich mineral plateau.

Saavedra's attempt to perpetuate himself in office led to split within his own party, with the dissenting group combining with the Liberals to bring to the presidency Hernando Siles in December, 1925. However, like his predecessors, Siles resorted to loans to maintain himself in office. These, facilitated by the recommendations of the American Kemmerer Commission, employed by Siles to make a survey of Bolivia's resources, paved the way in 1928 for Dillon, Read and Company to extend a $23,000,000 loan to the government. Bolivia also secured from the British armament firm of Vickers-Armstrong a loan of $9,000,000 believed by some to have had some relation to Bolivia's preparation for the growing conflict with Paraguay over the Chaco. Both the English and the American loans were used in considerable part to purchase military equipment.

The steady construction of Bolivia's railroads advanced by the loans of the 1920's gave impetus to the country's mineral production. Chief among these was tin, whose development after 1905 went rapidly forward in the hands of Simón Patiño, who over a period of years had secured title to the bulk of the known tin deposits of the country. During World War I Patiño, while maintaining control over his properties, made agreements with British tin smelting interests in Liverpool which thereafter, because of their previous ownership of Malayan and Dutch East Indian tin mines, exercised a virtual monopoly on the world's supply of manufactured tin.

Because after World War I the United States was the world's greatest consumer of tin, American companies sought a foothold in Bolivian production. The most important advance was the purchase of the National Lead Company in 1924 of a third interest in the Patiño holdings in tin mines and railroads, since the Patiño interests by that date accounted for 80 per cent of Bolivian tin production. Other American companies secured lesser holdings. The British, while holding the smelting monopoly, also dominated the small but rich Aramayo Company, headed by a Bolivian. The Hochschild interests, later associated with Swiss capital, composed the third group of what eventually became known in modern Bolivia's history as the Big Three. It was estimated that by 1928 American concerns held a large part of the $77,000,000 investment in Bolivian tin.

The demand for petroleum after 1900 by the leading industrial nations led oil companies to explore the possibilities of Bolivia. Almost at the same moment when Patiño was securing control of his vast tin holdings, small Bolivian oil companies began operations in the trans-Andean areas. There, in the departments of Sucre, Chuquisaca, Tarija, and Santa Cruz in southeastern Bolivia adjoining Argentina, the richest fields were located, although some oil zones were found near Lake Titicaca. By 1916, when more than 7,500,000 acres of oil lands had been ceded outright, Bolivia nationalized its oil. But this law was set aside in 1920 to encourage foreign investment in the trans-Andean area.

In the following year under the new law, Spruille and William Braden and Bolivian capitalists secured in eastern Bolivia over 5,000,000 acres of oil lands. At about the same time the American Richmond Levering Company was holding over 1,000,000 acres. When in 1922 both groups sold out to Standard Oil, that company became the largest single holder of oil lands in Bolivia. While oil and tin were the leading minerals in which Americans invested in Bolivia, other American companies secured concessions to lands holding lead, antimony, copper, and wolfram. Thus from an investment in 1913 by American companies in Bolivia's minerals, the total grew to some $133,000,000 by 1929. European including British investments raised the total foreign holdings in that country to about $150,000,000.

The Depression and the Chaco War, 1929–1936. The rapid expansion of Bolivia's economy in the 1920's, nourished by American loans, came to an abrupt halt with the depression of 1929. Her exports, which totaled over $50,000,000 in 1929, dropped by 1932 to slightly more than $10,-000,000; her imports, from a high of over $25,000,000, to less than $5,000,000. Her foreign debt in 1930, which reached about $60,000,000 with interest payments of about $6,000,000 annually, found the state's income from all sources barely $16,000,000. With the disastrous decline of her export trade, the principal source of income, unemployment spread rapidly in the mining areas, bankruptcies occurred, the nation's financial structure collapsed, and inevitably riots and revolts broke out against the government.

Soon investigation showed that Siles and his supporters had diverted much money from the loans to their own enrichment. His attempt to increase taxes to meet current expenses proved to be the final straw. A revolt in May, 1930, overthrew his government to place in power a military junta. By March, 1932, with the support of the Patiño interests, Daniel Salamanca, who had long before opposed the program of reform initiated by Montes, became the next dictator. As conditions continued to get worse, the Salamanca government sought a solution for its difficulties in seeking an outlet through the Chaco, a policy which with other causes provoked the Chaco War.

The Chaco War, 1928–1938. The area in dispute between Paraguay and Bolivia was the Chaco Boreal, some 115,000 square miles of subtropical forests and plains suitable for cattle grazing, besides its oil-rich lands. Its principal product was quebracho wood, valuable for its tannin. Paraguay had colonized in the Chaco area with the aid of foreign capitalists, mainly British, Argentine, and American companies interested in developing the quebracho forests as well as cattle and agricultural industries along the Pilcomayo River and interior plains. Bolivia had nothing in the way of occupation except some small towns on the upper headwaters of the Pilcomayo. Standard Oil fields far to the east of these were in the territories of Tarija, Chuquisaca, and southern Santa Cruz.

The causes of the Chaco War arose out of (1) a boundary dispute between Paraguay and Bolivia, (2) the need of an outlet, intensified by the loss of her Pacific littoral, for Bolivia to the east for her oil and other products, and (3) the danger of revolution among the Bolivian and Paraguayan people, engendered by the suffering dating from the 1929 depression. The boundary dispute had existed since the independence of the two nations. In the late nineteenth century Bolivia and Paraguay, as noted above, had attempted treaty negotiations, which, beginning in 1879, had continued until 1913. After that date diplomatic exchanges went forward, but in 1928 these collapsed. When in that year both countries moved troops into the disputed area, violent clashes occurred and continued until 1932 when the war broke out.

The need for an outlet became particularly important after Standard

Oil interests had begun to develop the properties in eastern Bolivia purchased in 1922. By 1930 Standard had invested over $54,000,000 and was producing from a number of wells, Argentina, backed by British oil interests, imposed tariffs against the import of Bolivian oil. Since it was practically impossible for Standard to pipe oil back over the Andes to the Pacific, development was stymied. President Salamanca stated the case for Bolivia in 1932 when he wrote that the "natural and logical remedy would be to construct a pipeline to the Paraguay River. But there lies the Republic of Paraguay disputing the territory of Bolivia, and also closing the Pass. Bolivia cannot resign [itself] to live miserably as a country isolated from the world."

The demand for an eastern outlet was greatly stimulated after 1929 when the final settlement of the Tacna-Arica question excluded Bolivia from the Pacific Ocean. Perforce she had to turn to the east. At the moment oil had become of paramount import since it promised to provide a new source of income to the Bolivian state, as well as becoming a means of opening up eastern Bolivia to colonization and the development of other sources of wealth.

The danger of revolutionary movements existed in both countries. While the depression nourished a liberal movement in Asunción among students, intellectuals, and labor, who demanded reforms, that world disaster had a greater impact on Bolivia. As the export of tin and other metals declined, the mining companies closed their properties and threw large numbers of Indians out of work. Simultaneously the government retrenched so severely that hundreds of schools were forced to close throughout the country.

These events gave rise to the growth of a vigorous labor movement, whose origins can be dated back to a mutual society founded in 1906. In the depression of 1921, after World War I, union organization made rapid strides among teachers, railroad workers, tin miners, and others. In 1930 during the great depression the Workers' Federation of Bolivian Labor met in Oruro in their Fourth Congress to demand and voice freely revolutionary doctrines. Two years later, as the discontent grew, Salamanca took advantage of the breakdown of the Washington Chaco Conference to attack Paraguay.

The actual fighting lasted four years from 1932 to 1936. The campaigns took place in the disease-ridden jungles of the Chaco. Bolivian soldiers from the rarefied atmosphere of the highlands suffered disastrously, their losses reaching some 60,000. The Paraguayans, accustomed to the environment, fared better. Neither side had difficulty in purchasing war materials, since the great industrial countries were glad to find an active market in the doldrums of the depression. This international interest for years blocked attempts to mediate the conflict. The League of Nations' investigating commission failed to get results in 1932, and the Seventh International Conference of American States, meeting at Montevideo in December, 1933, secured an armistice for only about two weeks. After the war resumed its course, the scandal of munition shipments had roused world opinion by the spring of 1934. The British government then proposed to the League of Nations an embargo on arms to the two countries. The United States cooperated with the League when Congress authorized a similar embargo. However, both the Bolivian and Paraguayan governments, still uncertain of their capacity to prevent revolt at home, sought arbitration from the League, a step which set aside the League's authority to enforce the arms embargo. The war therefore continued for another year.

By June, 1935, Paraguay was in possession of the bulk of the territory, but she was unable to launch an invasion of Bolivia to end the war. This stalemate became the basis for new efforts at peace led by the United States and five Latin-American countries, Argentina, Chile, Peru, Uruguay, and Brazil. In June, 1935, the representatives of these countries, meeting in Buenos Aires, secured an armistice. For the rest of the year the delegates of Bolivia and Paraguay met with those of the six American nations at the peace conference, also held in Buenos Aires. By January 21, 1936, an accord was reached by which both Paraguay and Bolivia agreed not to reopen hostilities, to renew diplomatic relations, and to exchange prisoners of war. The end, however, was not yet in sight. Political changes in both countries, of which the Bolivian are discussed below, caused delays until July, 1938, when the two nations finally agreed to abide by an arbitration decision on their respective claims to be handed down by the presidents of the original six American nations involved in mediation. The settlement, achieved July 21, 1938, provided (1) for the drawing of a definite boundary line through the disputed area, (2) the awarding of slightly more than 90,000 square miles of the region to Paraguay, and (3) provision for a strip of land for a port on the Paraguay River for the use of Bolivia.

Part II. THE STRUGGLE FOR DEMOCRATIC INSTITUTIONS SINCE 1936

The Immediate Effects of the War on Bolivia. The war, which fell with crushing weight upon the Bolivians, produced the first significant social and political reforms in that country's history. With hostilities ended in 1936, the Workers' Federation of Bolivian Labor in May demanded reforms and improvements in working conditions in the mines. Calling a general strike, they quickly found support in the Bolivian Socialist party, among the underpaid younger officers of the Bolivian army, and among the unemployed Chaco veterans. In the same month these groups overthrew the government of President Tejada Sórzano, who had succeeded Salamanca in June, 1934. The leaders, Lieutenant-Colonel Germán Busch and Colonel David Toro, established a military junta from which Toro emerged as president on a Socialist platform on May 19, 1936. In these years two new political parties in Bolivia's history made their appearance. One, the party of the Revolutionary Left or PIR, headed by Antonio José Arze, was socialist with strong Marxian leanings. The other, the National Revolutionary Movement or MNR, while socialist in its program, was dominated by a strong nationalistic fervor. Labor, too, in 1936 combined in the Confederation of Union Workers of Bolivia.

Reforms, 1936–1940. The Toro government set aside the constitution drawn up in 1880 and governed by decree to effect the reforms demanded by its supporters. These decrees provided for a minimum wage law, an increase of 100 per cent in wages in the mining industry—a raise which, in fact, meant an increase in the daily wage from thirty-five cents to seventy cents—and union organization. But the action of the Toro government that attracted the greatest attention was the expropriation in 1937 of the petroleum properties of the Standard Oil Company in Bolivia on charges of having aided Paraguay in the Chaco War. Standard denied all accusations, but to no avail. When shortly thereafter Toro was overthrown in a revolt, Germán Busch, still popular with the veterans of the Chaco War and the newly organized labor unions, assumed power on July 13, 1937. He, too, ruled by decree and launched even more farreaching reforms than Toro.

For labor, Busch's principal support, the dictator decreed a social security system. He instituted a retirement fund for government employees and education for children and all adult illiterates. To make public officials more responsible, he required all officeholders to declare their wealth before and after taking office. His most drastic innovation was a mining census, which called upon all owners to state the nationality of the ownership of mines, taxes paid, income of the property, sources of materials, and the financing of mining operations. These measures stirred the opposition of the Big Three, who cut off tin production to embarrass the government. To replace these revenues, Busch made a series of treaties with Bolivia's neighbors, Argentina, Brazil, and

Chile, granting them concessions to Bolivian raw materials. As has been noted, he also concluded in July, 1938, the treaty with Paraguay under which, while Paraguay received the bulk of the disputed area, Bolivia did secure a strip of land for a custom house on the Paraguay River and access to the Atlantic Ocean.

The Constitution of 1938. Enjoying great popularity among the workers, Busch next promulgated a new constitution on October 30, 1938, to replace that of 1880. This document was not implemented, but it does reveal Bovilian ideas of modernizing the country. For education it established a free public school system and a special Indian education program which reflected the influence of Mexican reforms in Indian education. For labor it provided a fair wage, outlawed illegal labor, and recognized collective bargaining, the right to strike, and the right to organize unions and cooperatives, particularly in the rural areas. Taxes were to be levied according to the ability to pay, and all mineral wealth and natural resources were declared the property of the nation. Finally, property was held to fulfill a social function, a provision undoubtedly reflecting the influence of the 1917 Mexican constitution and that of Chile of 1925.

The constitution became the fulcrum for a comprehensive reform program, including a labor code. These measures the conservative groups of the country attacked so vigorously that Busch set aside the constitution itself and established a dictatorship in April, 1939, based, he stated, upon the economic and social needs of the country. In August of that year Busch jailed Hochschild for violations of the labor code. On August 23 Busch died under mysterious circumstances.

The violence of public reaction to Busch's death led his successor, General Carlos Quintanilla, to declare that the dead president's policies would be continued. Restrictions were taken off political parties in preparation for a new election. Arze, back from exile, headed the PIR. Victor Paz Estenssoro led the MNR, which was intensely nationalistic along with its socialist doctrines. A new party, the Authentic Republicans, combined the liberal middle class and conservative landowners under the leadership of General Enrique Peñaranda, who was elected president in March, 1940. With him conservative control returned as World War II began to affect the economy of Bolivia.

World War II and Bolivia. World War II made Bolivian minerals of vital importance to United States industries. The stockpiling program of the Reconstruction Finance Corporation, operated through the Metals Reserve Corporation, agreed with the Bolivian tin interests to take 18,000 tons of tin for three years, that is, one-half of the Bolivian production. In 1941 the United States next contracted for all Bolivian tungsten for three years for $25,000,000. At the Rio Conference in 1942 the foundation was laid for a settlement of Standard Oil's claims for its expropriated properties. Later in 1942 the United States made a further agreement with the tin groups not only to take larger amounts, but to pay an increase in price from forty-seven and one-half cents to sixty cents a pound.

The war had an adverse effect upon Bolivia's working population. Shortage of transportation and manufactured goods sent prices of essential commodities soaring. This increase in the cost of living, together with dissatisfaction with conditions of work in the mines, led to a widespread strike to secure a 100 per cent increase in wages, that is, from seventy cents a day to $1.40. The tin interests refused to make the concessions demanded. A protest meeting of the miners and their families at Catabi was dispersed by gunfire, with many killed and wounded. The most important immediate effect of the event was to pave the way for a Nazi movement to seize control of the government. Taking advantage of considerable anti-American sentiment in the country, and supported by Nazi espionage groups and the Argentine government, the MNR, led by Paz Estenssoro and General Gualberto Villarroel, carried out a *coup d'état* in December, 1943, ousted Peñaranda, and placed Villarroel in as president.

Villarroel sought recognition from the United States, which, after three cabinet members associated with the Nazis were dropped, was extended in July, 1944. With the ending of the war in 1945, tin from Malaya and the decline for the demand for the metal led the Big Three to close their mines in Bolivia. Villarroel tried to force the reopening of the industry, for unemployment, rapidly mounting, was undermining the government's control of the nation. However, the move failed and the mines remained closed. To maintain itself in power, Villarroel's government next turned to a program of reform and sought support for it among the miners and native industrial groups. At the same time it carried out a ruthless suppression of its critics. Gradually the various political parties coalesced into what was called the Bolivian Democratic Union. In July, 1946, students, businessmen, and others, leading a revolt characterized by great violence, overthrew the Villarroel government and drove Paz Estenssoro into exile in Argentina.

The Herzog Government, 1947–1949. A provisional military government, headed by Nestor Guillén, promised elections for the following

January. By that date Monje Gutiérrez, who had succeeded to the leadership of the junta, withdrew his candidacy in favor of Enrique Herzog of the Socialist Republican Union, the landowners' party. Opposing him was Fernando Guachalla, a coalition candidate of conservative business groups which hoped to attract the voters of the PIR and the MNR, both of which were excluded from participation in the election. Herzog won by a narrow margin and took office in the following March, 1947, with Guachalla as his foreign minister.

In power, the new government deported the remaining MNR leaders on charges of subversive activity. However, the administration, intent upon securing a new agreement with the United States for tin, had little time to meet the fundamental needs of the country. Thus in October, 1948, Herzog declared a state of siege to round up once more the PIR and MNR political leaders who had secretly returned and who were charged with attempts to overthrow the government. Before the spring elections in April, 1949, the army had occupied the principal mining centers of Catavi, Llallagua, and Siglo Veinte, principally Patiño mines, to put down labor protesting low wages and the high cost of living.

Hoping to appease the opposition, Herzog permitted the MNR to present candidates in the spring election. While the government won, Paz Estenssoro's party, to the surprise of everyone, won eleven seats. Charges of fraud and violence succeeding the elections brought on another state of siege. In the following month, May, Herzog suddenly left the country while the vice-president, Mamerto Urriolagoitia, took over.

The Urriolagoitia Government, 1949–1951. The new president outlawed the MNR and threw into jail Juan Lechín, the leader of the tin miners' union, and others accused of fomenting revolution. In spite of these measures, the MNR staged a successful revolt for ten days in Santa Cruz, Cochabamba, and Oruro, with Paz Estenssoro at the head. Put down with a loss of 350 killed, the government resorted to still more violent reprisals against the captured rebels. Continued opposition from the MNR led to another state of siege declared in January, 1950.

Throughout the spring, crisis succeeded crisis. In April the Communist party was outlawed, while in May a teachers' strike for higher pay and better working conditions forced the government to declare a state of emergency. In the same month the Confederation of Bolivian Workers called a nation-wide strike which resulted in 60 per cent pay increases for teachers and 30 per cent for workers. Plots nevertheless continued to be hatched, the product of a miserable standard of living.

Thus in June, 1950, both the leftist PIR and the rightist Socialist Falange, the Catholic party, were charged with subversive action. Three months later a demonstration of students at the University of San Andrés was put down. In the following December new plots involved the MNR and the Falange and led to the latter charging the government that its state of siege was to hide its own inefficiency and growing unpopularity.

In this tense atmosphere the end of the year saw Bolivian political parties preparing for the presidential elections to be held in May, 1951. Significantly, as lines began to be drawn, organized labor began to consolidate its power. The strong Factory Workers' Union and the railroad unions planned to affiliate with the Bolivian Confederation of Workers, the bulk of whose numbers were revolutionary in outlook and supported either the PIR or the MNR. Exiles abroad—university professors, students, journalists, and members of the Bolivian congress—in an effort to make the Bolivian government more democratic, called upon the United Nations to use its influence to this end.

Seemingly the government responded to the pressure of the labor unions when in April, 1951, it suddenly granted a 30 per cent increase in wages to railroad workers and made similar concessions to factory and mining laborers. Even the powerful Patiño mines awoke to the necessity of improving Bolivian agriculture to augment the country's poor food supply and of developing other mining resources than tin. For this purpose it proposed a ten-year plan with the expenditure of several millions of dollars. These were recognized as last-minute moves to influence the election, which everyone privately conceded Paz Estenssoro would win if the election were held and the votes counted.

Such in fact turned out to be the case when the results of the balloting were announced. Paz Estenssoro had won 46 per cent of the votes cast, but did not have, as the constitution required, a clear majority over the other three candidates. The decision, therefore, as the law required, was referred to congress. When it was evident that congress would award the presidency to Paz Estenssoro, Urriolagoitia promptly resigned and turned over the government to a military junta consisting of three generals and seven colonels. Determined that the MNR candidate should not become president, the junta declared the election invalid and announced a state of siege.

The Ballivián Dictatorship, 1951–1952. The head of the junta, General Hugo Ballivián, dispatched the army into key centers which headed off any revolutionary protest at the cavalier treatment of the electorate. In spite of this attack upon the democratic process, the junta was recognized by various governments in Latin America and by the United States, the latter having a policy for Latin America in this respect based upon recognizing any government which maintained order, demonstrated a capacity to govern, and recognized its international obligations.

The Ballivián government made no pretense about holding further elections. It was simply a military dictatorship aimed at maintaining the Bolivian oligarchy in power, and guaranteeing the continued ownership of the country's mineral resources in the hands of the Big Three mining companies. Against a constantly growing wave of protest, strikes, revolts, and plots, the Ballivián government held to its course for the next eleven months.

On April 9, 1952, the MNR, which had carefully organized its forces, suddenly revolted in all the major cities: La Paz, Oruro, Cochabamba, Potosí, Trinidad, Sucre, and Santa Cruz. When on April 11 the rebels captured the air base at La Paz, the government fled. Siles Suazo, nominated vice-president in the preceding May elections, assumed control until Paz Estenssoro arrived from Uruguay, whence he had been exiled from Argentina, to be sworn in as president on April 15, 1952.

The Paz Estenssoro Government, 1952 to the Present. Paz Estenssoro who had served in the Villarroel government, undoubtedly had the overwhelming support of the Bolivian underprivileged. He took a series of decisive steps in the next six months to destroy the feudal agricultural economy of Bolivia and end the dominance of the Big Three in the control of the tin resources. Attacking first the traditional army, the government exiled the high ranking officers and disbanded the bulk of the armed forces to replace them with the revolutionary troops that had put Paz Estenssoro in power. By the same token, the officers of the MNR army assumed the leading positions in the new Bolivian armed forces. The president ousted the supreme court justices and replaced them with judges favorable to the ideas of the government. The chief opposition newspaper, *La Razón,* was closed and taken over, an action which gave the government, already in possession of *La Nación,* control over the dissemination of news.

Having made its position virtually impregnable, the new government turned its attention immediately to Bolivia's most urgent problem— an adequate food supply. The shortage of food arose from the emphasis put upon mineral production, particularly tin. Little attention had been paid to lift Bolivia out of its primitive Indian methods of land cultivation. The growing industries, moreover, in the leading cities had steadily increased the urban population, thus adding to the pressure upon the food supply. La Paz, for example, which had a population in 1900 of some 52,000 had by 1950 more than 300,000. Basic foods, maize, potatoes, rice, sugar, were all imported, absorbing in fact some 35 per cent of the national income for that purpose. However, prices were so high that the low wages of the miners, factory workers, and other labor groups could never bridge the gap between adequate food and stark starvation. They made up the deficiency by chewing coca leaves, the cocaine of which gave them an astonishing strength while in their prime of life, but eventually reduced the user to a pitiful shell of humanity.

The rural population never had sufficient food for itself, for owners of agricultural estates naturally shipped the bulk of the production to the cities, where high prices prevailed. At the same time the Bolivian landowner bitterly resented all proposals to change the system of production, since any improvement inevitably meant the introduction of technical education among the Indian farmers, or rather agricultural workers, that is, the establishment of schools.

The Paz Estenssoro government proposed to solve the agricultural problem by expropriation of lands for distribution among Indians who previously were bought and sold with the lands. After considerable research, involving dispatching land commissions into various parts of Bolivia and preparing surveys, the Agricultural Reform Plan was inaugurated in August, 1953. Its main features included returning land belonging to all towns before 1900 for the use of the local population; converting all forests of gum and nut trees in eastern Bolivia into public domain for the benefit of workers cultivating those products; making available for all Bolivians land in tracts of 123 acres in the east; and expropriating large food-producing estates in the plateau area for division among agricultural workers and urban laborers. Outstanding was the seizure of some thirty-five properties for mining workers in Oruro, Cochabamba, Potosí, and Chuquisaca.

Expropriation, of course, did not produce the food which Bolivia chronically lacked. Because of Communist agitation among the rural hungry, the government appealed immediately after expropriation to the United States for food imports. The Eisenhower administration responded at once with agricultural products to the value of $9,000,000. At the same time the United States assured Bolivia she understood the emergency, which needed the "assistance of friends." Bolivia also concluded agreements with Argentina, Paraguay, and Brazil to exchange food and other commodities, with few restrictions, between their respective border towns. By 1954 the land reform program had created some 2,500,-

000 landowners, mostly in the plateau region. But scarcity of land there led the government to plan for large-scale colonization of Indians in the unpeopled fertile areas of eastern Bolivia.

Strengthened by the recognition of the United States, the Bolivian government executed its second major reform—the nationalization of the tin mines. Since tin is the principal export of Bolivia, the basic objective of this reform was to secure funds to modernize the entire economy: to introduce scientific agriculture and diversification of crops, to achieve self-sufficiency in food, to develop hydroelectric projects for industrial power, to construct roads and highways, to exploit oil, other minerals, and forests, and to educate the masses. In common with his contemporaries, Betancourt and Gallegos in Venezuela, who proposed "ploughing the oil," Paz Estenssoro saw for tin a comparable role in Bolivia.

Unable to come to a satisfactory agreement with the owners, the government on October 31, 1952, nationalized the bulk of the tin mines held by native and foreign corporations. Outstanding were the Patiño holdings, in which United States investors held a 28 per cent interest. The decree provided for compensation, although the government entered a large claim against the tin groups for unpaid taxes and back wages for miners. To continue tin mining and exploitation of other minerals, the government created the Bolivian Mining Corporation to centralize management and control production, refining, and marketing. The United States, deeply concerned over the expropriation, nevertheless continued to buy Bolivian tin both for stockpiling purposes and to keep Bolivia out of the Soviet orbit.

Besides these measures affecting agriculture and tin, the Paz Estenssoro government supported industrial development, the search for oil and other minerals, and construction of highways and railroads. As a primary undertaking, an excellent highway between Santa Cruz and Cochabamba, completed in 1954, linked eastern Bolivia with the plateau region. This highway also fulfills the important role of tying in the railroad, constructed by Bolivia and Brazil from Corumbá to Santa Cruz, with the railroads at Cochabamba, thus bringing into being a transcontinental line from Santos on Brazil's Atlantic coast to Arica on the Chilean Pacific.

The Paz Estenssoro government launched special efforts to develop eastern Bolivia, of which the city of Santa Cruz is the center. Near-by colonies of Indians have been given land. Coffee plantations are established. To the south are the principal oil fields at Camiri, Sanadita, and Bermejo. From the Camiri fields a pipeline furnishes oil to refineries in

Sucre and Cochabamba, which by 1954 were supplying the country's needs and providing exports to Chile and Argentina. In the south, too, in Tarija province, bordering on Argentina, the government granted an extensive concession to the McCarthy Oil Company of Texas, which has opened a number of wells. These, together with the petroleum fields of the government, raised Bolivian production by 1956 to about 3,000,000 barrels a year. Development of other mineral resources are also under way, particularly tungsten, lead, zinc, wolfram, and sulfur. Radioactive ores are reported in eastern Bolivia.

As part of this changing Bolivian picture, the government has shown an interest in basic democratic institutions. Significant in this respect was the decree in 1952 establishing universal suffrage for all Bolivians over twenty years of age. Equally striking are the efforts to build schools. These consist in a national program to abolish illiteracy, placing schools for Indians in rural areas, an enlarged teacher training program, construction of technical institutes, and provisions for higher education. In this picture, too, is a rapidly increasing inflation deriving from the necessity of importing food and raising the wages of labor to meet the costs of living. Pointing to a solution of this basic difficulty is the new farm program, the expansion of the oil industry which is furnishing a new source of income, and the help of the United States by loans and the continued purchase of tin.

Bolivia is at the point of converting her economy from a feudal to a modern one. While democratic practices and institutions are still in their infancy, prospects seem fair that these will become part of the new state.

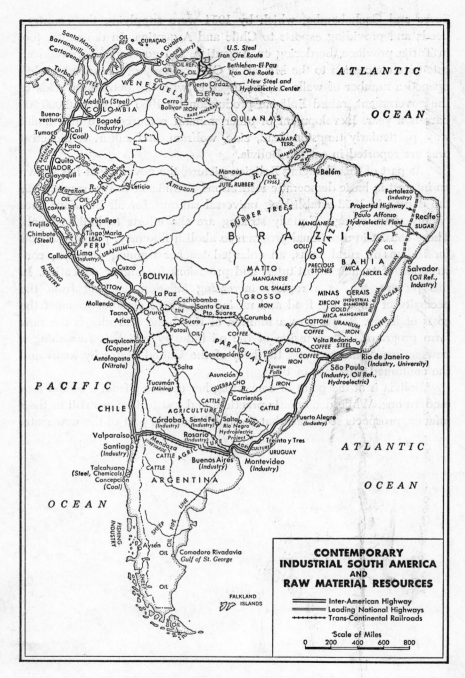

Map labels (reading roughly top to bottom, left to right):

OIL REF.
CURAÇAO
La Guaira
Santa Marta
Barranquilla
Cartagena
Caracas (Industry)
U.S. Steel Iron Ore Route
OIL
OIL REF.
OIL
Bethlehem-El Pau Iron Ore Route
Turbo
COFFEE
VENEZUELA
Puerto Ordaz
El Pau
New Steel and Hydroelectric Center
ATLANTIC OCEAN
OIL
Medellín (Steel)
Cerro Bolívar IRON
IRON
RARE MINERALS
COLOMBIA
Buenaventura
Bogotá (Industry)
GUIANAS
Tumaco
Cali (Coal)
Pasto
Quito
ECUADOR
Guayaquil
Napo R.
Iquitos (Shipping Port)
AMAPÁ TERR.
MANGANESE
BANANA COCOA
COTTON
Marañon R.
Ucayali R.
Leticia
Amazon
Manaus
JUTE, RUBBER
R. OIL (1955)
Belém
Fortaleza (Industry)
OIL
OIL
OIL
COPPER
IRON
Trujillo
Chimbote (Steel)
Pucallpa
Tingo María
LEAD
PERU
Callao
Lima (Industry)
URANIUM
Cuzco
SUGAR
COTTON
Mollendo
Tacna
Arica
Oruro
TIN
Potosí
OIL
BOLIVIA
La Paz
Cochabamba
Santa Cruz
Pto. Suárez
Sucre
COPPER
Corumbá
RUBBER TREES
BRAZIL
MANGANESE
GOLD
GOIAZ
MATTO GROSSO
MANGANESE
OIL SHALES
IRON
PRECIOUS STONES
Projected Highway
Paulo Affonso Hydroelectric Plant
Recife
SUGAR
São Francisco R.
BAHIA
MICA
NICKEL
OIL
Salvador (Oil Ref., Industry)
MINAS GERAIS
ZIRCON
INDUSTRIAL DIAMONDS
GOLD
MICA MANGANESE
COTTON
URANIUM
IRON
Volta Redonda STEEL
COFFEE
COFFEE
COFFEE
RIO-BAHIA HIGHWAY
SUGAR
COFFEE
Chuquicamata (Copper)
Antofagasta (Nitrate)
Salta
PARAGUAY
COFFEE
Concepción
Asunción
QUEBRACHO
Paraná R.
Iguaçu Falls
GOLD
IRON
COFFEE
IRON
Rio de Janeiro (Industry, University)
São Paulo (Industry, Oil Ref., Hydroelectric)
PACIFIC
CHILE
Tucumán (Mining)
CATTLE
AGRICULTURE
Corrientes
CATTLE
Puerto Alegre (Industry)
Córdoba (Industry)
Santa Fe (Industry)
Salta Rio Negro Hydroelectric Project
SHEEP
URUGUAY
Treinta y Tres
Valparaíso
Santiago (Industry)
Rosario (Industry)
Mendoza
VINEYARDS
AGRICULTURE
Buenos Aires (Industry)
Montevideo (Industry)
ATLANTIC OCEAN
Talcahuano (Steel, Chemicals)
Concepción (Coal)
CATTLE
CATTLE
ARGENTINA
OCEAN
FISHING INDUSTRY
SHEEP
PIPE LINE
OIL
OCEAN
Aysén
OIL
Comodoro Rivadavia
Gulf of St. George
SHEEP
FALKLAND ISLANDS
OIL

CONTEMPORARY INDUSTRIAL SOUTH AMERICA AND RAW MATERIAL RESOURCES

——— Inter-American Highway
———— Leading National Highways
++++++ Trans-Continental Railroads

Scale of Miles
0   200   400   600   800

PERU

Part I. FEUDAL ANARCHY, 1822–1920

The Character of Peruvian History. The history of Peru reflects a strong feudal background. The landholding system of the colonial period intrenched an agrarian aristocracy and a powerful church. After the Wars for Independence the leading families, occasionally displaced by *mestizo* leaders, struggled for the control of the presidency of the new republic. In the midst of the incessant military struggles a middle class began to emerge. After 1900 little-taxed foreign investment and harsh dictatorships engendered radical ideas of reform among the Peruvian people. In these same years foreign businesses gave opportunity for further growth of the Peruvian middle class. Thus while the latter opposed radical reforms, they supported national policies, which, while encouraging continued foreign investment, protected their own growth.

Dominance of Military Governments, 1822–1845. The congress of 1822 appointed a governing junta which, soon overthrown by the army, led the congress to seek the aid of Bolívar. After he ended this conflict, Peru adopted a constitution in 1825, which preserved the form of a republic but placed essential power in the hands of the wealthy. Besides provision for a president and vice-president, elected every four years, who were to be assisted by ministers of state, a conservative senate supervised the execution of laws. Voting rested with literate married males who could show ownership of property. The Catholic religion was recognized as the only one of the state.

Bolívar, who had gone to Bolivia, returned to Peru in 1826, set aside the new constitution, and imposed one modeled upon that of Bolivia. Late in that year uprisings, which called him to Venezuela, were the signal for Peruvian militarists to renew their struggle for power. General Andrés Santa Cruz first established his authority as president in 1826, but, shortly driven out, retired to Bolivia where he became dictator. In the next ten years violent struggles between militarist presidents paved the way for the return of Santa Cruz, who established a

Bolivian-Peruvian confederation. When he was overthrown in 1839 by Chile and Argentina, Peru returned to its civil wars.

Ramón Castilla, 1845–1860. In 1845 a small middle class put in power a *mestizo,* Ramón Castilla, who, outside the coterie of militarist families, established orderly government and began developing Peru's guano resources. Elected to office for a term of six years, he temporarily ended the civil wars and respected the authority of congress and the rights of individuals. In 1847 he called an American congress to meet in Lima with the idea of forming a league against European invasion, threatened at the moment by an Ecuadorean, General Juan José Flores. This congress, with representatives from five South American states, drew up conventions which called for defense, but these were not in fact ratified by their governments.

To develop a new source of income for the government, Castilla exported guano from the Chincha Islands and nitrate beds of southern Peru. With the proceeds he built roads, a railroad, and a telegraph line to connect Lima and Callao. He encouraged immigration, reorganized finances, and began to make payments on loans contracted during the Wars for Independence.

Castilla's successor in 1851, General José Rufino Echenique, inspired a contemporary to write that "all pernicious tendencies, intrigues, imposture, fraud, deceit, bad faith and treason were put into play to exploit this rich vein of corruption [the treasury]." The results were revolts which within three years brought Castilla back to the presidency for a second term (1855–1862). Two humane measures stand out during this period, namely, the abolition of slavery and the ending of colonial tribute still being paid by the Indians. Too, the middle class leaders successfully called a national convention in 1856 which gave for the first time formal expression to liberal ideas in Peru—the abolition of capital punishment, ecclesiastical and military privileges, and compulsory tithing—and promulgated a constitution, the most significant provisions of which restored municipal government and granted universal male suffrage.

However, the traditions of militarism were too deeply intrenched. The army, antagonized by loss of its privileges, joined Castilla to overthrow the constitution. With the conservative forces in power, a new document was drawn up in 1860 which lasted until 1920. This constitution provided for a president with a first and second vice-president, elected indirectly for four years, and a bicameral legislature. The senators were elected by the departments into which the country was divided. Since the Creoles dominated the local governments in the de-

partments, this arrangement assured the continuance of feudal control
in the national government as well. So, too, the lower House of Deputies,
whose members were chosen by an electoral college in the departments,
represented powerful families. Numerous qualifications limited suffrage
to the few; the Catholic religion was again decreed the state religion;
a bill of rights provided for was soon forgotten.

Foreign Interest in Peru, 1862–1904. The rivalries of the militarists
who followed Castilla weakened Peru in the face of the Spanish invasion
in 1864. This war upon her former colony arose from the hopes of Isabella's corrupt government to quiet internal discontent by a foreign
adventure, by diverting attention from her failure to lead the invasion
of Mexico in 1861, and by the hope of rehabilitating an empty treasury
from the wealth of the guano deposits. The conflict opened with the
Spanish seizure of the Chincha Islands and the threat of war. When
President Juan Antonio Pezet signed a treaty essentially conceding the
Spanish demands, his countrymen drove him from office and placed in
power General Mariano Ignacio Prado. In spite of British pressure upon
Peru the new president declared war on the invader and sought an
alliance with Bolivia, Chile, and Ecuador. The Spaniards thereupon
bombarded the port of Callao. Chile's protest against this action turned
the Spanish fleet upon that country to attack brutally the city of Valparaíso. A revolt displaced Prado in Peru, but local resistance at Callao
forced Spain, troubled at home with impending revolt, to abandon the
undertaking in May, 1866. The fact that the war did little to develop
nationalist sentiment in Peru stands in strong contrast to the effects
of the contemporary French invasion of Mexico.

Loans and Railroads. Internal conflicts at the end of the invasion
brought José Balta to the presidency in 1868. This figure had some importance in Peru's economic growth during his administration (1868–
1872). He opened Peru to foreign capital, made necessary by the financial
crisis brought on by the war with Spain. His measures were to negotiate
loans and grant concessions to foreigners in the guano region. Outstanding was the loan made by the Dreyfus House in Paris, which received
as security a monopoly on guano exports annually to the extent of
2,000,000 tons until its loan was repaid.

Instead of using the money secured by the loan to meet obligations,
Balta and the new Peruvian capitalists diverted the funds to the construction of railroads and other undertakings. For the former the president employed Henry Meiggs, an American adventurer who had established his reputation by the construction of railroads in Chile. To do the

work, Meiggs imported Chinese laborers and Chileans, who, under stupendous difficulties, built lines from Lima to the central sierra, from Cuzco to Juliaca, and from Arequipa to Lima. Balta also began a program of public works and the construction of a breakwater and mole to improve the Callao harbor. These undertakings proved more costly than originally anticipated, so that new loans were sought. In 1870 one for about $6,000,000 was secured in London and another for $75,000,000 followed two years later, both being devoted to railroad building. Then, to amortize the foreign debt, still another loan by the state was contracted for, amounting to more than $100,000,000.

Peru's small but wealthy middle class businessmen elected in 1872 a successor to continue Balta's policies, Manuel Pardo, who had founded a new political party, the Civilian party. He continued the construction of the railroad system begun by Balta. At the same time he tried to reduce the power of the militarists by strengthening the municipalities where the emerging middle class had its strength. To encourage the economic development of the country, he founded a mining school and expanded the curriculum of the University of San Marcos to include political science and other courses needed in the growing economy.

The enormous debts contracted proved a heavy burden upon the state. By 1872 the service on the foreign debt alone amounted to $12,-000,000 annually. Moreover, Peru's income suffered a blow from the competition of Chile in the sale of nitrates on the world market. This rivalry, straining the relations of the two countries, led Pardo to sign an offensive and defensive alliance with Bolivia in 1873, the latter being also disturbed by Chile's aggressiveness. To bolster the shaky financial condition of the country, Pardo in 1873 expropriated the nitrate holdings of Chilean companies in Peruvian territories as part of a program to create a state nitrate monopoly. The final blow fell in 1874 when the world depression of that year made it impossible for Meiggs and the Peruvian government to secure new loans. By the end of Pardo's administration in 1876 the country was bankrupt.

Peru and the War of the Pacific. Since the War of the Pacific has been surveyed in the history of Chile, it is important here only to see the effects of the conflict upon Peru. Pardo's successor, General Mariano Prado, trying unsuccessfully to meet the financial situation by the issue of inconvertible paper, increased discontent with the government. The army, resorting to force, assassinated former President Pardo. Thus bankrupt and torn with internal conflict, Peru was catapulted into the War of the Pacific in 1879 by the action of Bolivia in seizing the Chilean installations at Antofagasta. Prado, knowing the weakness of his country, tried to mediate between the two nations, but Chile rejected his offer, an action which left Peru with no alternative but to honor her treaty of 1873 and declare war.

The defeat of the Peruvian forces and the harsh terms offered by Chile forced the resignation of Prado, who fled the country. On October 20, 1883, when General Miguel Iglesias, who had assumed the presidency, signed the Treaty of Ancón, he, too, was forced out of office. Refusing to accept the terms for the Peruvians, General Andrés Cáceres continued resistance and was elected to the presidency (1886–1890).

Economically, the war was a devastating blow to Peru. The outright loss of Tarapacá and the plebiscite agreement which gave Chile control of both Tacna and Arica deprived Peru of an important source of income upon which to rebuild her finances. Moreover, the bulk of Peru's guano deposits were hypothecated to Dreyfus House and her industries ruined by the war. Finally, the war added to the public debt, already swollen by the reckless spending of the loans contracted in the previous decades for railroad construction. The autocratic structure of Peru's society made impossible levying taxes upon landholders to share the burdens. Among these were many foreigners who had secured sugar plantations along the coast, including Japanese companies which between 1889 and 1909 brought over 6,000 Japanese workers into Peru as laborers.

In these dire circumstances Cáceres sought means to meet the payments due on the public debt. The result was virtually to turn Peru over to foreigners through an agreement reached with the bondholders. These, British, French, and Dutch, who held almost $270,000,000 in bonds, formed themselves into the Peruvian Corporation in London. To this corporation Cáceres agreed to give control of the state railroads for sixty-six years, concessions to export up to 2,000,000 tons of guano, from which the corporation was to receive annually £80,000 and, finally, control of the navigation of Lake Titicaca.

The news of this agreement provoked strong criticism in Peru. Some of the younger men who had served in the War of the Pacific and had lost faith in the Civilian party now organized the Democratic party and the Civil party for the elections of 1890. However, Cáceres was able to dictate the election of his successor. Four years later, when the arrangements for a plebiscite over Tacna and Arica fell through owing to the Chileanization of the two provinces, Cáceres, in spite of popular indignation, returned to the president's office.

Between the years 1895 and 1904 it appeared for a moment that the growing middle class would establish its control in Peru's government. With Nicholás de Piérola and Eduardo López de Romaña in office in these years, Peru encouraged foreign investment, particularly in the development of copper and silver mines and in the rapidly growing rubber industry. But in the election of 1904 the conservative landowners, the church, and the military recovered control of the government with the election of José Pardo (1904–1908).

The Return of the Militarists and Loss of Territory, 1904–1914. More concerned with strengthening its political position throughout the provinces of Peru, the conservative party under Pardo treated lightly the importance of the trans-Andean region, rapidly becoming the scene of keen competition for the rubber-tree areas. Into this territory Brazilians had penetrated, but there was, in fact, no well-defined boundary between Peru and Brazil. After 1890, when both Peruvian and Brazilian groups sought out rubber areas in the vast Acre territory, each claimed ownership on behalf of their respective countries. By 1896 the Peruvian rubber hunters had pushed their way from the Ucayali Valley into the Acre region along the tributaries of the Surúa River. In 1901 they were operating on the upper Purús River, meeting Brazilians, with whom conflicts frequently arose.

Meanwhile, in 1903 Brazil, as noted already, negotiated with Bolivia the Treaty of Petropolis, under the terms of which she secured title to some 191,000 square kilometers of territory in the Acre River basin. But to this region Peru had already entered claims. Arbitration of the question in 1909 led to a treaty under which, out of the total of 442,000 square kilometers involved, Brazil succeeded in winning 403,000, while Peru gained the remaining 39,000. Thus the undemocratic structure of Peruvian society and government made it possible for her statesmen to sign away practically unnoticed one of the choicest possessions of the country.

With Pardo's successor, Augusto B. Leguía (1908–1912), militarism continued in the saddle while nascent political parties of some democratic color declined. Their lack of influence was testified to in the overthrow of Pardo's successor, Guillermo Billinghurst (1912–1914), whose humane efforts to alleviate the unconscionable exploitation of the rubber workers in the Putamayo region stirred revolt against him. The leader of the uprising, Colonel Oscar R. Benavides, later to become one of Peru's dictators, occupied the presidency until Congress, dominated by the small, conservative clique, selected again José Pardo as president on August 10, 1915. The chief concession to the growing liberal movement was an amendment to the constitution granting religious freedom; but this freedom remained, in fact, illusory.

World War I and Peru, 1914–1918. On the eve of World War I Peru's finances were once more in a state of collapse. The loss of the trans-Andean territory bankrupted native rubber companies. The Peruvian Corporation drained away the income of the state pledged to it besides controlling the nitrate production. The price of sugar declined rapidly as Cuban sugar reached the world markets in cheaper prices. From taxes the state derived little benefit. Those on certain state monopolies, such as alcohol, matches, salt, tobacco, and opium, were collected through a private company which enjoyed huge profits but left little for the national treasury. Export taxes were purposely held at a low figure to encourage foreign investment in coffee, sugar, cocoa, and petroleum. No income or real estate taxes existed. Thus the most important sources of income, derived from taxes levied upon the necessities of the desperately poor, were totally inadequate to meet the needs of the government.

Upon this bankrupt and militarist-ridden state, World War I descended. Loss of markets, as occurred elsewhere in Latin America in 1914, was immediate. With the rapid decline of her export trade, customs revenues fell 30 per cent in 1914 and to over 60 per cent by 1916. Schoolteachers and other government workers went unpaid. Unemployment on the estates and in the cities mounted. The government declared a moratorium on the payment of debts, closed banks, and mortgaged some of its monopolies, notably tobacco, to secure funds. Unwilling to levy taxes upon the wealthy, it raised those on the necessities of the working class.

After the opening of the Panama Canal and the entry of the United States into the war, Peruvian raw materials were sought. American capital, encouraged by Pardo's policies, found its way into Peru's silver and copper areas, and construction was begun on new railroads to facilitate the export of these minerals. To favor the exports through the ports of Lima, that is, Callao, and others, Pardo launched a program to exterminate mosquitoes on the coastal area. However, this period of prosperity was short. The sudden ending of the war in November, 1918, threw Peru once more into a state of collapse. Unemployment became practically universal in the copper, oil, and sugar industries and in the urban export businesses associated with the handling of these raw materials. Revolts followed and a new dictatorship appeared, but at the same time movements to democratize Peru also emerged from World War I.

Peruvian Cultural Development. The background of this concern for democracy stemmed from the determined efforts of nineteenth century liberals to alter the clerical-militarist character of Peru. At the end of the century several figures appeared to give a new impetus to this drive. In the field of literature was Manuel González Prada. Although he had no Indian blood, Prada advocated reforms from which Indians were to be the chief beneficiaries. His attacks upon the government of Peru and the country's leading families were merciless; he characterized them as "echoes of men." He demanded seizure of government power by intellectuals, Indians, and laborers, for he believed no change could come by peaceful means. His most famous books, *Hours of Battle, Pages of Freedom,* and *Propaganda and Attack,* gave Peruvian liberals the ammunition to fight for land reform, the end of Indian abuses, improvement of labor's lot, and political responsibility through representative government. His other works, particularly his poetry of perfection, mark him a forerunner in the modernist movement and establish his reputation as one of Peru's great writers.

A contemporary of Prada, José Carlos Mariátegui, came from the other end of the social scale, a *mestizo* from Lima's slums. Self-educated and suffering from a knee injury which never healed, Mariátegui forced recognition of his great writing talent. A period of study in Europe took him to Russia, where he became a Marxist. His leading work, *Seven Essays on Peruvian Reality,* outlined a program of land reform and called for dissolving the alliance between Peru's landowners and foreign mining groups. This solution, he insisted, combined with redistribution of the land to the Indians and amelioration of urban labor conditions, was the only one for Peru's salvation. Mariátegui's ideas on agricultural reform influenced the later *aprista* movement, which, however, abjured his Communist beliefs.

Contributing to the emphasis upon Indian culture and hence focusing the attention of liberal leaders upon Indian emancipation was the work of two other figures, neither of whom had the least interest in reform movements. The first of these was Julio Tello, Peru's internationally known archaeologist. A full-blooded Quechua Indian himself, Tello was educated in part by his family at great sacrifice, proud of their son's genius. When their resources failed them, he found employment in the National Library. Winning several degrees at the university, he studied abroad in the United States and Germany. His great work consisted in giving scientific direction to the recovery of Peru's ancient Indian civilizations. He himself excavated many undreamed of ruins, great Indian cemeteries, and other monuments which have given pre-Incan history a new interpretation.

High in the ranks of Peru's literary figures is the great traditionalist, Ricardo Palma. World-famous is his creation of a new type of literature, part folklore, part history, and part fantasy, in his monumental, ten-volume *Tradiciones Peruanas (Peruvian Traditions)*. Palma's work has been a source of inspiration for the study of the Indian-Spanish colonial period, whose picturesque life he has welded together in a literary form that has defied classification. Palma profoundly disagreed with González Prada, but he aided him as he did Tello, finding for the latter employment in the National Library of which he was the director.

In the decades after 1920 other gifted writers also explored the culture of the Indian and interpreted his spirit. Whitman-like José Santos Chocano (1873–1934), a defender of the Indian and a critic of the United States in the 1920's, presented in his poetry a vast panorama of New World life. In the present day, also preoccupied with the Indian, is the highly regarded novelist, Ciro Alegría (1909–   ). In his well-known book, *Broad and Alien is the World,* Alegría combines his indigation at the exploitation of the natives with a profound understanding of their traditions and their significance as a cultural force in the nation's development. This is the mark of the indigenous writer, no longer European in his emphasis.

Part II. ATTEMPTS TO ESTABLISH DEMOCRATIC INSTITUTIONS, 1920–1956

The Leguía Dictatorship, 1919–1931. The long-term effects of World War I were to bring into prominence a wealthy middle class. Though small in numbers and nourished by American capital invested in Peru, it soon assumed a place in power alongside the traditional oligarchy. Equally long-term, as we have noted, was the intellectual upheaval in the train of the war which became linked after 1920 with the efforts of a handful of liberals to improve the condition of both urban labor and the leaderless Indian masses—the *aprista* movement. But in those years the intellectuals, labor, and Indians were no match for the skilled and experienced leaders of the oligarchy and the new figures of the economic-minded middle class.

The oligarchy was content for the Indian to remain in his historic subjection. But the new businessmen looking out upon Peru saw the possibilities of its vast resources. Huge agricultural areas along the coast awaited irrigation; others, stretching between Lima and Cuzco and from Arequipa to Trujillo, needed but the plow directed by modern science. At its different geographic and climatic levels, ranging from Arctic to semitropical, the country could produce anything: wheat, sugar, cotton, coffee, fruit, cattle, fertilizer in huge deposits of guano; while its unending mountain ranges hid untapped wealth in virtually every important mineral—coal, iron, oil, copper, silver, gold, vanadium, antimony, and a myriad of others. Beyond the Andes were vast timber reserves and undiscovered resources.

In office, Leguía, in a harsh dictatorship (1919–1931), crushed all opposition, destroying local self-government, in particular the popularly elected municipal councils. With control securely lodged in his hands, he invited foreign capital, principally American, to begin the exploitation of Peru's enormous wealth. The process was facilitated by the sale of Peruvian bonds and by British and American loans which added to the already large national debt of $100,000,000. At the same time the resulting investment and construction did begin to change Peru from its essentially feudal character into a modern state, without, however, accompanying political rights. Railroads begun before World War I were extended and new ones were planned to aid the export of coal, copper, and silver from the fabulous Cerro de Pasco area. Leguía also added paved highways and roads, the latter built by Indian labor working for a pittance under a labor tax requiring each to contribute yearly fifteen days on road construction.

Significant in opening new areas was the establishment of communications between Lima and the Peruvian Amazon at Iquitos. Sugar and coffee plantations developed, while an attempt was made to revive the rubber industry. The most neglected area of the country—the vast coastal region from Túmbez to the Chilean border—saw irrigation projects begun by using the waters of the Cañete River. Outside of Lima on the Pampas del Imperial extensive irrigation projects opened up some 17,000 acres. By 1931 Peru had invested more than $10,000,000 on these and other land reclamation projects. Cotton from these and older lands provided new and cheaper supplies for the growing Peruvian textile industries.

The growth of urban labor in the new factories brought attempts to unionize, harshly suppressed by the government. But Leguía saw the necessity for better housing and began in Lima a program of modern low cost dwellings for labor. The larger cities, too, saw the introduction of modern conveniences, sewage systems, utilities, and paved streets.

Politically, the dictatorship took cognizance of the new ideas emerging in Peru, although Leguía gave but lip service to the constitution. Promulgated in January, 1920, it called for compulsory primary education, arbitration of industrial disputes, the adoption of an income tax, religious toleration, stronger local self-government, extension of the suffrage, and a one-term presidency. In 1924 Leguía amended the document to provide for his re-election, the basis for his continued dictatorship. Meanwhile his political secret police destroyed individual liberties, throttled the press, and arrested nonconformists. In education the dictatorship recognized the importance of technically trained personnel for the new economy and provided scholarships for young Peruvians to study in the United States. The close association of the church with the government, however, continued control of education in its hands, particularly over higher education at the University of San Marcos.

The suppression of the freedom to teach awoke a violent opposition among students in universities. From a revolt at San Marcos emerged a figure, Haya de la Torre, destined to become world-famous for his struggle against Leguía, but more important for his efforts to improve the lot of the Indian. Exiled in 1924, Haya de la Torre nevertheless created in his secret visits to the country a political party, the APRA (the Alliance of American Revolutionary Parties). It had as its original objectives opposition to the dominance of foreign capital; the nationalization of the large estates of the oligarchy and their distribution among Indians; the industrialization of Peru; state agrarian enterprises; comprehensive reclamation and irrigation projects; revision of the tax structure; and equal rights for women. His proposed foreign policy was the creation of similar revolutionary parties in all Latin-American countries in which Indians were the dominant population element, the internationalization of the Panama Canal, and an unalterable opposition to Communism. In opposition to Mariátegui, Haya de la Torre regarded the doctrines of Marx as a body of political and economic ideas alien to the culture of Peru. Later the APRA, in the face of the Axis threat of the 1930's, abandoned its opposition to "Yankee" imperialism and the proposal to internationalize the canal. The APRA's chief contribution to the present has been to serve as an important vehicle for the spread of democratic ideas within Peru's feudal structure.

The Dictatorship of Sánchez Cerro, 1931–1933. By 1931 the Leguía dictatorship, shot through with corruption, came to an end. Hastening its fall was the world depression of 1929 which, denying further loans to the dictator, threw the country into bankruptcy and brought the repudiation of its foreign debt. The army, first to feel the shortage of funds, revolted in 1931. It put Colonel Sánchez Cerro in power, whose role was to save the country from *aprista* reform and Haya de la Torre, who had returned to Peru in the moment of freedom following the fall of Leguía. Facing serious problems of unemployment, loss of markets, and the consequent decline of the national income, Sánchez Cerro was helpless. To distract attention from his failures, he dramatically seized the town of Leticia on the Amazon River, previously awarded to Colombia. This blatant appeal to nationalistic feeling also failed when Peruvians, desperate under his military dictatorship, assassinated him in April, 1933.

The Dictatorship of Benavides, 1933–1939. The congress promptly chose a more stable figure from the oligarchy, General Oscar Benavides, who remained in office to finish the unexpired term of Sánchez Cerro in 1936. To his credit, Benavides, in cooperation with Colombia, peacefully settled the Leticia incident, returning the town to Colombia. The new president joined his policies to those of the more forward-looking middle class and revealed an interest in basic social problems. From the beginning of his administration he recognized that the solution for the depression in Peru lay in re-employment of workers in mines and industries, provided funds for this purpose could be found. His first step in this direction was to secure a loan from the International Petroleum (Standard Oil) Company, which had extensive holdings in Peru. Seeking an understanding with the investors of the 1920's, whose bonds had been repudiated or in default since 1930, he opened the way for securing loans from the United States government, itself anxious to find new markets to relieve the depression there.

With these funds he launched a comprehensive building program, essentially a continuation of the constructive work of the Leguía dictatorship. Notable was the completion of the Pan-American highway, a project in which the United States was interested. In various cities he established large numbers of workers' homes, and decreed mild social legislation including compulsory insurance for workers. How badly this was needed was evident in the wage rate, forty to sixty cents a day, for workers on highways and in foreign-owned mines.

Aiding in building up the treasury was a thriving trade developed with Germany, Japan, and Italy, all anxious to exchange goods for goods. An admirer of Italy's Fascism, Benavides invited an Italian military mission to reorganize the Peruvian army and instruct his secret police in Fascist methods of suppressing opposition. Considerable Italian investments found their way into Peruvian industries and raw materials. Japan on her part found a market for her low-cost goods among the depressed Indians, unable to buy higher-priced American products.

Politically, Benavides reflected the intense opposition to the *apristas*. He jailed Haya de la Torre for a year and kept him thereafter under rigid surveillance. Haya de la Torre, refusing to resort to revolution as a means of winning power, attempted in 1936 to reach the presidency by constitutional means. However, antagonism toward him in conservative ranks was so intense that he withdrew in favor of Dr. Luís Antonio Eguiguren, a liberal-minded but strongly Catholic candidate. When, however, the counting of the votes showed clearly that Eguiguren was defeating Benavides' choice, Dr. Jorge Prado, the president converted the election into a fiasco by declaring that *aprista* votes cast for the opposition were illegal. With the election thus set aside, the congress extended Benavides' term until December, 1939, during which time he ruled consistently by decree.

The Prado Administration and World War II, 1939–1945. Benavides, who did not have the complete support of the reactionary groups of Peru, threw his influence to elect Manuel Prado Ugarteche. Assuming office on December 8, 1939, Prado had long been interested in public affairs and was undoubtedly more national-minded than any of his predecessors. Coming from an old aristocratic family, he had been in his youth a leader in the international Latin-American student movement, where he absorbed an essentially liberal outlook. As a wealthy, successful businessman, he appreciated fully the possibilities of Peru's natural riches. Thus his natural inclination when World War II broke out was to sympathize with the Allies and shift Benavides' emphasis away from the Axis.

The outbreak of the war reduced Peru's markets in Europe, but this was compensated for somewhat by her expansion of trade with neighboring countries. Petroleum, cotton, and sugar went to Chile, Argentina, Bolivia, Brazil, and Uruguay. Later the bulk of her oil was diverted to the United States. Loss of rice sources in the Orient forced Peru to turn to Ecuador for that commodity, while the latter bought cotton textiles and other products. Colombia relied on Peru for cotton while sending coffee. But the United States came to consume the bulk of her raw materials, oil, copper, silver, and vanadium. For this reason for the first time in the history of her relations with the United States, Peru agreed to a commercial treaty in May, 1942. Under other agreements the United States also purchased all Peru's surplus cotton, flax, rubber, and quinine for the war period.

These close economic relations with the United States became the principal reason for Peru's breaking diplomatic contact with the Axis on February 15, 1942. Under the new policy Prado properly ended the activities of Axis nationals in the country, confiscated their property, and, to facilitate the development of strategic materials, signed a Lend-Lease agreement. These favorable relations in turn paved the way for new loans to forward the expansion of Peru's resources begun by Leguía and continued by Benavides.

The emphasis was put now upon industrialization. Greatly aiding Prado in his program was the support of the *apristas* who had long advocated industrialization as a means of raising the standard of living. With their support the Prado administration carried forward three great projects: (1) construction of new roads and highways to tap resources; (2) the establishment of a major hydroelectric project on the Santa River to irrigate coastal lands and furnish power; and (3) the construction of a steel plant. With all three went social programs to improve the condition of labor in the cities and efforts to raise the Indians out of the dark serfdom of the great estates.

Among the road building projects, that of connecting the coast with the Amazonian territories had the greatest interest for Peruvians. Benavides had taken the first steps in 1938. By 1944 the highway, completed from Callao to Pucallpa and 525 miles in length, required but five days' travel to reach the Amazon post on the Ucayali River. Besides reducing the long route through the Panama Canal and the Amazon River, the new highway contributed to the unity of the nation. Beyond the Andes, where the highway descended to the valley of Tingo María, an agricultural settlement for small farmers was established to facilitate travel and develop local resources. From the new route opened, Amazonian products —rubber, sugar, quinine, and timber, as well as agricultural foods—became available and a vast virgin territory was made ready for exploitation.

On the northwest coast and along the upper reaches of the Marañon River, Peru took the first steps to develop an industrial base for the nation. The work began with the construction of a hydroelectric station on the Cañon del Pato (Duck Canyon), long the dream of a Peruvian engineer, Dr. Santiago Antúnez. Raw materials for the undertaking Peru had in abundance: oil, coal, iron, lead, antimony, magnesium, tungsten, copper, zinc, limestone, cinnabar, nickel, and vanadium. The project, directed by the Santa Corporation founded in July, 1942, began work at Huallanca on the Santa River, which flows through Cañon del Pato and has a capacity of 125,000 kilowatts daily, capable of being produced at an extremely low cost.

Not far away at Chimbote on the coast, plans were made in 1942 to construct a steel mill. To aid as part of Peru's war effort, the United

States extended a loan of $25,000,000. The rich iron deposits south of Lima and excellent anthracite coal beds to the north made the venture a success from the beginning. Near-by other industries became possible— fertilizer, chemical, cement—supported by the future steel of Chimbote and the power from Huallanca. By 1945 Peru was planning national electrification with new plants, one at Mantaro, south of Lima, to embrace that area; a second near the ruins of Macchu Pichu to provide power for the Cuzco-Apurimac region; and a third near Borja on the Marañon River to embrace the region of the north.

As workers crowded into the new and old urban centers, an expanded educational program became imperative. During the six years of the Prado administration, the government constructed 3,962 primary schools, with 5,435 teachers looking after 717,612 pupils, a 29 per cent increase over 1939. In addition the universities received increased subsidies, while establishment of national high schools, normal schools, a music school at Arequipa, a school of veterinary science, as well as nineteen technical educational centers, vocational, agricultural, and industrial, began to round out the educational picture. Important was Prado's decree in 1944 launching a national literacy campaign and supplementing it with a second to teach Spanish to the millions of Indians speaking only Quechua. With these advances the democratic groups of the country were delighted; the conservatives, disturbed.

Causing similar feelings was the improved status of labor under Prado, who encouraged unionization. By 1944 the major unions of the country united to form the Confederation of Workers of Peru. The numerous strikes of the same year testified to the growing demands for improved working conditions, housing, and wages. A further sign of health in the social structure was the concern of the unions with the low state of the agricultural laborers.

Thus as a result of the impetus of World War II, Peru's projects of highway building, hydroelectric undertakings, steel, and other industries gave labor greater employment at higher wages than ever before and to greater numbers. The development of union organization and the broad educational program, accompanied by greater political freedom, was launching Peru at last on the road to a normal democratic evolution.

That Prado anticipated the force of the new political power was apparent in his decision not to violate the constitution and seek a second term. He even went so far as to give Peru in 1945 the only free election held in its history. The conservative forces, unreconciled to the changing economy, advanced as their candidate in the election General Eloy Ureta. The liberal opposition, composed of varied democratic groups, organized a Democratic Front under the leadership of Peru's widely respected poet, Dr. José Gálvez. The *apristas* entered the Front under a new name, the People's party. Haya de la Torre, so deeply feared by the conservatives, tactfully remained aside as a candidate. The Democratic Front nominated instead Dr. José Luis Bustamante, a conservative Catholic, but one who understood the need of supporting reforms necessary to modernize Peru's still feudal social structure. Not surprisingly, General Benavides supported Bustamante.

Accepting the nomination, Bustamante declared that democracy must be firmly implanted in Peru and without delay. When the votes were counted Bustamante had won with an overwhelming majority and carried with him the Democratic Front candidates for congress to gain control of that body. Significantly, APRA members so elected entered Peruvian official life for the first time, assuming three cabinet positions in the new government.

The Administration of Bustamante, 1945–1948. The Bustamante administration continued the main lines of development begun under the preceding governments. New highways were built; the Cañon del Pato hydroelectric project carried forward; port works at Chimbote were expanded, while the construction of the steel industry continued. In addition the government launched the great coastal development, irrigation, and mechanization of agriculture so long desired by the *apristas*. In an attempt to reduce Peru's dependence upon foreign-owned oil wells, Bustamante created the National Petroleum Corporation for exploration and development of national oil fields. Extensive housing projects were begun in the larger cities. Education was extended by increasing the kindergartens 50 per cent; enrolling a larger number of students in the secondary schools; and making more available to students and the public the resources of Peru's universities.

These normal advances both in the modernization of her economy and the broadening of her democratic base were rudely interrupted by a rightist revolt in 1948. The causes leading to this misfortune were many. The government had all the weaknesses of a coalition. Peru's history of dictatorship had prevented the bulk of her people from gaining political "know-how." Thus the attempt of Bustamante's government to fix solidly democratic institutions by restoring local self-government found inexperienced local boards, appointed to draw up new voters' lists, colliding with skilled conservatives intent upon preserving local provincial control.

This blow, aimed at the base of conservative power, was paralleled by an attack at the top with legislation proposing to lower the retirement age of high army officers and raise the pay of the lower ranks. The law, defeated in congress, left militarist leaders in key positions from which they overthrew the government itself.

Hastening the rightist revolt was the fear of Bustamante's government securing large loans from the United States if it could settle the claims of American bondholders, a heritage of the Leguía regime. Since such funds would, in part, go to expand the social reform program, conservative senators in Congress blocked all efforts of the government to reach a settlement. Adding to Bustamante's difficulties was inflation, brought on by the huge expenditures, on the one hand, for the vast industrialization projects and, on the other, by lack of adequate income, since Peru's wealth—oil, gold, silver, vanadium, and copper—lay mostly in foreign hands. Shortages in essential goods brought inflated prices. Government attempts to control both imports and prices resulted in charges in the conservative press of "socialism." When controls were taken off by a conservative finance minister appointed in desperation by Bustamante, prices skyrocketed while the poorer classes suffered and were encouraged to turn against the government.

In the heat of the political battle produced by these political and economic questions, the Democratic Front went to pieces. By early 1948 Bustamante was forced to govern without a congress when conservative senators went on strike. His attempt to call a national assembly was promptly declared unconstitutional by the supreme court. Thus by the middle of 1948, refusing to accept the socialization program as part of the democratic one and refusing conservative support at the price of ending his social reform policies, Bustamante had reached an impasse.

The crisis, apparent to both the *apristas* and the conservative oligarchy, meant that the time for a naked struggle for power was at hand. The *apristas* revolted on October 3, 1948, in an attempt to seize the Callao barracks. This move, more spontaneous than planned, bore no relation to the next uprising, the carefully thought out rightist revolt beginning in Arequipa under General Manuel Odría on October 29, 1948. This seizure of power assured the eclipse down to the present of Peru's promising democratic movement.

The Odría Dictatorship, 1948 to the Present. In control, the Odría dictatorship made its first order of business the extermination of all APRA organizations and the jailing, execution, and exiling of its leaders. Haya de la Torre fortunately made his escape to political asylum into the

Colombian embassy. Refusing him a safe-conduct out of the country, the Odría government continued to seek his release for execution on the ground of his being a common criminal. The Colombian government, to its great credit, stoutly honored its obligation. Finally, in April, 1954, Odría granted him a safe-conduct to Mexico.

In developing economic and social policies, the Odría government followed two major lines. Recognizing that the growing power of labor had to be met, it blunted its political demands by economic conces- sions: low-cost housing in key areas, wage raises, schools, improvement in working conditions, and health programs. Secondly, to continue the program of industrialization, the Odría government expanded the oppor- tunities for native Peruvian capital to invest in Peru's development, but relied most heavily upon foreign capital for this purpose. For the latter it extended inviting offers of lower taxes and longer terms for develop- ment of concessions.

The dictatorship continued the expansion of the Amazonian area. In the Tingo María region it secured the aid of Point Four funds to meet jungle health difficulties. Beyond, it supported the development of rubber plantations in the Hullaga River Valley, which by 1953, with other producing regions, was meeting the national needs. Throughout the area the government encouraged the immigration of skilled workers, trained Peruvian technicians, and European immigrants. Significantly, in 1953 the dictator visited Brazil to negotiate a series of treaties looking forward to their mutual cooperation in adjoining Amazonian territories. The chief features of these agreements involved making Manaus and Iquitos free ports, improving the navigation of the Amazon, joint exploration of natural resources, and exchanging frontier census data.

To facilitate exploitation of new resources throughout the country, the dictatorship constructed new roads, highways, and railroads. Im- portant was the modern highway completed from Lima to Ica and that linking the Puno region with the sea. In the south, too, the railroad begun in 1939 was completed to link La Joya with Matarani, a port north of Mollendo. In northern Peru, a railroad was under construction to connect the unfinished steel plant at Chimbote with Huayunca.

The Bustamante agricultural program was continued by Odría. Peru's population, now estimated at 8,500,000, had increased between 1940 and 1950 some 30 per cent, while food production rose only 20 per cent. Bustamante and the *apristas,* long aware of the problem, began developing the vast coastal areas, particularly a huge project on the Quiroz River, Piura Department in the north, and others at Chauvirú and in the Camaná Valley. With the Quiroz project completed in 1953, the government planned new agricultural undertakings northwest of Arequipa, and in 1954 opened an extensive irrigation system in the Junín Department, bringing 25,000 acres under cultivation. Contributing to the over-all picture has been the work of SCIPA (the Inter-American Cooperative Service for the Production of Food). Significant results—an increase of more than 25 per cent in food production—appeared at the end of the five years, 1950–1955.

To exploit Peru's valuable mineral resources, oil, iron, copper, silver, vanadium, and others, Odría attracted foreign aid with new oil laws and a revised mining code. The petroleum legislation provides for long-term concessions ranging from 50,000 acres up with favorable tax exemptions, in return for which Peru receives 50 per cent of the profits of the ventures. In a short time foreign oil companies including International Petroleum (Standard Oil) were bidding for approximately 15,000,000 acres of the rich Sechura coastal area north of Lima. By 1956 results appeared in an expanding production which reached about 17,000,000 barrels.

The new mining code also stimulated a search for minerals and especially aided native capital investment by assistance to Peruvian companies. In July, 1951, an important new discovery was the huge copper deposit in the Tacna Department, for the development of which the American Smelting and Refining Company received the concession. In the north large iron deposits at Marcona for the Chimbote steel mill were likewise being exploited by an American company.

Expansion of agriculture and mining activity provided the basis for Peru's manufacturing industries. In the cities, most importantly in Lima, the cotton and rayon textile industry, largely foreign-owned, employed some 35,000 workers. Other industries included paper mills, cement, tire, jute plants, piping and pharmaceutical factories. In these varied economic activities Peru had the benefit of American loans after the country's credit was re-established in 1952 under an agreement to liquidate the dollar debt outstanding from the Leguía dictatorship.

Foreign Affairs. Peru's foreign affairs under the dictatorship are closely linked with domestic policies. The exploitation of her varied resources broadened her foreign trade and facilitated commercial agreements with her neighbors, Ecuador, Brazil, Chile, and Argentina, and overseas with Italy, West Germany, Yugoslavia, and Japan. With the United States she signed in 1951 a Mutual Defense Pact. More important was the reciprocal trade agreement between the two countries which reduced duties on 90 per cent of Peru's imports into the United States and 50 per cent of those entering Peru from the United States.

Peru's interest in possible oil deposits in the Zamora Santiago region in the north kept alive her boundary dispute with Ecuador. Odría, to his credit, avoided stirring Peruvian nationalism over the issue, and moreover, showed a marked disposition to submit the question to abitration under the 1942 Rio de Janeiro Protocol. Too, in Peru's dispute with Colombia over the case of Haya de la Torre, the Odría government came to a peaceful solution in the face of strong domestic opposition. In another field of international affairs, however, Peru vigorously asserted her rights, supported by Chile and Ecuador, to territorial waters extending 200 miles offshore. When in 1954 a privately owned Argentine whaling fleet, under Panamanian registry, invaded these waters, she seized the ships and forced payment of a fine of several million dollars. However, the United States and Britain, disturbed by the far-reaching implications of Peru's action, strongly supported Panama's repudiation of the Peruvian claim. The three republics, nevertheless, remained adamant.

Social and Political Developments. The social and political aspects of the dictatorship present its weakest side. Huge sums spent on developing the industrial and mining undertakings left little for education, sanitation, public health, or any other of the most elementary needs of the population. The millions of Indians laboring on the plantations of wealthy Peruvians are sunk in illiteracy, superstition, and disease, the latter largely dietary. For these, education is considered dangerous. Illiteracy for the nation as a whole is above 60 per cent. In the urban areas emphasis is placed upon technical schools for the new middle class families. For labor and its children, education is kept at a minimum. Labor has benefited somewhat from low-cost housing largely confined to Lima, the principal industrial center. But with the right to strike suppressed, labor is helpless to seek its own improvement. Likewise, with suffrage denied, the legislative road is blocked.

Politically, the dictatorship concentrated in its first three years upon the destruction of the *aprista* and other democratic groups. Thus Odría had no opposition to his election as president in 1952. But with the approach of the presidential elections in 1956 the government has revealed within itself deep rifts. One group, stemming from the traditional colonial families, who have always ruled their domains through overseers while they fought among themselves for the presidency, opposed Odría's liberal economic policies. When, however, the government yielded to the pressure of world opinion and granted a safe-conduct to Haya de la

Torre, the Peruvian autocrats, headed by the powerful Miró Quesada family, attempted a revolt led by General Zenón Noriega late in 1954. The uprising was put down and Noriega exiled, but the lines were drawn tighter for the 1956 election.

Viewed as a whole, the history of Peru from independence to the end of World War I was the record of a feudal society. Into this economy World War I brought foreign investment which became the base for subsequent development of industrialization and a new growth in Peru's small middle class. World War I also brought new strength to liberal ideas advocated by Peruvian intellectuals throughout the nineteenth century. These ideas, finding expression in a native political movement, the *aprista,* made significant advances during World War II. The new dictatorship after that war continued the trend toward industrialization, but suppressed its concomitant democratic development. At present, rifts within the dictatorship may return Peru to the reform program advocated by liberals and expressed so vividly in the life of Haya de la Torre.

Chapter XXII

ECUADOR

Part I. THE CONSERVATIVE-CLERICAL STATE, 1830–1875

The Character of Ecuadorean History. Ecuador's history has been deeply affected by the mountainous character of her land. The colonial land grants in the deep valleys of the interior, where the bulk of the Indians lived, established the basis of the Ecuadorean oligarchy. The capital at Quito became naturally their principal stronghold. On the coast along the Gulf of Guayaquil, where colonial trade and commerce flourished, a middle class had its origins. After independence a liberal movement, mixed with the rivalries of the powerful families in Guayaquil, came into conflict with the clerical conservatives of Quito for the control of the country. By 1875 the tide turned in favor of Guayaquil liberal leadership, which steadily developed institutions to make Ecuador one of the democratic states of South America.

Conservative and Liberal Struggles, 1830–1875. General Juan José Flores, who led the revolt which separated Ecuador from Colombia in 1830, dominated the junta of churchmen and Creole landowners set up in Quito. In September of that year the junta proclaimed the first constitution without consulting Guayaquil leaders. The document, reflecting the oligarchic outlook of Quito, provided for a centralized republic with a single chamber, and set up qualifications for voting and holding office that only a few of the wealthy could meet. The Catholic religion was made the sole religion of the state with special provisions for its protection.

In Guayaquil, Bolívar's supporters organized a revolt to force the reunion of Ecuador and Colombia, but news of the Liberator's death ended their hopes. Flores won support temporarily for his government in Guayaquil when he took possession and occupied the Galápagos Islands, but promptly lost it when he surrendered to Colombia the territory of the Cauca Valley, over which the colonial presidency of Quito exercised jurisdiction. This event inspired liberals to assemble behind the leadership of Vicente Rocafuerte, a Quiteño, and Colonel José Hall, who had organized in the capital a society called *El Quiteño Libre*. Attacked by Flores, the little band retreated to an island in the Gulf where they set up a government of brief duration when Flores defeated them in the battle of Mirarica. Forced to recognize, however, the influence of Roca-fuerte, the two reached an understanding which paved the way for the latter to assume the presidency in June, 1835.

Rocafuerte, a scion of a wealthy family, had studied in Europe, met Miranda in Paris, and had become an ardent liberal in politics. He returned to his country eagerly looking forward to its progress as an independent state. Great was his disappointment when Flores, a brilliant and able leader, became the dictator of the nation upon independence. When he himself reached the presidency in 1835, he immediately began liberal reforms which included amending the constitution to provide two chambers, replacing the puppet judiciary with men of integrity, and seeking honest men for official posts in the government. He took the first steps in Ecuador's history to develop democratic institutions when he built more than eighty public schools, extended the suffrage, and reduced qualifications for voting.

Flores succeeded Rocafuerte in 1839 and promptly undid the work of the latter. He presented the country with a new constitution drawn up by hand-picked supporters, disregarding congress. The new document extended the presidential term to eight years and provided for re-election. As virtual dictator, he imposed extortionate taxes upon the Indians and lower classes. He sent aid to a clerical-conservative revolt at Pasto, New Granada against the Márquez government in Bogotá. These policies soon met the opposition of Rocafuerte, who had reassumed the governorship of the department of Guayas on the coast. In 1845 Rocafuerte and General Antonio Elizalde revolted and set up a separate government in Guayaquil. Flores, unable to put down the uprising, went into voluntary exile with schemes to return with foreign aid and set up a monarchy. His efforts failed, however, after elaborate preparations. Flores' successor, Vicente Ramón Roca (1845–1849), nevertheless had to face Flores, who, with Bolivian and Peruvian followers, next schemed to seize the governments of Bolivia, Peru, and Ecuador. When these projects, too, failed, Flores again fled into exile.

By the expiration of Roca's term in 1849 the commercial classes and intellectuals, mostly located in Guayaquil, and the Creole landowners and church leaders in Quito had resolved themselves into two political parties. The former composed the Liberal or Democratic party; the latter the Conservative. In the elections of that year the Liberals put forward

General Elizalde and the Conservatives, Diego Noboa. When the election, thrown into congress, could not be decided there, the country plunged into a civil war. The struggle resulted in a truce providing for a national convention, which selected Noboa as president. In power, the conservative forces erased the reforms of Rocafuerte and Roca drew up still another constitution which again restored the single chamber and high property qualifications for voting for representatives to this chamber. Other provisions fortified the position of the church, such as guaranteeing its ecclesiastical privileges or *fueros,* an independent system of courts and compulsory tithing for the entire population.

Not content with making reaction safe in Ecuador, Noboa tried to restore it in neighboring New Granada. The reforms there of President López had led to the expulsion of the Jesuits, who, taking refuge in Ecuador, received aid from Noboa to organize a revolt against López. To meet the challenge, the Granadine president prepared for war. But at this juncture General José María Urbina in Guayaquil, supported by liberal leaders including Generals Francisco Robles and Guillermo Franco, organized a revolt in Guayaquil to prevent the war with New Granada. The junta that was set up, after denouncing Noboa for destroying democratic institutions and risking war with López, appointed Urbina supreme commander to end the dictator's rule. At this moment the picture was further complicated by General Flores, who, viewing the conflict from Peru, collected some ships and soldiers of fortune to invade Guayaquil in 1852. The Guayaquil junta quickly defeated Flores, who escaped, and then called a national convention which selected Urbina as president on August 30, 1852.

Urbina returned the country to the liberal tradition. The Jesuits were expelled and a plan was drawn up to weaken the political activities of the church; but this was not effective. The president again began educational development with the founding of schools, aided the growth of Ecuador's foreign trade and native industry, and improved the administration of tax money. Controlling the election in 1856, the Liberal party put General Francisco Robles in power, who continued Urbina's program but who did not have the abilities of Urbina. The Conservative party, seeing their only hope in foreign assistance, sought the support of the Peruvian dictator, Castilla. The latter, hoping to secure Ecuadorian territory in return for his aid by settling a long-standing boundary dispute on the northern Ecuadorian-Peruvian frontier, blockaded Guayaquil and dallied over negotiations to give his Conservative allies in Ecuador time to organize their revolt.

The Dictatorship of García Moreno, 1860–1875. Out of the resulting conflict emerged Ecuador's most famous dictator, Gabriel García Moreno. In Quito he took the lead in a revolt which successfully drove Urbina and Robles into exile. However, in Guayaquil the Liberal general, Franco, came to terms with Castilla, who had arrived there with an army of 6,000 troops. Castilla readily recognized Franco as the head of the legal government of the country and signed a treaty with him in January, 1860, under which Ecuador agreed to certain commercial concessions and to salute the Peruvian flag in Quito. The Conservative party, not to be outdone by this maneuver, inflamed public opinion against Franco for his concessions to Peru, invited Flores back to Ecuador, and attacked Franco at Guayaquil. Successful, Flores occupied the city, whereupon the Conservative party called a national convention to elect a president. Because Flores was regarded in most circles as a traitor he was denied the presidency, which was placed in the hands of García Moreno in 1860.

Upon election to the presidency, García Moreno entered into negotiations with the Vatican for a Concordat. This action was the key to his basic outlook upon his role in the history of Ecuador. He believed that the state requires the discipline of the church. Under this Concordat the church became, in fact, the most powerful force in the country. García Moreno served as executor of its will. Thus papal communications entered the country without inspection; church courts received jurisdiction over all matters touching religious affairs, including the settlement of questions involving wills, marriages, inheritance, divorce, and crime. All education was placed in the hands of the religious orders; the Jesuits dominated the educational program. Harsh laws were passed to deal with the opposition. Unbelievers were harried out of the land; Masonic lodges were closed, liberal thinkers driven into exile. All books, magazines, and newspapers were subjected to church censorship. The most significant effect of this dictatorship was to drive the roots of liberalism deep into the soil of the country. Persecution only strengthened the faith of the liberals. Juan Montalvo and Eloy Alfaro grew up and fought for democratic principles in the shadow of the García Moreno dictatorship.

Other aspects of García Moreno's rule reveal a mind that appreciated the need of improving the material conditions of the country. He demanded improvement of the church's missionary program and the elimination of sinecures. He founded trade schools, extended both primary and secondary education, and advanced the study of medicine and astronomy. He reformed the prisons and established a school of art and music. Seeing the need of better communications between Quito and Guayaquil, he constructed the first highway to connect the two cities, and planned for a railroad to supplement the former. Elsewhere he supported a road building program.

Although former president Urbina attempted a revolt in 1864, García Moreno was able to dictate election of his successor, Jerónimo Carrión, in the following year. The latter served for two years, when he was succeeded by Javier Espinosa. By this date the Liberals were organizing to secure control of the country in the next presidential election in 1869. President Espinosa's too close association with the Liberal leaders led to his expulsion and the reassumption of power by García Moreno in 1869. Drawing up a new constitution which gave him wide powers, the president devoted himself more and more to the interests of the church, culminating in 1873 in the unusual action of dedicating the country to the "Sacred Heart of Jesus." This fanaticism, accompanied by harsher persecution of the Liberals, stirred them to extreme measures. Shortly after his next election in 1875, groups of students, citizens, and military figures, unable to bear the tyranny any longer, assassinated him in February, 1875. Juan Montalvo, Ecuador's great writer, claimed that his pen killed the dictator.

Part II. THE ESTABLISHMENT OF DEMOCRATIC INSTITUTIONS, 1875 TO THE PRESENT

Transition, 1875–1890. With the death of García Moreno, generals accomplished in brutality ruled the country until 1895. At the same time the weakness of the state, resting on nothing more than force, produced its counterpart in revolts led by the Guayaquil liberals. In this struggle, lasting fifteen years, emerged the next outstanding and the greatest figure of modern Ecuador, Eloy Alfaro. Alfaro represented in his career order based on liberty. He made no exceptions—individual liberty, freedom of conscience, political and economic freedom. Rarely did the nineteenth century democratic movement produce a more able exponent of its principles. Incorruptible personally, his administrations as president were models of integrity in financial affairs. Of the only financial abuse of which he was guilty, he was accused by his friend, Montalvo. Alfaro readily confessed that he had diverted some funds from a military expedition to publish a book—Montalvo's own famous work, *The Seven Treatises!*

Alfaro, born in 1842 of a middle class family in an Ecuadorean village, joined at the age of twenty-two Urbina's revolt against García Moreno, an uprising in 1864 to protest the dictator's plans to annex Ecuador to France. Exiled, Alfaro went to Panama, where, successful in business, he thereafter devoted his fortune to Ecuador's freedom. Fired by Montalvo, he himself led an expedition in 1875 to Guayaquil. Betrayed there, he was thrown into prison, but quickly converted his jailers to his cause. He escaped and returned to Panama. Feeling the need of military science, though he detested militarism, he studied tactics and strategy in foreign lands. Repeatedly he led expeditions to attack the succession of dictators after 1875. Between his attempts he recouped his fortunes by his unusual business abilities or wrote history in the archives of Peru. Liberal leaders in all parts of Latin America sought his counsel. When he was driven out of Colombia on one occasion, Costa Rica and Nicaragua opened their doors to him. When in 1895 a liberal revolt overthrew Luís Cordero, the dictator, the citizens of Guayaquil proclaimed Alfaro supreme head of the republic. Elected president in the same year, he assured Ecuadoreans he sought no revenge but only honorable reconciliation. But to no avail; he had to fight his way to the capital.

The Administrations of Alfaro, 1895–1901, 1906–1911. Alfaro's principal objective in his first administration was to seek a solution for the religious question. He avoided conflict with the clergy; he even called some of its leaders into consultation. Thus he succeeded in modifying García Moreno's Concordat and placed the patronage under the state. His constitution of 1897, besides providing for a democratic form of government, established religious toleration, while his efforts to secure a civil marriage law bore fruit in 1902. Leonidas Plaza Gutiérrez followed Alfaro in the presidency in 1901 and continued his religious reform program, in spite of the growing opposition of the conservative groups.

Returned to the presidency in 1906, Alfaro governed until 1911. This period saw his most constructive work. He established education on a compulsory and secular basis, founded normal and military schools, and established colleges. He tried to emancipate women and encouraged them to enter public life. He built asylums and hospitals. He began a public health program in Quito and Guayaquil with sewage and drainage systems. His business ability led him to reform and improve the taxation system, adopt the gold standard, and adjust the foreign debt. He made efforts to improve the condition of the Indians, protecting them from abuses and abolishing taxes previously imposed upon them. He drew up and promulgated enlightened penal, commercial, and banking codes and improved criminal procedures in the courts.

Alfaro's most important material contribution to Ecuador was his success in having constructed the Guayaquil-Quito Railroad. In spite of predictions of failure, refusal of support, and strong opposition, Alfaro went ahead almost single-handedly in his first administration to draw up plans, employ an American engineer, Archer Harman, and secure authority to spend some 12,280,000 sucres on the project. When he returned to his second administration he found the work little advanced. Putting his tremendous energy behind the project, he had the satisfaction of witnessing the first locomotive arrive in Quito from Guayaquil in July, 1908. For setting Ecuador on the road to freedom, Alfaro paid a martyr's price. To mediate a conflict after he left the presidency, he returned to Guayaquil. In spite of receiving assurances of his personal safety, he was shortly arrested and taken to Quito, where, thrown into prison, he was murdered in cold blood.

The Development of Modern Ecuador, 1912–1953. Alfaro's economic reforms and support of liberal movements aided the growth of a vigorous middle class in Ecuador's larger cities. Additional impetus to this growth was given by World War I. The export of raw materials and foreign investment in the country expanded rapidly. Banana, sugar, and cotton plantations, established along the west coast, and the exploitation of newly discovered oil deposits began the development of Ecuador's labor movement. Before 1914 the United States had about $10,000,000 invested in Ecuador, but by 1920 this had doubled. The bulk went into cocoa plantations, gold mining enterprises, utilities, and oil production. The British, too, invested in oil lands and had about 400 wells producing in the next decade. The influx of money contributed to the growth of native-owned industries in textiles, leather, buttons, soap, candles, pharmaceuticals, food processing, dairy products, baked goods, brewing, and the development of rice, cotton, and tobacco plantations, as well as sheep and cattle ranges. To improve public health and facilitate exports at Guayaquil, President Alfredo Baquerizo Moreno (1916–1920), with aid from the Rockefeller Institute, ended yellow fever in that port.

In 1920 the total population of the country was estimated at 2,000,000; by 1950 it had passed the 3,000,000 mark. Fully 75 per cent of Ecuador's people are Indians whose principal occupation is that of workers on the agricultural estates of the wealthy in the interior and along the coast. These natives live under conditions little changed from the serfdom of the colonial period. Among them illiteracy is virtually complete. Their small primitive villages are isolated communities whose people rarely have heard of cities such as Guayaquil, to say nothing of such an obscure figure as the president of Ecuador. Laboring as serfs, enjoying no political rights, defenseless against exploitation, and practicing a Catholicism interlarded with Indian superstitions, they represent Ecuador's most profound social problem.

Sensitive Ecuadorian intellectuals burn with indigation at this national disgrace. Indeed, Ecuador's literary productions describing this society are easily the most vigorous, hard-hitting, and uncompromising writings produced in Latin America today. Some of her men of letters have turned to Marxism for a solution to the problem. The bulk represent the fervor of crusading reformers so well known in the history of the United States and in the great revolutionary movements of Mexico. Outstanding are Jorge Icaza and Aguilera Malta. Icaza's *Huasipungo* (1934) reveals starkly the murder of Indians in their homes, the burning of their villages, and other horrifying details attendant upon their exploitation for the benefit of land speculators. Less harsh is the work of Malta's *La Isla Virgen,* the story of coastal natives hopelessly resigned to a life of virtual slavery to pay their debts.

The remaining 25 per cent of the population is composed of white families, descendants of the colonial Spaniards, and the mixed bloods or *mestizos,* the offspring of Indians and Spaniards. The landowning families, now largely dwellers in Quito and other interior cities, represent, along with the church, the intense conservatism of the country and offer the principal obstacle to efforts to improve the lot of the Indians and their urban counterpart, labor. The *mestizo* is the worker in the nation's factories, in transportation, on foreign-owned plantations, and in mines. Some, too, have found a niche in small businesses in towns and cities. The bulk of this *mestizo* labor, concentrated in Quito and Guayaquil, composes the principal support of liberal leaders from Eloy Alfaro to those of the present to modify Ecuador's rigid society.

The political history of Ecuador after 1920 saw new forces emerging. No longer, as before that conflict, was the political battle a clear-cut one between conservatives and liberals. On the contrary, the growth of labor, the importance of the middle class, the investment of foreign money, all gave rise to new political parties and alignments between the old. The end of World War I brought the first serious crisis with the collapse of Ecuador's foreign trade. The steady issuance of paper money, beginning in 1912, contributed to the high cost of imported necessities. Wages, on the other hand, declined and unemployment grew. Labor on its part resorted to widespread unionization, culminating in 1922 in the Confederation of Workers' Syndicates, which were strongly socialist in outlook. In 1922–1923 a series of strikes and riots resulted in an effort to improve conditions among the labor groups, and influenced the election of 1924. Dissatisfied when Gonzalo Córdoba was elected in that year, the left wing of the Liberal party, labor, and the younger army officers whose salaries were adversely affected by the large amount of paper money issued during the preceding administration, revolted and paved the way for a military junta to place in power Dr. Isidro Ayora in 1926, who governed the country until 1931.

President Ayora took the next steps after Alfaro to modernize Ecuador's economy. In 1928 labor was given its first code. Important financial reforms recommended by the American Kemmerer Commission and financial experts were made including the establishment of a central bank with the right alone to issue government notes, a new monetary law revaluing the sucre, the reorganization of the accounting system, revision of rural taxation, and the enactment of an income tax law. To aid the development of small farm ownership, the government gave a twenty-five year monopoly to the Swedish match corporation in return for a loan of $2,000,000 to establish a farm loan bank.

Ecuador and the Depression, 1929–1939. Hardly had these reforms time to take effect when the 1929 depression occurred. The workers, again thrown out of employment, turned to radical leaders who promised economic and political justice. Although Ayora was forced out in 1931 to be followed by several governments during the next four years, the political development of the country was steadily toward a more democratic state. Luis Larrea Alba, a radical with strong labor support, succeeded Ayora, but was soon overthrown. In 1932 Neptalí Bonifaz, a conservative, won the general election in October, 1931, when the liberal forces split. While a revolt against him, led by Ildefonso Mendoza in April, 1932, failed at Guayaquil, the Ecuadorian congress in August ousted Bonifaz on the ground of his Peruvian citizenship. The conservative forces, refusing to accept the defeat, revolted, but were unsuccessful. On October 30 and 31 peaceful elections placed Juan de Dios Martínez Mera in the president's office. By this date the depression had so adversely affected the country that riots took place in the principal cities, and Luis Larrea Alba led an attempt to overthrow the government in November. As the depression continued to deepen, protests against the government's inadequate measures to provide employment mounted. Internal politics were further complicated by the failure of the Martínez Mera government to secure the inclusion of Ecuador in the international conferences affecting the settlement of the Leticia question. This latter, discussed elsewhere, involved Amazonian territory to which Ecuador had entered a claim. The president, unable to answer the criticisms directed at his government was, on October 18, 1933, removed by congress from office.

For a moment the conservatives returned to power on December 14, 1933, when Velasco Ibarra carried the election. Hardly in office a year, he found opposition mounting over his failure to find a solution for unemployment and growing bankruptcies. His attempt to establish a dictatorship failed and forced his resignation on August 20, 1935. In the next four years the movement to democratize Ecuador steadily grew. The chief executives who held office during these years for short periods all contributed to this end.

Provisional President Antonio Pons, who resigned on September 26, was succeeded by Federico Páez. In his short rule until October 22, 1937, Páez recognized by law labor's right to strike, established a minimum wage law for commercial, manual, and agricultural workers, and endeavored to organize agricultural centers as a means of improving production of food. Resigning over opposition to his reforms, he was succeeded by General Alberto Enríquez G. from January 13, 1938 to August 8, 1938. In these few months he created a Council for National Economy to study means of developing national resources and investigating conditions of foreign ownership of these, and a Social Welfare Council to improve the administration of welfare agencies. Yielding to the expressed needs of the teaching profession, his government established in April, 1938, a National Union of Teachers to aid them in modernizing educational practices and improving their own economic status. In the latter respect their cooperative enterprises of both consumption and production were aided by the government with credits.

To expand trade, Ecuador negotiated on August 6, 1938, a reciprocal trade agreement with the United States under which many American manufactured items were permitted entry under lowered duties, while her own products, cocoa, coffee, bananas, tagua nuts, kapok, Panama hats, and balsa wood, found an expanding market in the United States. Two days later, August 8, encountering opposition, Enríquez resigned.

Temporary presidents held office until December 2, 1938, when Aurelio Mosquera Narváez became chief executive on the same day that the new constitution, extending the right to women to vote, went into effect. The early death of Mosquera and the outbreak of World War II paved the way for one of Ecuador's ablest executives, Carlos Arroyo del Río, to assume the office of president on September 1, 1940.

Ecuador and World War II, 1940–1945. Ecuador's marked tendency toward democratic government readily placed her on the side of the Allies in the world struggle. Her contributions were important, and benefits deriving from her actions rewarded her efforts. She readily granted naval bases and air bases to the United States along her coast and on the Galápagos Islands. These served the important function of guarding the southern approaches to the Panama Canal. From her balsa forests the United States derived the bulk of this valuable wood for airplane construction. Her basic products, cocoa, bananas, and coffee, were a further contribution. The sale of these and the necessary funds invested by the American government in the bases aided the program of internal development carried forward under the government of Arroyo del Río.

Early in 1941 the government secured a loan from the Export-Import Bank to construct needed highways through the rich agricultural region between Riobamba, Cuenca, and Loja and the coastal region, south of Manta. Besides opening new lands for cultivation, the highways made possible the expansion of mineral resources. The government also launched an extensive program of rural medical service. As funds continued to accumulate from the sale of her raw materials, Ecuador expanded her highway building program between El Oro and Loja to give the former a better outlet to the sea. Extensive health measures, a drainage system for Quito, various hospitals for tropical diseases in Guayaquil and an antimalarial campaign reflected the interest of the government in improving the health of Ecuador. Important in advancing the economic growth of the nation was the creation in 1943 of a national development bank and provincial development banks to provide credits for farm and livestock production, opening of new areas to cultivation, colonization of unused lands, irrigation, marketing, and loans to businesses of various kinds.

The emphasis Arroyo del Río had put upon the development of Ecuador had benefited largely industrialist and commercial groups. Labor had not fared so well. The high prices due to the inflationary effect of the war caused widespread discontent. The conservative land oligarchy, ever anxious to return to power, associated themselves with the extreme left in a Democratic Alliance and advanced former president Velasco Ibarra as their candidate. Arroyo del Río, sensing a *coup d'état*, arbitrarily imprisoned leaders of the opposition and built up the police force as a counterweight to the army. The opposition charged the president had sacrificed national interests in agreeing to the boundary settlement with Peru in 1944. That question had had a long history before 1942, when a tentative settlement in that year with Ecuador agreed to the arrangement made at the Rio de Janeiro meeting of the American foreign ministers. However, when the final settlement was agreed upon in 1944 which gave Peru the disputed territory, opposite interpretations of the final agreement kept the conflict alive.

The Velasco Ibarra Government, 1944–1947. In May, 1944, just before the presidental elections were scheduled, the army overthrew the government and placed Velasco Ibarra in power. His regime, lasting three years, was essentially a middle class government which recognized the need for a new and liberal constitution. This document was the principal achievement of the administration. An experiment in drawing up a constitution providing for a unicameral legislature was made in 1945, but was replaced by the present fundamental law in the next year, 1946. The constitution is significant in reflecting the body of democratic ideas that characterize present-day Ecuador.

Recognizing the sovereignty of the people, the document provides a bill of rights which includes the abolition of the death penalty and the recognition of rights of illegitimate children to education and inheritance of property. The framework of government has the familiar divisions, executive, legislative, and judicial, and the usual powers accorded to these parts of the government. The president holds office for four years by direct popular vote and has the right to appoint his own cabinet, but is ineligible for re-election. The senate is composed of forty-four members, with eleven selected by economic and cultural groups, labor, university and business organizations, and agricultural societies. Except for the eleven, selected by their own groups, the rest are elected by direct popular vote for four years, as are the members of the House of Deputies, who are elected for two-year terms. Local government functions under governors appointed by the president, but both the provincial legislatures and municipal councils are popularly elected.

The importance of labor as a social group is recognized in various provisions for minimum wages, the right to strike, and protection of minors and women in industry. The right to vote is given to men and, for the first time in the history of Ecuador, to women. Education is made free. Suspension of guarantees can only be by consent of congress or by the Council of State.

While the three years of Velasco Ibarra were filled with civil conflicts and attempts at revolt, the government did carry forward work on the Pan-American Highway and, in the south, a road to link Cuenca with Puerto Bolívar. Velasco Ibarra, too, joined with Colombia and Venezuela in the creation of the Gran Colombian Merchant Marine.

However, the refusal of Velasco Ibarra to embark upon a comprehensive program to meet the high cost of living, the need of labor for low-cost housing, and his disregard of the constitutional guarantees of freedom of the press and speech led to growing dissatisfaction. The end came on August 24, 1947, when Colonel Carlos Manchero, defense minister, revolted and drove the president from the country. This uprising, however, was a conservative one which promptly met opposition throughout the nation. After but nine days in office, Manchero fled to be succeeded by provisional president Mariano Suárez Veintimilla, who served simply to legalize the selection by congress of Carlos Julio Arosemena.

Under the latter's administration were held the next presidential elections. Leading figures were General Alberto Enríquez, nominated by the Liberal party, and Galo Plaza, strongly anticlerical, nominated by the National Civic Democratic movement, a combination of labor, intellectuals, and liberal businessmen. Plaza, who had been Ecuador's ambassador to Washington and had resigned in protests over Velasco Ibarra's undemocratic methods, was an admirer of the United States where he was educated. As a statesman, he had long advocated for Ecuador a modern economy.

The Administration of Galo Plaza, 1948–1952. Elected in June, the new president began his term on September 1, 1948. Galo Plaza proposed to attack the problem of food production by expanding highway building into new reclaimed areas, soil conservation, a broad program of land distribution, irrigation, and credits for farmers. For both industry and agriculture he urged a national electrification plan. Recognizing that Ecuador could not compete with highly industrialized nations, he insisted upon improving the production of its major mineral and agricultural resources, rice, coffee, cocoa, bananas, and diversifying food production for local consumption. He strongly urged mechanization of agriculture wherever possible. Coffee production, he believed, could be improved with the establishment of a Coffee Institute to study modern methods.

To bring these changes about the president foresaw the need of American loans. The necessity for land reclamation was evident in the fact that Ecuador's more than 3,000,000 population occupied but 15 per cent of its area, while some 40 per cent was unused for lack of communications. How sincere the president was, was evident, too, in his willingness to risk unpopularity. The test came in 1950 when the Shell and Esso oil companies withdrew from eastern Ecuador, announcing that this area had no future as an oil-producing region. The Ecuadoreans, deeply disappointed, were further shocked, though realistically, by Galo Plaza, who insisted that the dream of the east was not to be realized by patriotic feelings, but that Ecuadoreans should concentrate upon developing the known wealth in the west, in its valleys and coast.

To carry out his program, Galo Plaza established a National Institute for the Development of Production in 1949. Its duties were to redistribute land for small farmers, provide improved cottonseed and rice strains, establish breeding stations, and engage in soil conservation and reforestation. To aid this agricultural plan, the Rockefeller International Basic Economy Corporation worked out a program for an integrated, mechanized development of the Guayas River rice basin. To support the undertaking, Ecuador received from the Export-Import Bank a loan of $250,000 to purchase agricultural machinery. In 1951 the United States extended further aid under the Point Four program, made especially necessary when one-third of the port city of Esmeraldas was destroyed by fire in that year. Other aspects of Point Four were health and educational projects including one suggested by Galo Plaza himself in the form of aid to the Indian weaving industry, encouraging Indians to adopt a uniform color, pattern, and weave to make available this item for export.

The Galo Plaza government did much to open new lands by advancing highway construction, supported by loans from the Export-Import Bank. A major undertaking was a highway from Quito northeast to the port of Esmeraldas, opening up several thousand acres of new land. Others extended into the agricultural regions of Pichincha province and to the sulfur mining area near Quito. Besides aiding the Guayas River project and highway construction, the Export-Import Bank provided loans to buy railroad equipment, make airport improvements at Guayaquil and Quito, erect waterworks in a number of larger cities, and help to rebuild homes and cities damaged in the 1949 earthquake.

Galo Plaza's program for Ecuador went forward in the face of a lively political battle. He refused at the beginning of his term to make jobs for his followers where competent officials occupied office. He attempted to improve administration by insisting upon a full workday of eight hours from government employees and proposed a civil service based upon nonpolitical qualifications.

Probably the most striking policy, testifying to his essentially democratic outlook, was the refusal of Galo Plaza to make capital out of Ecuador's border dispute with Peru, the same one which contributed to the overthrow of Arroyo del Río. The president insisted upon Ecuador's rights in this dispute, which involved her claims in the Santiago-Zamora region in the south, significant because that territory gave Ecuador access to the Marañon River and thus an outlet to the Atlantic Ocean. At the same time he protected the national interests of Ecuador's fishing industry in the west with legislation declaring a twelve-mile territorial limit around the Galápagos Islands and along the coast.

The last two years, 1951–1952, of Galo Plaza's administration saw the various political parties preparing for the presidential struggle. In 1951 Liberal and Liberal-Radical parties won important municipal elections. In Guayaquil, however, where Velasco Ibarra had many supporters, a new party called the Concentration of Popular Forces elected Carlos Guevara Moreno mayor of that city. By the beginning of 1952 the various parties had chosen their candidates, of whom Ruperto Alarcón Falconí was the conservative candidate and Carlos Velasco Ibarra that of the Independent-Liberal party. In the struggle for votes Galo Plaza maintained a strict neutrality.

Before the campaign ended, it was evident that the choice was to be between Velasco Ibarra, whose strong methods had led him toward a dictatorship on two former occasions, and the conservative candidate, Alarcón Falconí, vigorously supported by the church. Probably the latter factor influenced strongly anticlerical Ecuadoreans to choose Velasco Ibarra rather than support the losing Liberal candidate. Galo Plaza himself had the satisfaction of being the first president in thirty years to complete his term of office when the June, 1952, elections gave the presidency to Velasco Ibarra.

This election has become the most significant in Ecuador's recent history in that it saw the largest vote cast, 340,000, while with few exceptions it was the most peaceful. Both facts testify to the maturity of Ecuador's democracy. Equally important in this respect was the character of the administration of Galo Plaza, which maintained individual rights, tolerated criticism of the government, and encouraged political activity.

The Administration of Velasco Ibarra, 1952 to the Present. Although Velasco Ibarra had pursued an anti-United–States line of attack in his political speeches and had revealed a marked sympathy for Perón's Argentina, it was obvious when he came to power on September 1, 1952, that neither of these were to be fundamental policies. In fact, with some changes, he carried on most of the economic programs launched by Galo Plaza for developing Ecuador.

Velasco Ibarra assumed office when many of the constructive measures of the preceding administration began to bear fruit. Bananas by the end of 1952 had doubled in value; rice exports had increased ten times. For these and other crops Ecuador received high prices, so that the year closed with a favorable balance of trade. The president continued the policy of negotiating trade agreements. With Argentina he bartered Ecuadorean petroleum for wheat; with West Germany, machinery for bananas, cocoa products, grains, fruits, tobacco, hardwoods, Panama hats, kapok, hides and skins, and other products. By 1953 Ecuador had become the world's largest exporter of bananas, selling some 15,000,000 to 16,000,000 stems which brought great prosperity to the Guayas coastal region. In the highlands, maize and barley crops were the largest on record, owing in part to the modern methods but recently introduced. The export trade, too, was further benefited by the president's improvement of customs administration, reducing and simplifying methods of tax collection.

For the internal development of the country Velasco Ibarra continued the improvement of transportation and other measures. However, in this matter he suppressed the Development Corporation created by Galo Plaza and extended authority rather to the National Development Bank and mortgage and commercial banks to make loans for projects, irrigation, reforestation, and importation of agricultural and industrial machinery. From the Export-Import Bank he secured a $2,280,000 loan to complete the Quevedo-Manta highway designed to open the former's rich agricultural areas to the coastal port. To secure funds to improve airports, highways, and roads, he imposed taxes on air travel and gasoline.

The new industries established under his predecessor continued to thrive. This prosperity enabled Velasco Ibarra to meet the attacks upon his government for favoring the business classes, but he also decreed a general raise of wages for all employees of private companies.

In foreign affairs the president continued Ecuador's traditional friendship for the United States, which, in fact, absorbed about 59 per cent of her major exports. In June, 1953, Ecuador negotiated with the United States a Mutual Military Assistance Pact. But she found herself in conflict with the United States diplomatically when she aligned her policy with that of Peru and Chile in maintaining the claim that their respective offshore jurisdictions extended 200 miles.

While the economic side of Velasco Ibarra's administration showed success, the political aspects presented in the first two years a dismal picture. Unlike Galo Plaza, who suppressed his personal dislikes to favor of aiding democratic practices, Velasco Ibarra revealed a bitter personal outlook. At the outset he dismissed civil servants, irrespective of their ability, to make place for his followers. He punished army officers who had displaced him in 1947, some of whom had been expensively trained in the United States for the Ecuadorean air force. His attitude toward the press, however, provoked the strongest criticism. For attacking his policies he seized Quito's liberal independent newspaper, *El Día* in 1952. For questioning this action the editor of Quito's *El Comercio* was jailed in spite of the fact that he was a member of the Freedom of the Press Committee of the Inter-American Press Association! When *La Hora* and *La Nación* took up the battle, all their executives were thrown into prison and the papers closed.

In the violent public debate that raged over these actions, rightist organizations, particularly the *Arnistas,* supported the government, while principal opposition came from the Student Federation. Inevitably the Radical-Liberal party, which had joined the government, withdrew its support. Before 1953 ended, Velasco Ibarra had lost most of those who had voted for him for president. Apparently recognizing that his choice lay between an attempt to establish a dictatorship or modify his course to conform to the country's democratic traditions, he chose the latter. In June, 1954, he made no effort to control the election of the membership of the House of Deputies, which was returned with almost a majority against him. Also revealing were his frequent declarations of the importance of liberalism and democratic government. To some extent he implemented these in his policy of land distribution in the departments of Santo Domingo and Quevedo. He continued, too, the now well-established program of building schools to reduce the nation's appalling illiteracy.

Thus Ecuador, with a huge body of Indians making up the majority of its population comparable in all respects to those of its neighbor Peru, has avoided resort to dictatorship to satisfy the small handful who profit so handsomely from exploitation of the helpless natives. On the contrary, the effectiveness of the reforms of Eloy Alfaro, reinforced by the excellent constitution of 1946, the growth of labor organization, and the work of its militant, liberal intellectuals, all give promise of strengthening the democratic institutions that Ecuador has created.

MODERN LATIN AMERICA

SECTION III

The Caribbean Republics
*Colombia, Venezuela, Cuba, Haiti, and the
Dominican Republic*

Chapter XXIII

COLOMBIA

Part I. THE LIBERAL-CONSERVATIVE STRUGGLE TO 1880

The Character of Colombian History. Geographically Colombia is dominated by the Magdalena River, which flows northward to the Caribbean between two ranges of the Andes, the Western and Eastern Cordilleras. Beyond the western range is the valley of the Cauca River, separated from the Pacific Ocean by coastal mountains. To the east, the Andes slope away to the Amazon basin, where Colombia has vast stretches of virtually unoccupied land. The agricultural regions of the Cauca and the southern Magdalena Valley provided a base for a colonial landholding oligarchy supported by Indians little removed from serfdom. To the north along the Caribbean coast, where trade was active in colonial times, the population felt the liberalizing influences of foreign ideas and international contacts. After independence the conservative oligarchy, intolerant of change, carried on a bitter struggle with the liberal leaders of Bogotá and the coast.

Between 1830 and 1880 the liberals made many important reforms in their efforts to advance the economic and political life of the country. After that date the conservatives, securing control, abolished most of these and maintained their power until 1930. In these fifty years, however, foreign interest in the territory and raw materials of Colombia brought a new element into the struggle between the two groups, the most outstanding event of which was the loss of Panama in 1903. After that date investment of foreign capital, the search for oil, the development of the coffee industry, and the extraction of minerals went rapidly forward.

When the depression of 1929 occurred, the liberals returned to power. They brought once more to Colombia a period of reform and economic growth which continued through World War II. After 1945 the conservatives, again in control, harshly persecuted the opposition but continued the economic expansion of the nation. The growth of democratic institutions, which seemed so fair in the 1930's, received a serious setback. But it would be foolish to believe that liberal Colombians, whose achievements in science, literature, and the arts, as well as in government, have come to the end of the road.

The Disintegration of Greater Colombia, 1821–1830. The career of Bolívar in Colombia after 1820 demonstrated the power of the feudal families. Bolívar was successful in war precisely because he had the support of the conservative groups. But when the common enemy, Spain, was removed, his conception of government crashed against the vested interests of provincial families whose vision hardly reached beyond the bounds of their own estates. In despair Bolívar cried out: "He who dedicates his services to revolution ploughs the sea!" The period of 1821–1830 is the history of the collapse of Bolívar's creation, the Republic of Greater Colombia.

The first defeat of the Liberator's ideas was in the Colombian constitution of Cúcuta in 1821. Provisions of the document confined control of the country to a few hands, and gave the president power to use force only in case of internal difficulties. The second major blow came in 1826 from Venezuela. Outraged at the opposition there, Bolívar exclaimed in anger that the inhabitants were no more than smugglers and that employees of the treasury were black marketeers. But the facts were otherwise. The Wars for Independence had destroyed the economy of the nation; agriculture lay in ruins and commerce declined; people were reduced to seeking an existence by any means. With no funds, for province after province in 1826 reported absolutely no income, Venezuela was unable to contribute taxes to the central government. Within this frame of poverty, agitation for separation from Colombia found supporters. The crisis came in that year when the Colombia congress ordered soldiers recruited for whom, in fact, there were no funds with which to pay them. The impetus to revolt gathered force when news arrived from Mexico of the adoption of a federalist constitution. Such a framework of government seemed the answer to Venezuelan woes.

Páez attempted at first to halt the movement, but soon placed himself at the head of it. Bolívar hurried back to Colombia from Peru and then on to Venezuela, where he rallied a strong nucleus of followers, granted amnesty to offenders, and for a moment succeeded in winning back Venezuela into the fold.

Hardly had he re-established his authority there, when the Colombian army itself in Peru mutinied in 1827, and demanded its return to Colombia. Disaffected over lack of pay and regarded as invaders by the Peruvians, they had no interest in maintaining Bolívar's control. The

Peruvians themselves took the initiative, overthrew the constitution that Bolívar had pressed upon them, and placed Santa Cruz in power. Simultaneously within Colombia revolts against the Liberator broke out. There the vice-president, Francisco Santander, led a coalition composed not only of those who hated Bolívar, but, more important, the dominating figures of the provinces.

In the meeting of the Colombian congress of 1827, Bolívar's opponents, having a clear majority, called a constitutional convention which drew up a new fundamental law. The provisions of this document, because they were repugnant to Bolívar, led his followers to withdraw from the congress and demand that he establish a dictatorship. Viewing the revolts in Peru, Ecuador, and Venezuela, the Liberator agreed. He set aside the new constitution, suppressed the vice-presidency, converted the prefects of the provinces into military governors, exiled the leaders of the opposition, suppressed the teaching of liberal ideas, and even showed signs of favoring a monarchy.

The Independence of Venezuela and Ecuador, 1830. Events, however, were beyond the Liberator's control. When what seemed to be the monarchical views of Bolívar became known in Venezuela, a revolt broke out in Caracas in 1829, when an assembly of notables announced the separation of the country from Colombia. Opposition to Bolívar within Colombia itself made useless the efforts of Sucre sent by Bolívar to Venezuela to win back support. Páez thereupon assumed the leadership in December, 1829, and called a convention at Valencia which took the final step of separation. In Ecuador at the same time, after Colombian troops had aroused antagonisms in that country, a junta led by General Juan José Flores established the country's independence of Colombia. Faced with this succession of failures, Bolívar in March, 1830, surrendered his office to depart for Europe. At Cartagena he received the crushing news of Sucre's assassination on June 4, 1830. As reports came in revealing the steady disintegration of his creation, he made a final halt at Santa Marta. There he died on December 17, 1830, leaving a plea to his countrymen to compose their dissensions and save the state from anarchy.

The Conservative-Liberal Struggle, 1830–1886. Bolívar's concept of a great Colombian state had diverted the normal political development of Colombia, Ecuador, and Venezuela. In all of these, Bolívar had many partisans, officeholders, military figures and favorites devoted to his interests. The local oligarchies in the three states, on the other hand, viewed with suspicion a centralized government they did not control.

When the Liberator disappeared from the scene, the states resumed their normal development. While Bolivia and Peru descended into reigns of military anarchy, characterized by practically no liberal tendencies until well after 1900, this condition was not true of Colombia, Ecuador, and Venezuela. All three nations created bases in the nineteenth century for the growth of authentic liberal movements which became significant in the twentieth.

In Colombia, after Bolívar's resignation, the constitutional convention, assembled in January of that year, selected Joaquín Mosquera, who served until 1832. On November 17, 1831, this convention defined the boundaries of the country as those of the former viceroyalty of New Granada, a name which it took for the new nation, and drew up a new constitution, promulgated in February, 1832. This document, representing the usual control by the landowning oligarchy, provided for a president and vice-president elected indirectly for four years, to be advised by a Council of Government and another of State, selected by congress. A bicameral legislature, with a senate whose members were elected indirectly for four years and a Chamber of Representatives, elected for two, was established. The document restricted suffrage to males over twenty-one years of age who could meet certain property qualifications. In the first election under the constitution, the groups representing the more liberal oligarchies and the middle classes won the presidency in the person of one of Colombia's great figures, Francisco de Paula Santander, whose victory was aided by his early opposition to Bolívar.

Liberal Advances, 1832–1857. Once in office (1832–1836), Santander proved his liberal leanings. In contributions to education and ideas he will undoubtedly take rank with Sarmiento. He established schools, public, professional, and scientific. He refounded the National Academy, encouraged the importation of French political writings, and reduced the influence of the church on education. Taking a generous attitude over the question of the debt of Greater Colombia, Santander opposed those who said the debt should be shared equally and insisted that Colombia with its larger population should assume half and the rest be divided between Ecuador and Venezuela. This policy made him enemies as did his harsh treatment of Bolívar's followers, so that his candidate lost in the next election.

However, the next president, José Ignacio Márquez (1837–1841), carried forward the liberal program against mounting opposition. In 1839 the church organized a revolt in the south at Pasto, accusing Márquez of participation in Sucre's assassination and attacking him for closing convents and extending public education. The powerful provincial families, resentful of the liberal program, joined the uprising. Significantly, among the revolutionary elements was Panama, which maintained its independence for two years, 1840–1841. While Márquez succeeded in putting down the revolt, he had to abandon any further liberal measures in this fight for life. The president who succeeded Márquez, General Pedro Alcántara Herrán (1841–1845), more conservative in outlook while favoring education and supporting the rebuilding of schools destroyed in the wars of the preceding years, permitted the return of the Jesuits who had been exiled by Charles III in 1767. To increase the authority of the president, he modified the constitution in 1843 to allow the chief executive to appoint provincial governors.

The liberal element returned to full control in the next presidential election with Tomás Cipriano Mosquera (1845–1849). Mosquera, from an influential Creole family, was essentially a military man, but aware of the economic needs of the country. The growing middle class particularly found satisfaction in his rule, for the president encouraged the growth of British and American trading interests, already making themselves felt in the Caribbean and Central America. The period saw the establishment of steam navigation on the Magdalena River and the reduction of the tariff for the benefit of the coastal businessmen. Prominent was the rapid expansion of the cultivation of tobacco, a monopoly of the government which during the years after 1833 was passing into the hands of private individuals. Within this framework of economic expansion, Colombia negotiated the Bidlack treaty with the United States in 1846, under the terms of which American imports were put on a par with the British, who were formerly favored. Of greater significance for the future, the United States was given the right of transit over the Panama area in return for a guarantee of Colombian sovereignty over the isthmus.

Mosquera likewise encouraged immigrants from Europe, many of whom were refugees from the defeat of the Revolution of 1848. From them stemmed the first movement among Colombian workers who organized clubs to voice demands for better working conditions and the abolition of slavery. Mosquera reduced the internal debt, stimulated mining and the tobacco industries by freeing them from restrictions, improved customs collections, and constructed roads. For education he founded technical schools and improved the National Library. Politically, the rule of Mosquera had significance, not only because he was the last of what might be described as the liberal *caudillos,* but because during his regime political parties sufficiently defined themselves to become known as Liberals and Conservatives.

The support that Mosquera gave to liberal development found fuller expression in the administration of his successor, José Hilario López (1849–1853), the leader of the Liberal party. He decreed the abolition of slavery and the death penalty, encouraged the economic growth of the country by making navigation of rivers free, ordered the first fairly reliable map of the nation, aided the establishment of a railroad line across Panama, and abolished the tobacco monopoly in 1850. In an effort to strengthen democratic institutions, López decreed absolute liberty of the press, provided for freedom of worship, and made education free and compulsory. Attacking the economic power of the church, he expelled the Jesuits, suppressed all ecclesiastical privileges, and put restrictions on other organizations of the church, measures reminiscent of those of his contemporary, Juárez, in Mexico.

The Jesuits, taking refuge in Ecuador, sought the support of President Noboa. Ecuadorean liberals frustrated this move, while in New Granada, López, in retaliation, withdrew the nation's representative at the Vatican. Threatened with excommunication for himself and his followers, the president exiled Archbishop Márquez of Bogotá and the bishops of Pamplona and Cartagena. Simultaneously, he asked for a law, enacted under his successor, providing for complete separation of church and state. Because of this church-state conflict, the López administration was especially significant in Colombian history, for the church soon afterward, as in Mexico, entered politics to become a principal supporter of the Conservative party.

Civil Wars, 1853–1888. López' liberal program was carried a step further by his successor, José María Obando. With López' and Liberal party support, Obando called a constitutional convention which promulgated a new fundamental law in 1853. This document incorporated the legislation abolishing slavery, separation of church and state, establishment of religious liberty, and freedom of the press and association. Under it public officials were elected by direct manhood suffrage. But its most important provision, decentralizing of power, enabled the provinces to elect their own officials and transferred to them the power over municipalities. In 1855 a further amendment permitted provinces to become federal states. In April of 1854 revolt against the government was successfully led by General José María Melo, supported by the church and the Conservative party. Obando, proving helpless in the struggle, saw himself displaced as the Liberal leader by Mosquera, who drove Melo into exile and paved the way for the succession to the presidency of the vice-president, a Conservative, Manuel María Mallarino.

By this date the Liberal party itself had split into two factions. One, called the Draconians, stood for the uncompromising separation of church and state; the other, the Gólgotas, were moderates. The latter had within their ranks the wealthier elements of the middle class, which during this decade was profiting from an active trade in tobacco after the abolition of the monopoly. Tending to become more conservative in outlook, they broke with the Liberals determined to bring about political reform. This conflict enabled the Conservative party to place Mariano Ospina in the presidency in 1857. In the following year, 1858, the Conservatives drew up a new constitution which, while preserving many of the features of that of 1853, abolished separation of church and state and gave Colombia the name of the New Granadine Confederation. This document, by conferring extensive power upon the states, favored the emergence of local dictators who, conspiring with the central government, prepared to dominate the election for the presidency in 1860. Mosquera, sensing the maneuver when Julio Arboleda was declared president in that year, revolted with General López and established liberal control. Exiling the Jesuits who had returned under Ospina, suppressing religious houses, and confiscating their property for the use of the government brought Mosquera into conflict with the church. To end it, Mosquera exiled Archbishop Herrán and other leading church officials. The Jesuits on their part sought the support of García Moreno in Ecuador who, when he invaded Colombia to restore them, was defeated.

But the most notable work achieved under Mosquera was the constitution of 1863, which lasted until the Liberals had been crushed and the Conservatives restored to power in 1886. This new document, like its predecessor, was federal in character with large autonomy left to the states. It contained a bill of rights, but prohibited ministers of any religion to vote. The presidential term was fixed at two years. The Liberals in drawing up this document hoped to weaken the influence of the church in national affairs, but by distributing power to the states they in fact established powerful bases for the growth of strong conservative centers, since the oligarchies in the various states came to control elections.

Mosquera served for two years under the new constitution to be succeeded by a Liberal, Murillo Torro. When under the latter the church and the conservatives showed signs of reviving their power, Mosquera returned to the helm in 1867. When he attempted to establish a dictatorship, he was exiled, later to become involved in the efforts of the Cubans to free themselves in their heroic struggle of the Ten Years' War.

In the next ten years Colombia saw itself plunged into a series of new civil wars. In 1877 a temporary peace was made after Aquileo Parra became president in 1876. His administration carried on the liberal tradition of developing the nation's economic resources. When tobacco export, which in the preceding twenty years had provided 70 to 90 per cent of the nation's exports, suddenly declined in 1875 in the face of Dutch competition, the government supported the expansion of the coffee industry, rapidly taking the place that tobacco formerly held in the exports of the country. Parra endeavored to recoup the country's finances by granting to the Universal Oceanic Canal Company of France a concession for $10,000,000 to build a canal across Panama. But the conservative forces, resenting his liberal reform program, particularly freedom of teaching in the schools, revolted. While he suppressed the uprising, the country was debilitated by the cost of the conflict. By this date the split in the Liberal party, which began under Obando, had become permanent. The moderates, led by Rafael Núñez, succeeded to the presidency to set the stage for the control of the country by the conservative groups.

Part II. DOMINATION BY THE CONSERVATIVES, 1880–1930

Núñez and the Constitution of 1886. Núñez, who started his political career as a Socialist, had a mystical spirit which eventually drew him into the ranks of the clerical-conservatives. His leadership in the Liberal party during the 1870's brought supporters to him from the moderate wing, which, dismayed by the destructive civil wars, was seeking a solution to the unending conflict. Primarily businessmen, they believed that stability of government was the first consideration. Upon this basis, with an appeal to elements in both the Conservative and Liberal parties, Núñez, after assuming office in 1880, formed a new party, the Nationalist party. Successful in holding power throughout his first term, he sought office and was again elected in 1884. By this date, with the Liberal party hopelessly split, Núñez was able to establish a dictatorship with Conservative support and restore the church to power more complete than it had enjoyed before Charles III expelled the Jesuits in 1767.

In 1886 the new order was consolidated in the constitution of that year, which has lasted down to the present with few amendments. The president and vice-president were chosen indirectly for terms of six years each. The cabinet was responsible to congress composed of a senate, with three senators from each department elected for six years, and a House of Representatives whose members were elected for four years. The essence of control, however, rested in the fact that the states, stripped of their powers and reduced to provinces or departments, were ruled by governors appointed and removable by the president. The control was further tightened by the power given congress to dictate the activities of the departmental assemblies, even though the latter were elected directly. The suffrage was carefully restricted to literate male voters twenty-one years of age who had a lawful occupation and an income of 500 pesos or real estate valued at 1,500 pesos.

Other provisions of the constitution declared Roman Catholicism the official religion under the protection of the state. Freedom of conscience was allowed where it did not conflict with Christian morals and law, and education was to be in accord with the teachings of the Roman church.

The other major change of the Núñez administration was the drawing up of a Concordat with the Vatican. Under the terms of this document the church was compensated for all losses suffered in the Liberal period and received back all its lands, buildings, and religious institutions; the clergy was excepted from the operation of the laws of the state, and church courts were permitted; and finally, the curricula of all educational institutions were to coincide with Catholic dogma.

In the next ten years, with Conservative control fastened upon the country, Liberal leaders were exiled, imprisoned, and in some cases executed. Inevitably, the Liberal party struck back in revolt. Characteristic was the War of One Thousand Days, which occurred in 1898. Led by an able and energetic figure, Rafael Uribe, the Liberals fought tenaciously for three years, a struggle which culminated in a bloody battle at Palo Negro in which the casualties were estimated at between 30,000 and 50,000. Forced to recognize Liberal strength concentrated in the coastal and northern part of the state, the Conservatives surrendered control of a number of provinces, as a result of which Liberal senators were elected to the national congress.

Loss of Panama, 1903. The violent civil war between the Liberals and Conservatives had hardly ended when the United States opened negotiations with Colombia to secure concessions for a canal across Panama. The Conservative government in power, wishing to recoup the state's finances that had been weakened by the conflict, readily agreed with the United States' proposal of $10,000,000 cash, an annuity of

$250,000, the right to construct and operate a canal, and full control of a strip of land three miles wide on either side of the canal route. The agreement negotiated by the Colombian *chargé d'affaires* in Washington was immediately opposed by the Liberals in the Colombian congress, who felt that the concessions were too generous in view of the world importance of the isthmian region. The impasse in Colombia led President Roosevelt to encourage revolt in Panama itself, which was successful and lost the territory to Colombia forever in November, 1903. The Conservative party, through suppression of discussion of its role in the loss of Panama, was able to turn national resentment away from itself and toward the United States. Under these circumstances it was able to secure the election of its candidate in 1904, Rafael Reyes, to the presidency.

Economic Growth of Colombia, 1904–1930. Reyes faced an economic situation of currency collapse and decline of exports as a result of the civil war. To rehabilitate the economy he reduced the amount of paper money and negotiated loans to build railroads, the most important of which was the beginning of a rail connection between Bogotá and the Caribbean coast. His administration benefited by a growing foreign investment in the country, made in banana plantations and minerals. Coffee plantations rapidly expanded, while the older areas increased their export. In foreign affairs Reyes sought reparations from the United States for the loss of Panama, negotiating a treaty which gave his country certain rights when the canal was built. But the clause in that agreement which provided for Colombia's receiving the first ten $250,000 rental payments in return for recognizing Panama's independence raised such a storm of protest that the president resigned in 1909.

World War I gave an extraordinary impetus to the expansion of Colombia's economic life. For the Allies she provided coffee, bananas, forest products, gold, silver, platinum, and other valuable raw materials. However, she maintained a strict neutrality, for her pride was still hurt by the American action in Panama in 1903. The most significant immediate effect of the war upon Colombia was to stimulate the search for oil. The demand for the liquid gold caused by the war impelled Colombia, doubtless influenced by contemporary events in Mexico, to declare title to subsoil riches vested in the nation. However, this law did not halt the efforts of oil companies to secure concessions, the most important of which was that belonging to Virgilio Barco. General Barco, who had commanded the Colombian Conservative army against the Liberals in the civil war ending in 1903, had been rewarded with a grant of 1,250,000 acres of jungle land in Santander province. This he sold to a British-American syndicate in 1916, dominated, however, by American capital. While this penetration was going forward, the American government under President Wilson entered anew into negotiations with Colombia, inspired by motives of doing justice to that country over the acquisition of Panama. However, this treaty of 1914 failed when influential Republican senators and Theodore Roosevelt campaigned against the clause expressing regret over the actions of the United States. Its defeat did not end the effort to compensate Colombia, although action was deferred until after the war.

When World War I ended, Colombia found itself launched upon a new career of economic expansion. The large amount of capital brought into the country to take out its raw materials had at the same time increased the wealth and influence of the Colombian businessmen, that is, the middle class. Consequently after the war, Colombia launched a successful campaign of advertisement in the United States to encourage the growth of Colombian-American trade and American investment in her resources as a vast virgin field. This expansion received an impetus by the successful negotiation of the Harding administration of a treaty (1922) which compensated Colombia to the extent of $25,000,000 for the loss of Panama and gave her the right to use the Panama Canal free of charge. In return Colombia modified her oil legislation and agreed to negotiate a boundary settlement with Panama.

The settlement of the differences between Colombia and the United States in 1922, the interest of the Colombian middle class in the development of national resources, and the needs of American industry for Colombian raw materials laid the basis for an astonishing growth of investment and trade. It is estimated that in 1913 the total investment of American capital in Colombia approached $2,000,000. By 1920 under the impetus of World War I, this total reached almost $30,000,000. Trade revealed a similar growth, namely, from $60,000,000 in 1913 to over $150,000,000 by 1920. Between 1920 and 1930 the growth of both trade and investment was phenomenal. Investment by the latter year was estimated at between $260,000,000 and $280,000,000, a figure representing an increase of over 12,000 per cent over 1913. Trade with other countries reached no such heights, that with Britain, next in importance, amounting to but $37,000,000 in 1929. Upon this basis of a steadily expanding economy, Colombia was able to negotiate loans. Municipalities, private companies, and her national government all borrowed heavily in the New York market. The income enjoyed under such prosperous conditions went

in part into the dredging of rivers and harbors; the construction of telegraph and telephone lines, highways, and public buildings; improvement
of coffee and banana plantations and the cattle and sheep industry; and
the establishment of scientific and technical schools.

This expansion of the economy of the country, however, affected its
various regions differently. The conservative groups had in considerable
measure turned to the production of coffee and textile manufacturing.
The coffee areas of Cundinamarca, Santander, Antioquía, and Caldas,
the latter two in the Cauca River Valley, received especially favorable
treatment from the Conservative governments of Pedro Nel Ospina, a
textile mill owner himself (1922–1926), and Dr. Miguel Abadía Méndez
(1926–1930). To strengthen their own interests the coffee growers organized in 1927 a Coffee Federation to advertise abroad and to improve
methods of production to meet competition in the world market. Because of the difficulty of transportation down the Magdalena to the
Caribbean ports, the Conservative governments before World War I,
influenced by the need of an outlet for the textiles of Medellín and the
coffee areas expanding southward along the Cauca River toward Cali,
had built by 1914 a railroad from Cali to Buenaventura, a port on the
Pacific coast. The fortunate opening of the Panama Canal in the next
year made Cali during the 1920's a major commercial city. As such it
became a Liberal stronghold in the center of what was formerly a clerical-
conservative region, typified by Popayán and even better by Pasto farther
south. On the northern side of the country and in the center, the development of the oil fields gave new importance to Barranquilla at the expense
of Cartagena, already injured by the diversion of the coffee traffic through
Cali.

These economic changes, increasing the importance of new commercial centers, created stronger Liberal groups whose nationalistic demands
opposed Conservative support of coffee and textile interests. The Liberals
insisted upon more attention to the development of Colombia's natural
resources by Colombians and less by foreigners, particularly oil companies. The Liberal criticism paralleled the attack by Socialists, labor
unions, and intellectuals upon the government's policy toward labor. The
Conservative government of Marco Fidel Suárez in 1918–1921 had responded to the demands of workers by enacting labor legislation, which,
however, not enforced in the 1920's, led to the famous strike of 1928. In
1927 the government answered the Liberal criticism by enacting oil legislation aimed at protecting the nation's rights in oil deposits and imposing

higher taxes as a means of deriving immediate benefit from the export of oil.

While the investment of foreign capital benefited certain regions and groups in Colombia, the bulk of the Colombian people remained outside its blessings. The population, estimated at about 4,000,000 in 1900, had reached 6,000,000 by 1929. The majority belonged to the working population on the plantations and docks and in transportation, utilities, factories, and other urban industries. While mostly mixed bloods or *mestizos* were in the interior, the coast had a Negro and mulatto population that, it has been estimated, made up fully 35 per cent of the total. Educational facilities in the rural, urban, and coastal regions were woefully lacking. By 1929 of the 6,000,000 total population, barely 170,000 children were enrolled in the schools. Girls were uneducated, while the total illiteracy was estimated at about 80 per cent. The standard of living was among the lowest on the South American continent. Wages on the coffee plantations, mostly owned by native Colombians, were the equivalent of a few cents a day. On the American and British-owned banana plantations and in the oil fields, wages ranged from $1.00 to $1.65 a day, but the actual situation of the workers was little better than that of those on the coffee plantations, since workers were required to purchase food, clothing, and other necessities at company-owned stores while they received their wages in scrip good only at the stores.

Under these circumstances radical movements developed among the workers in the 1920's. The Socialist party played a role in encouraging the establishment of unions among banana workers, on the docks, and in transportation. Strikes for higher wages and improvement of working conditions resulted. The most outstanding was that of 1928 when the Syndicalist Union of Workers of Magdalena, supported by the local Socialist party, struck to secure compliance with the national insurance law, one day's rest in seven, hygienic homes, more hospitals, increase in wages, and the abolition of scrip. Local businessmen and chambers of commerce of Santa Marta and Barranquilla supported the strike, for the use of scrip hampered the development of native businesses in the area. The strike was eventually broken by the use of government troops, but the company, after the struggle was over, did erect two hospitals, built a small number of schools for the workers' children, and raised wages. The event had the further significance of giving an impetus to unionization among other workers and bringing into prominence later the well-known Liberal leader, Jorge Gaitán.

Part III. GROWTH OF DEMOCRACY AND CONSERVATIVE
REACTION, 1929–1956

The Depression and the Olaya Herrera Administration, 1930–1934. The
depression of 1929 broke the hold of the Conservative party upon Colombia for sixteen years. Economic expansion of the country that began
with World War I contributed, as noted, to the rapid growth of the
Colombian middle class and the increase of the Liberal party, with a
strong nationalistic outlook. At the same time foreign investment in oil,
bananas, and minerals, together with the expansion of the coffee industry, greatly enlarged the number of workers who since World War I
had demanded improvement of their lot. These new forces by 1930,
when the next presidential election was scheduled, were prepared to
challenge the Conservative control. The latter suffered a damaging blow
when the depression created widespread unemployment and brought a
collapse of Colombia's foreign trade. Coffee was most seriously affected,
for it accounted for more than 60 per cent of the nation's income. In
these circumstances, with the Conservatives split over the question as to
what remedy to follow to meet the depression, the Liberal party won
the 1930 election with Enrique Olaya Herrera.

The new president, broad in outlook, made an effort to work out a
program which would relieve unemployment, place Liberal principles
into operation, and revive the coffee industry, the principal source of income. His first measures reduced expenditures of the government to meet
the interest payments on the loans contracted during the 1920's. He next
gave expression to the nationalistic feelings of the middle class by imposing control and restrictions on foreign businesses felt to be detri-
mental to the development of native capitalistic industries. The most
important of these were a series of laws which regulated industries,
made the employment of Colombians mandatory in the oil industry,
reduced the amount of land that could be given out in concessions, and
required that all oil companies submit to the decisions of Colombian
courts in disputes involving both native Colombians and the government.

On the positive side the government extended loans to businessmen,
notably coffee and banana planters, to tide them over the loss of foreign
markets. Linked with this aid was a program of road building to expand
the country's transportation system and provide easier access to markets.
At the same time the administration came to the rescue of labor with a
program of public construction in which road building played a prominent part. Unemployment was also reduced somewhat by enlarging the

Colombian army. This measure, however, was forced on Colombia by the irresponsible actions of the dictator of Peru, Sánchez Cerro, who in 1932 seized Leticia, a small village on the Amazon River claimed by Colombia.

The Leticia Incident. This incident ended a long history of boundary disputes in the upper Amazonian area among Brazil, Ecuador, Peru and Colombia. A major step toward settlement occurred in 1922 when the Salomón-Lozano treaty of that year awarded the territory on the Amazon, which included Leticia, to Colombia. Peruvian citizens there who numbered between 300 and 400 were naturally dissatisfied, but Peru itself had done nothing for the development of the territory, which lacked schools, roads, and any economic activity. Its importance to Colombia was that it provided a future outlet to the Amazon River. Although the treaty had been ratified by both countries, Sánchez Cerro, who, on August 25, 1932, overthrew the Leguía government, had no other program to remain in power but to appeal to Peruvian patriotism by suddenly seizing Leticia on September 1 and driving out all Colombian officials and armed forces stationed there. The Colombian government prepared to defend the territory and rejected Peru's proposals to withdraw in return for concessions. Colombia, to her credit, sought the aid of every international agency available to settle the dispute including the various inter-American organizations and the League of Nations.

On April 30, 1933, the assassination of Sánchez Cerro and the intervention of Alfonso López of Colombia opened the way for the success of the League's commission. This body, meeting with the representatives of Peru and Colombia in Rio de Janeiro under the presidency of Brazil's foreign minister, agreed to an apology by Peru and to the reoccupation of the territory when both countries ratified the agreement, as they did in 1935. Ecuador, ignored in the settlement, protested its terms.

The Administration of Alfonso López, 1934–1938. When the presidential election arrived in 1934, the Conservative party abstained so that Alfonso López, businessman and diplomat of broad humane outlook, from the liberal wing of the Liberal party, was elected. Under López and his successor, Eduardo Santos, Colombia began reforms which marked the first advance in Colombian democracy following the heroic efforts of the nineteenth century liberals to modernize the country's feudal structure.

López differed from Olaya Herrera, primarily interested in the planters and middle class, in his efforts to raise the standard of living of all Colombians, rural and urban. An advance in the democratization of the country came in 1936 with a series of amendments to the 1886 constitution, followed by similar changes in 1945. Under these, control of public schools, with primary education free and obligatory, passed to the state with a reduction of the influence of the Vatican exercised through the Concordat. Protestant organizations increased their numbers rapidly in the following years. In 1938 twenty Protestant groups working in Colombia had a total of about 9,000 converts; by 1947 this figure had increased to almost 26,000.

Socially, the amendments recognized labor's right to strike, except in public services, gave freedom of choice in professions and trades, postulated the social function of private property, and gave the government the right to intervene to direct production, distribution, and consumption.

In government, under the amendments, the most significant changes were the explicit adoption of the separation of powers principle and direct election of municipal councilors, departmental (state) representatives, national legislators, and the president. Improvements in taxation, with direct taxes upon real estate, increased the government income, but antagonized the wealthier elements of Colombia's society. By the end of the first two years of the administration, both national and municipal governments had balanced budgets.

To forward the economic development of the country, the López government assisted the coffee industry, the nation's most valuable crop, and extended technical and financial aid to increase the production of wheat, copra, cotton, tobacco, and rice. Similar measures helped the manufacturing industries, hampered by conditions of the depression, in their efforts to expand local markets. Important in this respect was the addition of almost 2,000 miles of roads and highways to the 2,400 existing when López took office.

For labor and education the López government did much. Noting more than 1,000,000 children with no schools, López began a building program, teacher training in normal schools, and broadening the scope of university education. Labor was encouraged to organize and help raise its own standard of living. Significant was the establishment in 1937 of a nation-wide union, the Confederation of Workers of Colombia, and that of the white-collar workers in a National Confederation of Institutions of Employees. Together these national unions strongly supported López' reform program.

The Administration of Eduardo Santos. In the 1938 elections, with the Conservatives again refraining from entering a candidate, the moderate wing of the Liberal party nominated and elected Eduardo Santos, a distinguished editor, on August 7, 1938. Santos continued the policies of his predecessor, in particular on the interior of the country. The Agrarian Credit Bank provided some 50,000 farmers with loans for machinery, fertilizer, tools, and other help. The government also aided the cattle industry through its National Cattle Fund, and with the Territorial Credit Institute gave aid to cooperative societies, which, from none in 1930 had grown to 165 by 1940. A National Social Security Fund was established for workers, as well as health clinics and child welfare institutions, the two latter of which included, for example, 50,000 free dental examinations and 1,800,000 bottles of milk distributed to 50,000 school children in 1939.

The administration carried on the construction of roads and development of ports. Highways by 1940 had brought all major isolated regions into contact with the rest of the country, while a general network tied in all departmental capitals with one another by 1941. Barranquilla, Cartagena, and Buenaventura, the major ports, had modernized their facilities by the end of the Santos regime.

The reorganized ministry of education (1938), concerned that only a third of the school population was housed, planned buildings for 20,000 primary schools to supplement the existing 9,200 which accommodated in 1940 but 600,000 pupils. Rural schools particularly benefited. The expansion of secondary schools and the establishment of a "University City" to supplement the three existing institutions were recognized as necessities for the cultural and technical education of Colombia's young people.

When the presidential elections came in 1942, World War II and the reform program of the Liberal party were the main issues. The twelve-year record of the Liberal party in giving Colombia a democratic orientation had prepared the majority of her people to accept the democratic principles involved in World War II. However, the essentially reactionary oligarchy, which had never accepted their defeat in 1930, turned a sympathetic ear to the Axis. Its antidemocratic slogans were trumpeted throughout the country by the Conservative leader, Laureano Gómez and the Falange, imported from Spain. Although the growing influence of Communism among Colombia's low-paid workers began a split in the Liberal party, the frightening possibilities of Conservative return to power assured the overwhelming election of Alfonso López on May 2, 1942.

Colombia and World War II, 1942–1945. In 1939 under Santos,

Colombia had ended possibilities of German sabotage of the Panama Canal by "Colombianizing" the German airlines, Scadta, replacing them with Avianca. Two years later, after Japan's attack at Pearl Harbor on December 7, 1941, Colombia promptly severed diplomatic relations with Japan and, before the year ended, with Germany and Italy. Her anger was further stirred early in 1942 by Germany's sinking two of her schooners, an action which paved the way for her declaration of war against the Germans in November, 1943. Shortly thereafter she took sharp measures against Axis aliens and their property. In other aspects of the war mutual cooperation between Colombia and the United States, markedly aided by President López' frank admiration for Franklin D. Roosevelt, facilitated American acquisition of valuable raw materials, coffee, minerals, and rubber. In return the United States, through the Export-Import Bank, extended loans totaling some $20,000,000.

Nationally, López continued his program of developing the human and material resources of Colombia. In 1943 his government launched a 60,000,000-peso bond issue to meet in part the deficits caused by loss of markets and to promote education, public health, social welfare, and a public works program, as well as to aid Colombia's industries, handicapped by the war, and expand its agricultural production. In the rural areas, where 70 per cent of the population lived, López secured in 1943 a new educational law requiring 33 per cent of the educational budget to be spent in support of primary schools and to supplement local revenues for school buildings and salaries of teachers. The Conservatives strongly opposed this legislation, not only as a measure to educate the masses, but because income and inheritance taxes were earmarked for the purpose.

The López administration, too, secured a land law in aid of small farmers calling for expropriation of unused lands and providing for government loans for tools, seed, and shelter on allotments ranging from 60 to 250 acres. Again the Conservatives found no comfort in this legislation. Aiding another sector of the population and incurring the displeasure of López' wealthy opponents, was an advanced labor law which, going into effect in 1945, provided for an eight-hour day for urban labor, a nine-hour day for rural, the right to organize unions, arbitration of disputes, equal pay for equal work, and paid yearly vacations. The low standard of living demanding these measures was apparent in the fact that wages, urban and rural, ranged in 1944 between twenty-five cents to a dollar a day.

While the López administration was particularly anxious to raise the standard of living of the most poverty-stricken, it also encouraged industries beneficial to the middle class and inevitably to the very wealthy. The steel industry received aid in the Santos administration through the Institute for Industrial Development. The first result was a steel mill established to exploit the huge iron deposits in the Medellín Valley. In 1944 a second steel mill was opened in Bogotá to produce rolling stock and precision tools. Industry as a whole grew rapidly, with over 600 companies, commercial and industrial, organized during 1942 and 1943. Aiding greatly the development of the Cauca and Medellín Valleys, cut off by the central range of the Andes from the Magdalena Valley, was the completion of the Cali-Buenaventura highway early in 1946.

The Liberal reform program, particularly the land, labor, and education laws, produced violent political conflict. López himself was elected in 1942, with part of the conservative Liberals opposing his candidacy. In office the fissure deepened as the more radical wing, growing in influence under Jorge Eliécer Gaitán, strongly supported labor's demands, some of which were sponsored by unions dominated by Communists. More than López himself, Gaitán incurred the enmity of the businessmen who made up the leadership of the Liberal party. To the Conservatives, Gaitán was unspeakable. By 1944, with the Gaitán Liberals insisting upon even greater reforms, the political struggle split the Liberal party. Evidence of Conservative feelings came in July of that year when an army officer kidnapped President López in a vain effort to launch a military uprising. López, hoping to quiet the harsh conflict, took a leave of absence leaving Darío Echandía as acting president from November, 1944, to May, 1945. On López' return he announced his desire to resign, but strong labor protest deterred him until July, 1945, when he tendered his resignation. His term was completed by a highly respected and able figure from the moderate wing of the Liberal party, Alberto Lleras Camargo. He served provisionally until the presidential election of May, 1946.

The Administration of Ospina Pérez, 1946–1950. With the Liberal party, led by Gabriel Turbay, hopelessly split, the Conservatives elected Dr. Mariano Ospina Pérez with but 40 per cent of the total vote. Inaugurated August 7, 1946, the president and his party persecuted their defeated opponents only to see the Liberal party win control of both houses in the 1947 congressional elections and repeat their success later in the year in the municipal elections. Unable to win legally, the government converted its persecution into virtual civil war, which enabled it to declare martial law.

In these distressing circumstances, the Ninth International Conference of the American States met in Bogotá in the spring of 1948. To the horror of the civilized world Gaitán was assassinated. The event immediately set off a city-wide riot. Before the violence had expended itself, 160 buildings had been either destroyed or seriously damaged with much loss of life suffered, while property loss ran into the millions. The government, charging Communist influence, broke relations with the Soviet Union, but subsequent history was to reveal that while the Communists exploited the unrest and the event, the explosion stemmed primarily from the violent character of the Liberal-Conservative conflict.

The Bogotá uprising led the Ospina Pérez government to seek a solution of the struggle. The elections of the following June, 1948, national and local, seemed a harbinger of a return to law and order when the Liberals won throughout the country. The event indeed forecast a Liberal return to power in the coming presidential election. Conservative fears of such an event probably accounted for the sharp rise in the number of political murders, expulsion of Liberal farmers from their homes, and a general collapse of Liberal and Conservative cooperation. The battle took a turn for the worse when in June, 1948, the most uncompromising of the Conservative leaders, Laureano Gómez, returned from Spain to become the Conservative candidate for president. In the next year, 1949, civil war became general throughout the country when it became apparent that Ospina Pérez was seeking to guarantee the election of Gómez. Congress attempted to circumvent the action by moving up the elections from May, 1950, to November, 1949.

By this date, however, Liberal participation in the election had become impossible: the Liberal congress was dissolved, Ospina Pérez ruled by decree and martial law was declared, followed by a state of siege, while the country was threatened by the army. In these circumstances the Liberal party boycotted the election, withdrawing its candidate, Darío Echandía. Laureano Gómez was declared elected on November 28, 1949.

After the election a state of siege and suspension of constitutional guarantees continued. Former presidents López and Santos both attacked the virtual dictatorship, while a new party, named after Gaitán, made its appearance. These events increased the tempo of the government's repressive tactics, arresting Liberals and supporting systematized attacks upon Protestant churches in the interior. By June, 1950, Liberal farmers, driven from their lands, took to arming themselves as a defense against wholesale arrests and outright murder. In these circumstances, disgraceful to Colombia's traditions, Gómez was inaugurated on August 7, 1950.

The Dictatorship of Gómez, 1950–1953. In office, Gómez continued suppression of newspapers and criticism of the government, refused to convene congress, postponed departmental assembly meetings (state legislatures), and returned control of public schools to the church. Against these acts the Liberal party issued a manifesto calling for civil opposition and abstention from voting. The continued violence and killings throughout the spring of 1951 brought unity to the Liberal party in its June national convention. It reaffirmed its decision not to participate in the congressional elections scheduled for September. Thus the Conservatives won when Liberal strongholds refrained from voting. When congress assembled it presented a picture of forty Conservative seats in the senate with twenty-two vacant; while the Chamber of Deputies showed seventy-one Conservative seats and fifty-one vacant.

After this election events began to shape themselves to terminate the bloody civil war, although two years were to elapse before the end came. A sign of the times came in October, 1951, when twenty-three retired generals signed a plea in the Liberal newspaper, *El Tiempo,* for the re-establishment of republican government to restore Colombia's prestige in the world, brightened only by the heroic bravery of Colombian troops on the Korean battle front.

Late in the year it was apparent that the dominant Conservative party was torn from within. The split was further aggravated by the sudden illness of Gómez, which led Dr. Roberto Urdaneta Arbeláez to assume the acting presidency in November, 1951. But the Conservative congress seemed determined to plunge the country deeper into conflict when it enacted a law providing for a constitutional assembly to meet in 1952. Constructively, it did take time out to create the sixteenth state of Colombia, Córdoba, on the Caribbean coast. Early in 1952 it was apparent how serious the revolt was when the government itself acknowledged that civil war existed in eleven of the sixteen departments.

Further evidence of the lengths to which the Conservative government was moving came in its decrees in July, 1952, which gave governors, appointed by the president, and mayors of municipalities the right to appoint individuals to all offices formerly elective. Designed to control the growing unrest among university students was another decree placing all provincial universities under the central government. Foreign reporters became liable for "tendentious" reporting. American newspapers condemned this action and charged the Conservative government with censorship as a means of hiding its responsibility for the political murders disgracing the nation.

Late in 1952 the Conservative party definitely split when Gilberto Alzate Avendaño joined the Liberals in demanding an end to press censorship. Seemingly in reply the government gave approval to mobs which destroyed the buildings of the two Liberal newspapers, *El Tiempo* and *El Espectador,* as well as the homes of former president Alfonso López and Carlos Lleras Restrepo, both of whom had to flee the country. By this date discussion was rampant in the country in an effort to find an escape from the struggle. Significantly, one proposal suggested formation of a military junta including General Gustavo Rojas Pinilla. Although the Conservative party again won in the March, 1953, elections when the Liberals and the Alzatista Conservatives abstained, the party became irrevocably split over the presidential elections scheduled for 1954. The more moderate group backed former president Ospina Pérez for the office, while the Gómez-Arbaláez faction began to smother the former's candidacy with all the restrictions formerly reserved for Liberals.

With powerful middle class support, Ospina Pérez threatened the control of the government, now a clerical-conservative one. To avoid such a disaster, Arbaláez appointed an assembly of supporters who drew up a new constitution so thoroughly reactionary in character as to guarantee the continuation of the Gómez regime. As this objective became clear to the country, the idea of turning to the army for relief from police atrocities and civil war rapidly gained ground. Thus on June 13, 1953, the military, led by General Rojas Pinilla, seized control with little opposition. Both Gómez and Arbaláez went into exile. By the same token the presidential elections were postponed.

The Government of Rojas Pinilla, 1953 to the Present. The new government restored to some extent the freedom of the press and other liberties, and declared amnesty for the Liberals who had taken up arms to defend themselves. Moreover, the government returned the farms to those Liberals who had been driven from them. With these terms satisfactory to the guerrillas, and with the army replacing the police, the Liberal fighters went to designated points to surrender their arms. In the subsequent weeks the thousands who appeared for this purpose revealed to the surprised Colombians how widespread had been the opposition to the Gómez regime.

In the following months the terrible tensions of the preceding years

slowly relaxed. The Rojas government permitted public meetings, reduced persecution of Protestants, and freed the press in foreign affairs
matters, though it moved more slowly in ending restrictions in internal
affairs. The Liberal party expressed confidence in the new government
and reunited early in 1954 under Carlos Lleras Restrepo, Alberto Lleras
Camargo, former director-general of the OAS, and former president Alfonso López.

When, however, the party sought representation in the government,
its hopes were quickly dashed by Rojas Pinilla, who called together a
constituent assembly with no election. Composed overwhelmingly of
Conservative party members, it promptly chose on August 3, 1954, General Rojas Pinilla as president for the term, 1954–1958. Liberal hopes
received a further blow when the assembly abolished in departments
and municipalities all locally elected bodies, which were replaced by
appointees of the president. Constructively, the assembly did extend the
right, to be exercised after 1958, to all women over twenty-one years of
age to vote and hold office. At its convention in December, 1954, the
Liberal party chose Alfonso López as chief, who demanded the restoration of normal democratic processes. But little hope was held out that
this would be done when Rojas Pinilla announced he would govern the
country during his term by martial law. Unhappy evidence of the growing severity of the dictatorship came in August, 1955, when the government forced the closing of *El Tiempo*, one of the best newspapers in
Latin America.

Economic Development since 1946. In spite of the civil war, fought
intermittently, the country saw marked economic advances after 1946.
The basic economy of Colombia rested upon the production and export
of coffee. Averaging over the years between 4,000,000 and 5,000,000
bags, this crop made up four-fifths of all exports. Ninety-three per cent
of the production went to the United States and was naturally the chief
source of income to the Colombian government. Other agricultural crops
were cotton, sugar, rice, and bananas. Supplementing these were the
minerals oil, copper, mica, iron, gold, lead, tin, and asbestos and precious
and semiprecious stones, with emeralds outstanding.

To develop these resources and add industrial undertakings, the
small middle class took a leading part. They received their first important
support in the administrations of López and Santos (1934–1945). The
Conservative government of Ospina Pérez (1946–1950) continued this
economic policy, having the added resource of a large gold reserve accumulated during World War II. Under Ospina Pérez a unified program

emerged when the government invited the International Bank for Reconstruction and Development to make a survey in 1949–1950. It outlined for the government the major changes and improvements needed in Colombia's economy to raise standards of living and to make the best use of its resources. After 1950 the administration began giving effect to many of the recommendations, aided by loans from the Export-Import Bank and from the World Bank itself.

In the central area including the region about Bogotá and Medellín to the west, hydroelectric projects and dams were built to develop power for the new industries and for irrigation of reclaimed land. To provide oil from the Barrancabermeja oil fields, a pipeline was constructed from Puerto Salgar to Bogotá, and another projected from Puerto Berrío to Medellín. Coinciding with the growing consumption of oil was the return in 1951, at the end of thirty years, of the De Mares oil concession to the Colombian government, formerly held by the Tropical Oil Company (Standard). This event marked the first time in history that an oil concession in an undeveloped country had been returned to a government upon expiration of the terms of the lease. Immediately the government launched a national program under *Empresa Colombiana de Pétroleos* to develop refineries and build new pipelines. Other industries were also established for production of consumer goods, and of special importance was a new steel plant at Paz del Río. A railroad projected along the Magdalena River, besides providing more rapid transport, will open about 3,000,000 acres of new lands to be put in the hands of small farmers.

Outside the central area of the Magdalena Valley have been important developments in the Cauca Valley, in the west on the Pacific littoral, and in the south. In the latter the modernization of the port of Tumaco has begun. To connect the interior with the west coast and furnish an outlet for the manufactures of Medellín, the industrial capital of the country, modern highways are under construction to reach Buenaventura from Buga. Outstanding in the north was the completion in 1955 of a highway from Medellín to Turbo on the Gulf of Urabá. Cauca Valley developments are also making possible for the first time the exploitation of huge coal reserves near Cali along with those in the Magdalena Department. For the country at large, Colombia has encouraged foreign capital to supplement native investment. To this end her commercial treaty with the United States guarantees equal treatment in industrial, commercial, and cultural matters, and provides for protection of property and persons, as well as recognizing the need for American investment in Colombia's development.

In the total view of recent Colombian history, it seems clear that the middle class and the growing labor movement will continue to increase their importance as social forces as industrialization continues. It would seem equally inevitable that these changes will bring Colombia back to the normal democratic orientation given the nation by López and Santos, descendants of the nineteenth century liberal tradition. However, it is also apparent that the basic political conflict remains unsolved: the reconciliation of the clerical-conservative fears of loss of privileges with the determination of the Liberals to raise the nation's standards of living and give life to democratic practices.

Colombian Cultural Life. Colombia's colonial cultural traditions gave it the title of the "Athens of South America." Before the Wars for Independence the new political ideas of the French Revolution activated the writings of Antonio Nariño and the classic prose of Camilo Torres. After that struggle was over, in Colombia as in other Latin-American nations, romanticism took a deep hold among its writers. However, little original contribution resulted because the Colombian romanticists remained too closely bound to their European models. Standing out, however, as the exception is *María,* the sentimental classic of Jorge Isaacs (1837–1895), probably the most widely read novel in Latin America. Adding a compelling charm to the story of love, life, and death are romantic descriptions of Colombia's sylvan landscape.

With the far-reaching changes, economic and social, affecting Colombia after the opening of the twentieth century, new writers emphasized the realities of man's struggle against both human greed and nature's malignant forces. Adept in working this lode, José Eustasio Rivera (1889–1928) created a remarkable novel, *The Vortex (La vorágine).* He described the cruel Amazonian forests, whose insects, wild animals, reptiles, and parasitic plants drag down to horrible deaths the rubber workers caught in the ceaseless warfare of the jungle. Thus far no writer has equaled Rivera in a fictional portrayal of the labyrinthian life of the tropics.

Other contemporary figures have set similar high standards in their fields. A leading modernist was the escapist poet, Guillermo Valencia (1873–1943). In historical writing Germán Arciniegas has won wide audiences both in the United States and Latin America. However, probably the best known literary figure Colombia has produced is Baldomero Sanín Cano (1861–   ). Acclaimed widely as Latin America's greatest teacher, he is an able essayist, literary critic and philosopher.

Chapter XXIV

VENEZUELA

Part I. THE ERA OF LIBERAL CAUDILLOS, 1830–1888

The Character of Venezuelan History. The colonial period fixed the basic framework of Venezuela's social structure and the organization of its economy. On the Orinoco Plains a cattle industry established itself. In the west in the coastal mountains and foothills of the Andes, a land-owning agricultural oligarchy became a second economic group. At Caracas and in the coastal cities, where trade flourished on the export of cotton, tobacco, and cattle, a commercial class had its beginnings. In common with most of the Latin-American countries the mixture of Spaniards and Indians produced a *mestizo,* the cowboy of the plains and the proletariat of the cities and towns. In the western area were *mestizos* and a considerable number of Indians, laborers on the estates of the oligarchy. Along the coast Negroes and mulattoes, as in Colombia, composed a considerable part of the population.

Colonial commercial activity, the export of sugar, cotton, and tobacco from the coastal plantations and hides from the interior, effected a junction of interests between the commercial groups of Caracas and the coast and the cattle and plantation owners. Late eighteenth century free trade ideas developed liberal and progressive attitudes among Caracas leaders in contrast to the rigid colonial outlook of the agricultural landowners in the west, known later as *Andinos.*

This economic division of the social groups of colonial Venezuela became the basis for the struggle after independence between the traditional liberal and conservative elements of the population. Between 1830 and 1888 the liberal *caudillos,* establishing dictatorships, dominated the development of Venezuela and began economic reforms beneficial to the growth of a commercial class. By 1888 rivers were open to traffic; colonial restrictions were removed; roads were improved and attempts made to introduce state education. A nationalistic feeling appeared which pitted Venezuela against British claims to Guiana territory. After 1888 conservative dictatorships continued to encourage foreign investment and culminated in that of Gómez. While destroying liberal advances of the nineteenth century, the Gómez regime gave a base to modernize the economy. With its overthrow in 1936 a renaissance in Venezuelan democracy attracted world attention with its advanced reforms until its progress was halted by a new dictatorship in 1948.

Páez and the Liberal Caudillos, 1830–1870. Páez himself and Monagas, a later political leader, both of whom entered the War for Independence landless, emerged among the richest landowners of the country. As such they represented a considerable body of new wealth unburdened by colonial tradition. The constitution of 1830, when Venezuela became independent of Colombia, accordingly reflected both restrictions which gave control to the wealthy and provisions which incorporated liberal ideas. The former was apparent in that the voters of the parochial districts had to meet property qualifications. Given the dire poverty of the bulk of the Venezuelans, only a handful in each district could qualify. Representative of the liberal ideas already manifesting themselves were the provisions which did away with the *fueros* or special privileges of the church. Unlike the first constitutions of the other Latin-American countries, Venezuela's did not provide the Catholic as the sole religion of the state.

When the government was formed under the new constitution, the discontent of rival *caudillos* and the opposition of the church manifested themselves in a revolt in 1831 which, however, Páez put down quickly. During his administration until 1835 Páez permitted freedom of the press and of elections. He devoted his energies to improving the economy of the country, ending restrictive colonial trade laws, freeing the tobacco industry from government monopoly, and negotiating commercial agreements with foreign nations.

When Páez' term ended in 1835, he was succeeded by José M. Vargas, head of the university. Revolt, however, drove him quickly from office, but Páez just as quickly restored him. Vargas soon resigned, for he found politics too rough for his scholarly soul. Carlos Sublette finished the term under peaceful conditions. In 1838 Páez returned to the presidency to govern until 1843. During this administration he reduced the influence of the church in Venezuelan politics and stimulated the economic development of the country. Over the protests of the American minister, he agreed with the British to abolish the slave trade. The British, too, negotiated a favorable treaty with Páez for the importation of their goods. He carried forward the road building program of his earlier administration, and had the satisfaction of seeing foreign commerce rapidly develop. Coffee revealed the most striking advance as the industrial cities of Europe provided a growing demand. From a trifle over 87,000 bags exported in 1831, almost 213,000 sacks were being shipped abroad by 1845. Similar conditions in the export of hides and tobacco brought prosperity both to the plantation owners and the commercial groups of Caracas and La Guaira. The condition of the poorer classes, however, in the cities and rural areas remained one of abject poverty. Unemployed agricultural workers, artisans, and escaped slaves caused constant disorders in their search for a bare existence.

By the time Páez' second administration ended, the country was beginning to develop liberal and conservative parties. These political groups, however, were composed of disparate elements. The conservatives rested principally upon the landowners; the wealthier commercial class tended to join them. The liberals found their support in the smaller bankrupt farmers, in the small businessmen, and often in the masses. Many intellectuals, frequently from the wealthy class, were supporters of democratic principles, and agitated for fundamental reforms. Their leader in these early years was Antonio Leocadio Guzmán, whose newspaper, *El Venezolano*, propagated liberal ideas and contributed to the formation of the Liberal party. The effectiveness of his work to make really democratic advances, however, was limited to a small group, so that in the election of 1846, in which he himself was a candidate against José Tadeo Monagas, he lost. The strength of the oligarchical control is seen in the simple facts that, of a total population estimated at about 1,275,000, only 60,000 voted. Moreover, if all registered voters had cast their ballots, the electoral college would have had 2,798 members, but in actual fact only 342 were elected. Guzmán, who attacked this control of the suffrage, was not only arrested but sentenced to death. Monagas, however, commuted the sentence to exile.

By 1847 the economic collapse in Europe, which was to bring the Revolution of 1848, affected the prosperity of Venezuela. Monagas, of humble origin, found in the distress of his friends his sympathies aligned with the commercial groups who demanded reforms rather than with the older landowning oligarchy. Accepting the Liberals' demand for the return of Guzmán, Monagas supported him for his election to the vice-presidency in 1848. Attacked by his former supporters, the Conservatives, Monagas declared a dictatorship, appointed Liberals to his cabinet, and exiled Páez when the latter tried to overthrow him. In the next election Monagas dictated the election of his brother, José Gregorio Monagas, who brought about the abolition of slavery in 1854, an action largely explained by the fact that many Venezuelans with Negro blood held important public offices and army posts under the Liberal regime.

José Tadeo Monagas again became president in 1856, drawing support from a faction of the Conservative party which joined the Liberals in the election. His support of proposals to re-create Bolívar's superstate met opposition in congress against granting the wide powers he asked. In the following year he secured congress' consent to draw up a new constitution which extended his term to six years and under which he was re-elected. However, in 1858 he was accused of giving in to British demands for territory on the Guiana frontier and driven from office by General Julián Castro. The event ended the domination of the Monagas brothers in the history of Venezuela.

Guzmán Blanco, the Last of the Liberal Caudillos. The next ten years saw Venezuela descend into bloody civil wars between the Liberal and Conservative *caudillos.* The new constitution of 1858, of liberal hue, provided for freedom of religion, but in conferring extensive powers upon the states, strengthened the power of the conservative landowners who dominated local politics in the interior. In 1859 Castro, a conciliatory figure, was set aside and a Conservative, Pedro Gual, became president, an event which immediately brought the Liberal forces to arms. Defeated on the battlefield, Gual was succeeded by Manuel Felipe Tovar, who invited Páez to return from exile to command the army. In September, 1861, Páez, elevated to the presidency, became a pillar of support for the conservative forces. His action, however, in setting aside the constitution of 1858 stirred the liberals to action under the leadership of General Juan Cristomo Falcón and Antonio Guzmán Blanco, son of the great liberal of the 1840's.

Páez, defeated, went into exile with honor to die a few years later in the United States. Falcón's presidency gave the country the constitution of 1864, which named the nation the "United States of Venezuela." But peace was not forthcoming. The president campaigned against the rebellious Conservatives, while Guzmán governed in Caracas. For a moment the Conservatives won power led by José Tadeo Monagas, whose early death brought his son, Rupert Monagas, to the head of the government. Guzmán Blanco, rallying the Liberals with the prestige of his great name, overthrew Monagas and assumed power in 1870.

The rule of Guzmán Blanco, who dominated Venezuela from 1870 to 1888, finds its chief explanation in the dictator's combining liberal policies with encouragement of foreign economic interest in the resources of Venezuela. He captured the imagination of the people by holding to the tradition of liberal reforms, and secured funds to maintain his military power, the army, by negotiating loans and granting concessions to European and American interests. Attempts to interest foreign companies in the resources of Venezuela found expression under Monagas in 1858 when he sought the assistance of German, French, and British companies, but unsuccessfully. Páez, in his administration of 1861, negotiated in England for a £1,000,000 loan, and Falcón, who followed him with Guzmán Blanco as vice-president, likewise opened negotiations in Britain for a loan of £1,500,000. However, difficulties with Britain over the boundary of the Guiana territory turned Guzmán Blanco after 1870 to Paris for his principal loans.

With a lavish granting of concessions and contracts to French, British, German, and American companies, Guzmán Blanco began the modernization of the country's economy. A vital railroad connected Caracas with La Guaira, the chief export city on the coast. Other lines ran between Puerto Cabello and Valencia and thence to the capital. Roads, bridges, and highways were built. In the principal cities, parks were laid out, streets widened, new public buildings constructed. While Guzmán Blanco boasted he would build a schoolhouse in every street in every town in Venezuela, some primary and secondary schools were in fact built, as well as professional colleges, particularly engineering schools. In the capital he improved the curriculum of the University of Caracas, encouraged the liberal arts, founded an Academy of Languages and opened a Municipal Theater. However, the literary figures of the day were permitted no criticism of the government, and those of independent mind faced exile and even imprisonment. Undoubtedly influenced by viewing Napoleon's impressive tomb in the Invalides in Paris, Guzmán Blanco converted a large church in Caracas into a magnificent Pantheon to hold the remains of Bolívar brought back from Colombia. Everywhere on bridges, buildings, and statues, a plaque reminded the Venezuelans that their benefactor was the "Illustrious American," Guzmán Blanco.

With the same energy the dictator attacked the problem of political and religious reform and contributed to the development of the liberal tradition. While most of his political reforms were aimed at consolidating his own power, his religious policy struck deeper. His measures were those of a representative of the middle class, which historically had attacked the monopolies of the church in land, education, and political power. Thus reflecting the usual practice of the nineteenth century European liberals, such as Cavour, Guzmán Blanco confiscated the property of the monasteries and put them up for sale to businessmen. His public school program found its counterpart in decreeing civil marriage laws and state control over registration of births and deaths. Characteristically, as in Mexico under Juárez in the preceding decade, Protestant missionary societies were invited into the country to evangelize among the primitive Indian groups. Further, his constitution of 1873 provided for freedom of worship. When these reforms stirred the church to opposition, Guzmán Blanco exiled the archbishop of Caracas. As the conflict grew bitter, the dictator threatened to sever relations with the Vatican and set up a national church whose officials would be elected by the laity. While the proposal died in congress, the idea was later revived, though ineffectively.

The economic prosperity of the country and his reforms were the basis of the dictator's political control over the state. After the first three years he was elected constitutional president in 1873 for the next four years. In 1874 he drew up a new constitution under which the president was to be directly elected for two years but with no immediate re-election. He was able to dictate the election of his successor, although in 1878 on his return from Europe he used harsh methods against his enemies who had pulled down some of his statues. This event led him to produce another constitution, the chief feature of which was a Federal Council in which representatives of each political administrative unit participated. In this way he congregated about him his principal supporters. Out of this council came the next president, General Joaquín Crespo, who served as a puppet (1880–1884), but who was destined to overthrow the dictator. That event took place in 1887 when Guzmán Blanco, faced with violent revolt within the country and British pressure to settle the Guiana boundary, resigned from Paris where he had established a comfortable bank account.

Part II. CONSERVATIVE DICTATORSHIPS, 1893–1936

Transition, 1888–1909. After the overthrow of Guzmán Blanco, Venezuela fell into violent civil wars out of which in 1892 Joaquín Crespo built a new dictatorship under the cry of *Legalismo*. Under a new constitution in 1893 he served until 1898. The document was significant in revealing a fundamental economic and political change coming over the country, largely the result of Guzmán Blanco's dictatorship. Its provisions limiting suffrage to those not condemned by the courts assured control in the hands of the landowners and wealthy commercial class that had profited under Guzmán Blanco, a group not unlike the *Científicos* under

Díaz in Mexico. These elements, accustomed by the previous dictator to accommodate the interests of foreign investors, eventually established absolute power under Gómez in 1909.

Crespo's administration saw a rapid expansion of British, American, and German interests in the country. German trade became significant, while a loan negotiated in Germany marked the beginning of German penetration into the country. However, the outstanding event of Crespo's rule was the culmination of the boundary dispute with Great Britain.

The Venezuela Boundary Dispute, 1895. The origin of the Vene-zuelan boundary dispute with Great Britain goes back to the colonial period. After the Wars for Independence Venezuela fell heir to the Spanish claims, although no boundary had been defined between the colony and Guiana. In 1840 the search by British prospectors for gold expanded British claims westward. From the beginning of her national period Venezuela protested British claims. Guzmán Blanco even con-sidered seeking protection from the United States by granting exclusive rights to the Orinoco River to American citizens. American interest in the region began during the Wars for Independence and by the time of Guzmán Blanco included navigation of the Orinoco, investments in gold mines, asphalt deposits, and trade and commerce. British claims and British-American rivalry over the navigation of the Orinoco River were, in fact, in the background of Olney and Cleveland's decision to force arbitration under the Monroe Doctrine to protect American interests as well as Venezuela's rights.

When the British refused to recognize the Monroe Doctrine as apply-ing to her dispute with Venezuela, Cleveland appealed to Congress to force the issue. The British, however, troubled in 1895 with a growing conflict with the Dutch in South Africa and rivalry with the French in the Sudan, agreed to arbitrate. The question was settled under unusual circumstances. The chairman of the arbitration commission, a Russian, delivered in the final stages of the discussion an ultimatum to the United States representatives which called for agreement on a line that awarded the bulk of the territory to the British. The American members felt that Britain had no right, in fact, to the amount of territory allotted her under the arrangement, but decided that since the mouth of the Orinoco remained in the hands of Venezuela, they would accept the proposal of the Russian chairman.

Juaquín Crespo was succeeded in 1898 by Ignacio Andrade, whose government was overthrown shortly by an outright bid for power by the landowning *Andinos* led by Cipriano Castro. By the device of proroguing congress, setting up new constitutions, and ruling the country with a ruthless hand, Castro dominated Venezuela for the next nine years and dissipated its wealth. A violent, sensual, reckless man, Castro was a disgrace to his country. In the shadows of his government was Juan Vicente Gómez, waiting for the opportunity to overthrow the dictator. The latter's rule not only produced one revolt after another, but brought claims against the government by foreign powers for damages suffered in the disorders. These Castro ignored.

The Venezuelan Imbroglio, 1902. In 1902 Britain, Germany, and Italy joined a blockade of Venezuelan ports to force payment of their claims. When Castro continued to defy the powers, the blockading naval vessels opened fire on the country's defenseless ports and cities, sank Venezuela's gunboats, and did other damage. Castro assumed a still more defiant attitude and sought arbitration of the conflict by the United States. President Theodore Roosevelt, at the moment deep in plans for a Panama Canal route, had no liking for the action of the British and Germans, whose activities of a similar nature a few years before had led to the seizure of Chinese territory. At the same time he raised no objection in principle to their method of collecting claims. However, in view of the American interest in Panama he urged arbitration. To effect this end a group of mixed claims commissions investigated the claims of the foreign powers, found them exaggerated, and reduced the amounts of all claims of foreign nations including those of the United States.

The event was noteworthy in the field of international affairs. As noted, Argentina, through her foreign minister, Dr. Luís Drago, rejected this method of collecting debts in the Drago Doctrine.[1] Britain's willingness to arbitrate rested upon her need of American goodwill in the face of growing German naval and military power. The Germans followed the British lead, for they had no confidence in the outcome of the political situation in England, where demands to arbitrate were threatening the stability of the Conservative government.

While Castro's defiance of foreigners stirred support for his administration, he soon lost it by his continued dictatorial national policy. In 1908, seeking medical treatment in Europe, he left the government in the hands of Juan Vicente Gómez, the next "Man of the Andes." Gómez' followers filled the army and the congress so that the latter in 1909, after repudiating Castro's protests over suspension from office, conferred the presidency upon Gómez. Thus began one of the most ruthless dictatorships in Latin America in the early twentieth century.

[1] See page 290.

The Gómez Dictatorship, 1909–1936. Gómez was a combination of animal brutality and financial genius. An illegitimate half-blood, he grew to manhood in the Andean mountains on the Venezuelan-Colombian border. From an early age he displayed a cruel nature, a capacity to make money, and such an unerring judgment of men that his neighbors credited him with a knowledge of the black arts. To these characteristics he added others that made him feared, a complete insensitiveness to human suffering, and a staggering capacity for immorality. Neither the number of his mistresses nor that of his illegitimate children is known, but the lowest estimate of the latter is 400.

On his assumption of power, Gómez assured foreign nations that Venezuela would meet her financial obligations. Turning to establish domestic control, he crushed revolts of Castro's sympathizers including Castro's own return to Venezuela in 1913 and attempt to seize the presidency. His rivalry with Castro settled, Gómez began the process of changing the constitution until he had created a completely undemocratic and centralistic government. Having established control in the states and municipalities, Gómez had the 1914 constitution drawn up under which the president was provided for a term of seven years, elected by congress, with no vice-president. Two senators from each state were chosen by the legislatures; members of the House of Deputies were elected on the basis of population, but with suffrage restricted by various qualifications; no one actually voted unless he supported the dictator. He created a single political party which he called the *Causa Rehabilitadora*. Elected under the constitution, Gómez served until 1922 when he was re-elected for two years, after which a new constitution provided for his election under which he served until 1929. At that time he refused re-election, so that the presidency went to a supporter, Dr. Juan Bautista Pérez, while Gómez remained the head of the army. When the 1929 depression occurred, Venezuela's foreign trade fell off and criticism of Pérez arose, followed by attempts at revolution. In June, 1931, Pérez was forced out of office by congress. Gómez accepted the call to become president again and served until his death in December, 1935.

The most important feature of Gómez' rule was the development of Venezuela's oil resources. World War I, giving an impetus to the search for oil, found the British as early as 1914 seeking concessions in the Maracaibo district where Guzmán Blanco had urged a search for petroleum. Three years later, when the Mexican constitution of 1917 seemed to put foreign oil companies in jeopardy, a flood of investment, encouraged by Gómez, turned to Venezuela. Gómez' oil legislation of 1920 guaranteed foreign property rights and provided for low export taxes. The effects were phenomenal. From an annual production of about 1,000,000 barrels in 1921, Venezuela jumped by 1928 to second place in world production with a total of over 137,000,000 barrels. By 1936 at the end of Gómez' rule, Venezuelan oil production reached almost 148,000,000 barrels annually. Under constant exploration of British and American oil companies the total area under concession included more than 22,000 square miles, with the greatest single field in the basin of Lake Maracaibo. The oil companies refrained from building refineries in Venezuela, but shipped the crude product for refining to the Dutch islands of Curaçao and Aruba off the Venezuelan coast.

The wealth that poured into Venezuela's coffers from oil taxes, ranging from $13,000,000 in 1921 to over $50,000,000 by 1936, was diverted by Gómez to support undertakings in which he and his supporters had interests. Few significant industries made an appearance, confined largely to a number of cotton mills, breweries, and match and cigarette factories. On the other hand, Gómez himself, through forced sales, became the largest real estate owner in the leading cities, in agricultural lands, and in the cattle plains of the Orinoco. To connect his vast holdings with the ports and the capital, he built railroads, but more especially excellent highways, which by the end of his reign exceeded more than 800 miles. These were effective, too, as military roads needed to control the population. Plantations in which he and his supporters invested expanded rapidly, producing sugar, cocoa, and coffee; and the cattle industry likewise began to be modernized by the introduction of scientific methods. In finance Gómez reduced the public debt to such a low point and established such financial stability that Venezuela was probably the only country in the world which survived the 1929 depression with no material ill effects.

However, the price paid in terms of human suffering for this gilded dictatorship was appalling. The destruction of democratic institutions was complete. Liberal leaders and others who opposed the dictator were, if caught, either executed without remorse, confined to seacoast dungeons where ocean tides flowed into the cells, or harried out of the land. Labor worked in the oil fields and on plantations at wages among the lowest on the South American continent; proscribed unions functioned underground. Secret police held the population in a grip of terror. Elections were lifeless, mechanical farces; civil liberties, nonexistent; and congress a rubber stamp. The church, too, suffered persecution when its leaders criticized the immoral life of the dictator. Gómez, his supporters who occupied the chief offices in the government, and foreign companies, principally oil, were the only ones that profited from the long dictatorship.

Part III.   DEMOCRATIC ADVANCES AND CONSERVATIVE REACTION SINCE 1936

López Contreras and the Beginnings of Democratic Reforms. When Gómez died the Venezuelan people at once revealed a mood that would not tolerate a new dictatorship. Fortunately, General Eleazar López Contreras, an able man with an understanding that the times called for democratic government, completed the dictator's term of office. In his first address to the nation López assured it that he would provide them with representative government. True to his word, he called a constitutional assembly which drew up and promulgated a new constitution in 1936. This document laid a basis for advancing Venezuela on the road to democracy to match the modernization that had begun under Gómez.

Under the new constitution the president served for five years with no immediate succession, but with the right to appoint and remove ministers of his cabinet, who were obliged to report annually to congress. Congress was composed of a senate and a house of deputies. Suffrage was extended to all males over twenty-one who could read and write. Significant provisions guaranteed individual rights and inviolability of life, property, correspondence, the home, petition, and assembly. Personal liberty was further protected in provisions against forced recruiting and slavery and guarantees of full freedom of thought, although Communist and anarchist doctrines were banned.

For labor the document provided a day of weekly rest, annual vacations with pay, and provisions for improvement of working conditions, both urban and rural. Conscious of the vast pool of illiteracy, estimated at the time at more than 70 per cent, the constitution makers made education free, obligatory, and controlled by the state. At the moment that the constitution became effective, a labor code amplified further the guarantees designed to bring labor out of its medieval status. It included sharing in the profits of enterprises, social insurance, an eight-hour day, trade union organization, collective bargaining, labor inspection, protection of women and children, and health programs.

López Contreras, elected president under the new constitution, served until May, 1941. In 1938 he launched a three-year program to improve the condition in general of all the Venezuelan people. Its main features included improvement of public health, education, and inexpensive housing for the masses. Other aspects looked to the development of the economy neglected under Gómez. Here measures were taken to improve port facilities, develop inland transportation, and build extensive public works. Available for these varied undertakings was the income of the state, principally royalties from oil, which in 1938 reached about $80,000,000. The educational features of the program achieved significant results. The number of public schools was doubled; professional and agricultural institutes and a huge national university in Caracas were laid out. This enterprise had the benefit of the advice of an educational commission from Chile, a country which by 1938 had had some thirteen years' experience in solving educational problems peculiar to South American nations. By 1941 it was estimated that illiteracy in Venezuela had dropped from 70 per cent to about 54 per cent.

The Administration of Medina, 1941–1945. Isaias Medina Angarita succeeded López Contreras in May, 1941. Medina completed the three-year plan and immediately launched a four-year one. This latter put the emphasis on the development of the interior of the country and far-reaching social programs to improve the lot of the population in general. As a costly undertaking but nevertheless vital to the nation, the importance of which was plainly perceived by the groups supporting the program of social reforms, it led the government to open negotiations with the oil companies for a fairer distribution of the wealth being extracted from Venezuela. For example, in that year, 1941, the production of oil constituted 88 per cent of Venezuela's exports and was valued at some $225,000,000, representing a production of over 227,000,000 barrels. The resulting legislation, known as the Petroleum Law of 1943, reiterated the constitution of 1936, which placed the subsoil riches in the hands of the nation. This provision became the basis of the law which governs the "terms under which the right to explore, exploit, refine, and transport petroleum may be exercised and provides basic petroleum taxation." In effect the law required oil companies to exchange their holdings for concessions to run forty years, made it possible for the government to collect the royalty in oil, and required the companies to establish refineries in Venezuela itself. Income tax legislation was adopted in 1943 which supplemented the government's income from royalties in such a way that Venezuela's return on oil production would "in no case be less than the net earnings of each company in Venezuela." Thus the state's income increases along with the income of the oil companies.

At the inception of the Four Year Plan, World War II reduced temporarily Venezuela's markets, so that the government sought and secured a loan of $20,000,000 from the United States. However, the demand for oil and minerals as the war progressed once more brought prosperity and the revival of the plan, only to be slowed down shortly thereafter by a shortage of needed manufactured goods. Much, nevertheless, was done. Highways were built into the interior, harbor development at La Guaira was begun, extensive low-cost housing projects in Caracas and Maracaibo were launched, and a far-reaching health program gotten under way.

In World War II Venezuela's new democratic orientation placed her on the side of the Allies, for whom her vast oil resources became available. After Japan's attack on the United States in 1941, Medina declared Venezuela's friendship for the democracies and froze Axis funds. The government, too, reached a friendly settlement with Great Britain over a dispute involving the area of the Gulf of Paria in the east, of which Venezuela received 5,600 square kilometers and the British 3,600. Possible oil deposits there gave the settlement particular significance. When German submarines threatened the oil refineries on the Dutch islands of Aruba and Curaçao, Venezuela cooperated with the United States in occupying the islands.

The Revolt of 1945. In spite of the marked progress of the country under López Contreras and Medina, the shadow of Gómez still lay over the land. Important figures in the Gómez regime remained in power. Various groups—labor unions, liberals, intellectuals, and others—attacked the government for its slow advances. Discontent was rife among the younger army officers because of low pay and limited possibilities for promotion. The war, having created a shortage of manufactured goods, had also sent the cost of living skyrocketing, so that labor suffered with all other low income groups. As the presidential election set for 1946 approached, many came to believe that some of the generals in the army and holdovers from the Gómez regime were preparing to establish a dictatorship. The liberals consolidated their forces under the leadership of a newspaperman exiled by Gómez, Dr. Rómulo Betancourt, who, with Rómulo Gallegos, had founded the Democratic Action party (*Acción Democrático Partido*) in 1941. This party, somewhat socialist but strongly nationalistic, advocated the government ownership of the transportation system and public utilities together with increased taxation of the oil companies to support an extensive program to expand education, develop agriculture, and lower the cost of living by creating a national industry to avoid importing high cost foreign goods.

On October 18, 1945, the revolt, aided by the younger army officers, was successful. A seven-man junta appointed Betancourt provisional president until elections could be held. When López Contreras, the army's commander-in-chief, and the archbishop of Caracas declared for the new government, the tenure of the junta was assured. Recognition by the United States was immediate. In preparing the election schedule for 1946, the provisional government enacted a law providing for direct suffrage to assure voting by all men and women, even though illiterate. Other significant measures were the restoration of constitutional rights, the calling of a constituent congress to draw up a new fundamental law, a 30 per cent increase in the pay of enlisted men and lower-ranking officers, and the first steps to establish a merchant marine.

The Betancourt-Gallegos Government, 1945–1948. The Betancourt provisional government remained in power until February 15, 1948, after which Rómulo Gallegos took over as duly elected president and served until November of that year, when a military revolt overthrew him. Gallegos carried on the program initiated by the Betancourt junta, so that the two governments are best considered as a unit. The junta planned immediately to call a constitutional assembly. For this purpose it registered Venezuelan citizens who were to exercise the suffrage granted to all, male and female, literate and illiterate. By 1946 when the election took place, more than 1,500,000 voters had registered. In the campaign for the assembly were fifteen recognized parties, among which the Democratic Action party was outstanding. Others of importance were the COPEI (Committee for Independent Political and Electoral Institutions), the Conservative, the Socialist Workers' party, and the Patriotic Junta, a businessmen's party. In the election the Democratic Action party received three times the number of votes cast for the others, possibly explained in part by the participation of women for the first time in Venezuela's history, who thus recorded their gratitude to the party granting them the suffrage. Interestingly, twelve of their number were elected to the assembly.

By the following July 5, 1947, the new constitution had been drawn up and promulgated. It guaranteed all the basic freedoms and the individual's right to education, employment, and health, while specifically protecting property rights. It recognized for the state a definite role in planning the development of the national economy. It prohibited monopolies, but permitted employers' associations and guaranteed a fair return on invested capital. For labor it recognized the right to organize and to strike, fixed labor's rights to paid vacations and to pensions, and included other modern practices. The form of government, executive, bicameral, and judicial, recognized the principle of separation of powers. The president, elected for four years, appointed the governors but could not seek immediate re-election.

Rómulo Gallegos, President and Writer, 1947–1948. The election held under the new constitution in December, 1947, resulted in the victory of Rómulo Gallegos, the nominee of the Democratic Action party. His choice as president had a special significance. He was the first civilian executive to fill the office since José M. Vargas in 1835. Greater interest attached to his role as Venezuela's most distinguished literary figure and one of Latin America's greatest novelists. In a series of novels of the dwellers of the plains, he revealed a profound knowledge of his country. Outstanding are *The Climber,* a detailed analysis of life on a coffee plantation, and *Cantaclaro,* the story of a troubadour on the Orinoco prairies.

Ranking as a classic in the Spanish language (and translated into English under the same title) is *Doña Bárbara,* the story of a woman, a ruthless creature, who is the owner of a great hacienda in the interior. His skill in revealing the ways in which this female *caudillo* used her beauty, wealth, and power to corrupt men makes her an unforgettable character. More important, however, she portrays the evils besetting the Venezuelan rural population, the venality of the landholding system, and the lawlessness of the plains as a refuge for criminals, a paradise for smugglers, and a breeding ground for irresponsible "strong men" who have dominated the interior. In Gallegos, Venezuelans found that rare combination of qualities insisted upon by the Uruguayan philosopher, Carlos Vaz Ferreira, namely, a man of thought who was also a man of action. As president, Gallegos took the lead in attacking the evils he so vividly portrayed in his novels. But within a year his work was cut short and he was driven into exile by the "strong men."

Reforms: Food, Oil, and Homes. The Betancourt regime had organized the Venezuelan Development Corporation, whose work Gallegos carried on. Its basic objectives were to aid existing industries, mineral development, and agricultural enterprises, as well as to finance food production, especially rice, corn, beans, vegetable oils, beef, fish, and milk. Its efforts brought marked improvements in the production of food and the expansion of industry. The basis for the financial support of the program lay in the income derived from oil. "Plowing the Oil" became, in fact, the watchword of the Democratic Action party.

Under the Petroleum Law of 1943 the government received a sixth of the profits of the oil companies. But a new law in 1946 enlarged the share of the Venezuelan government to the equivalent of 50 per cent of the profits of the oil companies, collected in taxes and royalties. The companies, thoroughly satisfied with the new arrangement, launched an extensive expansion program among the items of which was the construction of a $45,000,000 refinery at Punta Cardón in 1947 and a 175-mile pipeline from Cabinas to Amuay Bay, where extensive improvements were already under way. Important among the latter was a refinery built by the Creole Oil Company (Standard) on Amuay Bay, one of the largest in the world.

The government supported the demands of the Oil Workers' Federation including some 40,000 workers, which, after expelling Communists from its leadership, sought and received a collective contract with the various oil companies. Under it workers received increases in salaries and wages and vacations with pay and sick benefits. The government on its part, taking its royalties in oil, sold the product to the highest bidder, receiving thereby considerably more than the equivalent in cash. Brazil, starved for oil, found the Venezuelans willing to accept food in exchange for oil. Other purchasers were Italy and Portugal.

Another major achievement was the founding in 1947 with Ecuador and Colombia of a new merchant fleet, the Gran Colombian line, to escape the high freight rates imposed by foreign shipping companies. This fleet, operating along the Caribbean and Pacific coasts, also established lines to the United States. The government, too, aided the growth of the Venezuelan Navigation Company for coastal service and began extensive harbor improvements, especially at La Guaira, Guanta, Cumaná, and Carapano. At Maracaibo the greatest effort was made with the investment of $14,000,000 in port works in 1948.

To expand agricultural resources became a major objective. The government launched a program to educate and train 225,000 rural families in agricultural production, gave technical supervision to almost 400 rural cooperatives, and made some 3,000 small loans to individual farmers. It also opened up about 740,000 acres of public lands for distribution among the landless, part of whom were European refugees who by 1952 numbered several thousand. A large area set aside for distribution was the 163,086-acre estate of former dictator Gómez, on which a thousand new owners raised coffee and cattle and provided dairy products for near-by urban areas. By 1948, too, the government had established over 200 agricultural colonies of fifty families each. Receiving government support was the imaginative undertaking of the Rockefeller brothers, who sponsored the Venezuelan Basic Economy Corporation, which devoted itself to financing modern scientific agricultural undertakings, livestock breeding, and other productive enterprises.

To expand industrial possibilities, the junta launched a comprehensive plan of establishing hydroelectric stations in various parts of the nation, modernizing its telecommunication system and railroads, and constructing highways and bridges. Important aspects of the undertaking were the rebuilding of Caracas, particularly to provide a huge low-cost housing program for workers, a great University City, construction of public schools, and a Workers' University. Throughout the country the government carried on a campaign to reduce the illiteracy among the adult population, estimated to be as high as 68 per cent. In Maracaibo, the center of oil development, the junta constructed a Polytechnical Institute to meet the growing demand for trained technical personnel.

By the end of 1948 Venezuela reflected a growing and soundly based prosperity. Oil, which had traditionally held the balance of power, was being made to contribute its share in carrying the national burdens. At the same time the Betancourt-Gallegos governments had made a significant advance in establishing democratic institutions. It came doubly as a shock to the world, therefore, to learn that the Gallegos government had suddenly been overthrown by a military uprising in November, 1948. One reason for the action was the antagonism of the army to the Betancourt government, which had abolished compulsory conscription, a policy followed by Gallegos. More important was the statement of the military junta in indicating the reason for its action, namely, that the Gallegos government was endangering the military traditions of Venezuela. The conclusion, however, seems inevitable that the army, sensing its decline as a power within a growing democratic society, struck to halt the process.

The Venezuelan Dictatorship, 1948 to the Present. Upon assuming control, the military junta, composed of Lieutenant-Colonels Marcos Pérez Jiménez, Carlos Delgado Chalbaud, and Felipe Llovera Páez, resorted to suspending civil liberties, censoring the press, arresting all political opposition leaders, outlawing the Democratic Action party, and dissolving the national congress, all state legislatures, and all elected municipal councils. Subsequently it disbanded the powerful Venezuelan Workers' Confederation and confiscated union funds and membership rolls. Inevitably, it set aside the constitution of 1947 which guaranteed universal suffrage.

Promising free elections soon, the junta appointed a board to draw up a new electoral law, presented in May, 1950. Discussions on the new law were unhappily interrupted on November 13 when a personal enemy murdered the head of the government, Lieutenant-Colonel Carlos Chalbaud. To succeed him the junta on November 24 selected a civilian, Germán Suárez Flamerich, a political and diplomatic figure. While public attention was diverted for a moment by the event, it soon turned back to the proposed elections. With most of 1952 spent in again registering the voters, the elections were finally announced for November 30, 1952, with the Democratic Action party outlawed. The junta suffered a sad surprise on election day. The Democratic Action party members voted overwhelmingly for the Democratic-Republican Union (URD), whose basic principles included universal suffrage and a larger share of oil profits for the country. When it became evident that the URD was easily winning the election, the junta stopped counting the votes and announced that its party, the Independent Electoral Front, had won a majority of the seats in the constitutional assembly.

To insure its control, the junta moved quickly. It removed its civilian head, Dr. Flamerich, and set up an all-military group on December 2, 1952, headed by the chief of national defense, Lieutenant-Colonel Marcos Pérez Jiménez. The constitutional assembly next promulgated a new constitution on April 15, 1953, and named Pérez Jiménez president on April 19 to serve a five-year term. It also appointed all officials under the new constitution: both houses of the Venezuelan congress, the five judges of the supreme court and all other courts, all state legislatures, all municipal councils, the inspector of the army, and the attorney-general. Throughout these months the junta drove the leaders of the URD into exile. All semblance of democratic government disappeared. By largesse to the armed forces and measures to meet the minimum demands of labor for better housing, higher wages, and other improvements, it has thus far maintained itself in power.

Economic Development since 1948. Economically, the dictatorship has carried on the programs initiated by the Betancourt-Gallegos government. From the start Pérez Jiménez was favored by world events. The expansion of the oil industry was given an impetus by the outbreak of the Korean War in 1950. A year later the nationalization of Iranian oil on April 30, 1951, put the great Abadan refinery out of business and increased demands upon Venezuela. Through the following years production continued to rise until by 1956 it reached over 2,000,000 barrels daily.

However, clouds have appeared on the oil horizon. Powerful groups in the United States are proposing to restrict Venezuelan oil imports which compete with the coal industry. The seriousness of the threat is apparent in that Venezuela exports 90 per cent of its oil to the United States, from which she derives 34.5 per cent of all her revenue. Moreover, the return of the Iranian fields to production have threatened Venezuela's markets in the East while Canadian oil is invading the American market.

The dictatorship, too, fell heir to the policy of the Betancourt-Gallegos governments in aiding the United States in its search for iron deposits. Bethlehem Steel was the first major company to develop deposits at Pau south of the Orinoco River and ship iron ore in March, 1951, down the Orinoco River to the United States. In 1947 a spectacular discovery made by United States Steel revealed a hill, Cerro Bolívar, containing an estimated half billion tons of high grade ore. By January, 1954, the company, having built a railroad to Puerto Ordaz, some ninety miles north at the junction of the Orinoco and Caroní rivers, and dredged the Orinoco itself, began shipping the ore to the United States on ocean-going vessels.

Venezuela, stimulated by the possibilities of the new area, began surveys for its exploitation. Besides abundant fresh-water supplies and known iron reserves, other resources appeared in bauxite beds, gold deposits, and natural gas zones suitable for industrial use. By 1953 the Venezuelan Development Corporation had selected Puerto Ordaz for the site of the country's first steel mill and a huge hydroelectric plant on the near-by Caroní. In 1951 out of the enthusiasm came a new exploration of the Orinoco River itself to discover its headwaters (which proved to be in Venezuela and not in Brazil) and assess its scientific values. In a move of far-reaching implications, the Venezuelan government recently has questioned the boundary settlement of 1899, which grew out of the boundary conflict of 1895. The new wealth and consequent importance of eastern Venezuela undoubtedly are linked to the statement of the Venezuelan foreign office during the Caracas Conference in March, 1954, that concerning the boundary line of British Guiana, Venezuela was asserting ". . . its just aspiration that the damages then suffered (1899) by the nation be redressed through an equitable rectification . . ."

Throughout the country as a whole the dictatorship carried out further works. New electric plants and water supply systems were built in various urban and rural centers. Public health was improved by new hospitals, clinics, and dispensaries in most states, to add to the several hundred sanitary centers and rural medical stations. Other projects included lush military clubs for the officers of the armed forces, port improvements, and the expansion of Venezuela's own merchant marine after she withdrew from the Gran Colombian fleet in 1953. In agriculture the advances made by the Betancourt-Gallegos government became apparent in 1955 when sugar, corn, and rice became ample.

In the 1940's Venezuela began a comprehensive highway program to link the western with the eastern oil areas, and the new mineral regions beyond the Orinoco with the capital and coastal cities. The dictatorship continued this work, completing the Inter-American Highway connecting with Colombia and pushing forward the east-west communications. Uncertain for years whether railroads were suitable for the country, the Pérez Jiménez government finally decided in 1954 to launch a huge rail network to connect the agricultural, cattle, and mining areas of the interior with the larger cities and ports.

Probably the most spectacular building achievement of the dictatorship, but one which also rested upon the work of the previous administration, was the beautification of the capital, Caracas. Now completed, its vast civic center, fed by twenty-four broad avenues, gives the city a metropolitan air. Southeast of the capital, the government also brought to conclusion the modern University City conceived in 1943. Capping its building efforts was the completion in 1953 of a superhighway between Caracas and its port, La Guaira, which virtually makes the capital a seaside metropolis.

The dictatorship's housing program for the working classes, however, except for some showpieces in Caracas, fell far short of the needs of the people, and testifies to the incapacity of the government to meet this problem. The principal cause of the failure is the vast sums spent on housing the military. The officers' club in Caracas, with the furnishings of a palace and estimated to have cost some $10,000,000, stands in strong contrast to the shanties that cluster on the neighboring hills. Account, however, must also be taken of Venezuela's phenomenal increase in population. Between 1940 and 1950 the capital's inhabitants tripled in number; by 1955 they approached 900,000. The Federal District itself, which includes the capital, held a fifth of the country's population of 5,600,000.

Venezuela saw in the nineteenth century the beginnings of an authentic liberal movement. Ideas of democracy were firmly implanted in the minds of some of its intellectuals. Some political leaders made sincere efforts to reform its feudal economy. But with the appearance of the early twentieth century dictatorships, the country fell back into the category so sharply etched by Bolívar: "Venezuela is a barracks." Between the death of Gómez and the exile of Gallegos, Venezuelan leaders gave the world a startling example of what could be done with its rich resources to raise the standard of living of the people and advance democratic practices. But the return of the dictatorship again gave truth to Bolívar's aphorism, modified in only one respect, namely, that today the barracks are gold-plated.

Chapter XXV

CUBA

Part I. THE CUBAN REVOLUTIONARY MOVEMENT, 1808–1898

The Character of Cuban History. Cuba throughout the colonial period guarded the approaches to the Spanish empire, a role which early made it the objective of pirates, and in the later centuries the prize in international wars between Spain and England. The colonial social structure of masters and slaves left Cuban Creoles with little sympathy for the independence movement on the continent. After the New World did become independent, the United States, Britain, and France each feared the designs of the others upon the island. When, however, Spain continued to hold Cuba within the framework of her mercantile system, revolutionary sentiment grew rapidly. Until the middle of the nineteenth century Cuban patriots carried out filibustering expeditions to free the island.

Spanish oppression and failure of the American markets after the Civil War to take Cuban hides and cattle brought on the violent Ten Years' War (1868–1878), the first major attempt of Cubans to win freedom. After 1880 growing American investment continued to draw the island closer to the United States. Spain, attempting to halt this economic drift, inevitably forced the Cubans into a second attempt at independence in 1895. That conflict led directly to the Spanish-American War and the freeing of Cuba. With independence, American investment in Cuban sugar and utilities increased the importance of the middle class and Cuban labor. At the same time the Platt Amendment and the Machado dictatorship blocked the normal growth of democratic institutions. In 1934 the Good Neighbor policy finally set Cuba free to become master in her own house. Since that time middle class and labor parties have launched reforms aimed at social betterment, industrialization, and laying a base for a democratic state.

Failure of the Independence Movement, 1808–1821. Cuba and

533

Puerto Rico did not join the movement for independence (1808–1821). Whereas all classes in Santo Domingo reacted strongly to the influence of the French Revolution, Cuban Creoles feared the fate that befell the Haitian planters. Moreover, many Haitian Creoles took refuge in Cuba after 1804, where they added their influence to the conservative groups. Thus in 1812 the Cuban representatives in the Spanish parliament strongly opposed any separation of the island from Spain. More positively, Cuban prosperity discouraged change. Her trade had almost doubled, from $8,000,000 in 1805 to almost $13,000,000 in 1820, including that of Puerto Rico. Equally important in blocking any revolutionary movement was the inability of Cuban patriots to secure foreign aid because of international rivalry of the United States, Britain, and France over the island. Thus when Napoleon invaded Spain in 1808, Jefferson's cabinet expressed disfavor at Cuba falling into the hands of either France or Britain. Britain on her part warned Spain that the United States hoped to secure Cuba in much the same way she had the Louisiana territory. After the annexation of West Florida, American statesmen feared that Cuba in hands other than Spanish would became a "fulcrum" against the United States. After the Wars for Independence Cuban exiles and Bolívar favored the freeing of the island at the Panama conference in 1826. United States opinion, however, held that an independent Cuba would become either a republic of free Negroes or fall to Britain.

Spanish Oppression and Cuban Revolts, 1821–1851. In Cuba, Spain showed she had learned nothing; the colonial system on the island with all its abuses remained in full force. Spaniards continued to hold all the chief offices of government. A captain-general ruled under absolute authority, limited only by the powers of other Spanish officials. In military affairs the captain-general had supreme authority, although the navy was an independent command. Finances were in the hands of a superintendent who had succeeded the colonial intendant. The chief civil authority in internal affairs was the *Junta de Fomento*, or Council of the Interior, presided over by the captain-general.

The administration of the island was divided into three districts. The west included Havana, the capital; the central district had Puerto Príncipe as its head; in the east, Santiago was the center. The colonial court system headed by an *audiencia* exercised both judicial and administrative functions, a department of government in which corruption was the greatest. Local authority, such as was exercised by the *cabildos* on the continent, was nonexistent. The offices of the town councils or *ayuntamientos* were hereditary or purchased and could be presided over at will by royal authorities.

After Spain lost her mainland colonies, her imposition of taxes upon Cuba increased. Between 1830 and 1850 she extracted from the island some $50,000,000. The expanding trade of Cuba in these years and its steady increase in population made possible the levying of huge taxes. But as her trade inclined more and more toward the United States, Spain imposed restrictions after 1826. The most serious of these were upon the import of American flour, which fell from 100,000 barrels in 1826 to less than 1,000 in 1850. These measures stimulated smuggling and led to internal discontent, which in turn brought on the suppression of newspapers and the increase of naval and military forces. The island became a garrison state. Cuban exiles in New York in the 1830's and 1840's agitated for freedom, the predecessors of the *Cuba Libre* clubs of the 1890's. Within the island, too, slave revolts were frequent, the most serious of which was in 1843. On that occasion Captain-General Leopoldo O'Donnell ordered the execution of thousands of blacks, as well as a large number of whites who were believed involved in the uprising.

Given an impetus by the American action in annexing Texas, Cuban exiles in the United States carried on a propaganda for a similar move toward Cuba. American interest, favorably disposed, found expression in official proposals to purchase and in filibustering expeditions of individuals. Thus in 1848 after the war with Mexico, President Polk offered to buy the island from Spain for $100,000,000, but the latter sharply refused the offer. The discovery of gold in California in 1849 made Cuba, athwart the sea route to Panama, even more desirable. In this framework of enthusiasm for acquisition and Cuban desire for annexation came a series of filibustering expeditions led by Narciso López from American soil in 1850–1851. His first attempt in 1849 was blocked by President Taylor, but in the next year he left New Orleans with a force of 750 men and landed on the island. Lack of support forced him to retreat. Undiscouraged, López commanded in the following year a second expedition of 400 men. Spanish forces, however, captured the bulk of the filibusters including an American officer, Colonel Crittenden, as well as López himself. All were executed. The deed stirred American public opinion to free Cuba, which reached its height in 1854 when three American ministers in Belguim issued the famous Ostend Manifesto that Spain should either sell Cuba or the United States would have "by every law, human and divine, the right to take it."

The Ten Years' War, 1868–1878. The Civil War in the United States brought on a rapid decline of American interest in Cuba for annexation, and produced an economic revolution on the island. One change was the decline of Cuban coffee production as American imports from Brazil increased. Whereas in 1833 Cuba exported over 64,000,000 pounds, by 1862 she barely produced enough to meet her own demands. Too, the cattle industry, one of the oldest on the island, suffered a collapse as American cattle supplied hides. These changes brought ruin to some of the oldest families in Cuba, turning them to revolutionary undertakings to overthrow Spanish power. The resulting Ten Years' War (1868–1878) had as additional causes the long-standing abuses of the Spanish government in excluding Cubans from office and imposing heavy taxes. The immediate cause arose from the revolt in Spain, which, exiling Queen Isabella, gave Cuban patriots an opportunity to strike when Spain appeared weak. Led by a former coffee planter, Carlos Manuel de Céspedes y Castillo, the Cubans put an army of 15,000 men in the field, promulgated a constitution in April, 1869, and set up a government. Céspedes, elected president, sought aid abroad while he conducted operations against the Spaniards. Both sides, fighting with little thought of quarter, brought widespread destruction in lives and property. In the first three years of the war, Spain, torn by internal struggle at home, had little success, but many Cuban sugar planters, afraid of a republic in which slaves would be free, kept the Spanish effort going. After 1873 the tide turned. Ships bringing supplies to the Cubans were intercepted, the most famous instance being that of the *Virginius,* of whose crew and passengers fifty-three were executed. Its fate discouraged others. In 1874 Céspedes was captured and shot, while the other great Cuban leader, Máximo Gómez, was defeated. In the end, Spain used the most shocking methods to destroy the rebellion. Her policy drew strong protest from the United States, but forced the Cuban leaders to surrender. On February 10, 1878, the Treaty of El Zanjón ended the war, with promises to the Cubans of a general amnesty, the right to send delegates to the Spanish parliament, and political reform.

The Ten Years' War brought practically complete destruction of homes and plantations in the eastern end of the island from Camagüey to Bayámo. Negroes, emancipated for fighting on one side or the other during the war, saw the abolition of slavery by 1886, an event, however, also influenced by the change in the methods of producing sugar after the conflict. The war left, too, a huge debt which became a reason for Spain's imposing new and heavier taxes upon the island. Nevertheless, she did make some political reforms, giving Cuba representation in the Spanish parliament and including Cuba within the framework of the Spanish constitution. But the most significant effect of the war was the destruction of the coffee and cattle industries. Tobacco and sugar thereafter became the two principal raw materials upon which the Cuban economy came to rest.

Rise of the Sugar Industry and the Revolt of 1895. Although sugar soon became the principal crop of Cuba after 1878, it faced competition from the Polish and Russian beet sugar industries. Even Hawaii had begun by 1876 to send sugar, duty free, into the United States, while new methods of producing American beet sugar made that native product important. This competition in turn forced a change in the methods of Cuban sugar production. The chief ones were the creation of the "central" and the *colono* systems. The first involved the construction of railroads to tap outlying sugar plantations for transportation of the crop to a large central mill. More than 1,000 small mills closed in the country and made the owners of those that remained dependent upon the more powerful companies which controlled the "centrals." Under the *colono* system, an owner contracted to plant a certain part of his land to sugar and received advances from the mill owners for this purpose. These changes enabled great savings to be made in production, while modern machinery introduced into the "centrals" improved and reduced the cost of the refining process. In this new order a few native Cuban families as well as several American companies became prominent in the refining of sugar. The most important of the latter was the American Sugar and Refining Company, which emerged in 1890 from the combination of nineteen small .refineries. Other American interests purchased mineral rights in Cuba.

Equally significant was the rapid growth of American-Cuban trade after 1880. The close economic ties were greatly strengthened after 1890 when the United States put sugar on the free list. But for a moment this trade was endangered when Spain, to benefit Spanish shippers of manufacturers, added a 25 per cent duty on foreign goods entering Cuba. The United States responded at once in the McKinley Tariff by imposing duties on Cuban sugar. When the mother country faced a serious loss of income from the export tax, she hastened to conclude the Foster-Canovas reciprocity agreement in 1891. In 1894 Cuban sugar production, with 1,050,000 tons, reached the highest level in its history. But in that same year the United States, suffering from the depression of 1893, sought new revenues and reimposed the duty on raw sugar in the Wilson tariff.

The Revolt of 1895. The effects upon Cuba were catastrophic. Spain again levied duties from 25 to 125 per cent on foreign goods, while the loss of the American sugar market bankrupted the planters. At once all the antagonisms nursed by arbitrary rule flared out in revolution in 1895. With the battlecry, *"Cuba Libre,"* José Martí, a beloved figure and gifted poet who had long agitated for Cuban independence, led the patriots. Unfortunately, he was killed early in the revolt, to be succeeded by Cisneros Betancourt. Máximo Gómez commanded in the field with Antonio Maceo, a Negro of high ability and courage, who directed the war in the eastern end of the island. Tomás Estrada Palma represented the revolutionary forces abroad. Against the Spaniards Gómez carried on guerrilla warfare, a "scorched earth" policy of destroying plantations, public buildings, and all property useful to Spain in the war against the patriots. The Spaniards retaliated under General Weyler, whose concentration centers for civilians suspected of aid to the insurgents shocked the civilized world.

The war, endangering American lives and investments, then estimated by some at $50,000,000, although the British placed it at a lower figure, became a factor leading to the Spanish-American War. Equally important were the Wilson tariff and Spain's tariff decrees which wrenched Cuba's economy away from that of the United States. Only independence, it was felt by the Cubans, could restore the balance. Significant, too, in bringing about the war was propaganda. Ever since the end of the Ten Years' War, Cuban exiles, through *Cuba Libre* clubs in New York and other cities, had emphasized the worst side of Spanish rule in the island. Contributing to this propaganda was the rivalry between Hearst's New York *Journal* and Pulitzer's *World*. Striving to increase their circulation, both papers published horror stories on Cuba and frequently fabricated incidents. Outstanding in the list of causes that brought on the war was the remarkable book, *The Influence of Sea Power Upon History,* by Admiral W. T. Mahan, a distortion of history, whose thesis was that the greatness of a nation rests upon foreign commerce which in turn necessitates sea power with accompanying naval bases on islands of strategic importance. The book gave expression to a point of view held by influential American statesmen, somewhat bluntly stated by Richard Olney in 1895 in the Venezuela boundary dispute: "Today the United States is practically sovereign on this continent and its fiat is law upon subjects to which it confines its interposition." Theodore Roosevelt was the most able exponent of the doctrine.

The Spanish-American War, 1898. In this framework of Cuban hopes for freedom, the protection of American property and lives, and ambitions for empire, the blowing up of the battleship *Maine* in the Havana harbor on February 15, 1898, led directly to the war. The conflict, in fact, was unnecessary. During the Cuban revolt after 1895, the American government had laid down a barrage of notes to Madrid demanding reforms to restore peace on the island. Among these was an insistence upon the virtual independence of Cuba. By April, 1898, Spain had conceded all the American demands. Nevertheless, President McKinley sent his war message to Congress, which declared war on April 24, 1898.

While the American army was hardly prepared for its task, the navy under Admiral Sampson was ready to blockade Havana and to dispatch Admiral Dewey from Hong Kong to take Manila. At the same time the battleship *Oregon* at the Puget Sound naval base proceeded on a 15,000-mile journey around South America to join the battle in the Caribbean Sea. Its journey, highlighting for the American people the need of a canal, also revealed that the thinking of their statesmen had leaped beyond Cuba.

After spectacular examples of inefficiency, the American army, led by General Shafter, landed on Cuba and in Puerto Rico. The Spaniards offered little resistance. Within three months the fighting was over. At sea the collapse of Spanish power was equally swift. Admiral Cervera's fleet left its safe anchorage under the guns of El Moro Castle and was sunk in a running fight with Admiral Schley and Sampson. Puerto Rico fell without a struggle. In the Philippines, Dewey, cooperating with the insurgents led by Aguinaldo, forced the surrender of Manila. Thereafter Aguinaldo was disabused of the idea of immediate independence for the islands.

The terms of the peace treaty, signed in Paris and ratified by both countries in 1899, left Cuba free of Spanish control, ceded Puerto Rico and Guam outright to the United States, and provided for the payment by the United States of $20,000,000 to Spain for the cession of the Philippine Islands. Results, other than the treaty, were far-reaching. The successful conclusion of the war opened the way for large-scale American investment in Cuban sugar lands, railroads, utilities, and mineral deposits. It launched the United States on a career of colonial ownership in the Philippines and Puerto Rico. It created a demand for a canal to connect both oceans, and it opened the way for American economic penetration into all the Caribbean region including Central America.

American Military Government, 1898–1902. Upon the close of the war American forces under a military government headed by General Leonard Wood occupied Cuba until May, 1902. During this period much was done to reconstruct the ruined economy of the island. A sanitary program stamped out centers of disease by introducing modern methods of sanitation in Cuban cities. The most spectacular achievement was the elimination of yellow fever, brought about by following the theories of a Cuban doctor, Carlos Finlay, who had established that mosquitoes were carriers of the yellow fever germ. American physicians, notably Dr. Walter Reed, finding the assumption correct, directed a mosquito elimination program which ended the scourge. The military government revived Cuban economic life by construction of roads, improvement of harbors, and the granting of extensive concessions of sugar and tobacco lands to American corporations. In education the government established public schools based upon American methods and installed a large number of American teachers to initiate the program.

Part II. ECONOMIC GROWTH AND DICTATORSHIP, 1901–1933

The Administration of Estrada Palma, 1902–1906. As the well-being of the island revived, the American military government in 1900 called for an election of delegates to draw up a constitution. The document promulgated on February 21, 1901, provided for a republic with a president and vice-president elected every four years, a two-house legislature with a senate composed of four members elected from each of the six states, and a House of Representatives chosen on the basis of the population. The franchise was given to males over twenty-one. The colonial theory of local autonomy for municipal and state assemblies was recognized, but the president had the power to intervene to protect the republic from disorder. The church and state were separated and freedom of worship allowed.

Before the United States would permit the constitution to go into effect, however, it insisted upon the inclusion of the Platt Amendment. This demand the Cubans objected to on the ground that it infringed upon their sovereignty. But when it was made clear that the army of occupation would remain until the amendment was added, the convention complied. In brief the Platt Amendment provided for the sale or lease of Cuban territory to the United States for a naval base, namely, Guantánamo Bay on the eastern end of the island. Secondly, it gave the United States virtual control over Cuban foreign policy by prohibiting the Cuban government from making treaties with foreign powers which might affect the island's independence and from assuming a debt not justified by the revenues of the nation. But the most drastic provision gave the United States the right to intervene at will to preserve order. After the constitution was adopted and the new government established, the terms of the Platt Amendment were made effective by a treaty in 1903, drawn up between the United States and Cuba.

Elections held under the constitution gave Cuba its first national government, headed by Tomás Estrada Palma, on May 20, 1902. On that date the American military forces withdrew. Protected by the Platt Amendment, American investments in Cuba rose by leaps and bounds. The bulk went into railroad building, the sugar industry, tobacco, electrical installations, cattle raising, real estate, and utilities. From a bare $50,000,000 before 1898, American investments reached $200,000,000 by 1909. European capital, likewise reassured, rushed to invest some $400,-000,000. These huge sums found reflection in the phenomenal expansion of Cuba's trade. From $76,983,418 in 1904 her exports to the United States reached $160,000,000 by 1913, while her total world trade amounted by that year to almost $340,000,000, of which over $300,000,000 was with the United States. The bulk of the latter was in sugar, the basis of which was laid by the reciprocity treaty of 1903, an agreement that gave Cuban sugar a preference in the American market, opened Cuba's markets to the import of American goods, and, as noted, included the terms of the Platt Amendment.

The income of the Cuban government from this prosperous condition of her trade and internal construction meant lucrative positions for those who could win public office in the national government—the presidency, the congress, and governorships of the states. Estrada Palma, who alone among the early presidents retired from the presidency a poor man, was unwilling to see the government pass into the hands of men who he felt were corrupt. When he was re-elected in 1906, his opponents, who had founded the National Liberal and Republican parties, which were united in 1905 to form the Liberal party, claimed fraud and revolted under the leadership of José Miguel Gómez. Unable to put down the uprising, Estrada Palma appealed to the United States government, which sent Secretary of War W. H. Taft to the island in an effort to reconcile the parties. When this move failed, Estrada Palma resigned. Taft thereupon drew up a provisional government, headed by Charles E. Magoon, in September, 1906, and the first American intervention was under way.

The Magoon Government, 1906–1909. Magoon's administration has been criticized by some Cubans as corrupt, but no proof was ever advanced that he personally was other than an honest man. He spent the surplus in the treasury of about $13,000,000 and added a $12,000,000 public debt. But much of this money went into constructing some 400 miles of roads, a large number of public buildings, a sanitary program for smaller towns, improvement of transportation, increasing wages of Cuban labor, and, when the panic of 1908 occurred, aiding Cuban banks to remain solvent. A prominent figure in his administration, Colonel Enoch Crowder, drew up a code of administrative law and electoral machinery which was designed, but which later failed, to prevent fraud in Cuban elections. Connected with the inauguration of the new electoral code was a census taken in 1907 to provide new voting lists. On the other side of the ledger, however, was a waste of public funds used to employ politicians in jobs without duties and granting contracts which were not always carried out, although the work, supposedly done, was paid for. Too, many American concerns were favored with special privileges.

The Gómez Administration, 1908–1912. Before leaving Cuba on January 28, 1909, Magoon held the presidential election in which José Miguel Gómez won the office. During his term the president amassed a huge fortune. In contrast, the unconscionable exploitation of Cuban workers by native and foreign companies led to an uprising in 1911 among the Negroes in the eastern end of the island. Gómez rushed troops and the United States landed marines to quell the uprising. More than 3,000 Negroes were killed before conditions returned to their former status. Warnings at the time to the Cuban government that the United States would not tolerate electoral disturbances in the coming election, together with Gómez' ruthless use of troops to put down criticism, produced a peaceful election in 1912. General Mario Menocal, a conservative and the managing director of the Cuban American Sugar Company, won when the Liberal party split.

Cuba and World War I, 1912–1920. Menocal, one of the wealthiest planters in Cuba, put emphasis upon expansion of the sugar industry. In 1912–1913, the island suffered from a depression, but when World War I broke out, declining European beet sugar fields brought a steady rise in the price of Cuban sugar. Immediately large-scale planting expanded in the eastern end of the island, where thousands of acres of fine timber were burned over to make room for the cane. The Menocal government also gave sugar companies the authority to import thousands of Negroes from adjoining islands and Chinese labor from the Orient. These, when set to work with no thought of housing and sanitation, created a serious health problem and later contributed to the growth of the Cuban labor movement.

The war continued to put unprecedented demands upon Cuban sugar production. Tax money pouring into the government treasury intensified the desire of politicians to get into power by any means to share in the golden stream. Thus in 1916 Alfredo Zayas, the defeated Liberal candidate in 1912, supported by Gerardo Machado, Carlos Mendieta, and Gómez, were determined to revolt if Menocal, against his promise to retire, again became a candidate. When Menocal did run and won in the face of charges of corruption, probably correct, the Liberals, rising in revolt, captured Oriente province and its capital, Santiago. To block government attack, the insurgents tore up the Cuba Railway and destroyed telephone and telegraph lines. The United States sent marines to protect American property and lives. At the same time the Wilson government threw its support to Menocal, an action explained by the imminence of the war with Germany, the imperative need for continued production of sugar, and the Wilson policy of refusing to recognize revolution as a means of political change. By March, 1917, Gómez was captured and the other Liberal leaders had surrendered. On May 20, 1917, Menocal began his second term.

World War I brought great prosperity to the island. Menocal had declared war on Germany on April 17, 1917, so that Cuba had full status as an Ally. This fact and because her sugar economy was closely associated with the needs of the American war effort brought civilian control over prices. Refined sugar, fixed at nine cents a pound, met the demands of the American beet sugar producers, while the price of Cuban raw sugar, established at five and one-half cents per pound, left a margin of profit pleasing to the Cuban producers. With the cost of production, a bare four cents, the impetus to expansion of sugar planting was great. At the same time shipping, brisk trade, and higher wages brought great wealth to the island in which the Cuban business classes and small landowners shared handsomely.

The end of the war produced a fantastic wave of speculation in Cuban sugar and the businesses allied to it, particularly banking. During the war many Cubans amassed fortunes, which, when sugar was released in 1919 from international control, they invested heavily in new sugar lands. Europe's beet fields were still in ruins and those of Java were hampered by lack of shipping, so that Cuba remained the world's sugar center. Thus during 1919 sugar made up 90 per cent of the island's export trade, while prices climbed to phenomenal heights. Raised during

1918 and 1919 at a cost of less than five cents a pound, it sold at twenty-two and one-half cents by May, 1920. The value of sugar exports at that time was estimated at over one billion dollars. Sugar plantations were bought and sold at unbelievably high prices. Banks which had invested their funds in sugar saw their own stock rise rapidly and become the object of wild speculation. The frenzy became known as the "Dance of the Millions."

But the boom was building up for a collapse. High prices made it profitable to ship small amounts, in a steadily increasing stream, from all parts of the world to the American market. Beet sugar fields revived in Europe by the middle of 1920, while the same industry in the United States poured increasing quantities into the market. After May the price of sugar declined rapidly; by November it was back to five and one-half cents a pound, and in December a vast surplus in Cuba was going begging at less than four cents. The resulting collapse had far-reaching effects upon Cuba. Bankruptcies ruined thousands of businessmen. The high wages of the war had attracted workers from other islands, Spain, and Italy, all of whom, together with the native Cuban laborers, were thrown into unemployment. In protest against their suffering, the unemployed rioted in the larger cities, and listened to fiery orators proclaiming revolutionary ideas. In this confusion the Communist party organized itself in the island in 1921. Politically, the debacle led to the next American intervention.

The Administration of Zayas, 1920–1924. To relieve conditions, President Menocal appealed to United States bankers for a loan and declared a moratorium on the payment of debts. In the crisis the presidential election of 1920 approached. Menocal and the Conservatives supported Alfredo Zayas, who had split the Liberal party and founded a new one, the Popular party. The Liberals on their part supported former president Gómez. As the election neared, the United States warned the Menocal government that order must prevail. With this support Menocal, after counting the votes, declared Zayas elected. The Gómez party at once declared that fraud and violence had defeated them and appealed to the Crowder code to prevent fraud in elections.

At this juncture the president received the news that the Harding administration was sending General Crowder to Cuba to settle the crisis. Crowder first required the Cuban courts to decide the disputed election. When Zayas was again declared elected, Crowder insisted upon a new cabinet, called the "Honest Cabinet," and secured for Cuba a loan of $50,000,000 from the banking house of J. P. Morgan and Company at 5½ per cent. Under the watchful eye of Crowder, Cuba next made economies in the administration, began paying off her public debt, and repaid the loan made to her during the war by the United States.

When Crowder in 1923 was converted from his role as financial adviser to that of ambassador, Zayas immediately laid siege to the national treasury, appointed to high government office members of his own family, and filled the lesser ones with his hungry followers. In the next two years Zayas himself became immensely wealthy and his administration became known as one of the most corrupt and graft-ridden in Cuban history. The bulk of the Cuban people, particularly labor, received no benefits.

The Machado Dictatorship, 1924–1933. With the Liberals intrenched in the provinces, they nominated Gerardo Machado, a wheelhorse of the party, who defeated with ease the Conservative candidate, former president Menocal. By this date, 1924, American interest had become predominant in the island's economy. American sugar companies and banks had absorbed the bulk of the native-owned sugar businesses which had gone into bankruptcy after the collapse in 1920. By 1927 it was estimated that United States concerns owned 22 per cent, or slightly more than one-fifth, of the land of Cuba. Electric companies controlled 90 per cent of Cuban utilities. The Bethlehem Steel Corporation had acquired over 300,000 acres of mining lands, with deposits of iron estimated at over 300,000,000 tons. Other American mining companies owned lesser reserves. The Consolidated Railroads of Cuba after 1920 passed under the control of a New York City bank, with investments in the road estimated at $100,000,000. Six foreign banks, three American and three British, controlled about 75 per cent of the banking business. Many other small businesses also passed into the hands of Americans. From an estimated $200,000,000 in 1913, the total American investment in Cuba by 1929 had reached about $1,500,000,000.

Machado recognized these realities. Confident that the Platt Amendment was a guarantee against revolution, he launched one of the most brutal dictatorships in the history of Latin America. Cuban University students were among the first to protest when Machado, to prevent educational reforms, chiefly more autonomy for the university, placed one of his henchmen as rector of the University of Havana. Indignation meetings led to expulsion and even exile of many students. Their leader, Rafael Trujo, was assassinated and the university and normal schools throughout the island were closed. Labor likewise suffered persecution. Machado directed the assassination of prominent labor leaders, broke up unions, and ended labor's efforts to increase its low wages. How low this level was is apparent in the wages of sugar, sisal, and tobacco workers, who received thirty cents a day for ten hours' work. All persons low or high who dared to criticize the government were punished. By 1932 more than 1,000 Cuban exiles were living in Miami, Florida, including a former president, Menocal, mayors of Cuban cities, university professors, newspapermen, lawyers, labor leaders, and intellectuals.

Because of the continued depression of sugar prices in the world market and resulting unemployment on Cuban plantations, Machado launched two constructive projects. One was to grant concessions to American companies to build a 740-mile highway the length of Cuba, using for the work unemployed labor. The other, more spectacular, was the construction of a $20,000,000 capital building, which included even diamonds inlaid in the lobby. To carry out these projects and meet the interest on previous loans, Machado contracted huge loans in the New York market, so that by 1932 Cuba's foreign and floating debts reached almost $300,000,000.

On the other hand, to reduce the amount of sugar on the market, the Machado government cooperated in the enforcement of the Chadbourne Sugar Plan. This agreement among international sugar interests, drawn up in Brussels, Belgium, in 1929, had as its principal objective the limiting of production to maintain high prices, not for producers but for refiners. In detail it provided for the withdrawing from the world market of surplus sugar stocks, which in turn were to be disposed of over a span of five years, and secondly, to reduce immediate exports from the various sugar areas. For Cuba a special provision required her to assume a $42,000,000 burden to be paid for eventually by Cuban taxpayers. As the world's greatest producer of sugar, Cuba was forced by Machado to reduce output over 36 per cent, while the highest for any other country was but 15 per cent.

Fortified by loans, imported armored cars, and a ruthless secret police, Machado not only broke his promise not to run for re-election, but had the constitution altered to extend his term and those of his congressional supporters to six years. Hardly had he entered upon his second term when the world depression of 1929 struck Cuba, as it did all the Latin-American countries, with disaster. A cycle of bankruptcies occurred again, unemployment reached a new high, and revolts inevitably followed against the dictatorship. The rebellion broke out in August, 1931, led by former president Menocal. Its crushing was succeeded by the organization of an underground secret society called the ABC, made up of students and other patriotic Cubans. To hunt them down, Machado dispatched his secret police, called the *Porra*, which carried out a reign of terror that shocked the civilized world. When Franklin D. Roosevelt became president of the United States in 1933, Cuban patriots had good reason to believe that the new president would not long tolerate the Machado regime. They were not disappointed, for he immediately sent Sumner Welles to offer the good offices of the American government to the Cuban parties to end the violence. Welles urged Machado to re-sign, but the decisive event was a general strike called on August 4, 1933, followed almost immediately by a revolt. Machado, no longer able to depend upon American intervention to keep him in office, asked for a leave of absence from his congress, but, not waiting for an answer, fled.

Part III.   THE DEVELOPMENT OF DEMOCRATIC INSTITUTIONS SINCE 1933

The Beginnings of Reform, 1933–1939. The overthrow of the Machado regime brought to the surface in Cuba powerful revolutionary and nationalistic forces which aimed at economic and political reforms. At the same time the traditional conservative groups girded for battle to defend their sources of power. The revolutionary groups centered around the figure of Dr. Ramón Grau San Martín, a distinguished professor in the National University. Grau later founded the *Auténtico* political party, which claimed to represent the authentic revolutionary demands of the Cuban people. Opposed were the Conservatives, led by Menocal; the Nationalists, headed by Colonel Carlos Mendieta; and the Liberals, in disrepute since Machado had ruined the reputation of the party. However, the Liberals did retain the support of some native business interests, Spanish and Cuban, as well as commercial groups allied with American investments. Emerging as an influence in labor and a competitor of the *Auténticos* was the Communist party, led by Dr. Juan Marinello Vidaurreta.

The successor to Machado was the government of Dr. Carlos Manuel de Céspedes y de Quesada, an honorable and upright patriot, who had taken a leading part in the Revolution of 1895. However, his close association with Sumner Welles led his enemies to claim that his government was created by the United States. This feeling spread rapidly among the revolutionary groups who had sacked the residences of Machado and his followers and tracked down his henchmen for execution or exile. But when the ABC and other parties called for revolutionary measures by the government, Céspedes restored instead the constitution of 1901 and declared his government would meet its international obligations. Since the government, in fact, did little to relieve conditions of unemployment and hence suffering among the working classes, strikes and riots swept the country. In this situation a group of army sergeants, headed by Fulgencio Batista, rose in revolt, removed the officers from command of the army, and set up a new government under a five-man military junta on September 4, 1933. The army officers, resisting, barricaded themselves in the National Hotel in Havana.

While the new government could not secure the support of the conservative groups, it did have the allegiance of university students, whose organization, the Student Directory, had within it some of the later leading political figures of Cuba and outstanding intellectuals. The United States, fearing revolutionary action by the military junta, sent a fleet of battleships to the island, an action which gave clear indication that the sergeants' government would not get United States recognition. On September 10 the junta made Grau San Martín provisional president, an office he held until January 18, 1934.

The Government of Grau. Grau made every effort to secure American recognition and to maintain law and order. In October he ousted the army officers from the National Hotel and in the next month put down an attempt at revolt in the capital. He made significant and in part successful efforts to improve conditions among the unemployed, meet labor's demands, and carry out liberal reforms. Under his short administration the National University received complete autonomy; an eight-hour working day was decreed; minimum wages for sugar workers were set at seventy-five cents a day over the twenty to thirty paid under Machado; arbitration boards were set up to settle strikes; and legislation was enacted which required that 50 per cent of all employees of commercial, industrial, and agricultural companies, mostly foreign, must be native Cubans, except those engaged in technical capacities. The Grau government suspended all payments on the Chase National Bank loan pending investigation of expenditures made by Machado for highway construction and the building of the national capitol. It seized the properties of the Cuban American Sugar Company in the Oriente province because of labor trouble, but these lands were returned under a later administration. Finally, throughout his administration, Grau maintained service on all international obligations except the Chase loan.

The Grau government, in spite of these achievements, fell in January, 1934. The United States played a part in this change when on September

6 it assured the representatives of Chile, Brazil, and Mexico that it was looking for an alternative to intervention. Other factors within Cuba, however, were more significant. The Grau government from the beginning was a coalition; conflicts within its ranks led one group after another to withdraw its support. The Communists, strong in certain unions, criticized the government for being too conservative; the Spanish merchants, foreign interests, and Cuban conservatives felt it was too radical. Many university students were disturbed by Batista's influence in the government, fearing military domination of the country. When Grau resigned in January, Carlos Hevia served for three days before he, too, gave up the office to be followed by Carlos Mendieta as provisional president, January 18, 1934. In spite of its inability to maintain itself, the Grau government was significant in that it began both political and economic reforms, democratic in nature, upon which later administrations could build.

Conservative Government under Mendieta. Mendieta's election marked the return to conservative government, quickly recognized by the United States. Internally Mendieta undertook to block the growth of the political power of the National Confederation of Labor and took repressive measures against Grau and his followers, who had organized a new political group, the Cuban Revolutionary party *(Auténtico).* To meet the continued depression, he declared a moratorium on debts pending the accumulation of national revenues. However, the improvement in Cuba's economy came more from the effects of measures taken by the Grau government and from favorable actions toward Cuba by the United States. Prominent among the latter was the enactment of the Jones-Costigan Act of 1934, which assigned a quota of 1,902,000 short tons of Cuban sugar to the American market and the lowering of duties on sugar from two to one and one-half cents a pound. Finally, the two countries negotiated a Reciprocal Trade Agreement in 1934, under which the duty on sugar was again lowered to nine-tenths of a cent, while other Cuban products, rum, fresh fruits, vegetables, and tobacco, also enjoyed tariff reductions. Cuba on her part opened her markets wide to almost 500 items of American manufacture.

The Mendieta government, too, was the beneficiary of the new Good Neighbor policy of the Roosevelt administration, which invited Cuba to repeal the Platt Amendment, a decision strongly influenced by the long agitation of Cuban liberals. Under the new treaty of May 29, 1934, the "permanent treaty" of 1903 was ended, as was the right of the United States to intervene in Cuban affairs.

By 1935 the Mendieta government had revealed its antagonism to continued reform to improve the condition of Cuban workers and had resisted effort by Cubans to bring about the restoration of constitutional government. Batista, who had remained in control of the military forces, had greatly strengthened the army, but, as part of the government, remained adamant against agrarian and educational reforms advocated by many Cuban political leaders. In desperation in March, 1935, school-teachers, government employees, and organized labor joined in a general strike which promptly won the support of the ABC and Grau's new Cuban Revolutionary party. Batista attacked the strikers, destroyed the union's headquarters, jailed the leaders, and made free use of the "law of flight."

The strike being crushed, Batista installed virtual dictatorships in the provinces. With reform parties outlawed, Mendieta decreed an election for June, 1935. General Mario Menocal became the candidate of the National Democratic party, an offshoot of the Conservative, while Miguel Mariano Gómez, mayor of Havana, was nominated by a coalition of Nationalist and Republican liberal parties, likewise conservative in outlook. Mendieta, supporting Menocal, was forced to resign, so that the way was cleared for the election of Gómez on January 10, 1936. However, continued opposition filled the year of 1936 with continued crises. In despair, Gómez resigned on December 24, 1936.

Growth of Cuban Labor. By the date 1936 this new force in Cuban politics, organized labor, was making itself a power in the economic, political, and social life of the island. The beginnings of this movement go back to 1889–1890 when the tobacco and port workers set up the first labor organizations. The phenomenal expansion of sugar production after independence and the importation of workers, particularly during World War I, led to the growth of unionization and the emergence of the Socialist party under Diego Vicente Tejera, a poet and writer whose teachings injected a socialist influence into labor thinking which previously had been predominantly anarcho-syndicalist. After the war, the Communist party gave a further Marxist orientation of some parts of the Cuban labor movement. When Machado began his government in 1925, the Cuban Federation of Labor was organized, which by 1928 had over 70,000 members. In January, 1930, a general Congress of Workers met in Havana to demand immediate social legislation, universal education, social security for intellectuals, domestics, and labor in general, unemployment and accident insurance, arbitration of disputes, an eight-hour day, equal pay for equal work, better housing, annual paid vacations, and other similar benefits. The Machado government, of course, did not grant these, but their expression marked a step toward their later enactment and toward the growth of Cuban economic democracy.

In 1933 labor, which played a major role in the overthrow of Machado, secured from the succeeding Grau government many of their demands. When the Mendieta government attacked their powerful organizations, their resistance led Batista to make a military effort to destroy them. However, while military control was established throughout the provinces, the Cuban Federation of Labor rebuilt its strength and continued the struggle against the Gómez government which succeeded that of Mendieta. Batista, who had some of the insight of Vargas of Brazil, recognized the power of labor after his brush with them and began immediately to change his tactics. After the election he accepted one of labor's most insistent demands, the abolition of illiteracy. To this end he began a program of using the army to teach in the schools founded by the army itself. Gómez, opposed to this policy, resigned, to be succeeded by Federico Laredo Bru.

The Administration of Laredo Bru, 1936–1940. The Laredo Bru government enacted the necessary legislation to support the school program launched by Batista. Batista also sponsored a Three Year Plan for the development of Cuban agriculture, industry, and finance by limiting the profits of sugar and other industries and raising the wage scale of rural workers. To improve the standard of living in rural areas, he secured laws to distribute the land, not exceeding thirty-five acres to each tenant farmer. Other laws met the demands of the Workers' Congress of 1930 for safety appliances in industry, prison reform, and improvement of conditions of work in factories and on plantations. In foreign affairs the Laredo Bru government negotiated commercial treaties with Britain and Italy and showed marked cordiality toward the Mexican government of Lázaro Cárdenas and the Spanish Republic. Upon the outbreak of World War II in 1939 the Cuban Confederation of Labor declared for neutrality, a policy supported by Batista.

With the ground laid for labor's support, Batista resigned from the army, headed the Democratic party, and became a candidate for president on the basis of the Three Year Plan and promises of economic reforms including the regulation of foreign and Cuban banks, insurance companies, and other corporations, further extension of his agricultural program to include cooperatives, and a public works undertaking. He also promised neutrality in World War II. Capping his program was his pledge to draw up another constitution to include the advances made since Grau's government. Because he gave promise of being able to maintain law and order, seven parties besides his own nominated him including conservative ones, such as the Liberal, Nationalist, and National Democratic. Largely because of his stand on neutrality the Cuban Revolutionary Union (Communist) party also made him their nominee. These were sufficient to outweigh the Cuban Revolutionary party (*Auténtico*) led by Grau.

The Administration of Batista, 1940–1944. Although Batista won the presidency, Grau's party elected a majority of the members of the convention which was to draw up the new constitution. This document was promulgated in March, 1939, but bitter disputes between the parties delayed the presidential elections until July, 1940. Batista took over his duties on October 10, 1940.

The new constitution marked a definite step in the development of Cuban democratic institutions. It provided for a president and vice-president elected every four years by direct vote and a prime minister appointed by the president, with a cabinet responsible to congress. The congress is bicameral, with a senate of fifty-four members—nine from each of the six provinces—elected to serve six years and a House of Representatives elected for four years by direct popular vote on the basis of proportional representation. The judiciary consists of a supreme court and inferior courts with qualifications and membership fixed by law. The framers, influenced by the Argentine Sáenz Peña law, made voting compulsory for all citizens, men and women, of twenty years of age or over.

Striking evidence of the progress of Cuba toward economic democracy was the incorporation of the bulk of the recommendations of the Cuban Confederation of Labor, which by 1940 had a membership of 492,445. These measures included a forty-four-hour week, an eight-hour day, accident, old age and unemployment insurance, equal pay for equal work, annual paid vacations of four weeks, the right to organize and strike, collective bargaining, state encouragement of cooperatives, low cost housing, abolition of the land monopoly, aid to small landowners, and a merchant marine. The last item naturally had the support of Cuba's commercial classes.

Cuba and World War II. The outbreak of World War II had the same effects upon Cuba as elsewhere in Latin America—loss of markets, unemployment, government deficits, and distress among the general population. Axis influence attempted to stir up the latent antagonism to the United States, since Roosevelt's administration represented a danger to the Nazis in Latin America. Their major attempt at sabotage, the wrecking of the Havana Conference of 1940, failed. Conversely, the strong liberal and labor support in Cuba for Roosevelt's Good Neighbor policy and hemisphere defense provided a basis for Batista's close cooperation with American policy.

This teamwork was manifest on December 9, 1941, two days after Pearl Harbor, when Cuba declared war on Japan, and two days later when she followed with a declaration of war on Germany and Italy. She also granted air, naval, and army bases, and on her part received in 1941 a loan of $25,000,000 from the United States to meet the immediate needs of the government and for the construction of public works to relieve unemployment. Later the United States provided $11,000,000 to aid in grinding sugar while other large sums were granted to Cuba for defense purposes under Lend-Lease. In 1942 and 1943 the United States agreed to take the entire crop of Cuba's sugar, while in 1944 it contracted for 4,000,000 tons. For strategic minerals, important to the United States, Cuba received $20,000,000 as a loan to aid the production of nickel, manganese, and copper. Others mined were antimony, tungsten, and chromium. Facilitating the trade between the two countries was a new reciprocal agreement in 1942 which provided for the lowering of the tariffs of both countries to admit the goods exchanged.

As Batista's term neared its end, political maneuvering began. Batista and his Democratic party made alliances with the Menocal Republicans in the hope of heading off the election of Grau San Martín and electing Batista's choice, Dr. Carlos Saldrigas. Batista made no effort to control the election which, conducted peacefully, saw Grau win the coveted office.

The Administration of Grau San Martín, 1944–1948. The second administration of Grau had well-defined objectives. It encouraged industrialization linked to a diversified agricultural program. Leading features were tax reductions for industries which used Cuban raw materials, assistance to agriculture for the cultivation of corn, yams, sweet potatoes, rice, and peanuts, and aid to small farmers for the purchase of farm machinery. Stockbreeding, reforestation, and mineral production likewise were to receive special attention.

A significant beginning was made toward combating illiteracy and improving public health. A government survey in 1945 revealed that cities had a 10 per cent illiteracy rate, while rural areas showed over 35, and that, of the approximately 1,000,000 children of school age, 481,000 were not in school. These facts became the basis for plans for 3,000 rural schools and a nation-wide nutrition and health service for the schools.

In the field of public health, Dr. Grau, a physician, reorganized the general health office and combated malaria, typhoid, and other parasitic diseases by improving the water supply for cities and rural areas. The government also brought pressure to bear upon landowners and sugar companies to provide sanitary facilities for workers.

While the Grau government moved toward social improvement, the political life of most of its leaders left much to be desired. Graft, rampant in many departments, led to a hotly contested presidential election in 1948. Grau, head of the *Auténtico* party allied with the Republican, threw his support behind one of the founders of his own party, Carlos Prío Socarrás. However, the prevailing corruption in some quarters alienated sincere supporters, who, under the leadership of Eduardo Chibás, founded the party of the Cuban People (Orthodox) on July 14, 1946. The Liberal and Democratic parties formed a coalition which nominated Dr. Ricardo Núñez Portuondo, a man of rectitude. The Communist party, with strong labor support, put forward Juan Marinello. The campaign was bitter, but resulted in the election of Prío Socarrás. The election itself was peacefully conducted. Particularly heartening to Cuba's well-wishers was the large number of votes, almost 321,000, cast for Chibás out of a total of 1,954,972, attracted by his honesty.

The Administration of Prío Socarrás, 1948–1952. Prío Socarrás took office on October 10, 1948. At the outset of his administration he sought a $200,000,000 loan to build a "luxurious tourist city" to attract Americans, to make internal improvements, such as better port facilities, highways, irrigation canals, and aqueducts, and to give aid to agriculture and the growing fishing industry. However, the Machado regime had left a bad taste in the mouths of Cubans respecting foreign loans, so that strong opposition developed against the proposal. Grau himself, Batista, and other political groups took the position that Cuba's economy could not stand the burden of such a loan and that a tourist city was unnecessary. When finally the loan was secured from the Boston International Corporation it was for but $100,000,000, to be used primarily for highways and other improvements. The incident added to the split within the *Auténtico* party.

The most important problem of Cuba, sugar, got the bulk of the administration's attention. Cuba protested strongly that the United States sugar law of 1948, which gave the American Department of Agriculture the power to suspend trade with any country, was aimed at her specifically for the purpose of blocking Cuba's industrial textile growth. While the two countries entered into long negotiations over this question, they set the quota of Cuban sugar for the American market for 1949 at 3,092,000 tons. In the next year a serious sugar surplus developed which at once affected the Cuban industry with its 500,000 workers. The government took immediate action to prevent deflation and reduce prices. The most important measure was to support the demand of the sugar workers to maintain wages in the face of a falling world price. By 1950, however, the Korean War came to the rescue. The heavy buying of the United States converted Cuba's surplus into a shortage to such an extent that Cuba herself had to buy sugar back to meet her own needs! This sudden rise in the price of sugar gave a phenomenal boost to construction of new hotels, homes, and theatres and the purchase of American consumer goods, especially automobiles, while simultaneously sending the cost of living skyrocketing.

In the face of rising costs, labor in 1951, represented by the powerful Cuban Federation of Labor and supported by the government, negotiated agreements with the sugar companies which provided that wages were to be increased as the price of sugar rose, that the same number of workers should be employed despite mechanization of the industry, and that 1 per cent of the workers' wages be paid into the union fund. This latter provision greatly strengthened the Cuban Federation of Labor, whose chief concern became the elimination of Communist control from some unions.

The dependence of Cuba on sugar, ever since the overthrow of Machado, had turned the country's attention to alternatives. The chief proposals were to diversify agriculture and to stimulate manufacturing industries. The textile industry in particular had expanded rapidly, receiving tariff protection in 1949 along with industries producing nylon hose, braid, ribbons, and tires. In 1950 a national bank with government capital extended aid to native industry, commercial undertakings, and agriculture. In 1951 an agricultural and industrial government bank was established, primarily to foster agriculture and the industries. An index to the growing mechanization under the impetus of government encouragement was evident in the imports of agricultural machinery and implements. These had a value in 1939 of about $380,000; by 1947 they had risen to over $5,000,000. Programs, too, were developed to expand the production of kenaf, educate workers in the use of mechanical agricultural methods, and develop crops which had a ready sale in the United States, such as rice, peanuts, coffee, cocoa, and cocoanuts.

Paralleling these advances was progress toward native Cuban ownership of transportation lines. In 1951 a National Development Commission, backed by $200,000,000 in bonds sold to Cuban citizens, launched a program to dredge harbors, build roads, establish refrigeration plants for meats, vegetables, and fish, and provide waterworks for a considerable number of small towns. Industrialization was given added impetus by American purchase of nickel, copper, and manganese needed for the Korean war effort. This expansion of Cuba's economy was reflected in her growth of foreign trade, which had a favorable balance in 1937 of about $56,000,000 and by 1948 reached more than $182,000,000. The United States, Cuba's best customer, took over 75 per cent of all exports, although Britain, as a purchaser of sugar, was becoming significant in Cuban exports.

As the world crisis or "cold war" developed, the close cooperation between Cuba and the United States found expression in 1951, with the former granting two air bases for American jet planes and accepting an air mission to train Cuban pilots. The crisis also saw Cuban action against the Communist party. In 1949 Eusebio Muja, secretary-general of the powerful Cuban Confederation of Labor, launched a drive to combat Communism in labor's ranks. As the Korean War intensified feelings, the Cuban government in 1950 seized the Communist newspaper *Hoy,* closed the party's radio stations, and conducted raids upon its headquarters.

By the middle of June, 1949, the leading parties began maneuvering for positions to win the presidency in 1952. Outstanding was the split between Grau and Prío, although the *Auténticos* won control of congress and over 100 of the mayoralty contests in June of 1949. The following December, Batista announced his candidacy for the presidency on the platform of the Unitary Action party.

The Return of Batista, 1952 to the Present. Until the spring of 1952 the various parties continued making and unmaking coalitions. Their activities came to a sudden halt on March 10, when Batista, in a practically bloodless revolt, seized control of the country. He justified himself on the ground that Cuba was descending into a gangster state and that the Prío government was planning to continue itself in power. With the title of Chief of State, he permitted the opposition to go into exile but established firm control over the police, army, his own political party, and the powerful Confederations of Cuban Labor and the Sugar Workers. Cementing his position was the support of the United States by prompt recognition and the implementing of the Cuban-United States military aid pact concluded in the last days of the Prío regime. To govern until presidential elections could be held, Batista promulgated the Statutes of Government. These replaced the 1940 constitution and dissolved all political parties.

The most serious problem facing the new government was the sugar surplus accumulated after the end of the Korean War. To keep up prices for producers enabling them to pay the wages of sugar workers, Batista created the Sugar Stabilization Fund to withhold 1,750,000 tons from the market. Further, to prevent the reappearance of a surplus he restricted the 1953 crop to 5,000,000 tons, which actually fell somewhat under that figure. Additional strength was given Cuban sugar by the success of Batista's representative at the International Sugar Conference in London, July–August, 1953. There forty-four nations, reaching agreements, allotted to Cuba an export quota of 2,250,000 tons, with prices fixed to guarantee a substantial profit to producers. These measures, together with the 2,700,000 tons Cuba shipped to the United States, put a floor under Cuban sugar and solved for the time being her most pressing problem. The achievement naturally redounded to Batista's credit.

Building activities continued apace under Batista. Secondary road construction tied the interior of the island into the Central Highway. Adding to the nationally owned railroads was the purchase in 1953 of those belonging to the British. In Havana the government launched a $14,000,000 water system for the city. In 1954 Batista encouraged plans for a cross-Cuba canal between the city of Cárdenas on the northern shore and Cochinos Bay on the southern coast. Not only does the plan envisage opening new ports and providing extensive employment, but it will reduce the voyage from United States Atlantic ports to Panama by some 400 miles.

In other aspects of economic development Batista was at pains to support labor's efforts to raise the standard of living. To prevent employers from reducing wages, he froze those of the sugar workers, whose labor union is the most powerful one on the island. In 1953 he decreed that all employees in Cuba were to receive one month's annual vacation with pay. These and other prolabor measures, together with the favors shown the Cuban army, became the basis of his political control of the island. Both gave him overwhelming support against efforts to dislodge him between 1952 and 1954, and for his plans for re-election later in the year.

The first two years of his dictatorship were characterized by several small uprisings. A major one in July, 1953, resulted in the death of about 100 persons. After this revolt Batista censored the press and radio and set aside all freedoms for a period of ninety days. Contributing to the acceptance of these measures was his brilliant success at the International Sugar Conference, which won him the support of the conservative business groups. In October he restored the liberties under the Statutes but postponed elections until November 1, 1954.

Early in 1954 to facilitate campaigning, Batista set aside the Statutes of Government. In the following July he announced his candidacy for the presidency and resigned, putting into the office of president, his secretary, Andrés Domingo Morales y Castillo, long prominent in Cuban politics. While no one doubted that Batista would win, his way was smoothed by the opposition, which fell into warring camps. In September Grau y San Martín, the candidate of the *Auténtico* party, withdrew on the ground that his party had no representation on precinct electoral boards. Since he was the strongest opposing figure, the election, peacefully held on November 1, resulted in an overwhelming victory for Batista.

The election was construed as returning Cuba to constitutional government. Besides the office of president, more than 2,500 offices were filled from a list of more than 11,000 candidates who presented themselves from various parties. Early in January, 1955, mayors and councilmen were sworn into local government offices, and the congress met at the end of the month. In the latter the *Auténticos* were guaranteed eighteen of the fifty-four seats; in the House, the opposition captured sixteen of the one hundred and fourteen seats. Completing the restoration of the 1940 constitution, Batista was sworn in as president on February 24, 1955. Late in 1955 Batista extended amnesty to his political opponents, who had gone into exile. Chief among those returning to the island was former president Prío Socarrás.

Cuba, after almost 400 years of colonial subjection, found herself tied to the United States economically and politically at the time of winning her independence. She achieved her political freedom after 1933 with the advent of the Good Neighbor policy. Her economy, however, based on sugar principally consumed in the United States, has remained dependent upon her great neighbor to the north.

Within this framework and burdened by the colonial heritage of mass illiteracy, Cuban leaders since 1933 have sought to introduce modern economic and political reforms aimed at diversifying the nation's resources and training her citizens in the hard school of democracy. In both fields she has made notable advances, so that today defiance of democratic practices, such as that represented by Machado, is no longer possible. Powerful labor unions have won advances in material well-being for their members, education is universal, the freedom of the press is rarely infringed upon, and the right of suffrage, male and female, is guaranteed. Recalling that Cuba, unlike the rest of the New World nations, has had barely a half-century of independence and less than twenty-five years of undisputed political freedom, her progress toward establishing democratic institutions has been remarkable.

Cuban Culture. Although Cuba remained bound to Spain until the end of the nineteenth century, her writers and poets were all in the Latin-American tradition. In fact Cuba has the honor of claiming in José María Heredia (1803–1834) the first of the American romantic poets. Driven into exile by the Spanish government, as were so many of Cuba's intellectuals, Heredia wrote his *Niagara* in the United States, one of his most impassioned poems of nature. His famous contemporary was Cuba's first and highly respected philosopher, Father Félix Varela y Morales (1787–1853). Varela inspired a whole generation of Cubans with an awareness of their ignoble subjection to Spain. For his liberal thought and revolutionary influence he, too, was exiled, finding haven in the United States.

Exercising possibly an even greater influence on Cuban liberal development was Enrique Varona y Pera (1848–1933). His range of interests included every field of human endeavor. He was one of the first to urge Cubans to industrialize their country and thus make use of their natural riches. While he introduced Comte to Cubans, he escaped from Positivism to become a Spencerian evolutionist. In politics he rose to the office of vice-president. Public office for him, however, was but a platform from which to urge civic virtue upon his countrymen. A leading literary critic, his history of the literature of the United States still ranks as the best thus far written in the Spanish language.

The greatest Cuban of them all, poet, journalist, patriot, and statesman, was José María Martí (1853–1895). In his early youth a cruel experience at the hands of the colonial government drove him to seek freedom. He became thus in literature as in action a precursor of the modernist movement in Latin countries. Through his constant writing, in which the keynote was love of man for man, he sought not only to educate Cubans but the whole New World. He urged Mexican writers and artists to see in their own country a source of inspiration. Rubén Darío looked upon him as a teacher. Sarmiento sensed his greatness. In Spain his revolutionary poetry gave new meaning to the Spaniards themselves during their short-lived republic in 1873–1874. As the world spokesman for Cuba's efforts to win independence, Martí stirred his countrymen out of their apathy into an active devotion to the cause of freedom. During his residence in the United States, where he threw his immense energy into organizing support for the Cuban revolt of 1895, he interpreted in numerous writings the spirit of the great republic in the north to Latin Americans. It was Lincoln's America especially that inspired his admiration. From his writings, which fill some seventy volumes, Martí has emerged as a man who was selfless in his devotion to the ideal of human betterment. His death in battle in the Cuban revolt added a halo of martyrdom to a life of self-sacrifice.

In recent times Cuba, with Brazil, has given literary expression to the culture of the Negro. Nicolás Guillén (1904–   ), a mulatto, has given dignity to Negro street songs and dances. At the same time his poetry expresses a deep yearning for a humanity that knows no racial boundaries.

A profound student of Negro life in all its aspects is Fernando Ortiz (1882–   ). His investigations of the Negro in Cuba have taken him into African backgrounds and into the long history of the Negro in slavery, as well as his recent role as a free citizen. Ortiz has sought the Negro's expression of his African culture in religious survivals, in his social behavior, in his music, songs, dances, languages, traditions, legends, arts, games, and folklore. Probably no figure in either Anglo- or Latin America has made greater contributions to the understanding of the role of the Negro in American history than Ortiz.

Chapter XXVI

HAITI AND THE
DOMINICAN REPUBLIC

HAITI

Part I. CIVIL WARS AND FEARS OF CONQUEST, 1804–1915

The Character of Haitian History. The outstanding difference between the colonial background of the other Latin-American nations and Haiti is that practically all the people of this land emerged into independence from slavery. Haiti as a French colony had produced great wealth from its sugar plantations, especially valuable in the northern and central parts of the island. On them the bulk of the Negro population, estimated at over 500,000, lived as slaves. Important commercial cities and towns had grown up along the northern, western, and southern coasts, inhabited by an estimated 30,000 to 46,000 whites and 35,000 to 56,000 mulattoes. The white population after independence steadily declined from massacre and emigration.

Most of the mulattoes and freed Negroes engaged in trade or became small landowners in the coastal areas. Thus in the north and central interior the Negro predominated; along the coast, the mulatto. This rough distribution of the population became the basis for the nineteenth century conflicts between the north and the south, between urban and rural populations. These internecine wars added their destructive toll to the heritage of slavery, illiteracy, deep-seated superstitions, and uncontrolled tropical diseases. Moreover, civil conflict was constantly made worse by Negro fears of foreign conquest and return to slavery.

With practically no training in self-government, conscientious leaders of these people fought to overcome formidable obstacles. Understandably in the face of civil war and foreign meddling, little was done to advance the institution of democracy until well into the twentieth century. A period of United States control (1915–1935), while devoted primarily to nourishing American interests in the island, did leave behind democratic forms. Since 1935 Haiti has made significant efforts to create institutions foreshadowing representative government.

Dessalines, Christophe, and Petión, 1804–1818. Jean Jacques Dessalines, the leader of the successful revolt against France in 1804, made himself emperor in September of that year, and drew up a highly centralized constitution for the new state. The most important work of Dessalines was in the north, where he began to establish land titles and distribute the holdings of the expelled French to the mulattoes and Negroes. To revive agriculture successfully and to distribute its crops fairly to workers, landowners, and the state, he resorted to military rule. When the north was functioning, he launched a similar program for the south. But here opposition and widespread corruption in public office forced him to drastic measures which in turn produced revolt and his assassination in 1806.

In that year deputies drew up a constitution in Port-au-Prince which made Haiti a republic, limited the power of the president, and made the senate supreme. Henri Christophe, who became president, resented from the beginning the reduction of the power of his office. He attempted military conquest of Port-au-Prince, but met defeat at the hands of Alexander Sabes Petión. When he retreated north beyond the Artigonite River, where he set up his government (1807–1818), Haiti split into two separate states. In the north Christophe in 1811 proclaimed himself King Henri I and issued a new constitution which provided for a monarchical form of government and an aristocracy. He established law and order under a strong military government, revived agriculture, and began a program of building castles and palaces. Extraordinary was his castle atop the mountain, Laferriere, whose solid construction and vast proportions make it one of the wonders of the New World.

Petión, the mulatto, who had become president of Haiti in 1807, was a man of entirely different character. His policy was one of compromise rather than war. He sought and obtained honest men as his advisers, gave land taken from former French owners to veterans of Toussaint's army, encouraged the founding of schools, and established the National Lycée in Port-au-Prince. Re-elected in 1811 after an attempt at revolt by General Regaud, who had returned from France, Petión continued land distribution.

His land policy is considered a decisive factor in Haiti's later history. To his friends, mulatto aristocrats, he restored lands seized by Dessalines, and made titles secure by requiring registration under a government deed. He abolished the tax under which the government had received one-quarter of the crop, a measure to encourage sugar production on the large plantations. But Petión did not forget the little people. He placed lands in small acreages in the hands of virtually every citizen of the republic. To people too poor to buy them, legislation made a gift of state lands in small parcels. By the end of his rule he had converted the population of Haiti from serfdom to peasantry.

The effects of his reform were far-reaching. The great landowners found difficulty in securing labor to cultivate the sugar crop. The bulk of the population naturally desired to till their own plots for food. To meet this problem, the owners of sugar lands turned to share-cropping, similar to that later developed in the southern part of the United States. The system, however, did not produce the expected results, largely because the peasants were more satisfied to work for themselves. The effect was to bring about a startling decline in sugar production and eventually the break-up of the larger estates. Coffee, the second major crop, was also adversely affected. The tenants did not give the coffee trees the required attention but simply let them produce as nature dictated. The total result was to bring about a drastic decline of the government's income, largely dependent upon coffee and sugar, and the issuance of large amounts of paper money to meet mounting deficits.

Socially, the mulatto aristocracy experienced a disappointment in that their prestige, based upon ownership of land, became a hollow thing when everybody owned property. Petión, a highly cultured and sophisticated man, probably derived secret enjoyment from the discomfiture of his fellow mulattoes. For the people as a whole, the policy gave them a taste of freedom; they had food and they had happiness. Later writers, appalled by the condition of Haitian finances under Petión, condemned him for his uneconomic policies and his "false egalitarian and democratic ideas." But the people loved him.

In his second administration, beginning in 1816, he drew up a new constitution which lasted the country until 1867. Under it the president was elected for life, with a senate and house of deputies as advisory bodies. Its most important provision, however, was Article Seven which forbade foreign ownership of property in Haiti. In that same year, 1816, Petión, welcoming Bolívar in exile at Cayes, provided the Liberator with arms and ammunition in return for a promise for freedom for the slaves of Venezuela. Since his death in 1818 Petión has been regarded as one of Haiti's best presidents.

Civil Wars and Foreign Intervention, 1818–1867. Jean Pierre Boyer succeeded Petión, to rule until 1843. His first action was to unite northern and southern Haiti after the death of Christophe. In 1822, at the request of the Dominicans, now independent of Spain, Boyer extended Haitian control over them until 1843. In foreign affairs Boyer secured British recognition for his regime in 1825. With France he had difficulties. Governed by the restored Bourbons, France was determined to exact indemnities from Haiti for plantations confiscated during the struggle for independence, a policy aimed at rehabilitating the impoverished French aristocracy. Thus these remnants of the Old Régime advanced outrageous claims against the Haitian government. When these were refused in 1825, France sent a fleet to blockade the island and enforce a demand of $30,000,000. Boyer, with no alternative but to agree, later did secure a reduction to $18,000,000. Even this concession gave rise to plots against his government. Subsequently, Haiti was quite unable to make payments, so that in 1838 France sent a commission to review the claims with Haiti. Two treaties resulted. One extended recognition to Haiti; the other reduced the indemnity to $12,000,000, to be paid in yearly installments of $400,000 for a period of thirty years.

To meet the payments, Boyer reduced government expenditures and resorted to Christophe's policy of military supervision in rural areas to maintain agricultural production. In 1843 the rising resentment against his administration was added to by a devastating earthquake which partially or wholly destroyed towns and cities in the north. Cap-Haitien was leveled. Port-au-Prince suffered at the same time a great fire. Out of this distress Charles Riviere Hérard, a blond mulatto, led a revolt in Cayes which forced Boyer to flee to Jamaica. Later in Paris he died in 1850, to be regarded, like Petión, as one of Haiti's great presidents.

The overthrow of Boyer saw in the next four years four figures, all Negroes, succeed one another by the use of military power. In this confusion, moreover, Haiti lost Santo Domingo when that part of the island revolted and established once again its independence in 1844. The last of the four rulers, Jean Baptiste Riché, showed ability, but, old and infirm, died in less than a year after taking office. He left behind him, nevertheless, a monument in the form of a school for boys without homes, *Maison Central,* in Port-au-Prince.

Upon the death of Riché those who had feared the emergence of another Boyer selected as president, after a deadlock in the senate, an illiterate captain of the guards, a full-blooded Negro, Faustin Soulouque, who took office on March 1, 1847. Disconcertingly, the new president exhibited unexpected abilities. He set aside those who put him in power and attacked without mercy the mulattoes, whom he feared. In 1849 he abolished the republic and created a monarchy, complete with a nobility in imitation of Christophe, with himself as Emperor Faustin I. His coronation in Port-au-Prince in April, 1852, was attended with pomp and ceremony hardly equaled by similar events in Europe. For eight days and nights the city was brightly lighted. Vast sums were expended for the emperor and his empress. He clothed his nobility with brilliantly colored uniforms of the new imperial and military order of St. Faustin.

The emperor began at once an attempt to reconquer Santo Domingo. He sent a major expedition in 1849 but suffered defeat. In the next year France, Britain, and the United States interceded to end hostilities. But Soulouque took the position that if Santo Domingo's independence were recognized, it would mean opening the island to foreigners, who, developing the eastern end, would eventually destroy Haiti's own independence. When the negotiations broke down in 1855, Soulouque made a second attempt. That, too, failed for the Dominicans decisively halted the invasion with inferior forces. The foreign powers thereupon succeeded in bringing about a truce for two years. By 1858 the orgy of spending that accompanied the campaigns against Santo Domingo and the upkeep of the royal position had emptied the treasury. At the same time wild speculation by the commercial classes in coffee, a sudden collapse, high tariffs, and government monopolies affecting essentials brought widespread discontent. Soulouque's chief of staff, General Fabre Geffrard, who had distinguished himself in the retreat from Santo Domingo, led a revolt which in January, 1859, forced the abdication of the emperor, who escaped to Jamaica under British protection.

Geffrard, a mulatto, president from 1859 to 1867, was an able man, a strict disciplinarian, and an excellent administrator. He supported education, primary and secondary, public as well as private. To improve religious conditions, he negotiated a Concordat with the Vatican in 1860 under which priests and nuns were recruited in France. He founded colleges of medicine, navigation, and art, and sent students, Negroes and mulattoes, to study in Europe besides encouraging industrial training in the cities. He also made efforts to improve the health of the people by providing fountains in the leading cities, and aided agricultural development as well as the establishment of small industries in the capital. Aware of the importance of foreigners skilled in the development of backward countries, he tried unsuccessfully to modify the constitution to permit foreign land ownership.

In foreign affairs Santo Domingo remained the chief problem. The Dominicans, deeply disturbed by the efforts of Soulouque to conquer them, split into two parties, pro-Spanish and pro-Haitian. The former successfully persuaded Spain to annex Santo Domingo in March, 1861, as a means of protecting it from conquest by Haiti. The other retreated into Haiti, whence it carried on guerrilla warfare against the Spaniards. aided by Geffrard. The Spanish admiral, Rubalca, in retaliation, arrived at Port-au-Prince and demanded an indemnity of £200,000 and a salute of twenty-one guns. Geffrard, through mediation of the British consul-general, had the indemnity reduced to £20,000 and tendered the salute.

This event lessened the prestige of the president and encouraged General Sylvian Salnave to attempt a revolt at Cap-Haitien. The insurgents there attacked the British consulate, an action which led the British commander of the *Bull Dog* to bombard the city. Aided indirectly by the British attack on Cap-Haitien, Geffrard put down the revolt, but many Haitians believed he had foreign aid. The expense of suppressing Salnave's uprising, bad crops, and a major fire in Port-au-Prince forced Geffrard to economize in many branches of the government. Discontent, rising rapidly, forced his resignation and flight to Jamaica in 1867. In perspective, Geffrard's administration takes rank with that of Boyer and Petión as one contributing to the well-being of Haiti.

Dominance of the Commercial Mulattoes and Growth of Foreign Interest, 1867–1915. After Geffrard's overthrow Haiti descended into violent civil wars which eventually produced American intervention. Mulatto presidents from the commercial coastal classes, always favoring foreign aid, stirred the fears of the Negroes over a possible return to slavery. Opposition to any policy favoring foreigners found expression in revolt, which in turn, destroying foreign stocks of goods, brought threats of invasion. Sylvian Salnave, who held office for two years (1867–1869), saw the country plunged into a bloody conflict between the north and the south. The civil war was particularly severe from the practice of the élite politicians in Port-au-Prince of hiring *Cacos,* northern bands of peasants, who, in return for putting down Negro uprisings, were given a free hand in plundering towns and cities. Salnave attempted to suppress the activities of the *Cacos* and assembled his supporters in the south, called *Piquets.* Defeated, he was succeeded by Nissage Saget, who took over for four years (1870–1874). His administration, comparatively peaceful, was devoted to a revival of prosperity, retiring large amounts of paper money, and importing American silver dollars to stabilize the currency. In spite of his efforts, however, to meet payments for damages to foreign commercial houses, particularly German, Germany sent a fleet which seized Haitian ships in compensation.

At the end of his term, in fear of another Negro uprising, he gave the nomination to Michael Domingue, whose government was in fact under the domination of his nephew, Septimus Rameau, a man intensely antagonistic toward foreigners and whites. Under the pretext of improving the economy, Domingue negotiated two loans from France totaling $10,-000,000, but the proceeds were, in fact, divided among the members of the government, a scandal which caused his overthrow. His successor, Boisrond-Canal (1876–1879), who represented the growing mulatto middle class of merchants and liberals, attempted to improve the administration of finances and encourage democratic practices in government. However, fearing revolt of the Negroes, Boisrond-Canal resigned in 1879. In October of that year the National Assembly selected Lysius Salomon, the leader of the blacks, for the presidency (1879–1888). While he persecuted the liberal leaders of the commercial class, he nevertheless showed ability in trying to meet the needs of the country. He founded a national bank at Port-au-Prince, paid off the national debt, encouraged the sale of land to Negroes, and held an agricultural exposition to stimulate an understanding of methods of improving Haiti's crops. He also established schools in the rural areas and reorganized the army. Although re-elected in 1886, uprisings forced his resignation within two years.

The revolts continued and again plunged the country into a civil war between the north and the south. During 1888 General F. D. Légitime succeeded for several months in bringing order while he held the presidency and in paving the way for Florvil Hyppolite to assume the office. During the latter's administration (1889–1896) Haiti adopted a new constitution (1896). Aided by a capable minister of finance, A. Firmin, Hyppolite made an effort to bring order into the administration of the country. But American efforts to purchase Mole St. Nicholas as a coaling station stirred fears among the Haitians that the president was sympathetic to the sale of Haitian territory to foreigners. A revolt at Jacmel which he tried to suppress brought on his death by heart failure.

Tiresias Augustin Simon Sam succeeded to the office of president (1896–1902). While his government was characterized by reckless spending, he nevertheless began railroad construction from Cap-Haitien into the interior. His rule also marked a growth of German investment in Haiti and the establishment of commercial firms. The proprietor of one of these, one Emile Luders, mauled by some Haitian police, led Germany to demand an indemnity and send two war vessels to force collection. Sam's acquiescence touched off a revolt. Again the fear of foreign domination made an effective appeal to the masses. His departure from Haiti in 1902 left two figures, Antenor Firmin and Nord Alexis, fighting for the office of president. Nord Alexis, successfully destroying his enemy's

military supplies aboard a Haitian ship, took over the presidency and
served from 1902 to 1908. His administration concerned itself with efforts
to improve public works and investigate frauds in the previous government. The latter action led to the indictment of prominent Haitians,
Vilbrun Guillaume, Sam, Tancred Auguste, and Cincinnatus Leconte,
three of whom later were presidents of the country.

Part II. AMERICAN INTERVENTION IN HAITI, 1915–1935

American Intervention in Haiti: Causes. Beginning in 1908 with the
successful revolt of Sam, who became president in that year, Haiti
plunged into a civil war which brought on American intervention in
1915. The causes arose out of the American expansion into the Caribbean
area and the civil strife within Haiti itself. The unsettled condition was
evidenced by the fact that other than a few attempts to establish some
schools in the larger cities, nothing had been done for the rural areas,
or where beginnings had been made, recurring civil wars soon destroyed
them. Thus illiteracy among the almost 2,000,000 rural Haitians amounted
to nearly 95 per cent. Outside of the regulations governing the presidency, the legislature, and the council of state, all of which were used
by the educated élite to seize or hold power, the only constant factor in
the numerous constitutions was that which prohibited foreigners from
holding property. The élite knew that this provision made it impossible
for foreigners to secure a foothold and thus become their competitors,
while the Negroes believed it protected them from a return to slavery.

Nevertheless by the beginning of the twentieth century, foreign interest in Haiti had become a dominant factor in her political and economic life. French and German business houses largely controlled trade,
and under various devices had secured ownership of land through Haitian
citizens. When in 1914 Germany became involved in war, her interests
in Haiti were regarded with suspicion by the United States. The latter,
having already secured Puerto Rico and Guantánamo Bay in Cuba,
extended the Monroe Doctrine through the Roosevelt corollary to justify
intervention in the Caribbean countries if their conditions invited European occupation. The first step had been taken in 1905 with the establishment of a customs receivership in the Dominican Republic.

The "Ephemeral Governments," 1908–1915. The governments between 1908 and 1915, called "Ephemeral," were characterized by negotiations of extensive loans abroad and military uprisings. In 1910 under
President Simon the National Bank was reorganized with French, Ger-

man, and American participation, the latter represented by the National City Bank of New York. In August of the same year Haiti negotiated a loan for 65,000,000 francs with French, German, and American bankers. The National Bank was to receive tax money set aside to pay off the loan. In the following year, 1911, Cincinnatus Leconte, with *Caco* support, won control after a revolt. He made a serious attempt at reform with a program of reducing the army and building schools, but he also floated an internal loan of $674,000 at 6 per cent interest to pay the expenses of his own revolt. Soon thereafter an explosion in the National Palace killed him and brought Tancrede Auguste to power in August, 1912, but the latter died shortly, believed to have been poisoned. Three armies took possession of Port-au-Prince, out of which struggle Michael Oreste emerged as the next president in May, 1913. He floated an internal bond issue for $609,000, but, unable to put down his enemies, he resigned and fled the country after ruling nine months.

The presidency was next held by Davilmar Theodore, supported by a *Caco* army. He attempted to reintroduce military reforms, but after nine months found himself forced to resign and flee to Jamaica in January, 1914. Charles and Oreste Zanor, who likewise had behind them a *Caco* army, took possession of the government. To pay the leaders of his army and to meet government expenses, Charles Zanor floated another internal bond issue for $712,000. Six months later he issued still another, this time for $525,000. All these loans brought in far less than their face value and were held mostly by German business houses and banks, to which control of customs duties and concessions to raw materials were given for security. Still unable to meet expenses, Zanor next attempted to force the National Bank to turn over funds set aside to retire paper money. The bank refused and a revolt led by Davilmar Theodore drove Zanor from power in November, 1914. Equally without funds to pay his *Cacos* leaders, Theodore threatened to seize the bank's pledged funds, but the bank appealed to the United States, which sent a cruiser to Port-au-Prince, landed marines, and removed the $500,000 to New York City for safekeeping. Later in 1919, under other conditions, this money was returned to the Haitian bank.

Intervention. With World War I in progress, the United States was concerned to see stable conditions in Haiti. When it was obvious that Theodore could not put down the revolution led by Sam in the north, the Wilson administration dispatched Admiral Caperton with war vessels to the island. As Sam progressed down the coast, Admiral Caperton landed forces to prevent looting in the captured towns, an action which forced the two Haitian armies to confine their battles to the outskirts. When in May, 1915, Sam captured Port-au-Prince, the National Assembly elected him president. Shortly afterward another revolt broke out, led by Dr. Rosalvo Bobo. To crush it, Sam ordered the frightful massacre of 167 prisoners, many of whom were distinguished citizens, in the Port-au-Prince prisons. For this atrocity a mob stormed the palace, captured the wretched killer, and tore him limb from limb.

Haiti was now without a government. Acting on orders from Washington, Admiral Caperton landed forces in July, 1915, to protect lives and property and help the Haitians establish a stable government. In control, Caperton assumed the responsibility of directing the selection of a president whom the United States considered suitable. Senator Sudre Dartiguenave, proving satisfactory, was elected by the Haitian Congress in August, 1915. With American control a fact and with the principal source of income of the Haitian government, the customs houses, under American direction, the United States next pressed for a treaty with Haiti, signed and ratified on May 3, 1916. This agreement provided for an American receiver-general of the customs, a financial adviser, the creation of a Haitian constabulary, and measures to aid the island develop its agricultural, mineral, and commercial riches. While the majority of the élite saw the necessity of accepting American occupation, the marines had to invade the north to put down the *Cacos'* opposition. With order established, the American authorities turned to the matter of reorganizing Haitian finances. To that end Haiti agreed in 1919 to negotiate a loan of $40,000,000 to settle claims against the country.

While these matters were in progress, the American government urged upon Haiti the revision of her constitution to end the prohibition against foreign ownership of land. Opposition to the move was strong. The élite could see that their irresponsible control of internal affairs would be threatened, while the Negroes feared the change would open the way for a return to slavery. The United States on its part felt that the proposed $40,000,000 loan would be better secured with American landownership, that is by corporations, guaranteed. When opposition in the Assembly became too great, the marine head of the Haitian gendarmerie dissolved that body. The constitution, then submitted to a plebiscite, was adopted with a vote of 69,000 for and 339 against. The new constitution, in effect on June 19, 1918, provided for a president to serve four years, a two-house legislature, and a senate and Chamber of Deputies whose members were to be elected for six and two years respectively. Suffrage was given to all citizens over twenty-one and those naturalized after having lived in Haiti for five years. Other features of the document gave aliens the right to own land and provided for a Haitian constabulary in place of the former military organs of the state.

When the constitution was in effect the Americans began the reconstruction of Haiti, but conflicts soon arose. The efforts to build roads by the use of forced labor, a corvée system, resulted in a revolt in 1919, led by Charlemagne Peralte. The marines, forced to establish law and order, eventually killed Charlemagne, an event which led to widespread criticism of the United States and to a senatorial investigation. As a result of the inquiry the marine general, John H. Russell, was given civilian status as high commissioner in February, 1922, an action which transferred control from the War to the State Department. Although the constitution had been adopted providing for elections, none were held in 1922 when Dartiguenave's term expired. On the contrary, the Council of State selected Louis Borno, acceptable to the United States, as president. Under the circumstances the government of Haiti became in effect a dictatorship, ruled jointly by the president and the American high commissioner.

Economic Changes under American Control. In the next eight years a beginning was made in changing Haiti's economy. To provide funds for liquidating the public debt accumulated over the years, a loan of $40,000,000 was made with some protest on the part of the Haitians. Various other loans were floated to meet the internal debts. By 1930 the public debt was reduced from $24,000,000 to $12,500,000. But the diversion of so much of Haiti's income to debt service hampered the development of other needed services. Other financial reforms included the raising of the tariffs on luxury goods and imposing tariffs upon items which, when excluded, encouraged native Haitian industries, particularly tobacco. Efforts to reduce export duties were successful on bananas and salt. Little was done, however, to combat disease in the rural areas and to establish an adequate educational system.

Beyond expanding the acreage devoted to coffee production, the American occupation saw nothing done to develop other Haitian resources. In 1916 coffee exports made up 61 per cent of the total exports; by 1928 they had risen to 78 per cent. Some effort was made to encourage the peasants to diversify crops, but only tobacco production showed a significant increase. On the other hand, plans for the development of irrigation systems in the Artibonite River plain came to nothing. In the field of transportation about 1,000 miles of roads had been put into condition for use. But the trails leading from the country into the cities and towns remained the chief avenues for transportation of goods. Some advances were made in the larger cities, such as the construction of public buildings, municipal water systems, wharves, parks, and squares.

Probably the greatest failure came in the field of education. The value of Haiti's exports rose from $8,932,885 in 1916 to over $22,000,000 in 1928, but only 11 per cent of the government's expenditures went for educational purposes. Thus in 1928 there were but 1,087 Haitian-directed schools with about 85,000 pupils enrolled out of a total school population of over 400,000. Moreover, a large number of these were schools only in name. Exceptions were the few but excellent institutions established by the American Service Technique. Thus by 1930 the American occupation had done little to raise the material and moral condition of the Haitian population. Its chief contribution was stabilizing the government and providing a working financial system under which the bulk of the revenues went to retire loans held by American banks.

Political Changes under American Control. When the depression of 1929 came, Haiti suffered from loss of markets and a rapid rise in unemployment. These conditions produced strikes and revolutionary movements which were put down by the marines. The event, attracting widespread attention, led to an investigation by a presidential commission headed by W. Cameron Forbes, appointed by President Hoover. The commission, however, devoted the bulk of its time to the effort of finding a successor to President Borno, whose term expired in 1930. An agreement was reached by which Eugene Roy, a Haitian businessman, was selected by the Council of State. Roy convened a congress and then resigned to permit the election of a Haitian. The commission also laid down a new policy for the United States and Haiti under which the high commissioner's office was abolished, a regular minister was to be appointed, and steps taken to replace Americans in Haiti's administration with Haitians, that is, a Haitianization program was to lead to self-government. Finally, the marines were to remain until 1934. Under this agreement Stenio Vincent was elected president without American interference in 1930.

Part III. ECONOMIC AND SOCIAL IMPROVEMENTS, SINCE 1935

The Administrations of Vincent, 1930–1941. In the following six years Stenio Vincent carried out the Haitianization program in cooperation with the American minister. By 1933 Haitians had taken over public works, health, and agricultural service techniques. In the following year an executive agreement provided for the withdrawal of the last of the marines, who left the island in 1934. This event was followed by a second agreement reached by President Roosevelt and Vincent which ended the occupation in 1935, although an American fiscal representative remained until 1941 to supervise the collection of revenues to pay off the remaining $12,500,000 due on the 1922 loan.

President Vincent met the depression by launching a public works program and restoring Haitian control over all aspects of its economy. He negotiated a loan of 500,000 francs with France in 1935, but the drop in coffee prices made it necessary for him to seek a $5,000,000 loan in the United States to expand the public works program of constructing roads, bridges, irrigation works, and municipal water systems. In 1934 he succeeded in buying out the American interest in the National Bank. In the following year the Haitian congress restricted foreigners from engaging in retail trade on the ground that their activities were detrimental to the national economy.

As Vincent's term drew to a close, he had the constitution revised in 1935 to remain in office for five more years until 1941. Besides continuing the program of Haitianization, Vincent successfully met a difficult impasse with the Dominican Republic when the Dominican dictator, Trujillo, suddenly ordered a massacre of thousands of Haitians who had peacefully settled in the neighboring country. Avoiding a war and aided by pressure from the other American republics, Haiti successfully secured from Trujillo's government compensation for the Haitian families to the extent of $750,000. When Vincent's term expired in 1941, he stepped aside to permit the election of Elie Lescot, who cooperated closely with the United States during World War II.

Political and Economic Developments, 1941 to the Present. The Lescot government, besides engaging at the request of the United States upon rubber production, fibers, and vegetable oils, negotiated an agreement to aid agriculture. The United States, too, began a sanitation program to improve Haitian public health, and thus benefit the war effort in Haiti. However, the spending of considerable money in Haiti under these conditions encouraged black-marketing and profiteering, while the rubber growing program displaced thousands of Haitians. These conditions led to discontent which erupted in a *coup d'état* forcing Lescot out of office in January, 1946. A military junta, taking over, held elections for a congress which in turn selected in May, Dumarsais Estimé, a Negro, for president. Estimé's effort to alter the constitution to permit his re-election brought about his overthrow in 1950 and a new military government. The latter, holding a controlled election, placed in office as president in October, 1950, Colonel Paul E. Magloire, the head of the junta.

Magloire carried on Estimé's efforts to improve health conditions among the Haitians. Important in this respect was the work in 1949 of a commission of the United Nations which found health conditions so deplorable that it recommended immediate assistance through the World Health Organization. Approved and aided by funds from the United Nations, the World Health Organization in 1950–1954 inoculated the entire Haitian population with penicillin to combat yaws and syphilis; in the latter year the WHO launched a second major attack to eradicate malaria and yellow fever from the island. This humanitarian work pointed up sharply Haiti's most serious problems: abject poverty for 90 per cent of the people, lack of schools, an illiteracy beyond 90 per cent, and lack of any program on the part of the Haitian government to remedy these evils. Haiti's population of over 3,200,000 presents, except for the favored few, the most distressing picture of "man's inhumanity to man" to be found in any Latin-American country.

The basic economy of the country rests upon the export of coffee and sugar, with others, far behind, including rubber, bananas, cocoa, sisal, and tobacco. The Magloire administration launched many projects on paper to improve the economy, but these have advanced at a snail's pace because of corruption within the government and lack of any fundamental interest in the well-being of the population as a whole.

Shortly after election Magloire drew up a new constitution which encouraged foreign investment in Haiti's resources. A New Industries Law, enacted in 1949, drastically reduced taxes on industries established under its terms and permitted free importation of building materials. By 1954 a considerable number of foreign companies had taken advantage of the new legislation. The government continued the hydroelectric project in the Artibonite Valley, aided by an Export-Import Bank loan, and late in 1954 completed the large dam on the Artibonite River for irrigating some 77,000 acres. Other improvements included harbor dredging at Cap-Haitien, construction of highways, and encouragement of exploration for copper, lignite, and bauxite.

A Five Year Plan begun in 1951 to aid agriculture was far behind schedule in 1955. More success, however, attended a Point Four undertaking to expand food production and the export of coffee, sugar, cocoa, edible oils, and other crops. Important in the general picture of agriculture was the completion by SCIPA (Inter-American Cooperative Service for the Production of Food) of a dam at St. Raphael in northern Haiti to irrigate about 5,000 acres. Further American interest in Haiti was manifest in an agreement which guaranteed to protect investments of United States nationals from expropriation of their properties and from currency fluctuations. Early in January, 1955, Haiti signed a military assistance agreement with the United States, bringing to eleven the number of such pacts signed with Latin-American governments.

The government of Haiti remains virtually a dictatorship. Since World War II the United Nations has taken important steps to improve the health of its people and the United States has aided the improvement of food production. Responsible Haitians, to be distinguished from the leaders of its government, hope that democracy will find a foothold among them; today it is still a dream of the future.

THE DOMINICAN REPUBLIC

Part I. INDEPENDENCE AND FOREIGN DOMINATION, 1808–1904

Colonial Background and Independence. The Dominican Republic had a common origin with Haiti as Española in the colonial period. While Haiti in the west, under French control, developed an overwhelming Negro slave population, the Spanish end of the island remained predominantly European. The first formal division of the island came in 1697 with the Treaty of Ryswick, under which Spain ceded approximately half of the island to France. Thereafter the eastern end was called Santo Domingo. After the cession the two colonies had little contact with each other, although the cattle ranges of Santo Domingo provided hides and horses for the sugar plantations of Haiti. In 1795 under the Treaty of Basle, Spain ceded the rest of the island to France. The Dominicans resented the transfer, since France was extending citizenship and other rights to Haiti's dominant Negro population. In this year, too, Toussaint L'Ouverture began his meteoric career. In 1801 he took possession of Santo Domingo for France, where he freed the few slaves held by the Dominican Creoles. When Le Clerc's army was driven from Haiti, a small French force established itself in Santo Domingo and aided the Dominicans to resist Haitian attempts to conquer them. But the Dominicans, in fact, were not happy under French rule. Thus in 1808 with

British aid, they joined the mother country to revolt against Napoleon and return to Spanish rule.

The stage was now set for complete independence. The liberalizing influences of France and the examples of Spain's colonies winning their independence on the mainland led the Dominican Creoles to revolt in 1821. Successful under José Núñez de Cáceres, they drew up a constitution in the same year which created a republic with a captain-general at the head of the government. The country was divided into five departments which elected representatives to the Central Junta. Its political governor shared executive authority with the captain-general.

Conquest by Haiti, 1822–1844. The government had little time to function, however, for in 1822 Boyer, the Haitian leader, conquered the new state. The Dominicans, who feared Spanish reconquest, in fact offered little resistance. During the next twenty-two years, while Boyer ruled, the Dominicans remained under Haiti. Their willingness stemmed largely from his policy of noninterference in their affairs. But as the Dominicans came to be taxed for Haiti's benefit and unscrupulous governors found excuses to deprive white Dominicans of their lands, resentment grew. In 1838 Juan Pablo Duarte, a patriotic and gifted leader, taking advantage of the growing revolt in Haiti to Boyer's rule, organized a secret society on July 16, 1838, the *Trinitaria,* based on principles of sacrifice and denial. Working for independence, they were able to revolt by taking advantage of Boyer's overthrow and resulting civil war in Haiti. By 1844 the Dominicans had established their independence, recalled Duarte from exile, repelled a Haitian invasion, and begun again a career of independence.

Fears of Conquest. For the next seventeen years until 1861, the Dominicans were torn by fears of either Haitian or Spanish reconquest. The Central Junta, drawing up a new constitution on November 6, 1844, made a rich mulatto landowner, General Pedro Santana, president. In the following four years the Dominicans, led by Buenaventura Báez and President Santana, sought foreign recognition of their independent status in the hope of strengthening themselves against Haiti. When efforts to interest the United States failed, largely because the Mexican War was absorbing American attention, Santana turned to France and Spain. These moves stirred the fears of the Haitians, who under Soulouque led a major expedition in 1849 to conquer the eastern end of the island. Santana repulsed the invasion, while France, Britain, and the United States attempted to mediate the conflict.

Báez, defeating the Haitian attempt and succeeding to the presidency, continued negotiations in 1849 to place the country under France or the United States as a protectorate. In 1853, when Santana returned to head the state, he, too, directed his efforts toward the United States, for that country had become increasingly interested in securing a naval coaling station on Samaná Bay. The British and French, however, blocked this effort by threatening to stir up the Haitians and by appealing to the patriotism of the Dominicans. In the meantime, Soulouque, now Faustin I, had prepared and launched a new attempt at conquest, but again the Dominicans defeated the effort. Báez, who had played an important part in the defeat of the Haitians, took advantage of his popularity and patriotic fervor to force Santana out of office in 1856. His leanings toward Spain, however, shortly led to his own overthrow and the return of Santana to power in 1858.

The Spanish Reoccupation of Santo Domingo, 1861–1865. By this date the Republic was in dire financial straits; its obvious weakness made the Haitian threat of conquest seem great. Santana, looking for a way to avoid such a contingency, lost hope in the United States as that country was moving toward a great Civil War. As a last resort he adopted Báez' policies and turned to Spain. There an adventurer, Don Leopoldo O'Donnell, head of Isabella's ministry, welcomed the opportunity to annex the Dominican Republic to offset the criticism of the government over losses in Morocco. Thus on March 19, 1861, the Dominicans became once more colonials of Spain. But not all agreed; many fled to Haiti, where they were joined by Cubans fleeing from Spanish oppression in that island. Supported by the Haitian government, the patriotic Dominicans launched the "War of Restoration." So effective were their guerrilla raids that in the next four years Spain lost an estimated 10,000 men trying to hold the colony. By 1865, finding the expense too great together with her war in Peru, the mother country gave up the experiment and withdrew between May and July of that year.

The United States and Samaná Bay. Santana, who had served as Spain's captain-general for two years, died in 1864, so that when the provisional government established itself in the next year, Báez became president upon General Cabral's failure to organize the country. Haiti, fearing Báez' proforeign record, backed Cabral's revolt to return him to power in 1866. By this date American interests had grown rapidly through the influence of an American land speculating company whose officials easily persuaded Cabral, short of money, to seek an American loan of $20,000,000. He offered in return a concession to coal mines and a naval base on Samaná Bay. Báez at this juncture, taking a page from

Cabral's book, turned to Haiti for support, which, when forthcoming from General Salnave, overthrew Cabral.

But as soon as Báez reached the presidency in 1870, he immediately opened negotiations with the United States to cede Samaná Bay and propose annexation. In the meantime, General William L. Cazenau and Colonel Joseph W. Fabens, the ringleaders in the land speculation venture, had established contact with the important figures in the Grant administration through their Santo Domingo Company. Forwarding their plans at the moment was the interest of the naval officials in Samaná Bay as a coaling station. Thus Báez' proposal for annexation, falling on fertile ground, led President Grant to send a trusted friend, General Orville Babcock, to the Dominican Republic to negotiate a treaty of annexation.

The completed treaty provided for ending the existence of the Dominican government and the cession of all its rights and government property to the United States. It pledged the public lands to pay the public debt, and agreed to have the Dominican people express their ideas on the cession while the United States protected the country from interference with this expression. The United States on its part agreed to pay the Dominican government $1,000,000 after ratification of the treaty. This sum the Dominicans were to use toward retiring the national debt. Finally, a provision stipulated that in case of the failure of the treaty to secure ratification, the Dominicans agreed to let the United States acquire Samaná Bay for $2,000,000. A convention signed at the same time gave the United States a lease on the bay for ninety-nine years. When, however, the treaty came up for consideration in the United States Senate, the questionable activities of the American speculators and their influence over the Dominican government came out. Senator Sumner, chairman of the Foreign Relations Committee, turned against the treaty so that it failed of ratification in June, 1870.

Loans and Threats of European Occupation, 1870–1905. With the treaty dead, withdrawal of American forces led to the immediate overthrow of Báez. During the next ten years the Republic passed through a series of revolts which by 1880 brought a strong man to the presidency, Ulises Heureaux, who remained in power for nineteen years. During these years foreign economic interests grew rapidly. The most important of these were loans contracted recklessly by the Dominican governments. The most flagrant case was that of the Hartmont loan of 1869 under which the Hartmont Company was to raise £420,000 with £100,000 reserved to itself as a commission. The Dominican bonds floated were listed fraudulently on the London Stock Exchange, netting the company over £372,000, out of which the Dominican government received less than £40,000. Moreover, it was bound under the contract to pay back to the bondholders more than £800,000. A second loan, contracted in 1888 to pay off the Hartmont obligation, led to the founding of the Santo Domingo Improvement Company, an American concern. But the Dominican government, unable to meet payments on either, became bankrupt with a public debt of almost $20,000,000. In addition the government was besieged with claims for other obligations to individuals for unpaid bills.

Concessions to foreigners after 1880 affected both the economy and the social conditions of Santo Domingo. Most of the money invested went into the sugar industry. In 1880 the production of sugar reached about 4,000 tons; by 1905 the crop amounted to over 50,000 tons, produced principally by American and Italian companies. Sugar expansion brought on the importation of Haitians and Negro workers from other Caribbean islands at low wages, and the growth of large plantations at the expense of native small holdings. Thus with the best lands going into the hands of foreigners, who paid low taxes and barely a subsistence wage to Dominican labor, no wealth was produced to meet the payments on the huge loans contracted in the previous years. Heureaux had done nothing with the proceeds of the loans to improve the economy of the republic. Roads and highways became worse than they were in the colonial period. His ruthlessness in putting down revolts against his rule drove his enemies in despair to assassinate him in 1899. The resulting anarchy in the next five years, as one *caudillo* after another tried to seize power and negotiate new loans to bolster his weak government, sent the public debt up to some $32,000,000.

Part II. AMERICAN INTERVENTION AND THE TRUJILLO DICTATORSHIP SINCE 1905

American Intervention, 1905–1924. With industry in a state of collapse and trade declining, the government could not meet the interest on the national debt, to say nothing of making payments on the principal. France, Belgium, and Italy had claims and were demanding payment. American claims up to 1901 were better treated inasmuch as the Santo Domingo Improvement Company had the right until that year to collect customs revenues to repay its claim of about $1,000,000. After 1901, however, these funds were diverted from this purpose by successive *caudillos.* In the face of this condition, the United States appointed in 1904 a financial agent to take over the custom house at Puerto Plata. Before the year ended, France was threatening to seize the custom house at the capital, Santo Domingo, while Italy had dispatched a cruiser to the island.

With the country's credit gone and conditions of anarchy prevailing, President Carlos F. Morales turned to the United States and asked for protection in 1905 against the threatening attitude of the European powers. The appeal fell within the framework of American policy of expansion in progress since the end of the Spanish-American War. The Monroe Doctrine was now given a new meaning by President Roosevelt, whose Corollary, issued with the conditions of Santo Domingo in mind, stated in effect that it was the duty of the United States to maintain order in Caribbean countries to prevent foreign powers from occupying territory to collect debts and thus become a possible threat to the United States.

In pursuit of this thesis President Roosevelt proposed a treaty by which the United States would administer the custom house receipts and allot 45 per cent to the Dominican government's creditors. Signed on February 7, 1905, the agreement was rejected by the United States Senate. Roosevelt thereupon by executive order set up a *modus vivendi* by which the United States administered the custom house and effected a settlement with the country's creditors, after claims totaling $32,000,000 had been reduced to $17,000,000. This step was followed by an American loan of $20,000,000 to pay off debts and make internal improvements. On February 8, 1907, a convention, negotiated and ratified, gave the American president the right to appoint customs receivers and bound the Dominican government not to increase the debt.

In the following year, 1908, Morales ended his term to be succeeded peacefully by Raymond Cáceres, who served until 1911. Prosperity returned to the country, with Cáceres guaranteed the support of the United States against revolutionary disturbances. Dominican trade under the new dispensation jumped from about $10,000,000 in 1905 to $17,000,000 in 1911. Little was done, however, to improve conditions among the people of the Republic through encouraging native industry and education. On the contrary, American companies evaded their taxes while the Republic was flooded with American goods—even shoes which a Dominican leather industry could have well supplied from her own cattle ranges. In 1911 President Cáceres was assassinated as a result of his favoritism toward foreigners, the most flagrant case in point being the Agricultural Concessions Law of 1911 under which foreign sugar companies greatly expanded their holdings at the expense of small Dominican landowners, as well as producing wild speculation in land. The assassination plunged the country into civil war, which in turn led the United States, under President Taft, to send marines to protect the custom house.

American Military Government, 1916–1924. When order was restored, Archbishop Noel became president in March, 1913, but died shortly after assuming office. Civil war again broke out, but President Wilson, refusing to recognize any revolutionary government, exerted pressure to secure peaceful elections, which, supervised by three American commissioners, brought Juan Isidro Jiménez to power. Revolts, however, overthrew him a year later. In April, 1914, marines arrived again to maintain order, and Dr. Henríquez y Carvajal was made provisional president by the Dominican congress. When he refused, however, to accept an American demand that a new treaty turn over the customs collections to an American administrator, accept an American financial adviser, and establish a constabulary, the United States, represented by Captain H. S. Knapp, declared the Dominican Republic under military occupation. His purpose, he stated, was to carry out the convention of 1907. He dissolved the Dominican congress and, acting as governor-general, appointed American naval officers to positions held by cabinet members.

The American military government, which lasted eight years, constructed more than 400 miles of roads to facilitate the export of sugar plantations. Likewise it built a large number of bridges in the interior, new piers, and wharves and made other improvements at the capital, Santo Domingo. Of value to the Dominicans themselves was some improvement in education, although illiteracy was still at about the 50 per cent mark in 1924, and the introduction of modern sanitary methods benefiting public health.

On the other side of the ledger, however, the military government was guilty of injustices. American military courts wrongfully imprisoned many innocent people; civil and political liberties disappeared; censorship of the press was enforced to prevent all criticism of the government. Economically, Dominican labor and businessmen suffered. The average wage was sixty cents a day for labor, while the rapid growth of American goods in the country handicapped native industry. Simultaneously the phenomenal expansion of Dominican trade, which rose from some $17,-000,000 in 1911 to over $105,000,000 in 1920 under the stimulus of World War I, benefited chiefly foreign-owned sugar plantations.

By 1920 the Dominicans were demanding the end of the military government. The United States, under criticism throughout Latin America and at home during the 1920 presidential campaign, announced, after the election of Harding, that the time had come to withdraw the marines. In 1921 the first step was taken when Admiral S. S. Robison promised withdrawal within eight months upon Dominican acceptance of conditions submitted by the American government. These in the main provided that the military government's acts were to be ratified, that a new loan of $24,000,000 be negotiated in the United States, that an American receiver of Dominican customs be appointed who would have the authority to liquidate the new debt by using internal revenues if customs receipts were inadequate, and finally, that an American military mission be appointed to organize a native constabulary. The Dominicans refused these terms. A conference, next arranged in Washington in 1922, reached an agreement for the American withdrawal. It provided essentially for complete control of political affairs to be in the hands of the Dominicans and for Dominican authority over the police, with the understanding that the acts of the military government would be ratified, that the Dominican Republic would recognize the bond issues of 1918 and 1922, and that the treaty of 1907 would remain in force. In 1924 a convention, based upon the 1922 agreement, was signed after a presidential election, held in March, had placed Horacio Vásquez in the office of chief executive. In September, 1924, the marines left the country.

The Trujillo Dictatorship, 1930–1952. Vásquez' announcement of his candidacy for re-election in 1930 stirred discontent, which, combined with the suffering produced by the 1929 depression, led to revolts. Rafael Estrella Ureña established a provisional government in March, 1930, under which elections were held. On May 16 of that year General Rafael Trujillo Molina became president and established a dictatorship which has persisted down to the present.

Trujillo, from the lower middle class, had risen to power through the National Guard created by the American occupation. A man of harsh character and extreme energy, he launched immediately a reign of terror, which by 1936 had established a complete dictatorship. He drove opposing political leaders out of the country, destroyed the freedom of the press, smashed labor unions, imprisoned or shot their leaders, and reduced the wages of the sugar workers from forty to twenty-five cents a day. With the opposition dissolved, he created a single political party, the Dominican party, and set up a subservient congress to enact laws which concentrated power in his own hands. To glorify himself he changed the name of the ancient city, Santo Domingo, to Ciudad Trujillo.

Economically, the Trujillo dictatorship made progress in giving the

Republic a modern economy. Agriculture—the production of sugar, cocoa, coffee, and tobacco—remained the basic industry in the country. Sugar, far in the lead, accounted for almost 60 per cent of the exports. However, in 1934, after "re-election," Trujillo began a program of diversifying agriculture by leasing land to small farmers. By 1935 more than 30,000 farmers had been settled on about 150,000 acres. In 1937 he colonized a 26,000-acre tract in the north with some 300 Jewish refugees from Nazi Germany. But these people soon made efforts to migrate elsewhere. His small landholders' program, in fact, remained almost static after the first allotment. To bring additional acreage under cultivation, Trujillo began irrigation projects in Santiago province between 1930 and 1950. Irrigated land, as a result, rose from about 7,000 to almost 180,000 acres. The construction of the Navarrete Canal, still in progress, will bring, it is believed, an additional 31,000 acres under cultivation.

To relieve unemployment caused by the depression, Trujillo also launched a public works program—improvement of roads and highways, building of bridges, and port dredging, particularly of San Pedro de Macorís, from which the bulk of sugar was exported. In education he abolished academic freedom in the higher institutions and launched schooling in agriculture, cattle raising, manual training, and military training. School enrollment declined; in the higher levels it was catastrophic. The total number in the elementary schools in 1936 was 103,255, about the same as that in 1920, despite the increase in the population. Of those who completed courses, considerably less than 2 per cent continued on to the secondary schools. Night schools for adults reduced illiteracy, figures for which in 1935 were between 55 and 60 per cent.

Trujillo made efforts to reduce the foreign debt. The depression had created a financial crisis as exports fell off. A hurricane, destroying three-fourths of the capital city, added new burdens. In 1931 Trujillo enacted the Emergency Law which diverted funds from payments on the debt, $18,000,000, to run the government, but kept up interest payments. He negotiated in 1934 an agreement with the bondholders which extended the expiration dates of the 1922 and 1926 loans to 1962 and 1970, with corresponding reduction in the yearly payments. Finally, to strengthen the government's income, he levied internal revenue taxes on some 200 items consumed in the Republic, a precedent for which had been established by the American military government.

In international affairs Trujillo and President Vincent of Haiti settled the long-standing boundary dispute between their countries. But two years later relations were savagely broken by Trujillo in ordering the massacre of several thousand helpless Haitians who had entered the country in search of employment. At Haiti's protest the Dominican Republic compensated for the outrage to the extent of $750,000 with promises to punish the perpetrator!

When Trujillo's term ended in 1936, he selected one of his group, Dr. Jacinto B. Peynado, former secretary of police and war and vice-president, as president, who served until 1940, when he died. Dr. Manuel Troncoso de la Concha finished the term. In 1941 Trujillo had the constitution amended to provide suffrage for women and to extend the presidential term to five years. As the only candidate under the new constitution, he was overwhelmingly elected in 1942.

When World War II broke out in 1939, Trujillo benefited by the growing demand for Dominican products. From the increased income he was able in 1940 to end the American receivership by treaty, and, as the war continued to swell the revenues of the state, liquidate the Republic's outstanding bonds by 1947. The war found Trujillo cooperating with the United States in the struggle against dictatorship in Europe, and at the same time crushing opposition to his rule at home.

After World War II was over, sentiment against his dictatorship stirred attempts to overthrow him. These were organized abroad, particularly in Cuba, by the Caribbean Legion, composed of exiles from Latin-American countries and soldiers of fortune. In 1947 the Cayo Confites Expedition made an attempt to invade the Dominican Republic, but its departure was frustrated by the Cuban government. In November, 1949, Trujillo charged that new efforts were being organized in Cuba to unseat him; in January, 1950, he secured authority from his congress to declare war on any Caribbean country. Meanwhile, however, Trujillo himself was encouraging attacks upon neighboring governments, an activity which led Haiti to invoke the Rio de Janeiro Treaty of Reciprocal Assistance. Trujillo invoked the same pact against Guatemala, Cuba, and Haiti. The resulting investigation of the Organization of American States demanded that Trujillo deport all Haitians plotting against their government, exonerated Haiti of any blame, and warned Cuba and Guatemala to break up the activities of the Caribbean Legion on their soil.

In February, 1950, Trujillo again stirred fear among his neighbors by assuming full war powers and increasing his military budget. However, most observers believed the action was one connected with the suppression of the opposition to his re-election scheduled for 1952. In anticipation of this event, the Christian Democratic party in October,

1950, nominated its candidates for the office. In the following March, 1951, the Dominican senate announced that Trujillo's return to office was the hope of the nation.

Continuation of Trujillo Control, 1952 to the Present. When the time came for elections, May, 1952, Trujillo's brother, Hector Bienvenido, was the only candidate. Presented by the Dominican party, he was elected with more than 1,000,000 votes out of a total population of 2,121,000. Inaugurated on August 16, the new president declared he would continue the policies of his brother. The latter assumed various cabinet positions as well as that of representing the Republic at the United Nations.

The government early in 1953 launched a Five Year Program consisting of building schools, public buildings, low cost housing, and highways. Of the latter a major undertaking was linking Ciudad Trujillo with Santiago de los Caballeros in the north. Lesser roads were planned for the interior.

Other activities were aimed at increased agricultural production, notably sugar. Of its total 1954 production, 735,000 tons, Britain took about one-half, while the United States permitted the entry of but 27,000 tons. Other crops for export are coffee, cocoa, molasses, tobacco, rice, bananas, and sisal. A United States Point Four agreement entered into in March, 1951, has aided the production of better grades of tobacco. Too, expanding agriculture has been a policy of Dominicanization, that is, peopling the area along the Republic's border with Haiti.

The Trujillo government, anxious to release the country from foreign economic influences, succeeded in 1953 in paying off the external debt and subsequently the internal one. Much emphasis, too, has been placed upon developing industries to supply local demands for many industrial goods. These increased by several thousands between 1936 and 1955, and include the Río Haina sugar mill, one of the largest in the world. Because iron deposits have been found in the Río Haina area, the region is being considered suitable for establishing large-scale industries. Other undertakings include paper mills, to utilize bagasse as a raw material, and a hydroelectric plant. Begun in 1954, the latter is expected to double the production of electric power.

In international affairs the dictatorship re-established friendly relations with the Magloire government in Haiti. With the United States it signed a mutual assistance military pact in 1953, and granted bases for testing new weapons.

The harshness of the dictatorship had led to constant unrest on the island. Sugar workers, without political or other rights, have sought to better their lot by strikes. These have been crushed. Against Communists Trujillo has waged incessant warfare, although Dominican exiles insist that his campaign would be more effective if democratic institutions were re-established.

MODERN LATIN AMERICA

SECTION IV

Central America, Panama, and Mexico

Chapter XXVII

CENTRAL AMERICA AND
PANAMA

Part I. THE CENTRAL AMERICAN UNION AND FOREIGN
RIVALRY, 1823–1856

The Character of Central American History. Central America, the captaincy-general of Guatemala in the colonial period, maintained a unity until 1839, when it dissolved into the five Central American republics of Guatemala, Honduras, Nicaragua, El Salvador, and Costa Rica.

All inherited a colonial organization of society. Guatemala in 1821 had a population estimated at little more than 1,000,000. Its Maya Indians had a highly developed agricultural economy upon which the colonial Spanish families established a powerful feudal structure. El Salvador to the west, with its fine lands, partook of the character of Guatemala. However, a small, liberal, commercial group on the coast gave the country progressive ideas which became a source of conflict with the interior landholders.

Honduras, with its mountainous character and long, swamp-like Atlantic coast, provided less foothold for a strong landed gentry, while the smaller number of Indians and their extensive intermarriage with the Spaniards gave the population a dominant *mestizo* element. Nicaragua, geographically similar to Honduras, had the bulk of its population in the western highlands. More centrally located and with better facilities for trade along the San Juan River, Nicaragua developed at León a small but vigorous commercial class which constantly opposed the interests of the oligarchy in the interior city of Granada. The population, too, like that of Honduras, became predominantly *mestizo* in the course of the colonial period.

Differing sharply from the others was Costa Rica. Its small native population soon succumbed to Spanish colonizers, although intermarriage gave practically every Costa Rican Indian blood. The consequent lack of Indian labor provided no inducement for establishing a system of large landownership. On the contrary, Costa Rica attracted Spaniards with little capital who tilled the soil for themselves and laid a basis for a later democratic society.

The United Provinces of Central America, 1823–1839. In July, 1823, as has been noted, these five countries proclaimed their independence and created the United Provinces of Central America. But the preceding years of revolt against Spain and Iturbide had already divided the country into conservative and liberal groups. Throughout Central America a sturdy body of intellectuals and commercial leaders, influenced by the writings of Rousseau and other eighteenth century thinkers, advocated a federal form of government, the ending of ecclesiastical privileges, and land reforms. The conservative elements, frequently called the *Moderatos* or *Serviles,* stood for a strong centralized government, the continuation of the privileges of the church and military, and maintenance of the system of landholding.

When the constituent assembly convened in 1823 to draw up a constitution, the liberal forces dictated the provisions of the document. Promulgated on November 22, 1824, and modeled upon that of the United States, the charter called for a president, a bicameral legislature, and a judiciary, with the chief power in congress. Important provisions defined property rights, made the press free, as well as public education, regulated trade and finance, and abolished titles and colonial monopolies. While congress chose the president, election was by popular vote; the congress itself, composed of seventeen representatives, was chosen from the five states. Before the assembly adjourned, it enacted legislation ending slavery and gave freedom to fugitive slaves in Central America. This was the first instance of abolition of slavery in the New World, the work of Antonio Cañas.

On April 21, 1825, the first congress elected Manual José Arce president. The struggle between the liberal and conservative forces began at once. Arce, refusing to give an accounting of his spending of the British loan, threatened to dissolve congress, while throughout the country in the various states liberal programs were reducing the power of the church. In El Salvador, Juan Delgado, a priest who had liberal support, succeeded in having that state name him bishop. The action drew the wrath of the archibishop of Guatemala, also offended by anticlerical reforms and the growth of French liberal ideas in El Salvador. Urging Arce to action, the latter arrested the Guatemalan chief of state, Juan Barundia, and attempted to assemble an extraordinary congress under his control. With *Servile* support Arce invaded El Salvador, an action which brought the Honduran liberals into the resulting civil war.

By 1829 a new leader of the liberals, Francisco Morazán, a Honduran, took command. A man of superior intelligence and marked military ability, Morazán quickly defeated the armies of Arce and freed El Salvador. In Guatemala itself, in answer to appeals of liberals suffering from the arbitrary rule of the *Serviles,* Morazán invaded with aid from El Salvador, Nicaragua, and Honduras. Winning control of the country, he launched a reform program which included the expulsion of the archbishop and the leading *Serviles* and confiscation of church properties to secure funds for the depleted treasury. The proceeds soon found an excellent outlet in the hands of Mariano Gálvez, a great liberal leader who became chief of Guatemala in 1831. He built schools and hospitals and developed plans for a canal through Nicaragua. Civil marriage was made the law. The Louisiana Code, drawn up by Edward Livingston, whom Gálvez greatly admired, was introduced as part of the judicial reforms of the state. Priests were encouraged to marry; freedom of religion was decreed, and Protestant groups urged to enter the country. Other states of the Confederation enacted similar laws. Under the reforms agriculture revived and trade grew rapidly.

But in the midst of these changes inaugurated by Morazán, the Confederation was threatened by invasion when, in 1829, Spain launched her attack upon Mexico under General Barradas. Honduras took steps to protect her long coastline, while the conservatives in exile gathered behind Arce in Mexico and sought Spanish aid in Cuba. In El Salvador a conservative group revolted and withdrew that state from the Confederation. Out of fear of Spanish designs, both Nicaragua and Costa Rica gave Morazán support for his attack upon El Salvador. By 1832 his vigorous campaigns had overthrown the conservative threat, while the defeat of the Spanish forces in Mexico ended the danger in that quarter.

The peace was only temporary, for the church and the conservatives could never reconcile themselves to the loss of their privileges. Among the superstitious Indians, the priests stirred up a violent hatred of the liberals, a tactic which won success when a terrible cholera epidemic broke out in 1836–1837. The efforts of the government to stem its ravages among the Indians by sending doctors and medical students into the stricken areas failed. The Indians on their part, whipped into a frenzy by the priests, came to believe that the liberals were deliberately destroying them to turn their lands over to an English colonization venture in

Vera Paz. A general insurrection broke out with conservative support led by an ignorant *mestizo,* Rafael Carrera. With a rare gift of control over the Indians, Carrera was able to defeat Morazán in 1838, who fled to El Salvador and later to Chile, while Carrera proclaimed an end of the pact of Union in 1839.

Efforts to Restore the Union. For the next ten years Carrera, with the support of the Guatemala oligarchy, tried to extirpate the idea of a Central American Union. Morazán himself, returning from exile and landing in Costa Rica, was at first received well, but soon afterward seized and executed. With him passed the main hope of re-establishing a United States of Central America. In Guatemala, Carrera consolidated his power, but in the neighboring states of Nicaragua, Honduras, and El Salvador, liberal supporters of the idea of union fostered revolts against him. In 1849 he was forced from control, but returned again in a few months. His successor, Mariano Paredes, remained president, but the congress of the state conferred power anew upon Carrera to wage war upon the supporters of federalism. Thus in 1851 with a strong army, he defeated the combined forces of El Salvador and Honduras, a blow which destroyed the final hopes of the liberals to create their long-sought union.

Part II. BRITISH AND AMERICAN RIVALRY IN CENTRAL AMERICA, 1826–1856

Origin of Rivalry. Upon dissolution in 1839 the several states became involved in the imperial and commercial interests of Britain and the United States. Britain had from the seventeenth century a foothold in Central America at Belize. The establishment of independence opened this part of Central America to her trade. On the part of the United States the growth of American trade in the Caribbean had expanded to Central America even before the end of the Wars for Independence. The fostering of this interest found expression in a commercial treaty (1825) with the Confederation. Britain and America soon found themselves involved in seeking concessions for a canal route. The United States had already indicated its interest when it gave instructions to the delegates of the Pan-American Conference in 1826. President Arce on the part of the Confederation favored the Nicaragua route and tried to interest the United States in it. In 1835 the Central American Congress offered the United States a grant to construct such a canal. Thereafter, until 1848, American citizens, as well as British, French, and Dutch, advanced numerous projects for a canal.

In these same years, while Britain opposed the efforts of the United States to secure a concession from Nicaragua, she continued to hold the Mosquito Coast with a force at Bluefields, in spite of the Spanish-British Treaty of 1783. In 1830, with control of the coast assured, she was satisfied to see the dissolution of the Central American Union which threatened her interests. In 1838 the British actually expelled Central American authorities from the Bay Islands. Three years later Britain established the King of Mosquitia at the mouth of the San Juan River as an ally, drove out Nicaraguan officials, and rejected protests of their government. Nicaragua's appeal to the United States received in reply only President Polk's 1845 presidential message restating the Monroe Doctrine, that is, that the United States was opposed to the establishment of any European colony or dominion on the North American continent.

After the war with Mexico, Elijah Hise, the American minister to Guatemala, warned in December, 1848, that the British were trying to secure control of ports on both coasts while rejecting Nicaraguan demands to end British dominion over the Mosquitia area. Without authority Hise negotiated a treaty with Nicaragua, which, supporting the latter's claims to the Caribbean coast in defiance of the British, recognized the dominant interest of the United States in a canal route.

The discovery of gold in California in 1849 rapidly enlarged American activities in Central America. In that year Commodore Vanderbilt established the Accessory Transit Line along the San Juan River, crossing Lake Nicaragua, and continuing as a stage coach route to the coast at San Juan del Sur. E. G. Squier who followed Hise as minister, negotiated another treaty with Nicaragua in September, 1849, which, recognizing Nicaraguan sovereignty, guaranteed the neutrality of the canal route and gave exclusive rights to America to construct a canal. Britain, meanwhile, was not idle. Her consul ordered Tigre Island off the Honduran coast seized for claims against that country, but withdrew when Clayton, the American Secretary of State, recalled the American consul from Belize.

The Clayton-Bulwer Treaty, 1850. By 1849 the position of the two nations, Britain and America, had been defined. Great Britain under Palmerston did not want to build a canal, but she did wish to hold the Mosquitia territory and San Juan as bases for expanding her interest into Central America. The United States, for which a canal, after the gold discoveries in California, had become vitally necessary, wished the

Central American nations to have complete sovereignty over their territory as a prerequisite for treaties extending canal concessions. As these facts emerged from the discussion in London where, because of tense feeling between Great Britain and America, the American representatives were negotiating directly with Palmerston, the foundation was apparent for a settlement of differences, achieved in the Clayton-Bulwer Treaty of 1850.

Its main provisions were that neither nation would secure or maintain exclusive rights over the proposed Nicaraguan canal route; neither would erect or maintain fortifications commanding the vicinity of the canal; neither would occupy, fortify, colonize, or assume or exercise dominion over any part of Central America. Each party further agreed not to make use of any protectorate or alliance either might have to fortify or colonize; each agreed to invite the other nations to make similar treaties. Finally, and by no means of least import, both agreed to extend their protection to any other practical route through the isthmian area. The latter had special reference to the Tehuantepec and Panama routes.

The treaty did not end the conflict between the United States and Britain in Central America. For the next six years the five republics continued to find themselves the pawns of the imperial interests of the two great nations. Almost immediately upon signing the treaty, a dispute arose as to the meaning of its provisions. The British felt that the treaty confirmed their holdings in the area. In pursuit of that idea and possibly for the purpose of blocking the growing American activities, they annexed the Bay Islands in 1852. Protests of Nicaragua and the United States, however, led the British in 1860 to sign a treaty which restored Nicaraguan sovereignty over her eastern coast.

While the Central Americans were being forced into the pattern of British and American rivalry, they also found themselves in the midst of competing American groups for the control of the transportation through Central America, more particularly Nicaragua. Vanderbilt's Accessory Transit Company by 1854 had a monopoly upon all travel through Nicaragua. Adversely affected were the commercial groups, traders, and small landowners in liberal León. Anxious to share in the wealth that would come from accommodating Nicaragua to the needs of the growing volume of travelers on their way to California, the Liberal party struggled with the conservatives, then called Legitimists, for control of the national government. To strengthen their forces the Liberals sought to recruit American volunteers on promises of land. Their offers caught the attention of Vanderbilt's rivals in New York and San Francisco, who, to further their interests, enlisted William Walker, already known for his filibustering activities in Sonora. Walker himself, originally from Tennessee, believed that Central America should be annexed to the United States as a slaveholding area, a project that he saw would also open opportunities for himself to gain wealth from the commerce of the region.

Arriving in Nicaragua in 1855, he enlisted in the Liberal cause, defeating in the next year the Legitimists and becoming the military head of the Nicaraguan armed forces. Intent upon getting control of the transit route, he had Vanderbilt's concession canceled and transferred to a company in which he had a large interest. He was recognized by the United States as the chief of a *de facto* government largely because of American antagonism to British interests in Central America. Vanderbilt on his part supported Costa Rica and other governments in their protests against what they called the illegal overthrow of the Nicaraguan government by filibusters. To meet the combined forces directed against him, Walker had himself elected president of Nicaragua in 1856, but his army suffered severe setbacks from the able leadership of President Mora, who commanded the Costa Rican army. Eventually cut off from supplies, Walker left the presidency in 1857. Later, making two attempts to regain his power, he was killed on the second occasion in 1860 by a Honduran force.

Part III. LIBERAL TRENDS AND FOREIGN DOMINATION, SINCE 1856

The Character of Central American History. Between 1856 and 1890 the Central American countries plunged into what, on the surface, seemed to be meaningless struggles, but which in fact reflected differences over vital principles. Independence had brought union to the five provinces, and, among liberals and the commercial classes, the acceptance of democratic ideas. Strong-willed men, caught up by these ideals, fought and in many cases sacrificed their property and lives for them. While far from being established by 1890, the liberal tradition constantly reflected itself in the speeches of its leaders, in constitutions, and in the record of civil conflicts and international wars between the countries. After 1890 official American interest in an isthmian route and private investments in banana and coffee lands brought a strong conservative element into the traditional struggle. In spite of powerful opposition, or possibly because of it, liberal movements continued to struggle for democratic practices in the individual countries in the twentieth century.

NICARAGUA, 1856 TO THE PRESENT

Conservative Control to 1893. The occupation of the presidential chair by a foreigner seemed to have a sobering effect upon the Nicaraguan political parties. Following Walker's overthrow, General Tomás Martínez, who had performed brilliantly in the allied campaigns, became president with the support of both political parties. He began the reconstruction of the country under peaceful conditions until the end of his second term in 1867. He revived trade, arranged for the payment of the public debt, and presented the country with a new constitution in 1858. Until 1893 Martínez was followed by a succession of conservative presidents whose governments, with few exceptions, maintained the peace that Martínez had inaugurated.

Zelaya and Liberal Reforms, 1893–1909. The long dominance of the Conservatives ended in 1893. The commercial groups in León, stronghold of liberalism, led by José Santos Zelaya, gave expression to nationalistic feelings opposing foreign economic penetration. At the same time Zelaya's dictatorship, which lasted until 1909, improved and extended railroads and lake transportation, established schools, aided the coffee industry, beautified the capital, Managua, and sent Nicaraguan students abroad to study. Extravagance, ruthless punishment of his enemies, principally the conservatives of Granada, and disregard of personal rights marred his rule.

In foreign affairs Zelaya's policies antagonized Washington and brought Nicaragua within the orbit of its intervention. The first step occurred in 1906 when El Salvador, aiding a revolt against Estrada Cabrera in Guatemala, secured the support of the United States and Mexico to bring peace. Under the inspiration of the United States a conference met at San José to draw up an agreement guaranteeing the *status quo,* but Zelaya, opposed, placed his puppet, Miguel Dávila, in power in Honduras and stirred up a new revolt in El Salvador and other neighboring states to create, he claimed, a Confederation of Central American states.

The United States next invited all the Central American countries to send representatives to the Washington Conference of 1907. Their attempt to create a Central American Union failed, but the delegates agreed to refer disputes between them to a Central American Court of Justice established for the purpose in Costa Rica in the next year. They further agreed to neutralize Honduras, the scene of so many conflicts between the states, and to refrain from interfering in one another's affairs, or changing the fundamental law of any of their countries. Other agreements looked toward establishing identical values for currency, similar tariff regulations, and measures to facilitate trade and travel.

These agreements did not bring peace to Central America. Zelaya in 1909, trying to counterbalance the growing American influence in the region, negotiated a loan of £1,500,000 with a British business syndicate and made overtures to Japan to build a canal. When a revolution against him in that year occurred on the east coast, he crushed it, executing two Americans who had joined as volunteers. The United States, sympathizing with the rebels and sharply condemning Zelaya's action, forced him from office. When his successor, José Madriz, attempted to crush the revolt anew, American action prevented capture of the rebels' base at Bluefields. Juan J. Estrada, a Liberal, seized power, but when opposed by other candidates threatened to plunge Nicaragua into a new civil war. The United States intervened and brought about the Dawson Agreements in 1910, under which Estrada remained president for two years with his principal rival, Adolfo Díaz, as vice-president. In 1911 the Estrada government negotiated the Knox-Castrillo treaty providing for an American to collect custom house dues to guarantee payments on a loan proposed in the treaty. The United States Senate, however, refused ratification on the ground that American bankers had secured unjustified concessions. Nevertheless, Nicaragua secured a loan of $1,500,000 from an American bank, which placed an American agent in the office of collector-general of the customs to insure interest charges and repayment of the loan.

These events forced Estrada's resignation in 1911, to be succeeded by Díaz, a Conservative supported by a popular military figure, Emiliano Chamorro. Opposition nevertheless continued, and led Díaz to appeal for aid to the United States, which promptly sent a force of marines, who, controlling the election of 1913, placed Díaz in power. This event ended the hopes of the Liberals and opened the way for further favorable agreements with the United States. When Díaz assumed the presidency, the country was bankrupt. American bankers who had extended the loan to the Estrada government had secured control of the National Bank of Nicaragua to reform the currency and set up a Claims Commission, which recognized $1,750,000 owing to American citizens.

To relieve the difficulties, Díaz next proposed a canal treaty with the United States in return for cash. The negotiations were completed by his successor, President Chamorro, likewise put in office with marine support, and Secretary of State William J. Bryan, long a critic of imperialism. Under the Bryan-Chamorro Treaty, ratified and signed August 5, 1914, Nicaragua gave the United States exclusive rights and exemption from taxation to build a canal via the San Juan River and Lake Nicaragua or anywhere else. To protect the canal, Nicaragua provided bases for ninety-nine years to Great and Little Corn Islands on the east coast and the right to establish a naval base on the Gulf of Fonseca. In return the United States agreed to pay Nicaragua $3,000,000.

Opposition to the treaty in Nicaragua and the other Central American states was widespread. The latter claimed that it violated Costa Rica's rights in the San Juan River and those of Honduras, Guatemala, and El Salvador in the Gulf of Fonseca, since the waters of both were indivisible. Meanwhile, Nicaraguan Liberals, mostly businessmen, saw their future foreclosed by foreign control of the country's principal trade route and its greatest potential source of income. They also condemned the price paid, feeling that the canal route had a greater value. Their attitude became more antagonistic when creditors, mostly foreign, were paid $2,000,000, leaving the remaining $1,000,000 as the actual sum received by the country and that sum totally inadequate to meet her internal obligations.

To meet this problem of internal debt, the American and Nicaraguan governments agreed in 1917 to establish a high commission, with one of the three representatives a Nicaraguan. This commission and the American collector of the customs virtually ruled the country. The commission, of unquestioned integrity, in the next ten years reduced the nation's debt, met the interest on its foreign bonds, restored to Nicaragua the ownership of its railway and its National Bank, and made a number of improvements in road building and harbor improvements. While these achievements were beneficial, the Liberals still insisted that Nicaragua should run its own affairs.

The Conservatives continued in power after the election of 1920 when the president's uncle, Diego Chamorro, became chief executive (1920–1924). By the latter date, with a national constabulary established and the marines withdrawn, the Liberals won the election. However, the defeated Conservative candidate, Emiliano Chamorro, soon seized the government. The United States again intervened in 1926. But Juan Bautista Sacasa, the Liberal vice-president, refused to accept the decision of the State Department, the selection of the Conservative, Adolfo Díaz, as president. Leading a revolt, Sacasa established a government on the east coast at Puerto Cabezas and was promptly recognized by Mexico. The United States, condemning the Mexican action, sent marines to protect Díaz and the property and lives of its nationals.

By this date the whole of Latin America, supported by liberal circles in the United States, was rising in criticism of the United States action. The storm of protest forced President Coolidge in 1927 to send Henry L. Stimson to find a solution. He succeeded in persuading the Liberals to disarm, with but one exception, César Agusto Sandino, whose followers continued in revolt.

Sandino, besides expressing the ideas of many Nicaraguans who wished to see foreign control ended, attracted followers by his program of internal reform. He advocated the development of cooperatives to raise the standard of living and the breaking up of foreign ownership in land to create a small landholding class; and he emphasized the importance of developing Nicaragua's natural resources—forests, minerals, and agriculture. The strength of his support and the mountainous character of northern Nicaragua where he took refuge made marine campaigns against him useless. On the other hand, his resistance caught the imagination of Latin Americans, who by this time were strongly critical of United States policy in the Caribbean and Central America.

Under the Stimson arrangement Díaz served until 1928. In that year the presidential election, held under marine supervision, resulted, to the consternation of the State Department, in an overwhelming victory for the Liberals led by General Sacasa. In 1934, after President F. D. Roosevelt had withdrawn the marines, Sacasa sought an understanding with Sandino and invited him to the capital. There Sandino was assassinated, responsibility for which action was assumed by General Anastacio Somoza, commander of the National Guard, the former Nicaraguan constabulary. The event was in fact connected with Conservative fears of the Liberal reform program and foretold Conservative determination to establish a dictatorship. Thus when the 1936 elections came, Somoza, in control of the only significant force in the country, dictated his own election.

The Somoza Dictatorship, 1936 to the Present. During Somoza's long rule he has been at pains to maintain good relations with the United

States. On October 1, 1936, Nicaragua entered into a reciprocal trade agreement which admitted United States goods but also opened markets for her exports in the northern republic. This agreement aided Nicaragua to meet the depression and complemented Somoza's internal measures, the extension of government bank credits to businessmen, planters, and farmers and the absorption of unemployment in a public works program and highway construction.

Preparing for the elections of 1939, Somoza promulgated a constitution in March of that year, which, besides making him eligible for re-election, contained advanced provisions including freedom of worship, public education, protection of mothers and children in industry, regulation of labor, social security, and protection of property rights. Under this document Somoza was elected chief executive on March 30, 1939.

In World War II Somoza cooperated with the United States to secure aid for Nicaragua's development. Notable was the agreement of April 8, 1942, to build Nicaragua's portion of the Inter-American Highway, completed in 1948, and a new highway linking the Pacific and Atlantic coasts. In return the United States secured the right to develop a zone at Corinto for her Caribbean defense program and access to Nicaragua's raw materials.

Somoza, whose business acumen saw the necessity for schools, carried on a small but continuous building program. In September, 1945, he launched a campaign to abolish illiteracy. For that purpose the government provided traveling schools and supplies including primers and readers.

In 1947 Somoza retired from the presidency temporarily until 1950, permitting the election of Dr. Leonardo Argüello, who was inaugurated on May 4, 1947. The new president, proving too liberal in outlook, was removed before the end of the month. Provisional President Benjamín Lacayo Sacasa served until August 15, when Dr. Victor Román y Reyes took up the task. Upon Román's death in April, 1950, congress selected Somoza to finish the term. During this period Somoza evolved a formula for the elections under which, in agreement with the Conservatives, the Liberal party was to receive forty seats in congress while the Conservatives were guaranteed twenty. With no alternative, the Conservative leader, Emiliano Chamorro, accepted. Somoza, elected on May 21, 1950, put the new plan into effect. In November he promulgated a new constitution, confirming the arrangement in a provision calling for minority representation. Another provision fixed his term at six years. By dictatorial methods during the next five years he completed the process of virtually reducing Nicaragua to his private estate. In the spring of 1954, however, because of widespread opposition to his rule, he felt constrained to change the constitution to permit immediate re-election. Thus in 1955, maneuvering to divide the opposing groups, he set the stage for his return to the presidency.

As president after 1950, Somoza announced a very liberal program which, however, remained largely on paper. Its chief significance is its revelation of what the liberal forces in the country were demanding: mechanization of agriculture to achieve self-sufficiency, wage increases for urban labor, improvement of the status of rural workers, enforcement of the labor code, a social security program, more schools, hospitals, road building, and electrification of towns along the Pacific coast.

The measures carried out were naturally those which contributed to his own well-being and that of his supporters—landowners, industrialists, and the military. The less fortunate remained little changed in status. Teachers' salaries ranged between $23 and $35 a month; the average wage of urban workers was one dollar a day. The General Confederation of Nicaraguan Workers in fact declared that in 1950 rural labor was in about the same status it suffered in the colonial period. Attempts to improve wage and working conditions of rural, mining, and urban labor met repressive legislation. Indicative of basic conditions is the illiteracy rate, about 70 per cent, in a population of 1,530,000.

Among measures given effect that will in time benefit the country as a whole is a road building program. The most important project of all is the San Benito-Ramoa highway, begun under a United States-Nicaraguan agreement in 1942, which has been continued with $4,000,000 provided under the United States Federal Aid Highway Act. Other road building programs, aided by loans from the International Bank for Reconstruction and Development, are designed to link the interior with the capital, Managua, and the latter with provincial capitals, León and Granada, and with coastal towns. During the war years and subsequently Nicaragua enjoyed profitable exports from coffee, gold, rubber, cotton (somewhat mechanized), sesame, lumber, and cattle. Its population, however, as a whole suffered from high prices caused by shortages of basic foods. To meet this problem in some degree, Somoza, through Point Four, secured United States technicians to advise on improved methods of producing rice, corn, beans, and other foods.

In foreign affairs Somoza declared himself a partisan of Central American unity. He also aided the efforts of Castillo Armas to overthrow the Arbenz government in Guatemala. A more significant index to his

basic Central American outlook, however, appears in his active support
of exiles who attempted the overthrow of Costa Rica's democratic government in 1949 and again in 1955.

Nicaragua's history reveals a long record of foreign intervention
and internal dictatorship. Nevertheless, there have been attempts to
make its government more representative. These, in the past twenty years,
have been successfully blocked by the Somoza dictatorship.

GUATEMALA, 1839 TO THE PRESENT

Rafael Carrera, who had destroyed the Union of Central America in 1839
and established a dictatorship in Guatemala, provided that state with a
new constitution in 1851 which made it independent and sovereign. Its
other features included provisions for a president, a Council of State, and
a House of Representatives. Conferring citizenship only upon those who
had a profession, land, or business effectively confined political power
to the upper classes, excluded the bulk of the *mestizos,* and reduced the
Indians to their former status of serfdom. The actual selection of a president was restricted to an assembly of the lower house of congress, the
archbishop, the supreme court justices, and the Council of State. These
provisions successfully blocked any liberal movement until 1870.

Carrera, becoming president under the new fundamental law, remained in office until 1863. During these years Guatemala joined in the
overthrow of Walker, exiled its liberals, and did not hesitate to interfere
in other Central American countries to block attempts to re-create the
Union. When Carrera died in 1865, his successor, Vicente Cerna, held
office until 1871. In that year the Liberals captured control of the country
by a violent revolution to open a period of democratic growth.

Rufino Barrios, Founder of Guatemalan Democracy, 1873–1885. Two
figures at this moment, Miguel García Granados and Justo Rufino Barrios,
provided the vigorous leadership which broke down the feudal character
of the Guatemalan state. García Granados, provisional president until
1873, put down conservative uprisings and began the confiscation of
large landed estates for distribution among the predominant Indian
population. With order restored, Rufino Barrios became president in a
peaceful election on June 4, 1873. Barrios first directed the reform program at the dominant position of the church. He exiled the Jesuits,
suppressed compulsory tithing, ended all religious orders, and confiscated
the property of many of the latter. He abolished the special courts of

the church, requiring the clergy to subject themselves to the civil law, established complete freedom of religion, instituted civil marriage, and forbade all processions and the wearing of the clerical habit in public. Education he placed under state control. The constitution drawn up in 1879 separated church and state, a measure which, together with his decrees, not disturbed by later governments, effectively ended the church's political power in Guatemala.

Reorganizing the administration of the state, Rufino Barrios defined the functions of the governors, or *jefes políticos,* of the provinces. Their new authority gave them wider power to maintain order in the departments (provinces), to preserve peace between the Indians and the rest of the population, the *ladinos,* collect taxes, make education effective, foster agriculture, and draw up a census for the guidance of the national government.

To enrich the country's food resources and provide exports, Barrios outlined a land program which included free land to those cultivating cotton, rice, rubber, cocoa, and bananas. Trees and seed to cultivate plants providing drugs and herbs native to Guatemala, such as quinine and sarsaparilla, were offered free by the government. Carried out, this program made basic changes in Guatemala's economy. Linked to Barrios' agricultural plans was the construction of roads which connected the capitals of most departments with the national capital, Guatemala City. His highway construction took the first steps to connect the Atlantic and Pacific coasts. At the same time he developed plans for railroad building, improved harbors, and built bridges, municipal works, and telephone and telegraph lines. To provide eventually a literate population, Barrios established free public schools with compulsory attendance, besides a normal school, several superior (high) schools, and a military academy. The university, too, became a state institution.

To put a floor under his reform program, Barrios promulgated the constitution of 1879. This document, in common with the other liberal constitutions of Latin America, placed sovereignty in the people by providing for the election of the president and the congress by direct popular vote. Any citizen, moreover, not a member of the clergy could be elected to any office. The form of government was unitary in that while the three divisions, executive, legislative, and judicial, were provided for, there were no restrictions upon the central government in the exercise of its powers in the departments into which the country was divided. These powers of the central government, however, were qualified in a bill of rights which guaranteed complete freedom of education, speech, press, and religion. One provision was distinctive in that no person was required to testify against himself or his family. Separation of church and state was likewise provided for.

In international affairs, Barrios continued to uphold the ideal of a Central American Union. However, the strong opposition in the neighboring states led him to resort to force to achieve the union. In March, 1885, he led an army for this purpose into El Salvador, but in a battle on April 2 of that year, he was killed. The work of Barrios was carried on by his successors in office, although none of them fully observed the constitution of 1879. In 1891, when new elections were held to fill the office of president, María Reyna Barrios became chief executive to serve until 1898. Succeeding him on October 2 of that year was Manuel Estrada Cabrera, the second strong man in Guatemala's history, who held office until September, 1920.

Estrada Cabrera continued many of the aspects of the work begun by Barrios. He aided the development of agriculture, constructed highways and railroads, and gave considerable support to education, although teachers were forbidden to criticize his administration. Public health advanced with the generous support of the Rockefeller Foundation. In foreign affairs his administration continued the controversy over the boundary between Guatemala and British Honduras.

By 1920 his government had produced, through his arbitrary actions, a host of enemies who formed the Union party to overthrow him. The depression after World War I severely restricted exports and brought unemployment. Discontent gave rise to the Guatemalan labor movement, whose origin in various mutual societies dated from 1872. By 1910 many unions were established among the agricultural workers, who set up in 1912 the Federation of Workers' Societies. World War I gave the movement an impetus to the formation of the country's principal union, the Labor Federation of Guatemala for the Legal Protection of Labor. This body joined with the Union party to force the national assembly to call for Estrada Cabrera's abdication on April 14, 1920.

José M. Orellana followed the dictator in the presidency. He, too, was faced with financial chaos resulting from loss of markets and considerable reckless spending under his predecessor. He devoted his administration to revival of trade and employment. On his death in 1925 Lázaro Chacón followed as president to serve until 1930.

The depression of 1929, striking a new blow at the economy of Guatemala, brought to the presidency Jorge Ubico in February, 1930, to serve for six years. Ubico, taking advantage of the disorganization of the labor unions in the face of almost universal unemployment, established a harsh dictatorship which lasted until 1945. In common with many dictators, Ubico made his country safe for foreigners at the expense of the well-being of the Guatemalan people. During his rule foreign ownership of banana and coffee lands produced 90 per cent of the export of the country. The banana lands were American controlled; the coffee lands, German. The average wage for workers on the plantations was approximately fifteen cents a day, while dockworkers earned as high as seven to twelve cents an hour. These low standards naturally gave rise to discontent, which in turn was put down with repressive measures. The chief abuse was forced labor by Indians on plantations, together with a road building program which provided with forced labor some 3,000 miles of unpaved roads.

Ubico maintained his dictatorship through the use of a national police system which replaced local government. His own political party, called the Liberal Progressive, furnished the leaders for the urban and rural "front" organizations which demanded his re-election in 1940. However, no such election was held; Ubico merely continued in office, believing that any deference to democratic forms by this date was unnecessary. World War II brought prosperity to the country; its sale of products and the taxes on its exports provided funds for making his control more effective. Before the conflict ended, unemployment and falling government revenues prepared the way for a popular revolt on October 19, 1944, which drove Ubico from the country. The effects of the Ubico dictatorship, with its ruthless suppression of labor, opened the way for the entrance of Marxian ideas among its leaders. Moreover, the bulk of the intellectuals and businessmen, as well as some labor leaders returning from exile in the United States, were determined to make reforms in Guatemalan political and economic life.

Guatemalan Development since 1945. The leaders of the revolt put in power three men, a Committee of Liberation, to cleanse the country of Ubico's local despots and prepare for elections and a new constitution. By March, 1945, Juan José Arévalo, a former schoolteacher, was elected president and a new constitution adopted. This document, however, was set aside in 1954 in the revolution which brought Castillo Armas to power.

Arévalo began the construction of schools, improvement of sanitation, and low-cost housing for workers. He launched a campaign to

abolish illiteracy. Because of oppression under Ubico and the spread of
Soviet propaganda, Communism also secured a foothold among the proletariat. As a result, a number of leading labor organizations, dominated
by Communists, successfully elected some of their number to government
offices, both local and national. When presidential elections were held
in December, 1950, Jacobo Arbenz, supported by Arévalo, was elected
president. The new executive took office in the following March.

The Arbenz Administration, 1951–1954. The Arbenz government
drew its principal source of income from the export of coffee, which
in 1952–1953 produced the largest crop in its history, valued at $71,-
000,000, and which represented 80 per cent of Guatemala's exports.
Others were bananas, essential oils, cacao beans, and rice. The latter by
1953 provided an exportable surplus. Corn production was sufficient to
meet the nation's needs, but transportation, or rather the lack of it,
hindered distribution.

Labor organizations multiplied rapidly under the Arbenz administration and united themselves under Communist leadership into a nation-
wide organization, the Guatemalan Federation of Labor. The government
in general supported strikes for increased pay and improved working
conditions. Especially were the United States companies, the United
Fruit Company and Pan-American Airways, and the American and
British-owned International Railways of Central America beset with
strikes and walkouts.

However, the most striking action of the government which had
strong Communist support was legislation in 1952 expropriating large
estates for division among Indian peasants. In August, 1952, the government distributed lands held by Germans seized during World War II.
Early in 1953 it confiscated 225,000 acres of United Fruit lands on the
Pacific coast. The next startling development in May, 1954, was the
arrival at Puerto Barrios on the eastern coast of a ship from Poland
bearing 2,000 tons of arms for the Arbenz government. This event
had the double effect of alerting the United States to the danger of
Communism in Guatemala and giving stimulus to a revolt against the
Arbenz regime.

The Castillo Armas Government, 1954 to the Present. Washington
immediately sent military equipment to reinforce the armies of Honduras
and Nicaragua. At the same time a revolutionary movement took form
in June led by Colonel Carlos Castillo Armas. Within Guatemala, army
leaders, fearing distribution of the recently arrived weapons to workers
and peasants, supported Castillo Armas. Superior air power in the latter's

hands also proved a decisive factor. By the end of June the revolt had forced Arbenz out of office, leaving Colonel Elfego Monzón, an anti-Communist landowner, in control. After peace was re-established, Monzón was replaced by Castillo Armas as the head of a junta set up to rule Guatemala. In July he survived an effort of the army to oust him and in the following months successfully cleared the Communists out of the government and labor unions. In October a plebiscite confirmed his power and simultaneously chose members of a constituent assembly to draw up a new constitution. On November 6 Castillo Armas was sworn in as president of Guatemala to serve a five-year term (1954–1959).

As president, Castillo Armas attempted to rehabilitate the economy of the country. His greatest handicap was the lack of funds, for the treasury had been emptied by the revolutionary effort; many believed, too, that the Arbenz government had hidden funds abroad. The president's first efforts were directed to raising money by imposing an income tax. Because this tax was resented by the wealthier classes, an attempt was made, with army leadership, to oust the president in January, 1955, but it failed. The government came to an understanding with the United Fruit Company, returning to it the land confiscated under the Arbenz regime. The company on its part agreed to pay in taxes 30 per cent of its profits made in the country and to transfer to the government some 100,000 acres. Castillo Armas also extended liberal concessions to foreign companies exploring and developing Guatemala's oil resources.

Probably the most important work of the administration was the promulgation of a new constitution in 1956. This document proved surprisingly liberal. It guarantees freedom of worship. Juridical status is granted to all religious organizations so that the Catholic church for the first time since 1871 will be enabled to own property. On the other hand, members of the clergy are forbidden to hold political office. Suffrage is compulsory for literates and optional for those unable to read and write. Confiscation of property is forbidden, but expropriation of land not under cultivation is permitted. For labor, the constitution grants the rights to organize, to strike, to annual paid vacations, to equal salary for equal work, and a forty-eight-hour week and a minimum wage.

Guatemala has had a long history dating from Rufino Barrios, of liberal advances. Unfortunately the movement of reform after World War II became bogged down by Communist activity. From indications of the policies followed by Castillo Armas, the liberal movement still remains a powerful factor in shaping Guatemala's future.

HONDURAS, 1839 TO THE PRESENT

Honduras, in common with the other Central American states, joined the Union in 1824. At the same time a constituent assembly chose Dionisio Herrera, a Conservative, as chief of state and divided the country into seven districts. The Liberals, assuming that Herrera would resign upon ending the work of the assembly, revolted when he insisted upon continuing in office. But the Honduran conservatives had the support of Arce, president of the Confederation, as well as the church. During the next three years conflict between the two groups brought Morazán into power, who, establishing control of the Confederation after 1829, dictated the election of a Liberal government in Honduras. With Morazán's downfall, Honduras left the Union in a declaration of independence in October, 1838, reaffirmed the following month. In 1839 she adopted a new constitution, providing for a president to serve two years and a unicameral congress elected on the basis of population with voting restricted to those of eighteen years of age with a guaranteed income.

Under the new document Francisco Ferrera became president in January, 1841. Civil disturbances, largely due to the struggle between the Morazán Liberals and the Conservatives, were widespread. Ferrera spent most of his administration in the field, and after he was succeeded by Coronado Chávez in 1844, remained at the head of the army in the war against Nicaragua. Ferrera, refusing the presidency in 1847, put in Juan Lindo, a puppet, who declared war on the United States in June, 1847, for her invasion of Mexico. To continue in power, Lindo altered the constitution in 1848. In 1849 the Liberals revolted to overthrow him, but he was shortly returned with the aid of Conservative forces from El Salvador and Nicaragua. Upon being elected president in 1852, Lindo resigned, to be followed by Trinidad Cabañas, who defended the country from the encroachments and seizure of territory by Carrera in Guatemala. The Conservatives, however, aided by Carrera, overthrew Cabañas in 1855.

General Santos Guardiola, who had fought against Walker in Nicaragua, became the next president with Carrera's backing. Guardiola's principal achievement was to protect Honduran territory, with backing from the United States, against British attempts to seize strategic points. The interest of Britain dated back to the seventeenth century, when her logcutters and slave raiders established a post at Belize. After that date she steadily enlarged her holdings, while the government itself won, through treaties, recognition of ownership from Spain. When after 1850 the British tried to extend their possessions to include the Bay Islands and the Mosquito Coast, Honduras protested and eventually established recognition of Honduran ownership in a treaty with Great Britain in 1859.

Guardiola, succeeded by Victoriano Castellanos in 1862, cooperated with President Barrios in El Salvador against Carrera's efforts to overthrow their respective governments. Francisco Montes, who followed Castellanos shortly thereafter, was driven out in June, 1863, by the Honduran Conservatives, aided as usual by Carrera in Guatemala. With Senator José María Medina in as president, the Conservatives consolidated their power in October of that year in a new constitution which proscribed all religious bodies except the Catholic and concentrated power in the hands of the president and a Council of State. Medina dominated Honduras for the next ten years, doing nothing constructively for the country, but maintaining a harsh peace. In El Salvador leading liberals succeeded in overthrowing Medina in 1871 with the aid of Rufino Barrios. By 1873, with Medina driven out, Celeo Arías assumed power. A liberal constitution drawn up marked an effort to establish democratic practices, with provisions guaranteeing freedom of the press, rights of petition, and guarantees of life, liberty, and equality, as well as freedom to travel and assemble peacefully.

Arías did not prove to be a popular president. The Conservatives, taking advantage of discontent, kept up in the next five years constant disturbances which failed to return them to power but did lead to Medina's execution in 1878. Out of the conflict Marco Aurelio Soto became president in 1877, giving the country another constitution in 1880, also liberal in character but providing for a unicameral congress. He governed without serious disturbance until 1882. Luis Brogán, becoming president and sympathetic with Barrios in Guatemala, joined him in his effort to establish a union of Central America. Upon Barrios' death in 1885, Honduras quietly withdrew from the undertaking, negotiating a treaty of peace with El Salvador, Costa Rica, and Nicaragua.

During the next three decades Honduras continued to present politically the dreary picture of palace revolts among the wealthier families to place their respective sons, or rather fathers, in the presidential chair. The conflict threatened to become serious in 1907 when Zelaya of Nicaragua supported a revolt against the government of the then president, Manuel Bonilla. El Salvador, throwing her influence to Bonilla, brought

Guatemala into the controversy. At that point the United States and Mexico persauded the republics to join in the Washington Conference, dealt with elsewhere.

Economically, in this period Honduras became a major banana-producing area of Central America resulting from the investments of the American Fruit Company on the northern coast. There the company built railroads and improved ports. It also received concessions to land in the interior in return for promises to extend railroads to connect the coast with interior cities, particularly the capital, Tegucigalpa.

The interminable struggle for office after the Zelaya incident continued uninterrupted for another quarter of a century until a vigorous and somewhat ruthless general, Carías Andino, was elected by the conservative groups in 1933. Coming into power under depression conditions, Carías Andino met distress with a colonization plan in the rural areas and negotiated a reciprocal trade agreement with the United States in 1937 which enabled his country to find new markets for its products under favorable tariff reductions. However, the lack of liberty and unhappy effects of the depression stirred revolts of the liberal forces which were harshly put down. Under these circumstances the dictator maintained himself in power until 1948.

The Administrations of Juan Manuel Gálvez and Julio Lozano since 1949. Until this late date, 1949, Honduras, with a population estimated in 1950 at 1,533,625, predominantly *mestizo,* has remained an essentially feudal state. But inevitably the investment of foreign capital has created a middle class and labor group associated with the production of bananas, lumber, hemp, hides, gold, silver, and coffee. While these produce the principal sources of income for the government, the middle class, still tiny, has become conscious of the possibilities of exploiting the wealth of the forests of mahogany, cedar, sapodilla, pine, quebracho, and various rare woods. The new president, General Juan Manuel Gálvez, who took office in 1949 after Carías Andino retired, represented these new interests and took the first steps to modernize Honduran economy.

Recognizing that the first need was communications, the government laid plans in 1951 to connect Tegucigalpa and San Pedro Sula by highway with the rich lands of the west and with the Inter-American Highway. In 1952 the national legislature furthered the program by voting a bond issue of $10,000,000. In addition an all-weather road was projected to connect the capital with Puerto Cortés. In 1953 the program continued with a $4,000,000 bond issue to carry on work into 1954. In an effort to develop the resources opened up by the network of roads, the government created a Central Bank and Bank for Development, which were to extend loans to aid farmers and encourage scientific cattle breeding, forestation, and electrification. For this last in 1951 Honduras sought loans for a hydroelectric project on the Río Lindo. At the same time the government contracted to establish a modern telephone system in the two largest cities, Tegucigalpa and San Pedro Sula. Encouragement of industry brought the establishment by 1953 of a native-owned plywood industry at Puerto Castillo.

Significant of the new spirit of nationalism was the widespread but ineffective opposition in 1949 of businessmen and some landowners to the granting of a contract to the Tela Railroad Company (United Fruit) to develop palm oil, hemp, and cocoa plantations, on the ground that the resulting monopoly would be injurious to the nation's development. Even more striking evidence of nationalistic growth was the amendment to the constitution in 1951 extending Honduran jurisdiction seven and one-half miles offshore, with the further surprising declaration of control over the wealth of the continental underwater shelf, no matter how far that extended into both oceans from the nation's boundaries. In foreign affairs, too, Honduras has been willing to associate herself with her Central American neighbors in wiping out locust and other plagues, and in joining the Organization of Central American States.

To aid Honduran internal development, the United States Point Four program gave assistance in highway construction and in health and sanitation projects, besides expanding rural normal schools and agricultural agencies. Notable is the cultivation of unused lands with the aid of STICA, which in 1951 began the building of an agricultural school at Catacamas.

In 1951 a law benefiting the teaching profession also called for a basic study of educational needs. The necessity of the latter is evident in the government's statement in 1951 that Honduras had 306,725 children of school age, but educational facilities existed for barely 100,000. To remedy the lack the government planned extensive increases in both schools and in the number of teachers. In addition it established in Tegucigalpa a night school for adults and began plans for technical institutes. The United Fruit Company, to its credit, established in 1953 a school to abolish illiteracy among its workers, supplementing a program it had begun in 1951. The essential backwardness of the country's educational condition is apparent in its 45 per cent illiteracy rate.

The political condition of Honduras under Gálvez, in spite of his own generally liberal outlook, is a dictatorship of the Nationalist party, in power since 1933. In the presidential election of October, 1954, Carías Andino attempted to return to power. The election, eminently fair, resulted in a stalemate. Congress, summoned to decide, was blocked when the supporters of Carías Andino boycotted the session. However, with President Gálvez absent from the country, the first vice-president, Julio Lozano Díaz, assumed executive power.

Lozano, a successful businessman, has continued the policies of Gálvez and shown respect for constitutional government. His promise when he took power to direct the government toward "a normal democratic state" has been implemented by two important measures. One is the extension of political rights to all Honduran-born women; the other, legislation giving workers, for the first time in the history of Honduras, the right to form unions and strike, until a labor code, being drawn up with the assistance of international labor organizations, can be enacted into law.

Thus Honduras, with a colonial background and history of dictatorship almost identical with that of Nicaragua, seems to be seeking a more stable form of government by broadening the representation among its people.

EL SALVADOR, 1839 TO THE PRESENT

El Salvador, upon dissolution of the Central American Union, declared itself the Republic of El Salvador on January 30, 1841, and drew up a constitution in February of that year, conservative in character, for the state was dominated by Carrera in Guatemala and supported by Salvadorean conservatives and the church. Colonel Francisco Malespín succeeded in making himself president and shortly thereafter dictator in 1844. He restored ecclesiastical privileges, permitted the establishment of monasteries, and gave state support to church decrees. The liberals, unable to accept a clerical state, rose in revolt, driving Malespín out and exiling Bishop Viteri in 1847.

El Salvador now came under a liberal regime with Doneto Vasconcelos elected in 1848. His principal interest was an attempt to revive the union of Central America, while in foreign affairs he defended the country from efforts of the British to collect unjustifiable debts. When he attempted in 1851 to force Guatemala to join the union, war enveloped the three countries of Honduras, Guatemala, and El Salvador. During this struggle General Gerade Barrios, a liberal, emerged who fought against attempts of Carrera in Guatemala to dominate the country. By 1863, with Barrios defeated and fleeing the state, Carrera and the Salvadorean church placed Francisco Dueñas in power, imposing a strongly conservative constitution upon the nation.

The liberals, however, far from giving up the struggle, took advantage of Dueñas' war with Honduras in 1870 to revolt under General Santiago González. Overthrowing him, the liberals presented the country with a new constitution which revealed the developing liberal ideas in El Salvador. Adopted in October, 1871, the document provided for the usual framework of a republic—president, legislature, and judiciary. Other provisions called for freedom of assembly, speech, and press and freedom from illegal search. Primary education was made free and obligatory. While the Catholic religion remained that of the state, other Christian churches were tolerated. Suffrage had a broad basis, although military and church officials were neither allowed to vote nor hold office. Qualifications for holding office rested upon ownership of real estate, a fact not having the usual significance in Latin America, since much of the landholding was in small plots. The constituent assembly at the same time enacted important laws which provided universal suffrage, codification of the laws, and trial by jury. The president held office by amendment in 1872 for four years.

The González administration encouraged industries, extended public instruction, and improved the finances of the country. In 1876 reforms were halted when the country plunged into a war with Guatemala as a result of El Salvador's support of Honduras against the efforts of Rufino Barrios to bring about a union. El Salvador, defeated, signed a treaty which brought Rafael Zaldívar, a partisan of Barrios, to the presidency in July, 1876. He continued in office after the election of 1880, but his ardor cooled for Barrios' project for a union. Unfortunately, Barrios' threat of invasion drove him from the presidency and enabled General Francisco Menéndez to re-establish conservative control over the country.

When Barrios did invade in 1885 and was killed in battle, the conservatives were left with undisputed power to attempt to restore the usual feudal conditions characteristic of their outlook. Their new constitution, in deference to the liberal strength of the country, did not set aside all the features of that of 1871, and maintained the usual form of government, with a unicameral legislature, restriction of the president to one term of four years, and suffrage to citizens over eighteen or married, or who held a literary degree.

Between 1885 and 1898 the Conservative party consolidated its control, with the leading families agreeing among themselves to transfer power peacefully. Except for the assassination of a president in 1913, and an easily but bloodily crushed revolt in 1932, the Conservative government remained undisturbed. Outstanding in the El Salvadorean hierarchy was the Meléndez-Quiñones family whose power, broken in the late 1920's, opened the way for the virtual dictatorship of General Maximiliano Martínez (1932–1940).

By the end of World War II discontent with Martínez brought a violent military uprising and a general strike. Driven from power, he was succeeded by Salvador Castañeda Castro, elected in 1945. However, he, too, was removed in 1948 by another revolt, ending the constant siege under which he governed. The junta which took over in December, 1948, had the support of the liberal commercial class, slowly growing in numbers and wealth during the long winter of conservative control. By March, 1949, they had found their leader, Major Oscar Osorio, whom they put in the presidency and who also satisfied the more forward-looking landowners.

The junta first abolished El Salvador's long-standing 1886 constitution and held the March elections in which Osorio won as the candidate of the Revolutionary party of Unification and Democracy. The congress that was elected acted also as a constitutional assembly, which, drawing up a new fundamental law, put it into effect on September 4, 1950. Its chief provisions called for a six-year term for the president, gave women the right to vote, and offered protection to labor and small farmers.

The Administration of Oscar Osorio since 1949. The president taking office, called for the unification of Central America on a federal basis and appealed to his countrymen to make democracy a reality in El Salvador. The congressional elections of May, 1952, saw the government endorsed in a free election when its candidate polled over 700,000 votes after the oligarchy's candidate had withdrawn from the hopeless contest. In spite of this support, plots to overthrow Osorio continued throughout 1953.

The Osorio government launched a variety of undertakings to modernize its economy. Its most distinguishing feature is a hydroelectric project on the lower Lempa River, which flows along the northern boundary and turns south in the eastern part of the country to enter the Pacific Ocean. Completed in 1954, this undertaking is symbolic of the changes going forward in the country. Its power, aiding the establishment of new industries, will contribute to raising the standard of living. The waters stored up are to be used in irrigating some 85,000 acres to produce food, now imported, rather than coffee. Small landownership in this region is envisaged to meet the demand here, as elsewhere in Central America, for a more equitable distribution of land and wealth. The Osorio government, too, recognizing the need of combating the appalling illiteracy, about 80 per cent, has built since 1949 a large number of schools, trained more teachers, and greatly enlarged the budget for education.

Stimulating industrial development, the government with United Nations aid expanded the facilities on the Pacific coast port of Acajutla and its environs. The country's nationalism, like that of Honduras, found expression in the declaration of jurisdiction for 200 miles offshore, a claim rejected by Great Britain. Supplementing the economy were measures to pave the nation's main highways, improve roads, extend rural credits to farmers, electrify farm dwellings with Lempa power, and expand the national food supply.

To support these advances El Salvador depends for her principal source of income upon the export of agricultural products, cotton, coffee, and sugar. Of coffee, she produces annually almost 1,250,000 bags, while sugar, grown on 34,000 acres, represents an acreage six times that of ten years ago. The United States takes most of the coffee in its absorption of 80 per cent of the nation's exports. To diversify and improve agricultural production, El Salvador in 1951 made a Point Four agreement with the United States, the latter to provide financial and technical assistance. Need for this advice is evident in the fact that the country must import basic foods, corn, wheat, and milled rice.

In developing her foreign trade, El Salvador has negotiated free trade agreements with Mexico, Nicaragua, and Costa Rica. Increasing her potential trading capacity will be the new modern airport constructed in the capital. To facilitate further expansion of her industry, legislation enacted in 1951 and 1952 modified income tax laws to attract foreign and domestic capital.

In the midst of these constructive activities, in May, 1951, the whole southeastern area of the country was partially destroyed by an earthquake which leveled the city of Jacuapa, damaged other towns, and left 15,000 refugees under government care. Plans were immediately launched and put into operation in which the International Basic Economy Corporation Housing Authority (Rockefeller) participated to rebuild the area by consolidating the displaced urban dwellers in a single city.

In all these programs for the development of El Salvador, the

Osorio government kept labor, the largest element in the population, in view. Because of her comparatively small size, 13,176 square miles, and large population, 1,187,000, the country has consistently lost its nationals by emigration. To meet the needs of those remaining, the Osorio government in 1950 legalized collective bargaining for urban workers. Conservative landowners, however, prevented the extension of this benefit to the huge rural population. Moreover, the government does not permit congresses or national meetings of trade unions, which, nevertheless, are striving for modern labor legislation, the eight-hour day, limitation on child labor, a program of medium and low-cost housing, and other benefits.

Thus El Salvador since 1948 has been carrying forward the development of her natural resources, taking the first steps to recognize labor's role in the country's economy, and moving with free elections toward a democratic status.

COSTA RICA, 1825 TO THE PRESENT

Geography and People. Costa Rica's geographical position isolated her from the main conflicts that disturbed the other Central American republics. Her geography and conditions of colonization oriented her toward a democratic development in her later history. Under Spain, Costa Rica was not an area of large landholders. On the contrary, a hard-working farmer class, tilling comparatively small plots of land, and a small commercial group composed a population at once individualistic and self-reliant.

Costa Rica is dominated by a volcanic range, which in places rises as high as 6,000 feet. In the north the country widens to some 175 miles and narrows in the south to about seventy-five miles. The eastern side of the range slopes away to the humid lowlands of the Caribbean, where cocoa and banana plantations thrive and find their chief outlet at Port Limón, the Veragua of Columbus. In the north and west along the Pacific littoral are excellent cattle lands. But the heart of the country is in the central highlands where the capital, San José, the coffee city, Heredia, the colonial capital, Cartago, and Alajuela lie within a stone's throw of one another. Within this favored area of less than 1,000 square miles live over 500,000 of the 800,000 Costa Ricans.

The people of Costa Rica found few Indians to enslave. They themselves, accordingly, had to become tillers of the soil. While constant intermarriage took place with the natives, the bulk of the population derived from a nucleus of about fifty families who settled in Costa Rica in the late sixteenth century. After that date there was a steady but small stream of Spanish families moving into the country from Panama. Once in the valleys the settlers were cut off by Spanish policy from all communication with the outer world, except through official channels. Poverty was extreme and survival meant hard work. Out of this background emerged two central facts, significant for the later progressive development of Costa Rica: first, the homogeneity of the population, and second, the virtual absence of a powerful landholding oligarchy.

Costa Rica and the Union. In the struggle for independence Costa Rica joined the other Central American countries, but when Mexico's Iturbide sought to control the region, liberals vigorously defended the country and eventually defeated the effort. For the first twenty years of her independence Costa Rica enjoyed tranquillity. Her first president, Juan Mora, was able and liberal in outlook, serving two terms (1825–1833), and adding the territory of Guanacaste which had separated itself from Nicaragua. In 1829 Costa Rica seceded from the Central American Union to force reorganization of it. This purpose achieved, she returned in 1831. During his second administration Mora vigorously and successfully opposed the church, then trying to burn books of which it did not approve. The church, however, did not accept its proper place at once. In 1835 it stirred up a revolt over reforms which included the suppression of compulsory tithing and the reduction of the number of holidays, made by Braulio Carrillo (1835–1837), Mora's successor. The revolt had the interesting effect of strengthening San José's title to be the capital of the country. Carrillo, dissatisfied with the incompetence of his successor, Manuel Aguilar, overthrew him, an act which marked the first violent overturn of a Costa Rican government.

After the dissolution of the Union, Carrillo, altering his policy, secured conservative support to establish an illiberal regime under which the church received back a large part of its influence in the government. Politically, he set aside the 1825 constitution, establishing a virtual dictatorship in 1841. Economically, he encouraged Costa Rica's foreign trade, paying off a large part of the country's debt derived from its participation in the Union, from which it had withdrawn in November, 1838.

Mora and the Growth of Democratic Practices, 1842–1860. Liberal opposition steadily gathering united in 1842 when Morazán landed in Costa Rica came to the defense of her neighboring country. Mora him-

laws, and became the provisional head of the government, which called
a constituent assembly, in which Juan Mora, who had already served
two terms, took a leading part. The reappearance of Morazán in Central
America spurred conservatives in the other republics to support Carrera
in Guatemala in an attack upon Costa Rica. At the end of a series of
battles Morazán, considered the greatest of the Central American liberals,
was captured and executed on September 15, 1842.

When the conflicts attendant upon the country's withdrawal from
the Central American Union and the occupation of Morazán had ended,
Costa Rica turned to organizing a national government. Under José
María Alfora, the temporary president (1842), she received a new constitution in April, 1844, which, however, soon proving unsatisfactory,
was set aside in 1847. Under it Francisco María Oreamuno was elected
president, and served until the end of the latter year. Provincial rivalries
dictated the drawing up of a new constitution in that year, 1847, which
served the country until 1860. Its chief characteristic was the extension
of considerable autonomy to municipalities. Other provisions called for
a president and vice-president to be elected for six years, two ministers
of state, and a single house legislature consisting of ten deputies. The
franchise was extended to all citizens twenty years of age or eighteen
if married, who exercised a profession. As usual in conservative documents of this period, the Catholic religion was made that of the state,
the only one allowed.

Under the new fundamental law, José M. Castro became president
and Alfaro vice-president. The latter, dissatisfied with this office, resigned
to be succeeded by Juan Mora. When it had become apparent that all
attempts to revive the Central American Union had failed, Costa Rica
in 1848 officially declared her independence and sovereign standing as the
Republic of Costa Rica. She secured—the first of the Latin-American
nations to do so—the recognition of Spain and concluded a Concordat
with the Vatican. Besides negotiating commercial treaties with the leading nations, including the United States and Great Britain, she also
entered negotiations with Nicaragua and Colombia in efforts to settle her
boundaries. In 1849 Castro gave up his efforts to govern, resigned peacefully, to be followed in the presidency by Mora. In the next four years,
filled with political disturbances which at times threatened civil war,
Mora not only maintained control but was again re-elected in 1853, with
Francisco María Oreamuno as vice-president.

When in 1855 Walker, the American filibuster, invaded Nicaragua,
Costa Rica came to the defense of her neighboring country. Mora him-

self marched into Nicaragua in March, 1856, defeating Walker's forces at Rivas. After this battle he returned briefly to Costa Rica, where his enemies were plotting his overthrow. Before the end of the year he returned to make a successful attack on Walker's forces, depriving the filibuster of the use of the San Juan River, as a result of which the allies elevated Mora to the office of supreme commander. Shortly thereafter his direction of operations forced Walker to surrender and agree to leave the country.

Mora, greeted as a hero on his return to Costa Rica, was again elected to the presidency in 1859. His vigorous liberalism and his long tenure in office naturally made powerful enemies among the conservative forces, especially the church, which resented his exile of Bishop Lorente in 1859 who had ordered the clergy to refuse to pay taxes. Among his own followers, the commercial class, it stirred discontent when he chartered a state bank. The wealthy classes, fearing new reforms at his hands, took advantage of his loss of influence to organize a successful revolt, which in August, 1859, forced him to flee the country. They placed one of their members in the presidency, José María Montealegre, in 1860, the same year that Mora, believing he would be welcomed back into Costa Rica, landed in the north. Montealegre, acting swiftly, before Mora could gather a large force, attacked, captured, and executed him. The event shocked all of Central America. Mora, during his long prominence in Costa Rican history, had intrenched the liberal tradition and became for that reason one of its greatly respected figures.

Tomás Guardia: Liberal and Economic Advances, 1870–1882. The conservative constitution fixed upon the country in 1860 became the principal cause of violence and frequent changes of government until 1870, when a dominating figure, Tomás Guardia emerged from the chaos. He set aside the conservative document and presented Costa Rica with a constitution in 1871, which, with amendments, lasted more than forty years. Like that sponsored by Mora, it reflected liberal ideas as well as the progressive outlook of a growing commercial class. Besides the usual framework, executive, legislative, and judicial, the document contained a bill of rights and provided specifically for religious toleration, although the Catholic church continued to receive state support. A number of provisions encouraged foreigners to enter the country to carry on trade, develop industries, become citizens after a year's residence, and hold property. Guardia himself in the next eleven years broke the control of the handful of conservative families who had struggled against Mora and had dominated the early conservative governments. While many of his acts were dictatorial, his rule opened the way for further development of democratic government by reducing the power of the oligarchy.

Under his stimulus Costa Rica began its railroad development and the expansion of its banana and coffee plantations. Guardia himself had begun in 1871 the construction of railroad lines, of about ninety-eight miles, from Port Limón on the east coast to connect with the capital. In 1884 an American, Minor C. Keith, secured an agreement with the government to refund the foreign debt and to build the Costa Rica Railroad to the capital, San José. By 1890 the line was completed along the Reventazón River. The extension of the line from the capital to the Pacific coast, under government ownership, was authorized in 1879, but was not completed to Punta Arenas until 1909. The Costa Rica Railroad, however, did not serve adequately to develop the banana lands, so that short feeder lines were built for this purpose in the decade, 1890–1900.

With railroads available, coffee plantations expanded rapidly. Coffee reached Costa Rica in 1810; by 1829 it was the most important crop of the country. Twelve years later Costa Rican production reached almost 4500 tons. When the railroad opened Limón on the Caribbean coast to export, huge savings and profits were made by the banana growers, a fact which naturally stimulated a rapid development of banana plantations. In 1844 the total banana exports amounted to 420,000 bunches, but by 1899, when the United Fruit Company took over Keith's holdings, the export was almost 3,000,000 stems.

With these basic economic changes affecting the well-being of the population, political developments in the direction of greater democratic rule resulted. In 1886 an Organic Law provided for free, compulsory, and laical education, legislation which became the basis for an attack upon the illiteracy of the country. Three years later in 1889 a free election resulted in the elevation of José Joaquín Rodríguez to the presidency.

Until 1902 Costa Rican affairs were dominated by Rodríguez and Rafael Iglesias, who served two terms (1894–1902). Opposition to their control culminated in the election of Ascención Esquivel, who established democratic government that functioned until 1917, when Federico Tinoco overthrew it in opposition to the liberal reforms, direct property tax and progressive income tax, of President Alfredo González. The United States under the Wilson policy of denying recognition to governments winning power by force encouraged the opposition to overthrow Tinoco in 1919. Until 1948 Costa Rica earned the world's respect for its orderly government and democratic elections.

This respect was enhanced after World War II, when new crises found the Costa Ricans ready to resort to vigorous measures to protect their democracy. The danger came from the two extremes, right and left. The right opposed the government of Teodoro Picado (1944–1948), whose party won a slim majority in the 1946 elections on a platform advocating rights of labor to unionize and to strike, social security, and division of land, with financial aid to farmers along with proposals to industrialize and expand agriculture. The Communists, profiting from the liberal attitudes of the Picado government, wanted to push reforms further, electing two of their members to congress.

In the following months the registration of voters, about 100,000, took place in preparation for the presidential election of February 8, 1948. In this period armed clashes took place between the various political parties, among which were the official government party, the Republican-National, which named Calderón Guardia as its candidate, and the Democratic party, which nominated Otilio Ulate. In the election Ulate won, but congress annulled the voting and jailed Ulate. José Figueres, leader of the opposition parties, promptly revolted in March, 1948. The government, unable to crush the uprising, appealed to Somoza, dictator of Nicaragua, and secured aid from the dictator of the Dominican Republic. However, the Communists, supporting Picado in this crisis, split the government forces, hoping to win advantages in the final settlement. After sharp battles, Figueres, with popular support, forced the government to place Santos León Herrera, third designate under the constitution, in as acting president to serve until May 8. On that date a junta, composed of business and professional men and farmers, with Figueres at its head, served until November 8, 1949, when Ulate became president to complete the term to which he was elected in 1948.

During the period of junta rule Costa Rica advanced its democratic development with a new constitution, effective November 8, 1949. Permitting woman suffrage, the country removed itself from the small group of nations, Honduras, Nicaragua, Colombia, and Paraguay, which denied this right to women. It reduced the voting age to eighteen, forbade other Central Americans from voting until naturalized, made education the function of the state, and included a bill of rights. The junta made significant reforms including the nationalizing of the banks, a 10 per cent levy on capital, outlawing the Communist party, declaration of Costa Rica's sovereignty over the continental shelf within 200 miles of the coast, and plans for aiding small industries by developing the hydroelectric resources of the country. Outstanding was the extraordinary step of disbanding the Costa Rican army as a measure to reduce costs of government.

The defeated conservative candidate, Calderón Guardia, in the meantime secured the support of Somoza, war minister of Nicaragua, to invade the country and overthrow the junta. When the attack came early in December, Figueres promptly organized a volunteer army and appealed to the Organization of American States (OAS) to enforce the Rio Pact. The OAS sent a commission which forced Somoza to withdraw his troops and censured the Nicaraguan government for its action. In the following April, 1949, the junta crushed another revolt of the right.

With no further efforts to disrupt the government, Otilio Ulate became president, as agreed, on November 8, 1949. Ulate devoted his administration to establishing a sound economy for the country. A major source of income came from the increased tax on coffee exports. The new army built up to meet the Nicaraguan invasion was again disbanded, and legislation formally enacted in January, 1950, abolishing permanently the armed forces. Its appropriation thereafter was devoted to supporting education.

A national comptroller-general, appointed in January, 1951, with virtually dictatorial powers over nationalized banks, railroads, and hospitals, halted the rise in the cost of living and provided funds for the liquidation of Costa Rica's foreign debt and reduction of its internal one. To aid native businessmen, the government secured the termination of the 1936 trade treaty with the United States, which permitted competing goods to enter the country, and gave bank loans to assist farmers in improving agricultural production. Aiding the latter was a $4,000,000 loan from the World Bank. By 1953 Costa Rica had the largest surplus in its treasury in its history.

With large funds thus available, Ulate launched a broad program to improve the basic economy of the nation. Chiefly this included new highway construction, development of local airports—with a large international one at El Coco—building of public schools, and provision of water and drainage systems for towns. Outstanding in highway construction was the work to complete the Inter-American Highway, suspended in 1945, from San José, the capital, to the border of Nicaragua, to which the United States contributed $250,000 as compared with Costa Rica's $50,000. Greater difficulties were met in completing the highway through the rugged terrain to the south. The school program, pushed to end illiteracy in Costa Rica, now 90 per cent literate, was greatly aided by increased appropriations coming from former army funds. Plans were laid to double the number of schools in ten years and laying the foundations for a University City.

Other advances expanding the economy were the opening of a manganese mine in Guanacaste, the development of rubber plantations for the local market, establishing electric plants, and letting contracts to an American oil company for exploration in Guanacaste province on the west coast and Limón on the east. These measures, more beneficial to the commercial classes, planters, and foreign-owned companies than to the working urban and rural population, made the political life of Ulate's administration stormy. Figueres, who had nationalized the banks and threatened similar action toward the foreign-owned National Power and Light Company, steadily increased in popularity.

In these circumstances the country prepared for the presidential election to be held on July 26, 1953. Figueres, proposing new social reforms, was nominated by the National Liberation party. The opposition combined their forces in the National Union and Democratic parties to nominate a wealthy landowner, Fernando Castro Cervantes. The Independent Progressive party was refused permission to participate on the ground of Communist infiltration. The election revealed the excellent condition of Costa Rican democracy when, of the 294,000 registered voters, 270,000 appeared to cast their ballots, with women voting for the first time.

Costa Rica since 1953. Figueres, chosen by a large majority, was inaugurated November 6, 1953. Simultaneously the constitution was amended to permit incumbents of the presidency to become candidates after an intervening term had elapsed. In his inaugural address Figueres advocated encouragement of United States capital to enter Costa Rica and the expansion of the country's resources to make it less dependent upon foreign markets. To achieve the latter he proposed support for native capital investment in industry and agriculture, an objective which demanded expansion of schools to include technical, scientific, and business training. On the issue of nationalization of the United Fruit Company's properties, Figueres declared his opposition. In office, however, he succeeded in negotiating a new contract with the company under which it agreed to pay in taxes 30 per cent of its profits earned in the country.

The even tenor of Costa Rican affairs was again threatened early in 1955 when disappointed office seekers, former president Teodoro Picado and Rafael Angel Calderón Guardia, attempted to overthrow the Figueres government. As formerly, in 1949, they sought the help of

Somoza, now dictator of Nicaragua, who on his part had long been feuding with Figueres. The latter's leadership and the vigorous character of Costa Rican democracy were an inspiring example for patriotic Nicaraguans to end the Somoza dictatorship.

This time the revolt and invasion were more carefully planned. Not only did they consist of an incessant propaganda assault on Figueres, but huge amounts of war materials, planes, artillery, and other equipment, were gathered. When the invasion and revolt began, early in January, 1955, Figueres, as before, got together a small volunteer army to defend the border while he cabled the Organization of American States in Washington to investigate the attack. Costa Ricans themselves, meeting the invasion, succeeded in capturing a quantity of war materials plainly marked with the emblems and names of Nicaraguan military units.

The OAS on its part acted promptly. It secured from the United States five jet planes to send to Costa Rica to ward off Nicaragua's air power. At the same time it dispatched a commission chosen from the states of Mexico, Ecuador, Brazil, Paraguay, and the United States, with military advisers, to halt the war. With overwhelming evidence in the captured war equipment of Somoza's support of the revolt, the OAS representatives ordered the fighting ended. Once again, Somoza, indignantly denying he had anything to do with the uprising, withdrew Nicaraguan support of the rebels. These soon surrendered and the conflict came to an end. Costa Rica's democracy, along with that of Uruguay, is the chief contradiction of the belief held by some that democratic institutions cannot be established in Latin America.

Central American Unity. The dream of a United States of Central America has prevailed since the dissolution of the Union in 1839. The Inter-American Highway is in modern times a contribution of the United States to the present trend. But the Central Americans themselves have recently sought unified action in trade, agriculture, and education, all pointing toward eventual political union. Many of the countries have negotiated free trade treaties among themselves. In public health, Honduras, Costa Rica, El Salvador, Guatemala, and Panama have plans to study common nutritional problems, aided by the establishment in 1952 by the Pan-American Sanitary Bureau of a nursing education center in Costa Rica for all Central American students. In the same year the First Congress of University Students met in Guatemala City to secure recognition of student rights and standardization of curricula. That year also saw the Congress of Central American Journalists meet to found a

Central American School of Journalism in San Salvador with the distinguished Guatemalan writer, Flavio Herrera, as director.

The most striking step in unification came in 1951 when the five Central American government representatives met in San Salvador from October 8 to 14 to draw up the Organization of the Central American States, the statutes of which were called the Charter of San Salvador. Its purpose is to promote fraternity between the nations and study their common problems. The first meeting of their foreign ministers scheduled to meet in Guatemala City was postponed to be held in Managua on July 12, 1952. Guatemala in the meantime had withdrawn from the Organization, objecting to El Salvador's determination to secure a resolution condemning Communism.

At Managua the states adopted the Resolution of Managua, which declared democratic principles to be the basis of Central American republics; stated the need to improve social, economic, and cultural conditions to buttress democratic institutions; condemned Communism, and recommended adoption of means to prevent subversive activity of Communists in the various states. The defection of Guatemala, the subsequent revolt in that state, and the conflict between Nicaragua and Costa Rica temporarily halted the plans of the Organization proposed in 1953, to study the economic and political integration of the Central American states. The ideal, however, is not dead.

Central American Literature and Culture. Central America's long devotion to the idea of unity, dating from independence, has found literary expression among its poets and writers. More, her intellectuals in modern times have embraced horizons of world interest. The fact is not surprising since Central America is a link between two continents and is the highway between two great oceans.

Symbolically, Nicaragua gave birth to one of the world's outstanding figures in modern literature—Rubén Darío (1857–1916). Of Indian and Spanish parentage, Darío early in life showed his genius as a poet. By 1888 he had published the first of his greatest books, *Azure,* which, with his later works, *Profane Prose* and *Songs of Life and Hope,* established his place in poetry. They also created a new literary movement in Latin-America—modernism.

This movement was a complex of influences emanating in part from imitation of European styles, principally French. The imitation, however, was not slavish; rather it was the use of foreign literary forms within which Darío fashioned a poetry to express the feelings of the Latin-

American world. This world of ancient Indian cultures and strong Spanish traditions, deeply affected by the powerful influences of nineteenth century European and North American literatures, inspired the new poetry of modernism. The publication of *Azure* in 1888 is accepted as the date of the origin of the movement.

Among Latin Americans, Darío is regarded as their literary Bolívar— the man who gave them freedom to express their own originality. Darío himself exemplified the basic characteristics of modernism. Much of his poetry sprang from his desire to escape into an imaginary world. But his "Ode to Theodore Roosevelt," his "Song to Argentina," and his "Salutation to the Eagle" probed deeply into Latin-American economic, social, and international life. The influence of Darío extended beyond Latin America to Spain, where it has profoundly affected modern Spanish writers. To the world of poetry itself, Darío introduced free verse.

In Central America the powerful voice of Darío has carried down to the present. But its modern writers have eschewed the fanciful and emphasized the humanistic universalism implicit in the great master's work. More than in any other part of the New World, Central American writers, particularly poets, have sought to synthesize the literary trends of the world in a poetry which also reflects the American environment. Among the many outstanding poets of this spirit was the Nicaraguan, Joaquín Pasos (1905–1947).

Characterized, too, by a universal outlook is the Costa Rican, Joaquín García Monge, the world-famous editor of *Repertorio Americano,* published in San José. Distinguished by a profound faith in democracy and a warm humanity, García Monge has made his literary review the most important cultural periodical in Latin America. Having a strong sense of their debt to the great leaders of the American nations who have shaped Latin-American culture—Sarmiento, Lincoln, Martí, Bello, Walt Whitman, Hostos, Darío, Montalvo—García Monge has ceaselessly held before his audiences their great works to keep alive their teachings.

The *Repertorio,* too, has been a forum for the discussion of the world's chief literary, political, and artistic movements. Thus its columns have embraced all fields of the human intellect: literature, philosophy, science, art, and history. Not only have leading European and Oriental thinkers written for the review, but through its pages the writers of the United States have been received by Latin-American audiences. Every significant Latin-American figure in the last thirty-five years has contributed to the *Repertorio.* Many, in fact, got their first hearing in its columns through the aid and encouragement of García Monge.

The *Repertorio* has been more than just a literary journal; García Monge has been a powerful voice for the establishment of democratic institutions in Latin America. He has fought incessantly for the rights of individuals everywhere in the Americas and has fiercely defied the dictators. So deep is the devotion of his readers that, though the *Repertorio* is banned in some of the countries suffering from dictatorship, it has a way of reaching its subscribers. Exiles and political prisoners, frequently men of stature in their own countries, have been assured of a publisher in the *Repertorio* when no other journal would give them space. As a cultural force, with a continental outlook, *Repertorio Americano* under García Monge has no equal in the New World.

PANAMA, 1821 TO THE PRESENT

The Character of Panamanian History. The most recent of the Latin-American republics, Panama shared its colonial history with Colombia. Its isthmian character dominated its history throughout the colonial period by confining the population to both ends of the highway connecting the two oceans. The small colonial middle class that grew up in its principal city, Panama, after independence from Spain, looked forward to the development of the province as part of the new state of Colombia. A long history of resistance to the domination of Bogotá prepared Panama for its revolution in 1903, which made it an independent country. Emerging, however, into independence in the shadow of the United States, Panama's nationalistic spirit soon demanded release from the onerous burdens placed upon her by the treaty of 1903 with her big neighbor. Her aspirations reached culmination in 1936 when a new treaty freed her energies to exploit her own national resources with due consideration for the Panama Canal, the principal factor in her economy. Since that date Panama has been adjusting herself to the problems presented by a growing democratic labor movement and the demands of an agricultural population of small landowners.

Nationalism and International Influences, 1821–1903. Declaring independence on November 28, 1821, Panama attached herself to Bolívar's Republic of Greater Colombia. Five years later her capital became the site of the first Pan-American Conference in 1826. When the great state dissolved in 1830, Panama, in common with Venezuela and Ecuador, prepared to establish its independence, but concessions kept her within the new Republic of New Granada. Resisting the domination of Bogotá, she revolted in 1840 to remain independent for two years. By the middle 1840's she began to feel the influence of the great world powers, Britain and the United States, both interested in transit rights across the isthmus. Colombia, under the Mosquera government, fearing British imperial designs and British tolerance of the Colombian exile Flores' filibustering plans, accepted the Bidlack treaty with the United States in 1846 to protect her from Britain. This document guaranteed to American citizens a right of way over the isthmus, while the United States insured protection of free transit and support of the sovereignty of New Granada over Panamanian territory. The Clayton-Bulwer Treaty four years later provided for British-American joint control of any future canal built through Panama. With these agreements opening the way, Americans built the first railroad across the isthmus in 1855. The rush of gold seekers over the route to California led to conflicts with Panamanians, which, breaking out in the Watermelon War of 1857, caused the United States to land soldiers to protect the route of transit.

Panama, prospering, saw its territory made into a state in 1855 and given extensive local powers. Restrictions on these in 1859 led to revolts which again brought American troops to keep open the railroad. Colombia's constitution of 1863, restoring autonomy anew, produced violent civil war both in Colombia and Panama, with resulting occupation by the United States to maintain the operations of the railroad. New revolts flared again in 1885 and destroyed American property at Aspinwall, later Colón.

In 1879 French interest entered the picture when Colombia granted a concession to the Universal Oceanic Canal Company to construct a canal. Its undertaking failed by 1889. Significant were the thousands of workers, mainly Negroes, brought from the Caribbean to the isthmus, who thereafter became part of Panama's population. When conservatives won control in Colombia in 1885, revolts in Panama led to the burning of Aspinwall, later Colón, an action which brought American troops to the isthmus again. After 1886 the conservative government, depriving Panamanians of all rights, led them to join the liberals in the War of One Thousand Days in 1898. Thereafter until 1903 the fighting brought three more American interventions between 1900 and 1902. With this background of struggle against conservative Colombia, sentiment on the isthmus easily turned in favor of independence, a move encouraged by the United States.

The Independence of Panama, 1903. The acquisition of the Philippine Islands after the Spanish-American War made the United States particularly anxious for a canal through the isthmus to connect the east and west coasts and to open the way to trade with China. The Spooner Act of 1902, favoring Panama if French interests sold their holdings at a cost less than that estimated for a canal through Nicaragua, was the first significant step. Following was the Hay-Herrán Treaty on January 22, 1903, under which Colombia granted a right of way for $10,000,000 and an annual rental of $250,000; but the liberal businessmen of Colombia, through their representatives in the senate, refused to ratify the agreement as failing to recognize the strategic importance of the area and placing too low a value on territory connecting two great oceans.

With the treaty defeated in Bogotá, Panama sent Philippe Bunau-Varilla, the representative of the French interests, to the United States to secure support for a revolution, if such an event occurred. Evidently reassured, Panama revolted on November 2, 1903, under José Domingo de Obaldía and Dr. Manuel Amador Guerrero. Colombian troops, sent to put down the uprising, were prevented from leaving Colón by American forces landed from the U.S.S. *Nashville* and dispatched to protect the railroad. Having declared independence the same day, the revolutionary government, headed by Federico Boyd, Tomás Arias, and José Agustín Arango, received American recognition on November 6, 1903.

Independent Panama, 1903–1936. Panama began its history as a nation under the shadow of the Hay-Bunau-Varilla Treaty of 1903, which, with the constitution of 1904, fixed its course for the next thirty-three years. At the time of its independence the nation had an area of 32,383 square miles, not including the Canal Zone, with, however, but one-eighth of the territory occupied by its people and even less under cultivation. Its population, estimated at 300,000, was accurately determined in 1911 when a census showed 336,742 inhabitants including 38,742 Indians. The cattle industry was the most important one, but others included the production of cocoa, coffee, rubber, sugar, bananas, and timber in its forests, particularly mahogany. Pearl fishing dated from the colonial period. Of its mineral resources—coal, copper and gold— only gold was exploited. To this natural wealth after 1915 the canal added its value, becoming, in fact, the principal source of income.

The treaty of 1903 made the United States the guarantor of Panama's independence, for which the United States received in perpetuity the use, occupation, and control of a strip of territory ten miles wide with all lands lying outside the zone necessary for the construction of the canal. In addition, the United States was entitled to exercise sovereign powers in Panama over any matter affecting the maintenance and safety of the canal. As compensation, Panama received a sum of $10,000,000 and an annual rental of $250,000, financial terms identical to those earlier offered to Colombia. This document cleared the way for the construction of the canal, but became the source of continuous diplomatic conflicts between the two countries.

Construction of the canal got off to a slow start, but in 1907, when Colonel G. W. Goethals assumed direction, progress was marked. Overcoming the greatest obstacle, the slides in Culebra Cut, a huge force estimated at 50,000 workers, mostly Negroes from the Caribbean, carried the task to completion by 1914. When finished, the canal presented one of the world's great engineering achievements. Because of differences in the sea level between the Atlantic and the Pacific Oceans, three locks were constructed at each end of the canal to lift and lower ships to Gatun Lake, artificially created by damming the Río Chagres. Through this man-made channel the first ship passed on August 15, 1914, from Cristóbal on the Atlantic to Balboa on the Pacific.

The canal thereafter became a decisive factor in world development. The entire west coast of South and Central America was opened to new economic growth nourished by American capital. The west coast of the United States and the American gulf region rapidly expanded their industrial possibilities as new markets, brought nearer by the canal, opened unlimited opportunities. The shift in the world's trade routes brought the Orient closer to the United States, with a resulting growth of American influence in the far Pacific. Militarily, the American navy became a unit.

The constitution of 1904, adopted on February 13, provided both for the organization of the republic and incorporated Article 136 of the Bunau-Varilla Treaty, in essence the right of the United States to use force to maintain order in the republic. Its chief provisions established a single legislative body, the National Assembly, elected by direct popular vote given to all citizens over twenty-one, and an executive, similarly elected, with designates provided for in place of a vice-president. The country was divided into seven provinces and municipalities, the former ruled by governors appointed by the presidents, the latter by municipal councils elected for two years and presided over by *alcaldes* (mayors) appointed by governors of the provinces.

Manuel Amador Guerrero, the first president under the constitution, served from 1904 to 1908. Under him Panama constructed its first telephone and telegraph lines, began a public works program and initiated taxation on imports and liquor. Primary schools were established as well as a school of Arts and Trades, and a normal school to train teachers for instructing the Indians. With the advice of American canal authorities, Amador abolished the army and replaced it with a police force. In foreign affairs his government vigorously protested the American interpretation of the 1903 treaty to secure ports outside the Zone, apply American tariffs, and run postal services in Panama. Securing settlement of this dispute that she considered satisfactory, Panama thus began the defense of her sovereignty.

In 1908 the United States agreed to supervise the presidential elections, which resulted in the choice of José Domingo de Obaldía. Dying early in 1910, he was succeeded by designates until 1912, when the American-supervised election of that year placed Belesario Porras in power. During these first eight years, Panama took her first census in 1911, began development of the Chiriquí province on the southwest Pacific coast, entered protests against the American monopoly on transportation held by the Panama Railroad connecting her two coasts, and founded 242 schools.

President Porras, who dominated Panama's history for the next twelve years, did much to advance the economic growth of the country. By 1915 a short but important railroad connected the interior of Chiriquí province with the port of Pedregal. Colonization of vacant lands went forward under a liberal land policy, which, however, was not able to attract the bulk of the workers who were discharged when the canal was finished and who settled in Panama and Colón. To absorb these the Porras government began extensive public works in Panama, Ancón, Balboa, David, Portobelo, and Nombre de Dios, enacting for the first time an eight-hour day, with a day of rest, for Panamanian labor. Looking to the future, it reserved to the nation all petroleum deposits and natural gas fields, not given out in concessions. To improve administration, the government divided Los Santos in 1915 to create a new province, Herrera, in the south. By the end of his administration, Porras had brought the total number of schools up to 518 with 23,445 pupils attending. In the presidential contest of 1916, Porras dictated the election of Ramón M. Valdés, with the Conservative party refusing to participate.

Under Valdés, Panama declared war on the Central Powers, April 7, 1917, and placed her resources at the disposal of the United States. To meet growing political discontent, the constitution was amended in 1917 and 1918 to elect the president, vice-president, governors of provinces, and mayors of districts by popular vote. Valdés' death in 1918 brought Ciro L. Urriola to the presidency, who attempted unsuccessfully to postpone elections in 1920. These, held under American supervision, saw Porras again returned to office (1920–1924).

Porras continued to put emphasis upon internal development. He encouraged American investment and supported the American fiscal agent whose reforms had brought a surplus into the treasury. With these funds the president constructed roads and highways so that by 1931, from the bare 100 miles of roads in 1914, Panama had completed a 315-mile highway from Panama City to David and several hundred miles of dry season roads throughout the republic. In foreign affairs Porras actively resisted efforts of the United States to expropriate land for use of canal authorities. Outstanding was his success in saving Tabago Island, the chief health resort in the Gulf. In spite of his successes, the opposition, charging corruption in public works and fraud in politics, was able to win in 1924 when the United States refused to supervise the election. Rodolfo Chiari was elected and served from 1924 to 1928.

The new president continued to encourage American investment, built roads, opened new ports, dredged harbors, and installed waterworks in the leading cities. In foreign affairs the Chiari government negotiated a treaty with the United States in 1926, but the National Assembly, considering it too favorable to the latter country, rejected it on the eve of the 1928 presidential election. Becoming an issue, the treaty split the political parties, bringing to office Florencio H. Arosemena. On this occasion the United States refrained from interference, for by this date all political parties were against American supervision of elections.

During the decade 1920–1930, Panama experienced a prodigious growth of American investment. In the Canal Zone some $500,000,000 went to construct personnel quarters, hotels, commissaries, warehouses, public buildings, and schools. Private investment developed Panama's resources by expanding railroads to serve banana plantations and open up new sugar and tobacco plantations, as well as by financing agricultural colonies and the exploitation of timber lands and minerals. In the cities American banks and utilities were established. By 1929, from an investment of some $5,000,000 before World War I, the total reached $36,000,000. British investment lagged far behind, with $7,500,000 in mineral lands.

Panama's trade from the beginning of its history was unfavorable. Most of the cultivated lands were in bananas which made up 50 to 75 per cent of the exports; others were cocoa, coconuts, ivory nuts, hides, cabinet woods, pearls, and mother-of-pearl shell. However, the balance was redressed by money spent in Panama by canal employees and tourists and through exports to the Canal Zone. The government, unable to meet its expenses, resorted to foreign loans for railroads, highways, and public works. Thus by 1929 Panama had a national debt of over $18,685,000.

The 1929 depression reduced all sources of income, unemployment rose rapidly, and merchants faced bankruptcy. The government, failing to take adequate measures, encountered revolt on January 2, 1931, the first in its national history, led by the *Accional Communal,* organized for the purpose. Arosemena was removed and was replaced temporarily by Dr. Harmodia Arias, who resigned when Dr. Ricardo J. Alfaro took office to finish Arosemena's term. A year later, with the friendly cooperation of the United States military authorities, the election held in July resulted in the choice of Arias.

Panama, so completely dependent upon the United States, sent President Arias to Washington to secure aid to meet the depression and relieve Panama from the burdens of the 1903 treaty. One of these arose from the thousands of discharged workmen in the Canal Zone becoming indigent. What was equally serious, American commissaries in the Zone competing with Panama businessmen reduced the government's source of taxation and made her unable to meet the unemployment problem. The basic principles of the Good Neighbor policy of the Roosevelt government paved the way for a revision of the 1903 treaty, virtually a Panamanian Platt Amendment, and the root cause of Panama's grievances. Taking its place was the treaty of 1936, which abolished the guarantee of Panama's sovereignty and freedom, ended the right of intervention, and substituted mutual consultation in case enemy action endangered the canal. The treaty further met the economic complaints by restricting the privileges of purchasing goods in the canal's commissaries, regulating sales to ships and tourists, confining the use of the Zone's various facilities to canal personnel, and forbidding private firms from operating in the Zone. Other beneficial provisions included the surrender of the United States of the right to expropriate Panamanian property, but permitted her jurisdiction over land needed for the canal, and recognized the right of Panama to build a trans-isthmian highway to link Colón and Panama as well as the right to construct radio stations. Rent for the canal was to be paid in Panamanian money equivalent to the $250,000 agreed upon. The treaty, ratified by Panama in December, 1936, was also ratified by the United States Senate in 1939 when that body was satisfied that the right of the United States to take immediate action to protect the canal was assured.

Panama in these years also successfully concluded a treaty with Costa Rica, fixing the present boundary between the two nations. The final agreement in 1943 and the boundary commissions working under a Chilean arbitrator were hailed as a significant event in hemisphere cooperation.

Panama since 1936. Aiding Panama to meet the depression during the administrations of Arias (1932–1936) and Arosemena (1936–1939) were legislation providing funds for employment of workers in cities on public works projects and other laws to promote agricultural undertakings. The latter facilitated the growth in this period of a small landholding class. While the depression did reduce the educational program, Arias established on a modest scale the University of Panama on October 7, 1935. Various financial measures reduced Panama's indebtedness, foreign and domestic. Businessmen found relief in loans extended through government banks.

The official friendship in Panama for the United States after the ratification of the 1936 treaty made her a strong supporter of hemisphere defense when World War II broke out. Its capital was selected for the Declaration of Panama encircling the hemisphere with a neutrality zone. Upon the death of Arosemena, Julian Boyd served out the term until 1940. Arnolfo Arias, exploiting the latent antagonism against the United States, won the presidency in that year. His rule was short. His most striking action to reveal a pro-Axis outlook was his prohibiting by decree the arming of Panama's ships, many of which were American-registered under Panama's ultraliberal laws. When the Panamanian congress in 1941 proved unsympathetic to his policies, Arias left the country. In his absence congress selected Ricardo Adolfo de la Guardia as the chief executive.

The new president declared war on Japan the day after Pearl Harbor, rearmed Panamanian merchant ships, and granted bases to the United States for defense outside of the Canal Zone itself. The most important of these was the Río Hato air base south of the canal from which planes patrolled the southern exposure against submarine attack. In return, among other measures, the United States relieved Panama of repayment of the loan to the Export-Import Bank for road construction beneficial to the air base, and promised to return after the war all bases granted. Within the country, the president interned enemy nationals, froze Axis funds, and censored radio communications and cablegrams.

For the country as a whole during the war, the president made special efforts to broaden the nation's educational system, establish health and sanitary departments in rural areas, and extend the Pan-

American highway. Lack of shipping and shortages forced the country to expand its agricultural resources, achieving this by somewhat increasing the number of small landowners and aiding the development of small industries.

Panama's Postwar Problems. Freed of many of the restrictions on her growth by the 1903 treaty, and her gold reserve enlarged, Panama as a result of World War II, began earnestly to develop her national resources after the war. Of outstanding importance was the construction of a new highway between Colón and Panama City to reduce the cost of imported goods, increased previously by the monopoly of the Panama Railroad over rates. Widespread school building began in the interior, as well as construction of a normal school. Hotels, hospitals, and electrical plants were brought into operation, while plans of a more comprehensive nature for the interior were evolved. This program became the principal reason for the country's sharp opposition to the continuance of American-occupied bases outside of the Canal Zone. The issue came to a head in 1947 when the United States proposed that the continued use of these be formalized in a treaty. Refusal by the National Assembly forced the withdrawal of the American forces from the bases.

The nationalist feeling aroused over the event affected politics. After the war de la Guardia continued in office until May, 1945, after which Enrique A. Jiménez served as provisional president until 1948. In that year Arnulfo Arias, long an opponent of the United States in Panama, became a candidate, but Domingo Díaz Arosemena was declared elected, with Daniel Chanis as first vice-president and Roberto F. Chiari as second vice-president. Arias' followers, claiming fraud, revolted in July, but martial law maintained order, while a national election jury, recounting the votes, established Arosemena's right to the office. By the middle of 1949, however, Arosemena was forced out and Chanis became provisional president.

Chanis promised reforms, but government extravagance and failure to develop new sources of income led to strikes and general discontent. Chanis, becoming president in August, 1949, when Arosemena died, found himself attacked by Arias and Antonio Remón, chief of police and head of the only armed force, of 2,500 men, in the republic. With this support Arias was able to secure a recount of the votes of the 1948 election, whereupon it was discovered, so Arias claimed, that the greatest fraud in the history of the country had been perpetrated, namely, that Arias had won in 1948! He was accordingly installed as president.

Arias' rule was a short but stormy one. In this period two measures of economic importance to the country materialized, one of which was the opening of the Colón Free Zone in 1951 in which goods were stored for reshipment without paying duties and fees. Its opening increased the prosperity of Colón, which had declined after the war, so that it became a multimillion dollar center of business in the next three years. Of less permanent character was Arias' encouragement of foreign shipowners to register their vessels under Panama's loose laws to avoid the standards of employment set by the International Labor Union. It brought immediate funds into the national treasury, but also world-wide criticism upon the republic.

Politically, Arias did not wait long to begin his offensive with a demand for almost dictatorial powers from congress. Ostensibly he claimed to need them to fight Communism, but the National Assembly, suspicious of his intentions, believed he would use them to crush opposition to his rule, Alerted to the danger, the Liberal party in April, 1950, issued a manifesto signed by six former presidents calling for a general strike against the regime. On May 9, 1951, the opposition culminated in a revolt which drove Arias from office, after which he was found guilty of attempting to establish a fascist type of government and prohibited thereafter from ever holding office in Panama again.

Alcibíades Arosemena, chosen by the National Assembly, became president to complete the term until June, 1952. However, the evils of maladministration, avoidance of taxes by the wealthy, the rising cost of living, and growing unemployment brought protests and strikes. To solve the country's difficulties, five of the leading political parties gathered behind Police Chief Antonio Remón. The Liberal party, which included university students, supported Roberto F. Chiari, who claimed that the choice was between a militarist and a civilian. In the campaign Remón's wife distributed largess in the interior, while Remón himself kept watch in the capital. The election went in Remón's favor by a large majority.

Upon assuming the presidency on October 1, 1952, Remón promised loyalty to democracy, improvement of economic conditions, and respect for Panama's international obligations. The principal idea he developed to meet the country's needs was a revision of the treaty of 1936 to secure a higher rental, end discrimination against Panamanians in the Canal Zone, and win greater participation in the traffic passing through the canal. As president, Remón successfully negotiated a new treaty with the United States an January, 1955, which, incorporating these demands, raised the rent of the canal to $1,950,000 annually. Besides this achievement, Remón improved conditions by land reclamation, launched a public health program, founded schools, and aided industrial development.

Opposition to his regime existed. But most serious were the activities of certain politicians, who anticipated opportunities for graft in the greatly increased canal rent. The upshot of their plans involved the assassination of the president, which occurred on January 2, 1955. Investigation established one Rubén Miró as the murderer. His confession implicated the first vice-president, José Ramón Guizado, who became president, and who Miró claimed had promised him the office of ministry of government and justice, which controlled the spending of national revenues. Guizado, impeached by congress, was held for trial. The second vice-president, Ricardo Arias Espinosa, succeeded to the presidency. It is to be noted that with the exception of this assassination, the other features of this event—corruption in office and political intrigue—have always characterized Panamanian politics.

Viewed over the years, Panama has faced almost insuperable obstacles. Greatly handicapped in the first thirty-three years of its life by the inequalities of the 1903 treaty, it has only in the last two decades been able to develop its own natural resources. The political control by powerful families has been under attack only since the end of World War II. Most unfortunately, the able administration of Remón was cut short and the struggle to effect political reform thrown into confusion. However, with the greatly increased rental from the canal, patriotic Panamanians hope to carry forward the offensive against illiteracy, low living standards, and inadequate housing and develop new sources of wealth from Panama's almost untouched hinterland.

Chapter XXVIII

MEXICO

Part I. THE CONSERVATIVE-LIBERAL STRUGGLE, 1821–1854

The Character of Mexican History. The 300-year control by Spain in Mexico established a tradition of centralized government. At the same time the system of *latifundia* and peonage bespoke an essentially feudal structure of society. But pushing its way into this colonial pattern was a small but vigorous commercial class imbued with the liberal economic ideas of the late eighteenth century. Joining them were intellectuals drawn from all classes who embraced the principles of the French Revolution. These varied social elements after independence coalesced into liberal and conservative groups to give nineteenth century Mexico its distinctive history.

After an initial setback given them by Iturbide, the Mexican liberals controlled the central government until 1835. For the next two decades the conservative forces, aided by the opportunistic ambitions of Santa Anna, dominated to bring disaster—the Texas Revolution and the Mexican War—upon their country.

The turning point in Mexican history came with Juárez, who saved Mexico from French occupation under Maximilian. Equally important, his reforms broke the heart of the traditional Creole and church power, firmly established the liberal tradition, and opened the way for the growth of Mexico's new middle class. Under the Díaz dictatorship the normal political evolution set in motion by Juárez was blocked, but the economic changes implicit in the Juárez reforms found full expression. With foreign capital Díaz launched the modernization of Mexico's economy.

However, the dictator's suppression of human liberties brought reprisal: the Revolution of 1910. The liberal movement, thus renewing its march, came to flower in the constitution of 1917. That document, compromising the objectives of socialist labor and land-hungry Indians with the capitalistic interests of the middle class, has brought increas-

638

ingly stable government to Mexico and facilitated the growth of democratic institutions.

The Conservative-Liberal Struggle, 1824–1836. As soon as the super-
structure of Spain's authority collapsed under the combined blows of
Guerrero and Iturbide, the Creole landowners, as we have seen, attempted to seize control of the state. Iturbide's empire expressed their
determination to maintain their feudal *status quo.* The revolt against him
was a warning that the commercial classes and liberal intellectuals were
determined to make democratic principles effective. To call the resulting
struggle "anarchy" is possibly to miss the meaning of Mexican national
history at its beginning. The "anarchy" arose from the head-on collision
of two well-defined bodies of ideas: conservative and liberal. The wealthy,
particularly landowners who held the Indians in serfdom on their estates
and commanded local armies of *mestizos,* favored rule by the few, union
of church and state, limited education, and a strong standing army.
Supporting Iturbide's empire, they were known as Centralists, a mis-
nomer since their power was essentially feudal. Opposed with the
liberals, then called Federalists, who stood for *laissez-faire,* extension of
the suffrage, separation of church and state, public education, and the
federal form of government.

When Iturbide resigned on March 19, 1823, the congress turned the
executive authority over to Guadalupe Victoria, Nicolás Bravo, and
Pedro Celestino Negrete. The congress also adopted a flag, secured a
16,000,000 peso loan from a British firm, and called a constitutional convention. The new assembly, dominated by the Federalists led by Ramos
Arizpe, produced a document largely modeled upon the Spanish 1812
constitution and that of the United States. It provided for the organization of Mexico into nineteen states and four territories, and a central
government of a president, vice-president, bicameral legislature, and
judiciary. The president and vice-president elected by the state legislatures were to be chosen from the two candidates having the highest
number of votes. Two senators were chosen from each state, while one
representative from each 80,000 inhabitants made up the house of deputies. Other significant provisions made Catholicism the sole religion of
the state, but ended the Inquisition, prohibited such excessive penalties
for crimes as torture, and called for the development of agriculture,
industry and education.

The chief criticism directed against this document, made by Father
Servando Teresa de Mier, held that it decentralized the government of
Mexico, whereas Mexico had traditionally been centralized. This thesis,

accepted by later writers, overlooks the fundamental fact that the constitution of 1824 continued the tradition of establishing democratic principles in Mexican development, the ancestor of those thus far made effective.

Under the constitution Guadalupe Victoria and Nicolás Bravo became president and vice-president respectively on October 10, 1824. In the states where Creole landowners were powerful, armed conflicts occurred in the struggle to win control of state legislatures. In the capital and larger cities, there appeared the forerunners of the later conservative and liberal parties, two branches of the Masonic lodges—the York Rite and the Scottish Rite, called, respectively, the *Escoceses* (conservative) and *Yorkinos* (liberal).

The *Escoceses*, formed in Mexico in 1820, largely composed of Spanish royalists, the clergy, and wealthier Creoles, openly favored the return of the Spanish monarchy. In opposition were the *Yorkinos*, the followers of Hidalgo, Morelos, and Guerrero. Joel Poinsett, the American minister, by openly supporting them encouraged their democratic sentiments. When the congressional elections in 1826 went against the *Escoceses*, they turned to revolt, led by Father Joaquín Arenas and Generals Pedro Celestino Negrete and José Antonio Echararría, a Spaniard and a former official of Iturbide's empire respectively. When his revolt was nipped in the bud, Father Arenas was executed and the two generals exiled.

The rivalry of the United States and Britain in Mexico further embittered the political struggle. The British minister, H. G. Ward, seeking a trade treaty, endeavored also to block American expansion southward toward Mexico. Intimate with leading conservatives, Ward warned them repeatedly that the United States intended to annex Texas. The American minister, Joel R. Poinsett, sympathetic with the liberals, secured a treaty revising the boundaries fixed by the Adams-Onís Treaty of 1821. His success, however, came to nothing when the American Senate rejected the treaty. Subsequently a new treaty negotiated with the conservative government in power in 1829 recognized the existing boundaries. Two years later in 1831 a Mexican-American commercial agreement was also signed.

In the presidential election of 1828 the conservatives accused the Victoria government of tolerating Poinsett's political activities and suspending the payments on the British loan of 16,000,000 pesos. The attack turned to revolt when Victoria supported Guerrero, the popular leader of the Wars for Independence and a staunch liberal. Proclaiming the

Plan of Montaño, Vice-president Bravo led an uprising demanding the suppression of secret societies and the expulsion of Poinsett. Defeated, he went into exile, but his supporters, the *Escoceses,* joined the Conservative party in electing in 1828 Gómez Pedraza over Guerrero.

In power, the conservatives had Poinsett recalled in 1829, and set about to destroy the *Yorkinos.* Fighting back and charging fraud in the elections, Guerrero was determined that Gómez Pedraza would not take office. Santa Anna revolted in support in Perote but was put down. Shortly afterward in Mexico City a second revolt, headed by General Lobato, threatened congress, demanded the expulsion of the Spaniards, and proclaimed Guerrero president. Although this uprising was put down, feeling was running high against the Spaniards urging the restoration of the monarchy and congress was led to enact legislation forcing all Spaniards to leave the country within three months. Thereupon, Pedraza resigned and Guerrero was named president, with Anastasio Bustamante as vice-president, in April, 1829.

Spain, seizing upon the legislation as abuse of her nationals, sent to Tampico an expedition of 5,000 men from Cuba commanded by Brigadier D. Isidoro Barradas. Barradas, misled by the clergy into believing that the Mexicans would welcome him, made no preparations for defending his position. With news of the Spanish invasion, rival parties forgot their animosities. Their leaders hastened to enlist for service. Congress bestowed war powers upon Guerrero, while Santa Anna rushed to Vera Cruz, raised an army of 800 men, and marched to the aid of Tampico. Driven back by Barradas, he resorted to guerrilla tactics. Barradas, meanwhile, waiting for reinforcements that never came, saw the Mexican forces steadily increase while his own were decimated by yellow fever and malaria. Giving up his attempt as hopeless, he surrendered on September 11, 1829. Thus ended this effort of Spain to regain her lost Mexican jewel.

The affair ended unfortunately for Guerrero. His little part in the defense of Mexico weakened his prestige. His action in freeing the slaves in the country, won him the enmity of the coastal landowners. When the danger of foreign invasion ended, Bustamante, with Santa Anna and the clerical-conservatives in the background, organized a revolt to stop further reforms. Guerrero, defeated, was betrayed into the hands of his enemies and assassinated. The event produced an immediate revulsion of feeling. By December, 1832, Bustamante, who had seized the presidency, was ousted, this time by Santa Anna, ever keeping his eye on the main chance. Gómez Pedraza, now with but a few months left of the term to which he was elected in 1829, served until April, 1833.

Gómez Farías: the First Liberal Reforms, 1833–1834. The antagonism aroused by the execution of Guerrero brought the Federalists into power in April, 1933, with Santa Anna as president. Vice-president was Valentín Gómez Farías, an able and noted liberal. On discovering the determination of congress and Gómez Farías to launch basic reforms, Santa Anna promptly left town. In control of the executive power, the vice-president directed his chief legislation to end the special privileges of both the army and the church. The military reform reduced the size of the army and deprived officers of their privileges *(fueros)*. One of the most important of these was the right of trial in military courts for offenses against the civil law. Unfortunately, the immediate effect of this legislation was to turn loose on the country unemployed soldiers who were promptly organized into revolutionary groups by unemployed generals. This problem of militarism, closely associated with illiteracy, plagued Mexico until she found a solution in the twentieth century under Cárdenas.

The attack upon the privileges of the church was equally fundamental. To deprive the institution of its political power, the government secularized all the missions in the republic and nationalized their properties. Other legislation suppressed church courts, a privilege *(fuero)*, and ended compulsory tithing, also a *fuero*. The latter privilege liberals believed incompatible with the power of the state to tax. Voluntary tithing was not interfered with. Equally drastic was a measure which repealed all laws requiring compulsory fulfillment of the vows of monasticism; priests and nuns under this legislation were free to return to secular life.

Undoubtedly the chief measure in the series of reforms was the attack upon the patronage, that is, the right of the church to appoint its own officials. This power of the church, given its enormous financial and other economic resources and its independence of the laws of the state, gave its officials a standing comparable to that of the president and other high officers of the nation. This reform, then, was simply to end the status of the church as a state within a state. To effect the change, Gómez Farías invoked the state's highest power, sovereignty, in a decree which placed the power of appointment of church officials in the government and ordered all vacant curacies to be filled by the president and the governors of the states. Mexico thus assumed the patronal powers formerly exercised under the Laws of the Indies by viceroys, presidents of *audiencias*, and governors. These reforms, military and religious, the liberals regarded as normal in carrying out the promise of the War for Independence.

The conservatives, resisting these as attacks upon their intrenched positions, revolted under the slogan of "Religion and Privileges," with Santa Anna heading the movement. In power, he set aside the reforms, suspended congress, forced the resignation of Gómez Farías, dismissed state legislatures, overthrew governors, and ousted municipal bodies controlled by liberals. Thus ended the first major effort at liberal reforms after the constitution of 1824. Never enforced, they mark nevertheless a step in the growth of liberal ideas in Mexico.

The Conservative Constitution of 1836. By December, 1834, Santa Anna called a new congress which ended the constitution of 1824. With no authority from the voters in the nation, the congress, decreeing a new document called the Seven Laws, but derided by the liberals as the "Seven Plagues," promulgated it as the constitution of 1836. Giving perfect expression of the ideas of Mexican conservatives at this date, its primary object was to end the threat of the maturing liberal movement, not, as some have thought, simply to guard against the ambitions of Santa Anna.

The executive under the instrument was a two-headed one, a presidency and a weird institution called the Conserving Power *(Poder Conservador)*. Both of these offices were so hedged about with property qualifications that only the wealthy could qualify for them. The president, selected by a process deliberately complicated, served eight years. A presidential council, created by the constitution, together with the senate and the supreme court, each submitted a list of three names—nine altogether—from which the chamber of deputies chose three. Another organ created for the purpose, called the Departmental Assemblies, chose one of three, who became president.

This executive was subordinate to the Conserving Power, the source of all authority. Composed of five members, it could under the pretext of maintaining the equilibrium between the executive, the legislature, and the judiciary, set aside all laws, reverse court decisions, depose the president, suspend the congress, and charge any citizen with rebellion and treason punishable by death. Accountable to no one on earth, the Conserving Power did, however, recognize its responsibility to the Deity. Finally, under the constitution, all states were abolished and the country divided into military departments. The constitution was received by the liberals and many of the thoughtful conservatives for what it was—a monstrosity. Rebellions and insurrections were immediate in the various military departments. Among these the most serious, from the point of view of nation as a whole, was that in Texas.

The Revolt of Texas, 1836. The Texas Revolution, in the last analysis, rested upon the incompatibility of two differing cultures. After the United States had secured Louisiana from Napoleon in 1803, American settlers poured westward into these new acquired land. While Americans before 1820 had entered Texas mostly as horse traders, it was in that year that the migration of settlers began. Moses and Stephen F. Austin applied and received from Viceroy Juan Ruíz de Apodaca a land concession, which Iturbide's government confirmed under its original terms. These required American citizens to become Mexican citizens and accept the Catholic religion in exchange for land and deferment of taxes for a period of years. The migration grew rapidly; by 1827 fully 27,000 American settlers were in Texas.

Differences in cultures and international rivalries led to the revolt in 1836. After the signing of the Adams-Onís Treaty, public opinion in the United States demanded the "reannexation of Texas"; Poinsett, the first American minister, negotiated for its purchase; his successor, William A. Butler, hinted at bribery to secure it. Mexican fears were further stirred by Augustine Edwards, who, receiving a land grant adjoining the old settlement at Nagodoches, seized land belonging to Nagodoches citizens. Resenting the demand of the Mexican government to return the land, Edward led the Fredonian Rebellion, as it was called. Put down by the Mexican government with the assistance of Austin and other law-abiding colonists, the event, however, had sown seeds of distrust. The Texans on their part were disturbed by the Colonization Law of 1830, which encouraged the migration of Mexicans into Texas and ended any further immigration of Americans into the land. More upsetting was the abolition of slavery by Guerrero in 1829. Although the Texans secured modification of the law to except Texas, the event left them with a feeling of uncertainty. Again, in 1830 the Mexican government united Texas and Coahuila with the capital at Saltillo. The change caused many hardships in Texas legal affairs; the law's delay increased their impatience. On the other hand, the liberal government that came in with the constitution of 1824 and that of Gómez Farías had no thought of oppressing the Texans. They extended, in fact, the right of trial by jury to them, made the English language the equal of Spanish in the courts, and gave Texans important local rights in managing their own affairs. But after 1834, when Santa Anna arbitrarily dissolved the state governments and sent an army to patrol the border, the Texans considered these actions a threat to the rights guaranteed them under the constitution. When that document in turn was subverted by the clerical-conservatives in October, 1835, the Texans took steps to win their independence.

Forming an organization called the General Consultation which on March 2, 1836, declared the independence of Texas and made Samuel Houston commander-in-chief, the Texans prepared to defend themselves. Unfortunately, division within the Consultation led to a serious defeat at Goliad, followed by the invasion of Santa Anna. When on March 6 Santa Anna arrived at San Antonio with overwhelming force, Colonel William B. Travis defended the Alamo to the last man. This loss and that of Goliad left the Texans with no alternative but to begin a heart-breaking retreat eastward. Santa Anna, hastily pursuing what he believed to be a routed enemy, halted near the San Jacinto River. There Houston reorganized his forces and suddenly attacked the Mexican lines with such effectiveness that he won a complete victory including the capture of Santa Anna himself.

In spite of the slaughter at the Alamo, the Texans were generous to their defeated enemy, requiring Santa Anna, in return for his freedom, to sign the Treaty of Velasco on May 14, 1836, which recognized the independence of Texas and fixed the Rio Grande River as the boundary of the new state. Returning to Mexico by way of Washington and Havana, Santa Anna, safe in Mexico, repudiated the treaty, claiming he signed it under duress. Mexico therefore did not consider Texas as an independent state, but one temporarily out of relation to the central government.

Conservative Control, 1836–1844. The defeat of Santa Anna and the loss of Texas, together with the collapse of national finances, gave the liberals an opportunity to appeal strongly to the country in the 1837 election. Gómez Farías proposed to meet the financial problem by mortgaging the properties of the church. However, the latter, intrenched behind the constitution of 1836, was able to place Bustamante in the presidency. His hands were immediately strengthened by the recognition of the independence of Mexico by both Spain and the Vatican.

Bustamante, however, had no plan for developing the wealth of the country to escape bankruptcy. Unable to meet foreign obligations, he found himself faced in 1838 with French demands for a settlement of the claims of her nationals against Mexico. Failing to get satisfaction, France in 1839 landed troops to seize Vera Cruz. The incident, known as the "Pastry War," contributed to the downfall of Bustamante, and found

Santa Anna, ever ready, organizing an army, which, while not successful against the French, did uphold Mexican honor. Bustamante thereupon accepted British mediation in the settlement of French claims, whittled down from $800,000 to $600,000.

Bustamante's declining prestige gave the liberals once more an opportunity to appeal to the country. Fearful of their success, the conservative opposition supported General Mariano Paredes y Arillaga, who in 1841 presented the Plan of Tacabaya declaring the constitution of 1836 at an end, and called for a new congress to promulgate another. His supporters, organizing themselves into an "Assembly of Notables," named Santa Anna as president, who promptly took over when Bustamante fled to Europe in 1841.

Santa Anna, fully aware that the conservatives were depending upon him to block the Federalists, established a personal dictatorship. To give a color of legality to his government he promulgated in June, 1843, an extraordinary document, the "Organic Bases of the Mexican Republic," which conferred practically absolute authority upon him. Under it the country was divided into departments headed by Santa Anna's appointees. They in turn set up complicated election machinery which assured the selection of officials not tained with liberal ideas and loyal to Santa Anna. Over the central government Santa Anna himself presided with authority to veto without recourse any law of congress, enact legislation by decree, appoint all judges, and levy taxes without consent of congress. Santa Anna did not have to be corrupted by absolute power; he was already corrupt. This fact became evident in the extravagance of his administration. His cabinet officials paid their gambling debts out of the public treasury; and there were Bacchanalian feasts, immorality, justice by purchase, the whole supported by taxes arbitrarily imposed and ruthlessly collected.

The resulting discontent gave liberal leaders support even among some conservatives who had found their bargain with Santa Anna distasteful. Thus in December, 1844, the liberals succeeded by revolt in placing General José Joaquín de Herrera in the presidency, exiling Santa Anna "forever," which in this case proved to be about eighteen months. Herrera hardly had time to establish himself in office when Mexico suffered one of her great disasters, the annexation of Texas by the United States on March 3, 1845, followed almost immediately by war between the two countries.

The War with the United States, 1845–1848. The war with the United States was primarily the result of American expansion westward. This expansion followed territorial and commercial interests in Mexican territory. As we have noted, American migration into Texas produced a revolt in 1836, after which Texas applied for admission to the United States, delayed until 1845 by the internal conflict over the question of the extension of slavery. Paralleling this territorial advance were expanding commercial interests. In the 1820's caravans followed the Santa Fé trail from St. Louis to Santa Fé and to Chihuahua in northern Mexico. Carrying manufactured goods of all varieties, the owners, among them notably Josiah Gregg, had built up during the 1830's a business of over $1,000,000 a year. Traders from St. Louis also penetrated beyond the boundaries of the Louisiana Territory to seek furs in New Mexico, Arizona, California, and even Sonora. Another line of advance projected itself from New England around Cape Horn when Boston shipping companies brought back cargoes of whale oil, seal furs, and hides from the California and Alaskan coasts. From the Farallon Islands, opposite the mouth of San Francisco Bay, American traders secured in one year alone more than $1,000,000 worth of furs.

Giving spur to this interest in Mexican territory was American rivalry with Britain over Texas and California. Britain saw in Texas a state capable of blocking American southward expansion and an alternative source of cotton to the older southern states. In the northwest, fur brigades from the Hudson Bay penetrated into the Mexican territories of California and New Mexico. British trade on the California coast added to her interest in that distant land.

Political causes within the United States and Mexico played their part in bringing on the war. Both countries were divided over the question of Texas. In Mexico fears of American acquisition stemmed from the political cry north of the border of "reannexation" of Texas. After 1836 the Mexicans had their suspicions intensified by the active campaign in the United States to annex the area, a feeling sharpened in 1843 when Commodore T. A. Jones of the American navy seized Monterrey, the capital of Mexican California. The Mexicans retaliated by expelling all Americans from the northern provinces. By 1844 the Conservative and Liberal parties had adopted opposing positions on the question of Texas. The Conservative secretary of foreign relations in 1843 declared that the incorporation of Texas into the United States would be considered as a declaration of war against Mexico. The Liberals under Herrera, anxious to avoid war, agreed to an Anglo-French mediation proposal that Mexico would recognize Texas provided the two European powers guaranteed her independence.

In the United States, Texas fell into the broader struggle for control of the national government. The industrial north linked to the west feared that annexation would bring in more slave states and thus block its march to power. For this reason and because of fear of civil war, annexation was delayed for eight years after Texas proposed it in 1837. When, however, Tyler from Virginia became president, he began a vigorous campaign to annex the republic and settle the Oregon question. Spurred on by fear of British designs on both Texas and California, he secured the passage of the joint resolution annexing Texas on March 7, 1845. Polk next sent John Slidell to purchase the rest of the territory to the Pacific Ocean. However, Herrera dared not receive Slidell. In fact, the mere news of Slidell's arrival overthrew the Herrera government on December 31, 1845, and placed General Paredes in power.

The War. Late in March, 1846, Polk sent General Taylor, who took up a position between the Nueces and the Rio Grande rivers opposite Matamoros to repel "invasion." In Mexico, with no program for the country as a whole, the Paredes government turned to war on April 25, 1846. But with the conflict actually at hand, army leaders and others demanded the return of Santa Anna, then in Cuba. Cleverly outwitting Polk, Santa Anna secured from him a safe-conduct through the American squadron off Vera Cruz. In Mexico he assumed the presidency in September, 1846.

On April 26, 1846, a Mexican force crossed the Rio Grande and defeated a smaller American advance guard opposite Matamoros. Upon learning of the event, Polk sent a message to Congress stating war should be declared since American blood had been shed on American soil. Congress agreed, though courageous members like Abraham Lincoln wished to debate the question.

The war was fought in three major theaters. In the northeast of Mexico, General Taylor advanced across the Rio Grande River to occupy Monterrey and Saltillo, winning victories at Palo Alto and Resaca de la Palma en route. When Santa Anna arrived to attack Monterrey early in 1847, Taylor narrowly escaped defeat at Buena Vista. In the second theater, the West, Colonel S. W. Kearney invaded New Mexico, which he captured after a short negotiation with the Mexican governor. From Santa Fé, Kearney sent Colonel Doniphan southward with 900 men. Defeating two superior forces, he captured Chihuahua and turned eastward to join Taylor at Saltillo.

Meanwhile, in California, Captain John C. Frémont encouraged a revolt which established the Bear Flag Republic. With his eye on the presidency, Frémont hastened to the capital, Monterrey, but there Commodore J. D. Sloat had taken possession while the Mexican forces fled southward to halt near Los Angeles. Commodore R. F. Stockton shortly thereafter occupied the Los Angeles area. After all resistance had ended, except for local revolts, Stockton confirmed the treaty, negotiated by Frémont, under which California was annexed to the United States on August 13, 1846.

The third theater of operations involved an American invasion of Mexico at Vera Cruz, the expedition commanded by General Winfield Scott, with Mexico City as its objective. While Scott was taking Vera Cruz, which fell in 1847, Santa Anna had launched an attack upon Taylor in the north. Failing there because of a jealous rival, Ampudia, he returned to Mexico City. From the coast Scott advanced unhindered until he arrived outside of the capital. There he was stopped by Nicolas P. Trist, a representative of Polk, who arrived with authority to negotiate for peace. Santa Anna willingly discussed terms long enough to strengthen the defenses of the city. When the negotiations broke down, Scott, annoyed, renewed his advance against Chapultepec, where a small group of Mexican cadets made a heroic but hopeless stand. By September, 1847, the city was in Scott's hands with no help from Taylor.

The failure of Santa Anna to stop the enemy forced him from office, which now fell to Manuel de la Peña y Peña, who opened negotiations for peace. The Treaty of Guadalupe-Hidalgo (February 2, 1848), carried through with the cooperation of the Mexican Liberal government, resulted. One of the terms of this remarkable document transferred the vast areas of New Mexico, Arizona, and California to the United States, which on its part agreed to give up all claims against Mexico and compensate that country to the extent of $15,000,000. The treaty further fixed the boundary along the Rio Grande River to the Gila River and thence to the Pacific Ocean. Another clause fixed responsibility upon the United States for the actions of the Indians in the new territory. Significantly, the treaty gave the United States the right to transport troops across the Isthmus of Tehuantepec.

In the United States Senate the treaty met opposition and narrowly missed ratification on the ground that it was too generous toward Mexico! Many senators felt that since the United States had conquered and occupied northern Mexico, that vast region should also be surrendered. Too, it is worth noting that some conservatives in Mexico were willing to go even further than the most extreme American senatorial annexationists. A conservative group, hoping to set aside the Liberal government, offered Scott the whole of Mexico, asking only that he remain with his army and assure the safety of their lives and property! Individuals in this same group immediately after this date sought European intervention to preserve their privileges. Scott summarily rejected their offer and ended the American occupation in July, 1848.

The Effects of the Mexican War. Upon the United States the war exercised significant influences which have been obscured by the importance attached to the Civil War. The Mexican War did, of course, prove a training ground for officers who later played a leading part in that struggle; the question of slavery in the cession lands likewise influenced the development of the irrepressible conflict. But of equal significance to the development of the United States was the acquisition of the mineral resources of the Mexican cession, the lack of which before 1846 kept American industrial expansion in a strait jacket. The cession provided not only the gold and silver necessary for financing American industrial expansion, but as a more immediate by-product gave the north a financial power unknown in the south, for the latter neither had access to nor benefited from the new mineral discoveries in the west. During the conflict, for example, Nevada became the "Battle Born State" (1864), whose great Comstock lode helped to support the northern effort.

The Mexican War gave the United States the basis for its later position as a world power. Not only did the territorial acquisition extend American boundaries to the Pacific, but in California it opened the way for the subsequent growth of United States power in that ocean. A counterpart of this expansion was that southward into Central America and the Caribbean implicit in United States control of the northern rim of the Gulf of Mexico when Texas entered the Union.

With frontage on the Pacific and on the Gulf, the idea of connecting the two by an isthmian route received new impetus. Indeed, testimony on such a need had found practical expression in 1846, with the negotiation of the Bidlack Treaty with Colombia. Success in the war likewise made inevitable the Clayton-Bulwer Treaty of 1850, under the terms of which the British recognized the interests of the United States in Central America. Thus viewed broadly, the Mexican War had in international affairs the effects of ending British threats in Texas and California, raising the United States to a position of equality with Britain in Central America, and, in the Pacific, opening another branch of American expansion.

Throughout Latin America the Mexican War raised doubts about the Monroe Doctrine. The acquisition by the United States of 750,000 square miles of Mexican territory made it plain that the Doctrine was a restriction only upon European powers. Upon Europe, the war, ending successfully for the United States in 1848, had the interesting effect of stirring fears among the aristocratic classes, but giving hope to the democratic forces, which, defeated in the Revolution of 1848, considered American triumph over Mexico a liberal success, denied in Europe, against a clerical-oligarchic state.

In Mexico itself the war discredited the Conservative party, which collapsed as a force. Conversely, the liberals early in the 1850's succeeded under Juárez in launching the reform movement initiated by Gómez Farías and revived by Herrera just before the war. The conservatives, recognizing their helplessness, turned to seek foreign aid, so that a direct political relation tied the Mexican War to the French intervention in 1861. Aiding the liberal success and the growth of democratic ideas was the entrance of Protestantism into Mexico during the war. American army chaplains who brought the Bible to Mexico prepared the ground for the evangelical missionary movement of the 1850's.

Economically, the war deprived Mexico of approximately one-half of its territory, thereby bringing the American boundary far south to the Rio Grande. From this favorable base, economic penetration, evident early in the Juárez era, began to tap Mexico's vast storehouse of raw materials. Anticipation of this effect is seen in the debates in the American Senate over the treaty of 1848 for the annexation of northern Mexico, in the interest of transcontinental railroad routes through the same area, and in the provision of the Guadalupe-Hidalgo Treaty which gave the United States transit rights across Tehuantepec.

Decline of Conservative Power, 1848–1854. Immediately after the war, liberals and conservatives plunged the country into civil war. Santa Anna went into voluntary exile to await another call, while Herrera assumed the presidency. He began the construction of the country, but conservative uprisings hampered his work. In 1850 he was succeeded by General Mariano Arista. As a liberal president, his major reform was to reduce the size of the army as one means of rehabilitating the treasury. But the soldiers turned loose were quickly recruited by conservative leaders in a revolt in Guadalajara, which, supported by the church, drove Arista from power in January, 1853.

The conservatives, now desperate, saw no other solution except the usual one, another dictatorship. Lucas Alamán and others in contact with the Vatican, Spain, and other European monarchies, hoped to establish a royal house in Mexico. But the generals, more practical-minded, urged Santa Anna to return. Back in Mexico in December, 1853, he assumed the titles of "His Most Serene Highness and Perpetual Dictator." The final blow which ended Santa Anna's career was the sale of Mesilla Valley, the Gadsden Purchase, to the United States. The interest of the latter lay in a more suitable route for the Southern Pacific Railroad. Such an avenue had been discovered through the Mesilla Valley south of the border fixed by the Treaty of Guadalupe-Hidalgo. Successful with Santa Anna, Gadsden purchased the area for $10,000,000 and made the Indian control provisions of the 1848 treaty mutual.

Part II. JUÁREZ AND LIBERAL REFORMS, 1854–1876

The Revolt of Ayutla, 1854. The alienation of part of the fatherland, Mesilla Valley, stirred deep resentment among the Mexicans. They could overlook the fortunes of war which brought Santa Anna's defeats in Texas and in the Mexican War, but despoiling the nation for personal advantage was unforgivable. With the money, Santa Anna resorted to bribery to silence opposition, while he and his followers led a life of debauchery in the capital. Revolts soon broke out, the most significant one of which was led by Juan Alvarez, an old liberal leader, on February 20, 1854. Winning support of a group of veteran liberals, they met to proclaim on March 1 the "Plan of Ayutla" to overthrow Santa Anna and to assemble a congress to draw up a new constitution. Throughout the nation Mexicans rallied and forced the dictator to flee into exile for the last time on August 9, 1855. Alvarez assumed the presidency until December 1, when Ignacio Comonfort became the chief executive.

Juárez and the Laws of Reform, 1855–1856. At this point in the history of Mexico appeared the greatest of the Mexical liberals—Benito Juárez. A full-blooded Zapotec Indian, born in 1806 and educated in Oaxaca, Juárez' gifts for leadership were early recognized. A profound student of liberal principles, he entered public life in the Liberal party in his native state, served as governor, and became known for his incisive action on behalf of the Indian peasantry. Appointed minister of justice in Alvarez' cabinet, Juárez secured enactment of the *Ley Juárez*, legislation which suppressed all special courts except the military and church courts, and which deprived the latter of all civil jurisdiction. The second significant law, fathered by Miguel Lerdo de Tejada, *Ley Lerdo,* ended the power of civil and religious corporations to own property. This legislation forced the church to sell its lands, mostly at public auction, for which it received compensation. However, the law was immediately taken advantage of by speculators to denounce lands held by Indian villages. The third law, sponsored by José Iglesias, *Ley Iglesias,* threw safeguards around the civil rights of citizens to protect them from the more powerful and privileged. Other legislation defined the amounts that the church could collect as fees for baptism, funerals, and marriage.

The enactment of these laws, particularly the *Ley Juárez* and the *Ley Lerdo* drew conservative denunciation of both the Alvarez and Comonfort governments. In spite of this opposition, some of which even came from within the Liberal party itself, the government sought to enforce the Reform legislation. Meanwhile, stirring even greater conservative attacks was a new constitution then under debate. Upon its promulgation on March 11, 1857, the conservatives organized their forces and openly revolted the following December. Comonfort resigned and joined the opposition. The liberals thereupon, January 19, 1858, elevated to the acting presidency the Chief Justice of the Supreme Court—Benito Juárez. Under these circumstances the War of Reform began.

The Constitution of 1857. The constitution of 1857 takes rank with those of 1824 and 1917 as one of the three great Mexican contributions, of this character, to the development of Latin-American political thought. Its framework, patterned upon that of the United States, provided for a president with succession going to the president of the supreme court, a supreme court, a unicameral legislature and a judiciary. The president was elected for a term of four years, as were the senators (when a senate was added in 1878), two from each state, by the state legislatures. The house of deputies was chosen on the basis of the population and held office for two years.

The significant provisions of the constitution revealed the remarkable advances made in the thinking of the Mexican leaders as democratic philosophers. Suffrage was extended to all male citizens of twenty-one years of age, or eighteen if married. A bill of rights, freedom of speech and of the press, and the right of petition and assembly were guaranteed; inviolability of domicile was recognized, and imprisonment for debt ended. Its essentially middle class character was evident in the provisions incorporating the *Ley Lerdo,* depriving the church of its vast holdings in real estate in Mexico, abolishing monopolies, guaranteeing private property rights, and ending titles of nobility and hereditary privileges. In patterning itself upon the Constitution of the United States, it refrained from any mention of religion. Indeed, the constitutional requirement of oaths in state affairs consisted of a simple affirmation in court. A striking

Article, No. 128, testifying to the faith of the makers in the ultimate establishment of democratic institutions in Mexico, stated that in case the document were overthrown, those guilty were to be tried in accordance with its provisions when it was restored.

The War of Reform, 1857–1861. Félix Zuloaga, declared president by the conservatives, seized Mexico City and put in operation his "Plan of Tacubaya," which called for the setting aside of the constitution of 1857, the re-establishment of the jurisdiction of the church and military courts, and the ending of the three laws of *Juárez, Lerdo* and *Iglesias,* in short, a return to the feudal organization of Mexico. Juárez fled to the west to organize the liberal forces. There Santos Degollado, a staunch liberal, took command, while Juárez sailed via Panama to Vera Cruz to establish his government. In the north Santiago Vidaurri, an ambitious *caudillo*, tried to disrupt the liberal movement to carve out an independent republic for himself. That action was no aid to Juárez, but the conservatives derived no support for themselves.

In Mexico City Zuloaga soon revealed his incompetence either to conquer the liberal forces or to govern. The conservatives, recognizing his incapacity, overthrew him to place General Miguel Miramón in power. More able, the new leader defeated but did not destroy Degollado's forces in the west before he turned to attack Juárez at Vera Cruz in February, 1859.

Meanwhile, Juárez consolidated his position in traditionally liberal Vera Cruz, where its strong commercial class supported the government. Throughout the provinces along the coast, Juárez seized the revenues of the church and confiscated its lands, as well as those of the conservatives, to secure the sinews of war. Enforcing the constitution, he also implemented it with a body of liberal legislation such as ending the sales tax *(alcabala)* and the head tax on Indians. The cemeteries were secularized, and provision was made for civil marriage, establishment of schools, and the creation of a body of administrative officials to replace those customarily provided by the church.

These modernizing measures opened the way for the middle class to invest their capital in land and prepare plans for the construction of railroads and the expansion of trade and commerce freed from restrictions. Thus Juárez' position was firm in contrast to that of Zuloaga's and later Miramón's, who, having returned the land to the church, created antagonism within the ranks of those who had purchased it in good faith. The latter became the allies of Juárez in the territory of the enemy. Miramón attempted to destroy Juárez in 1858, but was defeated by the president's own generals and Degollado's rear attack. But with Juárez unable himself to capture Mexico City, the conflict became a stalemate.

In the midst of his difficulties, Juárez faced European creditors demanding payment of their claims. For aid he turned to the United States, which on its part, expanding its interests in California, in the Pacific, and in Central America, felt the need of an isthmian route through Tehuantepec. Reaching an agreement, the two countries drew up the McLane-Ocampo Treaty of 1859, under which the United States was to secure a perpetual right of way across the isthmus, with the right to intervene there to maintain order and enjoy exemption of its nationals from forced loans. For these concessions, Mexico was to receive $4,-000,000, with one-half of that amount retained to meet claims of American citizens against Mexico. Fortunately for Mexican-American relations, the American Senate failed to ratify the treaty.

Juárez' strategic location at Vera Cruz, the nation's port of entry, was indeed fatal to the Miramón government. Its inability to secure supplies sealed its fate. During 1860 in a series of battles, bitterly fought, Juárez' forces by December of that year overthrew the last remnants of conservative control. On January 11, 1861, Juárez, establishing his government in the capital, immediately put into force the constitution and all the laws enacted in Vera Cruz. Elected to the presidency on June 1, 1861, he faced, however, a country devastated by three years of war and an empty treasury. His own party was badly split over his expropriation policy, while the defeated conservatives ridiculed the Indian who was their president.

But towering above these difficulties was the threat of foreign intervention. In anger, Juárez had exiled the archbishop of Mexico and ordered the Spanish ambassador out of the country for their part in resistance to the government. Meanwhile, France, Britain, and Spain were demanding payment of debts, inflated beyond belief, due their nationals. Juárez negotiated with the three powers and succeeded in reducing their claims to reasonable figures; but when he was still unable to pay, he declared a two-year moratorium. The representatives of Britain, France, and Spain, however, demanded immediate settlement. Upon being refused, their governments launched a combined expedition to collect their debts.

The fundamental explanation of this action of Europe's powers is found in their determination to seize every opportunity to extend their imperial control. This objective of the European powers found sympathetic reception among the clerical-conservative leaders who, deeply resenting the aspirations of the Indians and Mexico's emerging middle class, had long sought foreign aid. Thus while Juárez was negotiating with Britain, France, and Spain, conservative agents, Gutiérrez de Estrada and José Manuel Hidalgo, were trying to persuade Spain, France, and the Vatican to establish a monarchy in Mexico.

French Intervention in Mexico, 1862–1867. Spain took the lead in England and France in propagating the idea of intervention; but Napoleon III, engaged in world-wide imperialism, provided the driving force. In London an agreement signed in 1861 between the three powers called for a joint expedition of intervention. Its declared purpose was to seize custom duties to apply on their respective debts. France claimed $16,800,000 based on debts to a Swiss, one J. B. Jecker who, through the Duc de Morny, became a French citizen. Of this amount Juárez recognized $2,860,000. To collect this flimsy claim the French, upon arrival in Mexico, revealed to their allies their intention to occupy the country. The Spaniards, disappointed in the hope of dominating the undertaking, departed. The British, after attempting to get a new settlement, likewise left. On April 20, 1862, the French opened hostilities by occupying Orizaba. Throughout the whole of these proceedings, the Lincoln government in the United States assured Juárez that it would give him any assistance it could.

Marching upon the capital, the French forces met a decisive defeat at Puebla on May 5, a date thereafter celebrated in Mexico as a national holiday. However, when Napoleon III sent over 30,000 troops to carry out the occupation, Juárez' army of a bare 6,000 abandoned the capital and moved to San Luis Potosí on May 31, 1863. With the French came the Mexican conservatives headed by General Juan Almonte to await the establishment of a European prince upon the Mexican throne.

Meanwhile Napoleon III, anxious to please France's middle class with raw materials from Mexico and hopeful of winning back papal support lost in aiding Cavour in Italy, believed an empire overseas would achieve both aims. Napoleon's choice for a puppet fell upon Maximilian of Austria, a man of principle and charm, but naive. On April 10, 1864, the two principals drew up the Convention of Miramar under which French troops were to be gradually reduced until 1867, while a force recruited among the Mexicans would replace them; secondly, to meet current expenses, Maximilian was extended a loan of 221,600,000 francs.

Maximilian and his empress, Carlotta, arrived in Mexico in June, 1864. The Mexican conservatives soon discovered to their sorrow that far from being a tool for their purposes, the emperor was a man of liberal tendencies, humane in outlook, and favoring a policy of kindness toward his enemies. He refused to return the lands of the church and he invited Liberal leaders to join his cabinet. Some accepted, but the majority indignantly refused. His wife, ambitious and imperious, endeavored to make up for his shortcomings as an emperor. But probably the most important reason for Maximilian's failure was his complete lack of understanding of the issues in Mexico, an understandable limitation, since there was nothing in the training of an Austrian prince to give an insight into Mexican political struggles. Evidence was his agreeing to sign the barbarous order of October 3, 1865, which characterized Juárez and his supporters as bandits and authorized their execution on capture without trial.

By this date, 1865, the French under General F. A. Bazaine had succeeded in establishing control only through the central part of the country. Juárez maintained his government in the north; his principal general, Porfirio Díaz, held the south. In spite of this incomplete control of the country, Maximilian made an effort to develop his new possession. He offered land to foreign immigrant companies on favorable terms. He supported a program to develop trade and commerce, an important item of which was supplying the Confederate states in their struggle against the Union blockade. But the obstacles to success were too great. Juárez' stubborn opposition placed a heavy financial burden upon the state. More decisive was the collapse of the Confederacy, which not only cut off an important source of income but threw the balance of the struggle in favor of Juárez.

The United States government, which had never recognized the French intervention, supplied Juárez with surplus war materials left over from the Civil War. More important was the large number of American volunteers who, in return for offers of land, joined Juárez' army. Some Confederate families, unwilling to accept the consequences of defeat, migrated, in return for land grants, to Maximilian's area, but these were not an addition to his military forces. The final blow came from Secretary Seward, who on February 12, 1866, demanded that Napoleon III withdraw the French troops. This diplomacy was backed up by the dispatch of several hundred thousand veteran troops to the Texas border. Napoleon III himself at the moment was under pressure at home to abandon the enterprise. The war with Juárez had prevented the French from securing the raw materials hoped for by her industries, while the maintenance of troops at great expense was a heavy financial burden. Finally, the success of Bismarck in unifying Germany after the defeat of Austria in 1866 stirred the nationalists in France to demand the return of the French forces in Mexico. Thus by March, 1867, the last of the French troops had left.

Maximilian now faced Juárez supported only by troops commanded by his conservative Mexican generals. The latter believed that by combining their armies at one point, Querétaro, with Maximilian at their head, they could defeat the liberal armies converging upon Mexico City. The choice of Querétaro was a poor one strategically. Juárez' forces, soon dominating the low surrounding hills, poured in a murderous fire and held the city in a grip of iron. In the south, Díaz' capture of Puebla ended all hope of reinforcements from that quarter. Desertions depleting Maximilian's forces left him with hardly 5,000 troops. When finally Juárez' army captured Querétaro's key defensive outpost, Maximilian marched out to surrender on May 15, 1867.

True to the constitution of 1857, Juárez ordered the emperor brought to justice in accordance with its provisions. The ablest liberal lawyers, among them Mariano Riva Palacio, defended the emperor, advancing the striking argument that the treatment accorded Jefferson Davis after the Civil War in the United States should be the precedent for the decision in Maximilian's case. The defect of the argument, of course, was that Davis was not a foreign invader. Thus the emperor was found to be a filibuster, an instrument of France for the overthrow of Mexico's constitutional government, guilty of treason and responsible for the infamous order of October 3, 1865. Pleas to save the life of the royal prisoner poured in upon Juárez from all parts of the civilized world. But the president was powerless. Mexican public opinion demanded the execution of Maximilian to serve as a symbol to all foreigners who sought to subject Mexica to their control. On June 19, 1867, Maximilian, with Miramón and Mejía, fell before the firing squad.

The Reconstruction of Mexico, 1867–1876. The years 1854–1867 saw the enactment of the Reform Laws, the 1857 constitution, the War of the Reform, the French intervention, and the Maximilian empire established in Mexico. What was the significance of these fourteen years? The meaning was simply that these events, representing the growth of a Mexican middle class and Indian demands for justice, were destroying the feudal structure of Mexican society. Juárez' laws, aimed at freeing the land for the benefit of the Indians, saw the bulk of this land, however, pass into the hands of speculators. Porfirio Díaz, a good example, became one of the new landowners during this long struggle. Businessmen saw trade flourish while Juárez controlled Vera Cruz. During the French intervention opportunities were many to supply the Confederacy, to trade with France, or to buy and sell the loot that fell into the hands of the commercial groups either from the Juarist or French soldiers.

When peace came in 1867 this new middle class wished to attract foreign capital, to exploit the wealth of their newly acquired lands, and to modernize the economy. No longer were the riches of Mexico to remain stagnant in the agricultural holdings of a feudal class and a medieval-minded church. Juárez' struggle had, in fact, broken the bonds of feudalism. With this break-up its political expression, the Conservative party, also disappeared, hastened to its end by the taint of treason. On the other hand, Juárez' own party, the Liberal, became hopelessly split between those, who, following Juárez' lead, wished to carry forward social reforms to improve the status of the Indians and the lower classes in general, and those whose first objective was economic reform to exploit the landlocked wealth of Mexico. The latter were soon to turn toward the United States, where a like-minded group, having won the Civil War, were engaged in exploiting the mineral wealth of the West, reconstructing the South for its raw materials for northern industry, and, reaching out, were seeking railroad concessions in Mexico and isthmian communications in Central America, while evincing an interest in the rich minerals of Mexico itself. The political struggle between 1867 and 1876, accordingly, has its meaning in this light.

In spite of the growing conflict within his party, Juárez was re-elected for a fourth term in 1867. He had already begun the administrative reconstruction by re-establishing the state governments, reorganizing the judicial system to secure enforcement of the laws, and cleansing municipal administrations. After he assumed the presidency he turned his efforts to reconstructing the country economically, planning the construction of railroads between the principal cities, attempting to revive agriculture, and establishing technical schools. In foreign affairs, in appreciation of the support he had received from the United States, he reached with that country an amicable settlement of claims against Mexico, and re-established relations with the leading European nations.

Attempting to reduce expenditures, he dismissed large numbers of soldiers and officers from the army, now that the main task was over. The effect of this measure, however, was disastrous, for many thousands of these men for some fourteen years had known no other profession. Discontented, they became the prey of conservative groups and those liberals who disagreed with Juárez' enforcement of the Reform Laws.

Military uprisings plagued the administration. State governments frequently defied the central authority in the matter of enforcing national laws. In an effort to win support, Juárez in 1870 issued a general law of amnesty benefiting adherents of the imperialist party and those who had conspired against his own government. The measure did contribute to the restoration of a semblance of law and order.

In 1872 Juárez again became a candidate for the presidency, for he felt that his great work of reform was just getting under way and needed his hand to guide it. But by this date, many, viewing his long tenure, believed he was trying to establish a dictatorship. Leading members of his own party opposed him, notably Sebastián Lerdo de Tejada, brother of the author of the *Ley Lerdo*, and Porfirio Díaz. The former was in the Juarist tradition of reform; the latter represented the new aggressive middle class which placed social reforms second, if at all, on their agenda. The election, which was close, was decided by congress in favor of Juárez. Díaz promptly revolted under the "Plan of Noria," which demanded among other things a new constitution in which the powers of congress would be confined to economic matters, the ending of burdensome taxes, and the enlargement of the powers of municipalities. In the midst of putting down the uprising, Juárez suffered a heart attack and died on July 18, 1872. The great man who had given the Mexican nation a new orientation was interred in the Pantheon of San Fernando, while the country stood in silent respect and mourning.

As the constitution provided, Lerdo, the chief justice of the supreme court, succeeded Juárez as president. In spite of Díaz' continuing revolt, Lerdo went on with the reform program, succeeding in getting congress to include all the Laws of the Reform in the constitution in May, 1874. The church was completely disestablished, freedom of worship was guaranteed, and marriage by civil contract became the law of the land. Between 1870 and 1876 more than 3,000 schools had been established. Against Díaz, too, Lerdo eventually succeeded. Thus by the end of his administration, peace, with minor exceptions, was the order of the day. In October, 1876, Lerdo, elected by congress, began his second term. But Díaz, carefully organizing his strength, again revolted under the "Plan of Tuxtepec," later supplanted by the "Plan of Palo Blanco," in which he attacked Lerdo's administration on the surprising ground, it turned out later, that the president was turning the nation over to foreign capitalists! Defeated, Lerdo left the country to live in New York City. Iglesias, who had revolted on the charge of electoral fraud, likewise found himself exiled by Díaz. The latter assumed the presidency provisionally until new elections could be held.

Part III. ECONOMIC CHANGES AND DECLINE OF LIBERALISM: THE DÍAZ REGIME, 1876–1911

The Economic and Political Bases of the Dictatorship. Porfirio Díaz' long dictatorship (1876–1911) opened the floodgates to foreign investment in Mexico. Native Mexican capitalists increased their own wealth through the opportunities that came with the consequent modernization of the economy. Upon the income derived from granting concessions, the small tax imposed upon the growing volume of exports, and the ending of taxes burdensome to the expanding middle class, Díaz developed sources of income not only new in the history of Mexico, but which far exceeded those derived formerly from internal taxation on a backward, agricultural economy. This income in turn became the base for establishing a peace with force. With it he purchased the services of generals who otherwise would have been competitors for the presidency. With it he paid the soldiers of the army regularly so that discontent among the military was unknown. With it he established a state police called the *Rurales,* many of whom were former bandits who, during the long period of disturbances between 1856 and 1876, had established virtual control in their respective areas. Their chieftains, becoming heads of the *Rurales* in the various states, maintained a ruthless, internal peace. Likewise Díaz made certain of his governors by providing them with an income and prerogatives hitherto unknown in the country's history.

With these weapons at hand, he persecuted without mercy those who had courage to maintain the political principles of the constitution of 1857. One of the most infamous examples of the terror exercised was the telegram to the governor of Vera Cruz in 1879 in which Díaz ordered all caught conspiring against him to be executed in cold blood. With the church Díaz made his peace. While he did not set aside the constitution or repeal the Laws of the Reform, where they touched the privileges of the church, he winked at their violation. Thus gradually the church by purchasing land became again a great property owner.

When Díaz' first term (1880–1884) ended, he placed in the presidency General Manuel González, who governed from 1880 to 1884. His administration saw the beginning of railroad construction on a large scale carried out by the Southern Pacific Railroad Company. With transportation available, foreigners began the opening up of mines in northern Mexico. The enthusiasm for the new ventures led to wild speculation in land values. The resulting criticism of Díaz officials who engaged in this practice inspired González to end the free press. Díaz occupied himself in this period as governor of Oaxaca, serving in the Mexican senate, and visiting the United States to encourage American investors to exploit the resources of Mexico. Just before González left office, Díaz secured an amendment to the constitution which permitted the re-election of a president who had already served one term. Later in 1888 and 1890 other amendments permitted continuous and legal re-election. Ambitious political leaders he eliminated by encouraging rival candidacies and offering himself at the last moment as the compromise candidate, or exiling them by ambassadorial appointments.

During his long reign from 1884 to 1911, Díaz continued the economic progress begun under Juárez of converting the state of Mexico from a feudal to a modern one. Unfortunately, however, he failed to carry forward the counterpart of economic advance, democratic growth, set in motion by Juárez. The principal figure in the dictatorship, who created new economic institutions and effected financial reforms, was José Ives Limantour, his secretary of the treasury. Frequently referred to as the Alexander Hamilton of Mexico, Limantour became minister in 1893. He abolished the sales tax *(alcabala),* ended in some parts of Mexico by Juárez, placed the country on a gold basis, established a central banking system, and funded the national debt. These measures stabilized Mexican currency and reduced the interest on national bonds, which became eagerly sought after by foreign banking houses. He augmented the income of the state by the imposition of new taxes, increasing the efficiency of collection, but kept taxes at a minimum on foreign enterprises under the theory that low taxation would encourage investment. Legislation, too, facilitated the purchase of land by foreigners, both from native owners and from the government. By 1911 the excellent financial condition of the country was attested to by its small national debt, some $438,000,000.

Limantour's reforms provided stability, and a policy of low taxation attracted capital, as did a vast body of cheap labor and inexhaustible mineral riches. Railroad building led the way. Mileage grew from about 460 miles in 1876 to over 16,500 by 1911. The main lines ran from El Paso, Laredo, and Tucson southward to Mexico City. Others connected the capital with the principal ports on the east and west coast as well as with the important state capitals. Feeder lines penetrated the northern mineral regions and the southern agricultural areas. These were all largely owned by American companies. Across the northern tier of states from New León to Sonora millions of acres of grazing lands passed into the hands of foreign companies, mostly American.

In the western mountain area, the leading American mining companies secured ownership of gold, silver, mercury, lead, copper, and other mineral deposits. In southern Mexico important agricultural land, producing principally cotton, sugar, coffee, and rice, became the property of American corporations or individuals who settled in Mexico. In the Yucatan peninsula a large foreign investment went into lands producing chicle, the chief ingredient of chewing gum. In other parts of the peninsula a leading Chicago concern secured extensive holdings on which henequén, a fibrous plant, was grown, valuable for the manufacture of rope, twine, cordage, and similar products.

In 1901 as a result of discoveries by Edward H. Doheny, the vast oil reserves of Mexico along the Gulf of Mexico opened a new era of wealth. By 1911 production was almost 13,000,000 barrels annually. In the intervening years, Standard Oil, Gulf, Sinclair, and lesser American companies had secured from Díaz concessions to the region between the Rio Grande and Vera Cruz. British oil interests held grants from Vera Cruz southward along the coast. By 1911 much of the area from the Bay of Campeche to the Rio Grande had passed into the hands of foreign oil companies.

In addition to investment in lands, foreign funds also went into the construction of utilities, chemical plants, hydroelectric installations, smelters, sugar mills, and other similar industries which brought the industrial revolution to Mexico. This foreign interest, of course, gave an impetus to the growth of native Mexican-owned industries, most of which were in textile, shoe, and pottery factories, in breweries, and in other similar businesses. Of the total investment the American was preponderant, estimated in 1913 at about $800,000,000. British companies had extensive holdings in mining and oil, ranking second with some $200,000,000 invested. Other foreign groups, Dutch, French, Spanish, German, and Italian, brought the total foreign investment to well over $1,250,000,000. The vast export flowing from this widespread extraction of raw materials reflected itself in the rapid expansion of the country's foreign trade. Estimated at 51,760,000 pesos in 1873, it reached a value of 499,588,000 pesos by 1910. Of this total, more than 328,000,000 were with the United States.

The Effects of the Dictatorship. The extraordinary economic expansion of Mexico, resting principally upon the exploitation of its riches, human and natural, produced deep antagonism among most Mexicans toward both Díaz and foreigners. Possibly the group most profoundly affected were the Indians, workers on the agricultural plantations and

in the mines. For the first time in the history of Mexico Indians were
extensively dispossessed of their lands. Thousands of Indians were driven
off their communal holdings, ploughed up to make room for huge sugar,
cotton, coffee, and other plantations. Others saw their ancient lands made
useless by the vast exploitation of oil along the coast. Many thousands
were driven bodily from their homes by the *Rurales* to provide unskilled
labor on railroads, in the oil fields, and in mines. Moreover, a system
of peonage existed. Union organization, on the other hand, was treated
virtually as treason. In factories long hours, low wages, and unhealthful
working conditions prevailed. Slum-housing, disease, and lack of schools
characterized urban environment. Strikes broke out in the cities; revolts,
in the rural areas. *Rurales* crushed the latter with appalling ruthlessness.
Yearning for the return of their lands, the Indians nourished a hatred
for Díaz and foreigners. Within the ranks of urban labor, ideas of socialism took hold.

Benefited was the new wealthy middle class. The coterie which
particularly surrounded Díaz, businessmen, government officials, lawyers,
were known as a group as the *Científicos*. The name derived from the
late nineteenth century exponents of the doctrine that science, applied
to Mexico's development, would create a modern state. Becoming immensely wealthy, this small but aggressive middle class invested their
money in native industries and became intensely nationalistic. While
approving the harsh methods to hold the Indians and labor in check,
they were simultaneously dissatisfied with the power exercised by foreigners in national affairs. The most serious obstacle to their growth
was foreign ownership of railroads. Díaz, bowing to their demands for
nationalization, quietly bought up in 1907 the majority control of the
Harriman-owned Mexican lines.

Part IV.   THE MEXICAN REVOLUTION: RETURN TO
DEMOCRATIC DEVELOPMENT, 1910 TO THE
PRESENT

1. THE REVOLUTION TO 1917

Causes. The Mexican Revolution, considered by Mexicans as still in
progress, had its origins in the efforts attending independence from Spain
to establish liberal institutions. Juárez' success in giving these a workable
basis was halted by the Díaz dictatorship. Don Porfirio, however, continued the economic progress demanded by Mexico's middle class. But
the methods followed by the dictatorship, as we have noted, dispossessed

Indians of their lands and created a major source of discontent. Suppression of labor turned that body of Mexicans to socialist solutions to escape their suffering. The church, failing in its mission to relieve suffering, came under attack. These are basic causes.

Discontent in the higher levels of Mexican society, however, set the revolutionary forces in motion. Díaz perforce antagonized wealthy and powerful figures that he kept from the presidency. Outstanding was the ruthless but able General Bernardo Reyes. Typical was his experience in 1904 when, believing he had Díaz' support for the presidency, he was dispatched on a mission abroad. His "Reyes Clubs" remained active in the hands of military figures, industrialists, lawyers, and others who foresaw that Díaz' advancing years would force his retirement. The *Ciéntificos* as a group feared for their investments in the face of growing discontent. In 1904 they persuaded Díaz, then seventy-four years old, to accept an amendment to the constitution providing for the office of vice-president. Ramón Corral, Díaz' minister of government, filled that office in the election of that year.

The next step came in 1908 when Díaz told James Creelman, the representative of *Pearson's Magazine,* that if an authentic opposition party should be formed and if the nominee of that party could win legally, he, Díaz, would retire in 1910.

The immediate cause of the Mexican Revolution was the work of a frail man but one touched with genius—Francisco I. Madero. In 1910 Madero published a famous book, *The Presidential Succession in 1910.* It criticized the Díaz regime, advocated democratic elections, and proposed political reforms which would provide powerful families, hitherto excluded, with entry into political life. The phraseology of the book was sufficiently democratic to attract the support of labor and the disinherited Indian masses. Madero's ambition, not to win a presidency, but to educate the Mexicans in democracy, drove him forward in the face of family opposition, persecution, and even threats against his life. As the candidate of the Anti-Re-electionist party in 1910, he campaigned vigorously. Huge crowds gathered to hear the little man. Díaz regarded him at first with tolerance, but, becoming suddenly aware of the danger, ordered his arrest. He then dictated his own re-election and that of Corral as vice-president. But the dictator had entered a world of illusions: Madero's campaign had touched off the Revolution.

The Revolution, 1910–1917. Madero escaped to San Antonio, Texas, on October 5, 1910, where he issued a call to arms in the "Plan of San Luis Potosí." Denouncing Díaz and Corral, he called for new elections and

armed revolt, and vaguely promised redistribution of the land and electoral reform. The aged Díaz neglected to send adequate forces against
the many uprisings in the north. The fatal blow fell on May 11, 1911,
when Villa, capturing Ciudad Juárez, gave the revolutionists access to
arms and ammunition from across the border.

Madero's promise to redistribute the land roused the Indians in the
south under Emiliano Zapata. Díaz, attempting to head off these gathering forces, conceded recognition to the rebels. He enacted a land bill to
divide up the large estates and a law prohibiting re-election. These
offers, interpreted as weakness, encouraged thousands to join Madero.
Díaz, recognizing the inevitable, resigned, surrendering the presidency
to Francisco de la Barra. On May 25 the old dictator left for France
never to forgive the Mexicans for their "ingratitude."

The Presidency of Madero, 1911–1913. In Mexico Madero received
a triumphal ovation. In October, as head of the newly created Constitutionalist party, he was overwhelmingly elected president, with José Pino
Suárez as vice-president. With Madero, landowners, industrialists, lawyers, and commercial figures came into power. Behind them were the
bulk of foreign interests. Excluded were the *mestizo* and labor elements,
represented after a fashion by Villa in the north, and the Indians under
Zapata in the south. Zapata, unlike Villa, sought no office; he asked only
that the promise be kept to return village lands. Madero's brothers, who
held high government positions, and their conservative friends, however,
wanted no disturbance of the social structure. Electoral reform, which
would give their group representation, was the limit of change they
sought.

Madero's proposals on land reform gave an excellent index to the
prevailing ideas of these middle class Mexicans. He himself thought in
terms of creating a class of small landowners; these would wipe away
the economic and social evils in the rural areas. Moreover, he believed
that such agrarian reform should be gradual, an evolutionary rather than
a revolutionary process. Nothing, in fact, was done under Madero to
effect land reform. Zapata, disillusioned, revolted in the south.

On this occasion Zapata promulgated his famous *"Plan de Ayala,"*
the first important document to express Indian ideas of land reform. He
advocated in brief that the people repossess immediately land taken from
them where they could show a title; for persons and villages without land
or title, expropriation of private properties, with indemnification in part
to the owners, should be carried out. Thus citizens would receive land,
and pueblos, *ejidos.* The *ejido* to which Zapata referred became the heart

of the later agrarian reform in Mexico. In Spain *ejido* meant the collectively held, untilled lands on the outskirts of an agrarian community. In Mexico *ejido* was eventually defined in the constitution of 1917, Article 27. Its intent, as Eyler Simpson states, was to give villages "any and all classes of 'waters, woods and lands' which they may need. These waters, woods and lands, title to which is vested (temporarily at any rate) in the village as a whole and which are enjoyed by the members of the village in common, are *ejidos*."[1] Madero sent his generals against Zapata in a fruitless campaign. More important, Zapata's unflinching policy finally brought into Madero's cabinet ministers who proposed what eventually became national policy, namely, the restoration of ejidal lands and the use of expropriation as a means to that end.

The Zapata revolt was paralleled in the center by an uprising of the displaced remnants of the Díaz regime, led by Díaz' son, Félix, and General Reyes, with church support. A third outbreak under Orozco and Villa, the original leaders, disaffected the north. Most serious for Madero was Díaz' attack on the capital, the "Tragic Ten Days," beginning on February 19, 1913. In desperation, Madero turned to Huerta, his chief of staff, but that personage was already scheming with Díaz, abetted by the American minister, Henry Lane Wilson, to oust the president. When the latter refused to resign, he and his vice-president, Pino Suárez, were arrested and promised a safe-conduct to exile. Both got as far as the gates of the federal prison, where they were brutally assassinated. The event shocked Mexico. Venustiano Carranza, governor of Coahuila, repudiated Huerta's request for recognition by the governors of the states. Villa rejected him, as did other leaders. In vain he tried to pacify the country. His downfall, however, came directly from American intervention, fortunately in the hands of President Woodrow Wilson. Horrified by Huerta's method of reaching the presidency, Wilson indignantly refused recognition, although such was advocated by Henry Lane Wilson, the American ambassador.

Huerta. To secure peace between the warring groups, Wilson sent a representative, J. Lind, an action resented by many Mexicans, who, even though they wished Huerta out of office, believed there should be no meddling in their affairs. The direct effect was to strengthen Huerta's position, so that he carried the elections held in October, 1913. Although powerful groups in the United States were demanding intervention to protect their investments in Mexico, Wilson adopted his famous policy of "watchful waiting."

[1] Simpson, *The Ejido, Mexico's Way Out,* Chapel Hill, 1937, p. 74.

Early in April, 1914, an incident at Tampico brought the long-expected American intervention. On that occasion some American sailors, arrested for entering a forbidden area, caused Admiral Mayo, in command of an American fleet, to demand an apology and a salute to the flag. Huerta refused the salute, but acceded to the other demands. Wilson thereupon ordered the occupation of Vera Cruz on April 21, 1914. The American president, not wishing to advance into the country and precipitate a war, asked the representatives of Argentina, Brazil, and Chile to meet with delegates named by Carranza and Huerta to find a solution. Over the protests of Huerta's spokesmen—for Carranza refused to participate—the members called for the resignation of the Mexican president. On its part the United States agreed to withdraw from Vera Cruz. Unable to maintain himself, Huerta resigned, leaving for Europe in July, 1914.

Mexico under Carranza, 1914–1920. With the overthrow of Huerta, Carranza continued middle class leadership of the Revolution. With him were associated two figures later dominant in Mexican affairs, Alvaro Obregón, his chief of staff, and Plutarcho Elías Calles, a wealthy landowner in Sonora. However, Indians and *mestizos* were to make their influence felt in the confusion following the fall of Huerta. From the south Zapata captured Mexico City and demanded land for the Indians. Upon his withdrawal, Villa entered the capital from his stronghold in the north. From March to July, 1914, Zapata reoccupied Mexico City, suffered defeat at the hands of Obregón, but extracted anew promises of land division.

In this turmoil Carranza took two important steps to consolidate support behind him. He appealed to Zapata's followers in the Decree of 1915, the first legal document to recognize that rural discontent stemmed from extensive loss of village lands under Díaz and to propose their return as the only way to insure peace and aid the poorer agrarians. Misinterpreting its meaning, many village communities seized lands, as did some unprincipled individuals. More important, the Decree, next in sequence to Zapata's *"Plan de Ayala,"* paved the way for more carefully worded provisions on land tenure in the constitution of 1917.

His second measure was to recognize the demands of labor. Freed from the ruthless Díaz suppression, urban labor had been openly organizing into unions since 1911. To these, in return for aid against Villa, Carranza promised legislation to protect their hard-won gains. Thus supported by Red Battalions, as they were called, he dispatched Obregón, whose forces, armed with machine guns, defeated Villa's dreaded cavalry.

Labor now looked to Carranza for fulfillment of his promises. Meanwhile, spreading conflicts in the rural areas over the interpretation of the Decree of 1915 demanded a basic settlement. To find a solution to these problems and others of equally far-reaching import to the nation, Carranza early in 1916 summoned a constitutional convention.

To an outsider Mexico in the latter part of 1915 seemed to be disintegrating. Zapata held the south; Villa menaced the north; Manuel Petaez, supported by foreign capital, occupied the Gulf coast; while Carranza dominated the center. But after Villa's defeat, Carranza was recognized by several Latin-American countries and by the United States government, which cut off Villa's imported supplies. Knowing that an attack on the United States would embarrass Carranza, Villa seized and executed some eighteen Americans at Santa Isabel in January, 1916. He followed this outrage with a raid upon the town of Columbus, New Mexico, killing a number of American citizens in the streets. This violent act precipitated the Pershing expedition into Mexico (March, 1916–February, 1917).

This undertaking had a more complex background than that arising from a border raid. From the beginning of the Revolution, powerful American and other foreign interests demanded intervention. When events drove out the clergy, threatened ownership of American properties, and gave recognition to the socialist doctrines of labor, pressure for intervention increased. On the other hand, the Wilson administration foresaw the possibility of the United States becoming involved in World War I and for that reason had no desire to be pushed into a war with Mexico. Just as strong were Wilson's own feelings that the Mexican people had a right to self-determination in their internal affairs. He adopted accordingly a policy of "watchful waiting," ridiculed by the interventionists. To avoid war with Mexico, Wilson hit upon the device of sending the Pershing expedition to cooperate with the Mexican government in the capture of Villa.

Villa, with his puny but reckless force in opposition, became at once a national hero. Carranza, out of deference to this public opinion, virtually refused to cooperate and eventually warned President Wilson to withdraw the American forces. Thus for eleven months the American forces pursued their fruitless quest. Finally, in February, 1917, at a cost of $130,000,000, the Pershing expedition returned. While not accomplishing its ostensible objective, the capture of Villa, it had served the more important purpose of warding off a war with Mexico.

Probably the most significant effect of the expedition was the influence it exercised upon the constitution makers. The spectacle of an American army marching across the north, no matter how well justified, strengthened the forces in the convention demanding a radical statement of Mexican ownership of her natural resources. The constitution was, in fact, promulgated on the very day that the last United States troops left Mexico on February 5, 1917.

The Constitution of 1917. The basic ideas of the constitution of 1917 sprang from the long struggle to establish democratic institutions and from the harrowing experiences of most of the Mexican people under the Díaz regime. After five and a half years of revolutionary struggle, the basis of cooperation between the chief groups had been laid. Together they produced a document expressing the fundamental interests of all. The Indians, dispossessed under Díaz, wanted land and the end of age-long abuses. They had the support of Mexican labor, which demanded reforms recognizing their rights and providing opportunities for their growth. Finally, the middle class, a significant force under Juárez, had greatly expanded its wealth and its numbers under Díaz, and had led the Revolution. Resentful of the control of foreigners over raw materials, oil, minerals, agricultural lands, industries, and other resources, they could join hands with the Indian and labor representatives in the convention to break the hold of the foreigner. Playing an important part in the work were intellectuals, who looked to reforms restricting the church and providing a modern system of education, sanitation, public health, and industrialization, all objectives, too, of the middle class. The 1917 constitution was, accordingly, the product of the joint efforts and compromises of these groups, all patriotically Mexican in outlook. As such it represented one of the major developments in Mexican democracy and had a profound influence in all Latin-American countries.

The document provided for the usual framework of a republican government. The president was elected by direct popular vote, with the right to choose his own cabinet, and served for four years. There was no provision for a vice-president. The congress was composed of two houses. The senate, comprising two senators from each state, was elected by popular vote for four years, while the members of the house of deputies, chosen by direct vote according to the population, served two years. A safeguard against presidential usurpation existed in a permanent committee which sat between sessions. The document further provided a supreme court and lower courts. The suffrage reached all male Mexicans twenty-one years of age who could show a legal occupation.

Reflecting the strong beliefs of the Indian, labor, and intellectual representatives, but vigorously opposed by some members of the wealthier middle class, was Article 27 which called for the ownership by the nation of all subsoil riches. Article 123, a Charter for Labor, provided for (1) a careful definition of the rights of labor including those to organize, strike, and bargain collectively, (2) minimum wages, and (3) a board with authority to enforce arbitration of industrial disputes. Other clauses carried enlightened measures to protect the social life of the people as a whole, placing education, socialist in character, in the hands of the state, separating church and state, ending the system of debt slavery or peonage, and confining the clergy to strictly religious activities by nationalizing all church property. Provision for making available land for the Mexican people was carefully drawn in clauses calling for the division of large estates, whether native, church, or foreign-owned. The constitution of 1917 prepared the ground for stable government in Mexico. Since its promulgation, the people of Mexico have shown themselves increasingly effective in developing democratic institutions.

This remarkable document not only laid the basis for the reconstruction of Mexico's national life; it also opened the way for a flowering of Mexican culture, which, in turn, has made significant contributions to world civilization. This movement in literature and art can best be appreciated by a brief survey of the work of its leading intellectuals since independence. Their writings and other expressions of cultural growth, it will be seen, have closely paralleled the social and political changes accompanying the great events of Mexico's national period: the Wars for Independence, the Liberal-Conservative struggle culminating in the era of the Juárez reforms, the Díaz dictatorship, and the Revolution of 1910.

2. LITERARY AND CULTURAL DEVELOPMENT OF MEXICO

Leading Figures, 1810–1910. The most significant literary figure of the Wars for Independence was Fernández de Lizardi (1774–1827), who wrote under the pen name of "The Mexican Thinker." His works do not cover the vast canvas of that struggle; rather he is remembered as the creator of the Mexican novel. His most famous work is *The Mangy Parakeet (El Periquillo sarniento),* a picture of Mexican life in the last epoch of the viceroys. It tells the story of an incorrigible youth, yet one honest and kindly, who moved through all levels of Mexican society. Fernández de Lizardi used his work to oppose vice, but the penetration of the author is so sharp and his types so lifelike that the novel gives of Mexican society a picture that has remained unequaled.

With independence the Liberal-Conservative struggle swept Mexican prose writers, poets, and dramatists into its vortex. The romantic movement, which followed a normal pattern of development elsewhere in Latin America, was in Mexico the weapon of the Liberals for an attack upon the conservative classicists. Important among the latter was José María Roa Bárcena (1827–1908), who wrote both prose and poetry. Fernando Calderón (1809–1845) and Rodríguez Galván (1816–1842) are recognized as the first of the romanticists. Of the two, Galván is considered one of the greatest of Mexico's lyric poets. The *Prophecy of Gautemoc* is his masterpiece.

The Liberal-Conservative struggle engulfed the Mexican historians of the early nineteenth century. Chief among these were Carlos María Bustamante (1774–1848) and Lucas Alamán, both conservatives. Bustamante, highly inaccurate and deeply prejudiced in favor of the colonial way of life, nevertheless rescued from obscurity the great colonial historians, Gómora and Sahagun among others, and preserved invaluable data on the national life of Mexico in the early nineteenth century. Unlike Bustamante, Lucas Alamán (1792–1853) was a disciplined historian who wrote in a vigorous and unadorned style. Equipped with a broad education in the sciences and humanities, he wrote two great works, *Dissertations on the History of Mexico,* covering the colonial period, and the *History of Mexico,* dealing with the period from 1808 to 1852. These volumes established, too, his place in Mexican literature. However, his strong party spirit gave his interpretation of Mexican history a flavor that made him a controversial figure. To the Liberals he stood as the defender of Bourbonism and all the evils of the colonial past; to the Conservatives he was above human frailties and dealt out judgments with an even hand.

Complementing Bustamante rather than Alamán was the liberal historian, Lorenzo de Zavala (1788–1836). Schooled in the masterpieces of the French Revolution, he embraced Liberalism with fervor. He dropped his pen at a moment's notice to take up the sword, and when the battle was over, returned to his manuscripts to rend his enemies. His *Historical Essay on the Revolution of Mexico* is filled with errors, but his sharp insights into the nature of the political struggle frequently illuminate a whole period. Indeed, the clarity of his vision defined questions which still agitate Mexico today.

With the restoration of the Republic in 1867, Mexican intellectuals made a conscious effort to forget their political differences and devote themselves to the development of Mexican culture. The leader in this unique movement was Ignacio Manuel Altamirano (1834–1893). An ardent supporter of the Reform and a soldier in the ranks, he came from a humble Indian family which had adopted a Spanish name. Altamirano received an excellent education by virtue of a law which favored promising young Indians. The War of the Reform, however, interrupted his studies in Mexico City and sent him to the battlefields in the South. After the war, elected a deputy to the Juárez congress, he was soon forced by the French intervention to take up arms again. Finally, in 1867 he began his brilliant literary career with the founding of a review, *The Renaissance.* He opened its columns to all ideas and all writers, liberal, conservative, and even imperialist (supporters of the French), in an effort to weld the antagonistic currents of classicism and romanticism into one national stream.

He himself wrote poetry of high quality, which significantly expressed the spirit of the Mexican people. His novels, moreover, are the first in Mexico to have artistic structure.

One of his great contemporaries was Justo Sierra (1848–1912), a man from whom all other Mexican writers of the period drew strength. Both a lyric poet in his own right and a great prose writer, Justo Sierra became the guide, critic, philosopher, historian, and inspirer of Latin-American writers on two continents.

By the end of the century French romanticism, deeply affecting the course of Mexican letters, gave rise to the movement of modernism. Its three chief figures were Gutiérrez Nájera, Amado Nervo, and Federico Gamboa. Nájera (1859–1895) was a lyric poet whose chief contribution, possibly, was the establishment of the *Azure Review* which resembled *The Renaissance* in its breadth of view. Amado Nervo (1870–1919) founded a few years after Nájera's death the *Modern Review,* which became the principal outlet for new poets breaking away from the Spanish tradition. His style in poetry, strongly influenced by French symbolism in its early stages, evolved a simplicity which Darío hailed as Nervo's greatest achievement. In addition to his novels, which take high rank in Mexican literature, Nervo was a prolific writer of essays, chronicles, and other journalistic articles.

French influence culminated in the work of Federico Gamboa (1864–1939). His contribution to Mexican letters was in the field of the novel, although his dramas were popular. His most famous work, *Santa,* was the life story of a courtesan. At the same time his autobiographical work, *Impressions and Memories,* is regarded as "the most beautiful Mexican book of its kind."

Besides the literary figures of this period, Mexico produced historians of the first importance. Manuel Orozco y Berra (1816–1881) pioneered in the study of prehistoric Indian civilizations. His great contemporary, Joaquín García Icazbalceta, devoted his life to the editing of rare and unknown books, manuscripts, and documents on Mexican history. His chief contributions were in the field of sixteenth century history, of which his greatest work is the magnificent *Bibliography of the Sixteenth Century*, a detailed catalog of books printed in Mexico between 1539–1600.

In the twentieth century Luis González Obregón (1865–1938) continued the high standard of historical investigation and writing set by García Icazbalceta. The author of numerous biographies, principally of the colonial period, he was a master in portraying the culture, manners, and customs of colonial life. His best works, based upon prodigious research, are those exploring the history of the capital, particularly his two-volume study, *The Streets of Mexico City*.

Revolutionary Literature and Art. The Mexican Revolution of 1910, an upheaval of the masses, met a stony silence from established Mexican writers, dominated by French influences and reared in Porfirian luxury. The Revolution in consequence produced its own singers. Among the first of these were street troubadours who invented with great facility *corridos* or ballads. These recorded a striking contemporary event, praised the heroes or ridiculed the enemies of the Revolution. Best known in the United States is *La Cucaracha*, the marching song of Pancho Villa's men.

In the literature of the Revolution two names are outstanding, Martín Luis Guzmán (1887–   ) in his principal work, *The Eagle and the Serpent*, glorified Villa, recounting in epic manner the incredible adventures of the famous chieftain. Of greater magnitude is the novel of Mariano Azuela (1873–   ), *The Underdogs (Los de abajo)*. Azuela, a physician by profession, exhibited from his student years a deep interest in Mexico's poor. Joining the Revolution as a supporter of Madero, he became a member of a small band in the mountain fastness of Jalisco, where he conceived the idea of *The Underdogs*. This novel, telling the story of a peasant driven from his plot of land and rising to the rank of a revolutionary general, was written and published in the heat of the struggle (1915). The usual reaction of the reader is that the Revolution was but an aimless slaughter carried on by leaders who little knew what they were fighting for and had no other objectives but to loot and murder. The merits of the novel, however, which give it its character as a masterpiece, are the lyric descriptions of the awe-inspiring terrain and the stark portrayal of the loves, hates, passions, and sufferings of the Mexican "underdogs." Recognized quickly as one of the great novels of modern times, *Los de abajo* has been translated into all major languages.

The Mexican Renaissance. The Revolution found its greatest cultural expression, not in literature, but in the achievements of a galaxy of painters whose work constitutes the "Mexican Renaissance." Its best known forerunners were José Guadalupe Posada, a lithographer, and Gerado Murillo, universally known under his adopted name, Dr. Atl (1877–   ). Posada foretold the Revolution in his irreverent caricatures of Díaz politicians. More important, his prints acidly illustrated Porfirian evils: the tinseled, imported culture of the wealthy and the tragic lives of the dispossessed. Significantly, his new and revolutionary forms of art influenced markedly many later Mexican painters, notably Diego Rivera and José Clemente Orozco.

The work of Dr. Atl, the chief prerevolutionary leader of the revolt of the artists, was of a different character. So offended was he with the imitation of imported European art work and artists that he abandoned his own name to adopt an Aztec one—Atl. His contribution to the Renaissance was his profound studies of native arts and crafts. These, he insisted, were the true sources of inspiration for Mexico's painters. Eventually his own great work was published in 1922, *Artes Populares en Mexico (The Popular Arts in Mexico).*

When the Revolution broke out in 1910 with shattering effect, Mexico's artists went off to fight in the revolutionary armies. Many of them for the first time saw the riches and beauties of their own land and observed the skill of Indian craftsmen. After the great effort had crystallized itself in the constitution of 1917, Mexico's political and artistic leaders supported, in fact demanded, a vast program of universal education. Above all, these leaders realized the need of giving visual expression to the broad objectives of the Revolution: land for the Indians, rights for the laboring masses, the overthrow of foreign and clerical domination, and the rebuilding of Mexico for the benefit of all her people. Such ideas could not be expressed on an easel board; great vacant spaces on public buildings were needed. But more important were the artists who could wield the brushes to paint the monumental figures demanded by the inspiring theme of Mexican liberation.

Fortunately, in the Obregón administration (1920–1924), José Vasconcelos, a philosopher, was minister of education. Beyond all others he had developed the basic ideas for the education of Mexico's illiterate millions. Into his sympathetic ear the artistic leaders poured their ideas for public murals which would express the new Mexican world. There was no lack of artists. But three or four stand out and even take rank among the world's masters. Of these considered by many the greatest is Diego Rivera (1886–   ).

To Rivera went the commission to paint the walls of the three floors of the ministry of education building. When finished he had protrayed there in overwhelming detail the Mexican people: full of life and energy, at play, at work, suffering abuses, escaping from their tormentors, celebrating their victories, and revering the great leaders of their past. As a unit, these powerful murals have no equal either in the Old or the New World. Elsewhere Rivera painted others of his now world-famous pictures. His murals at Chapingo in the National School of Agriculture, some critics acclaim as his most beautiful paintings. He himself, however, considers his best work is in the Court of the Detroit Institute of Art, where his frescoes caught the spirit of United States industrialism.

By some considered as great an artist as Rivera is José Clemente Orozco (1883–1949). An officer in the revolutionary armies, he portrayed at that time with frightening reality the horrors of war. In the 1920's Orozco, feeling that the new leaders were not achieving the ideals of the movement, painted on the walls of the University of Guadalajara huge frescoes of the long struggle begun by Hidalgo. At the end he etched with stark realism the starving and the naked, the inheritors of the Revolution. In the 1930's he again revealed his profound hatred of war on the walls of the Government Palace in Guadalajara. There, when the Axis was threatening a new holocaust, he painted his appalling figures of Europe and Asia's dictators reveling in a lust for war. Some have said that Orozco was a man without a philosophy; that he was not a moralist. His works hardly bear out such an interpretation. In portraying human goodness and evil on his canvases, Orozco showed himself the equal of Rivera. But his murals, always somber, have little of the genial, human warmth of Rivera's art.

Beyond these towering figures are others whose works at times equal those of the masters. Outstanding is David Alfaro Siquieros (1898–   ). His fiery, revolutionary spirit espoused the cause of the workers. He organized unions among artists; he was frequently jailed for opposing the government. But in a huge panorama of murals in the Electrical Syndicate Building, he portrayed with great power the life of the industrial workers, men and machines. Of more gentle nature is Rufino Tamayo (1889–   ). For a vast range of pictures of Mexican life, he derived his inspiration directly from long study of the work of Aztec and modern

Indian craftsmen. A strange figure among artists is Francisco Goitia (1882–   ). Although before the Revolution he had achieved an international reputation, suddenly, under the influence of the Mexican Renaissance, he abandoned painting to teach art to humble Mexican children. He now protests that he is not an artist, but his "Tata Jesu Cristo," a profoundly moving work, is a recognized masterpiece.

"While the Mexican artists have naturally been affected by the current drifts toward the abstract, it must be concluded that their particular genre has its roots not in European but in folk art. Summarized, though the techniques have been variously experimental, this bent is Indian, with a studied awkwardness, a massive blocking of form and color enormously moving even to the sophisticated palate." [1]

3. MEXICAN ECONOMIC AND POLITICAL DEVELOPMENT SINCE 1917

Carranza's Difficulties and Failures, 1917–1920. Carranza, faced by the necessity of securing funds for his depleted treasury, imposed decrees upon oil lands which oil companies claimed affected titles received before the constitution was promulgated. One of these, separating the surface tax from the royalties imposed on subsoil production and thus implying enforcement of Article 27, the companies refused to pay. This event became the first overt conflict between Mexico and the United States in regard to oil.

Besides the opposition of the powerful oil groups, Carranza faced difficulties imposed by World War I upon Mexico. His government had declared neutrality during this conflict largely because of the ravaged condition of the country after six years of civil war. The Germans, completely mistaking the reasons for neutrality, attempted to beguile Mexico into the conflict by the infamous Zimmermann note of March, 1917. In this strange document Mexico was invited to join the Central Powers and, in case of victory, was promised the return of the Mexican cession lost in 1848. Mexico, long engaged in a struggle to make democracy safe within her own borders, denied rightfully all knowledge of this weird brain-child of the German foreign office.

Carranza, a large landowner, did not have his heart in the provisions of the constitution calling for the distribution of land to the Indians. Most unfortunately, Zapata, the leader of the Indian masses, was treacherously murdered in 1919, a deed in which Carranza had no part. But his government, failing to distribute land, faced continuous Indian revolt in

[1] Muriel G. Thomas, Conversations.

the south. In the north, campaigns against the remnants of Villa's forces made life and property as unsafe at the hands of Carranza's troops as it was among those of Villa's. Discontent became open rebellion in 1920 when Carranza tried to impose his own candidate upon the country.

In March Calles, Obregón, and others, under the "Plan of Agua Prieta," declared Sonora a republic and invited neighboring states to join in overthrowing the government. After Adolfo de la Huerta, the leader of the Obregón forces, defeated an attempt of Carranza's army to invade the republic, the president resigned, accompanying his action, however, with a strong statement of the need of unquestioned acceptance of the principle of democratic elections and an end to military revolts. When his government, attempting to escape from Mexico City, was attacked by Obregón's army, Carranza was murdered on May 18. Obregón himself, a popular revolutionary hero and candidate for the presidency, was absolved of any complicity in the assassination, but the event shocked the Mexican people into a better appreciation of Carranza's efforts. His administration had seen, indeed, the promulgation of the constitution.

The Administration of Obregón, 1920–1924. On May 25, 1920, congress chose Adolfo de la Huerta as *ad interim* president who served until November when Obregón was overwhelmingly elected. A statesman-like and able man, Obregón encouraged the development of Mexico along the lines indicated by the constitution. He renewed the distribution of land to the Indians in villages, called *ejidos,* to agrarian collectives, and to those individuals who could prove—a simple matter in most cases— that Díaz had illegally seized their property. His administration accompanied the return of the land with a program of agricultural education, the establishment of ejidal (land) banks to finance purchase of machinery, and the sale of crops. His secretary of education, José Vasconcelos, launched Mexico's first major attack upon illiteracy, dispatching into the rural areas cultural brigades to teach Indians reading and writing, and give them fundamental training in hygiene, sanitation, manual skills, and art. Agricultural and technical schools were established in addition to several thousand primary and secondary schools as well as teacher training institutes. Hundreds of inexpensive editions of the classics were made into small libraries for distribution throughout the country. The program impelled thousands of enthusiastic volunteers to give their cooperation to the work.

Mexican labor, too, under the Obregón administration found support for its growth as provided for in the constitution. In 1918 the Regional Confederation of Mexican Labor (CROM) marked the first widespread movement of unionization. From some 50,000 members in that year, these combined regional unions grew to over 1,200,000 by 1924. They became the principal pillar for Obregón's program of low-cost housing, improvement of conditions in factories, and extension of benefits—accident insurance, pensions, and others—as well as the basis of a labor code promulgated later.

While Obregón's major objectives were to improve the domestic economy of the country, in foreign affairs he defended Mexican rights affecting subsoil and agricultural wealth. Upon Obregón's assumption of the presidency, American oil companies insisted upon a Mexican-American treaty to guarantee their rights acquired before May 1, 1917. Obregón's refusal led the Harding administration to deny recognition for more than three years. While the oil groups in the Harding cabinet remained adamant, American bankers, holders of large amounts of Mexican bonds issued under the Díaz administration, were anxious for recognition so that a basis could be laid for Mexico to resume payments. Thus in 1922 the first step in this direction was taken by the Lamont-Huerta agreement, which in essence provided that Mexico would make payments from money derived from royalties received from oil production. That the latter was significant at the moment was evident in the amount produced in 1922, namely, 182,278,457 barrels. This production, principally from foreign-owned wells, led the Mexican government to insist that foreign rights in oil were adequately safeguarded, pointing out further that the total capitalization of the oil industry was $1,050,532,434, 91 per cent of which was held by British and American interests, while Mexican ownership amounted to only 1.1 per cent.

The second step taken to resolve the conflict between the Mexican government and the oil companies came in the negotiation of the Bucareli agreements in 1923. Therein it was agreed that the expropriation of American agricultural properties would in the future be limited to about 4,000 acres, while, in the case of subsoil deposits, Mexico agreed to recognize a "positive act" taken before May 1, 1917, to exploit oil resources sufficient to guarantee protection against nationalization to the owner of the surface. Recognition of Obregón's government followed almost immediately.

The Administration of Calles, 1924–1928. In spite of the Bucareli agreements or possibly because of them, the Calles administration became involved in a serious diplomatic conflict with the United States over the question of oil. The agreements becoming known in Mexico, with many believing that they signified a halt in the distribution of the land, led

Adolpho de la Huerta to revolt late in 1923. The revolt was quickly crushed, however, so that Calles assumed office on December 1, 1924. Calles in fact belonged among the most conservative of the landowners, but his congress was determined to undo the Bucareli agreements and clarify with legislation the status of foreign companies under the constitution. Thus in December, 1925, congress enacted a Land Law and a Petroleum Law, both of which aimed at ending foreign ownership by making it Mexican.

The three principal provisions of the Land Law made it impossible for companies to hold land if foreigners controlled more than 51 per cent interest; it left foreign individuals undisturbed in their possession even though they owned more than 50 per cent, but required their heirs to dispose of all interest above that figure; and finally, it required corporations to dispose of all holdings over 50 per cent within a period of ten years. The Petroleum Law, equally comprehensive, made it mandatory that in accord with the constitution, all holdings in petroleum had to be exchanged for concessions which were to run for fifty years from the date of exploitation, even if this date were prior to 1917.

The laws precipitated a crisis in Mexican-American relations. Secretary Kellogg of the United States insisted that not only did the laws violate the Bucareli agreements but were retroactive in effect. Calles, strongly supported by Mexican public opinion, stated flatly that Mexico had the right to enact laws without outside interference. This *impasse* reached in 1926 was made worse by Mexico's recognition of the Sacasa government in Nicaragua. The United States, supporting that of the Díaz faction, charged Mexico with endangering American interests in Nicaragua. The drift toward war was fortunately halted by the United States Senate, which in January, 1927, unanimously called upon the Coolidge government to arbitrate all issues between the two countries. While not given effect by Coolidge, the action, reflecting the temper of the American people, halted the interventionist drive.

By 1927, too, Calles was making fundamental changes in domestic policy. A wealthy landowner himself, he had never taken kindly to the principle of land distribution to the Indians. Similarly, he had not given the support to labor that characterized Obregón. Moreover, under Luis Morones, the head of CROM, the leadership of that organization was being converted into a political machine closely associated with the control that Calles and Obregón had over state legislatures and governorships. In education Vasconcelos had been eliminated from the government for his expressed sympathy for the de la Huerta revolt of 1923. In short, the reform program of the Revolution was coming to a halt.

To answer the voices of discontent being raised, Calles, an extreme anticlerical, began persecution of the church. The latter had provided a legal base for action against it, but hardly persecution, by its refusal to obey laws which required it to register an inventory of its wealth with the government. Much was made of the fact that the Protestant churches had complied with this law. To bring pressure to have the laws changed, the hierarchy in August, 1926, ordered the priests to leave the altar. However, no significant protest followed except in the rural areas where the church organized the *Cristero* movement. Calles proceeded against the *Cristero,* punishing its leaders severely.

The unfortunate relations of the Calles administration with both the church and the United States suddenly took a turn for the better in 1927. Late in that year President Coolidge appointed Dwight W. Morrow, a prominent financial figure, as ambassador to Mexico. On his arrival Morrow refrained from public statements beyond expressing an intelligent interest in Mexico's prehistoric past. He was soon on amiable terms with Calles. The change in Mexico's policy was somewhat startling. The Mexican supreme court declared the Petroleum Law unconstitutional, and the government refrained from further enforcement of the Land Law. Calles' congress in 1927 further validated all titles in oil lands acquired before 1917; similar legislation affecting agricultural lands was not so successful. Morrow also used his influence to bring about an agreement with the church, ending the persecution. Under it priests chosen by the government would register with the authorities, and while church schools continued to be forbidden, instruction could be given in religious doctrine on the church premises.

When time came for the next election, however, the feeling in Mexico was growing that Calles' concessions were halting once more the progress of the Revolution. Congress, many believed, was hardly more than a rubber stamp. Charges of attempting to establish a dictatorship seemed substantiated by his decree in 1927, which, flying in the face of the constitutional prohibition of re-election, paved the way for the nomination of Obregón as the administration candidate. The constitution, too, was amended to extend the term of the president's office to six years. Revolts motivated by various reasons, important among them the fear of the Calles-Obregón clique perpetuating its power, broke out. Those led by Francisco Serrano in Mexico City and Arnulfo Gómez in

Vera Cruz in October, 1927, were quickly crushed, while their leaders and a large number of their followers were ruthlessly executed. In the following July, Obregón was elected without opposition, to take office the following December. However, a religious fanatic, unbalanced by Calles' earlier persecution of the church, assassinated Obregón in August.

Mexico and the Depression, 1929–1934. Since the constitution provided for no vice-president, the congress, after Calles refused to be a candidate, elected Emilio Portes Gil, Calles' minister of the interior, as provisional president to hold office until February 5, 1930, when a new election was scheduled. Portes Gil, an able man and a leading constitutional and corporation lawyer, was well known for his courageous campaign on behalf of temperance and temperance education. Behind the scenes Calles still hoped to establish a dictatorship, but the effects of the depression on Mexico blocked his best efforts. In November, 1929, the National Revolutionary party, the official party, put forward Pascual Ortiz Rubio, who had a mediocre career. The opposition to Calles coalesced into the Anti-Re-electionist party, which nominated José Vasconcelos, not only well known for his contributions to Mexican education, but a famous literary figure. Although vast crowds thronged to hear Vasconcelos, he secured but 20,000 votes; the controlled election gave Ortiz Rubio more than 1,000,000. Calles selected the cabinet for the new president, but his administration was short. The depression, closing in on Mexico, threw thousands out of work. Strikes forced the government to mollify labor by legislating an eight-hour day, the right to strike, and a minimum wage. Individual states took more drastic action, resorting to outright expropriation of lands and foreign industries to meet the demands of labor. The church, too, found new measures taken against it. Many states enacted laws severely limiting its activities, taking over church schools and restricting the number of priests. Vera Cruz permitted only one priest for every 100,000 inhabitants; Sonora expelled all members of the clergy.

Calles, blind to reading the signs of the times, drastically reduced the national budget by $32,000,000, cut school appropriations, and reduced health services and salaries of government employees. At the same time he negotiated a loan with American bankers for $16,000,000, and made new arrangements for payments on the debt including a moratorium in 1932. As labor continued to grow more restless in the face of widening unemployment, Ortiz Rubio, taking measures without consulting Calles, was quietly removed in September, 1932. Congress was summoned and selected one of Calles' closest collaborators, General Alberdo

L. Rodríguez, on September 3, 1932, to finish the unexpired term until 1934.

By this date, 1932, Calles attempted to head off revolt by himself proposing a far-reaching Six Year Plan to pave the way for socialism! This plan was adopted at Querétaro by a convention of the party in December, 1933, as well as in two amendments proposed for the constitution, later added. One of these extended the term of the president to six years without re-election and imposed the same restriction upon members of congress, state legislatures, governors, and mayors of cities; the other called for compulsory education upon a socialist basis. The new program was to go into effect with the presidential election of 1934.

The election of that year was a turning point in the history of Mexico. Calles apparently believed that his Six Year Plan, a concession to labor and the intellectuals of the party who wished to see the Revolution go forward, would ensure his continuation in control so long as he could choose the president. For this purpose he carefully selected as a candidate General Lázaro Cárdenas, who he believed would serve as a satisfactory puppet.

Cárdenas from an early age had fought against the *Rurales* of Díaz, and when the Revolution came, won the rank of colonel through sheer ability in Carranza's army. He had served in 1920 as provisional governor of his own state of Michoacán, where he was born on May 25, 1895. Elected governor of the state in 1926, he distinguished himself by his faithfulness to the principles of the Revolution, distributing land to the Indians and improving the health agencies and schools. His understanding was not born simply of good intentions, but rested upon a life-long study of the needs of Mexico and her people. The liberals of the Calles party had long admired Cárdenas for his achievements and incorruptibility. They offered no opposition to his nomination.

The Administration of Cárdenas, 1934–1940. Though Cárdenas' election was assured, he nevertheless campaigned from one end of Mexico to the other to acquaint himself first-hand with existing conditions and deepen his already extensive knowledge of the country. When he assumed the presidency on November 30, 1934, he probably had a better knowledge of Mexico than any other man who had served as chief executive. Fortunately, the long struggle since 1917 had produced a powerful labor movement and able leaders, upon whom Cárdenas could depend. In these circumstances Cárdenas carried out a series of reforms which strengthened Mexico's democratic institutions and opened up avenues for growth.

The Six Year Plan went into force with the election of Cárdenas. For agriculture the plan envisaged a greater distribution of land, the break-up of large estates, and the establishment of farming colonies provided with free housing, medical services, and schools. Agricultural labor was guaranteed a minimum wage. Lands not suitable for agriculture were turned to cattle raising and stock farms, with cattle provided by the government. Irrigation, too, was to be the special charge of the federal authorities over projects too large for local governments. Envisaged also were conservation of timberlands and the establishment of tree nurseries and national parks. Commerce was to be stimulated by aiding producers whose products found a ready sale abroad, and for this purpose trade treaties were to be negotiated.

Union organization, under the plan, was to receive government support and workingmen provided with old age and life insurance and assistance in home owning. Industrial schools were to be established, as well as sports programs. Unions were to have aid in solving disputes with capital. The plan's aims for the industrialization of Mexico were aid for manufactures of native consumer goods and government assistance for medium-sized industries, while monopolies were to be restricted. It demanded the nationalization of subsoil riches in accordance with the constitution, and proposed the prohibition of further acquisition of mining properties by foreigners. To provide power for industry, there was envisaged a national system of hydroelectric development. Closely integrated were provisions for airways and airfields, as well as for a merchant marine.

The plan proposed to increase the amount allotted for education in the national budget from 15 to 20 per cent to establish 5,000 rural schools by 1936, with state control of all private, primary, and secondary schools. Teacher training and agricultural and vocational institutes were provided for. Emphasis was to be given to sports to reduce use of alcoholic drink. To increase public health, special attention was devoted to the improvement of health of workers in industry in small rural communities. Included were plans to establish children's courts, reduce prostitution and the distribution of obscene literature, and encourage the entry into Mexico of certain classes of immigrants known for their stable social outlook.

In foreign affairs the plan strongly supported the Pan-American movement, denounced international wars, and advocated commercial and intellectual cooperation and the settlement of disputes by arbitration.

Cárdenas launched a vigorous offensive to carry out the plan in all its aspects. Not surprisingly, Calles and his clique planned a *coup d'état* in 1935. Waiting until he knew who was involved, Cárdenas suddenly seized the leaders including Calles, whom he had flown out of the country. With the strong support of the newly organized and nation-wide Confederation of Mexican Labor (1936), Cárdenas rooted out the Calles political machines in the various states. In 1938 he reorganized the old National Revolutionary party into the party of National Revolution, the PNR, which elected his supporters in national and state governments, as well as mayors of the principal cities. With them and the new labor organization, Cárdenas carried out the major policies outlined in the Six Year Plan.

In agriculture, the chief part of the plan, the Cárdenas government made giant strides by 1940, distributing almost 17,000,000 *hectares*, about 43,000,000 million acres, to over 1,600,000 individuals in *ejidos*. Accompanying this distribution was the construction of hundreds of schools and a National Ejido (Rural) Bank of Credit for cooperative undertakings. Land was taken in most cases from large landowners. Striking was the expropriation of about 300,000 acres in Durango to develop the Laguna District, an undertaking which included Palmito Dam impounding 3,000,000 cubic meters of water to irrigate some 5,000,000 acres. In Yucatan, where the peasants suffered from abuses on henequén plantations, the government seized 225,000 acres and turned them over to seventy-odd pueblos. In Morelos 200,000 acres were seized to become the basis for the Zapata Cooperative, the largest sugar mill in Mexico.

The *ejido* program in areas where agriculture already existed was paralleled by a herculean effort to reclaim by irrigation vast wastes in northern Mexico. In two years, 1935–1937, at a huge cost, the government launched more than forty major projects to build dams for irrigation and rural electrification. The bulk of these were in the states of New León, Chihuahua, Sinaloa, Hidalgo, Querétaro, San Luis Potosí, and Sonora, all northern states. Individual states with federal aid carried on hundreds of smaller projects, river control measures, and canal construction. Thus for the first time in her history Mexico moved to make the great northern deserts a new source of food for her population.

The Cárdenas government also attacked illiteracy. From a 70 per cent illiterate population in 1910, the figure had declined by 1940, with most of the change coming in the six years, 1934–1940, to between 45 and 50 per cent. In the same six years the government doubled the number of schools to 14,000 and quadrupled the number of teachers to about 45,000. More than 2,000,000 children by the latter date were receiving instruction.

Taking rank with other achievements of the Cárdenas administration was the rapid growth of labor organizations. The Confederation of Mexican Labor, the successor to the CROM, organized in 1936, had by 1940 almost 4,000 affiliated groups with a total membership of over 950,000. The older General Confederation of Workers, organized in 1921, had 600 unions with 270,000 members. Other labor groups brought the total up to about 1,500,000. Upon these the Cárdenas administration depended. In return it frequently supported strikes designed to improve living conditions and raise wages. How necessary was this combined effort appeared in the simple fact that between 1934 and 1940 it achieved a raise in the average annual wage in industry from twenty cents a day to one dollar a day. With this increase went the firm establishment of the eight-hour day, minimum wage laws, insurance against accidents, old age, and death, hospitalization benefits, housing, and sports programs. But Mexico still had a long way to go to win a comparable advance for her people as a whole. The Mexican census of 1940 revealed that more than 50 per cent of the population lived under virtually colonial conditions and that 40 per cent of the nation's habitations were but huts.

Expropriation of Oil, 1938. Out of the search of labor for a higher standard of living and nationalistic feeling against foreign ownership of raw materials, came the most striking action of the Cárdenas administration—the expropriation of oil. This event had its origin in the fall of 1936 in the oil workers' demands for increased wages, adequate housing, hospitals, and schools. By March, 1937, negotiations broke down; the companies capped their wells; the workers went on strike. When the crisis adversely affected the nation's economy, Cárdenas ordered the dispute settled by reference to the Industrial Arbitration Board set up under the constitution of 1917. The board, after examining the books of the various companies, returned a decision in December in favor of the union. The companies thereupon appealed to the Mexican supreme court, which upheld the constitutionality of the board. When the companies then refused to carry out the court's order, they were in effect defying the sovereignty of the Mexican state. Cárdenas had no alternative but to expropriate. Thus on March 18, 1938, the American, Dutch, and British companies were taken over and compensation promised which was subsequently paid.

The effects of the expropriation decree were far-reaching. Internationally, the fundamental issue at stake was the integrity of the nonintervention principle of the Good Neighbor policy. By prompt recognition of Mexico's right to expropriate, the Roosevelt administration cut the ground from under anti-United States Nazi propaganda in Latin America. Everywhere Nazis had predicted that the United States would march into Mexico in the same way that Hitler had marched into Austria, March 12, just six days before expropriation. Further, the refusal of Roosevelt to take such action won for the United States the widespread support it enjoyed in Latin America after Japan attacked at Pearl Harbor in 1941. Probably no other single event in the early history of the Good Neighbor policy had such a profound effect in altering attitudes in Latin America toward the United States.

Upon Mexico the effects of the expropriation were electric. The sudden realization among the people that the oil was theirs gave rein to the wildest enthusiasm. From every walk of life they came forward to offer their most precious possessions, even wedding rings, to help pay the compensation promised by the government. The total amount volunteered was small, less than $500,000, but the gesture revealed for a moment an unbelievable unity among the Mexican people. To them Mexico had taken a long step toward economic independence.

Mexico did pay for the oil properties after extended negotiations fixed their value at $130,339,000. Of this sum the United States companies received their compensation in 1947; the rest of the debt, the larger part owed to British concerns, will be extinguished by 1962. To administer the oil industry, the government created a state corporation, *Petróleos Mexicanos*, or Pemex. Prediction was widespread that Mexicans did not have the technical competence to operate the oil industry, but time has since proved otherwise.

Upon Latin America the effect of Mexico's action was significant. Oil companies everywhere began to make immediate improvement in their relations with labor. Wages were raised, adequate housing planned, and other needs met. The Latin-American nations themselves began petroleum legislative programs which aimed at securing fairer distribution of profits from foreign oil companies. Today in the cases of Venezuela and Peru, laws require petroleum corporations to pay 50 per cent of their profits, made in the country, into the national treasury. Practically all Latin-American countries in which oil is produced have established refineries or require oil companies to establish them on the national domain. The Mexican expropriation, in fact, completely altered the outlook of all, not just oil, corporations toward the Latin-American countries in which they operate. Today they take as a matter of course their responsibility to contribute to the improvement of the standard of living of their workers.

World War II and Mexico. When World War II broke out in 1939 Cárdenas threw his support to the Allies. He likewise gave full cooperation to the policy of hemisphere defense and opened Mexican resources to the United States for stockpiling raw materials. In 1940 Cárdenas retired from the presidency in accordance with the constitution.

General Manuel Avila Camacho, the candidate of the party of the National Revolution, conservative in outlook, won the presidency with little opposition and served throughout the war until 1946. Assuming office on December 1, 1940, the new president followed a policy of consolidating the gains made under Cárdenas. He continued the program of land distribution, but modified it by legislation which gave titles to land as soon as practicable to dwellers on *ejidos*. The laws carried provisions which protected the new owners from land speculators. The policy did not mean that ejidal lands were to be broken up; on the contrary, large landed estates continued to be distributed to villages whose peasants worked on them. The most famous case occurring during the Avila Camacho regime was the expropriation of over 130,000 acres of Hearst lands, distributed among eleven *ejidos*.

With regard to labor, the president assured the country that the gains made under Cárdenas would be protected. But he made it known that he would not tolerate unnecessary strikes, and warned that employers must observe labor laws already in existence. Several factors contributed to the success of his domestic policies. Vicente Lombardo Toledano, the fiery leader of the Confederation of Mexican Labor, withdrew from the headship of that organization. But more important was World War II, which brought increased employment and a high demand for Mexico's raw materials including oil. The resulting prosperity did much to ease the tensions created by the reforms of the Cárdenas administration.

In foreign affairs Avila Camacho continued the policy of friendship toward the United States and supported with enthusiasm the program of hemisphere defense. After the Japanese attack on Pearl Harbor, Mexico immediately made her vital resources available for the American war effort. In 1942, besides the final agreement to compensate the oil companies, she signed a reciprocal trade agreement with the United States. The latter extended to Mexico a loan of $40,000,000 to facilitate the extraction of raw materials and improve the Pan-American Highway. Other agreements provided for the United States purchase of $25,000,000 worth of silver each month, while Mexico reached an understanding with American agricultural groups to pay for properties expropriated in the early years of the Revolution. In May, 1942, as a result of German submarines sinking Mexican vessels, she declared war on the Axis. In 1943 because of the shortage of labor in American agricultural areas due to the draft, Mexico agreed to provide workers in the Southwest. By 1945 more than 115,000 Mexicans had entered the United States to engage in this important work. Mexico dispatched millions of tons of minerals and other raw materials to American factories, including mercury, tungsten, cobalt, zinc, lead, copper, and tin; her field and forests provided henequen, sisal, medicinal products, and vegetable oils. Just before the war ended in 1945, Mexico City was the choice of the American states in which to hold the Inter-American Conference on War and Peace.

Upon Mexico itself, the war had significant effects. With the sale of raw materials she built up the largest gold reserve in her history. With funds derived from the expanding volume of taxes, the government established her new oil industry, Pemex, on a firm basis. Large funds went into needed highway construction, extension of railroad lines, improvement of harbors, and the expansion of low-cost housing and school building programs. But the most imaginative achievement of the Avila Camacho administration was to launch a new attack upon the problem of illiteracy. The need was great. Mexico's rapidly growing industries demanded trained personnel; labor unions wanted schools for their children; teacher and women's organizations saw that health improvement required a literate population. Moreover, the dream of mass education had existed since Gómez Farías and Juárez. Vasconcelos gave it impetus in the 1920's with culture brigades; Cárdenas advanced it with schools in the 1930's. World War II, with its emphasis upon democracy as a way of life, brought the problem into sharp focus.

Supporting his brilliant minister of education, Jaime Torres Bodet, Avila Camacho secured a law which required the registration of all unable to read and write, and further required each literate Mexican to teach at least one illiterate. To carry out the work, published instructions in methods of teaching and vast supplies of inexpensive materials were put into the hands of unions, women's organizations, business clubs, schools, and other similar bodies. The president himself launched the program by instructing an illiterate Indian for an hour each day. Beginning in March, 1945, the program has been continuous and thus is ending one of Mexico's oldest problems.

The Administration of Alemán, 1946–1952. Miguel Alemán, who had been governor of Vera Cruz, a senator, and secretary of the interior under Avila Camacho, was the candidate of the dominant party of Revolutionary Institutions. An able businessman of liberal outlook, he was elected overwhelmingly. His term was characterized by a well-integrated program to expand agriculture, industry, mineral development, and communications. The government retained direction of major projects, railroad and highway construction, irrigation and reclamation, oil and hydroelectric power, at the same time encouraging foreign and native investors to establish industries, commercial undertakings, and agricultural products.

By 1951 the secretary of agriculture was able to announce that farm products increased in value 2,000,000,000 pesos annually, that cultivated land amounted to 4,250,000 acres, and that 62,742 families had received some 1,336,000 *hectares* (about 3,340,000 acres). This advance sprang from a vast irrigation program carried on by the construction of small and large dams to bring new land under production. The huge Morelos Dam brought 700,000 acres under cultivation near Mexicali in Lower California and in northern Sonora. Rapid colonization of the former led to the establishment of the northern region into a new state. The southern part remained a district. A second major project in Sonora was the building of the great Alvaro Obregón Dam to irrigate some 500,000 acres and provide for the development of electric power. A third was the Falcón Dam on the lower Rio Grande, built in cooperation with the United States. In Nayarit and Michoacán other significant projects improved food production in an area of about 18,000 square miles.

Prominent in agricultural development was La Laguna region in Coahuila, where 147 agricultural cooperatives, with government aid, produced a variety of crops, principally wheat and corn. In the south the Alemán administration began the development of the Papaloápan River basin to bring into production some 17,000 square miles of land in Oaxaca and Vera Cruz. There dams and hydroelectric stations on the Papaloápan and Tonto Rivers will affect approximately 150,000 acres of land already the source of cattle, rubber, cocoanuts, pineapples, tobacco, and varieties of hardwoods. Threaded by the Southeastern Railroad and numerous highways, the region holds considerable promise as a new industrial center. The results of this work in food production were significant in that by the end of Alemán's administration Mexico was producing food products almost adequate to meet the national demand. In the cattle industry alone the country suffered a severe setback from the hoof and mouth disease. When this was finally brought under control in 1952, with United States cooperation, Mexico's losses stood at almost 700,000 animals, but 60,000,000 were saved by vaccination.

Keeping pace with agricultural growth was Mexican industrialization. Government funds, foreign loans, and bonds sold to the Mexican people provided the chief source of support. Mexico City became the outstanding industrial region, with the bulk of its thousands of new industries in Tlalepantla on the outskirts. So rapid was growth that industrial production in 1949 exceeded in value that of agriculture for the first time in Mexican history.

Vital to industrial expansion was the production of minerals—gold, silver, copper, zinc, lead, coal, sulfur, iron, and tungsten. Above all others, petroleum expansion became the object of the herculean efforts of Pemex, the government-owned corporation directed by Antonio Bermúdez. Production in 1946 stood at over 49,000,000 barrels; by 1955 it was almost 100,000,000. Besides actual oil production, Pemex constructed pipe and gas lines to feed the industries at the capital, built refineries, purchased a fleet of tankers, paid off the American oil companies for oil expropriated in 1938, and came to an agreement with the British to extinguish the oil debt by 1962. These achievements in turn created a climate in which American oil companies returned to Mexico under agreements with Pemex to explore offshore along the coasts of southern Vera Cruz and Tabasco, where fields promised to equal those of Venezuela.

Integrated with industrial and agricultural growth were improved communications. Besides a multitude of lesser projects, the Alemán administration in 1951 brought to completion the Pan-American Highway to the Guatemalan border, and constructed an isthmian highway, Salina Cruz to Coatzacoalcos, across Tehuantepec. Besides beginning the rebuilding of her 9,500 miles of railroads, the Mexican government purchased the Southern Pacific of Mexico in the west and the British-owned line, Vera Cruz to Mexico City. In the south she completed the Southeastern Railroad through the Papaloápan area in 1952.

Under Alemán Mexico began modernizing her important harbors: Mazatlán, Acapulco, and Tobari on the west coast and Frontera, Tabasco, and Tuxpan, Vera Cruz, on the east, as well as beginning the construction of a merchant marine. Air transport to stimulate tourist trade saw construction of airports in eleven areas to supplement her older ones. The expansion and facilities developed for her economy were reflected in a growth of foreign trade. With a deficit of $200,000,000 in 1947, restrictions on imports to save dollars, the ending of the reciprocal trade agreement with the United States, the devaluation of the peso, and the negotiation of treaties with eleven European nations, besides those with Japan, Canada, South Africa, and the Belgium Congo, produced a favorable balance of trade by 1950.

Alemán and the progressive-minded middle class of Mexico readily recognized the importance of education, for which, by 1952, the country was spending some $50,000,000 annually. All children through the age of fifteen years were being accommodated in her schools; 1,000 new teachers were being trained annually for outlying districts, while the government built 965 new schools between 1946 and 1952. The dream of a national university became a reality in 1952 when, 70 per cent complete, that institution was opened. Built upon a wasteland of lava rock about ten miles south of the city, it serves about 25,000 students who pay an annual tuition fee of twenty dollars. The most modern in the Western Hemisphere, its architecture incorporates modern designs with Aztec tradition. All major fields are represented in the curricula, including studies involving laboratories for nuclear fission and cosmic energy. At the other end of the educational scale, the Alemán government continued the campaign against illiteracy begun by Avila Camacho.

Finances for these varied undertakings, administered by the treasury under Ramón Beteta, derived from taxes collected under improved methods, loans from the Export-Import Bank, the World Bank, and private banks, bonds, and an important source, tourist dollars.

The Administration of Ruiz Cortines, 1952 to the Present. Urged to become a candidate in 1952, Alemán, obeying the constitution, refused, but conducted the presidential election in such a manner that every Mexican cast his ballot without interference. Opposing the dominant party of Revolutionary Institutions, which nominated Adolfo Ruiz Cortines, were principally the Federation of the People's party, led by General Henríquez Guzmán, the National Action party, with Efraín Gonzáles as its candidate, and the Popular party, headed by Vincente Lombardo Toledano. Cortines was overwhelmingly elected, supported by the powerful union, peasant organizations, and middle class groups, which had profited by Alemán's constructive work.

Upon inauguration on December 1, 1952, Ruiz Cortines pledged his administration to reduce the cost of living, distribute the wealth more equally, and carry on the work of improving agriculture, expanding industry, and developing transportation and education, insisting only that a balance be kept between them. A man gifted in administration and of sterling character, Mexico has had high hopes for an improvement in political morals under Ruiz Cortines. From the beginning of his rule he gave wing to these hopes with a vigorous attack upon corruption. He secured a law requiring every public official to declare publicly his own and his wife's wealth upon assuming office; in case of an unaccountable increase in wealth, the officeholder would find himself subject to punishment. In answer to demands, the administration confiscated lands in Tamaulipas belonging to close friends of his predecessor and launched a campaign against vice centers in the capital and other cities. He vigorously aided the United States in its effort to halt the illegal narcotic traffic between the two countries.

In line with previous administrations, President Cortines pushed an aggressive agricultural program. A major event was the opening in 1954 of the great Falcón Dam on the lower Rio Grande River destined to irrigate some 700,000 acres in Mexico. But the year 1954 marked, in fact, a turning point in the agricultural history of Mexico: maize and wheat, traditionally imported, produced a small surplus above consumption. Many other basic foods, beans, rice, garden produce, barley, cocoa, were also rapidly approaching the same point. Sugar had met national needs in 1947 and had become, after maize, wheat, and beans, the fourth most important agricultural product. Its rapidly growing surplus makes it an important export item. Coffee cultivation, too, had met the country's needs. By 1955 Mexico, after Brazil and Colombia, had become the world's third largest coffee grower. This achievement in self-sufficiency in food has confounded some observers who had predicted that the rapid increase of Mexico's population, now 29,000,000, would always outrun the production of food. Proper significance had not been attached by these observers to the vast program, begun under the Cárdenas administration, of reclaiming the northern deserts.

Mexico's industrialization, keeping pace with agricultural advance, was likewise making the nation by 1956 virtually self-sufficient in essential goods. Indicative of this success was the manufacture in sufficient quantities of refined petroleum products, previously imported at heavy cost, to meet national demands. Equally striking were plans for the building during 1956 of the first atomic-electric plant in Latin America.

In politics, Alemán withdrew from any attempt to influence the policies of the new administration. General Guzmán, however, continued such violent opposition that his People's party, described as subversive, was outlawed in 1954. Simultaneously, legislation, which will undoubtedly contribute to the stability of the nation, required all political parties to show a membership of at least 75,000. Marking a new advance in Mexico's democracy is an amendment to the constitution permitting women not only to vote but to hold office including that of the presidency.

Mexico's heroic struggle since independence to establish workable democratic institutions has given her a distinguished place in the roster of American nations. In Latin America she has become a leader. Her long history of artistic and architectural achievement before Cortés touched her shores has found a rebirth in the new freedom since 1917. Her gifted people give promise of more significant contributions to world development.

INTER-AMERICAN AFFAIRS

Chapter XXIX

INTER-AMERICAN AFFAIRS

Part I. THE RELATIONS OR THE UNITED STATES AND
LATIN AMERICA

Colonial Origins. The origins of our relations with Latin America are
colonial. Spain's colonization of most of South America, Central America,
Mexico, the larger islands of the Caribbean, and Florida gave her a vast
empire. From it she extracted incalculable wealth in minerals, gold, silver, mercury, pearls; in tropical plantation crops, sugar, indigo, and
tobacco; and in forest products, mahogany and cabinet woods. Routed
back to Spain through the Caribbean, this wealth became the object
of attack by British, French, and Dutch pirates. This illegal commercial
activity began the New World struggle for trade. More, as the discoverers
of uncolonized lands, pirates became the forerunners of British, French,
and Dutch colonial undertakings of the seventeenth century.

By the eighteenth century New England commerce reached the West
Indies. Fashioned into a "three-cornered" trade, its base rested upon the
Caribbean. In 1766 more than 1,400 ships entered American ports from
the West Indies. This contact began the commercial relations between
the areas of the later United States and Latin America. Paralleling this
growth in trade was a territorial expansion which carried the British
south along the Atlantic seaboard toward Florida and into the Caribbean,
with the founding of the Bahamas, Jamaica, British Honduras, Barbadoes,
British Guiana, and other island settlements.

While these Caribbean colonies became the highwater mark of British expansion in the West Indies, on the mainland she had by 1763
annexed Florida and the territory east of the Mississippi River. Spain on
her part, holding up the British advance in the Caribbean, expanded her
own control over the continent to include the vast area from California
to the Mississippi-Missouri Rivers, St. Louis and New Orleans.

By the late eighteenth century Anglo-Spanish rivalry had become a
struggle for trade, for territory, and for control of the seas. In to this

empire rivalry, the revolt of the thirteen English colonies projected itself. Spain, appreciating to the full the significance of the revolt, promptly gave aid to the colonies—loans to Virginia, haven to American privateers in New Orleans, arms, ammunition, and supplies to George Rogers Clark to conquer the West, and finally, pursuing her own policy of driving the British out, she captured Mobile and Pensacola to erase British control in that area. Her next move, an attack upon British Caribbean possessions, halted when the armistice ended hostilities.

The Revolutionary War had a major importance in the relations of the United States and Latin America. It eliminated Britain as a rival of Spain, but the new states took the former's place from the moment the treaty of 1783 was signed. Secondly, Britain herself found her former colonies, now an independent nation, a rival which threatened the role she had so long held in the struggle for trade and territory in the New World. Of more profound significance, the Revolutionary War projected democratic ideas into the colonies of Spain, which were to become soon the new independent states of Latin America.

Between 1783 and 1823 the United States continued the colonial tradition of expansion of trade and territory into the Latin-American area. Revival of trade was rapid in the Caribbean. From nothing in 1783 it had reached, by 1809, with the Swedish colony of St. Bartholomew, over $3,600,000; by 1807, with the Danish islands, over $3,000,000; by 1799, with the Dutch islands, over $9,000,000, although it declined rapidly after this date; by 1800, with the French sugar islands, almost $14,500,000; by 1800, with the Spanish colonies, almost $19,000,000. Paralleling this growth was the territorial advance toward Florida and Louisiana. Spain's loss of the latter to Napoleon and its almost immediate acquisition by the United States in 1803 was a blow to Spanish power on our frontiers. It carried the United States to the Gulf of Mexico, with a major port, New Orleans, as a window looking toward Spanish colonies farther south and west. After 1803 official American interest doubled its efforts to secure Florida, while individual Americans crossed into Texas. Such was the strong position of the United States in the Caribbean trade and on the mainland in 1808 when the Spanish colonies revolted against the motherland, Spain.

Before 1808 our relations with the Latin-American area had been either through Britain, as colonies, or as an independent state through Spain. After 1808 our relations had a double aspect: official efforts aimed to secure Florida and a boundary line to the Louisiana Purchase from Spain, while individual Americans aided the revolt of the Spanish colonies. By 1821 the objectives of both the United States and the Spanish colonies had been achieved: the former had secured Florida and a boundary to the Purchase, while the latter had won their independence.

Three centuries of New World colonial history had created the main factors in inter-American relations: a struggle for trade, for territory, a fear of European reconquest, and the influence of democratic ideas. All these forces were to affect the future development of inter-American relations.

The Independence of Latin America: the Monroe Doctrine, 1823. The independence of Latin America was the basic cause for the promulgation of the Monroe Doctrine in 1823. This independence led the Quadruple Alliance in Europe in 1822 to propose aid to Spain to reconquer her colonies. This proposal was a disturbing one to the British. Reconquest would threaten the large investment she had made in the success of the movement for independence and close Latin-American ports to her lucrative trade. On the other hand, Britain was equally disturbed by the giant strides taken by the United States since 1783 toward Latin America: the revival of trade with the Caribbean, the acquisition of Louisiana, the purchase of Florida, the extension of American boundaries along the border of Texas and as far as the northwest Pacific coast.

In these circumstances the natural response of the British to the Quadruple Alliance was to propose a joint British-American declaration. On the one hand, it would block aid to Spain for reconquest of her colonies, and on the other, would tie the hands of the United States in its program of expansion. The character of this proposal, made by Canning, the British foreign minister, was clearly recognized by John Quincy Adams, who combated its acceptance in the Monroe cabinet. Fortunately, at the moment Russia, issuing in 1823 a ukase extending her boundaries southward along the northwest Pacific coast, gave the United States the opportunity to issue the Monroe Doctrine as a national policy.

Because the Monroe Doctrine remained the keystone in United States-Latin-American relations until 1932, its basic principles are important: (1) the New World, free and independent, was no longer open to colonization; (2) the United States would not tolerate any attempt of European powers to extend their political system to any part of the Western Hemisphere, but existing colonies would not be disturbed; (3) the United States would not permit any intervention for the purpose of oppressing any American governments or controlling them by any European power; (4) the United States would not interfere in the internal concerns of European powers; (5) with "movements in this hemisphere, we are of necessity more immediately concerned."

The Independence of Latin America: the Origins of the Pan-American Movement, 1826–1868. While the United States laid down the unilateral policy of protecting herself from European intervention, the Latin Americans proposed a policy more comprehensive in principle, Pan-Americanism. As the product of its struggle for independence, it went beyond the negative conception of resistance to foreign intervention to advance more positive principles. Because these have come to take the place of the Monroe Doctrine as an inter-American testament, they deserve careful study: (1) the recognition of the political independence of the New World from Europe; (2) the recognition that the New World has a community of political ideals; (3) the principle that the New World should recognize law in place of force; (4) the belief that nonintervention should be a principle of American states with regard to one another; (5) the recognition of the principle of equality of these states among themselves; (6) the recognition of the principle of cooperation both to resist European aggression and to aid one another's development.

The United States did little to implement the Monroe Doctrine until late in the century; the Latin Americans, on the other hand, held their first conference to begin the history of the Pan-American movement in Panama in 1826. Called by Simón Bolívar, the purposes of it were to free Cuba from Spain and to lay the basis for inter-American cooperation. While only delegates of the states of Greater Colombia (Venezuela, Colombia, and Ecuador), Central America, and Mexico attended the conference (the delegates of the United States arrived after it was over) it began the tradition of Pan-Americanism.

A second Pan-American conference was held in Lima, Peru, in 1847, with the idea of forming a league against European invasion, threatened at the moment by the activities of an Ecuadorean, General Juan José Flores, who purchased ships, enlisted Spanish troops, and proposed to place a Spanish prince on the throne of Peru. The congress, with representatives from five South American states, drew up conventions which called for defensive measures and trade agreements, but these were not ratified by their respective governments. The next conference (1864), also held in Lima, had representatives from Guatemala and from all South American countries, except Brazil, Uruguay, and Paraguay. Its object was not to defend against invasion, but to implement the other principles of Pan-Americanism, cooperation, arbitration, establishment of peace, and organization of a union of the Latin-American states.

Besides the efforts of Latin-American nations to make the ideas of Pan-Americanism effective, individuals throughout the nineteenth century frequently proposed plans for inter-American cooperation. Illustrative is that of the Chilean thinker, Francisco Bilbao. In 1856 he suggested a plan for a Federal Congress of Republics which would establish an international American citizenship, American international law and an international tribunal, a common system of weights and measures, the abolition of custom duties, universal education, intellectual cooperation, the settling of boundary disputes, an American university, and a federal congress to represent American states in a world federation.

The conferences of 1826, 1847, and 1864 failed of their immediate objectives, while proposals for other conferences by Colombia, Argentina, and Mexico did not materialize. But they represented a tradition of thought, contributed to by individuals with their programs such as those of Bilbao, which kept alive the basic principles conceived by Bolívar. There existed a base, therefore, for the growth of these ideas into significant institutions when the United States in 1889 finally joined the Latin Americans in calling conferences to make inter-American cooperation effective.

Nineteenth Century Expansion of the United States in Latin America. While in the field of inter-American relations the Latin Americans were fostering the ideas of Pan-Americanism, the United States in the nineteenth century was engaged in territorial and commercial expansion. The growth of trade in the Caribbean rapidly extended itself after 1800 to include the coasts of northern South America, Panama, and Central America. Other trade in the next decade from New England and Baltimore began pushing down the east side of South America to enter the Río de la Plata and go beyond through the Strait of Magellan into the Pacific as far north as Alaskan waters. Signalizing this expansion were a series of treaties marking the territorial growth and commercial interests of the United States westward to the Pacific coast and southward to Central America and Panama.

The first of these, the Bidlack Treaty with Colombia in 1846, gave the United States a right of way across the isthmus of Panama and equality with the British in Colombia's trade. In the same year negotiations with Nicaragua resulted in the Squier Treaty in 1849 looking to rights for a canal route. The success of the United States in the war with Mexico, ratified in the Guadalupe-Hidalgo Treaty of 1848, contained a provision for American use of the Tehuantepec isthmian route. This same treaty, giving up a base on the Pacific coast with the acquisition of California and coinciding with our growing commercial interests in Central America, paved the way for the negotiation of the Clayton-Bulwer Treaty of 1850. This document recognized American interests, as well as British, in possible canal routes through Panama, Nicaragua, and the Tehuantepec region. Our commercial interests with Cuba fostered filibustering expeditions in 1849–1851 and a demand for its annexation in 1854.[1]

After 1850 the process of commercial expansion continued unabated. In 1851–1853 we dispatched the Herndon-Gibbon expedition to explore the headwaters of the Amazon for the purpose of investigating the commercial possibilities of the region. This interest played a part in Brazil's decision to open the Amazon River to world trade in 1867. Land speculators and possibilities of a naval base led the United States to negotiate a treaty, which failed of ratification, with Santo Domingo in 1878 for the acquisition of Samaná Bay. This broadening of commerce and investment in the islands and along the northern coast of South America, particularly in Venezuela, alerted the United States to the threat of English efforts to extend her Guiana possessions. Upon Venezuela's appeal the United States insisted upon arbitration of the boundary dispute in 1895, saving thereby the mouth of the Orinoco River for Venezuela and American commercial interests in that region.

Inter-American Cooperation: Beginnings, 1889–1932. These economic interests in Latin America led the United States to the understanding of the need of a formal organization among the American states to facilitate the exchange of goods, avert war, and adopt means of cooperation. The first step, taken in 1881 by James G. Blaine, failed to materialize, but subsequent legislation enacted by the Congress of the United States led to the first meeting of the American states, held in Washington, D. C., in 1889–1890. Besides initiating the movement, this conference achieved an outstanding result in the organization of the Commercial Bureau of the American Republics, the forerunner of the Pan-American Union. This Bureau and later the Union accumulated and published a huge body of information about Latin America affecting its political, social, cultural, and economic life.

---

[1] The major aspects of the relations, referred to throughout Part I of this chapter, between the United States and individual Latin-American countries are discussed in the survey of each country concerned. Thus, for example, for a discussion of the Bidlack Treaty, the Guadalupe-Hidalgo Treaty, the Clayton-Bulwer Treaty, and our interest in annexing Cuba, mentioned in this paragraph, consult respectively the surveys of Colombia on p. 491; Mexico on p. 649; Nicaragua on pp. 593–594; and Cuba on p. 535.

After this date, 1890, conferences were held in Mexico City in 1901–1902; in Rio de Janeiro in 1906; and in Buenos Aires in 1910. World War I postponed further meetings until 1923, when the next conference met in Santiago, Chile. The Sixth Pan-American Conference convened in Havana, Cuba, in 1928. All of the meetings confined themselves largely to the consideration of very practical matters, customs and postal regulations, sanitation matters, trade marks, commercial agreements, copyrights, and other questions of this character. Occasionally, rumblings of discontent among the Latin-American delegates burst out in the later conferences demanding discussion, rigidly excluded by the United States, of compulsory arbitration of inter-American disputes, the high American tariff, limitation of military expenditures, and the policy of the United States in the Caribbean and Central America.

Once the policy of conferences began, a myriad of vital matters put in an appearance which could be discussed only by specialized groups. As a result there sprang up over the years many important subsidiary inter-American organizations which have contributed to the slow building of the present-day inter-American edifice. Among these were judicial, medical, scientific, financial, educational, and municipal congresses; others dealt with questions of public health, child welfare, commerce, agriculture, highways, and many other subjects of vital concern to all American states.

Continued United States Expansion in Latin America: New Policies, 1898–1932. While inter-American conferences were giving the future a bright look, full cooperation was hampered by new United States policies after 1898. The industrial power of the great country in the north, nourished by nineteenth century expansion and a flood of immigrants from Europe, demanded ever greater amounts of raw materials. At hand in Latin America were vast storehouses. Minerals abounded: oil, copper, tin, nitrates, gold, silver, bauxite, mercury, lead, zinc, iron. Tropical products were equally plentiful: sugar, coffee, bananas, cocoa, tobacco. Forest products were inexhaustible: mahogany, balsa wood, cabinet woods, varieties of nuts and fibers.

The acquisition of these raw materials for United States industrial needs demanded an investment of capital in a variety of undertakings. Most important were construction of communications, railroads, highways, and steamship lines; improvement of health conditions in port cities; docks and warehouses; urban facilities, utilities, sewage plants, paving of streets, modern office and public buildings. By 1929 investment of capital in all of Latin America, with two-thirds concentrated on

Mexico, Central America, and the Caribbean countries, had reached the total of $5,587,494,100, the largest single investment of American capital outside of the United States.

This basic economic situation fashioned the political policies of the government. The first, intervention for protection of life and property, appeared in the Platt Amendment to the Cuban constitution in 1903. A second, the acquisition of naval bases for the protection of commerce and the United States, also appeared in the Cuban treaty under which Guantánamo Bay was ceded for this purpose. Both these policies found expression also in the Panama Treaty of 1903. In 1902 in Venezuela and in 1904 in Santo Domingo, when Europeans threatened the area of investment and military bases by sending fleets, the Roosevelt government issued the famous Roosevelt Corollary to the Monroe Doctrine. It stated in effect that it was the duty of the United States to maintain order in Caribbean countries to prevent foreign powers from occupying their territories to collect debts and thus become a possible threat to the United States. Thus occupation became the next policy developed in this period.

Occupation found further expression in 1915 when President Wilson ordered the taking over of Haiti, which had become involved over debts with European creditors. But the most striking example of the policy of intervention and occupation came in Nicaragua during the years 1912–1928. In addition in 1917 the United States secured by treaty with Nicaragua rights to build a canal and establish naval bases on each side of the country. The crisis of World War I brought the next statement of policy when Woodrow Wilson refused to recognize Huerta as president of Mexico because he had secured the office by force. The application of this policy of nonrecognition of governments coming into power by force applied to the Costa Rican Tinoco government in 1919, and resulted, as in the case of Huerta, in its overthrow.

With these policies in force throughout this period (1898–1932) inevitably blocking developing reform movements, Latin Americans resented the Monroe Doctrine, which they frequently referred to as a shield for American investment. The refusal, moreover, of the United States to permit discussion of political questions, the high American tariff, and intervention in the Caribbean and Central America added to their frustration at the Pan-American conferences. By 1928, however, when the Havana Conference convened, these matters finally came in for discussion. As a major result of this meeting, the way was opened for a Conference of American States on Conciliation and Arbitration in the next year, 1929. Modeling their work upon the Gondra Treaty of 1923, which provided for commissions of inquiry with no power, the 1929 conference produced the treaties of that year called the Inter-American Arbitration and Conciliation Treaties. Together they outlawed war as an instrument of national policy and provided for arbitration of all questions arising between two American nations but which did not fall within the field of diplomacy.

Part II. INTER-AMERICAN RELATIONS

Inter-American Cooperation, 1933–1948. While the Havana Conference broke the tradition of nonpolitical discussion, the decisive turning point in inter-American affairs came with the depression during the years 1929–1932. The collapse of international trade and the necessity of reviving American industry and Latin-American raw material production demanded a completely new policy in inter-American affairs. The Hoover administration made some progress in this direction. The election of Franklin D. Roosevelt in 1932 produced the Good Neighbor policy, which ended all the unfortunate policies developed during the "big stick" era.

Recognizing the need of ending resentment among the Latin-American nations by frankly admitting their equality as states and recognizing their need for markets as well as our own to recover from the effects of the depression, Roosevelt gave voice to the principles of the Good Neighbor policy in his address on Pan-American Day, April 14, 1933. The political principle stated that no American nation henceforth should intervene in the internal affairs of another American nation. The second, or economic, stated a policy of inter-American reciprocal trade agreements. Under these the high American tariff was to be reduced at specific points upon executive agreement, authorized by Congress, while Latin-American nations would reciprocate by admitting American manufactured products into their markets.

The political principle of nonintervention was implemented at once by the United States by inviting Cuba to repeal the Platt Amendment to her constitution ending the right of the United States to intervene in Cuban affairs, by withdrawing the marines from all Caribbean and Central American countries, and by negotiating a new treaty with Panama in 1936, ending certain privileges of Americans in the Canal Zone and defining more clearly Panama's rights over its own territory. The most striking occasion, however, of the application of the nonintervention principle came in 1938 when the United States refused to inter-

vene in Mexico upon the latter's expropriation, as an internal affair, of
foreign-owned oil wells.

Reciprocal trade agreements implemented the economic side of the
Good Neighbor policy. Begun in 1934 with Cuba, such treaties were
eventually signed by most of the Latin-American countries, Argentina
being a notable exception. These agreements met expectations in bringing a huge increase in inter-American trade in the following years. Significantly, in the world picture of the time, both the new principles were
decisive factors in influencing the majority of the Latin Americans away
from the acceptance of Nazi propaganda, except in Argentina, against
democratic government.

Inter-American Conferences, 1933–1938. With the meeting of the
Seventh Congress in Montevideo in December, 1933, inter-American
cooperation became a solidly established principle. There the United
States accepted the resolution of the conference that "no state has the
right to intervene in the internal or external affairs of another state."
The basic principle of the Good Neighbor policy thus became an inter-
American one. Other accomplishments of the conference included the
bringing together of the various treaties, the Gondra Treaty of 1923, the
Argentine anti-war pact, which included the doctrine of nonrecognition
of territory acquired by force, and the Arbitration and Conciliation
Treaties of 1929. Since one country or another had signed all of these,
the effect was to bring about the universal recognition of the principle
of arbitration. The conference also arranged an armistice in the Chaco
War and agreed to accept the principle of reciprocity as a means of
improving trade relations.

The great importance of the Montevideo agreements became at
once apparent, for in Europe Hitler and Mussolini were moving in ex-
actly the opposite direction from peace. By 1936 Hitler had taken the
grave steps of withdrawing from the League of Nations, rearming
Germany, invading the Rhineland, and sending military planes to aid
Franco to overthrow the Spanish Republic. Mussolini had invaded
Ethiopia and dispatched troops and warships to Franco's Spain. These
events, foretelling war, led Roosevelt to propose an *ad interim* meeting
of the American states at Buenos Aires for 1936.

The Buenos Aires Conference agreed, in view of the world situation, to three major peace proposals. One was a convention for the
maintenance of peace, providing that in case of a threat to the New
World, the American states would consult together to maintain peace.
To give this effect, a permanent body was established consisting of the

foreign ministers of each state. The second agreement established procedures to be followed in relation to the treaties brought together at Montevideo: a six months' consultation period before resorting to hostilities in case of a conflict between two American countries, or in case hostilities broke out, the adoption of neutrality by the other American states to prevent the spread of the conflict; and measures defined for states to use including denial to belligerents of supplies, military and financial. The third agreement was the reaffirmation of the principle of nonintervention.

When two years later the European world was plunging ever faster toward war, the Eighth Inter-American Conference convened in Lima, Peru, in 1938. Here the American states, in spite of disruptive efforts of Argentina, built upon the achievements of the two preceding meetings to secure the Declaration of Lima. It provided for consultation procedures, namely, that any foreign minister of any American state could call a meeting of all American foreign ministers at a designated capital. The conference, too, in view of the apparent incapacity of Europe to maintain its peace, drew up a Declaration of American Principles defined as essential to preserve world order under law. These principles consisted of outlawing intervention and the use of force, settlement of disputes by arbitration, accepting the principles of international law as a guide to relations between powers, respect for treaties, and the recognition of the role of intellectual and economic cooperation as a means of bringing about world peace.

Inter-American Relations and World War II: the Panama Meeting. Hardly had the ink dried on the Lima documents when Hitler plunged the European world into World War II on September 1, 1939. The crisis made mandatory the establishment of a system of hemisphere defense in the New World, the basis for which had already been laid by the conferences between 1933 and 1938. Within three weeks the foreign ministers of the American republic had arrived in Panama to hold their first consultation on September 23, 1939. The outstanding result of this meeting was the issuance of the Declaration of Panama, declaring the neutrality of the American nations and extending around the hemisphere from Canadian waters southward a neutral zone 300 miles wide from which all belligerent activity was excluded on pain of penalties. Recognizing that the war would adversely affect the economic and financial structure of the Latin-American countries through loss of markets, the foreign ministers laid down the first measures to be taken for inter-American cooperation in these fields.

The Act of Havana, 1940. The progress of the war in Europe by the summer of 1940 had brought the overthrow of the Netherlands and France. At once the possibility presented itself of Nazi seizure of French and Dutch Guiana and the Caribbean possessions of these two countries. To forestall any such eventuality, the foreign ministers held their second meeting in Havana in July, 1940, where they agreed to resist any attempt to transfer sovereignty over these possessions. Besides this statement of policy, the conference drew up the Act of Havana which gave any single country the right to act immediately in case of necessity to defend the French and Dutch possessions. This act was simple recognition of the fact that the United States would so act in any event. Interestingly, the conference was giving effect to Bolívar's conception of inter-American cooperation against European aggression.

The Rio de Janeiro Conference, 1942. The action of Japan in attacking at Pearl Harbor on December 7, 1941, produced the next development in inter-American relations. At once all the agreements reached in the earlier meetings came into operation. The United States called the third meeting of foreign ministers in Rio de Janeiro on January 15, 1942. There they recognized that Japan's act was an aggression against one of the American nations, and therefore against all. The ministers recommended, accordingly, that all American states break diplomatic relations with the Axis powers. This action had, in fact, already been taken by Costa Rica, which declared war on Japan before the United States did. She was followed by eight other American nations within a week—Cuba, the Dominican Republic, Guatemala, Haiti, Honduras, Nicaragua, Panama, and El Salvador. Since all but two of these had been victims of the earlier "big stick" policy, their prompt action was striking testimony to the effectiveness of the Good Neighbor policy. By January, 1943, all except Argentina had either broken relations or declared war on the Axis. Argentina refrained until March, 1945, when there was no doubt of the defeat of Germany.

The ministers also provided machinery for an Inter-American Defense Board, recommended the boycott of all Axis firms and banks, and laid the basis for the economic collaboration of the American nations. Finally, foreseeing the end of the war, the ministers recommended that the Inter-American Juridical Committee, created in 1939 at Panama, formulate recommendations for a new American international organization.

Wartime Cooperation. With this foundation, American nations achieved an extraordinary unity of action during the war, marred only by

Argentina. Brazil and Uruguay granted naval and air bases to the United States, which played a significant role in eliminating the submarine menace in the South Atlantic in cooperation with the Brazilian and Uruguayan military forces. The base at Recife in Brazil was a large factor in the success of the North African campaign of 1942–1943. Brazil, too, sent an expeditionary force to Italy. On the other side of the continent Ecuador and Panama also granted air and naval bases to the United States to protect the southern approaches to the Panama Canal. Bases granted by Nicaragua and Cuba fitted into the defense program of the Caribbean. Practically all countries accepted American naval, military, and air missions to aid the development of their own forces.

The United States on its part extended Lend-Lease agreements to all but Panama, which was unnecessary in view of the American military forces stationed there, and Argentina, which allowed German sabotage operations against the United Nations. Through the Export-Import Bank the United States lent money to practically all the Latin-American countries to stabilize their currencies and assist developing their industries to meet shortages created by the war. Other agencies, the Metals Reserve Corporation, the Rubber Reserve Company, and others, purchased huge quantities of raw materials, tin, copper, rubber, industrial diamonds, quartz crystals, quinine, balsa wood, and mercury—all needed in the war industries in the United States.

Important in effecting the extraordinary cooperation achieved was the influence of the great Latin-American labor organizations. Their members, numbering in the millions, produced the minerals, harvested the plantations, and loaded the ships. Their fear of the fate which befell European labor under Hitler and Mussolini and their hope that the war would open new opportunities for extension of democratic practices made them willing workers in the common effort. The Atlantic Charter, calling for freedom of speech and religion and freedom from fear and want, expressed ideas they had long fought for themselves.

The Chapultepec Conference, 1945. World War II made clear that postwar Latin America would present new problems. Foreseeing these, the American states held the next meeting in Mexico City in February, 1945, called the Inter-American Conference on Problems of War and Peace, and commonly referred to as the Chapultepec Conference. Of immediate importance was the effort to get Argentina back into the inter-American organization from whose work she had been largely absent during the war. The conference invited her to return, but laid down requirements for her to meet, namely, declaration of war on the

Axis and ending the activities of German spies. Her declaring war in March, 1945, was sufficient to readmit her and therefore to be sponsored by the United States to become a member nation of the United Nations which opened its conference the following June in San Francisco.

The most important work of the conference, however, concerned affairs of long-term significance. One of these was the promulgation of an Economic Charter of the Americas. It presented a blueprint for such important matters as raising the standard of living in Latin America, increasing the productive capacity of the masses of the people, improving the general level of public health, and protecting women and children from industrial exploitation. To make its principles effective the conference created the Inter-American Economic and Social Council, replacing the Financial and Economic Advisory Committee set up in 1939 at Panama.

To maintain peace after the war and meet situations created by Argentina during the war, the conference also drew up the Act of Chapultepec, a foundation stone in inter-American efforts to maintain peace. After reiterating principles accepted since 1933—nonintervention, refusal to recognize territory acquired by conquest, and interdependence implicit in consultation—the act further stated that an attack of a state against the integrity, territory, sovereignty, or political independence of an American state would constitute an act of aggression against all other American states. An act of aggression received partial definition as consisting of an invasion of armed forces trespassing boundaries already established by treaty. The driving force behind this remarkable statement was the determination to protect governments against overthrow by invasion from within or without the Americas. Finally, the conference recommended the conclusion of a treaty among the states to define procedures to meet acts of aggression. Thus the stage was set for the next major achievement: the Inter-American Treaty of Reciprocal Assistance, usually referred to as the Rio Pact.

The Rio Pact, 1947. Signed at Rio de Janeiro on September 2, 1947, the Rio Pact condemned war as an instrument of national policy and provided for peaceful measures to settle controversies among American states. Its significant article is the third: ". . . an armed attack by any State against an American State shall be considered as an attack against all American States, and consequently, each one of the . . . parties undertakes to assist in meeting the attack in the exercise of the inherent right of individual and collective self-defense, recognized by Article 51 of the Charter of the United Nations." The article then goes on to provide for an Organ of Consultation consisting of the foreign ministers of the American states to decide upon the manner of fulfilling the obligation thus assumed. The area defined in which the pact applies is the Western Hemisphere from pole to pole and includes Greenland.

What is significant about this agreement is that it is *not* a mere resolution or recommendation—it is a *treaty* signed by governments of the American states. Its sanctions to secure enforcement, including almost everything from recall of ambassadors to the use of armed forces, may be applied by a two-thirds vote, and therefore do not require unanimous consent, as is the case in the Security Council of the United Nations. Ratified by the United States in December, 1947, the treaty became effective on December 3, 1948, when fifteen states had adhered to the pact. Its effectiveness as a means of preserving the peace in the Americas was demonstrated when it was invoked in the case of the Nicaraguan invasion of Costa Rica in 1949 and 1955, and in the dispute which arose between the Dominican Republic and its neighbors in 1950.

The Organization of American States: the Bogotá Conference, 1948. By 1948 the effects of the ending of the war were being felt throughout Latin America. All nations had seen their industries stimulated by the demands of the war. Their representatives at Bogotá hoped that the internal development of their respective nations could be further carried forward by establishing a common fund of $500,000,000, to which the United States as the wealthiest member would naturally be the largest contributor. Their purposes were to stimulate agriculture and irrigation, meet problems of housing the poorer masses, improve communications, and continue establishing and expanding native industries. The United States on its part was more interested in providing funds, proposed by President Truman to the extent of $500,000,000, which would be devoted more to the extraction of raw materials directly beneficial to the industries of the United States. The United States wished guarantees in addition against expropriation of foreign-owned property, provided for in one form and other in most Latin-American constitutions.

The ultimate result was that on these vital matters of a common fund or pool and guarantees, no agreement could be reached. The Latin-American delegates were further incensed by the fact that in view of their contribution to the common war effort, the expenditures of the United States in Europe under the Marshall Plan, while rejecting an essentially modest contribution to aid internal development in Latin America, seemed definitely a neglect of common interests. Nevertheless, the fifty-nine-year history of inter-American cooperation had so firmly fixed the tradition that the conference, the ninth, was not a failure. Before it adjourned, it had reorganized the structure of the Pan-American Union. More, it had placed this new body on a treaty basis to make the settlement of disputes more effective, as provided for in the Chapultepec Conference and carried out in part in the Rio Pact of 1947.

This new institution, replacing the Pan-American Union, is the Organization of American States (OAS). Its Charter consists of three parts. Part I, reiterating the fundamental rights and duties of the states, is the foundation of the entire structure. From treaties, declarations, and resolutions of past conferences, Part I drew the bases for social, cultural, and economic cooperation, for the obligation upon the states to settle controversies by peaceful means, and for reciprocal aid in case of attack against any American nation.

Part II states the chief features of the Organization through which it functions. They are (1) the International Conference of American States, the supreme authority on all matters relating to the relation among the states; (2) the Meeting of Consultation of Ministers of Foreign Affairs, which meets to consider questions of an urgent character, particularly affecting the peace of the Americas; (3) Specialized Conferences dealing with specific technical matters for purposes of cooperation among two or more nations; (4) Specialized Organizations, which are intergovernmental bodies established by multilateral agreements and have "specific functions with respect to technical matters of common interest to the American states"; (5) the Council; and (6) the Pan-American Union.

The Council of the Organization of American States replaced the Governing Board of the Pan-American Union to become the permanent executive council of the Organization itself. The organs through which the Council functions are the Inter-American Economic and Social Council, the Inter-American Council of Jurists, and the Inter-American Cultural Council.

The Pan-American Union became the general secretariat of the Organization. This body ties together the entire work of the Organization in that it is a clearing house for information concerning all aspects of the work of all activities of the OAS. Over the Pan-American Union, a permanent day-to-day organ, presides the Secretary-General, whose office rotates every ten years, and an Assistant-Secretary General, the latter of whom is the Secretary of the Council. Appointed as the first Secretary-General was Dr. Alberto Lleras Camargo, former president and distinguished statesman of Colombia.

Part III of the Charter states that nothing in the Charter conflicts with the obligations of American nations which they owe as members of the United Nations, and provides further for ratification and amendment.

Almost immediately after it began to function, the Organization of American States proved its value in keeping the peace. Hardly, in fact, had the Charter been ratified by the necessary number of states when Costa Rica called upon the Council of the OAS to repel the Nicaraguan invasion of 1949. This difficulty was barely settled when the Council's aid was again sought in 1950 to end a dispute between the Dominican Republic and its neighbors. Success attended this effort also. Once more in January, 1955, the OAS warded off a new war which was rapidly developing between Nicaragua and Costa Rica. These achievements have greatly increased the prestige of the world's most successful international organization.

The Technical Assistance Program and Latin America since 1948. Although the United States at the Bogotá Conference rejected the Latin-American proposals of an inter-American pool, their significance was clear in the light of world-wide demands for aiding underdeveloped areas. Indeed, less than a month later, President Truman in his inaugural address of January 20, 1949, enunciated the now famous Point Four program:

What we envisage is a program of development based on the concepts of democratic fair-dealing. . . . Greater production is the key to prosperity and peace. And the key to greater production is a wider and more vigorous application of modern scientific and technical knowledge. . . .

This policy became the basis of the Technical Assistance Program to Latin America. Under it missions were sent to practically all the southern nations to give advice and provide assistance in education, scientific agriculture, cattle raising, and other activities aimed at modernizing their economies.

Paralleling the United States program were the technical assistance undertakings provided by the OAS itself. In 1954 at the Rio de Janeiro inter-American economic meeting, the OAS reorganized its activities under the OAS Program of Technical Cooperation and provided it with adequate funds. Thus far it has established technical training centers for students brought from the various American countries. Upon this basis specific projects of vital importance to each country have been and are being carried forward.

Supplementing Point Four and the OAS Program have been other United States agencies, governmental and private. The Export-Import Bank, the International Bank for Reconstruction and Development, the Pan-American Sanitary Bureau, and private organizations, such as the Rockefeller, Ford, Guggenheim, and Kellogg Foundations, Protestant and Catholic missions, and others, are all engaged in efforts to raise the standards of living in their own spheres in cooperation with governments or private business organizations in Latin America. The total activities cover a host of subjects: loans to governments to establish industries, build communications, develop agricultural resources, conduct campaigns against tropical diseases, and carry on cultural undertakings ranging from support of purely scientific activities to the Cultural Institutes maintained by the Department of State. All of these agencies are proving their worth in creating good-will, aiding Latin-American economies, and opening markets for American goods.

Inter-American Cooperation since 1948. The Technical Assistance Programs of both the United States and the OAS, together with the above-mentioned activities of governmental and private agencies have, however, fallen far short of meeting the needs of Latin America. Moreover, in the last two decades profound economic and social changes have intensified these needs and created almost insoluble problems for every Latin-American nation. The most striking of these changes is the rapidity of population growth. The world rate is estimated at 1.2 per cent increase annually, but in Latin America the rate is more than double this figure, exceeding 2.5 per cent. Indeed, in this respect, Latin America is the fastest growing area in the world. In 1941–1943 its population was estimated at 133,000,000; today it is more than 170,000,-000. At its present rate of growth, which may even increase because of advances in modern medical science, careful students have estimated that by the year 2000, Latin America will have considerably more than 400,000,000 people.

Tied in with population increase is the second major change, namely, industrialization in all the great urban centers in Latin America. People crowd into the cities because they find more job opportunities there than in the rural regions. The steady increase in the number of workers in turn provides a vast reservoir of cheap labor for expanding industrial development. Together these two forces have created demands for food on a scale hitherto unknown in Latin America. Everywhere, excepting Argentina, Uruguay, and Mexico, agricultural production lags behind population increase and makes necessary huge imports of basic foods.

The reasons for the shortage are various. Unfortunately, the bulk of arable land in practically all countries is devoted to crops primarily destined for export. Erosion, a problem that Latin America is just beginning to attack, affects adversely agricultural production. Inadequate transportation systems play their part. Even in those parts of Latin America where surplus food exists, lack of transportation—railroads and highways—makes it impossible to get the food to the great industrial centers. This inadequacy of transportation hinges on the fact that railroads and highways were originally built with an eye to the export of raw materials, rather than to tap areas for food for the people of the various nations.

Within the rapidly growing cities themselves are compelling needs. All cities, large and small, desperately need programs of sanitation and fresh water; educational, housing, and medical facilities; transportation systems; and centers of amusement, parks, beaches, playing grounds, and theaters. But the comparatively sudden increase in urban populations in the last decade has left Latin-American cities struggling in an almost losing battle to meet these needs.

The pressures for improving agriculture, building highways and railroads, and solving the complex problems of metropolitan centers have placed a heavy burden upon the financial resources of Latin-American countries. These are further strained by the necessity of importing huge amounts of food, agricultural and transportation machinery, industrial equipment for rapidly growing factories, and, except for Mexico, Venezuela, Colombia, and Bolivia, oil. For these materials the Latin-American nations must pay the high prices demanded by industrial nations. On the other hand, they sell their raw materials in markets in which prices fluctuate. The result of this imbalance is to make Latin-American currencies unstable. Even Venezuela, which has a stable currency based upon taxes derived from export of oil, has been unable to meet the housing, transportation, and food requirements of its people, which, incidentally, next to El Salvador, has the highest rate of population growth, over 3 per cent, of any Latin-American country.

The Caracas and Petropolis Conferences, 1954. In March, 1954, the Organization of American States convened for its first general meeting under the Charter at Caracas, Venezuela, in the Tenth Inter-American Conference. There the delegates of the Latin-American countries arrived, obsessed with their internal problems of inflation, expanding populations, soaring costs of living, and need for a huge investment of capital. They hoped to lay the basis for a vast economic aid program. The United

States, on the other hand, engaged in a world-wide struggle against Communism, felt that the first order of business should be suitable action by the OAS to meet the menace of Communism in Latin America. Prevailing in its objective, Washington secured the adoption of the Caracas Resolution, which in essence stated that Communist political control of any American nation is foreign intervention and a threat to the peace of the hemisphere. As such it automatically called for action under the Rio Pact. Argentina and Mexico refrained from voting on the ground that the resolution endangered the inter-American principle of nonintervention. Costa Rica had not attended the conference as a protest against the unrepresentative character of the Venezuelan government. Guatemala voted against the resolution.

After this action several Latin-American countries, notably Chile, advanced anew demands originally made at Bogotá for greater economic aid. The United States opposed the specific proposals, particularly the establishment of a Latin-American bank. Agreement, however, was reached to hold a separate meeting later to consider economic questions.

In November, 1954, in accord with the recommendation of the Caracas meeting, the American Finance and Economy Ministers met at Petropolis, Brazil, to discuss the Latin-American proposals raised at the Tenth Conference. Led by Argentina and Chile, they asked for larger United States loans from both private and public sources for the development of their respective countries. They also sought support for stabilizing prices of the raw materials upon which their economies depend. They urged the United States to lower or abolish income and other taxes on profits to encourage more of its citizens to invest in Latin America. Finally, they proposed the establishment of an Inter-American Bank.

The United States agreed to support more liberal policies on the part of the Export-Import Bank and recommend legislation to Congress to reduce taxes on income from Latin-American investments. On the other hand, the United States felt that an Inter-American Bank was not feasible and that no hope could be held out for action to stabilize prices of raw materials.

Conclusion. The century and a half of history of the relations of Latin America and the United States have shown a steady growth toward the acceptance in both areas of a common set of international principles. The basis of this structure was laid in the Monroe Doctrine and in the Bolivarian conception of inter-American cooperation. With the calling of the Pan-American Conference in 1889 by the United States, the first step was taken to unite the two currents of New World relations, which previously had little in common. By 1933 the announcement of the Good Neighbor policy prepared the way for inter-American cooperation based on principles of nonintervention and mutual economic assistance. This union found a solid basis in American international law in the Treaty of Reciprocal Assistance of 1947 and the Pact of Bogotá, 1948, which created the present Organization of American States.

By the middle of the twentieth century the first great problem of inter-American relations had apparently found permanent solution, namely, cooperation between American states to maintain peace and protect the New World from war and aggression. There now remains the second major problem, which is best expressed in the words of the distinguished Uruguayan statesman José A. Mora:

> The advances made in the maintenance of peace have permitted substantial parallel progress in economic and social cooperation. The unlimited opportunities opened up by economic development of the Americas become plainer every day.
>
> In turn, the OAS Council is beginning new studies of a legal and political nature, thanks to the topics referred to it by the Inter-American Conference in Caracas. While new formulas on the procedure of pacific settlements are being considered, research is also advancing on the protection of human rights. . . . All this gives us hope that our organization will continue to develop, that it will widen the area of its operations, to benefit the peoples and governments of America. . . .[2]

[2] José A. Mora, "Moving Ahead," *Américas,* Vol. 7, No. 3, March, 1955, p. 5.

BIBLIOGRAPHY

BIBLIOGRAPHY

This bibliography is designed (1) to acquaint the student with the leading works in the field and (2) to aid instructors (other than those familiar with the Hispanic-American area) in the selection of key books and periodicals for their library for Latin-American courses they may be called upon to teach.

I. BIBLIOGRAPHIES, REVIEWS AND GENERAL WORKS

Bibliographies and Guides

Behrendt, R. F. W., *Modern Latin America in Social Science Literature*, Hamilton, New York, 1949.

Butler, Ruth Lapham, ed., *Guide to the Hispanic-American Historical Review, 1918–1945*, Durham, 1950.

Clark, Thomas D., ed., *Travels in the Old South: A Bibliography*, 2 vols., Norman, Oklahoma, 1956. (Includes Spanish travelers.)

Economic Literature of Latin America, a Tentative Bibliography, 2 vols., Cambridge, Mass., 1936.

Handbook of Latin American Studies, Cambridge, Mass., and Gainesville, Fla., 1937. (Most comprehensive guide to all fields of Latin-American life; includes items published annually in the United States, Latin America, and Europe.)

Hilton, Ronald, ed., *Handbook of Hispanic Source Materials and Research Organizations in the United States,* Toronto, 1942.

——, ed., *Handbook of Hispanic Source Materials in the United States,* Stanford, 1956.

Humphreys, R. A., *Latin America: A Selective Guide to Publications in English,* London, 1949.

Inter-American Review of Bibliography, Pan-American Union, Washington, 1951.

Jones, C. K., *A Bibliography of Latin American Bibliographies,* Washington, 1942.

Pan American Union, *Bibliografía de las conferencias interamericanas,* Washington, 1954. (A mimeographed guide to the documents of the first nine Pan-American conferences and other materials.)

——, *Selected List of Books [in English] on Latin America,* Washington, 1939.

United Nations, *Latin America, 1935–1949, A Selected Bibliography,* New York, 1952. (Over 4,800 items on various social sciences; history, government, and international relations include about 1,000 items.)

Who's Who in Latin America, ed. by Ronald Hilton, 3rd ed., rev. Stanford, 1945–1951.

Wilgus, A. Curtis, "Bibliographical Essay on Leading Works in Various Languages Dealing with Hispanic America Printed Since the Year 1800," in A. C. Wilgus, *The Development of Hispanic America,* New York, 1941, pp. 856–911.

——, comp., *Doors to Latin America,* University of Florida, Gainesville, 1954. (A quarterly; brief evaluations of current books and pamphlets dealing with Latin America.)

Reviews, Bulletins, and other Journals

American Journal of International Law, The, Washington, 1907. (Invaluable for technical discussions of inter-American problems.)

Americas, The, Academy of American Franciscan History, Washington, 1944. (A learned historical journal of the Franciscan order; quarterly.)

Hispanic American Historical Review, The, Duke University Press, Durham, 1918. (This *Review,* published quarterly, is the principal learned journal on Latin-American history; see Butler, *Guide,* under "Bibliographies and Guides" above.)

Hispanic American Report, ed. by Ronald Hilton, Stanford, 1948. (The first two volumes are entitled *Hispanic World Report;* a monthly survey, chiefly on current Latin-American events; excellent for economic data.)

Inter-American Economic Affairs, ed. by S. G. Hanson, Washington, 1947.

(Quarterly; confined chiefly to current problems.)

International Labor Review, Geneva, 1921.

Pan American Union, *Américas,* Washington, 1949. (Successor, with *Annals,* to the *Bulletin* of the Pan American Union; a monthly; popular, accurate, and valuable.)

———, *Annals of the Organization of American States,* Washington, 1949. (Official documents of the Organization of American States; quarterly.)

———, *Bulletin,* 82 vols., Washington, 1893–1948. (An invaluable storehouse of materials on Latin-American life.)

Revista de historia de América, Comisión de Historia, Instituto Panamericano de Geografía é Historia, Mexico, 1938. (Published twice a year; a major learned journal in the Latin-American field.)

United Nations, *Monthly Bulletin of Statistics,* Statistical Office, New York, 1947. (Vital and other basic statistics on Latin America.)

General Works: Colonial

Bolton, Herbert E., and Marshall, Thomas M., *The Colonization of North America,* 1492–1783, New York, 1925. (Still the basic work on Spain and other powers in North America for colonial period.)

Diffie, Bailey C., *Latin American Civilization: Colonial Period,* Harrisburg, Pa., 1945. (Invaluable; an original presentation of the material.)

Haring, Clarence H., *The Spanish Empire in America,* New York, 1947.

Holmes, Vera D., *A History of the Americas: From Discovery to Nationhood,* New York, 1950.

Merriman, Roger B., *The Rise of the Spanish Empire in the Old World and in the New,* 4 vols., New York, 1918–1934.

Priestley, H. I., *The Coming of the White Man,* 1492–1848, New York, 1929.

Wilgus, A. Curtis, ed., *Colonial Hispanic America,* Washington, 1936.

General Works: Colonial and Modern

Bannon, John Francis, *History of the Americas,* 2 vols., New York, 1952.

Chapman, Charles E., *Hispanic America: Colonial and Republican,* New York, 1947.

Christensen, A. N., ed., *The Evolution of Latin American Governments,* New York, 1951.

Crow, John A., *The Epic of Latin America,* New York, 1946.

Davis, Harold E., *The Americas in History,* New York, 1953.

Galindez, Jesús de, *Iberoamerica, su evolución politica, socio-economica, cultural é internacional,* New York, 1954.

Herring, Hubert, *A History of Latin America from the Beginnings to the Present,* New York, 1955.

Inman, Samuel G., *Latin America, Its Place in World Life,* rev., New York, 1946.

Jones, Tom B., and Beatty, W. Donald, *An Introduction to Hispanic American History,* rev. ed., New York, 1950.

Jorrín, Miguel, *Governments of Latin America,* New York, 1953. (Good for functioning.)

Keen, Benjamin, *Readings in Latin American Civilization,* 1492 to the present, New York, 1955.

Kirkpatrick, F. A., *Latin America, A Brief History,* New York, 1945.

MacDonald, Austin F., *Latin American Politics and Government,* New York, 1949.

Navarro y Lamarca, Carlos, *Compendio de la historia general de América,* Dos tomos, Buenos Aires, 1913. (One of the best surveys in Spanish.)

Rippy J. Fred, *Historical Evolution of Hispanic America,* 3rd ed., New York, 1945.

Robertson, William S., *History of the Latin American Nations,* 3rd ed., New York, 1943.

Schurz, W. L., *Latin America, A Descriptive Survey,* rev., New York, 1941.

———, *This New World: The Civilization of Latin America,* New York, 1954.

Wilgus, A. Curtis, *The Development of Hispanic America,* New York, 1941.

Williams, Mary W., *The People and Politics of Latin America,* rev. by R. J. Bartlett, New York, 1945.

Geography

Carlos, F. A., *Geography of Latin America,* 3rd ed., New York, 1952.

James, Preston, *Latin America,* rev. ed., New York, 1950.

Whitbeck, R. H., and others, *An Economic Geography of South America,* rev. ed., New York, 1940.

Wilgus, A. Curtis, *Latin America in Maps,* New York, 1943.

Interpretations

Arciniegas, Germán, *The State of Latin America,* New York, 1952. (Critique of the present.)

Bolton, Herbert Eugene, *Wider Horizons of American History,* New York, 1939. (Basic.)

Bryce, James, *South America: Observations and Impressions,* New York, 1917.

Duggan, Stephen, *The Two Americas: An Interpretation,* New York, 1934.

Jayne, Cecil, *Liberty and Despotism in Spanish America,* London, 1913.

Mijares, Augusto, *La interpretación pesimista de la sociología hispano-americana,* 2nd ed., Madrid, 1952. (A significant work; critical of many prevailing conceptions.)

Reyes, Alfonso, *The Position of America and Other Essays,* tr. by Harriet de Onís, New York, 1950. (By a universally reversed philosopher.)

Whitaker, A. P., *The Western Hemisphere Idea: Its Rise and Decline,* Ithaca, 1954.

(*Note:* For General Bibliographies on modern Latin America, see p. 740; on modern South America, pp. 740–741; on the Caribbean, pp. 751–753; on inter-American relations, pp. 764–766.)

Zavala, Zilvio, *New Viewpoints in the Spanish Colonization of America,* Philadelphia, 1943. (By a leading Mexican historian.)

II. BACKGROUND AND COLONIAL PERIOD

CHAPTER I: INDIAN CULTURE

Bennett, Wendell C., and Bird, Junius B., *Andean Culture History,* New York, 1949.

——, *Ancient Arts of the Andes,* New York, 1954. (Magnificent illustrations.)

Bingham, Hiram, *Lost City of the Incas: The Story of Machu Picchu and Its Builders,* New York, 1948.

Blom, Frans, *The Conquest of Yucatan,* Boston, 1936.

Collier, John, *The Indians of America,* New York, 1947.

Doering, Heinrich U., *The Art of Ancient Peru,* New York, 1952.

Gann, T., and Thompson, J. E., *History of the Mayas,* New York, 1937.

Goetz, Delia; Morley, Sylvanus G.; and Recinos, Adrián, *Popol Vuh: The Sacred Book of the Ancient Quiché Maya,* Norman, 1950.

Handbook of South American Indians, J. H. Steward, ed., 6 vols., Washington, 1946–1950. (A monumental work.)

Harcourt, Raoul d', *Primitive Arts of the Americas,* New York, 1950.

Hewett, Edgar L., *Ancient Andean Life,* New York, 1939.

Macgowan, Kenneth, *Early Man in the New World,* New York, 1950.

Martin, Paul S.; Quimby, G. I.; Collier, D., *Indians Before Columbus,* Chicago, 1947.

Mason, Gregory, *Columbus Came Late,* New York, 1931.

——, *Silver Cities of Yucatan,* New York, 1927.

Mayas and Their Neighbors, The, New York, 1940. (Has an extensive bibliography.)

Means, Philip A., *Ancient Civilizations of the Andes,* New York, 1931.

Morley, Sylvanus G., *The Ancient Maya,* 2nd ed., Stanford, 1947.

Osborne, Harold, *Indians of the Andes, Aymaras and Quechuas,* Cambridge, Mass., 1952.

Radin, Paul, *Indians of South America,* New York, 1942.

Roys, Ralph, *The Indian Background of Colonial Yucatan,* Washington, 1943.

Tax, Sol, ed., *The Civilization of Ancient America,* Chicago, 1951.

Thompson, J. Eric, *The Rise and Fall of the Maya Civilization,* Norman, 1954.

Tozzer, Alfred M., ed., *Landa's relación de las cosas de Yucatan,* Cambridge, Mass., 1941. (Authoritative translation.)

Vaillant, G. C., *Aztecs of Mexico, Origin, Rise and Fall of the Aztec Nation,* New York, 1950.

Van Hagen, V. W., *The Aztec and Maya Papermakers,* New York, 1944.

Weatherwax, Paul, *Indian Corn in Old America,* New York, 1954.

Weltfish, Gene, *Origins of Art,* Indianapolis, 1953.

Wissler, Clark, *The American Indian,* New York, 1927.

CHAPTER II: EUROPEAN BACKGROUND AND COLUMBUS

Altamira y Crevea, Rafael, *A History of Spain,* tr., by Muna Lee, New York, 1949.
Baker, J. N. L., *A History of Geographical Discovery and Exploration,* London, 1937.
Beazley, Charles Raymond, *Dawn of Modern Geography,* 3 vols., Oxford, 1897–1906.
Cary, M., and Warmington, E. A., *The Ancient Explorers,* London, 1929.
Chapman, Charles E., *History of Spain,* New York, 1927.
Cheyney, E. P., *The Dawn of a New Era,* New York, 1936.
Hart, Henry H., *Sea Road to the Indies,* New York, 1950. (Vasco da Gama.)
——, *Venetian Adventurer; the Life and Times of Marco Polo,* Stanford, 1943.
Jayne, Cecil, ed., *The Voyages of Christopher Columbus,* London, 1930.
Klein, J., *The Mesta: A Study in Spanish Economy, 1273–1836,* Cambridge, Mass., 1920.
Lane-Pool, Stanley, *The Moors in Spain,* New York, 1886.
Lea, H. C., *History of the Inquisition in Spain,* 4 vols., New York, 1906–1907.
Livermore, H. V., *Portugal and Brazil, An Introduction,* Oxford, 1953.
Merriman, Roger B., *The Rise of the Spanish Empire in the Old World and in the New,* 4 vols., New York, 1918–1934.
Morison, Samuel E., *Admiral of the Ocean Sea: A Life of Christopher Columbus,* 2 vols., Boston, 1942.
——, *Christopher Columbus, Mariner,* New York, 1955.
——, *Portuguese Voyages to America in the 15th Century,* Cambridge, Mass. Mass., 1940.
Newton, A. P., ed., *Travel and Travellers in the Middle Ages,* New York, 1930.
Nowell, Charles E., *The Great Discoveries and the First Colonial Empires,* Ithaca, 1954.
——, *A History of Portugal,* New York, 1952.
Nunn, George E., *Geographical Conceptions of Columbus,* New York, 1924.
Olsen, J. E., and Bourne, E. G., *The Northmen, Columbus and Cabot,* New York, 1906.
Prestage, E., *The Portuguese Pioneers,* London, 1933.
Reparaz (Hijo), Gonzalo de, *La época de los grandes descubrimientos Españoles y Portugueses,* Barcelona, 1931. (A scholarly and valuable summary.)
Sanceau, Elaine, *Henry the Navigator,* New York, 1947.
Thacher, John Boyd, *Christopher Columbus,* 3 vols., New York, 1903–1904.

CHAPTER III: COLONIZATION: THE CARIBBEAN AND NORTH AMERICA

Exploration: North America

Archaeological Survey in the Lower Mississippi Alluvial Valley, 1940–1947, by Philip Phillips, James A. Ford, and James B. Griffin, Cambridge, Mass.,

1951. (Valuable De Soto interpretations; see Swanton, *Final Report,* below.)

Bishop, Morris, *The Odyssey of Cabeza de Vaca,* New York, 1933. (Reliable.)

Bolton, Herbert E., *Coronado on the Turquoise Trail: Knight of Pueblos and Plains,* Albuquerque, 1949. (The authoritative work on Coronado.)

Brebner, John Bartlett, *The Explorers of North America, 1492–1806,* New York, 1933. (Excellent, scholarly work.)

Day, A. Grove, *Coronado's Quest: The Discovery of the Southwest States,* Berkeley, 1940.

Hallenbeck, Cleve, *Alvar Núñez Cabeza de Vaca, The Journey and Route of the First Europeans to Cross the Continent of North America, 1534–1536,* Glendale, California, 1940. (The authoritative work on Cabeza de Vaca.)

Hobbs, William Herbert, "The Track of the Columbus Caravels in 1492," *The Hispanic American Historical Review,* Vol. XXX, February, 1950. (A new and significant interpretation of Columbus' 1492 exploration.)

Penrose, Boies, *Travel and Discovery in the Renaissance, 1420–1620,* Cambridge, Mass., 1952. (Good for travelers in the Western Hemisphere; scholarly, and an excellent bibliography.)

Swanton, John R., Chairman, *Final Report of the United States De Soto Expedition Commission.* House Document No. 71, 76th Congress, 1st Session (10328), Washington, 1939.

Colonization: North America and the Caribbean

Aiton, Arthur Scott, *Antonio de Mendoza: First Viceroy of New Spain,* Durham, 1927.

Bancroft, Hubert H., *History of Central America,* 3 vols., San Francisco, 1886–1887.

——, *History of Mexico,* 6 vols., San Francisco, 1883–1888.

Blom, Frans, *The Indian Background of the Conquest of Yucatan,* Boston, 1936.

Bolton, Herbert E., *The Spanish Borderlands, A Chronicle of Old Florida and the Southwest,* New Haven, 1921. (A leading work.)

Bourne, E. Gaylord, *Spain in America, 1460–1580,* New York, 1906. (Invaluable.)

Braden, Charles S., *Religious Aspects of the Conquest of Mexico,* Durham, 1930.

Chamberlain, Robert S., *The Conquest and Colonization of Honduras [1502–1550],* Washington, 1953.

Chudoba, Bohdan, *Spain and the Empire,* Chicago, 1952. (Outstanding.)

Connor, Jeannette, *Pedro Menéndez de Aviles, Adelantado, Governor and Captain-General of Florida,* Deland, Fla., 1923.

Díaz del Castillo, Bernal, *The Discovery and Conquest of Mexico, 1517–1521,* ed. by Genaro García, tr. by A. P. Maudslay, Mexico, 1942. (American edition, New York, 1956, with an Introduction by Irving A. Leonard.)

Geiger, Maynard, *The Franciscan Conquest of Florida (1573–1618),* Washington, 1937.

Gibson, Charles, *Tlaxcala in the Sixteenth Century,* New Haven, 1952.

Hammond, George Peter, ed., *Narratives of the Coronado Expedition, 1540–1542,* 2 vols., Albuquerque, 1940.

———, and Agapito Rey, *Oñate, Colonizer of New Mexico, 1595–1628,* Part ·I and Part II, Albuquerque, 1953.

Hanke, Lewis, *Bartolomé de las Casas,* Philadelphia, 1952. (The authority on Las Casas.)

———, *The First Social Experiments in America,* Cambridge, 1935.

Kelly, J. E., *Pedro de Alvarado, Conquistador,* Princeton, 1932.

Kerrigan, Anthony, *Barcia's Chronological History of the Continent of Florida,* Gainesville, 1951.

Lewis, Clifford M., and Loomie, Albert J., *The Spanish Jesuit Mission in Virginia, 1570–1572,* Chapel Hill, 1953.

Lowery, Woodbury, *Spanish Settlements within the Present Limits of the United States, 1513–1561,* 2 vols., New York, 1901–1905.

Madariaga, Salvador de, *Hernán Cortés, Conqueror of Mexico,* New York, 1941.

Maynard, Theodore, *De Soto and the Conquistadores,* New York, 1930.

Means, Philip A., *The Spanish Main, Focus of Envy, 1492–1700,* New York, 1935.

Mecham, J. Lloyd, *Francisco de Ibarra and Nueva Vizcaya,* Durham, 1927.

Morris, J. Bayard, tr., *Hernando Cortés, Five Letters, 1519–1526,* New York, 1929.

Moses, Bernard, *The Establishment of Spanish Rule in America,* New York, 1898.

Oré, Luis Gerónimo, *The Martyrs of Florida (1513–1616),* tr. and ed. by Maynard Geiger, New York, 1936.

Powell, Philip W., *Soldiers, Indians and Silver,* Berkeley, 1952. (The advance into northern Mexico.)

Prescott, W. H., *The Conquest of Mexico,* 3 vols., New York, 1843. (The classic account; many later editions.)

Priestley, Herbert Ingram, *Tristán de Luna, Conquistador of the Old South,* Glendale, Calif., 1936.

Richman, Irving B., *The Spanish Conquerors,* New Haven, 1921.

Robertson, Henry Morton, *Stout Cortés, a Biography of the Spanish Conqueror,* New York, 1931.

Scholes, France V., and Adams, Eleanor B., *Don Diego Quijada, Alcalde Mayor de Yucatan, 1561–1565,* 2 vols., Mexico, 1938. (Basic on the founding of Yucatan.)

Shiels, W. Eugene, *Gonzalo de Tapia (1561–1594),* New York, 1934. (Jesuit beginnings on the west coast of Mexico; a significant work.)

Varner, John Grier, and Johnson, J., tr. and eds., *The Florida of the Inca* by Garcilaso de la Vega, Austin, 1951.

Wright, Irene A., *The Early History of Cuba, 1496–1586,* New York, 1916. (Authoritative.)

CHAPTER IV: CONQUEST AND COLONIZATION OF SOUTH AMERICA

Exploration

Anderson, Charles L. G., *Life and Letters of Vasco Núñez de Balboa,* New York, 1941.

Arciniegas, Germán, *Amerigo and the New World,* New York, 1955. (Vespucci.)

Bandelier, Adolph F., *The Gilded Man,* New York, 1893.

Greenlee, William Brooks, tr. and ed., *The Voyage of Pedro Alvarez Cabral to Brazil and India, from Contemporary Documents and Narratives,* London, 1938.

Levillier, Roberto, *America la bien Llamada,* 2 vols., Buenos Aires, 1948. (Vespucci in a new light, by a well-known authority.)

Medina, José T., *The Discovery of the River of the Amazons,* New York, 1934.

Parr, Charles McKew, *So Noble a Captain: The Life and Times of Ferdinand Magellan,* New York, 1953. (An excellent study, but many questions unanswered.)

Penrose, Boies, *Travel and Discovery in the Renaissance, 1420–1620,* Cambridge, Mass., 1952. (Includes Western Hemisphere travelers.)

Romoli, Kathleen, *Balboa of Darién: Discoverer of the Pacific,* New York, 1953. (Vigorous writing; at times unhistorical.)

Zahm, J. A. (H. J. Mozans), *The Quest of El Dorado,* New York, 1917.

Colonization

Arciniegas, Germán, *Germans in the Conquest of America, A Sixteenth Century Venture,* New York, 1943. (Venezuela and New Granada.)

——, *The Knight of El Dorado,* tr. by Mildred Adams, New York, 1942. (The life of Quesada.)

Boxer, C. R., *Salvador de Sá and the Struggle for Brazil and Angola,* London, 1952. (Scholarly.)

Graham, R. B. Cunninghame, *The Conquest of New Granada, Being the Life of Gonzálo Jiménez de Quesada,* London, 1922.

——, *The Horses of the Conquest,* ed. by R. M. Dernhardt, Norman, 1949.

——, *Pedro de Valdivia, Conqueror of Chile,* New York, 1927.

Kirkpatrick, F. A., *The Spanish Conquistadores,* London, 1934.

Marchant, Alexander, *From Barter to Slavery, the Economic Relations of Portuguese and Indians in the Settlement of Brazil, 1500–1580,* Baltimore, 1942. (A basic work.)

Markham, C. R., *A History of Peru,* Chicago, 1892.

Menas, Philip A., *Fall of the Inca Empire and Spanish Rule in Peru, 1530–1780,* New Haven, 1928.

Ober, F. A., *Pizarro and the Conquest of Peru,* New York, 1906.

Prescott, W. H., *The Conquest of Peru,* New York, 1908.

Shay, F., *The Incredible Pizarro,* New York, 1932.

Verrill, A. Hyatt, *Great Conquerors of South and Central America*, New York, 1943.

Zarate, Agustín de, *A History of the Discovery and Conquest of Peru*, London, 1933.

Zimmerman, Arthur Franklin, *Francisco de Toledo, the Fifth Viceroy of Peru, 1569–1581*, Caldwell, Idaho, 1939.

CHAPTERS V–VI: ORGANIZATION: POLITICAL, ECONOMIC, AND SOCIAL; COLONIAL CULTURE

Political and Economic

Aiton, Arthur S., *Antonio de Mendoza, First Viceroy of New Spain*, Durham, 1927.

Barber, Ruth Kerns, *Indian Labor in the Spanish Colonies*, Albuquerque, 1932.

Bolton, Herbert E., *Texas in the Middle Eighteenth Century, Studies in Spanish History and Colonial Administration*, Berkeley, 1915.

Borah, Woodrow W., *New Spain's Century of Depression*, Berkeley, 1951.

Chevalier, François, *La formation des grands domaines au Mexique. Terre et Société au xvie–xviie siécles*, Paris, 1952. (Origin of hacienda.)

Cunningham, C. H., *The Audiencia in the Spanish Colonies*, Berkeley, 1919.

Fisher, Lillian E., *The Intendant System in Spanish America*, Berkeley, 1929.

———, *Viceregal Administration in the Spanish-American Colonies*, Berkeley, 1926.

Hamilton, Earl J., *American Treasure and the Price Revolution in Spain, 1501–1650*, Cambridge, Mass., 1934.

Haring, Clarence H., *Trade and Navigation Between Spain and the Indies in the Time of the Hapsburgs*, Cambridge, Mass., 1918.

Hill, Lawrence F., *José de Escandón and the Founding of Nuevo Santander, A Study in Spanish Colonization*, Columbus, Ohio, 1926.

Howe, Walter, *The Mining Guild of New Spain and Its Tribunal General, 1770–1821*, Cambridge, Mass., 1949. (Scholarly.)

Humboldt, Alexander von, *Personal Narrative of Travels to the Equinoctial Regions of America during the years 1799–1804*, 3 vols., London, 1881.

———, *Political Essay on the Kingdom of New Spain*, tr. and ed. by John Black, 4 vols., London, 1811.

Hussey, Roland Denis, *The Caracas Company, 1728–1784*, Cambridge, Mass., 1934.

Juan, Jorge, and Ulloa, Antonio de, *A Voyage to South America*, 2nd ed., 2 vols., Dublin, 1765. (Many later editions.)

———, *Noticias Secretas de America*, 2 vols. in one, Londres, 1826. (An abridged translation of Part Two of the *Noticias Secretas* was published in Boston, 1851; on authorship of the original, see A. P. Whitaker, "Antonio de Ulloa," *The Hispanic American Historical Review*, Vol. XV, May, 1935, pp. 155–194.)

Mecham, J. Lloyd, *Francisco de Ibarra and Nueva Vizcaya*, Durham, 1927.

Moore, J. P., *The Cabildo in Peru under the Hapsburgs*, Durham, 1954.

Moses, Bernard, *The Establishment of Spanish Rule in America*, New York, 1898.

——, *The Spanish Dependencies in South America*, 2 vols., New York, 1914.

Parry, J. H., *The Audiencia of New Galicia in the Sixteenth Century: A Study in Spanish Colonial Government*, Cambridge, Mass., 1948.

——, *The Spanish Theory of Empire*, New York, 1940.

Priestley, Herbert I., *José de Gálvez, Visitor-General of New Spain, 1765–1771*, Berkeley, 1916.

Roscher, William, *The Spanish Colonial System*, tr. by E. G. Bourne, New York, 1904.

Schurz, William L., *The Manila Galleon*, New York, 1939.

Service, Elman R., *Spanish-Guaraní Relations in Early Colonial Paraguay*, Ann Arbor, 1954.

Simpson, Leslie B., *The Encomienda in New Spain; Forced Labor in the Spanish Colonies, 1492–1550*, rev. ed., Berkeley, 1950. (A basic work.)

——, *Exploitation of Land in Central Mexico in the Sixteenth Century*, Berkeley, 1952.

Smith, Don E., *The Viceroy of New Spain*, Berkeley, 1913.

West, Robert C., *Colonial Placer Mining in Colombia*, Baton Rouge, 1952.

——, *The Mining Community in Northern New Spain: The Parral Mining District*, Berkeley and Los Angeles, 1949. (Excellent.)

Whitaker, Arthur P., *The Huancavelica Mercury Mines*, Cambridge, Mass., 1941.

Social and Cultural

Adams, Eleanor B., and Scholes, France V., "Books in New Mexico, 1598–1680," *New Mexico Historical Review*, XVII, 1942.

Braden, Charles S., *The Religious Aspects of the Conquest of Mexico*, Durham, 1930.

Coester, A., *Literary History of Spanish America*, New York, 1946.

Ercilla y Zúñiga, Alonso de, *La Araucana, the Epic of Chile*, ed. by Walter Owen, Part I, Buenos Aires, 1945.

Espinosa, G., tr., *History of New Mexico, by Gaspar Pérez de Villagrá Alcalá, 1610*, Albuquerque, 1933.

Gage, Thomas, *A New Survey of the West Indies, 1648*, ed. by A. P. Newton, New York, 1929.

Griffin, Charles C., ed., *Concerning Latin American Culture*, New York, 1941. (Essays.)

Hammond, George P., and Rey, Agapito, eds., *New Mexico in 1602*, Albuquerque, 1938.

Hanke, Lewis, *Bartolomé de las Casas, Bookman, Scholar and Propagandist*, Philadelphia, 1952.

——, *The First Social Experiments in America*, Cambridge, Mass., 1935.

——, *The Spanish Struggle for Justice in the Conquest of America*, Philadelphia, 1949.

Jacobsen, Jerome V., *Educational Foundations of the Jesuits in Sixteenth-Century New Spain*, Berkeley, 1938.

Kubler, George, *Mexican Architecture in the Sixteenth Century*, 2 vols., New Haven, 1948.

Lanning, John Tate, *Academic Culture in the Spanish Colonies*, New York and London, 1940.

———, *The University in the Kingdom of Guatemala*, Princeton, 1955.

Lea, H. C., *The Inquisition in the Spanish Dependencies*, New York, 1922.

Leonard, Irving A., *Books of the Brave*, Cambridge, Mass., 1949.

———, *Don Carlos Sigüenza y Góngora, A Mexican Savant of the Seventeenth Century*, Berkeley, 1929.

———, *Romances of Chivalry in the Spanish Indies*, Berkeley, 1933.

Mecham, J. Lloyd, *Church and State in Latin America*, Chapel Hill, 1934.

Moses, Bernard, *Spanish Colonial Literature*, New York, 1922.

Motten, C. G., *Mexican Silver and the Enlightenment*, Philadelphia, 1950.

O'Neill, George, *Golden Years on the Paraguay. A History of the Jesuit Missions from 1600 to 1767*, London, 1934.

Prado y Ugarteche, Janvier, *Estado Social del Peru durante la Dominación Española*, Lima, 1941.

Priestley, Herbert I., *The Coming of the White Man*, New York, 1929. (Early chapters on Spanish colonies; excellent.)

Rippy, J. Fred, and Nelson, Jean Thomas, *Crusaders of the Jungle*, Chapel Hill, 1936. (Mission life; somewhat critical.)

Royer, Franchón, *The Tenth Muse*, Paterson, New Jersey, 1952. (Biography of Sor Juana Iñes de la Cruz.)

Ruiz, Hipolito, *Travels of Ruiz, Pavón and Dombey in Peru and Chile (1778–1788)*, tr. by B. E. Dahlgren, Chicago, 1940.

Scholes, France V., *Church and State in New Mexico, 1610–1650*, Albuquerque, 1937.

Spell, J. R., *Rousseau in the Spanish World Before 1833*, Austin, 1938.

Torres-Rioseco, Arturo, *The Epic of Latin American Literature*, New York, 1942.

Weismann, Elizabeth Wilder, *Mexico in Sculpture, 1521–1821*, Cambridge, Mass., 1950. (Authoritative.)

Whitaker, Arthur P., ed., *Latin America and the Enlightenment*, New York, 1942. (Essays.)

CHAPTER VII: EXPANSION AND RIVALRY IN THE CARIBBEAN AND NORTH AMERICA

The Caribbean

Bell, Douglas H., *Elizabethan Seamen*, Philadelphia, 1926.

Bourne, Ruth, *Queen Anne's Navy in the West Indies*, New Haven, 1939.

Burns, Sir Alan, *History of the British West Indies*, London, 1954. (Detailed; scholarly.)

Crouse, Nellis M., *French Pioneers in the West Indies, 1665–1713*, New York, 1943.

Exquemeling, Alexandre Olivier, *The Buccaneers of America*, ed. by W. S. Stallybrass, London, 1924.

Gomara, Francisco López de, *The Conquest of the Weast India (1578)*, tr. by Thomas Nicholas, New York, 1940.

Gosse, Philip, *Hawkins, Scourge of Spain*, New York, 1930.

Haring, Clarence H., *The Buccaneers of the West Indies in the Seventeenth Century*, New York, 1910.

Harlow, V. T., *Colonising Expeditions to the West Indies and Guiana, 1623–1667*, London, 1925.

Hart, Francis R., *The Disaster at Darién*, Boston, 1929.

——, *The Siege of Havana*, Boston, 1931.

Mims, Stewart L., *Colbert's West India Policy*, New Haven, 1912.

Newton, Arthur P., *The Colonising Activities of the English Puritans*, New Haven, 1914. (Puritans in the Caribbean.)

——, *The European Nations in the West Indies, 1493–1688*, London, 1933.

Pares, Richard, *War and Trade in the West Indies, 1739–1763*, Oxford, 1936.

Pitman, F. W., *The Development of the British West Indies, 1700–1763*, New Haven, 1917.

Roberts, W. A., *Sir Henry Morgan, Buccaneer and Governor*, Kingston, Jamaica, 1952.

Wafer, Lionel, *A New Voyage and Description of the Isthmus of America*, ed. by George P. Winship, Cleveland, 1903.

Williamson, J. A., *English Colonies in Guiana and on the Amazon, 1604–1688*, Oxford, 1923.

Wood, William, *The Elizabethan Sea-Dogs*, New Haven, 1918.

North America

Baegert, John Jakob, *Observations in Lower California*, tr. by M. M. Brandenburg and C. L. Baumann, Berkeley, 1952.

Bailey, Jessie B., *Diego de Vargas and the Reconquest of New Mexico, 1692–1704*, Albuquerque, 1940.

Bolton, Herbert E., *Arredondo's Historical Proof of Spain's Title to Georgia*, Berkeley, 1925.

——, *Rim of Christendom: A Biography of Francisco Kino, Pacific Coast Pioneer*, New York, 1936.

——, *Texas in the Middle Eighteenth Century*, Berkeley, 1915.

——, and Ross, Mary, *The Debatable Land*, Berkeley, 1925. (The Georgia-Florida frontier in the eighteenth century.)

Boyd, Mark F., and others, *Here Once They Stood: The Tragic End of the Apalachee Missions*, Gainesville, 1951. (Excellent cooperative work.)

Castañeda, Carlos E., *Our Catholic Heritage in Texas, 1519–1782*, 4 vols., Austin, 1936–1939.

Chatelain, Verne E., *The Defenses of Spanish Florida, 1565–1782,* Washington, 1940. (A detailed, documented study.)

Crane, V. W., *The Southern Frontier, 1670–1732,* Durham, 1928.

Dunn, William Edward, *Spanish and French Rivalry in the Gulf Region of the United States, 1678–1702,* Austin, 1917. (Authoritative.)

Dunne, Peter M., *Black Robes in Lower California,* Berkeley and Los Angeles, 1952. (Includes discussion of Jesuit expulsion.)

———, *Early Jesuit Missions in Tarahumara,* Berkeley and Los Angeles, 1948.

———, *Pioneer Black Robes on the West Coast,* Berkeley, 1940.

———, *Pioneer Jesuits in Northern Mexico,* Berkeley, 1944.

Espinosa, J. Manuel, *Crusaders on the Rio Grande,* Chicago, 1942. (Vargas reconquest.)

Folmer, Henry, *Franco-Spanish Rivalry in North America, 1524–1763,* Glendale, 1953.

Ford, Lawrence Carroll, *The Triangular Struggle for Spanish Pensacola, 1698–1739,* Washington, 1939.

Griffith, William J., *The Hasinai Indians of East Texas as Seen by Europeans, 1687–1772,* New Orleans, 1954.

Hackett, Charles W., *Revolt of the Pueblo Indians of New Mexico and Otermíns Attempted Reconquest,* 2 vols., Albuquerque, 1942. (Standard authority.)

Hughes, Anne E., *The Beginnings of Spanish Settlement in the El Paso District,* El Paso, 1935.

Lanning, John Tate, *The Diplomatic History of Georgia: A Study of the Epoch of Jenkins' Ear,* Chapel Hill, 1936.

———, *The Spanish Missions of Georgia,* Chapel Hill, 1935.

Leonard, Irving A., *Spanish Approach to Pensacola, 1689–1693,* Albuquerque, 1939.

McCarthy, Edward J., *Spanish Beginnings in the Philippines, 1564–1572,* Washington, 1943.

Mood, Fulmer, *The English Geographers and the Anglo-American Frontier in the Seventeenth Century,* Berkeley, 1944.

Morfi, Juan Agustín, *History of Texas, 1673–1779,* tr. and ed. by Carlos E. Castañeda, 2 vols., Albuquerque, 1935.

New Spain and the Anglo-American West: Historical Contributions Presented to Herbert E. Bolton, Lancaster, Pa., 1933.

Pénicaut, André, *Fleur de Lys and Calumet,* tr. and ed. by R. G. McWilliams, Baton Rogue, 1953. (Spanish-French rivalry, 1598–1721.)

Pfefferkorn, Ignaz, *Sonora, A Description of the Province,* tr. by Theodore E. Treutlein, Albuquerque, 1949.

Priestley, Herbert I., *Tristán de Luna, Conquistador of the Old South,* Glendale, Calif., 1936.

Thomas, Alfred B., *After Coronado, Spanish Exploration Northeast of New Mexico, 1696–1727,* Norman, 1935.

———, *The Plains Indians and New Mexico, 1751–1778,* Albuquerque, 1940.

Vargas, Diego de, *First Expedition of Vargas into New Mexico, 1692,* tr. and ed. by J. Manuel Espinosa, Albuquerque, 1940.

CHAPTERS VIII–IX: SOUTH AMERICA; REORGANIZATION AND DECLINE OF EMPIRE

South America

Dampier, William, *A New Voyage Around the World, 1700–1703,* London, 1927.

Hernández, Alfonso Luis, *Virreinato del Perú,* Madrid, 1930.

Jorge, Juan, and Ulloa, Antonio de, *A Voyage to South America,* 2nd ed., 2 vols., Dublin, 1765.

Koebel, W. H., *British Exploits in South America,* New York, 1917.

Kubler, George, *The Indian Caste of Peru, 1795–1940: A Population Study Based on Tax Records and Census Reports,* Washington, 1952.

La Condamine, C. M., *Relation abregée d'un voyage fait dans l'interior de l'Amerique méridionale . . .* Paris, 1788.

Levene, Ricardo, *Investigaciones acerca de la historia económica del Virreinato de la Plata,* Buenos Aires, 1952. (A revised edition of this basic work.)

Means, Philip A., *The Fall of the Inca Empire and Spanish Rule in Peru; 1530–1780,* New Haven, 1928.

Mörner, Magnus, *The Political and Economic Activities of the Jesuits in the La Plata Region; the Hapsburg Era.,* tr. by Albert Read, Stockholm, 1953.

Moses, Bernard, *South America on the Eve of Emancipation,* New York, 1908.

———, *Spain's Declining Power in South America, 1730–1806,* Berkeley, 1919.

———, *Spanish Dependencies in South America,* 2 vols., New York, 1914.

Stackpole, Edouard A., *The Sea Hunters,* Philadelphia, 1953. (Scholarly; 1635–1835.)

Tibesar, Antonine, O. F. M., *Franciscan Beginnings in Colonial Peru,* Washington, 1953.

Von Hagen, Victor W., *South America Called Them,* New York, 1945. (Great scientists, including La Condamine and von Humboldt.)

Reorganization and Decline of Empire

Abernethy, Thomas P., *The Burr Conspiracy,* New York, 1954.

Anderson, Conwell A., *Spanish Caribbean and Gulf Defense, 1763–1783,* University of Alabama, 1954. (Unpublished doctoral dissertation.)

Beaglehole, J. C., *Exploration of the Pacific,* London, 1934.

Bemis, Samuel F., *The Diplomacy of the American Revolution,* Vol. I, *The Foundations of American Diplomacy, 1775–1823,* New York, 1935.

———, *The Hussey-Cumberland Mission and American Independence,* Princeton, 1931.

Bolton, Herbert Eugene, *Anza's California Expeditions,* 5 vols., Berkeley, 1930.

———, *Athânese de Mézières and the Louisiana-Texas Frontier, 1768–1780,* 2 vols., Cleveland, 1914.

———, *Font's Complete Diary, A Chronicle of the Founding of California,* Berkeley, 1931.

———, *Fray Juan Crespi, Missionary Explorer, 1769–1774*, Berkeley, 1927.

———, *Outpost of Empire*, New York, 1931. (Colonization of California.)

———, *Pageant in the Wilderness, The Story of Escalante . . . 1776*, Salt Lake City, 1951. (Spanish exploration, New Mexico, Arizona, and Utah.)

———, *Palou's New California*, 4 vols., Berkeley, 1926.

Brooks, Philip C., *Diplomacy and the Borderlands: The Adams-Onís Treaty of 1819*, Berkeley, 1929. (Authoritative.)

Burns, Sir Alan, *History of the British West Indies*, London, 1954.

Carrington, H., *Life of Captain Cook*, London, 1939.

Caughey, John W., *Bernardo de Gálvez in Louisiana, 1776–1783*, Berkeley, 1934.

———, *History of the Pacific Coast*, Los Angeles, 1933.

———, *McGillivary of the Creeks*, Norman, 1938.

Chapman, Charles E., *A History of California: The Spanish Period*, New York, 1922.

———, *The Founding of Spanish California*, New York, 1916.

Cox, Isaac Joslin, *The West Florida Controversy, 1798–1813: A Study in American Diplomacy*, Baltimore, 1918.

Darling, Arthur Burr, *Our Rising Empire, 1763–1803*, New Haven, 1940.

Gálvez, Bernardo de, *Instructions for Governing the Interior Provinces of New Spain, 1786*, ed. by Donald E. Worcester, Berkeley, 1951.

Greater America: Essays in Honor of Herbert Eugene Bolton, Berkeley, 1945.

Hackett, Charles W., *Pichardo's Treatise on the Limits of Louisiana and Texas*, 4 vols., Austin, 1931–1946. (Monumental.)

Hart, Francis Russell, *The Siege of Havana, 1762*, Boston, 1931.

Houck, Louis, *The Spanish Regime in Missouri*, 2 vols., Chicago, 1909.

Jacobs, James R., *Tarnished Warrior: Major-General James Wilkinson*, New York, 1938.

James, James Alton, *The Life of George Rogers Clark*, Chicago, 1928.

Johnson, Cecil, *British West Florida, 1763–1783*, New Haven, 1943.

Kinnaird, Lawrence, ed., *Spain in the Mississippi Valley, 1765–1794*, Annual Report of the American Historical Association for the Year 1945, Vols. II, III, IV, Washington, 1949.

Lockey, J. B., *East Florida, 1783–1785*, Berkeley and Los Angeles, 1949.

Nasatir, Abraham P., *Before Lewis and Clark, 1785–1804*, 2 vols., St. Louis, 1952. (A basic work.)

Priestley, *José de Gálvez, Visitor-General of New Spain, 1765–1771*, Berkeley, 1916.

Richman, *California under Spain and Mexico, 1535–1847*, Boston, 1911.

Robertson, James A., *Louisiana under the Rule of Spain, France and the United States*, 2 vols., 1911.

Stephens, Henry M., and Bolton, Herbert E., *The Pacific Ocean in History*, New York, 1917. (Essays.)

Thomas, Alfred B., *Forgotten Frontiers, A Study of the Spanish-Indian Policy of Juan Bautista de Anza, Governor of New Mexico, 1777–1787*, Norman, 1932.

————, *Teodoro de Croix and the Northern Frontier of New Spain, 1776–1783,* Norman, 1941.

Whitaker, Arthur P., *The Mississippi Question, 1795–1803: A Study in Trade, Politics, and Diplomacy,* New York, 1934.

————, *The Spanish-American Frontier, 1783–1795,* Boston, 1927.

CHAPTERS X–XI: COLONIAL BRAZIL

Calógeras, João Pandiá, *A History of Brazil,* tr. and ed. by P. A. Martin, Chapel Hill, 1939.

Costa, L. E., da, *Rio in the Time of the Viceroys,* tr. by Dorothea Momsen, Rio de Janeiro, 1936.

Freyre, Gilberto, *Brazil, An Interpretation,* New York, 1945.

————, *The Masters and the Slaves: A Study in the Development of Brazilian Civilization,* tr. by Samuel Putnam, New York, 1946. (A Brazilian masterpiece.)

Kiemen, Mathias C., O.F.M., *The Indian Policy of Portugal in the Amazon Region, 1614–1693,* Washington, 1954.

Livermore, H. V., *A History of Portugal,* Cambridge, England, 1947.

————, *Portugal and Brazil, an Introduction,* Oxford, 1954.

Magalhães, Pedro de, *The Histories of Brazil,* ed. by J. B. Stetson, Jr., 2 vols., New York, 1922.

Manchester, Alan K., *British Pre-eminence in Brazil: Its Rise and Decline,* Chapel Hill, 1933.

Marchant, Alexander, "Aspects of the Enlightenment in Brazil," in A. P. Whitaker, ed., *Latin America and the Enlightenment,* New York, 1942.

————, *From Barter to Slavery, the Economic Relations of the Portuguese and Indians in the Settlement of Brazil, 1500–1580,* Baltimore, 1942.

————, ed., *International Colloquim on Luso Brazilian Studies,* Nashville, 1953.

————, and Smith, T. Lynn, eds., *Brazil: Portrait of Half a Continent,* New York, 1951. (Essays.)

Mawe, John, *Travels in the Interior of Brazil,* 2nd ed., London, 1821.

Nash, Roy, *The Conquest of Brazil,* New York, 1926.

Normano, J. F., *Brazil: A Study of Economic Types,* Chapel Hill, 1935.

Nowell, Charles E., *A History of Portugal,* New York, 1952.

Prestage, E., *The Portuguese Pioneers,* London, 1933.

Smith, T. Lynn, *Brazil, People and Institutions,* Baton Rouge, 2nd ed., 1954.

Southey, Robert, *History of Brazil,* 3 vols., London, 1810–1819.

Varnhagen, Francisco Adolphe de, *História geral do Brasil,* 3rd ed., 5 vols., São Paulo, 1927–1930.

Walsh, Rev. R., *Notices of Brazil in 1828 and 1829,* 2 vols., London, 1830. (Has data on colonial period.)

Watson, Robert G., *Spanish and Portuguese South America during the Colonial Period,* 2 vols., London, 1884.

Williamson, J. A., *English Colonies in Guiana and on the Amazon, 1604–1688*, Oxford, 1923.

Wiznitzer, Arnold, *The Records of the Earliest Jewish Community in the New World*, New York, 1953. (Brazil, seventeenth century.)

III. THE INDEPENDENCE OF LATIN AMERICA

CHAPTERS XII–XIV: WARS FOR INDEPENDENCE

General Works

Angell, H., *Simón Bolívar*, New York, 1930.

Armitage, J., *The History of Brazil from 1808–1831*, 2 vols., London, 1936.

Belaunde, Victor Andrés, *Bolívar and the Political Thought of the Spanish-American Revolution*, Baltimore, 1938.

Fisher, Lillian Estelle, *The Background of the Revolution for Mexican Independence*, Boston, 1934.

Frank, Waldo, *Birth of a World: Bolívar in Terms of His Peoples*, Boston, 1951.

Graham, R. B. Cunninghame, *José Antonio Páez*, London, 1929.

Hasbrouck, A., *Foreign Legionaries in the Liberation of Spanish America*, New York, 1928.

Humphreys, R. A., *Liberation in South America, 1806–1827; the Career of James Paroissien*, London, 1952.

Lansing, Marion, *Liberators and Heroes of South America*, Boston, 1940.

Masur, Gerhard, *Simón Bolívar*, Albuquerque, 1948. (A leading study.)

Metford, J. C., *San Martín*, New York, 1950.

Mitre, B., *Emancipation of South America*, tr. by W. Pilling, London, 1893. (A condensed translation of Mitre's *San Martín*.)

Moses, Bernard, *The Intellectual Background of the Revolution in South America, 1810–1824*, New York, 1926.

Parra-Pérez, Caracciolo, *Bolívar: A Contribution to the Study of His Political Ideas*, tr. by N. Andrew N. Cleven, Pittsburgh, 1930.

Paxson, Frederick L., *Independence of the South American Republics*, Philadelphia, 1903.

Robertson, William Spence, ed., *The Diary of Francisco de Miranda, Tour of the United States, 1783–1784*, New York, 1928.

———, *The Life of Miranda*, 2 vols., Chapel Hill, 1929.

———, *The Rise of the Spanish-American Republics as Told in the Lives of Their Liberators*, New York, 1918.

Schoellkoph, Anna, *Don José de San Martín*, New York, 1924.

Selected Writings of Bolívar, comp. by Vicente Lecuna and ed. by Harold A. Bierck, Jr., 2 vols., New York, 1951.

Sherwell, G. A., *Antonio José de Sucre*, Washington, 1924.

Thorning, Joseph F., *Miranda: World Citizen*, Gainesville, 1952.

Trend, J. B., *Bolívar and the Independence of Spanish America*, New York, 1948. (Balanced and popular.)

Turnbull, A. D., and Van der Veer, N. R., *Cochrane, the Unconquerable,* New York, 1929.

Ybarra, T. R., *Bolívar, the Passionate Warrior,* New York, 1929.

International Aspects of the Wars

Bemis, Samuel F., *Early Diplomatic Missions from Buenos Aires to the United States, 1811–1824,* Worcester, 1940.

———, *The Latin American Policy of the United States: An Historical Interpretation,* New York, 1943.

Bernstein, Harry, *Origins of Inter-American Interest, 1700–1812,* Philadelphia, 1945.

Brooks, Philip Coolidge, *Diplomacy and the Borderlands: The Adams-Onís Treaty of 1819,* Berkeley, 1929.

Fisher, Lillian Estelle, *The Background of the Revolution for Mexican Independence,* Boston, 1954.

Griffin, C. C., *The United States and the Disruption of the Spanish Empire, 1810–1822,* New York, 1937.

Kaufmann, William W., *British Policy and the Independence of Latin America, 1804–1828,* New Haven, 1951.

Keen, Benjamin, *David Curtis de Forest and the Revolution in Buenos Aires,* New Haven, 1947.

Lockey, Joseph Byrne, *Essays in Pan-Americanism,* Berkeley, 1939.

———, *Pan-Americanism: Its Beginnings,* New York, 1920.

Manning, William R., *Diplomatic Correspondence of the United States Concerning the Independence of the Latin American Nations,* 3 vols., New York, 1925.

Perkins, Dexter, *Hands Off: A History of the Monroe Doctrine,* Boston, 1941.

———, *The Monroe Doctrine, 1826–1867,* Baltimore, 1933. (Basic.)

Rippy, J. Fred, *Rivalry of the United States and Great Britain over Latin America (1808–1830),* Baltimore, 1929.

Robertson, William Spence, *France and Latin American Independence,* Baltimore, 1939.

Rydjord, John, *Foreign Interest in the Independence of New Spain,* Durham, 1935. (Scholarly; good bibliography.)

Tatum, Edward Howland, *The United States and Europe, 1815–1823, A Study in the Background of the Monroe Doctrine,* Berkeley, 1936.

Temperley, H. W. V., *The Foreign Policy of Canning, 1822–1827; England, the Neo-Holy Alliance, and the New World,* London, 1925.

Warren, Harris Gaylord, *The Sword Was Their Passport: A History of American Filibustering in the Mexican Revolution,* Baton Rouge, 1943.

Webster, Charles K., *Britain and the Independence of Latin America, 1812–1830,* London, 1944.

———, *The Foreign Policy of Castlereagh, 1815–1822, Britain and the European Alliance,* London, 1925.

Whitaker, Arthur P., *The United States and the Independence of Latin America, 1800–1830,* Baltimore, 1941.

IV. MODERN LATIN AMERICA
General Works

Bernstein, Harry, *Modern and Contemporary Latin America*, New York, 1952.

Davis, Harold E., *Latin American Leaders*, New York, 1949. (Judicious.)

———, *Makers of Democracy in Latin America*, New York, 1945.

Clagett, Helen L., *The Administration of Justice in Latin America*, New York, 1952. (An administrative study.)

Dunne, Peter M., *A Padre Views South America*, Milwaukee, 1945.

Editors of *La Prensa, Defense of Freedom*, New York, 1952.

Fitzgibbons, Russel H., *The Constitutions of the Americas*, Chicago, 1948.

Galindez, Jesús de, *Iberoamerica, su evolución politica, socio-economica, cultural é internacional*, New York, 1953. (Invaluable.)

Gordon, Wendell, *The Economy of Latin America*, New York, 1950.

Hanson, Simon G., *Economic Development in Latin America*, Washington, 1951. (Excellent.)

Harris, Seymour, *Economic Problems of Latin America*, New York, 1944.

Howard, George P., *Religious Liberty in Latin America*, New York, 1944.

Hughlett, Lloyd J., *Industrialization of Latin America*, New York, 1947.

Humphreys, R. A., *Evolution of Modern Latin America*, New York, 1947.

Leonard, Olen, and Loomis, Charles P., eds., *Readings in Latin American Social Organizations and Institutions*, Lansing, 1953.

Linton, Ralph, ed., *Most of the World: The Peoples of Africa, Latin America and the East Today*, New York, 1949. (Valuable for discussion of *mestizos* and Brazil.)

Martin, P. A., *Latin America and the War*, Baltimore, 1925.

Mecham, J. Lloyd, *Church and State in Latin America*, Chapel Hill, 1934. (Basic.)

Mulhall, Michael G., *The English in South America*, Buenos Aires, 1878. (Banks and other economic data.)

Poblete Troncoso, Moises, *El movimiento obrero latinoamericano*, Mexico, 1946. (The only adequate summary in any language.)

Rippy, J. Fred, *Latin America and the Industrial Age*, New York, 1944.

Rydell, Raymond A., *Cape Horn to the Pacific: the Rise and Decline of an Ocean Highway*, Berkeley, 1952.

Wilgus, A. Curtis, ed., *Hispanic American Essays: A Memorial to James Alexander Robinson*, Chapel Hill, 1942. (Essays: colonial Mexico and Central America.)

———, ed., *Modern Hispanic America*, Washington, 1933. (Essays.)

Wythe, George, *Industry in Latin America*, sec. ed., New York, 1949. (Authoritative.)

South America

Akers, Charles Edmond, *A History of South America*, new ed., New York, 1930.

Bain, H. F., and Read, T. T., *Ores and Industry in South America*, New York, 1934.

Beals, Carleton, *Fire on the Andes,* Philadelphia, 1934. (Indian movements.)

Carter, Albert E., *The Battle of South America,* New York, 1941. (Acute.)

Crow, Carl, *Meet the South Americans,* New York, 1941.

Cutright, Paul R., *The Great Naturalists Explore South America,* New York, 1940.

Dawson, T. C., *The South American Republics,* 2 vols., New York, 1903–1904.

Domville-Fife, C., *The States of South America,* London, 1920.

Forbes, Rosita, *Eight Republics in Search of a Future,* New York, 1933. (An acute British observer.)

Ford, Guy S., ed., *Dictatorship in the Modern World,* Minneapolis, 1939.

Frank, Waldo, *South American Journey,* New York, 1943.

Grubb, Kenneth G., *The Northern Republics of South America, Ecuador, Colombia and Venezuela,* London, 1931.

Herring, Hubert, *Good Neighbors,* New Haven, 1941. (Economic and social conditions.)

Ireland, Gordon, *Boundaries, Possessions and Conflicts in South America,* Cambridge, Mass., 1938.

Jenks, Leland H., *The Migration of British Capital to 1875,* New York, 1927.

Jones, Tom B., *South America Rediscovered,* Minneapolis, 1949.

Osborne, Fairfield, *Our Plundered Planet,* New York, 1950. (Erosion.)

Peck, A. S., *Industry in South America,* New York, 1927.

Phelps, Dudley M., *Migration of Industry to South America,* New York, 1936.

Plenn, Abel, *The Southern Americans,* New York, 1948.

Republics of South America, The, Royal Institute of International Affairs, London, 1937. (Has important discussion of land systems.)

Rippy, J. Fred, *South America and Hemisphere Defense,* Baton Rouge, 1941. (Excellent.)

Ryan, Edwin, *The Church in the South American Republics,* Milwaukee, 1932. (Catholic.)

Von Hagen, Victor W., *South America Called Them, Explorations of the Great Naturalists,* New York, 1945.

Whitaker, Arthur P., *The United States and the Northern Republics of South America,* Cambridge, Mass., 1945.

Wilgus, A. Curtis, ed., *Argentina, Brazil and Chile Since Independence,* Washington, 1935. (Essays by authorities.)

——, ed., *South American Dictators During the First Century of Independence,* Washington, 1937. (Essays by authorities.)

Cultural

Arciniegas, Germán, ed., *The Green Continent: A Comprehensive View of Latin America by Its Leading Writers,* tr. by Harriet de Onís, New York, 1944.

Crawford, William Rex, *A Century of Latin-American Thought,* Cambridge, Mass., 1944. (An invaluable summary.)

Henríquez Ureña, Pedro, *Literary Currents in Latin America,* Cambridge, Mass., 1945.

Hespelt, E., and others, *An Outline History of Spanish-American Literature,* New York, 1941.

Oglesby, C., *Modern Primitive Arts*, New York, 1939.

Menéndez y Pelayo, Marcelino, *Historia de la poesía Hispana-Americana*, ed. by Enrique Sánchez Reyes, 2 vols., Madrid, 1948. (The 1911 edition; little-changed, still basic work.)

Onís, José de, *The United States as Seen by Spanish-American Writers*, New York, 1952.

Reulet, Aníbal Sánchez, *Contemporary Latin-American Philosophy*, Albuquerque, 1954.

Slonimsky, Nicholas, *Music of Latin America*, New York, 1945.

Smith, Robert C., and Wilder, Elizabeth, *A Guide to the Art of Latin America*, Washington, 1948. (A *Guide* by two leading authorities.)

Spell, Jefferson Rae, *Contemporary Spanish-American Fiction*, Chapel Hill, 1944.

Torres-Ríoseco, Arturo, *The Epic of Latin American Literature*, rev. ed., New York, 1946.

Twelve Spanish-American Poets, An Anthology, tr. and ed. by H. R. Hayes, New Haven, 1944.

(For further references, see individual countries.)

THE ATLANTIC REPUBLICS: ARGENTINA, URUGUAY, PARAGUAY, AND BRAZIL

CHAPTER XV: ARGENTINA

Alberdi, Juan Bautista, *Bases y puntos de partida para la organización política de la República Argentina*, Buenos Aires, 1943.

Alexander, Robert J., *The Perón Era*, New York, 1951. (An able survey.)

Beaulac, Willard Leon, *Career Ambassador*, New York, 1951.

Bernstein, Harry, *Modern and Contemporary Latin America*, New York, 1952. (Chapters on Argentina.)

Blanksten, George L., *Perón's Argentina*, Chicago, 1953. (Good statement of Perón doctrine.)

Bruce, James, *Those Perplexing Argentines*, New York, 1953.

Bunkley, Allison, W., *The Life of Sarmiento*, Princeton, 1952.

——, *A Sarmiento Anthology*, Princeton, 1952.

Burgin, Miron, *The Economic Aspects of Argentine Federalism, 1820–1850*, Cambridge, Mass., 1946. (A basic study.)

Cady, John F., *Foreign Intervention in the Río de la Plata, 1838–1850: A Study of French, British, and American Policy in Relation to the Dictator Juan Manuel Rosas*, Philadelphia, 1929.

Cowles, Fleur, *Bloody Precedent*, New York, 1952. (The wife of Rosas and the wife of Perón.)

Denis, P., *The Argentine Republic*, London, 1922.

Editors of *La Prensa, Defense of Freedom*, New York, 1952.

Flores, María, *The Woman with the Whip*, New York, 1952. (Life of Eva Perón; reliable.)

Greenup, Ruth and L., *Revolution Before Breakfast: Argentina, 1941–1946*
    Chapel Hill, 1947. (A good account by two newspaper correspondents.)

Haring, Clarence H., *Argentina and the United States*, Boston, 1941.

Herring, Hubert, *Good Neighbors*, New York, 1941. (Chapters on Argentina.)

Herron, Francis, *Letters from Argentina*, New York, 1943. (Penetrating.)

Jefferson, Mark, *Peopling the Argentine Pampas*, New York, 1926. (Basic.)

Jeffrey, William H., *Mitre and Argentina*, New York, 1952.

Keen, Benjamin, *David Curtis De Forest and the Revolution in Buenos Aires*, New York, 1947.

Kirkpatrick, F. A., *A History of the Argentine Republic*, Cambridge, England, 1931.

Levene, Ricardo, *A History of Argentina*, tr. by W. S. Robertson, Chapel Hill, 1937. (A leading work.)

MacDonald, A. F., *Government of the Argentine Republic*, New York, 1942.

Nichols, Madeline, *Sarmiento: A Chronicle of Inter-American Friendship*, Washington, 1940.

Pendle, George, *Argentina*, London, 1956.

Perón, Eva, *My Mission in Life*, New York, 1953. (Pathetic.)

Phelps, V. L., *The International Economic Position of Argentina*, Philadelphia, 1938. (Basic for period.)

Rennie, Ysabel F., *The Argentine Republic*, New York, 1945. (A superior history.)

Rowe, Leo S., *The Federal System of the Argentine Republic*, Washington, 1921.

Smith, O. Edmund, Jr., *Yankee Diplomacy: United States Intervention in Argentina*, Dallas, 1953. (Critical.)

Taylor, Carl C., *Rural Life in Argentina*, Baton Rouge, 1948. (A basic work.)

Weddell, A. W., *Introduction to Argentina*, New York, 1939. (A diplomat's introduction.)

Weil, Felix J., *Argentine Riddle*, New York, 1944.

Whitaker, Arthur P., *The United States and Argentina*, Cambridge, Mass., 1954. (Scholarly; a careful analysis of conditions.)

Whitbeck, R. H., *Economic Geography of South America*, 3rd ed., New York, 1940.

White, John, W., *Argentina: The Life Story of a Nation*, New York, 1942. (Newspaper man's account; well done.)

Wilgus, A. Curtis, ed., *Argentina, Brazil and Chile Since Independence*, Washington, 1935. (An excellent presentation by Professor J. Fred Rippy.)

Willis, B., *A Yankee in Patagonia*, Stanford, 1947.

Cultural

Coester, A. L., *A Tentative Bibliography of Argentine Belles-lettres*, Cambridge, Mass., 1933.

Frank, Waldo, ed., *Tales from the Argentine*, tr. by Anita Brenner, New York, 1950.

Güiraldes, Ricardo, *Don Segunda Sombra: Shadows on the Pampas,* tr. by Harriet de Onís, New York, 1935.

Hudson, W. H., *Green Mansions,* New York, 1943. (A modern classic.)

——, *Tales of the Pampas,* New York, 1939.

Nichols, Madeline Wallis, *The Gaucho: Cattle Hunter, Cavalryman, Ideal of Romance,* Durham, 1942. (Scholarly; delightful.)

Sarmiento, Domingo F., *Facundo: Civilización y barbarie en la República Argentina,* Madrid, 1916. (First edition, Santiago, Chile, 1845.)

Tinker, Edward Larocque, *The Horsemen of the Americas,* New York, 1953. (The gaucho and others; excellent bibliography.)

CHAPTER XVI: URUGUAY

Browning, W. E., *The River Plate Republics,* London, 1928.

Clemenceau, Georges, *South America Today,* New York, 1911.

Fitzgibbon, Russell H., *Uruguay, Portrait of a Democracy,* New Brunswick, N. J., 1954. (Deservedly praised.)

Gordon, Ross, *Argentina and Uruguay,* New York, 1916. (Social and economic.)

Graham, R. B. Cunninghame, *Conquest of the River Plate,* New York, 1924.

Hanson, Simon G., *Utopia in Uruguay,* New York, 1938. (Scholarly; popular.)

Hudson, W. H., *The Purple Land,* New York, 1885.

Koebel, W. H., *Uruguay,* New York, 1911.

Pendle, George, *Uruguay, South America's First Welfare State,* London, 1952. (Detailed economics; seen through British eyes.)

Taylor, Philip B., *The Executive Power in Uruguay,* Berkeley, 1951.

CHAPTER XVII: PARAGUAY

Barrett, William E., *Women on Horseback,* New York, 1938.

Box, Pelham Horton, *The Origins of the Paraguayan War,* Urbana, 1927. (Scholarly.)

Browning, W. E., *The River Plate Republics,* London, 1928.

Dombrowski, Katharina von, *Land of Women,* Boston, 1935. (A novel; influence of women; historically accurate.)

Elliott, Arthur Elwood, *Paraguay, Its Cultural Heritage, Social Conditions and Educational Problems,* New York, 1931.

Fretz, J. W., *Pilgrims in Paraguay,* Scottsdale, 1953. (Mennonites.)

Graham, R. B. Cunninghame, *Portrait of a Dictator,* London, 1933. (Francisco López.)

Grubb, W. B., *An Unknown People and an Unknown Land,* New York, 1914. (Indians.)

Insfran, Pable Max, ed., *The Epic of the Chaco: Marshal Estigarribia's Memoirs of the Chaco War, 1932–1935,* Austin, 1950. (A basic work.)

Kerr, John G., *A Naturalist in the Gran Chaco,* London and New York, 1950.

Koebel, W. H., *Paraguay,* London, 1917.

Masterman, George F., *Seven Eventful Years in Paraguay*, London, 1869. (Francisco López period.)

Pendle, George, *Paraguay, A Riverside Nation*, London, 1954. (Good treatment of recent events.)

Robertson, J. P. and W. P., *Francia's Reign of Terror*, London, 1839.

———, *Letters on Paraguay*, 2 vols., London, 1838. (Basic for Francia.)

Warren, Harris G., *Paraguay: An Informal History*, Norman, 1949. (Scholarly; authoritative.)

White, Edward L., *El Supremo*, New York, 1916. (Dr. Francia in fiction.)

CHAPTER XVIII: BRAZIL

Armitage, J., *The History of Brazil from 1808–1831*, 2 vols., London, 1835–1836.

Barlow, Frank D., Jr., *Cotton in South America*, Memphis, 1952. (Accurate information.)

Bernstein, Harry, *Modern and Contemporary Latin America*, New York, 1952. (Chapters on Brazil.)

Braga, Ernesto, and Grubb, Kenneth C., *The Republic of Brazil: A Survey of the Religious Situation*, London, 1932. (Primarily Protestantism.)

Brazil, ed., by Lawrence F. Hill, Berkeley, 1947. (Essays.)

Brazil, 1939–40; An Economic and Geographical Survey, Ministry of Foreign Affairs, Rio de Janeiro, 1940.

Brazil, 1943, Resources and Possibilities, Ministry of Foreign Affairs, Rio de Janeiro, 1943.

Brazil: Four Papers Presented in the Institute for Brazilian Studies, by Charles Wagley and others, Nashville, 1951.

Brazil: Four Papers Presented in the Institute for Brazilian Studies, by James B. Watson and others, Nashville, 1953.

Calógeras, João Pandía, *A History of Brazil*, tr. and ed. by P. A. Martin, Chapel Hill, 1939. (A leading survey.)

Camacho, J. A., *Brazil: An Interim Assessment*, London, 1952. (Good for recent conditions.)

Coleman, William J., *The First Apostolic Delegation in Rio de Janeiro and Its Influence in Spanish America: A Study of Papal Policy, 1830–1840*, Washington, 1951. (Scholarly.)

Cooke, M. L., *Brazil on the March, A Study in International Cooperation*, New York, 1944. (Data on agriculture.)

Cooper, C. S., *The Brazilians and Their Country*, New York, 1917.

Correa da Costa, Sergio, *Every Inch a King*, New York, 1950. (Dom Pedro I.)

Denis, Pierre, *Brazil*, 6th ed., London, 1937.

Department of State, *Documents on German Foreign Policy, 1918–1945*, Series D (1937–1945), No. 4964, Vol. V. (Important data on Germans in Brazil.)

Eubank, Thomas, *Life in Brazil: A Journal of a Visit to the Land of the Cocoa and the Palms*, New York, 1856.

Gates, R. R., *A Botanist in the Amazon Valley*, London, 1927.

Guenther, R., *A Naturalist in Brazil*, New York, 1931.

Hambloch, Ernest, *His Majesty, the President*, London, 1935. (Satiric, but informing.)

Herndon, William Lewis, *Exploration of the Valley of the Amazon*, ed. by Hamilton Basso, New York, 1952.

Herring, Hubert, *Good Neighbors*, New Haven, 1941. (Chapters on Brazil.)

Hill, Lawrence F., *Diplomatic Relations between the United States and Brazil*, Durham, 1932.

Hunnicutt, Benjamin H., Brazil, *World Frontiers*, New York, 1949. (Forty years in Brazil.)

Institute of Inter-American Affairs, Foreign Operations Administration, *The Development of Brazil*, Washington, 1954. (Report of joint Brazil-U. S. commission.)

James, H. G., *Brazil After a Century of Independence*, New York, 1925. (Chiefly government before the Vargas period.)

——, *The Constitutional System of Brazil*, Washington, 1923. (Pre-Vargas.)

James, Preston, *Brazil*, New York, 1946. (Geography.)

Jobim, José, *Brazil in the Making*, New York, 1943. (Nationalist, but accurate.)

Kelsey, Vera, *Seven Keys to Brazil*. New York, 1943. (Descriptive.)

Kidder, Daniel, and Fletcher, J. C., *Brazil and the Brazilians*, Philadelphia, 1857.

Linton, Ralph, ed., *Most of the World: The Peoples of Africa, Latin America and the East Today*, New York, 1949. (Valuable for the Negro in Brazil.)

Livermore, H. V., *A History of Portugal*, Cambridge, England, 1947.

Lock, C. G. W., *Coffee, Its Culture and Commerce in all Countries*, London, 1888.

Lowenstein, Karl, *Brazil under Vargas*, New York, 1942. (Sympathetic treatment.)

Manchester, Alan K., *British Pre-eminence in Brazil: Its Rise and Decline*, Chapel Hill, 1933.

Maurette, F., *Some Social Aspects of the Present and Future Economic Development of Brazil*, Geneva, 1937. (Labor.)

Modern Brazil: Resources and Possibilities, Ministry of Foreign Affairs, Rio de Janeiro, 1949. (Concise, informative.)

Nabuco, Carolina, *The Life of Joaquim Nabuco*, tr. by Ronald Hilton, Stanford, 1951.

Nash, Roy, *The Conquest of Brazil*, New York, 1926. (A basic work.)

Normano, J. F., *Brazil: A Study of Economic Types*, Chapel Hill, 1935.

Nowell, Charles E., *A History of Portugal*, New York, 1952.

Oliviera Lima, M., de, *The Evolution of Brazil Compared with that of Spanish and Anglo-America*, Stanford, 1914. (Old, but thought-provoking.)

O'Neill, M. Ancilla, *Tristão de Athayde and the Catholic Social Movement in Brazil*, Washington, 1939.

Pearson, Henry C., *The Rubber Country of the Amazon*, New York, 1911.

Pierson, Donald, *Negroes in Brazil: A Study in Race Contact at Bahia*, Chicago, 1942. (Scholarly.)

Prewett, Virginia, *Beyond the Great Amazon,* New York, 1953. (Brazil's interior, by a competent observer.)

Ramos, Arthur, *The Negro in Brazil,* tr. by Richard Pattee, Washington, 1939. (By a leading authority on the Brazilian Negro.)

Reuss, Percy A., *The Amazon Trail,* New York, 1954.

Simonsen, Roberto C., *Brazil's Industrial Revolution,* São Paulo, 1939.

Smith, T. Lynn, *Brazil: People and Institutions,* 2nd ed., Baton Rouge, 1954. (Standard authority.)

———— and Marchant, Alexander, eds., *Brazil: Portrait of Half a Continent,* New York, 1951. (Essays by authorities, including one by Ramos on the Negro in Brazil.)

Spiegel, Henry Wilson, *The Brazilian Economy: Chronic Inflation and Sporadic Inflation,* Philadelphia, 1949.

Wagley, Charles, *Amazon Town: A Study of Man in the Tropics,* New York, 1953. (By a recognized authority.)

Wilgus, A. Curtis, ed., *Argentina, Brazil and Chile,* Washington, 1935. (Section on Brazil by P. A. Martin.)

Williams, Mary Wilhelmine, *Dom Pedro the Magnanimous, Second Emperor of Brazil,* Chapel Hill, 1937. (Exhaustive.)

Wythe, George, *Brazil, and Expanding Economy,* New York, 1949. (Authoritative.)

Zweig, Stephan, *Brazil,* New York, 1941. (Enthusiastic.)

Cultural

Azevedo, Fernando de, *Brazilian Culture: An Introduction to the Study of Culture in Brazil,* tr. by William Rex Crawford, New York, 1950. (Monumental.)

Cunha, Euclydes da, *Rebellion in the Backlands,* tr. by Samuel Putnam, Chicago, 1944.

Driver, David Miller, *The Indian in Brazilian Literature,* New York, 1942.

Ellison, Fred P., *Brazil's New Novel,* Berkeley, 1954.

Freyre, Gilberto, *Interpretation of Brazil,* New York, 1945.

————, *The Masters and the Slaves,* tr. by Samuel Putnam, New York, 1946. (Brazilian culture by its foremost authority.)

Goldberg, Isaac, *Brazilian Literature,* New York, 1922.

Luper, Albert T., *The Music of Brazil,* Washington, 1943.

Machado, José Bettencourt, *Machado of Brazil: Life and Time of Machado de Assis,* New York, 1953.

Machado de Assis, Joaquim Maria, *Don Casmurro,* tr. by Helen Caldewell, New York, 1953.

————, *Epitaph of a Small Winner,* tr. by W. L. Grossman, New York, 1952.

Portinari, Cândido, *Portinari, His Life and Art,* Chicago, 1940.

Putnam, Samuel, *Marvelous Journey: Four Centuries of Brazilian Literature,* New York, 1948. (Highly praised.)

Verissimo, Erico, *Brazilian Literature: An Outline,* New York, 1945. (An outline by a gifted story-teller.)

THE PACIFIC REPUBLICS: CHILE, BOLIVIA, PERU, AND ECUADOR

CHAPTER XIX: CHILE

Arana, Diego Barros, *Historia Jeneral de Chile,* 16 Tomos, Santiago, 1884–1902. (Standard.)

Bernstein, Harry, *Modern and Contemporary Latin America,* New York, 1952. (Chapters on Chile.)

Bowman, Isaiah, *Desert Trails of Atacama,* New York, 1924. (Geography.)

Bulnes, Gonzalo, *Chile and Peru: the Causes of the War of 1879,* Santiago, 1920. (A Chilean view.)

Butland, Gilbert J., *Chile: An Outline of Its Geography, Economics and Politics,* London, 1941. (Competent survey.)

Clissold, Stephen, *Chilean Scrapbook,* New York, 1952. (Descriptive; sensitive.)

Dennis, William J., *Documentary History of the Tacna-Arica Dispute,* Iowa City, 1927.

———, *Tacna and Arica,* New Haven, 1931.

Edwards, Agustín, *The Dawn,* London, 1931. (Interpretative.)

Elliott, G. F. S., *Chile, Its History and Development,* New York, 1927.

Elliott, L. E., *Chile Today and Tomorrow,* New York, 1922.

Ellsworth, Paul, *Chile, An Economy in Transition,* New York, 1945.

Evans, Henry Clay, Jr., *Chile and Its Relations with the United States,* Durham, 1927.

Fergusson, Erna, *Chile,* New York, 1943. (Descriptive.)

Fetter, F. W., *Monetary Inflation in Chile,* Princeton, 1931.

Finer, Herman, *The Chilean Development Corporation,* Montreal, 1947. (Use with care.)

Galdames, Luis, *A History of Chile,* tr. by I. J. Cox, Chapel Hill, 1941. (Best available in English.)

Hanson, Earl Parker, *Chile: Land of Progress,* New York, 1941.

Herring, Hubert, *Good Neighbors,* New Haven, 1941. (Chapters on Chile.)

Jefferson, Mark W., *Recent Colonization in Chile,* New York, 1921.

Lindsell, Harold, *The Chilean-American Controversy of 1891–1892,* New York, 1943.

McBride, George M., *Chile: Land Society,* New York, 1926. (Still basic.)

Maúrtua, V. M., *The Question of the Pacific,* New York, 1921. (A Peruvian view.)

Millington, Herbert, *American Diplomacy and the War of the Pacific,* New York, 1948.

Nelson, Edna Deu Pree, *O'Higgins and Don Bernardo,* New York, 1954. (Historical novel; substantial work.)

Roberts, Sarah Elizabeth, *José Toribio Medina, His Life and Works,* Washington, 1941. (Medina was one of the great authorities on New World bibliography.)

Shaw, Paul Vanorden, *The Early Constitutions of Chile, 1810–1833,* New York, 1931.

Sherman, William Roderick, *The Diplomatic and Commercial Relations of the United States and Chile, 1820–1914,* Boston, 1926.

Stevenson, John R., *The Chilean Popular Front,* Philadelphia, 1942.

Stewart, Watt, *Henry Meiggs, Yankee Pizarro,* Durham, 1946. (Chilean railroads.)

Stuart, Graham H., *The Tacna-Arica Dispute,* Boston, 1927.

Subercaseaux, Benjamin, *Chile: A Geographic Extravaganza,* New York, 1943.

Wilgus, A. Curtis, ed., *Argentina, Brazil, and Chile,* Washington, 1935. (The section on Chile was written by Professor I. J. Cox.)

——, *South American Dictators,* Washington, 1937.

Yrarrázaval Larraín, José Miguel, *El Presidente Balmaceda,* 2 vols., Santiago, 1940. (The best biography.)

Cultural

Blest Gana, Alberto, *Martín Rivas,* New York, 1918.

Edwards, Agustín, *My Native Land,* London, 1929.

Mistral, Gabriela, *Desolación,* Poemas, New York, 1922. (For a brief study and bibliography of Gabriela Mistral, see *Bulletin* of the Pan-American Union, Vol. 80 (January), 1945, pp. 29–33, by Fernando Alegría.)

Torres-Ríoseco, Arturo, *The Epic of Latin American Literature,* rev. ed., New York, 1946.

CHAPTER XX: BOLIVIA

Argüedes, Alcides, *Historia general de Bolivia, 1809–1921,* La Paz, 1922. (Standard.)

——, *Pueblo Enfermo,* 3rd ed., Santiago, 1937. (Analysis and interpretation; strongly critical.)

——, *Raza de Bronce,* Valencia, 1923. (A celebrated novel; pro-Indian.)

Cleven, N. Andrew N., *The Political Organization of Bolivia,* Washington, 1940.

Fortune Magazine, Article "Tin," Vol. 5, May, 1932.

Leonard, Olen E., *Bolivia: Land, People and Institutions,* New York, 1952. (An excellent treatment.)

McBride, George M., *The Agrarian Indian Communities of Highland Bolivia,* New York, 1921.

Marsh, Margaret, *The Bankers and Bolivia,* New York, 1928.

Osborne, Harold, *Bolivia, A Land Divided,* London, 1954. (Brief, scholarly.)

——, *Indians of the Andes: Aymaras and Quechuas,* Cambridge, Mass., 1952.

Walle, Paul, *Bolivia, Its People and Its Resources, Its Railways, Mines and Rubber Forests,* London, 1914.

Whitaker, Arthur P., *The United States and South America: Northern Republics,* Cambridge, Mass., 1948.

Wilgus, A. Curtis, *South American Dictators,* Washington, 1937.

CHAPTER XXI: PERU

Basadre, Jorge, *Historia de la Peru, 1822–1908,* 2 vols., rev. ed., Lima, 1949. (A leading work.)

Beals, Carlton, *Fire on the Andes,* Philadelphia, 1934. (Indians and the APRA.)

Belaunde, Victor Andrés, *La vida internacional del Peru,* Lima, 1942.

Bernstein, Harry, *Modern and Contemporary Latin America,* New York, 1952. (Chapter on the APRA.)

Borchard, *Opinion on the Controversy between Peru and Chile . . .* Washington, 1920. (Tacna-Arica controversy.)

Bowman, Isaiah, *The Andes of Southern Peru,* New York, 1916. (Geography.)

Burgess, Eugene W., and Barbison, F. H., *Casa Grace in Peru,* Washington, 1954. (W. R. Grace and Company.)

Davis, William C., *The Last Conquistadores,* Athens, Ga., 1950. (Spain in Peru and Chile, 1863–1866; scholarly.)

Dennis, William J., *Documentary History of the Tacna-Arica Dispute,* Iowas City, 1927.

———, *Tacna and Arica,* New Haven, 1931.

Duffield, A. J., *Peru in the Guano Age,* London, 1877.

Haya de la Torre, Victor Raúl, *Adonde va Indoamérica,* 2nd ed., Santiago, 1935. (The leader of the APRA movement; statement of principles.)

Kantor, Harry, *The Ideology and Program of the Peruvian Aprista Movement,* Berkeley and Los Angeles, 1953. (Scholarly.)

Kubler, George, *The Indian Caste of Peru, 1795–1940: A Population Study Based upon Tax Records and Census Reports,* Washington, 1952.

Leonard, Clark, *The Rivers Ran East,* New York, 1953. (Travel in Peruvian jungles; excellent.)

Markham, Sir Robert, *A History of Peru,* Chicago, 1892.

Maúrtua, V. M., *The Question of the Pacific,* New York, 1921. (A Peruvian view.)

Millington, Herbert, *American Diplomacy and the War of the Pacific,* New York, 1948.

Pan American Union, *The Peruvian Economy,* Washington, 1950.

Rowe, Leo S., *Early Effects of the War upon the Finance, Commerce and Industry of Peru,* New York, 1918.

Squier, Ephraim G., *Peru,* London, 1877.

Stewart, Watt, *Chinese Bondage in Peru, A History of the Chinese Coolie in Peru, 1849–1874,* Durham, 1951.

———, *Henry Meiggs, Yankee Pizarro,* Durham, 1946. (Peruvian railroads, nineteenth century.)

Stuart, Graham H., *The Governmental System of Peru,* Washington, 1925.

Tuedla, Francisco, *The Controversy between Peru and Ecuador,* Lima, 1941.

Wiesse, Carlos, *Historia del Peru: la Republica,* 4 vols., Lima, 1937–1941.

Wilgus, A. Curtis, *South American Dictators,* Washington, 1937.

Cultural

Alegría, Ciro, *Broad and Alien Is the World,* tr. by Harriet de Onís, New York, 1941.

———, *The Serpent of Gold,* tr. by Harriet de Onís, New York, 1943.

Leavitt, Sturgis, E., *A Tentative Bibliography of Peruvian Literature,* Cambridge, Mass., 1932.

Palma, Ricardo, *The Knights of the Cape,* tr. by Harriet de Onís, New York, 1945. (Selections from Palma's famous *Tradiciones Peruanas.*)

Torres-Ríoseco, Arturo, *The Epic of Latin American Literature,* rev. ed., New York, 1946.

Valcárcel, Luis, *La ruta cultural del Perú,* Mexico, D. F., 1945.

CHAPTER XXII: ECUADOR

Bemelmans, Ludwig, *The Donkey Inside,* New York, 1941. (Delightful travel book.)

Blanksten, George I., *Ecuador: Constitutions and Caudillos,* Berkeley, 1950.

Browning, Webster E., *The Republic of Ecuador: Social, Intellectual and Religious Conditions Today,* New York, 1920.

Franklin, Albert B., *Ecuador: Portrait of a People,* Garden City, New York, 1943. (The best modern study.)

Enock, C. R., *Ecuador,* New York, 1914.

Hassaurek, F., *Four Years Among the Spanish-Americans,* New York, 1867. (García Moreno and Indians.)

Linke, Lilo, *Ecuador, Country of Contrasts,* London, 1954. (Brief; excellent.)

Pattee, Richard, *Gabriel García Moreno y el Ecuador de su tiempo,* Quito, 1941.

Reyes, Oscar Efrén, *Breve historia del Ecuador,* 3rd ed., Quito, 1949. (Standard.)

Sáenz, Moises, *Sobre el Indio Ecuatoriano,* Mexico, D. F., 1933. (By a Mexican Indian authority.)

Santovenia y Echaide, Emeterio Santiago, *Eloy Alfaro,* n. p. 1935.

Tuedla, Francisco, *The Controversy between Peru and Ecuador,* Lima, 1941.

Von Hagen, Victor Wolfgang, *Ecuador and the Galápagos Islands,* Norman, 1949.

———, *Ecuador the Unknown,* New York, 1940.

THE CARIBBEAN REPUBLICS: COLOMBIA, VENEZUELA, CUBA, HAITI AND SANTO DOMINGO

General Works

Arciniegas, Germán, *The Caribbean: Sea of the New World,* tr. by Harriet de Onís, New York, 1946.

Bates, Marston, *Where Winter Never Comes: A Study of Man and Nature in the Tropics,* New York, 1952. (Excellent; by a trained scientist.)

Blanshard, Paul, *Democracy and Empire in the Caribbean,* New York, 1947. (A basic work.)

Bonsal, Stephen, *The American Mediterranean,* New York, 1912. (Not scholarly.)

Burns, Sir Alan, *History of the British West Indies,* London, 1954.

Callcott, Wilfrid Hardy, *The Caribbean Policy of the United States, 1890–1920,* Baltimore, 1942.

Critchfield, George W., *American Supremacy,* New York, 1908.

Davis, Hassoldt, *The Jungle and the Damned,* New York, 1952. (Exploration of the Maroni River in French Guiana; reliable.)

Follick, W. M., *The Twelve Republics,* London, 1952. (Mexico, the five Central American and the Caribbean republics; a British view.)

Fox, Annette, B., *Freedom and Welfare in the Caribbean,* New York, 1949.

Froude, James Anthony, *The English in the West Indies,* New York, 1888.

Hill, H. C., *Roosevelt and the Caribbean,* Chicago, 1927.

Howland, Charles P., ed., *American Foreign Relations in the Caribbean,* New Haven, 1929.

Inman, Samuel G., *Trailing the Conquistadores,* New York, 1930.

Ireland, Gordon, *Boundaries, Possessions and Conflicts in Central and North America and the Caribbean,* Cambridge, Mass., 1941.

Jones, Chester L., *Caribbean Backgrounds and Prospects,* New York, 1931.

——, *The Caribbean Since 1900,* New York, 1936.

——, *Costa Rica and the Civilization of the Caribbean,* Madison, 1935.

——, and others, *The United States and the Caribbean,* Chicago, 1929.

Latin American Institute, 1943, *Economic Problems of the Caribbean Area,* New York, 1943.

Macmillan, W. M., *Warning from the West Indies,* London, 1938. (Re the British colonies.)

Mahan, Alfred T., *The Interest of America in Sea Power,* Boston, 1898.

Munro, Dana G., *The United States and the Caribbean Areas,* Boston, 1934.

Poole, Bernard L., *The Caribbean Commission,* Colombia, S. C., 1950. (A study of underdeveloped areas.)

Pratt, Julius W., *Expansionists of 1898,* Baltimore, 1936.

Proudfoot, Mary, *Britain and the United States in the Caribbean,* New York, 1954. (Case studies re underdeveloped areas.)

Ragatz, Lowell, Jr., *The Fall of the Planter Class in the British Caribbean, 1763–1833,* New York, 1928. (An important study.)

Rippy, J. Fred, *The Caribbean Danger Zone,* New York, 1940. (The Caribbean with World War II in the offing.)

Roberts, W. A., *The Caribbean: The Story of Our Sea of Destiny,* Indianapolis, 1940. (A good survey.)

Surinam: Recommendations for a Ten Year Development Program, International Bank for Reconstruction and Development, Baltimore, 1952. (Indication of resources and possibilities.)

William, Eric, *The Negro in the Caribbean,* Albany, 1942.

Wilgus, A. Curtis, ed., *The Caribbean Area*, Washington, 1934. (Essays by authorities.)

——, *The Caribbean: Contemporary Trends*, Gainesville, 1953. (Essays by authorities.)

——, *The Caribbean: Its Economy*, Gainesville, 1954. (Essays by authorities.)

——, *The Caribbean: Peoples, Problems and Prospects*, Gainesville, 1952. (Essays by authorities.)

——, *The Caribbean at Mid-Century*, Gainesville, 1951. (Essays by authorities.)

CHAPTER XXIII: COLOMBIA

Bernstein, Harry, *Modern and Contemporary Latin America*, New York, 1952. (Chapters on Colombia.)

Bushnell, David, *The Santander Regime in Gran Colombia*, Newark, 1954. (Reliable.)

Cochrane, James S., *Journal of a Residence and Travels in Colombia during the Years 1823 and 1824*, 2 vols., London, 1825.

Crist, Raymond E., *The Cauca Valley, Land Tenure and Land Use*, Baltimore, 1952. (Excellent; by a trained geographer.)

Gailbraith, W. O., *Colombia, A General Survey*, New York, 1953. (Brief.)

Gibson, William, *The Constitutions of Colombia*, Durham, 1948. (Invaluable.)

Henao, J. M., and Arrubla, G., *A History of Colombia*, tr. by J. Fred Rippy, Chapel Hill, 1937. (Best general survey in English.)

International Bank for Reconstruction and Development, *The Basis of a Development Program for Colombia*, Baltimore, 1950. (Detailed, valuable.)

López, de Mesa, Luis, *De Cómo se ha de formado la nacion Colombiana*, Bogotá, 1934.

Ospina, Eduardo, *The Protestant Denominations in Colombia*, Bogotá, 1954. (A Catholic defense.)

Parks, E. T., *Colombia and the United States, 1765–1934*, Durham, 1935.

Parsons, James J., *Atioquía Colonization in Western Colombia*, Ibero-Americana: No. 32, Berkeley, 1949. (Detailed, scholarly.)

Rippy, J. Fred, *The Capitalists and Colombia*, New York, 1931.

Romoli, Kathleen, *Colombia, Gateway to South America*, New York, 1941. (Delightful.)

Scruggs, W. L., *Colombian and Venezuelan Republics*, Boston, 1905.

Wheeler, W. Reginald, and Browning, Webster E., *Modern Missions on the Spanish Main*, Philadelphia, 1925. (Protestant.)

Whitaker, Arthur P., *The United States and South America: The Northern Republics*, Cambridge, Mass., 1948.

Wilgus, A. Curtis, ed., *South American Dictators*, Washington, 1937.

Williams, Mary W., *Anglo-Isthmian Diplomacy, 1815–1915*, Washington, 1916.

Cultural

Coester, A., *Literary History of Spanish America*, New York, 1916.

Isaacs, Jorge, *María*, New York, 1922.

Karsen, Sonja, *Guillermo Valencia: Colombian Poet, 1873–1943*, New York, 1951.

Leavitt, Sturgis E., and García-Prada, C., *A Tentative Bibliography of Colombian Letters*, Cambridge, Mass., 1934.

Rivera, José Eustacio, *The Vortex*, tr. by Earle K. James, New York, 1935.

Torres-Ríoseco, Arturo, *The Epic of Latin American Literature*, rev. ed., New York, 1946.

CHAPTER XXIV: VENEZUELA

Allen, Henry J., *Venezuela: A Democracy*, New York, 1940.

Arcaya, P. M., *The Gómez Regime and Its Background*, Baltimore, 1936. (A supporter.)

Fergusson, Erna, *Venezuela*, New York, 1939.

Gil Fortoul, José, *Historia constitucional de Venezuela*, 3 vols., 3rd ed., Caracas, 1942. (Standard.)

Graham, R. B. Cunninghame, *José Antonio Páez*, London, 1929.

Grummond, Jane Lucas de, *Caracas Diary*, Baton Rouge, 1954.

——, *Envoy to Caracas: The Story of John G. A. Williamson, Nineteenth Century Diplomat*, Baton Rouge, 1951. (Valuable.)

Leonard, J. M., *Men of Maracaibo*, New York, 1933.

Lieuwen, Edwin, *Petroleum in Venezuela: A History*, Berkeley, 1954. (Scholarly.)

Rourke, Thomas, *Gómez, Tyrant of the Andes*, New York, 1936. (Uncritical; worth reading.)

Scruggs, W. L., *Colombian and Venezuelan Republics*, Boston, 1905.

Watters, M., *A History of the Church in Venezuela*, Chapel Hill, 1933. (Scholarly.)

Wilgus, A. Curtis, ed., *South American Dictators*, Washington, 1937.

Wise, George S., *Caudillo: A Portrait of Antonio Guzmán Blanco*, New York, 1951. (Scholarly.)

Cultural

Gallegos, Rómulo, *Doña Bárbara*, tr. by Robert Malloy, New York, 1948. (A famous novel of Venezuelan social conditions.)

Pietri, Arturo Uslar, *Letras y Hombres de Venezuela*, Mexico, D. F., 1948.

Ratcliff, D. F., *Venezuelan Prose Fiction*, New York, 1933.

Ybarra, T. Y., *Young Man of Caracas*, New York, 1941.

CHAPTER XXV: CUBA

Beals, Carleton, *The Crime of Cuba*, Philadelphia, 1934.

Buell, Raymond Leslie, *Problems of the New Cuba*, Report of the Commission on Cuban Affairs, New York, 1935.

Caldwell, R. G., *The López Expedition to Cuba, 1848–1851*, Princeton, 1915.

Chadwick, F. E., *Relations of the United States and Spain*, New York, 1911.

Chapman, Charles E., *History of the Cuban Republic*, New York, 1927.

Chester, Edmund A., *A Sergeant Named Batista*, New York, 1954. (A sympathetic view.)

Clark, S. A., *Cuban Tapestry*, New York, 1936.

Fergusson, Erna, *Cuba*, New York, 1952. (Descriptive; reliable.)

Ferrara, Orestes, *The Last Spanish War: Revelations in "Diplomacy,"* tr. by William E. Shea, New York, 1937. (The Spanish-American War; absorbing.)

Finlay, C. E., *Carlos Finlay and Yellow Fever*, New York, 1940. (The great Cuban doctor.)

Fitzgibbon, Russel H., *Cuba and the United States, 1900–1935*, Menasha, Wis., 1935.

Guggenheim, H. F., *The United States and Cuba*, New York, 1934.

International Bank for Reconstruction and Development, *Report on Cuba*, Washington, 1951.

Jenks, Leland H., *Our Cuban Colony*, New York, 1928.

Lockmiller, D. A., *Magoon in Cuba: A History of the Second Intervention, 1906–1909*, Chapel Hill, 1938.

Millis, Walter, *The Martial Spirit: A Study of the War with Spain*, Boston, 1931. (Realistic.)

Nelson, Lowry, *Rural Cuba*, Minneapolis, 1950. (By a trained sociologist.)

Portel Vilá, Herminio, *Historia de Cuba en relaciones con Los Estados Unidos y España*, 3 vols., Havana, 1938–1939.

Rauch, B., *American Interest in Cuba, 1848–1855*, New York, 1948.

Roberts, W. Adolphe, *Havana, The Portrait of a City*, New York, 1953. (Excellent.)

Rubens, H. S., *Liberty, The Story of Cuba*, New York, 1932.

Strode, Hudson, *The Pageant of Cuba*, New York, 1934.

Wallich, H. C., *Monetary Problems of an Export Economy: The Cuban Experience, 1914–1947*, Cambridge, Mass., 1950.

Wright, Philip G., *The Cuban Situation and Our Treaty Relations*, Washington, 1931.

Cultural

González, Manuel Pedro, *José Martí, Epic Chronicler of the United States in the Eighties*, Chapel Hill, 1953. (Scholarly.)

Lizaso, Félix, *Martí, Martyr of Cuban Independence*, tr. by Esther Elise Shuler, Albuquerque, 1953.

Mañach, Jorge, *Martí: Apostle of Freedom*, tr. by Coley Taylor, New York, 1950.

Ortiz y Fernández, Fernando, *Cuban Counterpoint: Tobacco and Sugar*, tr. by Harriet de Onís, New York, 1947.

CHAPTER XXVI: HAITI AND THE DOMINICAN REPUBLIC

Alexis, Stephen, *Black Liberator: The Life of Toussaint Louverture*, New York, 1949. (Dispassionate.)

Balch, Emily Greene, *Occupied Haiti*, New York, 1927.

Bellegarde, Dantes, *La nation Haitién*, Paris, 1938. (Standard.)

Bird, Mark B., *The Black Man, or Haytien Independence*, New York, 1869. (Sound.)

Brown, Jonathan, *The History and Present Condition of Santo Domingo*, Philadelphia, 1927.

Buell, Raymond Leslie, *The American Occupation of Haiti*, Foreign Policy Association, New York, 1929.

Craige, John H., *Black Bagdad*, New York, 1933.

Davis, H. P., *Black Democracy: The Story of Haiti*, rev. ed., New York, 1936. (Best study.)

Du Bois, W. E. B., *Black Reconstruction*, New York, 1935. (By an American Negro leader.)

Herskovitz, Melville J., *Life in a Haitian Valley*, New York, 1937. (Sensitive; by a leading anthropologist.)

Johnson, Sir Harry, *The Negro in the New World*, London, 1910.

Léger, J. N., *Haiti, Her History and Her Detractors*, New York, 1907.

Leyburn, James G., *The Haitian People*, New Haven, 1941. (Scholarly.)

Loederer, Richard A., *Voodoo Fire in Haiti*, New York, 1935.

Logan, Rayford W., *The Diplomatic Relations of the United States with Haiti, 1776–1891*, Chapel Hill, 1941. (Scholarly.)

MacCorkle, W. A., *The Monroe Doctrine in Relation to the Republic of Haiti*, New York, 1915.

Marshall, Harriet Gibbs, *The Story of Haiti from the Discovery of the Island by Christopher Columbus to the Present Day*, Boston, 1930. (Elementary text.)

Millspaugh, Arthur C., *Haiti under American Control, 1915–1930*, Boston, 1931.

Mission to Haiti, Report of the United Nations Mission of Technical Assistance to the Republic of Haiti, Lake Success, 1949. (Invaluable.)

Montague, Ludwell Lee, *Haiti and the United States, 1774–1938*, Durham, 1940. (An outstanding study.)

Niles, Blair, *Black Haiti, A Biography of Africa's Eldest Daughter*, New York, 1926. (Popular.)

Rodman, Selden, *Haiti: The Black Republic*, New York, 1954. (An excellent survey.)

St. John, Spencer, *Haiti*, London, 1889. (Reliable; British observer.)

Seabrook, William, *The Magic Island*, New York, 1929.

Steward, T. G., *The Haitian Revolution, 1791–1804*, New York, 1914.

Stoddard, T. Lothrop, *The French Revolution in Santo Domingo*, Boston, 1914.

Tansill, Charles C., *The United States and Santo Domingo, 1798–1873*, Baltimore, 1938.

Treudley, Mary, *The United States and Santo Domingo, 1789–1866*, Worcester, 1916. (Thorough, scholarly.)

Waxman, Percy, *The Black Napoleon: The Story of Toussaint Louverture*, New York, 1931.

Williams, J. J., *Voodoos and Obeahs, Phases of West Indian Witchcraft*, New York, 1933. (A careful study by a recognized authority.)

Vandercook, John W., *Black Majesty: The Life of Christophe, King of Haiti*, New York, 1928.

The Dominican Republic

Ariza, Sander, *Trujillo: The Man and His Country*, New York, 1939. (By an admirer.)

Hazard, Samuel, *Santo Domingo, Past and Present, with a Glance at Haiti*, New York, 1879. (Sound.)

Henríquez Ureña, Max, *Los Estados Unidos y la República Dominicana*, Habana, 1919. (Best for period before 1916).

Hicks, Albert, *Blood in the Streets: The Life and Rule of Trujillo*, New York, 1946.

Knight, Melvin M., *The Americans in Santo Domingo*, New York, 1928.

Nanita, A. R., *Trujillo, a Full-Size Portrait*, Santiago, 1939.

Pierce, E. L., *Memoirs and Letters of Charles Sumner*, 4 vols., Boston, 1877–1893.

Schoenrich, Otto, *Santo Domingo—a Country with a Future*, New York, 1918. (Basic.)

Stoddard, T. Lothrop, *The French Revolution in Santo Domingo*, Boston, 1914.

Tansill, Charles C., *The United States and Santo Domingo, 1798–1873*, Baltimore, 1938.

Waxman, S. M., *A Bibliography of the Belles-Lettres of Santo Domingo*, Cambridge, Mass., 1931.

Welles, Sumner, *Naboth's Vineyard: The Dominican Republic, 1844–1928*, 2 vols., New York, 1928. (A basic work.)

THE REPUBLICS OF CENTRAL AMERICA, PANAMA, AND MEXICO

CHAPTER XXVII: CENTRAL AMERICA AND PANAMA

Central America

Beals, Carleton, *Banana Gold*, Philadelphia, 1932.

Biensanz, John and Mavis, *Costa Rican Life*, New York, 1944. (Excellent.)

Burgess, P., *Justo Rufino Barrios*, Philadelphia, 1936. (Reliable.)

Caiger, Stephen L., *British Honduras,* London, 1951.

Carr, Archie, *High and Low Jungles,* Gainesville, 1953. (Biologist; good account of Honduran and Nicaraguan life.)

Chamberlain, Robert S., *Francisco Morazán, Champion of Central American Federation,* Miami, 1950.

Cox, Isaac J., *Nicaragua and the United States, 1900–1927,* Boston, 1927.

Cramer, Floyd, *Our Neighbor Nicaragua,* New York, 1929.

Department of State, *A Brief History of the Relations between the United States and Nicaragua, 1909–1928,* Washington, 1928. (Official.)

Deutsch, Herman B., *The Incredible Yanqui: The Career of Lee Christmas,* London, 1931.

Gann, Thomas, *Ancient Cities and Modern Tribes,* New York, 1926.

Fergusson, Erna, *Guatemala,* New York, 1937.

Greene, Laurence, *The Filibuster: The Career of William Walker,* Indianapolis, 1937.

Hill, Roscoe R., *Fiscal Intervention in Nicaragua,* New York, 1933. (Authoritative.)

Holleran, Mary P., *Church and State in Guatemala,* New York, 1949.

International Bank for Reconstruction and Development, *The Economic Development of Guatemala,* Washington, 1951.

———, *The Economic Development of Nicaragua,* Baltimore, 1952.

Ireland, Gordon, *Boundaries, Possessions and Conflicts in Central and North America and the Caribbean,* Cambridge, Mass., 1941.

Jones, Chester Lloyd, *Costa Rica and the Civilization of the Caribbean,* Madison, 1935.

———, *Guatemala, Past and Present,* Minneapolis, 1940.

Keasby, L. A., *The Nicaragua Canal and the Monroe Doctrine,* New York, 1896. (A valuable study.)

Kelsey, Vera, and Osborne, Lilly de J., *Four Keys to Guatemala,* New York, 1940. (Sensitive and accurate description.)

Kepner, Charles David, *Social Aspects of the Banana Industry,* New York, 1936. (Important.)

———, and Soothill, Jay H., *The Banana Empire, A Case Study in Imperialism,* New York, 1935. (Critical.)

Martin, Percy F., *Salvador of the Twentieth Century,* New York, 1911.

May, Stacy, and others, *Costa Rica: A Study in Economic Development,* New York, 1952. (Valuable.)

Montúfar, Lorenzo, and Maestre, Rivera, *Reseña histórica de Centro America,* 5 vols., Guatemala, 1878. (Basic for period.)

Munro, Dana Gardner, *The Five Republics of Central America,* New York, 1918. (Still the leading study.)

Scruggs, William O., *Filibusters and Financiers: the Story of William Walker and His Associates,* New York, 1916.

Silvert, K. H., *A Study in Government: Guatemala,* New Orleans, 1954. (Local and national; penetrating.)

Squier, Ephraim G., *Honduras,* 1870.

———, *Nicaragua, Its People, Scenery, Monuments, and the Proposed Inter-Oceanic Canal,* 2 vols., New York, 1852.

———, *Notes on Central America,* New York, 1855.

———, *Travels in Central America,* 2 vols., New York, 1853.

Stephens, John L., *Incidents of Travel in Central America, Chiapas and Yucatan,* new ed., by R. L. Predmore, New Brunswick, New Jersey, 1949.

Tax, Sol, *Penny Capitalism: A Guatemalan Indian Economy,* Washington, 1953.

Tumin, Melvin M., *Caste in a Peasant Society,* Princeton, 1952. (Study of a community.)

United Nations, *The Population of Central America (Including Mexico) 1950–1980,* New York, 1954. (An important scientific analysis and projection.)

Wallich, Henry C., and Adler, John H., *The Economics of Public Finance in El Salvador,* Cambridge, Mass., 1951.

Wilgus, A. Curtis, *The Caribbean Area,* Washington, 1934.

Williams, Mary W., *Anglo-Isthmian Diplomacy,* Washington, 1916. (A basic work.)

Wilson, Charles W., *Empire in Green and Gold: The Story of the American Banana Trade,* New York, 1944.

Cultural

McMichael, Charles B., *Prosas Profanas and other Poems,* New York, 1922. (Darío.)

Selva, Salomón de la, *Eleven Poems of Rubén Darío,* New York, 1916.

Torres-Ríoseco, Arturo, *Rubén Darío, Casticismo y Americanismo,* Cambridge, Mass., 1931.

Panama

Bunau-Varilla, P., *Panama, Creation, Destruction, and Resurrection,* New York, 1914.

DuVal, Miles P., *And the Mountains Will Move,* Stanford, 1947.

———, *Cadiz to Cathay: The Story of the Long Struggle for a Waterway Across the American Isthmus,* Stanford, 1940. (Thorough.)

Ealy, Lawrence O., *The Republic of Panama in World Affairs, 1903–1950,* Philadelphia, 1951.

Geothals, G. W., *The Panama Canal,* New York, 1916.

Johnson, W. F., *Four Centuries of the Panama Canal,* New York, 1906.

McCain, William D., *The United States and the Republic of Panama,* Durham, 1937.

Mack, Gerstle, *The Land Divided: A History of the Panama Canal and Other Isthmian Projects,* New York, 1944.

Miner, Dwight Carroll, *The Fight for the Panama Route: The Story of the Spooner Act and the Hay-Herrán Treaty,* New York, 1940. (A good summary.)

Munro, Dana G., *The Republics of Central America,* New York, 1918.
Padelford, N. J., *The Panama Canal in Peace and War,* New York, 1942.
Siegfried, André, *Suez and Panama,* New York, 1940.
Wilgus, A. Curtis, *The Caribbean Area,* Washington, 1934.

CHAPTER XXVIII: MEXICO

Anderson, Edgar, *Plants, Man and Life,* New York, 1952. (Botanist; chapter on maize.)
Beals, Carleton, *Porfirio Díaz, Dictator of Mexico,* Philadelphia, 1932. (Only recent full-length biography; based on inadequate sources, but instructive.)
Bernstein, Harry, *Modern and Contemporary Latin America,* New York, 1952. (Chapters on Mexico.)
Booth, George C., *Mexico's School-Made Society,* Stanford, 1941.
Brenner, Anita, *The Wind That Swept Mexico: The History of the Mexican Revolution, 1910–1942,* New York, 1943. (An important study of the recent period.)
Call, Tom C., *The Mexican Venture,* New York, 1953. (Newspaperman's report on Mexican industrialization.)
Callcott, Wilfrid H., *Church and State in Mexico, 1822–1867,* Durham, 1926. (Basic.)
——, *Liberalism in Mexico, 1857–1929,* Stanford, 1931. (Basic.)
Caruso, John A., *The Liberators of Mexico,* New York, 1954. (Scholarly; biographies.)
Corti, Egon Caesar, *Maximilian and Charlotte of Mexico,* 2 vols., London, 1929. (A leading work.)
Cotner, Thomas Ewing, *The Military and Political Career of José Joaquín de Herrera, 1792–1864,* Austin, 1949. (Scholarly; valuable.)
Creel, George, *The People Next Door,* New York, 1927.
Cumberland, Charles C., *Mexican Revolution: Genesis under Madero,* Austin, 1952. (A study of Madero and beginnings of the Revolution.)
Elliott, C. W., *Winfield Scott, The Soldier and the Man,* New York, 1937.
Fischer, Louis, *Oil Imperialism,* New York, 1926. (Data on Mexican oil.)
Gardiner, C. Harvey, "Survey: Foreign Travelers' Accounts of Mexico, 1810–1910," *The Americas,* Vol. VIII, January, Washington, 1952. (Valuable bibliography.)
Gibbon, Thomas Edward, *Mexico under Carranza,* New York, 1919.
Gill, T., *Land Hunger in Mexico,* Washington, 1951. (Solid scholarship.)
Gordon, Wendell C., *The Expropriation of Foreign-Owned Property in Mexico,* Washington, 1941. (Oil and other property.)
Gruening, Ernest, *Mexico and Its Heritage,* New York, 1928. (Valuable study of the Revolution.)
Hasbrouck, Louise S., *Mexico from Cortéz to Carranza,* New York, 1918.
Henry, Robert S., *The Story of the Mexican War,* Indianapolis, 1950. (Popular, reliable.)
Herring, Hubert, *The Making of a Nation,* New York, 1942.

Herring, Hubert, and Weinstock, Herbert, *Renascent Mexico*, 1935. (For the period, a valuable set of essays by authorities, Mexican and United States.)

Infield, Henrik F., and Freier, K., *People in Ejidos*, New York, 1954. (A valuable study of a problem undergoing change.)

International Bank for Reconstruction and Development, *The Economic Development of Mexico*, Baltimore, 1953. (Excellent, detailed data.)

Johnson, Richard A., *The Mexican Revolution of Ayutla, 1854–1855*, Rock Island, Ill., 1939. (Scholarly.)

Jones, C. L., *Mexico and Its Prospects*, New York, 1921. (Díaz material.)

———, *Mexico and Its Reconstruction*, New York, 1921. (The Revolution.)

Kirk, Betty, *Covering the Mexican Front*, Norman, 1942. (One of the better news correspondent's accounts.)

Knapp, Frank Averill, Jr., *The Life of Sebastián Lerdo de Tejada, 1823–1889: A Study of Influence and Obscurity*, Austin, 1951. (An excellent study.)

Lewis, Oscar, *Life in a Mexican Village: Tepoztlán Restudied*, Urbana, Ill., 1951. (Careful; detailed. See Redfield, *Tepoztlán*, below.)

López Aparicio, Alfonso, *El movimiento obrero en Mexico*, Mexico, 1952. (Labor.)

McCaleb, W. F., *The Public Finances of Mexico*, New York, 1922.

Mayer, Brantz, *Mexico As It Was and As It Is*, Baltimore, 1944. (New edition of this near classic.)

Millan, Verna C., *Mexico Reborn*, Boston, 1939. (Cárdenas; sympathetic.)

Mosk, Sanford A., *Industrial Revolution in Mexico*, Berkeley, 1950. (A basic work.)

O'Flaherty, Daniel, *General J. Shelby, Undefeated Rebel*, Chapel Hill, 1954. (Data on Confederate colony in Mexico.)

Parkes, Henry Bamford, *A History of Mexico*, Boston, 1938.

Pinchon, Edgcumb, *Zapata, the Unconquerable*, New York, 1941.

Plenn, J. H., *Mexico Marches*, New York, 1939.

Portes Gil, Emilio, *Conflict between the Civil Power and the Clergy*, Mexico, 1935. (By a former president.)

Priestley, Herbert I., *The Mexican Nation, A History*, New York, 1924.

Redfield, Robert, *Tepoztlán*, Chicago, 1930. (Basic community study.)

Rivera, Diego, and Wolf, Bertram, *Diego de Rivera*, New York, 1937.

Robertson, William Spence, *Iturbide of Mexico*, Durham, 1952. (Portrait by a master.)

Roeder, Ralph, *Juárez and his Mexico*, 2 vols., New York, 1947. (The best study.)

Ross, E. A., *Social Revolution in Mexico*, New York, 1923.

Ross, Stanley R., *Francisco I. Madero*, New York, 1955.

Simpson, Eyler, *The Ejido: Mexico's Way Out*, Chapel Hill, 1937. (Cf. above, Infield, *People in Ejidos*.)

Simpson, Lesley Byrd, *Many Mexicos*, Berkeley, 1952. (A general survey.)

Strode, Hudson, *Timeless Mexico*, New York, 1944. (A general survey: high literary qualities.)

Tannenbaum, Frank, *The Mexican Agrarian Revolution*, New York, 1929.

———, *Mexico, the Struggle for Peace and Bread,* New York, 1950.

———, *Peace by Revolution,* New York, 1933.

Townsend, W. C., *Lázaro Cárdenas: Mexican Democrat,* Ann Arbor, 1952. (A sympathetic account by a shrewd observer.)

United Nations, *The Population of Central America (Including Mexico), 1950–1980,* New York, 1954. (An important scientific analysis and projection.)

Ward, H. G., *Mexico,* 2 vols., 2nd ed., enlarged, London, 1829. (Basic to period.)

Whetten, Nathan L., *Rural Mexico,* Chicago, 1948. (Invaluable land study.)

International Relations

Barker, E. C., *Mexico and Texas, 1821–1835,* Dallas, 1928.

Batchelder, Roger, *Watching and Waiting on the Border,* Boston, 1927.

Callahan, James Morton, *American Foreign Policy in Mexican Relations,* New York, 1932.

Callcott, Wilfred H., *Santa Anna,* Norman, 1936.

Castañeda, Carlos E., *The Mexican Side of the Texas Revolution,* Dallas, 1928.

Cline, Howard F., *The United States and Mexico,* Cambridge, 1953. (Brief bibliography.)

Daniels, Josephus, *Shirt Sleeve Diplomacy,* Chapel Hill, 1947. (Basic to study of Cárdenas administration.)

Devoto, Bernard, *The Year of Decision, 1846,* Boston, 1943.

Dunn, Frederick Sherwood, *The Diplomatic Protection of Americans in Mexico,* New York, 1933.

Feller, A. H., *The Mexican Claims Commission, 1923–1934,* New York, 1935.

Fuller, John D. P., *The Movement for the Acquisition of All Mexico, 1846–1848,* Baltimore, 1936.

Garber, Paul N., *The Gadsden Treaty,* Philadelphia, 1923.

Hackett, C. W., *The Mexican Revolution and the United States, 1910–1926,* Boston, 1926. (A brief but valuable study; includes important documents.)

Inman, Samuel G., *Intervention in Mexico,* 2nd ed., New York, 1919. (First edition is more valuable.)

Jay, William, *A Review of the Causes and Consequences of the Mexican War,* Boston, 1849.

MacCorkle, Stuart A., *American Policy of Recognition towards Mexico,* Baltimore, 1933.

Manning, W. R., *Early Diplomatic Relations between the United States and Mexico,* Baltimore, 1916.

Morton, O., *Terán and Texas: A Chapter in Texas-Mexican Relations,* Austin, 1948. (Impartial.)

Nicholson, Harold, *Dwight Morrow,* New York, 1935.

O'Shaughnessy, Edith, *A Diplomat's Wife in Mexico,* New York, 1917. (Díaz, her god.)

———, *Intimate Pages of Mexican History,* New York, 1920.

Ramírez, José Fernando, *Mexico During the War with the United States,* ed. by W. V. Scholes, Columbia, Mo., 1950.

Rippy, J. Fred, *Joel R. Poinsett, Versatile American,* Durham, 1935.

———, *The United States and Mexico,* rev. ed., New York, 1931. (Best for the period, 1848–1920.)

Rives, G. L., *The United States and Mexico, 1821–1848,* 2 vols., New York, 1913. (Best for period.)

Romero, Matías, *Mexico and the United States,* Vol. I, New York, 1898. (Only one volume published; invaluable data on the Díaz period.)

Smith, Justin H., *The Annexation of Texas,* New York, 1941.

———, *The War with Mexico,* 2 vols., New York, 1919. (Authoritative.)

Tompkins, Frank, *Chasing Villa, The Story Behind Pershing's Expedition in Mexico,* Harrisburg, 1934.

Toulmin, H. A., Jr., *With Pershing in Mexico,* Harrisburg, 1935.

Turlington, Edgar, *Mexico and Her Foreign Creditors,* New York, 1930.

Williams, John Jay, *The Isthmus of Tehuantepec,* New York, 1852. (Basic for period.)

Wilson, Henry L., *Diplomatic Episodes in Mexico, Belgium and Chile,* New York, 1927.

Wyllys, Rufus Kay, *The French in Sonora (1850–1854),* Berkeley, 1932.

Cultural

Azuela, Mariano, *The Underdogs,* tr. by E. Munguia, New York, 1929. (Classic.)

Brenner, Anita, *Idols Behind Altars,* New York, 1929.

Calderón de la Barca, Madame, *Life in Mexico During a Residence of Two Years in That Country,* Introd. by H. Baerlein, New York, 1931. (Many editions of this famous classic.)

Cerwin, Herbert, *These Are the Mexicans,* New York, 1947.

Covarrubias, Miguel, *Mexico South: The Isthmus of Tehuantepec,* New York, 1947.

Flandrau, Charles M., *Viva Mexico!* New York, 1914. (Delightful.)

Goldwater, Robert, *Rufino Tamayo,* New York, 1947. (Excellent reproductions.)

González Peña, Carlos, *History of Mexican Literature,* tr. by G. B. Nance and F. J. Dunstan, Dallas, 1943. (A basic work; heavily colonial.)

Guzmán, Martín Luis, *The Eagle and the Serpent,* tr. by Harriet de Onís, New York, 1940.

Helm, MacKingley, *José Clemente Orozco, An Interpretative Biography,* New York, 1953.

———, *Man of Fire, José Clemente Orozco,* New York, 1953. (Outstanding.)

———, *Modern Mexican Painters,* New York, 1941.

Kneller, George Frederick, *The Education of the Mexican Nation,* New York, 1951.

López y Fuentes, Gregorio, *El Indio,* Indianapolis, 1936, tr. by Anita Brenner and illustrated by Diego Rivera.

Portrait of Mexico, paintings by Diego Rivera and text by Bertram Wolf, New York, 1937.

Radin, Paul, *The Opponents and Friends of Lizardi*, San Francisco, 1939.

Romanell, Patrick, *Making of the Mexican Mind*, Lincoln, Nebr., 1952. (Highly recommended.)

Sánchez, George I., *Mexico: A Revolution in Education*, New York, 1936.

Stevenson, Robert, *Music in Mexico*, New York, 1952.

Stewart, Virginia, *45 Contemporary Mexican Artists*, Stanford, 1951.

Tinker, Edward Larocque, *The Horsemen of the Americas*, New York, 1953. (Charros.)

Toor, Frances, *A Treasury of Mexican Folkways*, New York, 1947.

Wellman, Esther T., *Amado Nervo, Mexico's Religious Poet*, New York, 1936.

Wilson, Irma, *A Century of Educational Thought*, New York, 1941.

V. INTER-AMERICAN RELATIONS

CHAPTER XXIX: INTER-AMERICAN RELATIONS

The United States and Latin America

Beaulac, Willard L., *Career Ambassador*, New York, 1951.

Bemis, Samuel F., *American Secretaries of State*, 10 vols., New York, 1927–1929.

———, *The Latin American Policy of the United States: An Historical Interpretation*, New York, 1943.

Clark, Reuben J., *Memorandum on the Monroe Doctrine*, Washington, 1930. (A compilation.)

Cleland, R. G., *One Hundred Years of the Monroe Doctrine*, Los Angeles, 1923.

DeConde, Alexander, *Herbert Hoover's Latin American Policy*, Stanford, 1951.

Dietrich, Ethel B., *Economic Relations of the United States with Latin America*, Washington, 1941.

Hall, A. B., *The Monroe Doctrine and the Great War*, New York, 1920.

Lewis, Cleona, *America's Stake in International Investments*, Washington, 1938.

Manning, William R., ed., *Diplomatic Correspondence of the United States, Inter-American Affairs, 1831–1850*, 12 vols., 1932–1939.

Perkins, Dexter, *Hands Off: A History of the Monroe Doctrine*, Boston, 1941.

———, *The Monroe Doctrine, 1867–1907*, Baltimore, 1937.

Phelps, D. M., ed., *Economic Relations with Latin America*, Ann Arbor, 1940.

Robertson, W. S., *Hispanic-American Relations with the United States*, New York, 1923.

Stuart, Graham H., *Latin America and the United States*, rev. 5th ed., New York, 1955.

Tyler, Alice Felt, *The Foreign Policy of James G. Blaine*, Minneapolis, 1927.

Webster, Sir C. K., *The Foreign Policy of Palmerston, 1830–1841*, London, 1941.

(*Note:* For relations of the United States with individual countries, see appropriate chapter bibliographies. See note 1, p. 702.)

Winkler, Max, *Investments of United States Capital in Latin America*, Boston, 1929.

Inter-American Affairs

Aikman, Duncan, *The All-American Front*, New York, 1940.

Artucio, Hugo Fernández, *The Nazi Underground in South America*, New York, 1942.

Ball, Mary Margaret, *The Problem of Inter-American Organization*, Stanford, 1944.

Beckett, Grace, *The Reciprocal Trade Agreement Program*, New York, 1941.

Bibliografía de las conferencias interamericanas, Washington, Pan-American Union, 1954. (Mimeographed guide to the first nine conferences and the four meetings of the foreign ministers and other materials; invaluable.)

Bidwell, P. W., *Economic Defense of Latin America*, Boston, 1941.

Brown, William Adams Jr., and Redvers, Opie, *American Foreign Assistance*, Washington, 1953. (Data on United States spending in Latin America.)

Carter, Albert, *The Battle of South America*, New York, 1941.

Dávila, Carlos, *We of the Americas*, New York, 1949. (Good discussion of inter-American problems.)

Department of State, *Documents on German Foreign Policy, 1918–1945*, Series D (193701945) No. 4964, Vol. V., Washington, 1953. (Nazis in Latin America.)

———, *Peace in the Americas: A Résumé of Measures Undertaken through the Organization of American States to Preserve the Peace*, Washington, 1950.

Duggan, Lawrence, *The Americas: The Search for Hemisphere Security*, New York, 1949.

Economic Defense of the Western Hemisphere, The: A Study in Conflicts, Washington, 1941.

Foreman, C., and Raushenbush, V., *Total Defense*, New York, 1941.

Frazer, Robert W., "The Role of the Lima Congress, 1864–1865, in the Development of Pan-Americanism," *Hispanic American Historical Review*, Vol. XXIX, August, 1949.

Goetz, Delia, and Fray, Varian, *Good Neighbors: The Story of the Two Americas*, New York, 1939. (Compact information.)

Horn, P. V., and Bice, H. E., *Latin American Trade and Economics*, New York, 1949.

Humphrey, John P., *The Inter-American System: A Canadian View*, Toronto, 1942.

International Bank for Reconstruction and Development, The, 1946–1953, Baltimore, 1954. (Origins and operations.)

Kelchner, W. H., *Latin American Relations with the League of Nations*, Boston, 1930.

Martin, P. A., *Latin America and the War*, Baltimore, 1925.

Lockey, Joseph Byrne, *Essays in Pan-Americanism*, Berkeley, 1939.

Rowe, L. S., and others, *Latin America in World Affairs, 1914–1940*. Philadelphia, 1941.

Royal Institute of International Affairs, *Documents on Regional Organizations Outside Western Europe, 1940–1949*, London, 1950.

Scott, J. B., *International Conferences of American States, 1889–1928*, New York, 1931.

Scudder, Evarts Seelye, *The Monroe Doctrine and World Peace*, London, 1939.

Singer, K. D., *German Secret Service in South America*, New York, 1942.

Soule, George H.; Efron, David; Ness, Norman T., *Latin America in the Future World*, New York, 1945.

Stuntz, A. Edward, *To Make People Strong*, New York, 1946. (A reporter's sympathetic account of inter-American projects.)

Stuyt, A. M., *Survey of International Arbitrations, 1794–1938*, The Hague, 1939.

United Nations, *Economic Review of Latin America*, Economic Commission for Latin America, special issue, Bogotá, Colombia, August, 1955. (Important economic data, and significant interpretations of modern society.)

United Nations, *Economic Survey of Latin America, 1953*, New York, 1954.

——, *A Study of Trade Between Latin America and Europe*, New York, 1953.

United States Tariff Commission, *The Foreign Trade of Latin America*, Washington, 1942.

——, *Latin America as a Source of Strategic and Other Essential Raw Materials (1941)*, Report No. 144, Second Series, Washington, 1941.

Welles, Sumner, *The Time for Decision*, New York, 1944.

Whitaker, Arthur P., ed., *Inter-American Affairs, An Annual Survey*, Nos. 1–5, New York, 1941–1945.

INDEX